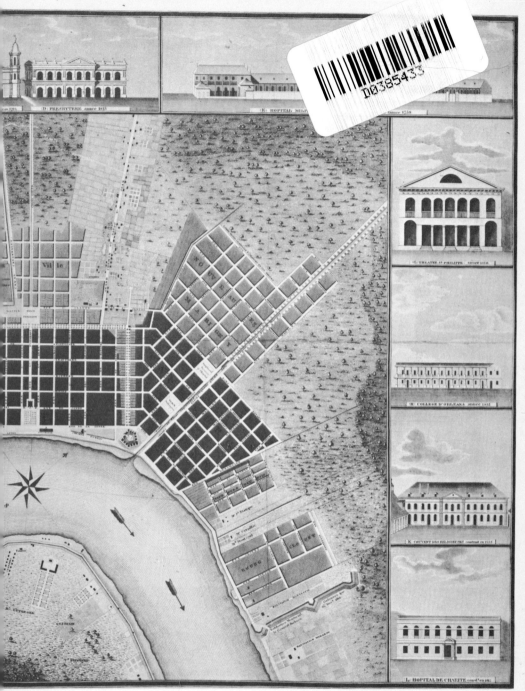

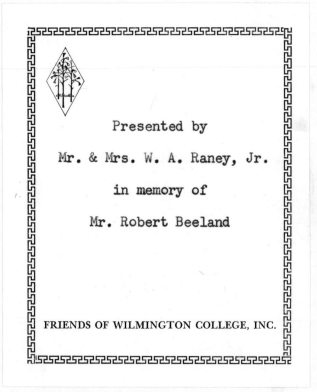

A HISTORY

OF THE

ENGLISH THEATRE

IN

NEW ORLEANS

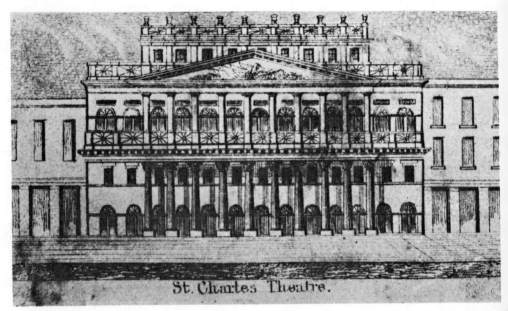

The St. Charles Theatre, built in 1835.

A HISTORY

OF THE

ENGLISH THEATRE

IN

NEW ORLEANS

Nelle Smither

Benjamin Blom
New York

Printed in U.S.A. by
NOBLE OFFSET PRINTERS, INC.
NEW YORK 3, N. Y.

Contents

Introduction

The record of the English stage at New Orleans constitutes an important chapter in the theatrical annals of America. Not only did the New Orleans stage at one time rank with the best in the country, but as the most important in the far South, it dominated the theatrical activity in the surrounding frontier sections. From this "emporium of the South and West" went out actors and stars to further the establishment of the professional theatre in places which hitherto had known only amateur organizations and "strolling players."

In 1806, when it witnessed its first English performance, New Orleans was still largely French. The three years under American rule had brought an increase in the American population; but according to Thomas Ashe, who visited the city in this year, the newcomers had been so occupied with politics and legislation that their minds had "never been sufficiently unbent to form a course of pleasure for themselves."[1] Scattered performances during the next eleven years indicate some theatrical activity, but not until 1818 was the English-speaking population of the city ready to support a full season of professional entertainment. Thereafter, with the exception of four or five seasons, the record is one of success for the English stage at New Orleans. The period between 1818 and 1842 saw a steadily increasing growth of interest in the English drama and the building of two theatres, said to be among the handsomest in the country. To these came the most distinguished stars of the day, and here excellent companies presented the current successes of the New York and London stages.

On the whole, the quality of the dramatic fare offered during these years appears to have been as high as that of the theatres in New York, Philadelphia, and Boston. Each season brought some of the most popular Shakespearian and eighteenth century

---

[1] *Travels in America, Performed in 1806*, 263.

plays; current successes in tragedy, comedy, melodrama, spectacle, and farce; and opera. Special entertainments such as the pantomimes of the famous Ravel family, the ballets of Celeste and Madame Lecompte, and the performances on the "elastic cord" by Herr Cline were also seasonal features.

An analysis of the records which are available today reveals the theatrical interests of the New Orleans audiences; however, it must be borne in mind that these records are incomplete and perhaps inaccurate because of last minute changes in program. So far as the existing data show, over nine hundred plays were given between 1806 and 1842 and of the various types of performance, exclusive of farce, comedy seems to have been the most popular, numbering some one hundred and forty-six titles. Melodramas come next with one hundred and fourteen, and drama is third with at least ninety being represented. Farces, of which over two hundred and fifty were given, have not been considered here, since in their capacity as curtain-raisers and afterpieces they almost invariably appeared in the bills.

According to our record, M. R. Lacy's comic opera, *Cinderella*, was the most popular production, being given some eighty-eight times between its introduction in 1833 and its last performance in 1842. M. G. Lewis' melodrama, *Timour the Tartar*, and T. H. Bayly's comedy, *Perfection*, were next in favor, each attaining sixty-one performances. The comedy, however, had not the long span of popularity that was the melodrama's, having been produced first in 1831. The first performance of Lewis' play was given in 1818, the last in 1842. Next came Bulwer Lytton's comedy, *The Lady of Lyons*, which attained sixty performances in its four years "on the New Orleans boards." Shakespeare's *Richard III* was played fifty-eight times, a record which entitles it to first place among the tragedies. Isaac Pocock's musical version of *Rob Roy* was presented some fifty-six times, and almost as popular was Richard Sheridan's excellent comedy, *The School for Scandal*, with fifty-five performances scattered over a period of twenty-two years. Another favorite of Sheridan's was his adaptation of Kotzebue's *Pizarro*,[2] which achieved forty-six productions during its long stay in the repertory.

The most popular of the dramatists represented on the New Orleans stage was William Shakespeare whose plays were presented for a total of three hundred and sixty-one performances,

---

[2] The newspaper notices of this play attribute it to Sheridan.

this exclusive of Garrick's version of *The Taming of the Shrew,* given twenty-seven times, and of the Dryden-Davenant adaptation of *The Tempest,* which reached thirteen productions. Of his plays, the tragedies were the favorites, *Richard III* being first with fifty-eight presentations, followed by *Hamlet* with fifty, *Macbeth* with forty-four, and *Othello* with thirty-seven.

Second in favor among the dramatists was John Baldwin Buckstone with three hundred and forty known performances of thirty-six plays. The most popular of his pieces were the farces, *The Dead Shot, A Husband at Sight,* and *Mischief Making;* and the spectacular *Ice Witch.* After him come several playwrights, all about even in popularity: J. R. Planché; T. H. Bayly; John Poole; and George Colman the younger. Not far below these was James Sheridan Knowles, who was represented by thirteen of his plays.

The intense rivalry which once existed between the American and French citizens of New Orleans may have been in part responsible for the enthusiastic reception accorded the works of native authors. The audiences of the English theatres welcomed the plays of both known and unknown playwrights, and the tag "by a gentleman of this city" could generally be counted on to insure a good house. Fifty-eight native writers were represented on the New Orleans stage between 1806 and 1842, the most prominent being William Dunlap, John Howard Payne, Robert Montgomery Bird, Samuel Woodworth, R. P. Smith, James N. Barker, Nathaniel Parker Willis, Mordecai Noah, John A. Stone, Charlotte Barnes, and N. H. Bannister. Nineteen of Bannister's compositions were given, a number equalled in the record by only Shakespeare, Buckstone, and Planché. Ten of John Howard Payne's plays were presented, his *Thérèse* leading the list of native compositions with forty-three productions. There were at least thirty-four performances of William Dunlap's *The Stranger,* thirty-three of Payne and Washington Irving's *Charles II,* and thirty-one of Mordecai Noah's *She Would Be a Soldier.*

New Orleans' interest in native writers is clearly demonstrated by the number of local playwrights who were given a hearing on its English stage. The record lists twelve of these, or nineteen if there may be included those actors whose plays were produced during their temporary residence in the city while members of the theatrical companies. Aside from the actor-play-

wrights, N. H. Bannister and J. M. Field, James Rees leads this
group with ten pieces, the most popular of which were *Charlotte
Temple* and *Lafitte, the Pirate of the Gulf.*

Approximately seven hundred players performed in New
Orleans between 1806 and 1842, among them many of the lead-
ing actors of the day. The "strolling players" of the first few
seasons were succeeded by excellent stock companies whose per-
sonnel included, at some time or another, names prominent in
theatrical history: Mrs. Entwistle, Mrs. Battersby, Mr. and Mrs.
H. A. Williams, Thomas Hilson, Mrs. Alexander Drake, Edwin
Forrest, James M. Scott, Mrs. Tatnall (later Mrs. Pritchard),
Joe Cowell, John Greene, H. G. Pearson, E. S. Conner, John
Gilbert, Jane Placide, Mr. and Mrs. George Farren, James Thorne,
James Murdoch, Thomas Bishop, H. J. Finn, Mrs. James Maeder
(the former Clara Fisher), John Latham, Charlotte Cushman,
John Mills Brown, Mr. and Mrs. George Barrett, and Mrs. Henry
Hunt (later the famous Mrs. John Drew).

In the early 1820's New Orleans became a part of the theatrical "circuit" and in rapid succession was visited by almost
all of the important stars of the day. Thomas A. Cooper led the
way, followed by Junius Brutus Booth, William Conway, Lydia
Kelly, Edwin Forrest, Mrs. Edward Knight, Clara Fisher, Mrs.
Duff, James Hackett, James Wallack, George Hill, Dan Rice,
Tyrone Power, Josephine Clifton, Ellen Tree, Mrs. Fitzwilliam,
John Baldwin Buckstone, and Fanny Elssler, to name some of
the most popular. Many of them came by sea from their runs
in the eastern cities or Charleston; others took the inland water
route, travelling by steamboat down the Ohio and Mississippi
rivers. The journey by either route was long and arduous, and
the fact that so many stars undertook it indicates that engagements in New Orleans were equally as profitable as those in the
eastern cities. "Mammon and fame led them on," asserted James
H. Caldwell in whose theatre many of them appeared.[3]

Until recently the historians of the American theatre have
paid little attention to the New Orleans stage. The only nine-
teenth century treatment of the subject, *The Drama in New
Orleans,* was written by an actor, John Gaisford, in 1849. Though
Gaisford had visited the city, his very brief account of the early
English and French theatres is full of errors. The twentieth

---

[3] James Rees, *Dramatic Authors of America,* 53.

century pioneer in the field of the English theatres at New Orleans has been Miss Lucile Gafford, who has written an unpublished Master's thesis, "Material Conditions in the Theatres of New Orleans before the Civil War," and an unpublished doctoral dissertation, "A History of the St. Charles Theatre in New Orleans, 1835-1843" The first, which is based on unreliable secondary sources, is of no value; the second presents in detail the history of one house during an important period in New Orleans' theatrical history. Within more recent years there appeared in *American Literature*, XI (May, 1939), an article by Dr. R. P. McCutcheon entitled "The First English Plays in New Orleans." *

The purpose of the present study is to record in some detail the history of the English theatre at New Orleans from 1806 to 1842. Theatrical annals of other American cities, books on the drama in general, and memoirs of those actors who visited New Orleans were consulted in the preparation of this work, but for the most part material was taken from the files of the New Orleans newspapers.

CHAPTER I

The Beginnings To 1818

THE FRENCH THEATRE

The first dramatic performance in New Orleans was given in the year 1791 when a group of French comedians, refugees from the Negro insurrections in Santo Domingo, came to the city.[1] They performed at first in halls, tents, or wherever they could find space and in 1792 established themselves in a house on St. Peter Street, between Royal and Bourbon. "La Salle du Spectacle" or "Le Spectacle de la Rue St. Pierre," as the theatre was called, had a checkered history, and several times during its early years the civil and military authorities ordered it closed. In 1807 the old building was renovated and designated as the Théâtre St. Pierre, but after three unsuccessful seasons it closed its doors forever.[2]

The erection of another French theatre early in 1808 was partly responsible for the failure of the St. Pierre. This was the "Théâtre St. Phillipe," a neat brick building located on St. Philip Street, between Royal and Bourbon. The house, which was said

[1] Alcée Fortier, *History of Louisiana*, II, 146.
[2] Nellie Warner Price, "Le Spectacle de la Rue St. Pierre," *Louisiana Historical Quarterly*, I, 3 (January, 1918) 221-223.
*Two Books on the New Orleans theatre have appeared since the present study was first published: John S. Kendall, *The Golden Age of the New Orleans Theatre* (Baton Rouge, 1952) and René J. Le Gardeur, *The First New Orleans Theatre, 1792-1803* (New Orleans, 1963).

to have cost $100,000, had a parquet and two rows of boxes and
could accommodate seven hundred people. To this stage in 1811
came William Duff, a pioneer in the English theatre in New Orleans, and here the American thespians gave performances "for
sweet charity's sake." Between 1817 and 1820 several American
troupes shared the theatre with the French companies, performing on alternate nights. The St. Philip was frequented by the
best French society during these years but after the opening of
the Théâtre Orleans in 1819 it ceased to be a fashionable resort
and though performances were given there until 1832, they failed
to attract those who had once patronized the house.

The Théâtre Orleans, erected in 1819, was the most famous
of the French theatres of New Orleans and the third of that
name. The first house, erected on Orleans Street, between Royal
and Bourbon, was constructed in 1809 and destroyed by fire in
1813. It was promptly rebuilt and enjoyed three successful seasons before it burned in 1816. Two years later John Davis erected
another building on the same site at a cost of $180,000.[3] The
interior and scenic arrangements of the house were excellent,
but the exterior with its unpretentious Roman Doric facade was
described as inartistic. In November 1819 Davis opened the
theatre with a company which he had brought from France and
here, during the next forty years, the creole families of New
Orleans saw the best in French opera and drama, presented by
actors recruited from the Parisian theatres.

THE ENGLISH THEATRE, 1806-1817

The first English theatrical performance in New Orleans
took place on April 29, 1806, just three years after the United
States had acquired Louisiana. On that evening in Moore's Large
Building on Chartres Street, a Mr. Rannie presented "A Theatrical Entertainment in three acts called *The Doctor's Courtship*
and two acts of the pantomime of *Don Juan*."[4] This "celebrated
performer from Europe and lately from the metropolis of the
United States" had arrived in the city over a month before, making his first appearance on March 14 in Tessier's Large Room at
27 St. Philip Street. Here he had displayed his "surprising Powers of Ventriloquism, the mimicking of various Birds and Beasts,
and also a larger variety of Philosophical and Magical Operations
than ever have been offered for public approbation."

---

[3] *Gibson's Guide and Directory of the State of Louisiana and the Cities of New Orleans and Lafayette*, 1838, p. 315.
[4] *Louisiana Gazette*, April 29, 1806.

The public must have been pleased with Rannie's entertainment. Subsequent advertisements record other evenings of ventriloquism at Tessier's and then on April 17, he moved to the city tavern in Moore's Large Building. "The room was handsomely fitted up for the occasion," reported the *Louisiana Gazette* of the 15th, "well illuminated and rendered cool and pleasant— with plenty of music." It is likely that Rannie included dramatic offerings in his bills soon after his removal from Tessier's, for on May 7 he announced Mrs. Rannie's benefit, an event which usually did not take place until the beneficiary was well known. The bill on this evening included Massinger's *New Way to Pay Old Debts;* a farce, *The Unfortunate Gentleman;* ventriloquism; and the "wonderful operation" of cutting off and then replacing a man's head without his feeling any pain.

On the 16th Rannie presented *The Battle of the Nile,* "at considerable expense and trouble." This spectacle, based on the naval engagement between Bonaparte and Lord Nelson, was to show "men sinking and swimming and Crokadiles *(sic)* molesting them and Whales, Sharks, Dolphins, Swords, and Flying Fish and Mermaids swimming on the surface of the water." The newspapers carry no notices of Rannie's activities after this performance, and it is impossible to say whether he left the city or merely ceased to advertise.

On April 23, 1811, William Duff announced in the *Louisiana Gazette* that by an arrangement with M. Coquet, the proprietor of the St. Philip, his American Company was to appear in the theatre once or twice a week during the season. Three nights later he gave the first performance, consisting of *The Unfortunate Gentleman, The Doctor's Courtship,* and bird imitations. Listed in the casts were Messrs. Wood, Wilcox, and Thompson.

Nothing is known of Duff's activities during the following month. On June 27 the *Louisiana Gazette* carried his announcement for the "English Theatre at the Grand Ball, Condé Street." He stated in this notice that he had spared no trouble or expense to make the theatre comfortable. For the opening performance on the 29th, he offered T. J. Dibdin's spectacle, *The Slaves in Barbary,* and a "number of operations, which for their singularity, have commanded the admiration of many eminent philosophers who took delight in the study of combination and the influence over the imagination by artful attractions and experi-

ments interspersed with logic." The cast of the play as given in
the *Louisiana Gazette* includes names omitted from Duff's earlier
notice: Wiles, Hamilton, Taylor, Carter, Spencer, Sanders, and
Briley.

On August 7 the "Society of Artists" united with Duff in a
performance which, originally scheduled for the 3rd, had been
postponed by bad weather. The newspaper notice mentions only
Madame Douvillier and M. Tessier, French actors who took the
leads in the pantomimes, *The Two Quakers* and *The Two Hunters
or The Dairy Maid.* Duff performed feats of balancing, danced
on the slack wire, and gave an imitation of a drunken man. With
this. performance Duff's name disappears from the newspapers.
Almost a year later we learn from the *Louisiana Gazette* (May
21, 1812) that he was still in New Orleans allied with an itinerant
acrobat, Siggismundi, and a Mr. Love. At a house on Bienville
Street, formerly used as a ballroom, they entertained with
balancing and "philosophical experiments." For May 24 they
announced a musical farce, *The Two Blind Fiddlers.*

Of greater importance than Duff's presentations are the
amateur performances which from 1812 to 1817 constituted the
only theatrical activity in English. The Thespian Benevolent
Society, composed of many of New Orleans' best-known citizens,
undoubtedly did much during these years to create an interest
in the English drama and to prepare the way for the professional
troupes which were to come. On January 24, 1812, at the St.
Philip Street Theatre the amateurs gave Colman's comedy, *John
Bull,* "to relieve the distresses of their fellow creatures." On
April 3, they brought out Colman's *Heir at Law* and James Ken-
ney's *Raising the Wind.* An editorial in the *Louisiana Gazette*
(April 6) tells of the success of this performance.

> We were again gratified on Friday last with the repre-
> sentation of a Comedy and Farce in the English language at
> the St. Philip Street Theatre. Whatever may be thought
> objectionable in the comedy, we cannot but say we were
> really gratified. And it surely must have given the gentle-
> men who for a moment "left their usual avocations for a
> path untrodden" the most pleasurable sensations in the recol-
> lections of the brilliance of the audience, of the thundering
> applause they received, of the cheering smiles and approba-
> tions of the fair, and in the sweet recollections that while
> amusing themselves they were largely contributing to the
> relief of distressed humanity.

The "pressure of the times" and the severity of the weather were said to be responsible for the appearance of the amateurs on January 23, 1813. On that evening their performance of *The Poor Gentleman* netted $426.50 to the Charitable Society of New Orleans.[5] The comedy was repeated on February 23 with J. T. Allingham's farce, *The Weathercock*, as an afterpiece.

The turbulent war years, 1814 and 1815, yield no newspaper announcements of either professionals or amateurs, and not until February 17, 1816, does the Thespian Benevolent Society again figure in the records. Their production of *A Cure for the Heartache* on that date was followed on March 28 by Colman's comedy, *Who Wants a Guinea?,* and Samuel Foote's humorous interlude, *Taste.* The mention in the announcement that Mr. Robinson was to take the part of Lady Pentweazle suggests that this actor was already well-known. On April 27 the bill at the St. Philip consisted of a French play entitled *Joueur* and Oulton's farce, *The Somnambula,* with Robinson as Somno. The notice does not state whether the latter was presented by the amateurs or by professionals. The next presentation of the Thespian Society came on November 21, 1816, when, "for the benefit of the sufferers by the late fire," they gave Charles Kemble's *Point of Honor* and Allingham's *'Tis All a Farce.* Again Robinson was the only member of the cast to be listed in the announcement.

The Thespians gave their first performance of 1817 on March 11, presenting for the benefit of the Female Orphan Asylum John Tobin's comedy, *The Honey Moon,* and the farce, *The Father Outwitted.* On the 28th they repeated the comedy and offered as an afterpiece Jackman's farce, *All the World's a Stage.* The day before the performance the *Louisiana Gazette* commented: "We are happy to find that the play of *The Honey Moon* is to be repeated. . . . From the few opportunities of rational amusement afforded to that portion of our fellow citizens who do not understand the French language, an English play is at all times a matter of interest."

It is strange that the writer of the above overlooked the following notice which had appeared in the *Louisiana Gazette* of March 22: "Rational Amusement. A. Cargill having taken the St. Philip Street Theatre, intends giving on Saturday evening, March 22, an entertainment to consist of a number of Moral,

---

[5] *Ibid.,* February 13, 1813.

Patriotic, and Humorous Recitations and Songs." There are no extant bills or newspaper notices giving the details of this or of the next few performances by Cargill; however, an announcement in the *Louisiana Gazette* of April 10 points to an early alliance with Robinson, the featured player of the Thespian productions. On that date Robinson informed the public that his benefit performance of Isaac Pocock's *The Miller and His Men* and the farce, *Animal Magnetism*, would take place shortly. The event did not take place until May 23, however, and then *The Weathercock* was substituted for Mrs. Inchbald's farce. The cast for the melodrama included Cargill as Lothair, Robinson as Karl, and a Mr. King as Grundoff. In the afterpiece Cargill was Old Fickle, Robinson, Briefwit, and Jones, "his second appearance," Tristram Fickle.

For his own benefit on June 2, Cargill presented *Othello* and William Macready's *Village Lawyer*. The explanation accompanying the announcement of the performance shows that Cargill may have had some doubts as to the public's reaction to his choice of *Othello*.

> In presenting this entertainment to the citizens of New Orleans, Mr. Cargill feels confident of giving at least as much satisfaction as has ever been experienced by an American audience in this place. The merits of the celebrated author of this piece, so justly termed the father of the English stage, are too well known to require any remarks on this occasion; and the weight of the piece depending principally on a small number of characters, it is conceived to be perfectly within the compass of the present society.[6]

Apparently the little company at the St. Philip Street Theatre disbanded soon after this. Except for the appearance of Cargill and Jones in a benefit for the French actor, Louis Douvillier, at the recently built Olympic Circus, on June 5, there is no further record of the troupe until fall. According to the notice in the *Louisiana Courier* of June 2, Messrs. Jones and Cargill, "amateurs," were to deliver all the English speeches in *The Battle of Bunker Hill, or The Death of General Warren*, "a great pantomime in 2 acts, intermixed with dialogues, etc." [7] The "new sceneries" were to be executed by Jones.

The American Theatre (the St. Philip Street Theatre) reopened "for one night only" on November 4, 1817 when Cargill,

---

[6] *Ibid.*, May 30, 1817.

[7] The newspaper notices do not indicate the author. The title resembles that of J. D. Burk's play on the same subject; however, his *Bunker Hill, or The Death of General Warren* is a five act tragedy, not a pantomime with occasional dialogue.

"having been dissatisfied in receiving his benefit last spring," offered the comedy *How to Die for Love,* Poole's interlude, *Intrigue,* and John Bray's farce, *The Toothache.* In December the Cargill troupe renewed its activities, advertising for the 5th the "celebrated tragedy of *Henry IV, or The Humours of Sir John Falstaff.*" Mr. Vos, "lately from the eastern Theatres," was Hotspur, Cargill was King Henry IV, Robinson was Prince of Wales, and Jones was Falstaff. Tickets and places were to be had from Jones at the theatre: Box $1.50; Pitt $1.00; Gallery $.50. For some reason the performance was postponed several times and did not take place until the 15th.

A critique in the *Louisiana Courier* of the 15th throws some light on the personnel of the little troupe.

We were greatly disappointed on Wednesday evening last at not receiving our anticipated pleasure in witnessing the performance of *Henry IV,* however as we are informed that great pains have been bestowed in bringing this admired piece forward we anticipate two-fold pleasure on this evening (when we understand the performance is to take place). We are promised the part of Hotspur by Mr. Vos, from the eastern theatres, who is said to be a "Theatrical Genius," and we may expect in *his* Hotspur, "Hotspur himself"—Mr. Jones as Falstaff will do justice to the character—Mr. Cargill is from Kentucky and to his talents we are no stranger—Mr. Robinson likewise claims our attention, without rivalry he is the first comic player in this part of the country, and in the afterpiece *(The Toothache)* he will have full scope for his abilities; the Amateurs no doubt will likewise obtain our approbation. Let us not dampen their exertions, but compose what is called a "GOOD HOUSE" and patronize the rising merit of our beloved country.

The performance seems to have been all that was predicted, for on December 18, "in consequence of the particular request of a number of the citizens of New Orleans," the "American Performers" announced a repetition of *Henry IV* to take place at the Olympic Circus. On the 26th at the St. Philip Street Theatre they gave two old favorites, *How to Die for Love* and *The Toothache.*

These presentations of Cargill's troupe at the St. Philip Street Theatre and the Olympic Circus bring to a close the first period in the history of the English theatre in New Orleans. With the new year came Noah Ludlow and a regularly organized company to present a sixteen-week season of tragedy, comedy, and farce.

CHAPTER II
Three Ventures 1818-1819

THE AMERICAN THEATRICAL COMMONWEALTH COMPANY, 1818

The season of 1818 is important in the annals of the early English theatre in New Orleans, for Noah Ludlow's company from Tennessee, while not the first professionals to give English performances in the city, was the first to give them regularly for an entire season.

Noah M. Ludlow had begun his career in 1813, at the age of eighteen, playing minor roles in the stock company of John Bernard of Albany. Two years later he joined a band of strolling players under the veteran manager, Sam Drake, Sr., and for the next few seasons played in Pennsylvania, Ohio, and Kentucky. In June, 1817, he and several of his fellow actors left Drake and formed a Commonwealth Company. They played their way through Kentucky and were enjoying a successful season in Nashville when Ludlow decided to try his fortune in New Orleans. In his *Dramatic Life as I Found It* he explains that this decision was prompted by the fact that no English-speaking company had appeared there, and that a letter to Richard Jones, an acquaintance of his in the city, had brought news not only of the excellent prospects for an American company but of a small theatre to be rented.[1]

Ludlow relates that his associates did not share his enthusiasm for the venture, but by the end of the Nashville season all except one, Aaron Phillips, had agreed to accompany him. Some, fearful for the success of the undertaking, withdrew from the commonwealth system under which they had started out the previous June, and in the reorganization, John Vaughan, Thomas Morgan, and Ludlow became the "sharers." Under this arrangement they were to reap the profits or the losses at the close of the New Orleans season while the other members of the company were to receive stipulated salaries.

The account which Ludlow gives of the journey to New Orleans differs somewhat from that which can be made up from the newspaper notices of the event. The company may have left Nashville around October 20 and played a fortnight in Natchez, as he says, but the New Orleans opening did not take place on December 24, 1817. The steamboat, *Orleans*, on which they made

---

[1] *Dramatic Life as I Found It*, 120.

the trip to Natchez, did not reach the city until January 7, 1818,[2] and the papers carried no announcement of the company until three days later.

The first announcement appeared in *L'Ami des Lois* on January 10.

> The American Theatrical Commonwealth Company having recently arrived in this place, take this opportunity to inform the patrons of the Drama that they have entered into an agreement with the proprietor of the St. Philip Street Theatre for the purpose of performing regular Dramatic pieces; and insure them that every exertion will be made to select such pieces as shall tend to render the amusement at the same time pleasing, moral, and instructive. The Theatre will therefore open on Tuesday Evening, January 13, 1818, with a celebrated comedy in five acts written by John Tobin, esq., called *The Honey Moon*. . . . The evening's amusement to conclude with an admired farce in three acts translated from the French of *Ruse contre Ruse* by Mrs. Inchbald called *The Midnight Hour or A War of Wits*. . . . Nights of performance, Tuesdays and Fridays. The doors will be open at 5 o'clock. Tickets of admission one dollar for box and pit—six bits for gallery. Children under twelve years of age, half price. As smoking is always disagreeable to ladies, 'tis to be hoped no gentleman will indulge in that practice while in the theatre. . . .

The cast for the opening night as given in this notice is not identical with that Ludlow recalls. Both the *Dramatic Life as I Found It* and the paper list Mr. and Mrs. Ludlow, Mr. and Mrs. Morgan, John and Henry Vaughan, Lucas, and Brainbridge, but in the notice Mrs. Cummins, and not Mrs. Vaughan, is cast as Juliana and among the actors are Messrs. Cummins and Hanna. Of the Mr. and Mrs. Jones and Mr. Plummer to whom Ludlow refers, no mention is made; nor do their names appear in subsequent notices.

The bill for the second performance on January 16 consisted of a novelty, William Dimond's *Foundling of the Forest,* and the familiar farce, *The Weathercock*. A gentleman who attended the theatre on this evening sent a communication to the editor of the *Louisiana Gazette,* who printed it in the issue of the 20th. For Ludlow, Mrs. Morgan, and Mrs. Cummins the critic had the highest praise. Ludlow, he reported, had an easy deportment, "a

---

[2] Registration of Steam Boats, Barges, Flatboats, etc., entering the Port of New Orleans. 1806-1812, City Hall Archives, New Orleans.

gentility of carriage which is the best feather in the cap of an
actor." He did not feel that Vaughan was entirely successful in
his personation of the Count de Valmont *(Foundling of the
Forest)* though he acted with "a tolerable grace." Lucas was
"too tame and actionless" in his role as the villainous Baron
Longueville, and Hanna not only suffered from "an unbecoming
shyness and stiffness of demeanor," but in many scenes his atti-
tude was one of stupid indifference. In spite of these weaknesses
the critic declared that he had been pleased with the performances.

The majority of the plays presented by the American Commonwealth Company were new to this city which had seen only
the limited repertoires of Messrs. Rannie, Duff, and Cargill. The
season continued with M. G. Lewis' *The Castle Spectre,* Goldsmith's *She Stoops to Conquer,* Home's *Douglas,* Charles Johnson's *The Farm House,* Shakespeare's *Merchant of Venice,* John
Tobin's *Curfew,* Thomas Morton's *Speed the Plough,* and William
Dunlap's *The Stranger.* The new farces included Charles Kemble's *Plot and Counterplot,* O'Keeffe's *The Rival Soldiers,* J. T.
Allingham's *Fortune's Frolic,* James Kenney's *Turn Out,* Thomas
Dibdin's *Of Age Tomorrow,* and Theodore Hook's *Darkness
Visible.*

The benefits began on March 6 when Morgan offered two
old favorites. The run of novelties was resumed on the 10th with
Vaughan's presentation of Shakespeare's *Romeo and Juliet* and
Andrew Cherry's *Miss in Her Teens.* Unfavorable weather, which
had caused many postponements, this season forced Ludlow to
take his benefit on the 17th, almost a week later than he had
planned. The novelty on this occasion was George Lillo's *George
Barnwell,* a tragedy which, in later years, became the standard
Christmas play. On his night Lucas offered Theodore Hook's
Tekeli with new scenery "by a distinguished artist of the city" and
O'Keeffe's farce, *The Irishman in London.*

A communication in the *Louisiana Gazette* of March 20 reveals that the public was indifferent to these performances. The
writer asserted that the American company would not remain
many weeks longer, owing to the lack of support. "The expenses
of a theatre here are great," he remarked, "and since their arrival
it is thought they have hardly made sufficient to defray them."

The last performances of the month featured Thomas Morton's comedy, *The Way to Get Married,* Colman's *The Mountaineers,* and Andrew Cherry's farce, *The Hotel.*

Now, as the season drew to an end, the newspapers announced the arrival of Mr. and Mrs. John Savage from Boston. They were to perform during the remainder of the company's stay in the city, four or five days at the most, stated the notices. Savage made his bow on April 2 as Pierre in *Venice Preserved* and on the 4th Mrs. Savage appeared as Lady Elizabeth in Marie Kemble's farce, *The Day after the Wedding.* The visitors continued in James Kenney's melodrama, *Ella Rosenberg,* Bickerstaff's farce, *The Romp,* Dunlap's *The Blind Boy,* and for their benefit, on the 15th, Frederick Reynolds' comedy, *Laugh When You Can,* and C. D. Dibdin's operatic farce, *The Waterman.* Their last appearance was advertised for April 18 but on the 17th the *Louisiana Gazette* reported their "sudden departure" and as a consequence an unavoidable change in the program originally announced.

The benefits commenced again after the departure of the Savages. The company volunteered their services for Richard Jones on the 21st, and on the 23rd assisted at a benefit for the French musician, M. Maurice, the bill on the latter occasion consisting of *The Birthday* and *Don Juan.*

The last benefit was that of Mrs. Vaughan on the 25th when she presented Mrs. Inchbald's drama, *Lovers' Vows,* and *Plot and Counterplot.* On May 1 the season came to a close with *The Castle Specter* and *A Miss in Her Teens.*

The company had not escaped criticism during this sixteen-week season, but in general their repertoire had been favorably received. The opinion expressed in a communication in the *Louisiana Gazette* of March 20 was doubtless shared by many.

> Now tho' the players here would not bear a comparison with those of London, New York, or Philadelphia, yet they are respectable in many walks of the drama. . . . They have done tolerable justice to some of the best comedies in the English language; and the public must indeed be fastidious when not pleased with most of their farces.

The season was a financial success. Ludlow recalls that after he and his two partners had paid the actors' salaries and the current expenses of their families, there remained over $3,000 in the treasury. This he regarded as "no contemptible profit."[3]

---

[3] Ludlow, *op. cit.,* 152.

The American Company under the direction of Cargill gave their first performance of 1818 at the St. Philip Street Theatre on January 5 when they presented *Othello*. Four nights later they appeared at the Olympic Circus in *The Duel,* an operatic comedy not previously seen in New Orleans, and in *The Toothache.* They repeated the farce on the 22nd in an evening's entertainment which included ropedancing, equestrian performances, and the pantomime, *The Tailor of Brentford,* given by the French troupe which occupied the Circus. For the 25th when Douvillier, manager of the Circus, took a benefit, the newspaper advertised "an entire new American performance called *The Watchword, or Quito Gate* got up by Mr. Jones."

The last announcement to list the names of all the principals of the troupe was that for Cargill's benefit on February 26. A communication printed in the *Louisiana Gazette* of this date suggests that the troupe had not been successful of late. "He has some claims on the public," said the writer of Cargill, "inasmuch as he has ever shown a willingness to give assistance when called on to exert his powers for a benevolent purpose. . . . We hope he will not be deserted on the present occasion when he asks for a small share of the public munificence."

Vos' benefit took place at the St. Philip Street Theatre on March 14 when, assisted by the American Commonwealth Company, he presented Shakespeare's *Richard III* and Greffulhe's farce, *The Budget of Blunders.* Included in the cast were the beneficiary, King, and Robinson, but not Cargill. On April 21, the Commonwealth Company again volunteered its services, this time for the benefit of Jones who offered William Dimond's melodrama, *The Doubtful Son.* There is no record of Robinson's benefit, and King's on April 7 had taken the form of a vocal and instrumental concert at the Orleans Ball Room. In a communication in the *Louisiana Gazette* of this date appeared a statement which is suggestive not only in its application to King but in the possibility that it was applicable to each member of the troupe with which he had been associated. The writer reported that King had been rather unfortunate during the winter, having been unable to procure employment, "however disposed to work."

Early in January a communication in the *Louisiana Gazette* had suggested that "the old and new companies coalesce," but apparently Ludlow and his partners had not thought favorably of the suggestion. The ultimate disbanding of Cargill's company was inevitable. The little troupe could not compete for long with the varied and extensive repertoire of the larger Commonwealth Company.

THE TURNER TROUPE, 1819

The only theatrical activity during the early months of the 1818-1819 season was in the French theatres. Noah Ludlow did not return to New Orleans, though his friend, Nathan Morse, had assured him of the support of the influential American citizens and had suggested the possibility of his sharing the new Orleans Theatre with the French troupe which was to occupy it on its completion.[4] In his *Dramatic Life as I Found It* Ludlow explains that the Commonwealth company had disbanded at the close of the last season and in the fall he had found it impossible to get together another company worthy of the discriminating New Orleans audience.

Early in March of 1819 appeared the first reference to an English performance that season. This was an announcement inserted in the *Louisiana Gazette* of the 2nd by Mr. Phillips, "from the Theatres of New York, Philadelphia and Charleston." He promised in the course of the next week "An Histrionic Divertissement or Evening's Dramatic Entertainment selected from the most approved authors, interspersed with satirical extracts from Alexander Stevens' celebrated Lecture on Heads and the most striking passages from some of our favorite Dramatic writers." The entertainment took place in the Orleans Ball Room on March 10 and was enthusiastically reviewed in the *Louisiana Gazette* of the 13th. This critic reported that well-deserved applause had greeted the performer, and added, "It gives us infinite pleasure to learn that an American Theatre will be established and conducted in New Orleans by a gentleman of his merit." Apparently Phillips, the same Aaron Phillips who had refused to accompany Ludlow to New Orleans the previous year, had changed his mind on hearing of his former associate's success and had decided to try his luck here. He remained a month during which he repeated the divertissement and played a short engagement with a little troupe of players that had arrived soon after he had. Most of his time, however, was devoted to effecting the necessary arrangements for the next season when he planned to return with his own company.

---

[4] *Ibid.*, 150.

The company which dominated the theatrical scene in 1819 was under the direction of William A. Turner, a pioneer manager of theatres in Pittsburgh, Lexington, Cincinnati, and St. Louis. The troupe consisted of Mrs. Turner, her young son and daughter, Mrs. Fitzallan, Messrs. Adams, Hanna, Melville, and A. Cargill. Aaron Phillips played a three nights' engagement with them the last of March, and in April they were joined by Abercrombie, "of the Philadelphia and Baltimore theatres."

They gave their first performance at the St. Philip Street Theatre on March 8. For that evening Mrs. Turner promised an address in defense of the drama; a variety of select pieces, recited and sung with the aid of Hanna and Cargill; the principal scenes in *Three Weeks after Marriage;* and as a concluding number, an "Ode on Jackson's Victory at New Orleans." During the latter there was exhibited a "Transparency, representing the Genius of America, crowning with laurels the Tomb of the Immortal Washington."

Mrs. Turner, "from the Theatre Royal, Bath, and Bristol," had made her New York debut in 1807 as Angela in *The Castle Spectre* and since then had played both comedy and tragedy. Melodramatic and tragic roles always remained her favorites, however, and figured prominently in her repertoire. She introduced the New Orleans audiences to Charles Maturin's *Bertram,* Young's *The Revenge,* Lewis' *Adelgitha,* John Brown's *Barbarossa,* Holcroft's *Tale of Mystery,* Sheridan's *Pizarro,* and Southerne's *Isabella.* In *The Revenge, Venice Preserved,* and *Adelgitha,* Phillips played opposite her.

Other plays introduced by the Turners were Hodgkinson's comedy, *The Man of Fortitude;* the burlettas, *Bombastes Furioso* by William Rhodes and *Tom Thumb* adapted from Henry Fielding by Kane O'Hara; and the farces, *Matrimony* by James Kenney and *The Prize* by Prince Hoare.

The last performance was announced for April 28, but when the vessel was delayed on which Turner had engaged passage for Liverpool, the season continued through May 17. The success of Turner's New Orleans venture is attested by his notice in the *Louisiana Gazette* of April 28.

> Mr. Turner, truly grateful to the citizens of New Orleans for their very liberal encouragement of the present small theatrical corps, respectfully informs them that he intends

in a few days, embarking for Europe for the express purpose of procuring a full company of comedians whose talents, as performers, and conduct, as public citizens, he sincerely hopes will entitle them to public notice and patronage.

With Turner and Phillips both scouting for companies, another season of English drama was assured.

CHAPTER III

The Coming of Caldwell 1820-1823

THE SEASON OF 1819-1820

The fall of 1819 brought several attempts to establish an American theatre but William Turner did not return, and Aaron Phillips, busy recruiting players in the East, delayed his return until December. By that time James H. Caldwell, manager of several Virginia theatres, had announced that he would bring a troupe to New Orleans, and the city was awaiting his arrival.

The first dramatic notice of the season tells of a performance of *The Vampire* at the "English Opera House" on November 22. There were no subsequent notices to disclose the identity of this theatre, the length of its season, or any details of its management. A communication in the *Louisiana Gazette* of November 23 refers only to the magnificent scenery and to the "rapturous applause" which greeted the play and the announcement of a repetition.

Two days later *L'Ami des Lois* informed its readers that Mr. Allen, "from the principal Northern and Southern theatres," intended to give shortly at the St. Philip Street Theatre an entertainment entitled *An Evening Brush to Sweep Away Care, or Dum Vivimus Vitamus*. "Mr. Allen," stated the notice, "contemplates opening the St. Philip Street Theatre for the season, the moment he can raise a respectable company; the above entertainment is intended to assist him in the undertaking. N. B. Particulars in future advertisements." It is possible that this performance never took place; no other mention of Allen has been found. Undoubtedly he was the famous Andrew Jackson Allen who, because he had appeared on the New York stage in 1787, styled himself the "Father of the American Stage."[1]

The first week of January, 1820, found two American companies in New Orleans. At the new Orleans Theatre was Aaron

---

[1] Henry Pitt Phelps, *Players of a Century,* 227.

J. Phillips with a hastily recruited company; at the St. Philip Street Theatre were James H. Caldwell and his company, recently arrived from Charleston. Phillips announced in *L'Ami des Lois* of January 3 that he would commence the regular dramatic season with an English performance early in the ensuing week. As a "native American"—Caldwell was English—he asked for the encouragement and support that would enable him "to claim the distinguished honor of being the first to effect a permanent establishment of the English Drama in this city on a firm basis and correct principles." Prices of admission were to be $1.50 for the first and second boxes, balcony, and private seats in the pit, and $1.00 for the gallery and pit.

Two days later Phillips announced Otway's *Venice Preserved* and Allingham's farce, *The Weathercock,* for the opening bill on January 7. Carpender, "from the New York and Charleston Theatres," was to take the role of Pierre assisted by the Jaffier of Bartow, "from the New York and Philadelphia Theatres," and the Belvidera of Mrs. Smith, "from the Philadelphia and Baltimore Theatres." In the farce Phillips and Mrs. Monier, also from the Philadelphia and Baltimore Theatres, were cast as principals. Others listed in the notice were Benton, Abercrombie, Wilkie, Turner, Scrivener, and Drummond. Carpender's "sudden indisposition" forced the company to postpone its début until the 8th when the Orleans Theatre was the scene of a "special celebration in commemoration of the glorious 8th of January, 1815."[2] Their presentation of T. Knight's *The Turnpike Gate* served as a curtain raiser for the opera, *Aline, Queen of Golconda,* given by the French company.

The second English performance at the Orleans Theatre on the 11th consisted of Home's tragedy, *Douglas,* and the younger Colman's farce, *The Review.* Mrs. Yates, "from the West Indies Theatre," made her appearance as Grace Gaylove in the latter.

Phillips now found it necessary to make a bid for public favor. "Understanding his first arrangement had not met, as he warmly anticipated, with their decided approbation and anxious in every point of view to meet their wishes," he announced a reduction in the admission: boxes and pit, $1.00; gallery for people of color, $.75. The new prices were to become effective

---

[2] On this date Andrew Jackson and his militiamen successfully defended New Orleans against a British force led by Sir Edward Packenham. Though the battle had no military value, peace having been signed on Christmas eve, the city always commemorated the event.

on the 15th, but the performance of that evening was postponed in consequence of the death of Mrs. Harris, a member of the troupe, and the "distressed situation" of Abercrombie, her brother.

Fortune had not favored Phillips since his arrival in New Orleans, and by this time he realized that he could not compete with the American company at the St. Philip Street Theatre. He had not been able to collect an audience; yet Caldwell's company was said to be "in full and successful operation."[3] In the *Louisiana Gazette* of January 19, Phillips announced that he and Caldwell had effected an arrangement in consequence of which he had been released from his previous engagement and would be given a benefit at the St. Philip Street Theatre on the 21st. With this performance he brought to a close his brief and unsuccessful career as an actor-manager in New Orleans.

The notice of a benefit performance, preserved in the Theatre Collection of Harvard University, reveals that some of Phillips' company were still in the city on June 10. Of their activity during the interim between the disbanding of the troupe and this benefit for an actress named Mrs. Wilkie, nothing is known. It seems unlikely, however, that this was the beneficiary's first appearance. The program on this night consisted of *The Gamester;* hornpipes by Wilkie; and *Sylvester Daggerwood.* The casts included the Wilkies, Scrivener, Richards, Reynolds, Walters, Kenny, Bolton, and Mrs. Davis.

AMERICAN THEATRE, ST. PHILIP STREET, 1820

James H. Caldwell, the manager of the American company at the St. Philip Street Theatre, was an English actor who had made his American début at Charleston in 1816. His managerial career began in Washington, D. C., a year later, and in 1818 he built a theatre in Petersburg, Virginia. In the same year his company performed in Alexandria, Norfolk, Richmond, and Fredericksburg. He continued to visit the Virginia theatres each summer until 1825 when he withdrew from them to extend his interests to towns in the Southwest.[4] To these towns, unfamiliar with anything but the crude fare of small companies, he brought

---

[3] Clipping from newspaper dated January 15, 1820, *In the Harvard Theatre Collection* .

[4] *In the Harvard Theatre Collection* there is a letter to William Tayleure, October 24, 1833, in which Caldwell gives the details of his career in this country.

competent actors in the best of the standard plays and current
novelties and soon made himself the most important figure in
the theatrical world of this section.

The company which Caldwell brought to New Orleans in
1820 was stronger than any that had preceded it. The manager
himself played the leads, both in tragedy and comedy, and Mrs.
H. A. Williams and Mrs. William Anderson appeared opposite
him. For the principal parts in opera and musical pieces he had
engaged Mrs. Jackson Gray, formerly Miss Trajatta of New York,
and Arthur Keene, an Irish tenor well known in the East. These
two had able support from the singing actors, Mr. and Mrs.
Richard Russell, Carr, Price, Boyle, Jones, and Petrie. The other
members included Mr. and Mrs. Joseph Hutton, Jackson Gray,
Thomas Fielding, Emberton, Master McCafferty, William Anderson, and Mrs. Price. When Phillips' company at the Orleans
Theatre disbanded, Entwistle and Mrs. Monier joined Caldwell.
Goll, a dancer from the Theatre Royal, Birmingham, and more
recently from the Park in New York, arrived late in January to
direct the ballets and entertain between the pieces with his comic
pas seul.

The American Company began its first season at the St.
Philip Street Theatre, on January 7, with Tobin's *The Honey
Moon* and Prince Hoare's farce, *The Three and the Deuce*. Caldwell's impersonations of the Duke Aranza and the Three Singles
were enthusiastically received. Said the *Louisiana Gazette* on
January 10: "Several good judges who have seen Mr. Cooper
in the Duke were heard to declare that the latter did not play it
so well; and in the cottage scene we are inclined to think it were
impossible to surpass Mr. Caldwell's acting." Evidently this
writer was not impressed by Mrs. Russell's Juliana or Mrs. Price's
Volante; he did, however, comment favorably on Mrs. Russell's
performance in the afterpiece as Taffline, "with the song of the
Silken Sash." On the second night, Mrs. Gray and Jones made
their bows as Rosina and Belville in Mrs. Brooke's musical drama,
Rosina. Mr. and Mrs. Anderson came out on the 10th in Maturin's
Bertram and on the 12th *Richard III* was given "for the purpose
of introducing Mr. Hutton." Commented "Dramaticus" in the
Louisiana Gazette of January 14: "These two tragedies did not
entirely satisfy the public." The fault, it seems, lay with Anderson and Hutton, who had elected to make their débuts in parts
which they could not sustain.

A more successful first appearance was that of Arthur Keene in Bishop's popular opera, *The Devil's Bridge*. Caldwell reappeared as Belcour in Cumberland's comedy, *The West Indian,* on the 15th, and on the 17th he essayed Hamlet. The French critic who reviewed the latter performance in the *Louisiana Gazette* (January 19) praised Caldwell's acting. He was surprised though that so little attention had been paid to the costumes. He notes that some of the Danish courtiers were dressed as Hussars and others as chevaliers, while the sailors wore the uniform of the United States Navy.

For his benefit on the 21st, Phillips, "late of the Orleans Theatre," played Romeo to the Juliet of Mrs. Williams and the Mercutio of Caldwell. Goll made his bow on this evening and the bill concluded with Charles Coffey's *The Devil to Pay,* a farce new to the city. These were interesting nights at the St. Philip Street Theatre. Entwistle came out on the 22nd as Tyke in *The School of Reform* and as Sam in *Raising the Wind.* The next evening brought the first native play of the season, John Howard Payne's *Brutus, or The Fall of Tarquin.* Another novelty was *The Green Man,* a comedy adapted from the French by Richard Jones. *Hamlet* was repeated on the 26th, Bartow, who had come to New Orleans in Phillips' troupe, making "his first appearance in this city" as the melancholy Dane. He appeared next as Young Norval and concluded his engagement with a benefit performance as Frederic Bramble in *The Poor Gentleman.*

Meanwhile the company continued to bring out pieces which were new to the city: *Guy Mannering,* with Keene as Henry Bertram; the melodramatic spectacle, *The Forty Thieves;* Holcroft's comedy, *The Road to Ruin;* and Dibdin's opera, *Lodoiska.* On February 5 came Cobb's *Paul and Virginia,* and in rapid succession followed *The Rendezvous,* a new operatic farce by Ayton, Thomas Morton's melodrama, *The Children in the Wood,* T. J. Dibdin's *The Lady of the Lake,* and Sheridan's *The School for Scandal.*

On February 14 Caldwell announced that "through the medium of his friends" he had arranged to use the Orleans Theatre. He had done this, stated the notice in the *Louisiana Gazette,* "in obedience to the wishes of many respectable families, and particularly with a desire on his part of gratifying the expectations of the French population." The move brought no change in the managerial policy. Doors opened at half past five;

the curtain rose an hour later. In this theatre, however, performances could be given only four times a week, Monday, Wednesday, Friday, and Saturday, since the French company occupied the house on the other three nights. For a short time he continued to use the St. Philip Street Theatre on Tuesdays and Thursdays, but these performances were not scheduled regularly.

Caldwell commenced his activities at the Orleans Theatre with the bill which had introduced his company, *The Honey Moon* and *The Three and the Deuce*. The first novelty was *Macbeth* on the 21st, followed by one of Goll's ballets entitled "The Jovial Millers." As the French company was using the theatre on Washington's Birthday, Caldwell took the company to the St. Philip Street house where they celebrated with Dunlap's *Glory of Columbia, Her Yeomanry;* a musical interlude, "The Feast of Apollo"; and a ballet. The novelties continued at the Orleans Theatre with Bickerstaff's *Padlock* and *Love in a Village;* Beazley's farce, *The Boarding House;* and O'Keeff's *Highland Reel.* Caldwell's benefit, on March 6, presented "for the first time in New Orleans" a harlequinade entitled "The House that Jack Built."

The most popular of the season's plays was M. M. Noah's *She Would Be a Soldier, or The Plains of Chippewa,* brought out on March 10. It was repeated the next night and by the end of the season had attained four performances. The critic "Wagstaff" in a communication printed in the *Louisiana Gazette* of the 16th expressed the belief that no other play had been received with such universal applause. "While our country can boast of such writers as Mr. Noah," stated the critic, "we see no necessity for our importing British Literature and British plays 'by the bale and by the hogshead'."

The benefits commenced on March 15 when Russell offered *The Rivals* and the melodrama, *The Honest Thieves.* Most of the pieces given on these nights had not been previously acted here. Fielding presented O'Keeffe's comedy, *Wild Oats,* and Mrs. Russell brought out three novelties: Mrs. Centlivre's *The Wonder! A Woman Keeps a Secret;* an alteration of Colman's *New Hay at the Old Market,* entitled *Sylvester Daggerwood;* and Prince Hoare's operatic farce, *Lock and Key. Much Ado about Nothing* and a revival of *Ella Rosenberg* comprised Mrs. Anderson's bill.

Goll offered a "first time" performance of Shield's tragedy, *The Apostle,* and T. J. Dibdin's *Don Giovanni,* "a comic, heroic, operatic, tragic, pantomimic burletta spectacular extravaganza taken from the celebrated pantomime of *Don Juan.*"

Gray introduced Thomas Morton's *Town and Country* on his night, and Master McCafferty's bill concluded with *The Forest of Bondy, or The Dog of Montargis,* a melodrama new to the city. According to the press this was a failure as the dog was overcome by a timidity which prevented its barking. More successful was the début of April 11 when "the living elephant" appeared in the melodramatic *Blue Beard* of George Colman the younger. For a month the beast had suffered the public gaze at Mr. Chardon's on Jefferson Street; consequently she performed with *"l'áplomb."*

Other important presentations of these last two weeks were J. N. Barker's spectacle, *Marmion* (April 12), Shakespeare's *As You Like It,* and Moore's tragedy, *The Gamester.* The notice of this last, on April 15, announced "in preparation for the benefit of Mr. Caldwell a new play called *The Bride of Lammermoor,* written by a gentleman of New Orleans." On the 19th, the night of the benefit and the last of the season, the play was again advertised. Almost a year later a communication in the *Louisiana Gazette* (March 1, 1821) mentioned that the piece had been postponed "under disagreeable circumstances" and as yet had not been given.

Reports differ as to the financial success of the season. Caldwell stated in a letter which James Rees published in the *Dramatic Authors of America* that after paying all of his expenses, including those of the voyage back to Virginia, he had a balance of $1,740.[5] A communication in the *Louisiana Gazette* of March 29, 1821, declared that Caldwell in his expense account for the 1820 season had charged a hundred dollars a night for his own personal services, "hence, deceptively lowering what he is pleased to call 'amount of profit.'" Continued the writer: "This for the twelve weeks which he played last season would be $4,800 which, added to what he shows as profit, would be $6,540, the clear gain carried away from the purses of the liberal, generous citizens of New Orleans."

Whatever the profits, they were large enough to convince Caldwell that New Orleans should be added to his theatrical

---

[5] P. 55.

circuit. Before he left with his company for the summer campaign in Virginia, he took a three-year lease on the Orleans
Theatre at $10,000 a year.[6]

Late in January of 1821 Caldwell and his company arrived
from Charleston. Of those who had appeared during the previous
season Mr. and Mrs. Price, Mr. and Mrs. Anderson, Mrs. Gray,
Boyle, Petrie, and Carr did not return. Their places were more
than adequately taken, however, by the new recruits, Mr. and
Mrs. Thomas Burke, Mrs. Entwistle, Mrs. Legg, Thomas Jefferson, Judah, Brennan, Hanna, and Miss Eliza Placide. Mrs. Burke,
who replaced Mrs. Gray, had been a popular actress at the Park
Theatre in New York and was still, in Noah Ludlow's opinion,
"unsurpassed in her singing of ballads or in English opera by
any one in the United States."[7] Mrs. Entwistle, formerly Mrs.
Mason, had also been a favorite at the Park, captivating all who
saw her in high comedy. Later she will figure in these annals
as Mrs. Crooke.

Caldwell opened his season at the Orleans Theatre on January
31 with *The Soldier's Daughter* and *The Liar*. In the former Mrs.
Entwistle appeared as the Widow Cheerly, a role which had been
associated with her name since her American début in 1809.
Caldwell enacted Frank Heartall and was Young Wilding in the
afterpiece. Mrs. Burke came out on February 5 in *The Devil's
Bridge* and *The Spoiled Child*. On her second night she enacted
Julia Mannering to Keene's Henry Bertram and Variella in the
afterpiece, *The Weathercock*. She was Rosetta in *Love in a
Village*, Maria in *Of Age To-morrow*, Agnes to Caldwell's Octavian in *The Mountaineers* and for her first benefit (February 23)
Araminta in O'Keeffe's musical farce, *The Young Quaker*. Meanwhile Mrs. Entwistle had played opposite Caldwell in *Much Ado
about Nothing*, *The School for Scandal*, and *Pizarro*. On the 24th
Colman's comedy, *The Jealous Wife*, was brought out, Mrs. Entwistle and Caldwell in the leads.

The first important novelty of the season was Sheridan
Knowles' tragedy, *Virginius, or A Roman Sacrifice*, presented on
February 26. The afterpiece on this evening was *Beaux Without
Belles*, a farce by an American, David Darling. For his benefit
on March 2, Caldwell offered *Lear* and a slack rope exhibition by

---

[6] *Ibid.*, 54.
[7] Ludlow, *op. cit.*, 216.

Williams. This was an unfortunate choice which led not only to
a severe criticism of the performance but to a general condem-
nation of the manager and the company. "Crito" in the *Louisiana Advertiser* of March 6 expressed displeasure that Caldwell
had permitted the exhibition immediately after the tragedy. Two
days later the *Louisiana Gazette* printed a reply to "Crito." Declared this commentator: "For ourselves as the Theatre has been
degraded, we hope Mr. Caldwell will do as he pleases. We be-
lieve the public would be pleased to see more of his Company on
the Rope, and we are certain that some of them would do it more
honor than they do the Drama."

The newspaper files for this season are woefully incomplete,
making it impossible to give a complete record of the performances. According to the extant advertisements, Caldwell turned
to lighter fare after his failure with *Lear*. The few notices of the
next two weeks show premières of Farquhar's *The Inconstant*,
Morton's musical *Henri Quatre*, and Pocock's *John of Paris*.

The outstanding event of the season was the visit of the
tragedian, Thomas A. Cooper. Caldwell says that he was engaged
at the enormous sum of $3,333.33 for sixteen nights, and that
the engagement was extended to twenty-four nights.[8] He made
his bow on March 23 as Macbeth and, assisted by Mrs. Entwistle,
went through a round of characters which had long been associated with his name: Leon in Beaumont and Fletcher's *Rule a
Wife and Have a Wife* ("first time in New Orleans"), Pierre to
Caldwell's Jaffier in *Venice Preserved*, Hamlet (to Mrs. Burke's
Ophelia), Virginius, and Othello. On his benefit night, April 9,
he played Bertram in Maturin's tragedy and recited the ode
"Alexander's Feast." Though he had been announced "for ten
nights only," on the 11th he began a second engagement as Marc
Antony in *Julius Caesar*, following it with *The Gamester, The
Robbers*, and *Virginius* (for the third time). The records of the
next five performances are missing, and as yet, there is no proof
that Cooper's engagement was extended to twenty-four nights as
Caldwell asserts.

On the evenings when Cooper appeared, the admission to the
boxes and parquet was raised to $1.50, an advance which Cald-
well said was "occasioned by the increased expenses of the manager's already heavy establishment attendant upon Mr. Cooper's

---

[8] Rees, *op, cit.*, 55.

engagement." When the indignant public asked for an accounting
of these expenses, a "particular friend" of Caldwell's tried to
appease them by explaining that the raise in price would prevent
the greasy Kentuckians and the rabble from leaning over the
backs of the boxes to the great annoyance of the ladies.[9] Two
days later the *Louisiana Advertiser* carried Caldwell's statement
that he had made the new price "to fill his coffers from the high
pitch of curiosity raised by the engagement of Mr. Cooper."

Several novelties were brought out in April: O'Keeffe's farce,
Modern Antiques, on the 4th and Dimond's opera, *Brother and
Sister,* on the 27th. In the afterpiece, *The Liar,* on the 27th,
Young Wilding was played by N. M. Ludlow "from the Western
Theatre." This actor had stopped in New Orleans on his way to
establish a theatre in Pensacola and, on finding that Caldwell
needed someone for juvenile tragedy and first genteel comedy,
had decided to remain.[10]

Mrs. Entwistle's benefit on May 2 presented, for the first
time in New Orleans, Colley Cibber's comedy, *The Provoked
Husband,* followed by *The American Captive.* Sometime within
two weeks of this performance her husband died and she was
allowed another benefit to help defray funeral expenses. She
had been a popular member of the company and one of the few
to win enthusiastic praise from French and English critics alike.
Now, however, she incurred displeasure by offering as the main
play on this benefit bill, Morton's comedy, *The Way to Get Married.* Noted the French critic in the *Louisiana Gazette* of May 18,
"Under the circumstances the play was badly chosen."

Keene selected *Laugh When You Can* and *The Lady of the
Lake* for his night, May 12. In the Scott adaptation he played
Allan Bane; Ludlow was Fitz-James, Mrs. Burke was Blanche of
Devon, and Mrs. Williams was Ellen. The advertisement of this
event stated that the season would end on Monday, May 14, with
a benefit for Mr. West. This actor had not been mentioned in
any of the other notices this season and of his offerings on the
14th nothing is known.

The incompleteness of the records for 1821 makes impossible
any statement as to the merit of the repertoire which Caldwell
offered during his second season in New Orleans. Caldwell him-

---

[9] *Louisiana Advertiser,* March 26, 1821.
[10] Ludlow, *op. cit.,* 215.

self dated his success in the South as beginning this year with the engagement of Thomas Cooper. He wrote James Rees in 1845:

> I conceived the idea of drawing our great tragedian, Cooper, to share with me in an engagement. . . . I succeeded and from that day the drama assumed a tone which has spread through the whole valley of the Mississippi. From that day I have wielded the tinsel sceptre and commanded to the South and West, every distinguished member of the profession who has sought these shores. . . .[11]

THE SEASON OF 1821-1822

Early in November of 1821 a company of comedians arrived in the city. The notice in the *Louisiana Gazette* of the 6th stated that they had been playing at Pensacola under the management of Mr. Allen and would open the winter campaign the next week in the St. Philip Theatre. It was reported that while the theatre was being altered and repaired, the managers were looking for actresses to fill the places recently left vacant by the deaths of Mrs. Price and Mrs. Vaughan, two of their number.

The next week saw a performance by one member of the little troupe. On Saturday, November 17, Vaughan ascended the rostrum in the "large room" of Mr. Elkin's Hotel in Chartres Street and delivered a "Serious, Moral, and Sarcastic Lecture— in three parts. Written to Dilate and Ridicule the Vices, Follies, Manners and Customs of the Mincing World; Interspersed with Serious and Comic Songs." The following Tuesday the *Louisiana Gazette* announced that Vaughan, Biglow, and Allen, "managers of the New Orleans Theatre, St. Philip Street," would open their doors in the course of the ensuing week. They promised tragedy, comedy, opera, melodrama, farce, pantomime, and the ballet by a company "in point of numbers capable of performing any piece and they trust, in point of talent, adequate to the attempt."

Apparently the prospective managers had not made definite arrangements with Coquet, the owner of the St. Philip, for the day after their announcement his card in the *Louisiana Gazette* informed the public that the St. Philip stage was being altered into a circus and "it was not contemplated or even possible to give scenic representations there for a month or six weeks to come." On the 24th Victor Pepin took over the theatre for his

---

[11] Rees, *op. cit.*, 53.

equestrian and gymnastic exercises. He did not remain there long, however, and in February after he moved into new quarters, the stage was again used for dramatic performances.

According to Paxton's *Directory of New Orleans,* published in 1822, the theatre was used by both English and French companies during the year. It is not unlikely that Allen's troupe returned to the city in the spring and occupied the theatre at this time. There seems to be evidence for this supposition in the *Louisiana Gazette's* announcement on April 23 that the players of "both American companies" had volunteered their services for a benefit to be held at the St. Philip Theatre on the 24th. The beneficiary was Mrs. De Grush, formerly the wife of Thomas Morgan, who had played here with Ludlow in 1818. It was said that she had come to New Orleans expecting to be engaged by Caldwell and had been disappointed.

AMERICAN THEATRE, ORLEANS STREET, 1821-1822

In attempting to trace the course of Caldwell's third season at the Orleans Street Theatre, we must turn to Ludlow's *Dramatic Life As I Found It* and to James Rees' *Dramatic Authors of America.* The only newspapers available for reference, the *Louisiana Gazette* and *L'Ami des Lois,* carry few theatrical advertisements and critiques.

The personnel of the company, as culled from the newspaper notices, included James H. Caldwell, Vaughan, J. M. Scott, Jackson Gray, Thomas Jefferson, Judah, James Scholes, Ludlow, Russell, Benton, McCafferty, Hughes, and Boyle, Mesdames Anderson and Russell and Misses Eliza Placide and Tilden. Except for the names of West and Mrs. Hughes, which are omitted here, the list coincides with that given by Rees.[12] Ludlow's roster of the company is valueless; it tallies in a few respects with the above, but the majority of those he names did not come to New Orleans until the fall of 1822.

As in the past, the American company shared the theatre with a French troupe and played only on Monday, Wednesday, Friday, and Saturday. The price of admission at the beginning of the season was $1.50, but after several months the old price of a dollar was reestablished. In a letter to the *Louisiana Gazette,* published in the issue of November 19, one who signed himself "Crito" had objected to the new price on the ground that three-

---

12 *Ibid.,* 58.

fourths of the audience would be composed of "that grade in society who have to depend upon their labour for obtaining their bread." He said that the chief support of the theatre came from greasy Kentuckians, Yankee dealers, shoemakers, tailors, carpenters, bricklayers, cabinet makers, hatters, blacksmiths, saddlers, clerks, customhouse officers, captains of vessels, sailors, and daily laborers.

The season at the American Theatre on Orleans Street began on December 10 with *The Honey Moon* and *The Three and the Deuce*. The next night H. M. Milman's tragedy, *Fazio,* introduced Mr. and Mrs. Hughes, the most important of the new recruits. Apparently Mrs. Hughes had been engaged to replace Mrs. Entwistle as leading lady. As Mrs. Young she had been well-known in Albany and New York. In later years she and her husband, a clever actor in heavy parts, were favorites at the Chatham in New York. On the 19th Thomas Hilson made his bow as Tyke in *The School of Reform* and as Somno in *The Sleep Walker.* Ludlow says that the comedian remained for a three weeks' engagement, playing each night to well-filled houses.

Junius Brutus Booth is the next star mentioned by Ludlow and Rees. Ludlow asserts that he made his New Orleans debut on January 11, opening, as was his custom, in *Richard III.* Other plays in which he is said to have appeared were the Younger Colman's *The Iron Chest; A New Way to Pay Old Debts;* and *The Distressed Mother,* a translation of Racine's *Andromache* by Ambrose Philips.

Thomas Cooper began an engagement on February 6 when he appeared as Richard III. According to Ludlow this was followed by *Othello, Virginius,* Shiel's *Damon and Pythias,* first time here, and *Rule a Wife and Have a Wife.* The newspapers refer to a performance of Lee's *Alexander the Great* and of *Zaire,* a translation from Voltaire by H. Hill, given for his benefit on March 27.

Apparently there were several nights in March when Cooper did not perform. A notice in the *Louisiana Gazette* of March 14 tells of a six nights' engagement with Victor Pepin and his horses. During this time Caldwell brought out *Timour the Tartar* and *Lodoiska,* and after Cooper's departure the horses were reengaged for other equestrian dramas.

Little is known of the last two months of the season. The benefits commenced early in March, says Ludlow, and his was about the fourth or fifth. It was on this occasion that he came out dressed in buckskin shirt and leggins, moccasins, and slouched hat, and to a familiar air sang Samuel Woodworth's "The Hunters of Kentucky." Shouts and Indian yells from the flatboatmen in the pit greeted the verses:

> For Jackson he was wide awake, and wasn't scar'd at trifles,
> For well he knew what aim we take with our Kentucky rifles;
> So he led us down to Cypress Swamp, the ground was low
>   and mucky
>
> There stood John Bull in martial pomp; *but here was old
>   Kentucky!* [13]

As the season neared its end, Caldwell began to plan for the establishment of a permanent American theatre in New Orleans.[14] This was not the first time the idea had been advanced. As early as 1819 it had been suggested that a theatre "in the upper part of the city" would draw the English-speaking population.[15] The following year Ludlow's friend, Nathan Morse, and "a number of respectable citizens" purchased land on the corner of Canal and St. Charles Streets, "with the sole object of erecting thereon a spacious and elegant theatre constructed in such a manner as will render it of public utility and an ornament to the city."[16] When the mayor and the city council refused to grant their request for an extension of time for the payment of the lots,[17] the plans for the theatre were abandoned. In the fall of 1821 there was again talk of building a theatre in the American section of the city, the Faubourg St. Mary,[18] but nothing came of it.

The success which attended Caldwell during his first three seasons in New Orleans proved to him that the Americans were eager for their own theatre and could easily support it. At the cost of $18,000 he purchased two lots in the Faubourg St. Mary, on the west side of Camp Street between Gravier and Poydras.[19] There on May 30, 1822, he laid the cornerstone of the "New American Theatre."[20]

---

[13] Quoted in Constance Rourke, *American Humor*, 35.
[14] *Louisiana Gazette*, November 19, 1821.
[15] *Ibid.*, March 19, 1819.
[16] Petition in Vol. III, Book III of the *Conseil de Ville*, Cabildo, New Orleans.
[17] Session of the *Conseil de Ville*, March 20, 1820, Vol. III, Book III, Cabildo, New Orleans.
[18] *Louisiana Gazette*, December 19, 1821.
[19] Notarial Acts of Hughes Lavergne, No. 1163, Court House, New Orleans.
[20] *Louisiana Gazette*, May 31, 1822.

The American company began its last season in the Orleans Theatre on January 4, 1823. Caldwell's lease on the theatre did not expire until June, and for that reason he had made no attempt to complete the "New American Theatre" on Camp Street.

The company was a large one, including among its members Caldwell, Russell, Ludlow, Gray, Benton, McCafferty, Petrie, Taylor, Scholes, Mesdames Russell and Higgins, and the new recruits Mr. and Mrs. Alexander Drake, Mr. and Mrs. Bloxton, William Forrest, Edwin Caldwell, Williams, Garner, Lewis, Hays, Mesdames Baker, Ludlow, and Noke, and the Misses Rosina Seymour (later Mrs. James Rowe) and Jane Placide. Richard Russell was stage manager; James Rowe, treasurer; John Higgins, prompter; and Noke, leader of the orchestra.

The opening bill, *The Road to Ruin* and *The Reapers,* introduced several of the new members. The *Louisiana Gazette* (January 6) in a critique of this presentation reported that William Forrest "sunk under the task" of performing the difficult role of Harry Dornton. This actor, the elder brother of Edwin Forrest and later a well known manager in Philadelphia, was just starting on his career and much unfavorable criticism was directed at his acting throughout this first season in New Orleans. Williams made a more successful début; his Silky "repeatedly exercised the risible faculties of the audience." But of all the personations in the comedy the *Louisiana Gazette's* critic regarded the Sophia of the newcomer, Jane Placide, as the best. He also praised Garner's performance as Belville in *The Reapers,* finding his voice "remarkable for the sweetness of its tones and harmony and albeit none of the strongest . . . infinitely more pleasing to our ears than the loud bawling and straining of other singers."

The second evening presented Mrs. Baker in the role of Miss Hardcastle, assisted by Williams as Tony Lumpkin and Caldwell as Young Marlow. In the afterpiece, *The Poor Soldier,* Mrs. Noke made her bow as Norah to Williams' Darby. The advertisements for this performance do not tell what role was played by Jane Placide, but according to the *Louisiana Gazette* of January 8, her "acting possessed, as usual, all the raciness of connoisseurship."

The first novelty of the season was Frederick Reynolds' *Folly as It Flies,* presented on January 10 with Caldwell, Jane Placide, and Rosina Seymour in the leads. In the *School for*

Scandal on the 11th, Lewis, "from the Western theatres," made
his first appearance as Joseph Surface to the Charles of Caldwell
and the Lady Teazle of Mrs. Baker. There was no afterpiece on
this evening but "at the solicitation of several families" Dr.
Preston exhibited nitrous oxide or exhilarating gas.

The operatic *John of Paris* was given on the 14th with
Garner in the name part, Miss Seymour as Rosa, and Jane
Placide as the Princess of Navarre. It has been said that of all
the players who came to New Orleans, whether as members of
the resident company or as stars, none was more popular than
Jane Placide. Knowing of her importance in the theatrical history of the city, one reads with especial interest the comments
which were printed in the *Louisiana Gazette* on January 17.

> Miss Placide . . . did not seem quite at home in mimick-
> ing the walk and gesture of royalty—the rolling motion
> which sets off a chambermaid does not become a queen. Miss
> Placide, we hope, will pardon these hints—they cannot affect
> the estimation which real merit has secured to her in the
> walks of the drama. With an eye full of meaning and a
> whole countenance equally expressive, Miss Placide may soar
> above opera singing. By a little care to study the proper
> attitudes and diligent study of the tragic muse, she would
> probably in Lady Macbeth, Cordelia, Jane Shore, and other
> similar parts, give as much satisfaction as she now does in
> light comedy.

Two novelties were offered on the 18th, M. M. Noah's
Wandering Boys and William Diamond's *The Lady and the Devil*.
Miss Seymour and Jane Placide made a hit in their portrayals
of the boys, Justin and Paul, and the piece became the most
popular of the season, attaining some five performances. Second
in favor was C. E. Walker's melodrama, *The Warlock of the Glen*,
presented first on the 20th and repeated on the 24th after a performance of *Hamlet*. With the last night of the month came another novelty, John O'Keeffe's comic opera, *The Agreeable
Surprise*.

The first week in February brought Arthur Murphy's comedy,
Know Your Own Mind, and Isaac Bickerstaff's *Lionel and
Clarissa*, an opera "now performing in northern theatres with
unbounded applause." On the 8th Mr. and Mrs. Russell made
their first appearance of the season, he as Timothy Quaint to her
Widow Cheerly in *The Soldier's Daughter*, and as Crack to her

Peggy in *The Turnpike Gate*. Two nights later Isaac Pocock's musical drama *Rob Roy Macgregor* was introduced with Caldwell in the title role and Jane Placide as Diana Vernon.

The company was now strengthened by the arrival of Mr. and Mrs. Alexander Drake, "from the Western Theatres." She made her début on the 12th as Portia to Caldwell's Shylock and as Lucy Racket to his Sir Charles in the farce, *Three Weeks after Marriage*. Drake appeared on the 14th as L'Eclair in *The Foundling of the Forest* and as Sharp in *The Lying Valet*. Mrs. Drake now played Mrs. Beverly in *The Gamester* and on her third appearance replaced Mrs. Baker as Helen M'Gregor in *Rob Roy*, her husband on the latter occasion following as Lingo in *The Agreeable Surprise*.

It was traditional with the American companies in New Orleans to offer special bills on national holidays, and on Washington's Birthday the management brought out Thomas Morton's *Columbus* and Isaac Pocock's *For Freedom Ho!*, a melodramatic opera which had been introduced at Caldwell's benefit earlier in the month.

As February drew to a close, Caldwell announced the engagement of Master C. F. Smith and his sister. The youthful star opened on the 26th as Frederick in *Lovers' Vows* and followed it with Romeo, Octavian *(The Mountaineers)*, Captain Flash *(Miss in Her Teens)*, Richard III, Selim *(Barbarossa)*, Young Norval, Darby *(The Poor Soldier)*, and *Hamlet*, this last for his benefit on March 12. Miss Smith made her bow as Juliet, thereafter playing opposite her brother in *The Mountaineers* and *Barbarossa*. On her night, the two enacted Rolla and Cora in *Pizarro*.

Caldwell planned a special bill for March 17, offering, "in compliment to the day so fondly cherished by a sister country," Mrs. Lanfau's comedy, *The Sons of Erin*, and Richard Sheridan's *St. Patrick Day*. John Dwyer, the light comedian, came on the 19th in *Laugh When You Can*. The announcement of the comedy stated that he was to perform only one night, his engagement having been "unavoidably though mutually curtailed." Apparently this was done that Thomas Cooper might begin his twelve night engagement on the 21st. The tragedian went through a familiar repertoire with the exception of *King John* on April 4 and *The*

Fair Penitent on the 11th. He had excellent support in Mrs. Drake, Jane Placide, and Mrs. Rowe (formerly Miss Rosina Seymour).

Cooper left for Natchez after his appearance at Caldwell's benefit on April 14 and with him went Mrs. Drake, Ludlow, and others of the New Orleans troupe under the direction of W. H. Benton. Both Ludlow and James Rees tell of this Natchez visit in their histories, but neither gives a complete account of the company. According to these authorities a large hotel room was the only convenient place that could be obtained; and here Caldwell sent the stars after they completed their New Orleans engagements.[21]

Dwyer returned on April 12 as Belcour in *The West Indian;* he was seen on the 23rd as Charles Surface and for the last time on the 30th as Young Rapid in *A Cure for the Heartache.* On the latter occasion John Dalton, "Principal Comedian of the Charleston, Savannah and Augusta Theatres," assisted as Frank Oatland and was featured in Mrs. Inchbald's *Ruse contre Ruse* which served as the afterpiece.

A more important visitor than either of these comedians was Thomas Phillips, the singing actor. On his opening night, April 14, he and Jane Placide were Count Belino and Rosalina in *The Devil's Bridge.* This was repeated on the 16th, and on the 18th, he introduced *Fontainbleau,* a comic opera by John O'Keeffe. As bad weather had kept many from attending the theatre during the first nights of his visit, he was reengaged for two more performances, appearing in *The Barber of Seville* and in Tom Moore's *M. P., or The Blue Stocking.*

The benefits this season began on May 2 with Master Smith's presentation of Thomson's tragedy, *Tancred and Sigismundi,* and *The Three and the Deuce.* Between the pieces the beneficiary recited Southey's poem, "Mary, the Maid of the Inn," and delivered a farewell address, written by himself. Of the other benefits only Drake's need be mentioned. On his night the comedian played Pizarro to the Rolla of William Pelby, "from the Philadelphia, Boston and New York Theatres," and the Elvira of Jane Placide. With Gray's benefit on May 9, Caldwell ended his stay in the Orleans Theatre. Henceforth this establishment was to be occupied only by French companies.

---

[21] Ludlow, *op. cit.,* 245; Rees, *op. cit.,* 59.

The New American Theatre on Camp Street was still unfinished when Caldwell opened it on May 14 with a performance
of *The Dramatist* and *The Romp*. He explained to the public in
the *Louisiana Gazette* (May 12) that he did this "in order to
avoid those defects which have been found to exist in many
theatres where the precaution has not been taken of ascertaining
how far the construction of the building was sufficient for a complete opportunity of seeing and hearing in every part of the house
devoted to the audience."

Caldwell offered excellent entertainment during these last
two weeks of the season. Such standard plays as *The Honey
Moon, The Mountaineers, The Wheel of Fortune,* and *A Bold
Stroke for a Wife*, were followed by popular farces featuring
Drake and Russell. Dalton made his second appearance on the
24th as Crack in *The Turnpike Gate*. On several nights, between
the play and the afterpiece, there was exhibited "an experiment
of the manner of lighting the theatre with gas." A benefit for
Master Smith ended the season on May 28. The program included
Lovers' Vows, Miss Smith as Amelia, and *No Song, No Supper*
with Garner as Frederick and Jane Placide as Margaretta.

In previous years Caldwell had taken the company to Virginia for the summer campaign. This year at the conclusion of
the Natchez season the New Orleans and Natchez troupes were
reorganized as one company and proceeded to Nashville under
the direction of Richard Russell.[22]

CHAPTER IV

The First Permanent English Theatre   1824-1833

The American Theatre on Camp Street, advertised' for a
short time as the New American, was formally opened on January
1, 1824. It was a building sixty by one hundred and sixty feet
with a seating capacity of 1,000 and had been erected at a cost of
$70,000. Joe Cowell described it as "one of the prettiest of the-
atres" and noted that it was better adapted to the peculiar climate
of New Orleans than any he had ever seen.[1] The only extant
picture of the theatre shows a substantial brick building, three

---

[22] Ludlow, *op. cit.,* 249.
[1] *Thirty Years Passed among the Players in England and America*, Part II, p. 95.

stories high, with a facade in the Doric order, a flight of marble steps extending across it. This was intersected by four marble piers upon each of which was a cast iron tripod supporting a brilliantly illuminated lamp.

The newspapers carried no descriptions of the building or of the interior decorations. There is only the statement in the *Louisiana Gazette* of January 3: "The audience part is neatly fitted up and when entirely oramented will, we think, be inferior to none in the U. S. The Chandelier is of very elegant construction and was splendidly illuminated with Gas—as were the footlights of the Stage."

Caldwell announced that the distribution of the house and the price of admission had been made "in compliance with the wishes of every part of the community." Boxes and parquet were a dollar; pit, seventy-five cents; and gallery, fifty cents. The left side of the third tier was "appropriated exclusively to the colored population" with boxes a dollar and other seats, twenty-five cents. Performances took place regularly on Monday, Wednesday, Friday, and Saturday, and sometimes on Thursday. During four weeks of the season they were scheduled for every night except Sunday. The doors opened at six; the curtain rose at seven.

The staff of the theatre consisted of Caldwell, manager; Richard Russell, prompter; John Varden, stage machinist; Symons, engineer of the Gas Department; and Antonio Mondelli, scene painter. In the resident company were Russell, Ludlow, William Forrest, Edwin Caldwell, Gary, Garner, McCafferty, Scholes, Mesdames Baker, Rowe, Russell, Higgins, Ludlow, Noke, and Bloxton, and Miss Jane Placide. New members were Joseph Page, Moses Scott, John Dalton, George Frethy, Samuel P. Jones, Edwin Forrest, and Mrs. Mongin.

The entertainment of the first evening, January 1, 1824, commenced with Caldwell's recitation of the prize poem written by Thomas Wells of Boston. The most interesting of its lines are the concluding ones which prophesy the future of the American drama.

On rapid wings still speeds the auspicious time,
When Bards our own the Olympic Mount shall climb;
When round their consecrated shrines shall throng
Our buskined Heroes, and *our* sons of *Song;*
In Attic pride *our* Drama then shall rise,
And nobly daring, claim the Thespian prize:
To classic height exalt the rising age,
And give, to peerless, lasting fame, the Stage.[2]

This was followed by the popular *Town and Country* and *Of Age Tomorrow.* The parts of Goody Hawbuck and Ross in the comedy were enacted by the new recruits, Mrs. Mongin and Scott. John Dalton made his bow, on the 3rd, as Tyke in *The School of Reform* and as Crack in *The Turnpike Gate.*

The first novelty of this season was Noah's *Marion, or The Hero of Lake George,* presented on January 8. Two days later came the première of Moncrieff's farce, *Monsieur Tonson,* and on the 12th, Holcroft's comedy, *The Deserted Daughter,* and O'Keeffe's *Sprigs of Laurel.* On this evening Joseph Page, a singing actor, "from the Charleston and Richmond Theatres," made his first appearance, playing Douglas in the comedy and Nipperkin in the farce.

William Pelby, the American tragedian, began an engagement on January 16 as Macbeth to the Lady Macbeth of Mrs. Baker. He enacted Virginius on the following night, and then appeared successively as Hamlet, Marc Antony, Damon, Petruchio, Brutus (in Payne's play of that name), and Rolla *(Pizarro).* In all of these except Petruchio he was supported by Jane Placide, who seems to have been promoted to the position of leading lady this season. On the 30th she and Caldwell personated Abaellino and Rosamonda in Dunlap's melodrama, *Abaellino,* and in *Guy Mannering* the next evening she was Meg Merriles, Mrs. Rowe making her first appearance of the season as Julia.

A new member of the company made his début on February 4, choosing Jaffier in *Venice Preserved* for his initial appearance. In the notices of this first performance he was listed as "E. Forrest, from the Ohio and Kentucky Theatres." Five years later he was to return to New Orleans heralded as "the greatest American tragedian." On his second appearance Edwin Forrest enacted

---

[2] Rees, *op. cit.,* 61.

Dorlin in the local première of John Howard Payne's *Adeline,* and
on his third he was Raymond in J. Stokes' *Forest of Rosenwald,*
another novelty.

Pelby returned on the 12th as Charles de Moore in *The
Robbers,* Edwin Forrest playing Francis de Moore, and Mrs.
Rowe, Amelia. The star next appeared as Bertrand in *The Foundling of the Forest,* and at Caldwell's benefit, on the 14th, he
played the name part in James Haynes' new tragedy, *Durazzo.*
It was announced that Pelby was detained in town by "an unavoidable accident" which had damaged the vessel on which he
was sailing for Charleston, and on the 24th he began a second
engagement. The benefit which concluded his stay on February
26 introduced *Riches, or Wife and Brother,* an adaptation of
Massinger's *City Madame* by Sir James Bland Burges.

Other novelties of this month were John Poole's popular
farce, *Simpson and Company;* George Soane's melodrama, *The
Falls of Clyde,* Edwin Forrest in the role of Edward Enfield; and
Charles Lamb's *Mr. H.*

March came in with the revival of *The West Indian* and
Douglas Jerrold's new burlesque, *Dolly and the Rat.* William
Dimond's melodramatic spectacle, *The Aethiop,* was brought out
on the 5th, with Caldwell in the title role and Edwin Forrest as
Almanzo. Alexander Wilson, "from the Western theatres," made
his bow the next evening in *Bertram* as Bertram to Jane Placide's
Imogine and as Monsieur Morbleu *(Monsieur Tonson).* During
his engagement Wilson appeared in *The Iron Chest, The Turn
Out, Alexander the Great, Who Wants a Guinea?,* and *Othello.*

On nights when Wilson was not performing, Caldwell sought
to attract the public with new plays. He brought out Isaac Pocock's musical farce, *Hit or Miss,* on the 12th; on St. Patrick's
Day the bill ended with O'Keeffe's *Love in a Camp,* a sequel to
The Poor Soldier. The offering on the 19th was *Richard III,*
"altered and amended from Colly Cibber's edition, and original
text generally restored by J. H. Caldwell." In this production
the manager's Richard had the support of Ludlow's Richmond,
Mrs. Baker's Queen, and Mrs. Russell's Lady Ann.

Mr. Symons, the engineer of the Gas Department, was given
a benefit on March 29; having completed the apparatus and carried the Gas Department "into full effect," he was now about

to depart for the North. Alexander Wilson volunteered his services, appearing as Cornet Ollapod in *The Poor Gentleman,* Caldwell being Frederick Bramble, Jane Placide, Emily Worthington, and Edwin Forrest, Sir Charles Cropland. After the play while Mrs. Noke sang "Auld Robin Gray," Symons exhibited the "novel spectacle" of a flower garden made of gas; and as a concluding feature he took the part of Mr. Belville, "for this night only," in the opera, *Rosina.* It is to be hoped that the people of New Orleans gave Mr. Symons a "bumper." The theatre was the first building in New Orleans to be lighted by gas, and the success of its lamps and those with which Caldwell lighted one side of Camp Street from the theatre to Canal Street was to result in the adoption of gas by the city several years later.[3]

April was ushered in with Joseph Addison's *Cato,* a tragedy which was not repeated. A more successful novelty was Isaac Pocock's melodrama, *Zembuca, or The Net maker and His Wife.* It ran from the 7th until the 15th when Mrs. Baker was given a farewell benefit. Her Angela in *The Castle Spectre* was supported by the Earl Osmond of Edwin Forrest and the Evelina of Mrs. Rowe.

The dancers, Monsieur and Madame Rousset and Mademoiselle Sophie, began an engagement on the 17th in the new ballet, "La Fille Malgardé." The cast included all the members of the dramatic corps, even Jane Placide who had appeared earlier in the evening as the heroine in *The Stranger.* On the 21st the dancers introduced the ballet "Annette and Lubin" and in *Zembuca.* on the 26th, Rousset and Mademoiselle Sophie executed a grand *pas de deux.*

The company benefits commenced with that of James Rowe on May 3. This had been advertised for April 30 but in consequence of the inclement weather had been postponed, "although contrary to the general rule." He offered *The Belle's Stratagem* with Mrs. Rowe as Letitia Hardy, a song by the six year old Miss Mongin, and the ballet, "Little Red Riding Hood," in which Jane Placide (Lubin) and Mrs. Rowe (Little Red Riding Hood) danced a *pas de deux.* On her night, Jane Placide presented Frederick Reynold's comedy, *The Will,* and revived Holcroft's *Tale of Mystery.* The beneficiary's impersonation of Albina Mandeville was enthusiastically commented upon in the *Louisiana Gazette* of May

[3] *Louisiana Gazette,* January 24, 1824.

7: "She promises in her profession on this side of the Atlantic what Mrs. Jordan (who first played the part) was on the other. She . . . wore the breeches with such effect that Mahomet himself, if a spectator, would have been deceived in her sex and given her a chance for a place in the Third Heaven."

Before the next benefit Caldwell brought out Moncrieff's burletta, *Life in London,* an adaptation of Pierce Egan's work which was to figure in the repertoire for many seasons. Ludlow introduced C. E. Walker's melodrama, *Wallace, or The Hero of Scotland,* on his night and between the play and the afterpiece sang "The Hunters of Kentucky." On this occasion Miss Mongin delivered an address written for her "by a gentleman of the city." The little actress had appeared only in roles suitable to one of her age, but in these she had shown a talent which the public felt was worthy of encouragement. At the benefit which Caldwell allowed her on the 15th, she sang "The Hunters of Kentucky," in character, and played Tom Thumb in Kane O'Hara's adaptation of the Fielding burlesque.

Edwin Forrest's benefit presented O'Keeffe's *Wild Oats,* Forrest himself appearing as Ephraim Smooth, Caldwell as Rover, and Jane Placide as Lady Amaranthe. The beneficiary also delivered an address written for the occasion by his fellow actor, Sam Jones, and Caldwell recited Sterne's story of "Le Fevre." On May 22 Mr. and Mrs. Noke offered *Richard III* with Edwin Forrest in the title role and Jane Placide as the Queen, a choice which suggests that the beneficiaries may have regarded young Forrest as a better tragedian than Caldwell, who had played the part earlier in the season. The joint benefit of Mr. and Mrs. Higgins on the 24th brought, among other entertainment, the local première of C. E. Grice's *Battle of New Orleans.* The 28th was announced as "Ticket Night" for the benefit of carpenters, callmen, billposters, captain of the supernumeraries, doorkeepers, and engineer of the gas department. On June 1, Mondelli, the scene painter, took his benefit, presenting *The Solitary of Mount Savage,* a melodrama translated from the French "by a gentleman of this place."[4] Again Miss Mongin offered a song and recitation between the plays and appeared as Helen in the afterpiece, *The Hunter of the Alps.*

---

[4] *Ibid.,* June 1, 1824.

A performance for the benefit of the Orphan Boys' Asylum brought the season to a close on June 8, and almost immediately Caldwell and most of the company left for Virginia. The others under Ludlow formed a commonwealth company to tour the South.[5]

AMERICAN THEATRE, 1825

The records for the second season of the American Theatre are few. Apparently Caldwell advertised in a newspaper which is no longer extant and though it has been possible to determine the personnel of the company from the scattered notices in the *Louisiana Gazette,* few of their presentations are known. Some information regarding the season is to be found in James Rees' *Dramatic Authors of America* and in William Alger's *Life of Edwin Forrest,*[6] yet without corroborative evidence this cannot be accepted as authoritative.

The theatre opened on January 3, 1825, with *The Soldier's Daughter* and *No Song, No Supper.* Caldwell played Frank Heartall in the comedy, and according to Alger, Forrest was Malfort Junior. A communication in the *Louisiana Gazette* the next day, our source of information for the performance, does not mention the cast except to express disappointment that Jackson Gray had not enacted the role of the Old Governor. Doubtless this part had been taken by one of the many new recruits, the most important of which were Alexander Wilson, the tragic star of last season, Mrs. Battersby, formerly of the Park, and Mr. and Mrs. John Greene. Other new members were Mr. and Mrs. Carter, Mr. and Mrs. Parker, John Moore, Lemuel Smith, Kelsey, Murray, and Barnett. Among those who returned were Caldwell, Mr. and Mrs. Russell, Miss Russell, Wm. McCafferty, Garner, Page, Gray, Moses Scott, Edwin and William Forrest, Mesdames Rowe, Higgins, and Bloxton, and Jane Placide.

Moncrieff's *Life in London* seems to have been the most popular presentation of the first month. The *Louisiana Gazette* contains notices of successive performances from January 16 through the 21st, Alexander Wilson playing Tom, Caldwell, Logic, and Russell, Jerry. William Alger records that Edwin Forrest took the part of the Master of Ceremonies. The newspaper notices list Forrest for the role, but it is impossible to say whether William or Edwin actually played it. Alger relates also

---

[5] *Ibid.,* January 1, 1825.
[6] I, 134-137.

that during this month Edwin played Adrian in *Adrian and Orilla*, Joseph Surface in *The School for Scandal*, and appeared in *The Falls of Clyde* and *The Aethiop*.

The next recorded performance is that of March 2 when William Conway, the English tragedian, began an engagement as Othello, Caldwell enacting Iago, Mrs. Rowe, Desdemona, and Mrs. Battersby, Emilia. The *Louisiana Gazette* of the 3rd notes that these parts were supported with much animation. "Since we have been in Orleans," concluded this writer, "we have not seen the piece so well sustained." During his stay of eight nights, the visiting tragedian appeared as Lord Townly in *The Provoked Husband*, Virginius (twice), Castali in the local première of Otway's *Orphan*, and for his benefit on the 14th as Heymey in *The Apostate*. Alger says that Edwin Forrest enacted Malcolm in the star's production of *Macbeth*, but of this performance we have no record.

Lafayette arrived in the city on April 9 and in honor of his visit to the theatre on the 11th there was presented, "for the second time in New Orleans," Samuel Woodworth's historical play, *Lafayette, or The Castle of Olmutz*. Caldwell recited an address written for the occasion and the farce *The Three and the Deuce* concluded the entertainment.

The benefits began sometime in April. At Wilson's benefit on the 18th, there was offered "for the first time the new American Drama written by an American Gentleman called *Percy, or The Hero of the North*." On the 23rd Russell presented *A Cure for the Heartache* and *The Spoiled Child* with Mary Ann Russell as Little Pickle. This young actress had made her stage début in New York the previous July. In Moncrieff's *Cataract of the Ganges* on the 30th she personated a Bayadère dancer. This novelty was brought out in great splendor with magnificent costumes and "a real stream of falling water; the first thing of this kind ever produced in New Orleans." According to Alger, Edwin Forrest's benefit took place early in May, when, after having been underlined for Lear, he appeared in *The Mountaineers* as Octavian.

The last notice to be found in the *Louisiana Gazette* is one on May 16, advertising for that evening Edward Fitzball's *Peveril of the Peak*. James Rees says that the season ended on May 28,[7] and Alger gives the additional information that on this occasion Edwin Forrest played Carwin in John Howard Payne's new drama, *Thérèse*.

---

[7] Rees, *op. cit.*, 64.

AMERICAN THEATRE, 1826

The American Theatre opened on January 24, 1826, several weeks later than Caldwell had originally planned. He had taken the company to Nashville for the fall season intending to return to New Orleans early in January; however, when the time came for the departure, the Cumberland River had become unnavigable and he was forced to take a longer route.[8] The company did not arrive in New Orleans until the 20th, and then the "impossibility of completing the new gas apparatus" caused another postponement of the opening.

The plays of the first night, *The Honey Moon* and *The Three and the Deuce,* reintroduced many of last season's company: Caldwell, Kelsey, Russell, Gray, Moses Scott, Moore, Higgins, Murray, Mesdames Russell, Rowe, Higgins, and Jane Placide. The recruits who made their bows on this evening were W. C. Drummond, "from the New York and Charleston Theatres," William Duffy, "from the Canada Theatres," De Grove, Lucas, Lowry, and Thomas Placide. This last actor, a brother of the famous Henry Placide and of Eliza and Jane, left soon after the beginning of the season. Before his departure he appeared as Campillo in *The Honey Moon,* Furst in *William Tell,* the second carrier in *Henry IV,* and a sailor in *Don Juan.* Ludlow records that Placide, having failed to secure an engagement with Caldwell, came to Mobile early in 1826 and was given a place in his company.[9]

Later bills of this season list Alexander Wilson, William Forrest, Parker, McCafferty, Mesdames Bloxton and Parker, and Miss Russell. Among the missing were Mr. and Mrs. Green, Edwin Forrest, Garner, Page, and Mrs. Battersby. Forrest had left the company at the conclusion of the previous season; Ludlow and Alger say that he had quarreled with Manager Caldwell.

The second night brought a novelty, Sheridan Knowles' *William Tell* with Caldwell in the name part, Mrs. Russell as Emma and Miss Russell as Albert. William Drummond appeared as Michael and as Caleb Quotem in the afterpiece, *The Review.* This actor who had been engaged to fill Edwin Forrest's place soon became a favorite. He was the Prince of Wales to Caldwell's Hotspur and Gray's Falstaff in *Henry IV,* on the 26th, following

[8] *Louisiana Advertiser,* January 10, 1826.
[9] Ludlow, *op. cit.,* 269.

it on the 27th with Bronzely in *Wives as They Were and Maids as They Are,* Corinthian Tom in *Tom and Jerry,* and Mr. Dearlove in Moncrieff's farce *The Secret.* A second important novelty was Shakespeare's *Merry Wives of Windsor,* presented on the 30th. Apparently Gray's portrayal of Falstaff had met with success.

Caldwell turned to melodrama the second week, bringing out *Zembuca, The Falls of Clyde,* and *Rob Roy.* A new recruit, Joseph Still, made his debut in the Scott adaptation as Osbaldistone. In *Matrimony,* the afterpiece of the evening, he was Delaval, Mrs. Russell playing opposite him as Clara. On February 6 they were paired as Belville and Rosina in the opera *Rosina,* and in *Guy Mannering* they were Henry and Lucy Bertram. Still was the principal singer this season and appeared regularly in the so-called operas and musical afterpieces. The *Louisiana Advertiser* of February 6 described him as possessing a sweet voice, good taste, and as being a better actor than was generally seen in the department of opera.

Alexander Wilson made his first appearance on the 13th as Octavian in *The Mountaineers,* the afterpiece being *The Forest of Rosenwald* with Drummond as Raymond and Mrs. Rowe as Agnes. In *The Aethiop* the next night Caldwell and Jane Placide took the leads. *Venice Preserved* on the 15th presented Caldwell as Jaffier to Wilson's Pierre and Jane Placide's Belvidera. A communication appearing in the *Louisiana Advertiser* of February 19 is a welcome one, for in previous seasons though criticism had often been directed at Caldwell's tragic impersonations, no definite faults were pointed out. Now we learn that Caldwell's impatience got the better of him in some scenes of *Venice Preserved.* "In fact," continued the writer, "the only things that Mr. Caldwell wants is a little more calmness and deliberation to render him a good tragedian."

The most popular comedy of the season was Bickerstaff's *Hypocrite,* introduced on February 17. In the *Louisiana Advertiser* of the 21st this was described as the most successful comedy since the opening of the theatre in 1824. A new historical play, H. J. Finn's *Montgomery, or The Falls of Montmorency,* was given on the 22nd and in the interval before the farce a transparency was exhibited. The performance of *Thérèse* on the 27th should not be overlooked, for the title role long remained one of Jane Placide's favorites.

Dr. Brown's celebrated tragedy, *Barbarossa,* was revived on March 6 that a "young gentleman of this city" might make his stage début as Selim. A month later the young gentleman enacted George Barnwell. It is likely that this amateur was the Mr. Watson who assisted at Wilson's benefit on May 5 and who, "although not upon the boards of the Camp Street Theatre," was given a benefit on the 24th. Stated a card in the *Louisiana Advertiser* on the latter occasion: "All his hopes (Watson's) of public favor arise from the generous sympathy that the considerate and enlightened lovers of the drama ever evince in behalf of a young performer commencing his theatrical career."

On March 8, Mrs. Johns, "from the Canada Theatre," made her first appearance as Angela in *The Castle Spectre* and as Little Pickle. The newcomer seems to have been engaged as "second comedy"; later she appeared as Lady Contest in *The Wedding,* Lady Elizabeth Freelove in *The Day after the Wedding,* Annelli in *William Tell,* Roxalana in *The Sultan,* and the first niece in *The Critic.*

The week of March 13 brought several novelties: Thomas Greenwood's skit, *Death of Life in London, or Tom and Jerry's Funeral;* Thomas Parry's farce, *Helpless Animals;* and the opera *Der Freischutz,* "with all the original music composed by the Chevalier Carl Maria von Weber." Earlier in the season an improvement in the musical department of the theatre had been noted, and now, on the day of the opera, a puff in the *Louisiana Advertiser* stated that never before had the orchestra been so well supplied or so replete with musical talent. In view of this it is interesting to read the comment of an English traveller who visited the theatre at this time.

> The late Carl von Weber would not have been delighted at witnessing the performance of his *Der Freischutz,* here metamorphosed into *The Wild Horseman of Bohemia.* Six violins which played anything but music and some voices far from being human performed the opera which was applauded; the Kentuckians expressed their satisfaction in a hurrah, which made the very walls tremble.[10]

Meanwhile Mathis, a Parisian Posture Master from the London Olympic Theatre, had begun a six-night engagement. He entertained with "grand lion leaps," posturing, bending, pitching, tumbling, flip flops, herculean feats, and tightrope

---

[10] Karl Post, *The Americans as They Are,* 184.

dancing. At his benefit, April 19, the bill concluded with a comic dance on stilts performed by the beneficiary and "a person belonging to the theatre." Mathis was the only visiting performer this season as Thomas Cooper and Robert Maywood, the English tragedian, failed to keep their engagements.[11]

Repetitions of *Der Freischutz, Sweethearts and Wives, La Perouse,* and *Don Juan* graced the bills of early April. On the 6th the afterpiece was a novelty, Poole's *Frederick the Great, or The Two Pages.* The next evening brought *The Talisman* by a "gentleman of this city"; this was repeated on the 10th, attracting, it was said, "a numerous and brilliant audience." A less important novelty was Pocock's *Robinson Crusoe,* given on the 8th.

Caldwell had a benefit on the 14th when he presented acts from five Shakespearian plays, Jane Placide supporting him in each. The popular musical farce, *The Children in the Wood,* concluded the bill. Managerial duties seem to have pressed heavily upon Caldwell this season causing him to appear less frequently than before. In a revival of *The Falls of Clyde* on April 17, Duffy replaced him as Malcolm. Earlier in the month the same actor had played Icillius *(Virginius)*, another of Caldwell's roles. The opening piece on the 17th was *Charles II* by John Howard Payne and Washington Irving, a comedy destined to figure in the repertoire for many seasons.

The most splendid of this season's novelties was the spectacular *Cherry and Fair Star, or The Child of Cyprus,* brought out on April 24 at a cost of $3,000. The scenery and machinery, on which Mondelli, McCafferty, and Varden were said to have spent three months, included a fairy grotto and views of the sea and the port of Cyprus. For this last the stage was entirely covered with water and down it sailed a splendid Grecian galley. The spectacle was enthusiastically received; it had a run of six nights and was brought back later for three more performances.

Comedies were a feature of the last month of this season. On May 2 Samuel Jones made his first appearance in two years as Governor Heartall *(The Soldier's Daughter)*. Russell initiated the benefits the next night with Thomas Morton's *A Cure for the Heartache,* "a gentleman" volunteering as Old Rapid, and Caldwell and Jane Placide assisting as Young Rapid and Miss Vortex.

---

[11] *Louisiana Advertiser,* January 21, 1826.

In *The Poor Soldier,* which served as the afterpiece on this evening, Miss Russell appeared as Darby. Jane Placide's benefit on the 10th offered *The Will* and *The Magpie and the Maid,* and between the pieces she sang, by particular request, "Home Sweet Home." "It is not too much to say," wrote a critic in the *Louisiana Advertiser,* "that she ranks with the first of the female performers in our country. She has appeared before us in every possible character and has always acquitted herself with applause." On Mrs. Russell's night her youthful daughter essayed Dr. Pangloss in *The Heir at Law,* and Ralph in the farce, *The Lock and Key,* was performed by the amateur who had enacted Old Rapid at Russell's benefit. In the afterpiece, *The Warlock of the Glen,* on May 13, A. J. Marks made his first New Orleans appearance as Andrew. Three nights later he personated Bailey Nicoll Jarvie *(Rob Roy),* one of Russell's old roles.

Only two of the other benefits need be mentioned. Mrs. Rowe's introduced Samuel Beazley's long popular opera, *Is He Jealous?,* and on her night Miss Russell appeared as Crack in *The Turnpike Gate.* On May 29 the season was brought to a close with *The Vampire,* erroneously announced as "the first time in New Orleans," and *Cherry and Fair Star.*

Caldwell had furnished good dramatic entertainment this season and with the exception of a few weeks, the theatre had been open every night but Sunday. Yet the *Louisiana Advertiser* of the 29th reported that he had lost $6,000 through "the effect of the present adverse times and the various accidents to which theatrical seasons are subject."

By 1826 Caldwell had given up his interests in the Virginia theatres and at the conclusion of this season he took the company to Huntsville, Alabama, to perform in a small theatre, which had recently been built there.[12] After five weeks the troupe proceeded to Nashville where they played in the old Cherry Street Theatre until they could occupy the new house which was being built for Caldwell.[13]

AMERICAN THEATRE, 1827

Caldwell promised to return to New Orleans early in 1827 and with this in mind he brought the Nashville season to a close on December 23, 1826.[14] Immediate departure was impossible,

[12] Rees, *op. cit.,* 64.
[13] *Ibid.,* 66.
[14] *Ibid.*

however, as the Cumberland River was again unnavigable. To the friends who were impatiently awaiting his arrival, he wrote on January 1:

> The ice is running down the river in acre-flakes—such a winter has never been known. I have made twenty attempts to get down, but in every one have been defeated—tomorrow morning we get into a keel to join the steamboat General Coffee and shall Heaven willing be in New Orleans by the 15th.[15]

Those who made the trip with Caldwell were Mr. and Mrs. Russell, Mr. and Mrs. Higgins, Gray, Kelsey, Duffy, Still, McCafferty, Moore, Lowry, Murray, Sam Jones, Mesdames Rowe, Bloxton, and Johns, and the new recruits Emberton, Mulhollon, Lear, Sandford, and Palmer. The company had lost Alexander Wilson, William Forrest, and W. C. Drummond but otherwise was little changed from that of last year. Later in the season Mr. and Mrs. Jackson, Mrs. Tatnall, Miss Carpenter, and Hartwig joined the forces.

The theatre opened on February 2, 1827, with Charles Dibdin's new comedy, *Paul Pry*, followed by *Of Age To-morrow* and *The Spoiled Child*. The first piece was an immediate success; Russell's personation of Paul Pry and later that of George Holland were to hold the stage for many years. On the second night *The Foundling of the Forest* introduced Lear, "from the Canada Theatre," as Bertram to the DeValmont of Caldwell, the Unknown Female of Jane Placide, and the Geraldine of Mrs. Rowe. The musical afterpiece, *Lock and Key*, featured Still as Captain Cheerly.

The first star to arrive was Lydia Kelly, a comédienne from the Theatre Royal, Drury Lane, and, for the past two seasons, the reigning favorite in New York. Se began her engagement on the 7th as Letitia Hardy in *The Belle's Stratagem*, followed it on the 9th with Beatrice in *Much Ado about Nothing* and Rosina in *Rosina*, and on her third appearance offered Donna Violante in *The Wonder! A Woman Keeps a Secret* and Caroline in *The Prize*. Thereafter, she was seen as the heroine in *The School for Scandal, Turn Out, As You Like It, The Honey Moon* (Juliana), *Of Age To-morrow, Wives as They Were, The Day after the Wedding,* and *The Jealous Wife.* Her benefit bill on March 12 presented her in *The Will* and *No Song, No Supper.*

---

[15] *Louisiana Advertiser*, February 1, 1827.

Miss Kelly performed only four times a week; on the other nights the manager revived such favorites as *The Aethiop, The Exile of Siberia, The Gamester,* and *Thérèse.* Caldwell appeared almost every night during this first month, playing the comedy leads opposite Miss Kelly and performing with Jane Placide in the melodramas.

On March 5 Miss Kelly reappeared as Bertha in *Des Freischutz* and as Mrs. Simpson in *Simpson and Co.* She also offered *The Soldier's Daughter* (Widow Cheerly), *No Song, No Supper,* and *Know Your Own Mind.* With the performance of March 10 the records of this second engagement end; the next available reference is to a bill of March 17, by which date Miss Kelly had departed.

Meanwhile, Mrs. Tatnall "from the northern theatres" had opened on March 8 in *Venice Perserved,* playing Belvidera to the Jaffier of Caldwell and the Pierre of Duffy. She was to have been introduced in *Pizarro* on February 27, but a sudden indisposition had prevented this. It is possible that on this occasion Jane Placide took her place as Elvira and that Hartwig "from the Boston theatre" made his début as Alonzo, the role for which he had been announced. In *Rob Roy* on March 3 Mrs. Tatnall made her third appearance as Helen McGregor and the next week she was Zorilda in *Timour the Tartar.* This was repeated with *The Magpie and the Maid* on the 24th; and for her benefit two nights later, she played Adelgitha and Umbra in *La Perouse.*

Since Mrs. Tatnall was soon to become a regular member of the company, a word as to her history may not be amiss here. She had made her stage début at the Olympic Circus in Philadelphia, where her second husband (Tatnall) was manager of the equestrian corps, and since then had appeared at the Park and Lafayette in New York. She played in tragedy, comedy, and equestrian drama and in all was eminently successful.

The last star of the season was the tragedian, Thomas Cooper, who began his engagement on the 28th with *Macbeth.* He went through a familiar round: *Hamlet, Virginius* (twice), *Damon and Pythias* (twice), *Richard III, Bertram, The Gamester, Othello,* and *Catharine and Petruchio.* Since the last visit the only additions to his repertoire were *Pizarro* and *William Tell,* the latter being given for his benefit on April 20.

Several new afterpieces brought novelty into the bills during Cooper's long engagement. On the 5th there was *The Irish Widow* of David Garrick with Mrs. Tatnall in the leading role. The evening before she had given her first performance as a regular member of the company, appearing as Calanthe in *Damon and Pythias.* On the 16th came George Macfarren's *Malvina, or The Hall of Fingal,* a "ballad opera," based on an older play, *Oscar and Malvina.* Richard Peake's new farce, *The Duel, or My Two Nephews,* was given several nights later.

After Cooper's departure Caldwell engaged the stud of horses belonging to the North American Circus Company and on April 23 he presented *Timour the Tartar* "in a style of splendor never before witnessed in New Orleans." Messrs. Gates and Green as well as others of the equestrian troupe supported the Timour of Caldwell and the Zorilda of Mrs. Tatnall. The theatre was closed on the 26th "in consequence of the necessity of a night rehearsal for *Blue Beard,*" in which Jane Placide enacted Fatima, and Kelsey, Abomilique. When the *Cataract of the Ganges* was revived on the 30th, these two again shared the leads; on its repetition the next night, it preceded Mrs. Inchbald's farce, *The Mogul Tale, or A Cobler's Flight in an Air Balloon,* "first time in New Orleans." It should be noted that on May 3 Mrs. Tatnall played Morgiana in *The Forty Thieves,* a role usually taken by Jane Placide, and that two days later she replaced Miss Placide as Zamine in *The Cataract of the Ganges.* For her benefit on May 8 she gave *Lodoiska,* the managers of the circus having very politely offered their horses. On this evening Miss Carpenter danced a *pas seul,* and *The Spoiled Child,* with the beneficiary as Little Pickle, concluded the bill.

Sakoski, an acrobat, made his first appearance on May 12 as Orson to the Valentine of Caldwell. The melodrama was repeated on the 25th and on the next evening when he volunteered for Still's benefit. Eugene Robertson, the aeronaut, came forward on May 16 to present his optical delusions or phantasmagoria. During this engagement of five nights he also exhibited an Automaton Trumpeter and Chinese Fire.

The benefits this season offered few new plays. On the 23rd Russell presented *Town and Country,* a gentleman volunteer appearing as Jacky Hawbuck, and *The Turnpike Gate* with Miss Russell as Crack. Mrs. Russell chose *The Soldier's Daughter* that she might enact Widow Cheerly, and Mrs. Higgins, on her night, appeared as Mrs. Malaprop. The bill on the latter occasion concluded with the ballet, "Little Red Riding Hood," Miss Carpenter and Mrs. Tatnall succeeding to the roles originally taken by Jane Placide and Mrs. Rowe.

On June 4 Jane Placide made her first appearance in over a month. According to a communication in the *Argus* she had lately been the victim of an unfortunate accident and now returned to the boards to take a farewell benefit. "Her retirement," said the writer, "will occasion a chasm in the female department of the theatrical corps which the manager will find difficult to fill."

On the 6th Mrs. Rowe revived Mrs. Inchbald's *Everyone Has His Fault* and *The Agreeable Surprise*, "not acted here in five years." Between the pieces a native of Scotland played national airs on a real Scotch harp. Caldwell's benefit on June 8, the last night of the season, brought the novelties, *Not at Home*, a new farce "by a gentleman of New Orleans," and Monk Lewis' *The Wood Daemon*, the latter with new scenery and decoration.

This year Caldwell had decided to extend his interests to St. Louis, a thriving little town where money was said to be plentiful. Early in May he sent carpenters and artists ahead to fix the theatre which he had leased [16] and three weeks after the closing of the American Theatre he and the company were in St. Louis.

AMERICAN THEATRE, 1827-1828

The theatre in St. Louis was a renovated salt house, none too comfortable in the hot summer weather, and though the New Orleans company offered "delectable amusement," the performances were not well attended. After two months the troupe proceeded to Nashville; but remembering the delays and difficulties of the previous winter journeys from that city to New Orleans, Caldwell arranged for an early departure. By December 18, he and the company were in New Orleans.

During the summer the American Theatre had undergone great alterations and now presented a "much lighter and better *tout ensemble* than it has ever yet done." Several new performers had been added to the company, among them Mr. and Mrs. Sol Smith, Mr. and Mrs. H. Crampton, Mr. William Anderson, a member of Caldwell's first New Orleans company, Mr. and Mrs.

---

[16] *Argus*, May 7, 1827.

Lemuel Smith, and a Mr. Jackson. These with Caldwell, Mr. and Mrs. Russell, Miss Russell, Mrs. Rowe, Mrs. Hartwig (formerly Mrs. Tatnall), Mrs. Johns, Mrs. Higgins, Jackson Gray, Sam Jones, John Still, Palmer, McCafferty, and Lear, formed a competent, though far from excellent, company. Mrs. Hartwig succeeded Jane Placide as the company's leading lady and though she never won the acclaim that had been Jane's, she managed to fill the "chasm" which had been occasioned by the loss of the favorite.

The season opened on December 21 with two novelties, Arnold's comedy, *Man and Wife,* and the younger Colman's farce, *X Y Z.* After the play "Little Wot Ye Wha's Comin'" and "Larry O'Gaff" were sung by Crampton, who was heard in Scotch and Irish songs from this day till the end of the season. The performances of the next night served to introduce Mr. and Mrs. S. Smith, "from the Western Theatres." She appeared as Diana Vernon in *Rob Roy,* and he as Billy Lackaday in the afterpiece, *Sweethearts and Wives.* Soloman S. Smith was twenty-seven at this time and had served an apprenticeship in the western theatres but as yet had not attained prominence as a low comedian. Russell and Crampton were the mainstays of this season's comic force, and Smith seems to have been engaged for utility work.

Caldwell brought out his novelties early this season. On December 24 came H. J. Finn's *Montgomery, or The Falls of Montmorency* with Caldwell in the title role. This was followed by an address and patriotic songs, all "in honor of the glorious 23rd of December, 1814," an anniversary which had been celebrated in the French theatre on the previous day. Christmas brought *Bertram* with Anderson in the name part and Mrs. Hastings as Imogine. This actor had been engaged for the "heavy business," and his name figures prominently in the melodramatic revivals of the season. On the 27th, he was Abaellino to the Rosamonda of Mrs. Rowe. The farce on this occasion was Richard Butler's *The Irish Tutor, or New Lights,* with Crampton taking the part of Jerry O'Rourke. The next night, in commemoration of another historical event of 1814, Noah's *Marion* and patriotic songs were offered. The afterpiece was one new to the city, Joseph Lunn's farce, *Family Jars,* with McCafferty as Diggory, Mrs. S. Smith as Lyddy, and Sol as Delph, a part which soon became a favorite with the public.

The spectacular *Cherry and Fair Star* was revived on the 29th. "That interesting child," Miss Russell, was Papillo; Mrs. Hartwig was Cherry, and Mrs. Rowe, Fair Star. A novelty for the New Orleans audience was E. P. Knight's musical farce, *A Chip of the Old Block,* in which Russell was Chip, the drunken cooper, Mrs. Russell was Rose, and Mrs. Rowe, Emma. On January 4, George Soane's melodrama, *The Innkeeper's Daughter,* was offered "for the first time in this theatre," Caldwell personating Richard and Mrs. Hartwig, Mary. Three or four days previous John Howard Payne's dramatic sketch, *Love in Humble Life,* had been introduced. The record of the first performance is missing, but the announcement of a repetition on January 7 lists Crampton as Ronstaus and Mrs. Russell as Christine. Sol Smith records in *Theatrical Management* that his was the role of Carlitz. The entertainment on January 8 commenced with M. M. Noah's play, *She Would Be a Soldier, or The Plains of Chippewa,* always a favorite on such days, and concluded with the anonymous *Nature and Philosophy* in which Mrs. Hartwig enacted Colin, the youth who had never seen a woman. To give *éclat* to these performances a "new and superb transparency" of General Jackson was exhibited after the play, and there were the inevitable address and patriotic songs. Two days later the transparency was still on exhibit and we read also of a perfectly equipped Frigate of War, which was drawn around the stage while Mr. Still sang "The Minute Gun at Sea."

First appearances were the feature of January 11, 1828, when H. N. Cambridge, "from the Boston Theatre," made his bow as Octavian in *The Mountaineers,* and the part of Jeremy Diddler in the afterpiece, *Raising the Wind,* was taken by Mr. Brady, "his first appearance on any stage." Cambridge had made his "fourth appearance on any stage" in New York the previous year—without acclaim. It is to be hoped that in New Orleans Mrs. Hartwig's Floranthe inspired him to better acting. On the 12th of January the city had its first glimpse of Charles Kemble's twenty-year-old drama, *The Wanderer,* Caldwell enacting Sigismond and Mrs. Hartwig, the Countess Valdestein. For the present this was the manager's last important role, as Junius Brutus Booth had arrived to take over the leads.

The tragedian opened on the 14th in his favorite character of Richard III and for his second performance appeared as Hamlet. *Othello,* with Caldwell as Iago, Mrs. Rowe as Desde-

mona, and Mrs. Hartwig as Emilia was the third offering; and
A New Way to Pay Old Debts, the fourth. Orestes in *The Distressed Mother*, Lear, to the Cordelia of Mrs. Rowe, and Reuben
Glenroy in *Town and Country* were enacted successively; and for
the last night of his engagement, January 28, he selected *Sylla*,
an adaptation from the French made expressly for him "by a
gentleman of New York." At his benefit on the 30th he appeared
as Shylock to the Portia of Mrs. Hartwig and as Jerry Sneak in
Samuel Foote's *The Mayor of Garratt*. The following night he
volunteered his services for the benefit of the Asylum for Destitute Orphan Boys, performing Sir Edward Mortimer in *The Iron
Chest*, Caldwell assisting as Wilford and Mrs. Rowe as Helen.
According to a notice which had appeared several times during
Booth's first week, his other engagements in the north would
prevent any re-engagement. Yet on February 2 Caldwell announced a re-engagement, and Booth stayed to repeat his favorite
Richard and to play opposite Mrs. Hartwig in *Bertram, Brutus,*
and *The Apostate*. As he was in New Orleans on February 13,
he "very generously offered his services" for Still's benefit, re-
appearing as Lear and as Sir Edward Mortimer, this time to the
Wilford of the beneficiary. It should be noted that on this night
the ever-versatile Mrs. Hartwig, fresh from her triumphs as
Imogine, Tullia and Florinda, danced a *pas seul* and appeared as
Mrs. Bromley in the afterpiece, *Simpson and Co.*

After Booth's departure Caldwell brought out more novelties.
On the 15th was performed M. R. Lacy's *Love and Reason*, announced as "a new comedy never acted in America," though it
had been given five months before at the Bowery Theatre in New
York.[17] It was repeated as an afterpiece on the following night
when the main attraction was a revival of *The Exile of Siberia*,
featuring Caldwell and Mrs. Hartwig and "a beautiful representation of a SNOW STORM." The same scenery was used in *The
Snow Storm, or Lorrina of Tobolsko*, which was given "for the
first time in this theatre" on February 22 and repeated on the
25th.

On February 18 was offered William Dimond's *Bride of
Abydos*, a spectacle which had cost the manager $1,000. For
four successive nights it was witnessed by crowded houses though
on two of these, February 19 and 21, Booth was performing in

---

[17] George C. D. Odell, *Annals of the New York Stage*, III. 329.

Racine's *Andromache* at the Orleans Theatre. While Mondelli prepared new and appropriate scenery for the next melodramatic romance, Richard Russell took a farewell benefit at which he appeared as Tyke in *The School of Reform*. There were repetitions of *Love and Reason, The Exile of Siberia,* and *The Bride of Abydos* and on February 28, *Tom and Jerry* was announced "for the only night this season." On the 3rd of March came the novelty which had been in preparation, *The Woodman's Hut,* by Samuel Arnold. According to the extant records, this was the most popular of the season's pieces, attaining at least six performances. Its success may have accounted for the revival of the *Falls of Clyde* and *The Forty Thieves* on March 6 and *The Forest of Rosenwald* on the 8th.

McCafferty's benefit (March 14) introduced William Barrymore's Grand Asiatic melodrama, *El Hyder.* Though this was generally staged as an equestrian piece, no mention is made of the horses. Is it possible that Mrs. Hartwig played Harry Clinton without "their powerful aid"? In the afterpiece, *The Turnpike Gate,* McCafferty essayed Crack with the song of "My Deary." On her benefit night (March 17) Mrs. Hartwig abandoned the role of Harry Clinton to enact Mrs. Oakley in *The Jealous Wife,* and Umba, "with an Indian dance," in the afterpiece, *La Perouse.* The historical pantomime was not new, but Mrs. Hartwig's Umba, assisted by the Ranko of "a gentleman of this city," and the Chimpanzee of Mr. Hunt, "of the circus," must have made this an interesting performance. After weeks of melodrama, Crampton's choice of *The West Indian* for his night (March 24) should have come as a relief to the audience—and to the actors. An added attraction was the appearance of the well-known citizen, Mr. Kenny Laverty, Esq., as Major O'Flaherty. After the play Sol Smith sang "The Beautiful Boy" and Mr. Crampton rendered his composition, "Blue Bonnets over The Border" and joined in a duet with Mrs. Crampton. Even Miss Charlotte Crampton, "a child only seven years old," contributed her musical bit. The bill ended with *The Highland Reel,* Crampton in the role of Shelty

The records of the next five performances are missing, but we know that one of these was Shakespeare's *Comedy of Errors,* a play which recently had proved successful in New York. For several weeks the newspapers had carried notices that it was "in preparation for Mr. Caldwell's benefit"; on the 31st it was

announced "for the second time in New Orleans." According to
this managerial notice in the *Louisiana Advertiser,* "a fashionable
and overflowing audience" had bestowed "unbounded applause"
on the initial presentation and there had been a "general request"
for a repetition. With this performance of March 31 the theatre
closed until Easter Monday.

Mrs. Rowe took her benefit when the theatre re-opened on
April 7. After she had enacted Letitia Hardy, with the song of
"The Mermaid," she sustained eight characters in George Mac-
farren's new farce, *Winning a Husband.* She was

> Miss Jenny Transit, a young lady who amplifies the
> mutability of human affairs; Margaret Macmuckleeanny, a
> learned lassie from the highlands, in which character she
> will sing a new song, called "Blue Bonnets o'er the Border";
> Miss Cornelia Clementina Clappergo, a voluminous and vola-
> tile literary spinster; Lady Dorothea Dashby, a lady of the
> town, with the celebrated song of "Bid Me Discourse"; Mrs.
> Deborah Griskin, a Pork Butcher's Widow, with more airs
> than graces; Madmoiselle Antoinette Marasquien, a French
> Figurante with a *Pas Seul;* Bridget Buckshorn, a rustic
> beauty with a red cloak; and Ensign Thaddeus O'Transit,
> of the Kilkenny Flamers.

During the calm before the next benefit, *The Honey Moon*
and *Rule a Wife and Have a Wife* were revived that Caldwell
might appear in his favorite roles of the Duke of Aranza and
Leon. Then, on April 11, Miss Russell bade farewell in one of
the season's most interesting benefits. Among the entertainments
offered by the young actress were her personation of Little
Pickle, a musical olio in which she gave "A Hit at the Law,"
"as sung by Mr. Sloman in the northern theatres," and *Tom
Thumb,* with Master Russell appearing in the title role, "for the
first time." But unquestionably the event of the evening was
the performance of *Tom and Jerry,* in which the part of Bob
Logic was played "by the master of an American vessel," O'Boozle,
"by the master of a British vessel," Corinthian Tom, "by the
gentleman who sung at Mrs. Russell's benefit," and Dusty Bob,
"by a Gentleman."

Mondelli's night (April 14) brought forth *The Blind Boy,*
an old melodrama "with new scenery," and the favorite comedy,
The Soldier's Daughter, Mrs. Russell as the Widow Cheerly.
Between the pieces a Mr. Jeandot played a concert on the flute.
On April 16, a benefit was tendered Victor Pepin, "formerly

manager of the Circus." As Mr. Pepin approached his fellow citizens "with the cap of necessity," it is to be hoped that a large and liberal audience was attracted by a bill which included three popular pieces, *Winning a Husband, Of Age Tomorrow* and *The Wandering Boys.*

For his benefit on the 17th Sol Smith offered *The Honey Moon* and *The Poor Soldier,* appearing as Jacques to his wife's Juliana in the first and as Darby to her Patrick in the afterpiece. Smith states in his memoirs that with the exception of the character of Delph *(Family Jars)* and Carlitz *(Love in Humble Life)* he did little this season except "walk in processions, sing in choruses, and shout in armies, besides fighting in all general battles." [18] He does not mention the many occasions on which he sang his comic songs; nor does he tell of his wife's activities. For further information concerning the young couple, we must turn to a communication in the *Argus* of April 17.

> As a general visitor of the theatre . . . I take the liberty of stating that there are not any of the whole Corps Dramatic, who possess stronger claims upon the generosity of the public than do Mr. Smith and his amiable wife. Mrs. Smith is surely the most admirable songstress that has ever graced our boards—and it cannot be denied that she has contributed no small share of the refined amusement which that portion of the audience have this season enjoyed. Mr. Smith in low comedy, has never failed to chase away the tragical gloom, often sending us away from the house with our sides aching with laughter at the truly comic performance of the "Beautiful Boy." . . .

Two more benefits and this season was to be brought to a close. To add novelty to a bill which included *Speed the Plough* and *The Critic,* Mrs. Higgins engaged the celebrated Mexican Dwarf, thirty-two inches high, and "upwards of fifty years old." He danced a Spanish Fandango, went through the manual exercises, and appeared in the afterpiece as Lord Burley. Caldwell, for his benefit on April 19, announced the "last new and highly attractive piece of *The Hundred Pound Note.*" In this farce of Richard Peake's, Russell played Billy Black, the part which Hilson and Barnes had taken in New York the previous year, and Mrs. Rowe was Miss Arlington, "with the original Bavarian Girl's Broom Song." After recitations of "Alexander's Feast" (Palmer), "Bucks Have At Ye All" (Caldwell), and the hum-

---

[18] Sol Smith, *Theatrical Management in the West and South for Thirty Years,* 49.

orous story of "The Kilkenny Cats" (Mr. Jarvis) came the *pièce
de résistance, Tom and Jerry,* with Corinthian Tom, Bob Logic,
and Dusty Bob enacted by those gentlemen who had appeared
at Miss Russell's benefit. This time, however, Corinthian Tom
was to sing "The Mill" and Dusty Bob was to dance a *Pas de
Deux* with African Sal, two features not mentioned in the notice
of the earlier performance. With this novelty the theatre closed,
and the company prepared to leave for the summer campaign in
Natchez and St. Louis.

AMERICAN THEATRE, 1828-1829

The American Theatre opened for one of its most successful
seasons on Wednesday, December 17, 1828. During the summer
extensive alterations had been made in the interior of the building, and it was reported that the house could now seat two thousand people. The pit had been converted into forty-two boxes,
which with the thirty boxes of the first tier accommodated nearly
six hundred. From an account of these improvements given in
the *Louisiana Advertiser* of December 19, we get the first and
only adequate description of the interior of the theatre on Camp
Street.

> The Pit (or parquet) Boxes are superbly fitted up,
> carpeted throughout and contain five mahogany chairs with
> stuffed seats and crimson coverings. . . . Each stage box is
> ornamented with a looking glass seven feet by three that
> affords a panoramic view, as it were, of the audience. These
> mirrors are tastefully decorated with blue damask and sur-
> mounted each by a large eagle in *or,* displaying the national
> flag in satin. . . .

> On entering the Boxes the first thing the eye rests upon
> is the majestic Proscenium of this theatre. It is an eliptic
> arch of thirty-eight feet span, supported by two Doric pil-
> asters in imitation of Scarcolina marble, reeded in gold, the
> bases and capitals also in gold, resting upon attic pedestals
> of *verd de mer* marble. . . . The dome or ceiling is painted
> in arabesque and has the appearance of a fan when open.
> The color is imitation of blue silk, surrounded by another
> resembling that of the morning's dawn. The centre is a
> canopy painted in light clouds, studded with silver stars.
> Here is suspended a beautiful cut glass chandelier nine feet
> in diameter.

> The decorations on the front of the boxes vary in every
> tier. The lower circle is set off with wreaths of roses and
> flowers, supported by golden zephyrs upon a prismatic
> ground with gold mouldings. The fronts of the second and

third tiers are in arabesque and gilt. Around the boxes are candelabras *(dores)* with three branches and large ground glass shades to soften the light. Every part of the house is brilliantly illuminated with gas.

The amphitheatre is divided from the lobby by a brick wall with doors leading to each box; and the parallel sides are thrown into large arches more convenient and salubrious in this climate, as a free circulation of air can be always commanded by opening several large windows in the main halls.

The partition of the Parquet boxes—the wall that encircles them, and supports the cast iron columns of the different tiers of boxes . . . are all, including the arches, of a delicate rose color, and thus seem well calculated to set off the fair complexions of the Ladies who may honour the really beautiful Theatre with their presence.

These improvements in the audience side of the house, however they may combine chasteness with splendor, are likely to be eclipsed in the stage department. The scenery is entirely new—each one covers nearly 1000 square feet of canvas, having 36 feet in width by 27 in height.

With the exception of Caldwell (Frank Heartall), Gray (Governor Heartall), Russell (Timothy Quaint) and Anderson (Mr. Malfort), the cast of the opening play, *The Soldier's Daughter,* was new: Henry G. Pearson, A. W. Fenno, Henderson, H. N. Barry, Kenny, Mrs. Lacombe, and Mrs. Edstram. The part of Widow Cheerly was taken by Mrs. Crooke, formely Mrs. Entwistle, who now returned to New Orleans after an absence of six years. Perhaps there is little need to record that her "fine recitation" gave great satisfaction to the "over flowing and brilliant audience" that witnessed this first performance. Mr. Crooke, "from the Dublin and Liverpool theatres," made his bow on the second night as Rolando in *The Honey Moon;* and in the operatic farce, *No Song, No Supper* a Mr. Carr was introduced as Frederick (with songs). According to his fellow actor, Sol Smith, Carr was a "kind of 'rough-shod' vocalist, a Cockney Jew, who could bellow out 'Oft in the Stilly Night' like a clap of thunder and warble 'Wha'll be King but Charlie?' like a bull."[19] Several other recruits were introduced on the third night of the season. Mrs. Petrie and Tatem made their first appearance as Ursula and Conrad in *Much Ado about Nothing;* H. A. Williams as Darby in *The Poor Soldier;* and between the play and the farce, George

---

[19] *Ibid.,* 55.

Hernizen sang a comic song "The Ring and the Countryman."
It should be noted that Sol Smith errs in stating that William
replaced Russell as principal low comedian.[20] Smith seems to
have forgotten that Russell after a summer in the East returned
to his old position in Caldwell's company. Also numbered among
the company were Lemuel Smith, Sam Jones, Morton, Kidd, Tyrone, Crampton, Lear, Jackson, and Mesdames John, Williams,
Higgins, and Kenny.

After the new members of the company had been introduced,
Caldwell brought out his first star, Mrs. Alexander Drake. It
may be remembered that she and her husband had been members
of Caldwell's company in 1823; now she was undeniably "the
first actress in the western country" and possessed of "a very
grand manner." She came out on December 20 as Lady Randolph
in *Douglas;* Miss Russell, also fresh from a short stay at the Park
Theatre in New York, played young Norval. Following this performance the star appeared as Elvira in *Pizarro,* Meg Meriles in
Guy Mannering, and on Christmas night she and Caldwell enacted the familiar story of Millwood and George Barnwell. On
the sixth night of her engagement she played Helen McGregor
to Caldwell's Rob Roy, Still making his first appearance of the
season as Francis Osbaldistone. An added attraction on this
evening was Payne's new drama, *'Twas I,* with the Delorme of
Crooke and the Georgette of Mrs. Russell. The 30th saw a repetition of *Douglas* as well as the third successive performance
of *'Twas I,* and the following day Mrs. Drake had her benefit.
Her Adelgitha was supported by Anderson, Pearson, and Crooke;
in the afterpiece, *The Hunter of the Alps,* Caldwell took the part
of Felix, Mrs. Crooke that of Helen, and Miss Russell was Julio.

"In commemoration of January 1, 1815," the new year was
ushered in with Samuel Woodworth's *Lafayette, or The Castle
of Olmutz.* Mrs. Drake returned on January 2, 1829 to play the
Queen to Caldwell's Hamlet. On the 3rd was presented the season's most popular play, *The Gambler's Fate, or A Lapse of
Twenty Years* (possibly by H. M. Milner[21]) with a cast which
included Crooke as Albert Germaine, Barry as Malcour, Mrs.
Russell as Henry Germaine, Miss Russell as Rose, and Mrs.
Crooke as Julia. It is not surprising that the play proved popular
in a city where the "most pernicious of vices" was publicly and

---

[20] *Ibid.*
[21] Allardyce Nicoll, *A History of Early Nineteenth Century Drama,* II, 347.

lawfully practiced. There is some doubt, however, as to its effects on the votaries of the roulette and the faro table. There are no records, or confessions, to prove that any of them saw it, though some ten performances were given before the end of the season.

After a run of three nights *The Gambler's Fate* was interrupted to allow Junius Brutus Booth to begin an engagement in "his own peculiar character of Richard." On January 9 Mrs. Drake made her final appearance as the Queen to Booth's Hamlet and Mrs. Crooke succeeded to the feminine leads. Performances as Sir Giles Overreach, Shylock, Macbeth, the Stranger, his first appearance in this character, King Lear, and Othello concluded Booth's engagement. On the 20th "at the request of many," he played Reuben Glenroy in *Town and Country*, depicting the generous mountaineer "with such force and simplicity of heart as makes vice shudder at its shadow and folly recoil at its own significance."[22] The benefit for the Catholic Association of Ireland, on January 24, brought him back as Octavian *(The Mountaineers)*, and the following day he left for Natchez. Sol Smith records that part of the company was sent to Natchez under Booth's direction, but he does not say which actors these were.[23] Only the names of Mr. and Mrs. Crooke disappear from the daily notices at this time.

On January 21, New Orleans witnessed the début of George Holland, the English comedian. He made his bow as Billy Lackaday in the comedy, *Sweethearts and Wives*, and in C. A. Somerset's imitative burletta, *A Day after the Fair*, in which he portrayed six characters and Mrs. Russell three. On the 26th he offered two favorite pieces, *The Secret* by John Poole, and the entertainment entitled *Whims of a Comedian*, "consisting of Ventriloquialism, etc., the whole . . . recited, acted, sung, and gesticulated by Mr. Holland alone." On the 28th John Poole's farce, *Deaf as a Post*, followed a repetition of the *Whims of a Comedian*, and on the 30th he enacted Paul Pry. Though Richard Russell had introduced the character in 1827, Holland disregarded this performance of what he referred to as the "Surry Theatre Comedy," and spoke of his presentation of Poole's *Paul Pry* as the first in New Orleans.[24] On his sixth appearance Holland repeated *As Deaf as a Post* (Tristram Sappy) and in *She Stoops*

---

[22] *Louisiana Advertiser*, January 21, 1829.
[23] Smith, *op. cit.*, 57.
[24] *Louisiana Advertiser*, February 4, 1829.

to *Conquer* as Tony Lumpkin he introduced the comic song
"Chump's Farm Yard" with imitations of cows, hens, sheep,
turkeys, etc. For his benefit on February 2, he played Timothy
Quaint in *The Soldier's Daughter* and repeated Somerset's burletta.

Before Holland completed his engagement, the celebrated
vocalist Mrs. Edward Knight, made her debut (January 27) as
Adela in James Cobb's comic opera, *The Haunted Tower*. The
next day the *Louisiana Advertiser* pronounced judgment: "Mrs.
Knight . . . fully realized all the anticipations which had been
formed of the surpassing extent of her vocal powers . . . as a
performer she is correct, natural, and pleasing." She enacted
Rosetta *(Love in a Village)* and Catharine *(Catharine and Petruchio)* on the 29th, but not until her third appearance did New
Orleans hear the songs which had made her famous. As Marianne
in *The Dramatist* she introduced "The Last Rose of Summer"
and "The Dashing White Sergeant"; as Margaretta in the afterpiece, *No Song, No Supper* she warbled "I've been warning,"
"With lowly suit and plaintive ditty," and "Across the downs
this morning."

Holland was re-engaged on February 4 and the following
day he and Mrs. Knight appeared in *Guy Mannering* as Dominie
Sampson and Julia Mannering and as Gregory and Marian Ram-
say in the after piece, *The Turn Out*. On this night Mrs. Sol
Smith made her first appearance of the season as Lucy Bertram.
On the 6th the Albina Mandeville of Mrs. Knight was followed
by the New Orleans première of Moncrieff's drama, *The Somnambulist*, a performance which featured another "first appearance this season," that of the popular Mrs. Rowe. The next night
the stars appeared as Diana Vernon and Bailie Nichol in *Rob
Roy*, and Holland and Mrs. Rowe were Watty Cockney and Priscilla Tomboy in the afterpiece, *The Romp*. For her benefit on the
9th, Mrs. Knight offered the opera, *Brother and Sister*, and Samuel Beazley's farce, *Gretna Green*, in which she enacted Betty
Finiken. Holland's engagement was now drawing to a close. On
the 10th he was Mr. Dingle in *Love and Reason;* and for his
benefit on the 12th, he appeared as Lapoache *(Fontainbleau)* and
Jerry *(Tom and Jerry)*.

The popular Mrs. Knight began a re-engagement on February
13. The manager announced that this had been requested by

"many respectable French families" who had been kept from the theatre by the very wet weather of the past two weeks. Her opening role was that of the Little Corporal in Thomas Morton's new play, *The Invincibles,* and so pleased was the audience with the songs and drills that the piece was given four times during the engagement. An interesting performance should have been that of the 18th when Mrs. Lacombe played Paul to Mrs. Knight's Virginia. For her farewell benefit on the 20th, Mrs. Knight introduced Charles Dibdin's opera, *The Lord of the Manor.* Need it be told that Annette sang "Coming through the Rye" and "The Dashing White Sergeant," or that the afterpiece was *The Invincibles?*

The day before Mrs. Knight's benefit, Booth returned from Natchez to begin his second and "positively his last engagement." His parts were Richard III, Sir Edward Mortimer, Brutus (Payne's tragedy), Bertram, and Malcour *(The Gambler's Fate),* and for his benefit on March 3, Orestes to Mrs. Drake's Hermione in *The Distressed Mother.* With Booth and Caldwell in the roles originally played by Crooke and Barry *The Gambler's Fate* proved even more attractive than the earlier representation. At the third performance on the 28th, it was played as a first piece in order that it might teach its lesson to the "juvenile branches of families."

The records of the first weeks in March are rich in the performances of stars. Cooper began an engagement on the 2nd as Virginius to Mrs. Rowe's Virginia; on the 4th his Damon was supported by the Calanthe of Mrs. Drake. The following day Mrs. Sloman, "the tragic actress from Covent Garden," and her husband, the "celebrated English Buffo Singer," made their débuts, she as Isabella and he as Sam Savoury in the farce, *The Fish Out of Water.* On the 6th, Booth, "reengaged in compliance with the general wish," was Iago to Cooper's Othello; the next evening he enacted the Stranger with the assistance of Mrs. Sloman. The bill for the 7th also included Sloman's personation of Delph *(Family Jars)* and several of his comic songs. On this occasion the admission to the parquet and dress circle was raised to $1.50, a price which Caldwell charged frequently during this month. When, on March 9, *Venice Preserved* was advertised with Cooper as Pierre, Booth as Jaffier, and Mrs. Sloman as Belvidera, the *Louisiana Advertiser* commented: "Seldom has an audience in America had a chance of witnessing so much histrionic ex-

cellence concentrated on a single piece. . . . Mrs. Sloman is unquestionably a first-rate tragedian, probably the best, for a female,
that has appeared on an American stage since the days of the
peerless Mrs. Wignell."

After a week of inactivity Mrs. Drake made her last appearance on March 10. In these days of another star's popularity,
the role in which she bowed herself out seems aptly titled; she
was the Unknown Female in *The Foundling of the Forest.*

The inimitable Jane Placide returned to the boards of the
American Theatre on March 12, her first appearance in almost
two years. Those who attended the theatre on this evening saw
a strongly cast *Pizarro,* Cooper playing Rolla, Booth, Pizarro,
Caldwell, Alonzo, and Miss Placide, Elvira. As an added attraction the management presented Richard Peake's new farce, *The
Haunted Inn.* Then on the 13th, while the tragedian rested, Mr.
Sloman assisted Caldwell as Don Ferola Whiskerandos in *The
Critic,* and Miss Russell led the Invincibles in their drills and
marches. For the 14th *Othello* was announced, Booth to enact
the title role supported by Cooper (Iago), Caldwell (Cassio),
Mrs. Sloman (Desdemona) and Jane Placide (Emilia). There
is a possibility that this performance was postponed, or that Mrs.
Drake played Emilia, as a notice of March 23 states that Miss
Placide, having recovered from her severe indisposition, was
ready for her "second appearance."

Mrs. Sloman's benefit, on the 18th, again brought forth the
constellation. Booth played Gloster, Cooper, Hastings, Mrs. Sloman, Jane Shore, and Mrs. Drake, Alicia. Mr. Sloman sang comic
songs after the play and assisted his wife and Caldwell in the
afterpiece, *Catherine and Petruchio.* For Cooper's benefit (March
19), Mrs. Sloman offered her services as Lady Macbeth. Two new
members of the company made their débuts on this night. Ross
was played by Mr. Watson and the part of Sophia in the afterpiece, *The Rendezvous,* by Mrs. Gray.

The parade of stars was not yet to end; the Slomans and
Cooper were re-engaged. On the 20th, Mrs. Sloman threw aside
her tragic mantle and essayed Lady Teazle; the 24th saw her
in *The Provoked Husband,* playing Lady Townly to Caldwell's
Lord Townly and surrounded by Russell, Gray, Mrs. Russell, and
Mrs. Rowe, the comic force of the theatre. This latter occasion
was Russell's benefit—and a proper time for Miss Russell to

show her filial devotion. To her belongs the honor of introducing John Poole's farce, *Old and Young, or The Four Mowbrays*. On the previous night Cooper had made his reappearance as Sir William Dorillon (in *Wives as They Were*), a role of his new to this city, and Jane Placide had returned as Miss Dorillon. Booth, too, had recovered from an indisposition, and on the 25th Caldwell again offered a combination of talent "greater . . . than has ever been presented at *any one time in any Theatre on the Continent.*" The performance was *Jane Shore* and with the exception of the role of Alicia, now played by Jane Placide, the cast was that of March 18.

Miss Russell joined the stars on March 26 when her young Norval, "no ordinary treat," had the support of Cooper (Glenalvon), Booth (Old Norval), and Mrs. Drake (Lady Randolph). A bill made up of *The Gamester* and *The Gambler's Fate* presented on the 27th "the united talents" of Cooper, Caldwell, Miss Placide, and the Slomans, but unfortunately there is no record of the parts they took.

March 28 offered the *Romeo and Juliet* of Booth and Mrs. Sloman and the first appearance of the infant prodigy, Miss Louisa Lane, later the famous Mrs. John Drew. This nine-year-old child sustained six roles in W. H. Oxberry's burletta, *Actress of All Work*, among them being that of Goody Stubbins, a deaf lady eighty years old! At Cooper's farewell benefit the next night the little actress shone in *Twelve Precisely*, a farce of H. M. Milner's which was new to the city. *Julius Caesar*, the main piece of the evening, presented the beneficiary as Marc Antony, supported by Booth (Cassius), Caldwell (Brutus), Pearson (Julius Caesar), and Mrs. Drake (Portia). On her third appearance (March 31) Miss Lane held the stage alone, enacting Dr. Pangloss and *The Four Mowbrays*. The *Louisiana Courier* (April 2) now made its report: "We are opposed to bringing girls of her age upon the stage, when they should be in a seminary cultivating their minds and inculcating fixed principles of virtue and religion. However, we are constrained to say that she is a most astonishing child, and far exceeds all the *Infant Prodigies* we have hitherto seen." For her benefit, April 7, the "astonishing child" appeared as Richard III to Booth's Richmond, and repeated *Twelve Precisely*.

As Miss Lane went through her repertoire, the Slomans prepared their farewell offerings. Mr. Sloman's benefit, on April 1,

presented the couple as Bob Acres and Lydia Languish, and introduced John Banim's new melodramatic piece, *The Sergeant's
Wife*. Another novelty introduced the following day must be
noted here. This was the "scenic burletta," *Paris and London, or
a Trip to Both Cities*, by Moncrieff. Its outstanding feature was
a Moving Diorama which represented a trip from Calais to
London, the work of the theatre's artists, Mondelli and Plissenau.
The piece was given for the fifth and last time on April 25, but
the diorama was exhibited on special occasions, until the end of
the season. For her night (April 4) Mrs. Sloman wisely returned to tragedy, offering for the first time in New Orleans
R. L. Sheil's *Evadne*, Booth appearing as Ludovico. Her husband
supplied the lighter touches as Tom in the farce, *The Intrigue*.

The most important event of the spring was the engagement
of Edwin Forrest, "the distinguished American Tragedian" who
had served his apprenticeship on the boards of the theatre he
now visited as a star. Jane Placide and Booth were re-engaged
to assist him, and on April 10 he commenced his engagement
as Damon to the Pythias of Booth, the Calanthe of Miss Placide,
and the Hermione of Mrs. Rowe. His second performance as
Virginius (April 13) called forth the following comment from
the *Louisiana Advertiser* of April 15:

> In *Virginius* . . . he produces frequently the deepest ef-
> fect, still on the whole, his Virginius is inferior to Cooper's.
> —Mr. Forrest wants that *ensemble* which the more mature
> judgment of Mr. Cooper gives to his acting—the former
> sometimes produces more *éclat*, he is frequently more flashy,
> but the latter throughout emits more heat. . . . We shall
> merely add that we entertain no doubt, that Mr. Forrest
> may, by incessant labour and judicious study, one day attain
> the highest pinnacle of histrionic fame.

On the 15th, Forrest enacted Othello to the Iago of Booth,
the Emilia of Miss Placide and, we imagine, the Desdemona of
Mrs. Rowe. His William Tell, on the 18th, was supported by the
Albert of Miss Russell and the Emma of her mother. *King Lear*,
with Mrs. Rowe as Cordelia, and a repetition of *William Tell*
concluded the first half of Forrest's engagement. *Brutus* with
Jane Placide in the role of Tullia, was his benefit offering on the
24th, and for Miss Placide's benefit he appeared as Rolla. *Pizarro*
was followed by *Hamlet, Venice Preserved, Richard III*, and for
his farewell benefit on May 6, he presented Mrs. Mitford's new
tragedy, *Rienzi*.

Information concerning this engagement is limited. The few extant critiques speak favorably but briefly of "the young and talented actor." The most illuminating of these is the puff which appeared in the *Louisiana Advertiser* on the day of his benefit.

> We do not profess ourselves to be among those who admire the versatility of Mr. Forrest's tragic powers; we think, that like all those in his line, his genius has its limits, and when confined within his own peculiar sphere, emits those vivid flashes which strike the audience with admiration and awe, and ever and anon calls forth bursts of unrestrained applause. It pours from his eloquent tongue and lightens in his expressive eyes—it is supported in his dignified and manly action and justly stamps him as the Kemble of America. Who that has seen this genius of native growth, in some of his splendid efforts, can withhold the tribute due to native talent and native worth? . . . Let us support this tender sapling and prove to the pedants of Europe that our soil is fertile in genius and that her children know how to cherish and reward it.

The papers reported full houses during the engagement, but it is impossible to estimate accurately either the attendance or the receipts. The only record is that of May 8 when Forrest performed Damon for the benefit of the Asylum for Destitute Orphan Boys. The receipts on that night were said to be $1,300.[25]

On those nights when Forrest was not playing, Booth appeared in familiar roles. Of these performances we need mention only that of April 16 when he enacted the Stranger to the Mrs. Haller of "a Lady of New Orleans, her first appearance on any stage." The *Louisiana Courier* the following day reported that this débutante had appeared quite disconcerted by the applause "constantly" bestowed upon her efforts, and that her attempt at the character was a failure.

The French dancers, Celeste and Constance, also made their first appearance on the 16th, appearing at the end of the play in a grand French *Pas de Deux*. Said the *Louisiana Courier* of the 17th: "They danced with much science and dexterity, and were loudly applauded. Some of the female spectators observed that they thought modesty had been left behind the scenes the while." On April 25, Celeste made her dramatic début as Myrtillo in *The Broken Sword* and followed it with Juliet in John Farrell's melodrama, *The Dumb Girl of Genoa,* and Julio in the Holcroft adap-

---

[25] *Ibid.,* May 12, 1829.

tation, *Deaf and Dumb*. These roles gave her excellent opportunities to display her exquisite grace and pantomimic ability
without making any demands on her limited knowledge of English. The benefit of "La Petite Constance," on May 9, offered
the romantic spectacle, *Valentine and Orson,* Celeste in the role
of Valentine and the beneficiary as Eglantine. This and *The
Dumb Girl of Genoa* concluded the dancers' engagement on
May 14.

Benefits were in order during the last two weeks of the season as the resident members of the company reappeared in their
favorite roles. H. A. Williams, Mrs. Russell, and Gray displayed
their talents in the old favorites, *The School of Reform, She
Stoops to Conquer, The School for Scandal,* and *The Belle's
Stratagem.* On May 15 Pearson offered C. P. Clinch's dramatization of *The Spy,* a novelty in which Caldwell played Harvey
Birch and the beneficiary Henry Wharton. The afterpiece, *Monsieur Tonson,* introduced Hosack, "from the Philadelphia, Charleston, and Baltimore Theatres." Caldwell's offering of *The West
Indian* and *Is It a Lie?* brought the season to a close on May 22.

This season, unlike the previous one, had presented the best
of the standard plays as well as several novelties. Though many
of the latter were trifles such as Lunn's *All on the Wing,* C. A.
Somerset's *The Poacher,* Brayley's *Wool Gathering,* Planché's
Half an Hour's Courtship and the anonymous *Touch and Take,*
they made for pleasant variety. It must be remembered, however, that the emphasis this season was not on novelties but on
stars. While New York complained of the lack of talent, Manager
Caldwell offered Cooper, Booth, Mrs. Sloman, and Mrs. Drake
in the same play. Taking it all in all, this was a good season.

AMERICAN THEATRE, 1829-1830

Caldwell and his company returned in December, 1829, to a
theatre which had undergone "numerous improvements" during
the summer. Of the nature of these nothing is known except that
the second tier had four additional boxes, "superbly furnished
and decorated." The extensive redecorating of last season and
of this can have been made with only one purpose in mind: Caldwell wished to number more of the "fashionable and fair" of the
American population among his audiences, and this, he thought,
was one way of attracting them. As a further inducement he
announced in the first notice of the season: "The regulations for

the representations have been made with care—men of firmness and of gentlemanly deportment will mildly point out venial infringements of the rules, but will assuredly exercise their power to put down every flagrant attempt to interrupt the general quiet."

The staff of the theatre included Richard Russell, Stage Manager; A. Mondelli, Principal Artist; J. Varden, Principal Machinist; and P. Lewis, Leader of the Orchestra. Jane Placide was again a regular member of the company, and among the familiar names are found those of Pearson, Gray, Morton, Clarke, Williams, Fenno, Hernizen, Kenny, Carr and Mesdames Russell, Rowe, Lacombe, Gray, Kenny, Carr, and Miss Russell.

Having announced his intention of "getting up the finest old comedies with judicious casts" and of introducing "new pieces of tried merit," Caldwell opened the theatre of December 7 with Buckstone's melodrama, *Luke the Labourer,* and Morton's *School of Reform.* Squire Chase in the melodrama and Lord Avondale in the comedy were played by John Gilbert, "from the Tremont Theatre, his first appearance in New Orleans." Gilbert, later to become one of the finest of our native comedians, was but twenty at this time and had been on the stage only a year. J. M. Field, "from the Tremont," and Miss Clarke, "from the Federal Street Theatre, Boston," were also introduced in these pieces. In the farce, *The Hundred Pound Note,* which concluded the evening's entertainment, Miss Clarke impersonated Miss Arlington "with the original Bavarian Girl's Broom Song." The next night in *Speed the Plough* a Mr. Marks, "from the Theatre Royal, London," made his first appearance as Sir Abel Handy. On December 11, Payne's opera of *Clari, the Maid of Milan* had its New Orleans première, Jane Placide in the title role. In the farce of the evening Miss Russell, now all of twelve, led the Invincibles in their exercises and sang, "Oh never fall in Love, dear Girls." Just five years ago she had been one of the children who took part in the first New Orleans production of the *Cataract of the Ganges.* Planché's new drama of *Charles XII* was the presentation of the 12th; on the 14th was introduced Douglas Jerrold's melodrama, *Ambrose Gwinett,* with H. G. Pearson as Ambrose. After Payne's farce, *The Lancers,* on December 16, the march of novelties ceased for a while.

On that day James Howard, the first star of the season, made his début. As befitted a vocalist, he opened a "short engagement" as Henry Bertram in *Guy Mannering,* numbering among his songs "Oft in the Stilly Night," "as sung by him 100 nights at Chatham Theatre, New York." Performances of *The Devil's Bridge,* Jane Placide as Countess Rosalina to his Count Belino, *Brother and Sister, Love in a Village, Sweethearts and Wives, John of Paris, Blue Beard,* and numerous musical afterpieces carry us up to his benefit on January 7.

Five days after Howard's first appearance, the tragedian, Thomas S. Hamblin, had begun his engagement as Virginius, the role of Virginia being played by Mrs. McClure. This lady was a new member of the company and with her husband had been introduced but two days before (December 19) in J. T. C. Rodwell's farce, *The Young Widow.* In the plays which followed, *Virginius, Macbeth, The Revenge,* and *George Barnwell,* Jane Placide supported the tragedian. For his benefit, on January 4, he offered *William Tell,* Albert being played by Miss Russell. Joe Cowell, the English comedian, commenced his engagement on this night, appearing as Crack in the farce of *The Turnpike Gate* and singing his celebrated comic song, "Gallamaufry or The Smokers' Club." The following day he appeared in *Paul Pry* and *Lock and Key,* two favorite pieces.

Miss Lydia Kelly had arrived by this time; on January 6 she enacted Letitia Hardy, "with a song," to Caldwell's Doricourt and appeared in the afterpiece, *Husbands and Wives.* At Howard's benefit on the 7th, this star shone again as Floretta in T. Dibdin's operetta, *The Cabinet,* presented for the first time in New Orleans. Cowell, in the role of Whimsicolo, sang two duets with Miss Kelly. On the following day, "in honor of that ever memorable day in 1815," was introduced the native play, *The Eighth of January.* It is perhaps worthy of note that the editor of the *Louisiana Courier* believed the author of the national piece to be "Johnny Wyers, the banker poet of New Orleans," and not Richard Penn Smith as announced in the bills. Mrs. LaCombe sang "L'Orleanaise, Hymne de Victoire," the composition of a Louisianian; and the entertainment concluded with *Much Ado About Nothing,* Miss Kelly playing Beatrice to Caldwell's Benedick.

Hamblin and Howard were now re-engaged to give "éclat" to several operas in which Miss Kelly was to appear, but the triumvirate was never to be. Her engagement was suddenly broken off and she did not appear again. For the next week Cowell and Hamblin played on alternate nights: Hamblin in *Damon and Pythias,* on January 11; Cowell as Mawworm in *The Hypocrite* on the 12th; Hamblin in *The Stranger* on January 13, followed by *The Turnpike Gate,* with young Cowell as Crack. An unusual attraction was presented on January 15, *The Merchant of Venice* with Hamblin enacting Shylock; Cowell, Launcelot Gobbo; Caldwell, Gratiano; Howard, Lorenzo, in which character he introduced two popular songs; and Jane Placide, Portia. The next day Cowell took his benefit, offering J. B. Buckstone's new piece, *The May Queen,* in which he was Caleb Pipkin. Young Cowell who had volunteered "his powerful aid," sang "The Coal Black Rose" and played Chip to his father's Robert in the farce, *A Chip of the Old Block.*

With this the Cowells departed, and tragedy and melodrama once more held sway. Hamblin appeared in Massinger's play, *The Fatal Dowry,* "first time in New Orleans"; in *Virginius,* "by particular request"; and for his farewell benefit, *Richard III* and *The Review* (Looney Mactwolter, "for this night only"). Communications such as the following in the *Louisiana Advertiser* of January 23 testify to the artistic success of Hamblin's engagement. "We have witnessed no instance in which Mr. Hamblin has not equalled, if not exceeded our expectations, and this is saying much, for we anticipated much." "Yet," continues the writer, "we are sorry that Mr. Caldwell has not been better paid for his devotion to the public, and hope his unwearied exertions to please, will in the future be better rewarded."

These hopes were realized with the engagement of the youthful Miss Clara Fisher. Gentlemen had been allowed to secure boxes for the whole of her twelve-night engagement, and all performances were played to "overflowing houses." On the opening night, January 25, after acting the part of Letitia Hardy, in which character she sang "I'm a brisk and sprightly lad," and "Poll dang it, how'd ye do," and danced a Sailor's Hornpipe, she went through the antics of Little Pickle. It must have pleased Caldwell to read in the *Louisiana Advertiser* (January 26) that a "brilliant assemblage of native belles and beaux" witnessed his representation of the polite and sensitive Doricourt. Perhaps

some of them returned the next night to see Jerrold's new melodrama, *Black Eyed Susan,* and to pay tribute to Howard, since
this was announced as his last appearance.

At her second performance Miss Fisher impersonated Albina
Manderville in *The Will* and the four Mowbrays in the afterpiece,
Old and Young. The *Louisiana Advertiser* of January 28 fails
to mention how many rounds of applause greeted her famous
song, "Hurrah for the Bonnets of Blue," but it gives a detailed
account of the farce.

> . . . Her inimitable representation of the Mowbrays was,
> beyond all doubt, the most perfect piece of acting of the kind
> we ever beheld in New Orleans. Master Hector stormed and
> hectored it about with all the mischievous humour of a rattle
> brained boy; and Master Gobbleton devoured with avidity
> the partridge pie of his uncle with the sang froid of a natural
> glutton, while the house rang again with burst of laughter
> and merriment. Master Fopping Mowbray was certainly a
> most exquisite hit at the foppling exquisities of the day. We
> thought indeed the charming little Clara had abandoned the
> stage, so unlike herself was she in those three characters,
> until we recognized her in the amiable and docile Matilda
> Mowbray at the closing of the piece.

The fair star played Beatrice to Caldwell's Benedick and sustained six characters in *The Actress of All Work* on her third
appearance. On January 30 she introduced Colly Cibber's comedy,
She Would and She Would Not, which was followed by that favorite of the last season, *The Invincibles.* The distinguished Henry
Clay witnessed this performance, doubtless receiving as much
pleasure from it as he did from the six rounds of applause which
greeted him on his entrance.[26]

A fine old comedy, a new farce, and the reappearance of Joe
Cowell made February 1 a memorable day for theatre-goers.
Clara Fisher's Lady Teazle was supported by Caldwell's Charles
Surface and Cowell's Sir Peter; in Buckstone's new farce, *The
Dead Shot,* Cowell was Mr. Timid, Clara Fisher was Louisa. The
second performance of the month was announced as "Howard's
benefit and last appearance." To date this was Howard's third
"last appearance," and several more were to be announced before
he departed with the company at the conclusion of the season on
May 22. As seems to have been customary with him on these

---

[26] *Argus,* February 1, 1830.

occasions, he enacted Blue Peter in *Black Eyed Susan* and sang
the lead in a musical afterpiece. Arnold's comedy, *Man and Wife,*
on February 3 introduced Clara Fisher as Helen Worrett; and
on the 5th she appeared in Mrs. Inchbald's *Lovers' Vows* and as
Arinette, a Little Jockey, in Dimond's *Youth, Love and Folly,* "a
new farce never acted here." Mrs. Inchbald's comedy, *The Country Girl,* "first time in ten years," presented the star as Miss
Peggy and that same evening she enacted Paul in the popular
afterpiece, *The Wandering Boys.*

The week of February 8 was an unusually interesting one.
It opened with Miss Fisher in *Wives as They Were* and *The
Actress of All Work;* on the 9th, Cowell appeared in *The Hypo-
crite* and in Barham Levius' farce, *Maid or Wife.* On Wednesday,
Master Russell enacted Tom Thumb after Miss Fisher had played
Juliet to the Romeo of Pearson and the Mercutio of Caldwell.
On Thursday, Miss Placide, "having recovered from her late
severe accident," returned to the stage as Madame Clermont in
Dimond's play, *Adrian and Orilla.* Clara Fisher's personations
of Clari, Arinette, Rosalind, and Moggie McGilpin *(The Highland
Reel)* brought the eventful week to a close. The star concluded
her engagement the following Monday as Violante in *The Wonder! A Woman Keeps a Secret* but returned as a volunteer at
young Cowell's benefit on February 17 when she appeared as
Little Pickle and as Peggy in *The Turnpike Gate.* When her
departure for Charleston was delayed, she performed Lady Teazle
for the benefit of the Orphan Boys' Asylum on the 18th.

Herr Cline, the celebrated artist of the Elastic Cord, began
a short engagement on February 19, but after two performances
illness forced him to postpone his next appearance until March.
Herr Cline's dances on the cord and his "unequalled display of
Gladiatorial Attitudes" were received with great favor. Reported
the *Argus* of February 20: "Herr Cline has the merit of originality and in him we no longer see a common rope dancer. . . . He
paints in turn, filial affection, love and anger; the most tragic
passions he also delineates with the greatest fidelity, and in his
jealous and furious transports he might be mistaken for Othello
or Orestes. . . ."

On Monday, February 22, the city was to have had its first
glimpse of Madame Feron, "from the Grand Theatre San Carlos
at Naples, La Scala at Milan, Italian Opera at Paris, Drury

Lane, London, and Park Theatre, New York." But Madame Feron was "indisposed" and her début was necessarily postponed. In the interim before she could begin her engagement, Caldwell presented several novelties. Peake's popular new musical farce, *My Master's Rivals,* was performed on the 25th; on the 27th among the entertainments offered at Caldwell's annual benefit was "The Coal Black Rose" arranged as a duet with young Cowell as Sambo and young Russell as the dark-hued Rose. By March 1 Herr Cline had recovered sufficiently to make a grand Ascension from the stage to the gallery, "upwards of forty-five feet in height." The performance of *The Maid and the Magpie* the following day was enlivened by the *Pas de Deux* of the Corps de Ballet which had been performing at the French theatre. This little troupe consisting of Benoni, Feltman, Madame Feltman, and Virginia Benoni presented during their short engagement at the American Theatre, *Osmar and Arsana,* a ballet pantomime "never acted in this country," and the new melodramatic ballet of action, *Jocko, or The Monkey of Brazil.*

Madame Feron, having recovered by this time, made her début in *The Barber of Seville* on March 3. The critic in the *Argus* of March 5 was not enthusiastic about the long awaited event: "Madame Feron had a thousand difficulties to contend with; she found herself placed along side of actors, who, to say the least were below mediocrity in the opera, and but little capable of feeling the sublime inspiration of Rossini. She had to contend against an orchestra badly directed, although composed of some good musicians. . . . Yet she astonished and delighted all who heard her. . . ." Alas for the operatic aspirations of poor Cowell (Figaro) and Howard (Count Almaviva).

Her second performance, which included *The Cabinet* and the musical farce of *The Prize,* in which she was Caroline with a "French Mock Bravura and an Italian Cavatina," was presented to an audience which was predominately French. Madame Feron was a brilliant soprano, but at the American Theatre she had not the support needed for more ambitious pieces. She was forced to appear in those operas and melodramas which were familiar to the company, *Rob Roy, Love in a Village, John of Paris, The Sultan,* etc. True, on March 15 there was presented for the first time *The Libertine,* "a literal translation of Mozart's celebrated opera of *Il Don Giovani (sic)* with music by H. B.

Bishop." Yet even into this was introduced "The Dashing White Sergeant." For her benefit she offered Mozart's *The Marriage of Figaro*, and John Walker's new melodramatic anecdote, *Napoleon, or The Emperor and the Soldier*. On the 26th she was Carolina in Dimond's operetta, *The Young Hussar*, "first time in New Orleans." At Howard's benefit, on March 31, she played Catharine in the "grand melodramatic poetic spectacle," *The Exile*, numbering among her songs, "The Arab Steed" and "Once on a Time a Pert Young Ape." On April 3, Madame Feron made her last appearance in *The Castle of Andalusia*, an opera of O'Keeffe's which was new to the city. Her engagement cannot have been a profitable one, as recurrent articles speak of the small patronage which she received. The comic trifles of Clara Fisher and Joe Cowell had set the musical standard at the American Theatre this season, and to that may be attributed the lack of enthusiasm which greeted the Italian airs of this more talented singer.

Though Madame Feron played to thin houses, certain of the March performances must have won public favor. There was the farewell benefit of the Cowells on March 16, when Young Cowell and Young Russell enacted the two Dromios in the *Comedy of Errors*, and sang the now famous duet, "The Coal Black Rose," Howard obliging with the equally familiar and popular "Savourneen Deelish." Two days later Caldwell presented a new skit, *Paul Pry at Dover;* the moving Diorama from last year's popular *Paris and London;* and Moncrieff's melodrama, *The Lear of Private Life* adapted from Mrs. Opie's novel, *Father and Daughter*. The latter evidently "took," for it was presented twice during the following week. *The Comedy of Errors* was repeated for the benefit of the young Russells on March 20. A splendid Drop Scene painted by Mondelli on 1500 square feet of canvas was exhibited on the 23rd; and "in compliment to the New Orleans Jockey Club," Caldwell appeared as Goldfinch in *The Road to Ruin* on March 25.

Mlle. Celeste and Constance began a starring engagement the day before Madam Feron's benefit, and until May 1 these two delighted crowded houses with displays of French dancing, grand ballets of action, and their acting in new and spectacular melodramas.

The most important novelties of this season seem to have been reserved for the last two months. On April 6 Caldwell brought out *Irma, or The Prediction*, a new tragedy "by a very

young gentleman of our city," James M. Kennicott. This had
won the $300 premium offered by the manager the last year;
and though the critics of New Orleans found it faulty in plot
arrangement, a defect which they attributed to the author's un-
familiarity with scenic representations and stagecraft, they
praised its originality, declaring that in incident and highly
wrought scenes it was inferior to no production of modern
date.[27] Jane Placide played Irma, who was brought to her ruin
by Remington's prediction that she would become a murderess,
and Caldwell was "the audacious Remington." The critics reported in detail on the first two performances of this native play.
According to "M.D.S." in the *Louisiana Courier* of April 7, Caldwell was incapable of doing justice to his part. "Mr. Caldwell
was not intended for a tragedian and especially not for such a
one as last night's piece required." Yet "Z" of the *Louisiana
Advertiser*, April 12, saw "some peculiar touches" in the manager's delineation and several very fine imitations of Charles
Kemble which could not fail to please. The character of Irma
suited the talents of Jane Placide, said the critic, and when
better acquainted with it she would make it "more than interesting." "Z" was especially pleased with Field as that actor appeared to have overcome "the affected and boyish manner of
speaking through his nose" which characterized his other parts.
The critics who attended the second performance of *Irma* on
April 12 found more to condemn. Not only was the beautiful
poetry of the author "mangled" by the principal characters but
"an episode of a most indecorous character" was introduced in
one of the scenes between Pearson and Field. The *Argus* of
April 13 reported that Field had forgotten his lines and had
retired from the stage in confusion when Pearson broke into
the prompter's words with "Speak, Sir, I've given you your cue!"
According to the *Courier* of April 19, Pearson himself had been
at fault several times in the past few weeks; in fact on one
occasion had saved himself from disgrace only by leaving the
stage in the midst of a speech and returning to read it with a
book in his hand.

There is no question that the actors had too many new
lines to learn these days. Celeste's benefit on the 17th introduced
the grand historical drama, *Masaniello, or the Dumb Girl of
Portici*, "Translated from the French by H. H. Milner, music and

---

[27] *Louisiana Advertiser*, April 6, 1830.

overture by Witt, scenery by Mondelli, Machinery by Varden, Dresses by Ammerman, Properties by Lewis, and the whole produced under the direction of Celeste." The character of Masaniello, the humble fisherman of Naples, was represented by Pearson; that of his sister Fenella *(La Muete De Portici)* by Celeste. In the last act the audience looked on "A View of the Bay of Naples, bordering on Portici and Tore Del Greco. VIEW OF VESUVIUS. Terrific explosion!! Forked lightnings rend the sky; the Burning lava impetuously flows down the side of the mountain, and the whole country becomes AWFULLY ILLUMI-NATED. Popular tumult and Death of Masaniello." A Mr. Jones, referred to in the advertisements as the celebrated singer from the Bowery Theatre, rendered comic songs after this exciting scene, and as a grand finale, Celeste, in male attire *à la Chevalier de France,* executed a great variety of French dancing with the "pretty little Constance." Newspapers reported that the receipts of this night were $1020. Celeste was immediately re-engaged for four more nights of *Masaniello.* At Constance's benefit on April 24, after a variety of dances and the petite comedy, *Paul and Peter Shack (My Master's Rival),* the last act of *Masaniello* was given. For their farewell benefit on May 1, the dancers offered the "Grand Asiatic Ballet of Action, *The Caliph of Bagdad,"* with splendid dances, dresses and decorations. . . . As performed at the Bowery Theatre." It would be interesting to know who supported Celeste (Islam, the Caliph) and Constance (Zetulbe). The cast of the ballet called for nine dancers.

On April 26, came "a new national melodrama," Captain Stephen Glover's adaptation of *The Last of the Mohicans.* The notices stated it had been played with distinguished success at Baltimore and Charleston; New York was not to see it until December, 1831. The cast included Pearson as Magua, Old Gray as Hawkeye, Russell as Gamut, and Mrs. Rowe as Cora. Pearson was the star of the presentation, depicting Magua so faithfully that the author and "competent judges" said the role could not have been bettered by Forrest himself. At the fourth performance, on April 30, Miss Clarke was forced to take the place of Mrs. Rowe whose absence was occasioned by the sudden death of a little daughter. Though she was "quite too fair, too fascinating and too timid for the stern, unbending and dignified dark-haired Cora," her acting was praised as being natural and affecting.

As early as April 1 "Old Gray" had taken his benefit, giving "in honor of the day" Reynolds' comedy, *Folly as it Flies*. Now benefits and novelties followed fast on one another. On Russell's night the city was introduced to Cumberland's comedy, *The Jew*, Russell enacting the role of Sheva and Master Russell that of Jabel. This was Russell's eighth successive season in New Orleans, and we may be sure that on this occasion a large audience paid homage to his merits as a "general and useful comedian" and as stage manager. On the 30th, "Old Gray" distinguished himself as Jonathan Postfree in *The Honest Yankee*, a piece by L. Beach which, though introduced in 1807, had never been given here. Mrs. Rowe revived John Millingen's *Ladies at Home* for her return to the boards on May 3 and enacted Christine in the long popular *She Would Be a Soldier*. *Pizarro* was presented for the first time this season at Pearson's benefit on May 5, Howard assisting as the High Priest. After the play Hernizen sang a new comic song, "A Hit at the Fashions of New Orleans." The Clarkes' benefit on the 8th brought out two pieces "never acted here": H. M. Miller's comedy *One Hundred and Two* and T. J. Dibdin's *The Sea Serpent*, a nautical pantomime in which Miss M. E. Clarke, as the Fairy of the Main, made her first appearance on any stage.

Jane Placide's benefit on May 10 offered both the old and the novel. After *The Soldier' Daughter*, with the beneficiary as Widow Cheerly, Caldwell as Frank Heartall and Mr. Langton, "from the New York, Philadelphia and Boston Theatres," as Malfort, Jr., there was presented the grand romantic drama, *Alonzo the Brave and the Fair Imogine*. Mondelli appears to have surpassed himself in the scenery for this play of Thomas Dibdin's. "The last scene represents a CEMETERY BY MOONLIGHT. The whole stage is occupied by tombs, graves, etc., . . . the shadows of Imogine and Alonzo are seen ascending in the CHARIOT OF DEATH, surrounded by CLOUDS. As it rises the surrounding tombs open, and the skeletons rise to look upon the passing scene. The whole is illuminated with a blue vapour, and the Curtain falls." Needless to say, the play was repeated.

All of the Russells lent "their powerful aid" at Mrs. Russell's benefit on May 12. After Russell had played Tony Lumpkin to his wife's Miss Hardcastle, the two younger members of the family sang, accompanying themselves on the Piano Forte. As a grand finale Miss Russell sustained six characters in the American première of R. Haworth's one act piece, *The Disguises*.

And still the novelties came. Mondelli's benefit on the 15th featured "A Splendid Naval Exhibition of the Glorious Feats of the American Navy against Tripoli in 1803," a representation of the naval action itself, by combination of Painting and Machinery. A new play, Planchè's *Green Eyed Monster*, was given on May 17; on the 18th and two days thereafter was exhibited a railroad and steam carriage, "its first appearance on the stage." Even the joint benefit of Mesdames Gray and McClure with the Naval Exhibition and Mrs. McClure's personation of Harry Clinton *(El Hyder)* pales before the stage début of this 1830 steam carriage.

Caldwell's benefit ended the season on May 22. On this occasion the manager sustained five characters in Mrs. Centlivre's comedy, *A Bold Stroke for a Wife,* and introduced Knowles' "Hibernian melodrama," *Brian Boroihme.* Howard sang the popular "Savourneen Deelish," thus bringing to a close his engagement of nine nights which had begun on December 16.

This had been a good theatrical season. James Howard, the first star to appear, had remained all season. Hamblin, Cowell, Miss Kelly, Miss Fisher, Herr Cline, Madame Feron, and Celeste and Constance had followed in rapid succession. Forty novelties had been introduced, among them the plays of five native writers. The editor of the *Louisiana Courier* (May 22) may act as spokesman for those who frequented the theatre this season: "When we recollect with what unremitting assiduity Mr. Caldwell has devoted his time and talents to amuse the public and contribute to the refinement of the age, and improve its taste, and above all keep up a proud national feeling, we cannot but award him our united approbation."

AMERICAN THEATRE, 1830-1831

The American Theatre, "improved and newly and splendidly decorated," opened for the eighth season on December 15, 1830. Though several favorites were missing from the company, even more capable performers had been engaged to replace them, and in continuation of the policy initiated in 1829, Manager Caldwell promised that the "first talent of the country" would be brought forward in regular succession.

In honor of "the recent and glorious Revolution in France," the entertainments of the opening night began with a display of the Tri-Colored Flag and the singing of "The Marseillaise Hymn" by the entire company. Caldwell and Jane Placide appeared as Benedick and Beatrice in *Much Ado About Nothing;* and Sol Smith, who now returned after an absence of two years, delighted "the respectable though not fashionable audience" with his performance in Thomas Dibdin's new musical farce, *The Two Gregories.* Mrs. Sol Smith, also making her first appearance in two years, assisted with songs and glees through the evening.

The stars came out early this season. George Holland opened his engagement on the second night with the favorite pieces, *Paul Pry* and *A Day After the Fair*, and continued in *Sweethearts and Wives, The Secret, Whims of a Comedian, She Stoops to Conquer, The Honest Thieves,* and *Deaf as a Post.* For his benefit on December 30 he enacted Jacky Hawbuck in *Town and Country,* a part which had not been among those offered during his first visit in 1829.

Thomas Morton's farce, *A Roland for an Oliver,* was introduced on the 17th. On the 20th Mr. and Mrs. Joe Cowell made their first appearance as Sir Peter and Lady Teazle; Cowell also played Crack in *The Turnpike Gate.* The Cowells had been engaged as regular members of the company this season, Joe to replace Richard Russell as stage manager and low comedian, Mrs. Cowell to perform the comedy leads, and Young Cowell to fill in whenever he was needed. James M. Scott, the tragedian from the Bowery Theatre in New York, made his bow on December 22 in *William Tell.* *She Stoops to Conquer,* on the following day, reintroduced two old favorites who had not been seen for seven years, Mr. and Mrs. Noah Ludlow. The cast included Ludlow as Young Marlow, Holland as Tony Lumpkin, Mrs. Ludlow as Mrs. Hardcastle, and Mrs. Cowell as Miss Hardcastle.

The combined force of tragic and comic talent drew a "full house" on December 24 when Scott played Charles DeMoor to Mrs. Rowe's Amelia in *The Robbers,* and the afterpiece, *The Honest Thieves,* enlisted the services of Holland, Cowell, and Ludlow. The *Louisiana Courier* reported the next day that these comedians "amused the risible faculties of the audience to such a degree . . . that the very walls rang again with the boisterous plaudits of the assembled multitudes." On Christmas night the management presented *George Barnwell* as a "beacon to the rising generation whereby they may learn to avoid the rocks and shoals on which so many promising youths have been shipwrecked

in their voyage of life." At the conclusion of Lillo's sad tale **Mr.**
Brown, the celebrated professor of Grecian exercises, went
through his amusing Christmas gambols, and Holland and the
Cowells appeared in the burletta, *Bombastes Furioso,* young Cowell taking the part of the General.

The veteran Cooper came the last of December "to add fresh
laurels to his hoary fame." His opening performance as Damon
on the 27th was supported by the Pythias of Scott, the Calanthe
of Jane Placide, and the Hermione of Mrs. Rowe. He was Othello
to Scott's Iago, Mrs. Rowe's Desdemona, Jane Placide's Emilia,
and Caldwell's Cassio. The performance of *Virginius* on his third
night introduced in the role of Icillius E. S. Conner, a new member
of the company. Inclement weather kept many from seeing *Hamlet,* performed on January 3 with a strong cast which included
Cooper in the title role, Caldwell as the Ghost, Scott as Horatio,
Cowell as the Grave Digger, Jane Placide as Ophelia, and Joseph
Page, "first appearance in three years," as Polonius. On the 5th
the star appeared as Sir John Falstaff in *King Henry IV, Part I,*
and though the character was out of his line, his interpretation
was heralded as "a *chef d'oeuvre* of the ironic art and every way
worthy of Shakespeare and his distinguished representation."[28]
In the cast were Scott (King Henry IV), Ludlow (Prince of
Wales), Cowell (Francis), Holland (First Carrier), and Edward
Raymond (Hotspur), a new member of the company who had
made his début on January 1 as Rolla *(Pizarro).*

The roles which followed Falstaff were familiar ones:
Beverly in *The Gamester,* Lord Hastings in *Jane Shore,* Marc
Anthony, Shylock, and Pierre in *Venice Preserved.* For his farewell benefit on January 17 he offered *Henry VIII,* a play not
previously seen in New Orleans. He portrayed Cardinal Wolsey;
Scott was King Henry, Ludlow, Cromwell, Jane Placide, Queen
Katharine, and Mrs. Rowe, Ann Bullen. Ludlow recalls that tears
flowed from Cooper's eyes in the scene between Wolsey and Cromwell at the close of the third act and that he could not restrain
his as he thought of the past days when Cooper had "trod the
ways of glory."[29]

There were other stars at the theatre during these weeks.
On December 28 William Pelby had begun a short engagement as
DeValmont in *The Foundling of the Forest* and followed it with

---

[28] *Louisiana Courier,* January 6, 1831.
[29] Ludlow, *op. cit.,* 371.

personations of Reuben Glenroy in *Town and Country*, Rienzi, and Brutus in Payne's play of that name. He had been re-engaged to appear with Cooper in *Venice Preserved* and in *Henry IV*.

Holland's engagement had ended on January 1, but he, too, had been reengaged and for the remainder of Cooper's stay the two played on alternate nights or Holland appeared in the after-piece. The comedian's roles were familiar ones except for Gaby Grim in the younger Colman's interlude, *We Fly by Night*, and Verges in Clara Fisher's opening performance of *Much Ado About Nothing* on January 19. His benefit bill, on the 20th, was made up of *Frederick the Great; Whims of a Comedian;* Brown's Grecian Exercises; Madame Edouard's dancing; and R. J. Raymond's farce, *Cherry Bounce*. Two days after this, Holland began a third engagement as Dan in Colman's *John Bull;* Scott played Peregrine, Cowell Dennis Brulgruddery, and Frederick, a recent addition to the company, was Frank Rochdale. During this engagement the star appeared in several new roles: as Soto in *She Would and She Would Not*, Stephen Harrowby in *The Poor Gentleman*, Brusque in *The Invincibles*, and Billy Black in *The Hundred Pound Note* (February 7).

Comedy was the standard fare these nights. Clara Fisher, who had begun her engagement in *Much Ado About Nothing* on January 19, followed it with *The Will, Old and Young, She Would and She Would Not,* and *The Spoiled Child.* She had added to her repertoire since the last visit and on her fourth appearance introduced Thomas Bayly's petite comedy, *Perfection.* Her Kate O'Brien with the songs, "Kate Kearney" and "Hurrah for the Emerald Isle" won immediate favor, and the piece was repeated three times. Another novelty was John Faucit's melodrama, *The Miller's Maid*, in which she played Phoebe to the Giles of Scott. Other new parts for her were Miss Arlington in *The Hundred Pound Note*, Lady Restless in *All in the Wrong*, Clari in Payne's play of that name, Catherine in Buckstone's new comedy, *A Husband at Sight*, Harriet in *Is He Jealous?*, and for her benefit, on February 17, Betty Finiken in *Gretna Green*.

On "off nights" when neither Clara Fisher nor Holland performed, Caldwell introduced several important novelties. The first of these, on January 29, was *Paul Jones*, a nautical melodrama which W. H. Wallack had adapted from Cooper's novel, *The Pilot.* Scott enacted Long Tom Coffin, a role that had been

associated with his name since he played it in the New York
première in 1824. Tryon was Barnstable, Field, Captain Bor-
oughcliff, Anderson, the Pilot, and Mrs. Rowe, Kate Plowden.
"Rapturous applause" greeted the first two performances though
it was felt by several that the actors had been miscast. Said
"Romeo" in the *Louisiana Courier* on January 31: "Mrs. Rowe's
Kate Plowden was very spirited and such a girl as her Kate would
never have run away with such a lieutenant as Mr. Tryon's
Barnstable." Though the play appealed to the patriotic citizens
of New Orleans, it was reported that the extreme cold weather
kept many from attending its third performance on February 3.
The afterpiece on this night was *The Rendezvous,* mentioned here
only because it introduced Miss Mary Vos, the daughter of John
Vos who acted in Cargill's little troupe in 1817.

Another native play, the anonymous *Miantonimoh, or The
Wept of Wish-ton-Wish,* was presented on February 5 with the
author in the role of Matacom, a Wampanoag Chief. According
to an announcement which appeared in the *Louisiana Advertiser*
on January 18, this play had been introduced in Richmond and
was not the *Miantonimoh* which had been given in New York.
Holland's benefit on the 10th brought out another novelty, *The
Hamlet Travestie,* written "by the author of the rejected ad-
dresses" stated the advertisement. It is easy to imagine the
laughter which must have greeted the Hamlet of young Cowell,
the Ophelia of Holland, and the "Grand Set To—Anglaise" of
the last scene.

A melodrama, *The Avenger,* was introduced at Scott's benefit on February 12. This was announced as his last appearance
but on the 22nd the play was repeated with him still in the title
role. "A thin but very attentive and discriminating audience"
saw a revival of Kennicott's *Irma* on the 15th. One of this body
commented in the *Louisiana Advertiser* the next day: "The part
of Irma by Jane Placide was one of the most powerful efforts
we have witnessed in a long while; it can only be compared with
the Imogine of Mrs. Duff in *Bertram.*". Tragedy was the offering
of February 16 when, for Cowell's benefit, Clara Fisher enacted
Juliet to the Romeo of Edward Raymond, the comedian appearing as Peter. A grand "Dramatic Masquerade" concluded the bill.

When Clara Fisher left for Natchez on February 18, her
place was taken by Mr. and Mrs. Cramer Plumer who had just

returned from there. This year Caldwell had decided to reopen the Natchez theatre for a short season, and sometime around January 21 Ludlow and a small troupe left New Orleans.[30] In his account of the season Ludlow lists as his associates Mr. and Mrs. Sol Smith, Mrs. McClure, McCafferty, and Miss Petrie.[31] Sol Smith refers to his brother Lemuel as one of the group.[32] Other members of the company were John Gilbert, E. S. Conner, and Marks.[33]

The "fatal glance" of Kate Kearney was not forgotten even after Clara Fisher's departure and for a while the Plumers played to thin houses. They opened on the 18th in *The Devil's Bridge* and *Winning a Husband* and continued in *Love in a Village*, *The Turn Out*, *Rob Roy* (with Scott replacing Caldwell in the title role), *Of Age Tomorrow*, *The Cabinet*, Poole's *Scape Grace*, "never acted here," *The Soldier's Daughter*, and *Rosina*. After a two-day rest during which the management introduced Douglas Jerrold's interlude, *The Smoked Miser*, and Charles Kean made his bow, the Plumers continued in musical pieces, playing now on alternate nights to the young tragedian. They were Donna Isadora and Don Sylvia in *Brother and Sister;* Patrick and Dermont in *The Poor Soldier;* Diana Vernon and Francis Osbaldistone in *Rob Roy;* Lucy and Henry Bertram in *Guy Mannering;* and Justine and Colonel de Courey in *Rencontre*, a French adaptation by Planché. Mrs. Plumer was also featured as Letitia Hardy, Lady Teazle, Miss Arlington *(The Hundred Pound Note)*, Clari, Juliana *(The Honeymoon)*, and Don Giovanni *(Giovanni in London)*. On March 21 the vocalist gave *The Marriage of Figaro* and *Love and Mercy* and departed for Mobile.

The receipts from Charles Kean's "overflowing houses" may have compensated for the "empty benches" during the Plumers' engagement. The young star had won immediate favor in his opening performance of *Richard III*, and with his second appearance as Sir Giles Overreach his reputation was established. Later parts for him were Sir Edward Mortimer *(The Iron Chest)*, Reuben Glenroy *(The Mountaineers)*, The Stranger, Brutus (in Payne's tragedy), Felix *(The Hunter of the Alps)*, and for his last appearance on March 22, Othello.

---

[30] The names of Ludlow and several of his fellow actors disappear from the New Orleans notices after this date. W. B. Gates in his article, "The Theatre in Natchez," gives January 26, 1831 as the opening date of the Natchez season. *The Journal of Mississippi History*, III (April, 1941), 89.

[31] Ludlow, *op. cit.*, 373.

[32] Smith, *op. cit.*, 69.

[33] Gates, *loc. cit.*, III, 90.

Clara Fisher returned as Kean prepared to leave for Natchez and on the 23rd enacted Lady Restless in *All in the Wrong* and Louisa in *The Dead Shot*. At Caldwell's benefit on the 25th she offered the popular *Perfection*. Her first appearance as Alice in *Love and Reason* called forth the following comment from the *Louisiana Advertiser* (March 29).

> The character of Alice is most beautifully characteristic of Miss Fisher's style of acting, which is mainly conspicuous for the continued play of her intelligent features, over which every shade of feeling or passion, whether of archness or anger, hope or fear, follows each other in rapid succession, yet reflecting the image of each with all the softness of shade and distinctness of coloring of the summer stream which reflects the clouds, the skies, and the foliage about it. Other characters which she now impersonated for the first

time in New Orleans were Lydia Languish, Mrs. Simpson, Elizabeth Freelove *(A Day after the Wedding)*, Bisarre *(Wine Does Wonders)* and Thérèse. For her benefit on April 11 she was Viola in the local première of *Twelfth Night* and Miss Arlingtor in *The Hundred Pound Note*. The *Louisiana Courier* of the 12th reported that the house had been "filled almost to suffocation," but the performances were "no more than respectable."

The last week in March was a busy one at the American Theatre. On the 24th came the world première of Captain Stephen Glover's new play, *Rake Hellies*. Only a "thin house" witnessed this dramatization of Cooper's *Lionel Lincoln*, but it is gratifying to read in the *Louisiana Courier* of March 25 that these few "seemed pre-disposed to be pleased with it, as every American audience should, with every American play on its first production." Two nights later the play was repeated as the afterpiece on a bill which featured the theatrical début of a young gentleman of the city. This gentleman won no praise for his performance as Zanga in *The Revenge*, and when he essayed Jaffier *(Venice Preserved)* on the 31st, he failed miserably. Those who witnessed his second attempt may have derived some entertainment from a new afterpiece, *Pop! Sparrow Shooting*, introduced on this evening.

The most ambitious spectacle of the season was J. R. Planché's melodrama, *The Brigand*, presented on April 5. Caldwell and Jane Placide enacted the leads amid scenery which had been four months in preparation, yet the play was not the success

the management had anticipated. A third representation, with
the added attraction of G. H. Rodwell's new farce, *Teddy the
Tiler,* was announced for the 13th, but the bill was postponed
and the theatre closed until the 16th "in consequence of the indisposition of several of the performers and the great and continued inclemency of the weather."

The stars were again in possession when the theatre reopened. Kean and Fisher had been brought back for a joint
engagement and Mr. and Mrs. Plumer were to fill the alternate
nights with music. The youthful stars made their first appearance in *Romeo and Juliet* and were "eminently successful." Indeed, continued the *Louisiana Courier* of April 19, "The immortal
bard himself would have joined . . . in the well merited plaudits
that were rendered to his representatives, although they were
applauded to the very echo." They also appeared as Durimel
and Bertha *(The Point of Humor)*, Sir Edward Mortimer and
Wilford *(The Iron Chest)*, Hamlet and Ophelia, Reuben Glenroy
and Rosalie Somers *(Town and Country)*, and as Carwin and
Thérèse. On the last night of the engagement (April 29) Kean
enacted the Duke Aranza to Clara Fisher's Juliana. Though
many felt it a "hazardous experiment" for the young actor to
try the role before an audience familiar with Caldwell's personation of it, he succeeded admirably.

The *Louisiana Courier* of April 30 throws some light on the
performance.

> The only fault that could be found with him (Kean)
> was, that he allowed his gravity to be overcome by the mock-
> gravity of Mr. Cowell, as the would-be duke; but the out-
> raged Juliana was also obliged to resign her fury for a
> moment, while a hearty laugh illuminated her previously
> vengeful countenance—a strong proof of the irresistible
> drollery of that genuine Son of Momus.

The Plumers must not be overlooked. Their opening performance of *Rencontre* and *The Poor Soldier,* on April 19, was
followed by the usual round of operas and musical pieces. Of
these *The Barber of Seville, No Song, No Supper, Henri Quatre,*
and *Paul and Virginia* had not been numbered among the offerings of the earlier engagement. Two novelties gave variety to
an otherwise familiar repertoire. On April 26 the vocalists introduced *The Beggar's Opera* by John Gay. For Gray's benefit on
the 30th they offered Dimond's operatic melodrama, *The Peasant*

Boy, "first time in New Orleans." Previous to her performance as Julian the peasant boy, Mrs. Plumer enacted Cicely Homespun in *The Heir at Law.*

The closing weeks of the season brought more benefits. On May 2 for the sake of the Orphan Boys, Kean and Clara Fisher reappeared in *Romeo and Juliet* and the Plumers gave *Winning a Husband.* The *Louisiana Courier* of the 4th says the receipts amounted to $1,200. For her night (May 6) Mrs. Cowell offered *Perfection* with Clara Fisher as Kate O'Brien and two novelties, Buckstone's comedy, *The Happiest Day of My Life,* and *Rap Van Winkle,* possibly the adaptation by John Kerr. One cannot help wishing for a more illuminating comment than that in the *Louisiana Courier* of the 7th: "The play did not seem to answer the high expectations that had been created in its favor by its success at New York."

The most varied of the benefits was Mondelli's on the 7th. The ever popular *Rob Roy* was followed by Hernizen's comic song, "The Fashions of New Orleans," Madame Edouard's French Dancing, the exhibition of an entire new scene representing New York, and the opera of *Rosina.* But this was not all; in the lull before the afterpiece a Mr. Cops exhibited his beautiful serpents, the anaconda and the boa constrictor!

Mrs. Carr's benefit on May 13 introduced Mr. and Mrs. Pearman in the operatic *John of Paris* and *Brother and Sister.* Now that the Pearmans had arrived, as early as January 18 the *Louisiana Courier* had stated that they were expected daily, they added their songs to those of the Plumers. They were Figaro and the Countess Almaviva in *The Barber of Seville* and in *The Marriage of Figaro,* Henry Bertram and Julia Mannering in *Guy Mannering,* and Mr. Scamper and Caroline in the farce, *The Effect of Endorsing.* A repetition of *John of Paris,* on their benefit night, presented Pearman in the name part, Plumer as Vincent, Mrs. Plumer as Rose, and Mrs. Pearman as the Princess of Navarre. The *Louisiana Courier* of May 21 reports that on this occasion the Pearmans supplemented the orchestra with "several amateurs and professors . . . to the end that the delightful melody of their own voices may suffer no abatement, by being intercepted by the villanous 'discord of sweet sounds' that are wont to issue from that department."

F. F. Cooper's burletta, *The Elbow Shakers,* was introduced
on May 19 and in order that it might be properly appreciated
The Gambler's Fate, which it parodied, preceded it on the bill.
On their night (May 24) Field and Hernizen called in Mr.
Brown's "unrivalled troop of horses" to assist with *The Forty
Thieves.* With the horses came Mrs. Sergeant (Zelie), Wells
(Selim), and Keyl (Ganem), three equestrians connected with
Brown's amphitheatre. The bill concluded with *The Tragedians,
or Business and Pleasure,* a new petite comedy written by Mr.
Rawlinson, "a gentleman of this city." Nothing is known of the
play beyond the mention of the cast in the notice of the perform-
ance.

A tragedy, *The Bohemian Mother,* and Soane's melodrama,
Aladdin, were the novelties offered by Jane Placide on the 25th.
First appearances marked the performance of *Speed the Plough*
given by Raymond and Morton on their night, the 26th, Gerald
being played by Charnock "from the Boston and New York
theatre" and Dame Ashfield by Mrs. Higgins, who now returned
after several years' absence. On the 30th Caldwell revived *The
West Indian,* "first time this season," and introduced *The Highland Widow, or The Woman of the Tree,* a new drama taken from
Scott's celebrated novel, *The Chronicles of Canongate.* This was
apparently the work of a local playwright; no other dramatization of the tale is recorded until 1836 when Edinburgh saw it.[34]

With this performance the American Theatre ended another
successful season. Whatever the evils of the starring system it
seems to have brought full houses to Caldwell's theatre. Though
records of his receipts are missing, the fact that he continued to
bring forward "the first talent of the country" shows that the
system was profitable for him. It should be noted also that the
stars brought about a change in the tastes of the New Orleans
audiences. The renewed interest in the legitimate drama this
season may be attributed to the presentations of these visitors.

This June Caldwell took his company to Cincinnati for the
summer season.[35] The St. Louis venture proving less successful
than he had anticipated, Caldwell had decided it would be well
to transfer his activities to another western city. Here the New
Orleans company was to play for the next two summers while
the Nashville theatre, which he had built in 1826, was leased to
other managers.

---

[34] Nicoll, *op. cit.,* II, 468.
[35] Rees, *op. cit.,* 70; Ludlow, *op. cit.,* 381.

The American Theatre opened on November 23, 1831. It had been repainted during the vacation and the seats recovered. Doors had been placed at each side of the entrance that the cold, as well as the noise from the stairway, might be excluded from the boxes.

The company consisted of Caldwell, Jane Placide, Mr. and Mrs. Cowell, Mr. and Mrs. Gray, Mr. and Mrs. Carr, Mr. and Mrs. Higgins, Edward Raymond, Joseph Page, George Hernizen, Morton, Field, Charnock, Frederick, and Madame Edouard, the dancer. Raymond apparently left the troupe for Mobile some-time in March, for his name disappears from the bills at this time and the *Bee* of the 21st in noting his appearance in Mobile refers to him as "late of the Camp Street boards." The new members were Mr. and Mrs. H. A. Williams, last here in 1829, Mr. and Mrs. Charles E. Muzzy, Messrs. Houpt and Madden, and Miss Eliza Petrie. Though there can be no question as to the excellence of this aggregation, Caldwell undoubtedly overesti-mated it when he declared that the company was not surpassed in any theatre of the United States.[36]

The opening performance of O'Keeffe's *Wild Oats* and the popular *No Song, No Supper* and the bills of the first few days served to introduce the new players and to display the strength of the company. The first novelty was Buckstone's *Popping the Question,* given as an afterpiece on the 29th; the next evening *Snakes in the Grass,* another of his recent farces, was presented as the curtain raiser. On December 3 came Douglas Jerrold's melodrama, *The Drunkard's Fate.*

The first visiting performer was John Herbert "from New York, Philadelphia, and Boston," an English actor who had made his American debut in 1817 as Sir Abel Handy in *Speed the Plough.* He opened on December 5 in this comedy and in *Animal Magnetism.* Afterwards he appeared as Governor Heartall, to the Widow Cheerly of Jane Placide, Sir David Dunder *(Ways and Means),* Sir Robert Bramble to the Emily Worthington of Miss Petrie *(The Poor Gentleman),* Job Thornberry *(John Bull),* Restive *(Turn Out),* Christopher Cosey *(Town and Country),* Brummagen *(Lock and Key),* and Bonus *(Laugh When You Can).* At his benefit on December 19 he was Sir Peter to the Lady Teazle

---

[36] *Louisiana Advertiser,* November 21, 1831.

of Mrs. Cowell. Young Cowell entertained between pieces with a new comic song and "Jim Crow," and G. W. P. Curtis's drama, *The Eighth of January,* concluded the bill.

On the 22nd Herbert began a second engagement during which he impersonated Sir Anthony Absolute (twice), Lazarillo *(The Hotel),* Sir Soloman Cynic *(The Will),* Sir Peter Teazle, Toby Allspice *(The Way to Get Married),* and Sir Adam Contest *(The Wedding Day).*

Meanwhile the visiting performers had been introduced. Carle Von Blisse, the Swiss minstrel, made the first of several appearances on November 28 when he sang "The Tyrolese Song of Liberty" in the true Tyrolese style, "introduced 600 years ago by the celebrated Professor and Composer Hirdwick." Millis, the American Fire King, was featured on December 6 and again on the 9th and the 14th. Promised the notices for these dates: "He will take a plate of Live Coals of Fire of which he will make a hearty supper, with as much *Sang Froid* as an epicure would swallow a bowl of Turtle Soup. He will also regale himself with a dish of Playing Balls, composed of Brimstone and Rosin." On the 13th came Peters, the Great Antipodean. He walked on the ceiling head downward, performed on the slack rope, and went through his Grecian Exercises during a three night engagement.

Melodramatic novelties now graced the bills. *The Courier of Naples, Will Watch, or The Black Phantom,* and *Melmouth, or The Horrors of the Inquisition* followed one another in rapid succession. A more important novelty was *The Two Gentlemen of Verona* introduced on December 28. This was the American première of the Shakespearian comedy, antedating by fifteen years the New York production which Joseph Ireland claimed as the first in this country.[37]

During the Chirstmas holidays Caldwell opened the theatre on Sundays that he might not lose the large receipts which were generally his on Christmas, New Year's, and the 8th of January. He presented traditional fare on these nights: *George Barnwell* and *The Gambler's Fate* on December 25, *She Would be a Soldier* on January 1, and *The Glory of Columbia* on January 8.

The curtain raiser on January 9 was Caroline Boaden's popular *William Thompson.* The 13th brought another new farce,

---

[37] *Record of the New York Stage from 1750 to 1860,* II. 466. Odell also gives October 6, 1846, as the date of the first New York performance. *Op. cit.,* V, 250.

Benjamin Webster's *High Ways and By Ways,* and on the 16th was staged Captain Stephen Glover's "new nautical play," *The Cradle of Liberty, or Boston in '75.* This play, like his *Rake Hellies* of the previous season, is based on Cooper's *Lionel Lincoln* and may have been a reworking of the earlier piece.

Henry J. Finn, the Boston comedian, began an engagement on January 19. He went through a round of characters familiar to the low comedians of his day: Bailie Nicol in *Rob Roy,* Billy Black in *The Hundred Pound Note,* Bean Shatterly in Poole's *Married and Single,* "never acted here," Dr. Lenitive in *The Prize,* Mawworm in *The Hypocrite,* Philip Garbois in *One Hundred and Two,* Sir Peter Teazle, Somno in *The Sleep Walker,* Billy Lackaday in *Sweethearts and Wives,* and Donald in *The Falls of Clyde.* On his benefit night, February 1, he enacted Lord Oglesby in Garrick's *Clandestine Marriage,* a comedy new to the city, and sang an original composition entitled "The New Orleans Firemen." He was immediately re-engaged and now came forward in several new roles: Dr. Pangloss *(The Heir at Law),* Bob Logic *(Tom and Jerry),* Tony Lumpkin, Paul Shack *(My Master's Rival),* Sir Edward Mortimer *(The Iron Chest),* Ephraim Smith *(Wild Oats),* Buskin *(Killing No Murder),* and Richard III.

William C. Forbes was featured on the "off nights" during the first part of Finn's engagement. He opened on January 24 as Sir Giles Overreach and on successive nights enacted Lieutenant Worthington to Finn's Dr. Ollapod *(The Poor Gentleman),* Macbeth, Damon, and Hamlet, the last for his benefit on February 4.

Forbes was succeeded by William Keppell, from the Theatre Royal, Covent Garden, an actor who had recently acted at the Bowery in New York. His was a Shakespearian repertoire: *Richard III, Much Ado About Nothing, Romeo and Juliet* (twice), *Hamlet, Macbeth,* and Garrick's adaptation, *Catharine and Petruchio.* It would be interesting to know what the New Orleans critics thought of this actor, for it was he who played Fazio to the Bianca of Fanny Kemble on her American début the following September and nearly ruined the performance. Said Miss Kemble of him: "The poor man is under strong mental delusion; he cannot act in the least."[38]

---

[38] For an account of Keppell and the Kembles see Odell, *op. cit.,* III, 605-607.

The next star was Master Joseph Burke, the youngest and the most popular of the visiting performers this season. On his opening night, February 24, he portrayed Young Norval in *Douglas* and Terry O'Rourke in *The Irish Tutor* and between the plays led the orchestra in the overture to *Guy Mannering*. The next night he was Sir Abel Handy *(Speed the Plough)* and Looney Mactwolter *(The Review)*. After his performance in *The Merchant of Venice* (Shylock) and *Whirligig Hall*, the *Louisiana Advertiser* (February 28) reported that the people of New Orleans were bewitched by his enchantments." On each night of the engagement Master Burke acted in both the play and the afterpiece. By March 10 he had appeared as Doctor Pangloss *(The Heir at Law)*, Richard III, Murtock Delany *(Irishman in London)*, Dr. Ollapod *(The Poor Gentleman)*, My Lord Duke *(High Life Below Stairs)*, Romeo, Lingo *(An Agreeable Surprise)*, Dennis Brulgruddery *(John Bull)*, Master Socrates Chameleon *(The March of Intellect*, a new afterpiece), Tristram Fickle *(The Weathercock)*, Major O'Flaherty *(The West Indian)*, Paul Pry, Hamlet, and Patrick *(The Poor Soldier)*. The notice of *The Death's Head, or The Disguise*, "a new farce never acted here," does not tell which was his role.

The young star began a second engagement on March 12 with *The Prize* and *Young Napoleon, Duke of Reichstadt*, announced as a new drama "never acted in any theatre." In addition to repetitions of earlier roles he now appeared as General Bombastes, Crack *(The Turnpike Gate)*, Cornelius O'Dedimus *(Man and Wife)*, and Jobson *(The Devil to Pay)*. The twentieth and last appearance on March 17 presented him as Barney Brallaghan in the farce of that name.

James H. Hackett, the American comedian, came out on March 19 as Nimrod Wildfire in J. A. Stone's alteration of Paulding's play, *The Lion of the West*. On the 21st he offered his adaptation of Colman's *Who Wants a Guinea?* entitled *Jonathan in England;* the next night he appeared in *Rip Van Winkle*, in *Down East*, and in the farce, *Monsieur Tonson*. In the interlude, *Sylvester Daggerwood*, on the 23rd, he gave imitations of Kean, Macready, Hilson, and Barnes; on the 24th, he impersonated Industrious Doolittle, "a busy talkative speculating Yankee," in *The Times, or Travels in America*. For his benefit on March 26, *Rip Van Winkle*, *Down East*, and *The Lion of the West* were repeated "in compliance with the wishes of various applications."

Thomas Cooper began an engagement of eight nights on March 28. Opening as Virginius, to the Appius Claudius of Houpt, "his first appearance in New Orleans," Cooper went through a familiar round of characters until his benefit on April 9. On that occasion he offered a "detached portion" of *The School for Scandal*, appearing himself in the role of Sir Peter.

George Holland was also filling an engagement during this time. His *Whims of a Comedian* followed Cooper's Hamlet on March 30, and for the remainder of his stay he and the tragedian generally performed on the same evening. On April 3 he played Valianto in Edward Fitzball's *Joan of Arc*, a popular melodrama which had been introduced earlier in the season. He appeared in one other new role when, on April 11, he acted Peter Pickwell in the first American showing of R. J. Raymond's farce, *P. S. Come to Dinner.*

Master Burke returned the day after Holland's benefit and in rapid succession repeated ten of his most popular roles. April 16 brought a new role, Sir Callaghan O'Brallaghan in *Love á la Mode,* and several novel features. Among other musical feats, he composed an extempore overture on the stage, "giving the parts to each instrument *with his voice* and enabling the orchestra to perform a perfect Overture without Books!" With Burke's farewell benefit on the 17th the theatre closed for the Easter recess.

The theatre reopened on April 23 with two novelties, Moncrieff's comedy, *Rochester, or King Charles' Merry Days,* and Buckstone's operetta, *33 John Street.* A new melodrama entitled *Charles the Terrible* was presented on the 26th and on the following night came Caroline Boaden's farce, *The First of April.*

Barton, the last of the visiting performers, began an engagement on April 25 as Lear to the Cordelia of Mrs. Rowe. On his second appearance he offered *Macbeth,* Jane Placide playing opposite him. Other parts were Zanga in *The Revenge,* Virginius, Werner in the play of that name which Macready had adapted from Byron's poem, Rolla in *Pizarro,* and for his benefit on May 12, Jaffier, Petruchio, and Paris in a sketch from Massinger's *The Roman Actor.* He volunteered his services at several of the company benefits. He repeated Lear on Mrs. Rowe's night and for Jane Placide he appeared as Carwin and Lord Townly to her

Thérèse and Lady Townly *(The Provoked Husband)*. At Mrs. Carr's benefit on the 16th he and Mrs. Rowe were Doricourt and Letitia Hardy.

Only Caldwell and Old Gray presented novelties during this benefit season. The comedian offered Frederick Reynold's *Management* and Buckstone's farce, *Mischief Making*. For his benefit on the 19th Caldwell advertised C. A. Somerset's *Maurice the Wood Cutter*. With this performance the theatre closed for the summer, and soon after Caldwell and the company left for Cincinnati.

AMERICAN THEATRE, 1832-1833

The season which opened on November 21, 1832, was Caldwell's last as manager of the American Theatre and one of the most brilliant he ever presented. The company was stronger than that of the previous year, including among the recent recruits James Thorne, a singing actor from the Park Theatre in New York, James M. Scott, J. M. Field, late of the Richmond Hill Theatre, New York, and John Gilbert, who returned after an absence of several years. Other new members were Mrs. Ludlow, Miss Coleman, "from the Philadelphia and New York Theatres," Schoolcraft, Coney, Lyne, Auguste, Brown, Powell, Gaskill, Eversull, Johnson, Richings, and Mesdames Caines and Roberts. The return of Richard Russell and his family compensated for the loss of the Cowells, and Hugh Reinagle, formerly scene painter at the Park, replaced Mondelli. In the opinion of Manager Caldwell his was the "best regular stock company in the union."

The bill of the opening night served to reintroduce Mr. and Mrs. Russell as Widow Cheerly and Timothy Quaint in *The Soldier's Daughter* and to present Jane Placide as the heroine in Buckstone's new drama, *Victoire, or The Orphan of Paris*. The next night Barton began an engagement as William Tell, Master Russell appearing as Albert. James M. Scott made his bow on the 23rd as Bertram in *The Foundling of the Forest,* and as Michael in *The Adopted Child,* and on the 24th was Pierre to the Jaffier of Barton. On this evening James Thorne was introduced as Looney Mactwolter in *The Review.*

Thomas Hilson came out on the 26th as Robert Tyke and Somno, and on the 28th Mrs. Hilson made her New Orleans début as Lady Teazle and Clari, the Maid of Milan, to the Sir Peter and

Rolamo of her husband. *Isabella* on the 27th had introduced Mrs. Mary Duff, a star of even greater magnitude than the Hilsons, and for the next few weeks the scene was dominated by the visitors. Mr. and Mrs. Hilson appeared together as Paul Pry and Harry Stanly; Martin and Rachael Heywood in *The Rent Day*, Jerrold's new domestic drama; Adam Brock and Eudiga in *Charles XII;* Captain Bertram and Charlotte in Dunlap's comedy, *Fraternal Discord;* Dogberry and Beatrice; and Sir John Falstaff and Mrs. Page, the last being for Hilson's benefit on December 19. Mrs. Hilson was seen as Mary in *The Innkeeper's Daughter*, Russell taking the part of Richard; as Francis De Foix in the Fanny Kemble tragedy, *Francis the First of France*, "first time in America"; and as Mrs. Banter in *Ladies! Do Not Stay at Home*. Hilson appeared in *Sprigs of Laurel, Paul the Poacher, Tis All a Farce, The Happiest Day of My Life, John Bull,* and *The Agreeable Surprise*.

Barton and Mrs. Duff played on alternate nights, appearing as the Stranger and Mrs. Haller, Beverly and Mrs. Beverly, Macbeth and Lady Macbeth, Lord Hastings and Jane Shore, Rolla and Elvira, and for Barton's benefit on December 15, as Lear and Cordelia. James M. Scott played opposite Mrs. Duff in *Adelgitha, The Robber's Wife, The Apostate, Bertram, The Bohemian Mother, Evadne, Adrian and Orilla,* and *Thérèse*.

As Mrs. Duff prepared to leave, Mrs. Knight, a favorite of five seasons ago, began an engagement. She opened on December 28 as Miss Hardcastle and Victoire *(The Invincibles)*, following it on the 31st with Marianne in *The Dramatist*, and a repetition of *The Invincibles*, "by desire." Her engagement was interrupted on January 1 to allow for the New Orleans première of Mrs. Caroline Lee Hentz's *Lamorah! or The Western Wild*, a play which did not prove so successful as the native pieces of recent years. The popular George Holland made his bow on this evening in the burletta, *The Day After the Fair*. He remained through the 26th, repeating roles in which he had appeared on previous visits.

On January 2, 1833, Mrs. Knight sang Susannah in *The Barber of Seville*, assisted by the Figaro of Thorne, the Count Almaviva of Field, and the Countess Almaviva of Mrs. Rowe; in the afterpiece she was Kate O'Brien. Her other parts were Diana Vernon in *Guy Mannering*, Rosina, Ophelia, and Pauline in

Auber's opera, *The National Guard.* Her benefit on January 11 presented her as Rosalie Somers and as Fanny Bolton in the local première of O'Keeffe's musical burletta, *The Grenadier.*

Two other visitors of early January were Monsieur Gouffe, the celebrated "Man Monkey," and Fletcher, "the Venetian Statue." On the 3rd, Gouffe made his bow in *Jocko, the Brazilian Ape,* and Fletcher exhibited his statues; thereafter, they appeared together in the pantomimes *Jack Robinson and his Monkey, Pitcairn's Island,* and *La Perouse.* On their benefit night, January 24, Fletcher presented twenty-eight models of ancient statuary and Madame Gouffe made her American début as Myssa to her husband's Jocko.

W. C. Forbes opened as Hamlet on January 7 and continued as Sir Edward Mortimer and Virginius, sharing the stage on these nights with Messrs. Gouffe and Fletcher. On the 15th he played the title role in *Eugene Aram,* a dramatization of Bulwer's novel said to have been made by Caldwell.[39] Mrs. Knight began a second engagement on January 17 with the local première of Pocock's opera, *Sweet Home! or The Rans des Vaches,* and *The Turn Out.* On the 19th the cast of *The Merchant of Venice* enlisted Forbes as Shylock, Jane Placide as Portia, Holland as Launcelot Gobbo, and Mrs. Knight as Jessica. The bill for the 21st included *Thérèse,* Forbes enacting Carwin, *Paul and Virginia,* with Mrs. Knight in the role of Virginia, and *Jack Robinson and His Monkey.* On the 23rd, *Guy Mannering,* with Mrs. Knight as Julia and Holland as Domine Sampson preceded William Diamond's, *Abon Hassan.* This novelty was repeated for Holland's benefit on the 26th with J. T. Haines' *The Idiot Witness, or a Tale of Blood,* and *Ramfylde Moore Caren,* a new Christmas Harlequinade featuring dancing, "curious tricks," mechanical changes, and a splendid display of fireworks.

Meantime the Hilsons had returned, and on the 28th Sheridan Knowles' new play, *The Hunchback,* was presented with Hilson as Master Walter, Forbes as Sir Thomas Clifford, Jane Placide as Julia, and Mrs. Hilson as Helen. Mrs. Duff had also been reengaged and she and Forbes appeared as Albert Germaine and Julia on the 29th; the next evening she was Mary to Scott's Will Watch, the opening pieces on both of these occasions being *The Hunchback.*

---

[39] Rees, *op. cit.,* 42.

Caldwell now engaged the stud of horses from Brown's circus and turned to equestrian drama. *Timour the Tartar* was given on February 1 with Scott replacing Caldwell as Timour and Master Russell as Agib, a role once taken by his sister. Forbes made his last appearance on the 6th as Iago to Barton's Othello, Mrs. Hilson's Desdemona, and Mrs. Duff's Emilia. On the 11th, Jane Placide, having "availed herself of the last day of the Hilsons' stay in New Orleans," offered *The Hunchback*. This was followed by *Blue Beard* with Miss Petrie, Scott, and the horses. In the farce, *The Lady and the Devil*, on the 12th, Miss Coleman made her first appearance as Zephyrina. The next night she played the Countess Wintersen to the Stranger of Caldwell and the Mrs. Haller of Mrs. Duff. What was destined to be one of the most popular of equestrian pieces had its American première on the 13th, *Mazeppa, or The Wild Horse*, with Field in the title role and Mrs. Rowe as Olinska. For his benefit on the 15th Brown offered a variety of entertainment which included exhibitions on the *cord volante*, Chinese Juggling, *The Lady of the Lake*, with an original scene by the equestrian corps, and *Timour the Tartar*. In these Charles Webb made "his first and only appearance in New Orleans," as Rhoderic Dhu and Timour.

The most ambitious of this season's spectacles was Rophino Lacy's *Cinderella, or The Little Glass Slipper*, brought out on February 18. The spectacle won immediate favor and was repeated on six successive evenings. Commented the *Bee* of February 27:

> Scarcely ever has so much igenuity and splendor been exhibited on the stage in this city in machinery and decorations. . . . The singing is not entitled to as much praise but that it should be first rate cannot be expected since the company was not selected for operatic pieces, and besides it is not to be forgotten that the pieces are such as offer great obstacles to the first singers of Europe. The choruses are well sung generally. Messrs. Caldwell and Thorne are entitled to the first rank as musicians in their company.

The piece was interrupted on February 26 so that Mrs. Duff, "having recovered from her late severe indisposition," and Master Russell might enact Lady Randolph and Young Norval in a performance of *Douglas* which had been postponed from the 16th. On March 4 the spectacle made way for a novelty, *Washington at Valley Forge*, "by two gentlemen of New Orleans." James Rees claims the play as his, and it is possible he was the chief collaborator; however, the announcement of the fourth performance on March 16 reads, "for the benefit of the authors." *The Hunchback* was now revived with a cast which included Caldwell as Sir Thomas Clifford, Scott as Master Walter, and Mrs. Rowe as Helen. When the play was performed for the seventh time on March 8, it preceded Shannon's new farce, *My Wife or My Place*. A less successful farce was C. A. Somerset's *Shakespeare's Early Days*, given as the curtain raiser on the 11th.

James W. Wallack made his New Orleans début on March 18 as Rolla in *Pizarro* and as Dick Dashall in *My Aunt*. The bill was repeated on the 20th when Jane Placide, "having recovered from her indisposition," replaced Mrs. Rowe as Elvira. The star continued as Don Felix in *The Wonder! A Woman Keeps a Secret*, Michael in *The Adopted Child*, Hamlet, Martin Heywood, "as originally played by him," Rattle in the farce *Spring and Autumn*, Richard III, Allesandro in *The Brigand*, Walter in *The Children in the Wood*, and Bob Honeycomb in T. E. Wilks' new farce, *The Wolf and the Lamb*. Among the roles which he offered for his benefit on April 1 was that of Benedick in *Much Ado About Nothing*.

Mrs. Knight returned on the 2nd as Cinderella. Her next offering, *Abon Hassan*, preceded Thomas Dibdin's *The Heart of Midlothian*, which, advertised for March 15, had been withdrawn in consequence of Jane Placide's illness. On the 5th the star was Ariel in the Davenant-Dryden version of *The Tempest*, "first time in New Orleans." Wallack began a second engagement on the 8th, succeeding Scott as Master Walter in *The Hunchback*. He now came out as Macbeth, as Don Vincent D'Almanza in Rodwell's new comedy, *My Own Lover*, and with Mrs. Knight he appeared in *The Mountaineers* (Octavian and Agnes) and in *The Honeymoon* (Duke Aranza and Juliana). His benefit and last appearance before his departure for Europe presented him as Mike Mainsail, "first time", in Captain Glover's *Cradle of Liberty*, Captain Glover himself enacting Captain Noodle for the "first time."

After Wallack left, the management brought out the second elaborate spectacle of the season, *The Flying Dutchman or The Phantom Ship* by Edward Fitzball. More interesting to the historian of the American drama is the novelty which came on the 29th, Captain Glover's new national play, *The Banished Provin-*

cial or Olden Times. According to a preliminary notice in the *Bee* of April 15, the play contained some excellent hits at foreign travellers such as Basil Hall.

The benefit of comedian Hernizen on April 30 should be noted. He promised to exhibit "the great natural curiosity, the Ourang Outang," and to conclude the entertainment by appearing as Richard III in the fifth act of the play.

Edwin Forrest began an engagement of seven nights on May 1. With him was Andrew Jackson Allen who played Kaneshine in the performance of J. A. Stone's prize tragedy, *Metamora*, on the opening night and impersonated the Doctor in *Animal Magnetism*, the afterpiece on the 2nd. The star continued in *Damon and Pythias*, *The Gladiator* of Robert Montgomery Bird, *William Tell*, and *Virginius*. The engagement was extended an extra night in order to comply with the general wish that he appear in *Othello*, and on the 15th he volunteered his services for Mrs. Russell's benefit, enacting Brutus to her Tarquinia in Payne's play. During this visit Mrs. Russell had been called on to support him in many of his roles as Jane Placide had sailed for Liverpool soon after his arrival.[40]

Two benefits of early May produced interesting novelties. On May 7 J. M. Field presented acts from the popular *Washington at Valley Forge* and introduced Jerrold's *John Overy* and his own satirical farce, *Tourists in America*. As this sketch was received "with shouts of approbation" Mrs. Ludlow offered it as the concluding piece on her night. On this occasion Ludlow made his only appearance of the season, as Sharp in *The Lying Valet*. He relates in his *Dramatic Life* that he had left the theatrical profession this winter and engaged in business with a cousin in New Orleans.[41]

Madame Brichta, the celebrated Prima Donna of the Italian Opera in New York, arrived from Havana on May 10 and was immediately engaged. She made her début as Cinderella, singing in addition to the original music an Italian Bravura. She was Rosina on May 16, with Thorne as Figaro and Field as Count Almaviva; and for her benefit on the 18th she apeared in *The Lottery Ticket* and *The Prize*.

The celebrated acrobats, the Ravels, were introduced on May 17. For six nights this family delighted with their tightrope

---

[40] *Louisiana Advertiser*, May 8, 1833.
[41] Ludlow, *op. cit.*, 483.

walking, herculean feats, pantomine ballets, and *tableaux vivants*. On these evenings the resident company offered a farce or light comedy.

Page and Field took a joint benefit on May 24 since inclement weather had kept Field's first night from being productive. The entertainments offered on this night were *The Pilot*, Field's new farce, *Coming Out*, and a Grand Masquerade in which the members of the company were "to mingle in the scene and support a variety of favorite characters." Tickets to the boxes with the privilege of the stage and use of dress were listed at $2.00; the price of admission to the boxes only remained the same.

The season ended on May 28 with Caldwell's benefit. For his last appearance as manager of the American Theatre he selected his favorite character, Belcour in *The West Indian*. George Holland made his appearance after the comedy, singing a comic song, and the entertainment concluded with tightrope walking and a new pantomime ballet by the Ravel Family.

There is little that needs to be added to what the records show of Caldwell's activities as manager of the American Theatre on Camp Street. His companies during many of these ten years were among the most competent in the United States, and each season he brought to New Orleans whatever stars he could engage. The repertoires with their generous sprinkling of novelties show him to have been untiring in his efforts to gratify the wishes and tastes of the public. Under his management the English theatre at New Orleans had become firmly established.

CHAPTER V

Under New Management   1833-1835

AMERICAN THEATRE, 1833-1834

The American Theatre opened on November 27, 1833, for its first season under the management of Richard Russell and James S. Rowe. By the terms of the contract with Caldwell, the new managers leased the theatre in New Orleans, the New Cincinnati Theatre, and the New Nashville Theatre, for a five-year period at $12,000 a year. They purchased outright, for $5,000, the stock wardrobe, books, and music belonging to the American Theatre.[1]

---

[1] Notarial acts of Boswell, May 13, 1833, Court House, New Orleans.

Russell continued in his old position as stage manager and Rowe as treasurer. The announcements of the first few performances show that with the exception of James Caldwell, Jane Placide, and James M. Scott, the stock company had suffered no notable losses. Joseph M. Field, James Thorne, John Gilbert, Jackson Gray, George Hernizen, Mr. and Mrs. Russell, Master Russell, Mrs. Rowe, Miss Petrie, and Mrs. Higgins were again members of the company. Among the new performers, pronounced "excellent in their line," were H. G. Pearson and Mrs. Crooke, two favorites of past seasons, S. Pearson, T. Pearson, Waldron, Hunt, Simonds, (A. J.) Marks, Corri, Mrs. Salzman, and the dancers, Mr. and Mrs. Gay. Early in March, Thomas Hilson, Spencer, "from the New York, Philadelphia and Boston Theatres," and Rice, "from the Tremont," joined the company. James Scott returned at this time and remained until the end of the season.

Managers Russell and Rowe were proud of their company and of the visiting performers whom they had engaged, and when a critic denounced the theatre, they replied in the *Louisiana Advertiser* of January 24:

> Now, if the public will pardon our boasting, we pronounce our stock company equal to any in the United States, and on this we offer a bet of $500. We also offer the editor, or author of the article under the editorial head of the *Courier* of the 22nd inst. in relation to the American Theatre, a further bet of $1,000 that he cannot name any theatre since the drama has been known in the United States that has even produced the same amalgamation of talent, called Stars, as is now in this city.

The opening performance on November 27 presented Mrs. Knight, the first of the season's many stars. She went through a familiar round of characters: Letitia Hardy, Clari, Kate O'Brien, Miss Hardcastel, Margueretta in *No Song, No Supper,* Miss Dorillon, Widow Cheerly, and Julima in *Abon Hassam.* In many of these she played opposite J. M. Field who had succeeded Caldwell in the high comedy leads. On her benefit night, December 3, she appeared in *The Marriage of Figaro* as Susannah to Thorne's Figaro and as Ariel in *The Tempest.*

Clara Fisher opened an engagement on December 5 in *The School for Scandal* and *The Actress of All Work.* She introduced nothing new during this first engagement, appearing as Juliana in *The Honey Moon,* Little Pickle, Albina Mandeville in *The Will,* Priscilla Tomboy in *The Romp,* Rosalind in *As You Like It,* Beatrice, to the Benedick of H. G. Pearson, Letitia Hardy, Donna Violante in *The Wonder! A Woman Keeps a Secret,* and other roles equally as familiar.

A third star emerged before Clara Fisher took her benefit. This was "Gentleman George" Barrett, the light comedian, who began his engagement on December 10 in *The Dramatist* (Vapid) and in *Raising the Wind* (Jeremy Diddler). Mrs. Barrett joined him on his second night when the two enacted Sir Thomas Clifford and Julia in *The Hunchback* and introduced J. R. Planché's new farce, *The Dumb Belle.* Among their next offerings were several other novelties: Sheridan Knowles, latest tragedy, *The Wife;* S. J. Arnold's farce, *Free and Easy;* and M. R. Lacy's adaptation from Scribe, *The Two Friends.* They also appeared as Corinthian Tom and Kate in *Tom and Jerry,* as Charles Paragon and Kate O'Brien in *Perfection,* and on their last night, December 28, as Charles Surface and Lady Teazle, Barrett also playing Narcissus Stubble in the afterpiece, *High Ways and By Ways.*

The new managers were taking no chances this first season. The Barretts had hardly begun their engagement when another star was brought out. This was the tenor, John Sinclair, who made his début on December 16 as Henry Bertram; Mrs. Knight, who had been re-engaged to assist him, enacted Julia Mannering. On alternate nights to the Barretts the vocalists were Prince Orlando and Floretta in *The Cabinet* and Frederick and Maria in William Murray's *No! or The Glorious Minority,* a musical farce not previously seen here. On the 20th Sinclair acted Francis Osbaldistone *(Rob Roy),* and in the afterpiece, *Is He Jealous?,* Clara Fisher reappeared as Harriett.

A union of the starry forces was inevitable. On the "glorious 23rd," Clara Fisher, Mrs. Knight, and Sinclair offered the local première of Dimond's comic opera, *Englishmen in India.* Following this came Bernard's new farce, *The Four Sisters,* with Clara Fisher in the multiple name part. On December 27 the trium-virate repeated *Englishmen in India* and appeared in the operatic *Rosina,* Clara Fisher in the role of Phoebe. As their engagement drew to a close, the vocalists appeared together in *Love in a*

Village, Sinclair concluding the bill as Apollo in Kane O'Hara's burletta, *Midas.* Mrs. Knight continued in oft repeated roles while Clara Fisher was featured in the afterpiece.

George Barrett joined the stars on January 2, 1834, reappearing as Pedro to Mrs. Knight's Cinderella and Sinclair's Prince. This popular spectacle, "with new and splendid scenery" by Reinagle, was repeated for Mrs. Knight's benefit on January 10 and for Barrett's on the 17th. During the second engagement Barrett supported Mrs. Knight in *She Stoops to Conquer* and played opposite Clara Fisher as Young Mirabel in *Wine Does Wonders,* as Mr. Belmour in *Is He Jealous?,* and as Charles Paragon. In *The Hunchback,* on January 11, he played Sir Thomas Clifford to the Julia of Jane Placide and the Helen of Mrs. Russell.

The performance of Jane Placide, the first since her return from Europe, brought forth the following comment from the *Louisiana Advertiser* of January 15:

> Her trip . . . has been of service to Miss Placide. Her personal appearance is improved and her style of acting, we think, chastened. It has always been conceded that but few actresses were superior to Miss Placide in portraying the stronger passions, but in Julia, in the critical scene with the secretary, she drew tears from those who are not wont to shed tears freely.

On January 13 came Mrs. Austin, the most celebrated of the season's vocalists. Her opening role as Ariel was followed by Rosina in *The Barber of Seville,* Countess Almaviva in *The Marriage of Figaro,* and Margaretta in *No Song, No Supper.* Sinclair returned on the 20th to appear as the Prince to her Cinderella.

George Handel Hill, the delineator of Yankee character, made his bow on the 21st, and for the next two weeks he and the vocalists performed on alternate nights. On the evening that he opened as Soloman Swap in *Jonathan in England,* Jane Placide made her second appearance in Jerrold's *The Housekeeper, or The White Rose,* a comedy which had never been acted in the United States. The 25th brought Hill as the Yankee servant Jedediah Homebred in J. S. Jones' play, *The Green Mountain Boy,* and Jane Placide in *Thérèse.* Except for his personation of Mawworm in *The Hypocrite,* Hill appeared only in those plays

which featured the Yankee type. He was Joshua Horsereddish in
East and West, Jonathan Ploughboy in Samuel Woodworth's
Forest Rose, and Zachariah Dickerwell in Woodworth's *Foundling
of the Sea.* As Jonathan Ploughboy he delivered his favorite
Yankee story, "Jonathan's Visit to the Genessee Country" and
sang "A Hit at the Fashions."

There were few starless nights this winter. On January 27
the management announced that new engagements had been
concluded with Mrs. Austen, Clara Fisher, and Sinclair. They
made their re-entry in *The Beggar's Opera,* Mrs. Austen as Polly,
Sinclair as Captain MacHeath, and Clara Fisher as Lucy. On
January 29 Mrs. Austen and Sinclair were paired as Henry
Bertram and Julia Mannering and as Belville and Rosina. *Cinderella, Rob Roy,* and *John of Paris* with Clara Fisher as Vincent
take us to Sinclair's benefit on February 10. On this occasion
Masaniello presented him in the title role assisted by Mrs. Austen
as the Princess and Clara Fisher as Fenella. He was re-engaged
immediately, and the play was given nightly until Mrs. Austen's
benefit on the 14th when she was Annette and Sinclair, Truemore
in *The Lord of the Manor.*

James Caldwell began an engagement on February 17 in
Laugh When You Can and *Of Age To-morrow.* Clara Fisher, who
now returned to play opposite him, was Juliana to his Duke
Aranza and Jane Placide's Volante in *The Honey Moon,* Lady
Teazle to his Charles Surface, Kate O'Brien to his Charles Paragon, and Ophelia to his Hamlet. Meanwhile several novelties had
been brought out. The 22nd witnessed the staging of *Washington,
or The Retaliation,* a new play by "a gentleman of this city," John
Dumont.[2] On the 24th came Dr. Arne's opera, *Artaxerxes,* and
on the 27th, for Jane Placide's benefit, Buckstone's domestic
drama, *The Wreck Ashore,* "first time in America."

After the departure of Mrs. Austen and Clara Fisher early
in March the interest centered in the new members of the company. On the 7th Thomas Hilson made his bow as Paul Pry, and
the afterpiece reintroduced James M. Scott in a favorite role,
that of Long Tom Coffin. Charles Hodges and Miss Nelson, whom
Caldwell had engaged in England the previous summer, came
out at this time, he as Count Belino in *The Devil's Bridge* and she
as Rosalind in *As You Like It.* Mrs. Knight returned on March

---

[2] *Bee,* May 14, 1835.

14 and with the aid of Hilson, Scott, Mrs. Rowe, and Sinclair, who seem to have been always near this season, the managers produced Cobb's operatic *Siege of Belgrade*. Mrs. Knight and Sinclair appeared frequently during the next six weeks, but of their presentations only Lacy's *Fra Diavolo* was new.

The middle of March brought Edwin Forrest and the Barretts. Mrs. Barrett had been re-engaged to play opposite the tragedian and her husband to appear in the afterpieces or whereever he was needed. Forrest opened on March 19 in *The Gladiator* and for the most part continued in familiar roles. His repertoire included only two new plays, *The Broker of Bogota* and *Oralloossa, the Last of the Incas*, both written for him by Robert Montgomery Bird.

An important event of the spring was the "Grand Dramatic Festival" given on April 14 for the benefit of Thomas Cooper and his children. Cooper had always been a favorite in New Orleans and now that he was in need, his friends planned a benefit such as had been tendered him in New York earlier in the year. Admission to the parquet and dress circle was fixed at three dollars, the second and third tier of boxes at two, and the gallery at one. The stars who were in New Orleans at the time volunteered their services. After the opening piece, *The Blue Devils*, with Hilson as Megrim and Mrs. Russell as Annette, Mrs. Barrett delivered a poetic address written "by a gentleman of this city." Then came the third act of *Othello* with Cooper in the name part, Forrest as Iago, and Mrs. Rowe as Desdemona. This was followed by *The Hunter of the Alps* in which Caldwell played Felix and Andrew Jackson Allen, Jeronymo. There were songs by Mrs. Knight, Mrs. Austen, and Sinclair and the fourth act of *Virginius* presented by Cooper and his daughter. The entertainment concluded with *The Dumb Belle*, Mr. and Mrs. Barrett in the leading roles.

Cooper was now engaged to play with Forrest and the two appeared on the 18th as Damon and Pythias. Successively Forrest enacted Othello to Cooper's Iago, Marc Antony to his Cassius, and Jaffier to his Pierre. At Forrest's benefit on the 23rd Cooper and Mrs. Russell enacted *Catharine and Petruchio*, and for the veteran star's benefit the next night, Forrest and Mrs. Rowe offered *Thérèse*. As he was still in the city on the night of Mrs. Russell's benefit, April 26, Forrest played Brutus to her Tarquinia in Payne's tragedy.

After Forrest's departure musical entertainment again dominated. Mrs. Austen now appeared as Julia Mannering to Hodges'
Henry Bertram and Mrs. Knight's Lucy. She enacted the Prince
in *Masaniello*, Zerlina in *Fra Diavolo*, and Alfred in the new
operetta, *Music and Prejudice*. In *The Beggar's Opera* she was
Polly, Hodges, Macheath, and Miss Nelson, Lucy. The performance was not favorably reviewed in the *Bee* of May 12. Hodges
was said to be the only one of the characters who was perfect in
his part. "As for Mrs. Austen," commented the critic, "as usual
she charmed us with her voice but as to the part of Polly she had
no idea of it." On the 9th of May this singer concluded her engagement in the local première of Boieldieu's opera, *The Caliph
of Bagdad;* however, she remained until the end of the season
assisting on benefit nights.

The benefit season brought new plays. The farce on Old
Gray's night was *The Miniature*, the authorship of which is
claimed by James Rees. On his night Field essayed Hamlet "for
the first time (by desire)" and impersonated Sylvester Daggerwood. Hilson's benefit presented him as Master Walter *(The
Hunchback)* and Mrs. Hilson "having recovered from her recent
indisposition" made her only appearance of the season as Helen.
For Reinagle's benefit on May 17, James Rees dramatized Cooper's
novel, *The Headsman*. The artist produced an entire new set of
scenes for this and exhibited a new transparency of the Mazeppa
horse between the play and the farce. Apparently the transparency awakened memories; *Mazeppa* was revived on the 20th
with the aid of Brown's horses and ran for six nights.

With the performance of *The School of Reform* and *Mazeppa*
on May 27, the season came to a close. The new managers had
deviated little from the policy of their predecessor this season and
had presented good dramatic entertainment.

AMERICAN THEATRE, 1834-1835

In November of 1834 Richard Russell and James S. Rowe
returned to New Orleans for their second season as managers of
the American Theatre. The newly appointed stage manager was
James M. Scott; J. R. Smith was chief scenic artist; and Lefolle,
leader of the orchestra. Among the old members of the company
were Messrs. James Thorne, H. G. Pearson, Sidney Pearson,
Hodges, Marks, Carr, Corri, and Fielding; Mesdames Russell,
Rowe, Crooke, Carr, and Higgins; and Misses Petrie and Nelson.

Notable among the absentees were John Gilbert, Joseph M. Field, Jackson Gray, George Hernizen, and Thomas Hilson, who had died suddenly during the summer campaign. The new members included Messrs. George P. Farren, engaged to replace Gilbert, Williamson, a singing actor, Drummond, Philips, Judah, Stith, Fairchild, Walton, Keppel, Thomas Radcliffe, N. H. Bannister, Bristow, Delmon, Charles Muzzy, Hubbard, Brace, Manly and J. Warrell; and Mesdames Thomas Hilson, Hubbard, Muzzy, George Rowe, and Horne. Later in the season Mrs. Stone and Miss Rae were engaged.

The theatre opened on November 24 with an appropriate address written and delivered by N. H. Bannister. Then followed the opera, *Love in a Village*, and *The Young Widow*. The roles of Rosetta and young Meadows in the opera were to be played by Mrs. Knight and A. F. Keene, "his first appearance in thirteen years," but in a last minute change of cast Williamson was forced to enact the lead. In the continued absence of Keene who, according to the *Louisiana Advertiser* of November 28, was "still in lavender," Mrs. Knight turned to light comedy, appearing in *The Belle's Stratagem* and *As You Like It* opposite H. G. Pearson. On December 2 Keene made his bow as Henry Bertram to Mrs. Knight's Julia Mannering. Thereafter, until January 8 when they left for Natchez, the two vocalists appeared as young Meadows and Rosetta, Colonel Oswald and Gulnare in *Englishmen in India*. Jocoso and Clari, and Francis Osbaldistone and Diana Vernon *(Rob Roy)*. Hodges enacted the Prince to Mrs. Knight's Cinderella on December 12, and on its repetition (December 19) Williamson succeeded to the role.

Apparently Keene was more popular than Mrs. Knight. The *Louisiana Advertiser* of December 1 said he was "perhaps the best singing actor in the country." This critic thought Mrs. Knight "too much addicted to the mechanical style of singing . . . and too frequently she does not appear to understand what she utters. When singing the mermaid song last week, she shouted 'follow me-ee-ee-ee' through several bars and flights till she exhausted her own strength and the patience of her hearers."

Mrs. Alexander Drake had begun an engagement on November 26 and until December 10 she and the vocalists played on alternate nights. Her personations of Bianca in *Fazio*, Julia in *The Hunchback*, Evadne, Adelgitha were well received. Cried one enthusiastic critic, "Talk of Fanny Kelly, Fanny Kemble or Fanny Jarman as being superior artistes, we have a Fanny Drake outvies them all."

Mrs. Drake was succeeded by Mrs. Pritchard, who in 1828 had been known as Mrs. Tatnall, a member of the resident company. She opened on December 11 as Elvira and as Little Pickle, a choice which indicates that she felt as young and as versatile as ever. Commented the *Bee* on December 13: "She has a fine commanding figure—voice full and powerful but not smooth, wanting that mellow softness . . . which is pleasing to the ear. She seems admirabily calculated for those characters which require great physical power."

Her personation of Allesandro Massaroni in *The Brigand* was the most popular offering of the engagement. The critic who saw the third presentation of the piece on December 18, regretted that only ten ladies had witnessed her excellent waltzing scene with Miss Petrie. Other roles for her were Helen McGregor, Mrs. Haller, Madame Manette *(Mischief Making)*, Madge Wildfire, and Priscilla Tomboy *(The Romp)*. Twice during the holidays she acted in Sunday performances attracting "well-filled houses."

Native characters once again came into prominence during the engagement of George H. Hill. The opening play, *Jonathan in England,* on December 22 was followed by *The Green Mountain Boy, The Yankee Pedlar,* and *The Knight of the Golden Fleece,* a new piece written for him by J. A. Stone.

December 27 marked the first appearance of an important addition to the staff of the theatre. This was Mr. Reynoldson, an English actor who had taken James Thorne's place at the Park when he left for New Orleans in 1833. Reynoldson made his début as Dandini in *Cinderella* and appeared later in other roles; however, his official title was that of director of the music department. His arrival gave "Colley Cibber," the dramatic critic of the *Bee,* an excuse to ridicule the orchestra and its leader. He stated in the issue of December 29 that Lefolle's "worn out pieces" were "delightfully somniferous," and that the gentleman himself was little more than "an heirloom bequeathed to the theatre as a legacy from some good natured former manager."

The brightest star of this season was Tyrone Power, the Irish comedian whose representations of his countrymen are still regarded as among the best. Three times a week throughout

January he appeared in those roles which had made him a favorite in the East the previous year. There is no record of his opening bill on January 6; the second night he appeared as Dennis Brulgruddery *(John Bull)* and Teddy the Tiler. Other parts were Murtock Delany in *The Irishman in London*, Doctor O'Toole in *The Irish Tutor*, Mons. Morbleau in *Mons. Tonson*, Looney Mactwolter in *The Review*, and Sir Lucius O'Trigger. More interesting than these are the pieces which he introduced to the city: James Kenney's, *The Irish Ambassador;* W. B. Bernard's *The Nervous Man and the Man of Iron; The Irish Valet;* and his own works, *Born to Good Luck, Etiquette Run Wild*, and *Paddy Carey.*

Minor satellites of January were Mrs. Sharpe, the tragedian from the Park Theatre, and Herr Cline. The latter made occasional appearances during January, offering between the play and the farce his "numerous and extraordinary evolution, gymnastic exercises, and elegant dances on the cord." Mrs. Sharpe opened on the 2nd in *Fazio*, following in *The Hunchback* on the 8th. Other known roles were Kate O'Brien, Lady Teazle to the Sir Peter of Russell, and for her benefit, on January 19, Mrs. Haller and Cinderella (only the first act). Hodges played opposite her as the Prince, and Miss Nelson was the Fairy Queen. This young lady had just rejoined the company, making her first appearance on the 14th as Rosalind in *As You Like It*. From now until the end of the season she played such roles as Colin in *Nature and Philosophy*, Sophia in *The Rendezvous*, Paul in *The Wandering Boys*, Maria in *The Citizen*, and Eugenia in *Sweethearts and Wives.*

Tyrone Power left for Mobile after his benefit on February 2 and his place was taken by James Hackett. Two novelties were among the newcomer's repertoire: Bernard's revision of *The Kentuckian* and his comedy, *Job Fox, the Yankee Valet*. To the first performance of *The Kentuckian* on February 5 the managers "with their accustomed courtesy" invited the Governor, Senate, Representatives, Judges, Mayor, City Council, and Clerks of the Legislature.

By the second week in February Mrs. Knight, Keene, and Hill had returned to New Orleans, and H. J. Finn was in town for an engagement. On the 16th Finn performed Bailie Nicol Jarvie to the Diana Vernon and the Francis Osbaldistone of the vocalists. For his benefit, February 23, Hill enacted Billy Lack-

land, "for the first time," and offered a new farce, *Ovid and Obid,
or Yankee Blunders,* and *A Grand Masquerade.* The bill concluded with Finn as Dr. Lenitive in *The Prize.* On Finn's night,
February 25, New Orleans saw two of the comedian's new plays,
Kasper Hauser, and the farce, *Removing the Deposits,* neither of
which was performed in New York until the following September.[3]

Another successful novelty of this month was *Tutoona, or
The Battle of Saratoga* written by George Washington Harby, a
New Orleans schoolteacher and brother of the Charleston playwright, Isaac Harby. All that is known of the play comes from
a review in the *Louisiana Advertiser* of the 23rd. Reported this
critic:

> As a melodrama we find in it everything required to
> insure its success, a score of hair breadth escapes, a great
> deal of action, and interesting incident. As a tragedy we
> would criticise its many trivial passages, condemn its many
> extravagant tirades, and cry out against scalping, whooping,
> trotting Indians, but in a melodrama these are all very well,
> and in this piece have been combined together in a workman-
> like manner. . . . One thing requires unqualified praise and
> that is the Prologue. . . . It contains flowing lines and several
> most beautiful figures.

The last of February Hackett returned for a short engagement. He repeated several of his familiar roles and introduced
two new pieces: a farce, *Jonathan Doubikins,* and Moncrieff's
drama, *Monsieur Mallet.* The *Bee* of March 22 says that he
demanded $200 a night and that once he played to an audience of
only 122 people.

On March 9 Power returned and performed every night until
the 17th. During this engagement, his third in New Orleans, he
introduced his own comedy, *St. Patrick's Eve, or The Order of the
Day.* The bill for the 14th commenced with this play and ended
with a repetition of *The Adventures of a Sailor,* a new farce by
N. H. Bannister.

Mrs. Stone, "late of the Arch Street Theatre, Philadelphia,"
made her bow on March 17. Some may have remembered her as
Mrs. Legg, a member of Caldwell's company in 1821; and next
year she was to return as Mrs. Bannister. On the evening of her
début Bannister played St. Aldobrand to her Imogine. The after-

---

[3] Odell, *op. cit.,* IV, 71.

piece was *The Mistletoe Bough* by James Rees, a new drama
founded on the ballad of that name. The New Orleans Benefit
to John Howard Payne was the feature of the 18th with tickets
to the parquet and lower tier of boxes priced at $5. The opening
address, which had been written by Rees, was followed by *Thérèse*
with Jane Placide making her only appearance of the season in
the name part. Finn, who had recently returned from Natchez,
volunteered Captain Bopp *(King Charles II)*, and Tyrone Power
offered the popular *More Blunders than One*. The press described
the benefit as "a partial and impartial failure" though the receipts
were $1,000.

Charles Kemble Mason, the English tragedian, appeared on
the 19th, his Macbeth having the support of Mrs. Stone. Other
roles were Hamlet to Mrs. Knight's Ophelia, Julian St. Pierre in
The Wife, Petruchio, and Sir Giles Overreach.

Thomas D. Rice succeeded him on the 27th, making his bow
in a piece called *Life in Philadelphia*, written for him by Dr.
Burns of that city. During this first engagement in New Orleans
he introduced the new Aethiopian opera, *Oh! Hush, or The Virginny Cupid,* appeared as Wormwood in *The Lottery Ticket,* and
"jumped Jim Crow." On his benefit night, April 6, he essayed
the Ghost in *Hamlet* with the assistance of Mrs. Knight and J. J.
Adams, an old actor from the Park Theatre who was in New
Orleans lecturing on elocution.

The chief attraction at this time was Meyerbeer's opera,
Robert le Diable, which, on March 30, was presented for the first
time in America. A communication in the *Louisiana Courier* of
this date notes that Reynoldson had procured a copy of the original score from Pierce Butler of Philadelphia and had curtailed
the parts of those instruments which were not in the orchestra
of the New Orleans theatre. He was also said to have made the
translation from the French. Concluded the article: "Another
useful novelty has been introduced which deserves support. Pro-
grams of the songs and choruses are printed; and are for sale at
the door to all the liberally curious."

Finn came back on April 4 as Doctor Pangloss and continued
in a familiar round: Mr. Paul Popp *(Removing the Deposits)*,
Dr. Lott Whittle *(Kasper Hauser)*, Paul Shack *(My Master's
Rival)*, Philip Garbois *(Legion of Honor)*, Sir Peter Teazle, and
Caleb Pipkin *(May Queen)*. On the 17th he took a benefit and
departed.

The crowning event of the season was the engagement with the Barnes family. The performance of *Isabella* on April 20 introduced Mrs. Barnes to an audience which included the Honorable Thomas H. Benton and family. The next night she was joined by John Barnes who appeared as Governor Heartall to her Widow Cheerly and as Delph in *Family Jars*. The seventeen year old Charlotte made her bow as Juliet *(Romeo and Juliet)* on the 22nd; on the 27th she and her mother enacted Francis the First and Louisa in Miss Kemble's tragedy, *Francis the First*. The afterpiece on this night presented Barnes in one of his most famous roles, that of the Dromio of Syracuse, Thorne playing the Dromio of Ephesus. In *The School for Scandal* the family was again united, Charlotte playing Lady Teazle to the Sir Peter of her father and the Mrs. Candor of her mother. Mrs. Barnes was Evelina and her daughter Angela on May 1 while the afterpiece, *The Turnpike Gate*, featured Barnes as Crack. Between the play and the farce Rice "jumped Jim Crow." Miss Barnes continued as Julia to Pearson's Sir Clifford and as Miss Dorillon to the Sir William of Scott and the Lord Priory of her father in *Wives as They Were*. Her dramatization of *The Last Days of Pompeii* on the 7th featured each member of the family, and the next night they concluded their engagement with *The Belle's Stratagem*. They reappeared at Rice's farewell benefit, May 11, in *The Honeymoon*, Barnes playing Jacques, Charlotte Juliana, and Mrs. Barnes Volante. An interesting feature of this night was Rice's rendition of Jim Crow in French and English, "at the request of several French families."

The benefits of this season presented many interesting novelties. On April 24 J. R. Smith, the scenic artist, offered *Rathaimus the Roman*, a five act tragedy written by Bannister. Mrs. Hilson called in J. J. Adams on the 28th to assist her as Rolla *(Pizarro)*, and at Scott's benefit this visitor personated Alexander the Great. For his own benefit on May 12, Adams offered *Othello* with Pearson as Iago. At the benefit given John Dumont, the author of *Washington, or the Retaliation*, he introduced another of his pieces entitled *A Day in New Orleans*. Bannister brought out two of his plays on the 16th, *Midnight Murder* and a national sketch, *Old Ironsides*.

Mrs. Russell's benefit was scheduled for May 18, but on that day and the succeeding one the theatre was closed owing to the death of Jane Placide and Mrs. Rowe. Jane Placide had been in ill health for several years, but Mrs. Rowe had appeared just four days before. In light of this we read with interest the statement in the *Louisiana Advertiser* of May 18 that she died "from debility consequent on overexertion while in a delicate state."

George Farren's night (22nd) marked the return of Mrs. Pritchard who assisted him in a performance of *The Tour de Nesle*. This was said to be Farren's revision of a translation made from the French by Frank Haynes, a young gentleman of the city. So successful was the piece that Russell included it among the pieces offered at his benefit on the last night of the season.

It must have been with some reluctance that Russell and Rowe drew the curtain on May 28, for after only two seasons their monopoly of the English drama in New Orleans was at an end. James Caldwell had decided to return to his old profession and earlier in the month he had laid the cornerstone for a new theatre to be opened in the fall.[4]

CHAPTER VI

The Rivals   1835-1836

AMERICAN THEATRE, 1835-1836

The American Theatre opened on November 19, 1835, under the management of Richard Russell. James Rowe had died of a self-inflicted wound in Nashville early in October[1] and his position as treasurer of the theatre was now filled by a Mr. Graham. It is not known whether the newcomer entered into partnership with Russell or shared the managerial duties as Rowe had.

The company which was now reunited after campaigns in Nashville, Louisville, and Cincinnati[2] included among the old members Messrs. Russell, Hodges, Hubbard, Thorne, Farren, Williamson, Reynoldson, Scott, Fielding, Bannister, Carr, Radcliffe, Manly, Bristow, and Gray, Mesdames Russell, Hubbard, Carr, Higgins, Salzmann, and Horne, and Misses Rae and Nelson. The new members were Messrs. F. S. Hill, Maynard, Carlos, Forster, Smith, and Eversull, Mesdames Wallack and Kutz, and Misses Charlotte Crampton and Mary Ann Russell. Later in the season

[4] *Bee*, March 8, 1835.
[1] Letter from Robert H. Jones to James H. Caldwell, October 4, 1835, Court House, New Orleans.
[2] *Bee*, November 18, 1835

they were joined by Mr. and Mrs. J. Herbert, James Wills, Mrs. Keppell, Mrs. Cowell, and the dancers, Mr. and Mrs. Bennie. The orchestra was larger this season and among the members was Signor Gambatti whom Russell had engaged in New York. His trumpet solos were a feature of the musical entertainment given between the plays.

The theatre opened with *The Soldier's Daughter* and on the following evening Charles Eaton made his bow in *Richard III*. The third night brought Mrs. Drake as Julia to Eaton's Master Walter and F. S. Hill's Sir Thomas Clifford. The two stars appeared next as Julian St. Pierre and Mariana in *The Wife* and as Shylock and Portia. On November 27 Mrs. Drake and Scott enacted Margaret and Bouridan in a performance of *La Tour de Nesle* which was announced as George Almar's "with alterations by B. Parsons."[3] The play was repeated at Mrs. Drake's benefit with the afterpiece, *Victoire,* in which she enacted the name part assisted by Farren as Jean. He last appearance was in *Evadne* given for Eaton's benefit on December 1. After her departure Eaton played in *Hamlet* opposite Miss Nelson and in *The Iron Chest* opposite Mrs. Wallace.

The first important novelty was F. S. Hill's *The Shoemaker of Toulouse,* on December 4. It ran for three nights before making way for *Murrell, the Western Land Pirate,* a new melodrama by N. H. Bannister. In the past this young actor-playwright had been severely criticised for carelessness of speech and dress; this season he had been promoted to juvenile tragedian and was considered one of the best actors in the company.

Hodges rejoined the company on December 9 as Count Belino in *The Devil's Bridge,* and the stage was now set for the return of Mary Ann Russell. The young lady had been studying since she quit the New Orleans stage in 1830 and on December 14, designated "Opera Night," she made her bow as Rosina in *The Barber of Seville.* The cast included Williamson as Count Almaviva, Reynoldson as Dr. Bartolo, Hodges as Fiorello, and Farren as Basil. The début was not the success which had been anticipated, partly because Miss Russell was hoarse and, reported the *Bee* of the 22nd, "consequently produced many discordant sounds." While she recuperated from her cold, Russell brought out George Almar's *Schinderhannes* and *The Marriage Contract,*

³ *Ibid.,* November 27, 1835. Undoubtedly B. Parsons was the actor Charles B. Parsons.

a comedy which Bannister had submitted unsuccessfully for the premium offered by Caldwell for the best native play. On the 21st Miss Russell made her second appearance as Cinderella. The critics found her greatly improved in her singing, but they were not enthusiastic.

Cornelius A. Logan, a favorite comedian in the West, made his New Orleans début on December 23 as Wormwood in *The Lottery Ticket*. During this short engagement he also appeared as Captain Copp in *Charles II* and as Thomas in *The Secret*.

Christmas night brought a curious mixture of entertainment: Charles Selby's farce, *The Unfinished Gentleman*, Rees' *Mistletoe Bough*, Signor Gambatti on the trumpet, and a comic pantomime, *Harlequin and Mother Goose*. In the latter the Bennies were assisted by Charles Parsloe, a clown from Covent Garden. On the 30th Miss Russell sang Alice in *Robert le Diable*, "her last appearance but one." On New Year's Eve Walton, the tragedian, began an engagement as Hamlet, and Logan made his last appearance.

January was ushered in with another of Bannister's new dramas, *The Fall of San Antonio, or Texas Victorious*. In the course of the play a company of United States Troops appeared on the stage and Pasloe and Bennie executed an Indian War Dance. On the 6th Mrs. Drake and Charles Eaton reappeared as Evadne and Ludovico, Walton assisting as Colona. These were patriotic nights at the American Theatre. The profits on the 7th were appropriated to the Texas Cause. The 8th was glorified by a bill made up of *The Soldier's Daughter* and James Rees' new national sketch, *Washington Preserved*. On the 12th Miss Russell essayed Bianca to the Fazio of Walton and F. S. Hill's new comedy, *Opera Mad*, was introduced.

Charles Mason joined the ranks of the visiting tragedians on January 15, enacting Macbeth to the Lady Macbeth of Mrs. Drake. Hereafter the couple appeared together in *Pizarro, Rob Roy, Venice Preserved* with Eaton as Jaffier, and *Othello* with Eaton as Iago and Mrs. Russell as Emilia. The Shakespearian tragedy was followed by Benjamin Webster's melodrama, *The Golden Farmer*, Walton playing the title role and Thorne as Jemmy Twitcher. Mrs. Drake's benefit on the 22nd presented her in her favorite role of Madame Clermont in *Adrian and Orilla*, F. S. Hill playing Adrian and Walton, the Prince of Altenburg. In the afterpiece Hill was Petruchio to her Catharine. The next night she reappeared as Lady Teazle to the Joseph Surface of Mason, Farren replacing Russell as Sir Peter.

Manager Russell put his faith in native stars this season. On January 26, Charles B. Parsons, the western tragedian, came out as Virginius. Miss Nelson, who had succeeded to all of Mrs. Rowe's parts, was Virginia and Bannister, Icilius. Parsons' Macbeth had the support of Mrs. Drake and Waton (Macduff). He followed this with two novelties, Jonas B. Phillips' Indian tragedy, *Oranaska*, and William Barrymore's melodrama, *Gilderoy*. For Mrs. Drake's farewell benefit, on February 2, he played Bouridan in *La Tour de Nesle* and Shylock in the trial scene from *The Merchant of Venice*. The bill concluded with a repetition of Oxenford's *My Fellow Clerk*, a new farce which was given frequently this season.

Eaton now prepared to depart, offering as his last roles Sir Edward Mortimer, Sir Giles Overreach, and at his benefit on the 5th, Julius Caesar. In the new burletta, *Pig and Whistle, or Actors in Distress*, which followed the Shakespearian play on this night, the star gave imitations of celebrated actors. The same evening witnessed the first appearance of James Wills as Looney Mactwolter in *The Review*. This "volunteer" joined the company later in the season, achieving great popularity with his song, "Billy Barlow."

The announcement of the performance of *The Shoemaker of Toulouse* and *Paul Jones* (one act) on February 11 stated that Scott would make his first appearance since his return from Natchez. Apparently he had been away from New Orleans since the middle of January. His name does not appear in any of the daily notices between January 14 and February 11.

On February 17 Miss Russell essayed Miss Dorillon in *Wives as They Were*. Her repertoire of the previous two months had been limited to musical roles; now she turned to light comedy and melodrama, Donna Olivia in *A Bold Stroke for a Husband*, Kate O'Brien in *Perfection*, and Juliana in *The Honeymoon*, being among her early parts.

T. D. Rice made his reappearance on the 17th in the afterpiece, *The Virginia Mummy*. He remained through March 2, jumping Jim Crow and playing in the Aethiopian operas, *Oh! Hush* and *Bone Squash Diavolo*, the latter new to the city.

Mrs. Knight came out on the 18th as Letitia Hardy and as Gertrude to Thorne's Peter Spyk in *The Loan of a Lover*. Other early parts were Gulnare in *Englishmen in India*, Ariel in *The Tempest*, Cinderella, Laura in *Sweethearts and Wives*, and Polly in *The Beggar's Opera*. She remained in New Orleans until April 2 during which time she seems to have been regarded as a member of the company.

A popular novelty of this season was Buckstone's romantic drama, *The Ice Witch, or the Frozen Hand*, brought out on March 3 and given nightly until the 8th when Charles Mason and his sister began an engagement. This was Miss Mason's first appearance in the city; supported by her brother she played the heroine in *The Hunchback*, *The Wife*, *Bertram*, *The School for Scandal* (Mason as Sir Peter), *Romeo and Juliet*, and in Jerrold's melodrama, *The Mutiny at the Nore*. In addition to these performances Mason enacted the title role in John Walker's *Napoleon, or the Emperor and the Robber*, a play which he had introduced on an earlier visit.

The Ice Witch came back on the 16th as a feature of the benefit given for the children of the late James Rowe. It figured in the bills until the 21st when it made way for F. S. Hill's new melodrama, *The Six Degrees of Crime*. After its first presentation Hill's play was given without curtain raiser or afterpiece, "in consequence of its great length."

The benefits began early this season. According to an announcement in the *Bee* of March 26, Farren's took place on Sunday, the 27th. It is impossible to say whether this was one of many Sunday performances or the only one. However, it will be recalled that in previous years Sunday performances at the American Theatre had been given only during the Christmas holidays.

Scott bade farewell on the 28th, including among ,his offerings the old favorite, *The Pilot*. Mrs. Knight's benefit presented a novelty, Buckstone's musical, *Pet of the Petticoats*. Bannister followed with his newest tragedy, *Gaulantus the Gaul*, and Thorne's night featured *The Rake's Progress*, a melodrama by W. L. Rede.

Little Miss Meadows began an engagement on April 4 when she appeared in *The Four Mowbrays*. During her brief stay the young star impersonated Hecla in *The Ice Witch*, Little Pickle in *The Spoiled Child*, Variella in *The Weathercock*, and Catharine in *Catharine and Petruchio*.

An interesting benefit was Radcliffe's on April 7. The opening piece, *The Honey Moon,* was followed by *Oh! Hush* in which Joe Blackburn, a clown from Brown's Circus, played Sam Johnson, and by an act from *Richard III,* Blackburn enacting Richmond to the Richard of James Wills. For Mrs. Carr's night was announced *Harcanlack, or The Demon of the Serpent's Glen.* This may have been the play of Bannister's which James Rees in his *Dramatic Authors of America* lists as *The Serpent's Glen.* Williamson's benefit brought Charles Shannon's *The Youthful Queen* with Miss Russell as Christine and *Will Watch,* Miss Russell as Mary.

The management turned to opera on April 18 bringing out Bellini's *Sonnambula* with Miss Russell as Armina. It held the boards until the 23rd but according to the *Bee* of that date few witnessed its nightly representations. Miss Russell's benefit on the 24th featured a dramatization of *Charlotte Temple* made by James Rees especially for her. She seems to have been the favorite performer during these last weeks. Planché's adaptation of Scribe's opera, *The Jewess,* was brought out on May 3 with the young actress in the role of Rachel. The spectacle ran almost nightly until the end of the season, and many of those actors whose benefits fell within this period offered it in preference to other pieces.

The season came to an end on May 25 though three nights later the theatre was reopened that Treasurer Graham might have a benefit. Outstanding features of this season had been the excellence of the company and the popularity of several of the plays. The *Bee* of May 23 asserted that in relying on the strength and capabilities of his own stock company and by exhibiting them in good drama, Russell had succeeded beyond his expectations.

ST. CHARLES THEATRE, 1835-1836

The new St. Charles Theatre, which James H. Caldwell opened in the fall of 1835, stood on St. Charles Street between Poydras and Gravier and extended almost to Camp Street. Caldwell had purchased the site in Jane Placide's name in 1833,[4] when he was negotiating with Russell and Rowe for the lease of his theatrical circuit. The purchase at this early date and in a name other than his own would seem to indicate the correctness of

---

[4] Notarial Acts of William Boswell, March 7, 1833; Notarial Acts of William Cristy, May 14, 1835. Court House. New Orleans.

Ludlow's belief that Caldwell was not sincere in announcing his retirement and that it was but a ruse.[5]

The theatre, designed by A. Mondelli, was the most magnificent in the South and one of the largest in the country. It had a frontage of one hundred thirty feet, a depth of one hundred ninety, and a height of eighty-six feet. Ten Corinthian columns supported the portico which ran across the front between the second and third floors and over this was a balustrade decorated with statues of Apollo and the muses.

Fluted Ionic columns supported the vestibule on the main floor, and on either side were stairways leading to a similar vestibule above. The parquet held two hundred and the pit five hundred. There were five tiers of seats including the pit boxes and the gallery. Attached to the boxes of the first tier were boudoirs, eight feet square and ten feet high, where the ladies might dress or retire as they wished.

The proscenium arch rested on Corinthian columns and the stage, said to be the largest in America, was ninety-five feet by ninety. Back of this was a large scenery room and on either side a green room. Two straiways led to the twenty-six dressing rooms and the room for the wardrobe, properties, and scenery.[6]

The stage manager for the first three months was J. W. Forbes; on his departure in February he was succeeded by W. H. Latham. Mondelli was chief scenic artist; his assistants, J. R. Smith, J. Cowell, and Schinotti. J. G. Maeder was musical director, H. Willis, leader of the orchestra, and George Holland, secretary and treasurer.

The company included Messrs. H. J. Finn, John H. Barton, J. W. Forbes, Latham, Joe Cowell, Henry Hunt, Vincent De Camp, H. G. Pearson, Ben DeBar, Williams, Williamson, Spencer, Schinotti, Corri, Larkin, Burke, Ford, Loomis, Solomon, Stanley, Brace, Lenox, Benedict, Harris, Dennison, Markham, Scot; Mesdames Gibbs, Maeder (the former Clara Fisher), Kinlock, Thorne, Browne, Bannister (formerly Mrs. Stone), Burke; and Misses Louise Lane (in March she became Mrs. Henry Hunt), Charlotte Cushman, Pelham, Copeland, Verity, Graham, DeBar, Vos, Rhodes, and Henning. Before the season was far advanced James E. Murdoch arrived from Philadelphia, and during several

---

[5] Ludlow, *op. cit.*, 404.

[6] The *Bee* of April 7, 1835, contains a detailed description of the theatre.

months Mrs. Cowell played with the company. The orchestra was a large one of twenty-nine pieces and included such well-known musicians as J. T. Norton, trumpet, Signor Cioffi, trombone, J. K. Kendall, clarinet, and Signor Boucher, violincello.

The theatre opened on November 30 with a prize address, overtures by the orchestra, and the favorite plays, *The School for Scandal* and *The Spoiled Child*. In the comedy Vincent De Camp played Sir Peter, Barton, Charles, Forbes, Joseph, Cowell, Crabtree, Mrs. Maeder, Lady Teazle, and Louisa Lane, Maria. The afterpiece served to introduce Miss DeBar as Little Pickle.

The *Bee* of the next day states that a very numerous audience attended the opening "despite the reports that had been industriously and villainously circulated of its being likely to fall." This commentator had been very much pleased with the orchestral performance and the *"tout ensemble"* of the decorations, although they were unfinished. "But we cannot boast of anything else," he continued. "The house is at present cold and cheerless; and the members of the theatrical corps are not properly disciplined or accustomed to so large a theatre."

The second night brought *The Marriage of Figaro* with Mrs. Gibbs, the English actress, as Susanna, Charlotte Cushman as Countess Almaviva, Latham as Figaro, Hunt as Count Almaviva, H. J. Finn as Antonio, and Mrs. Maeder as Cherubino. After a second presentation the *Bee* (December 4) announced that it did not think much of Caldwell's operatic force. Mrs. Gibbs' voice was described as being soft and sweet and well adapted for ballads but lacking in volume, flexibility, and strength. "Still," commented this critic, "it is greatly superior to that of Miss Cushman, who made the worst countess we have had the honor of seeing for some time; she is scarcely a third rate songstress and we confess . . . we were much more pleased with the performance of Miss Verity as Bacharina." Hunt's voice was said to be "feeble, husky, and thin without much compass or control." Only for the orchestra did the critic have unqualified praise. He pronounced it a "credit to the theatre and with the exception of that at Orleans Street (the French theatre), . . . probably the best in the United States."

Barton and Mrs. Maeder were Duke Aranza and Juliana in *The Honey Moon* on the 4th and a Mr. Frimbley appeared after the play as the Living Statues. On the 6th *John of Paris*, with

Mrs. Gibbs as Vincent and Miss Cushman as the Princess of Navarre, preceded *Charles II* in which Mrs. Gibbs was Mary, Miss Copeland, Lady Clara, and Hunt, Charles II. Miss Copeland had made her New Orleans début only a few days before when she played the Queen to Forbes' Hamlet.

Mr. and Mrs. Ternan were the first stars to visit the new theatre. They opened a short engagement on December 7 in *The Hunchback*. Mrs. Cowell, making her first appearance in four years, played Helen to their Master Walter and Julia; Forbes was Sir Thomas Clifford, and Finn, Modus. In rapid succession the stars appeared as Jaffier and Belvidera, with Pearson as Pierre; Fazio and Bianca; Mr. and Mrs. Beverly in *The Gamester;* Sir John and Lady Restless in *All in the Wrong;* and Lord Henry and Lady Julia in *Personation.*

With the departure of the Ternans on December 12, Mlle. Celeste began an engagement which lasted throughout the month. Nightly she appeared in melodramas and ballets, introducing during her stay J. T. Haines' *The French Spy* and *The Wizard Skiff; The Wept of Wish-ton-Wish,* a spectacle written for her by W. B. Bernard; *The Dumb Brigand; The Moorish Bride* by Caroline Lee Hentz; and *The Devil's Daughter* by George Almar. These were preceded or followed by musical pieces and farces given by the company. On December 16 *The Poor Soldier* enlisted Miss Cushman as Patrick and Latham as Darby. On the 17th James E. Murdoch made his bow as Tristram Fickle in *The Weathercock* and the next night he played with Mrs. Maeder in *Perfection.* The songs and acting of Miss Meadows, "the juvenile vocalist," were featured on the 24th. Since her guardian, Mrs. Frederick Browne, was a regular member of the company, the youthful actress was called on throughout the season for songs and impersonations of the Four Mowbrays and Little Pickle.

For Christmas night were advertised *George Barnwell* with Murdoch and Mrs. Bannister; *Old King Cole;* Celeste's dances; Frimbey's living statues; and the appearance of J. Clayton, the Western Aeronaut, "should he arrive in time." This gentleman had ascended at noon in his balloon "inflated by Mr. Caldwell from the gas works of this city."

Miss Lydia Phillips, "the highly distinguished tragedian from the Theatre Royal, Drury Lane", succeeded Celeste on January 11. She opened as Juliet to Murdoch's Romeo and followed it on the

next night with Julia in *The Hunchback*. Thereafter, she enacted
Portia, Mrs. Beverly to the Beverly of Forbes, Mrs. Haller to the
Stranger of Pearson, Lady Macbeth, Mariana to the Julian St.
Pierre of Barton, Desdemona to the Othello of Forbes, and Lady
Townly to the Lord Townly of Barton. Her benefit on January
25 presented her as Belvidera, Pearson being Pierre and Forbes,
Jaffier. The bill concluded with a novelty, Planché's *Michel
Perrin*.

G. W. Hill began an engagement almost immediately and
ran through his usual repertoire of native roles. The only new
part was offered for his benefit, February 5, when he introduced
J. S. Jones' recent comedy, *The Adventure, or The Yankee in
Tripoli*. At Forbes' benefit and last appearance on the 6th Hill
volunteered as Jonathan Doubikins.

The Ternans reappeared on February 8. They now came out
as Pizarro and Cora *(Pizarro)*, Young Marlow and Miss Hardcastle, Luke Eveline and Sicily in T. J. Serle's piece, *The Shadow
on the Wall*, and Sir George Touchwood and Letitia Hardy in
The Belle's Stratagem. Mrs. Cowell's performance as Mrs.
Rackett in this latter comedy was her last on the St. Charles
stage. The following night she appeared at the American Theatre where she performed until the end of the season. On the 22nd,
at the benefit given Latham, the newly appointed stage manager,
the Ternans offered Knowles' new play, *The Beggar of Bethel
Green*.

A more popular novelty was the spectacular *Peter Wilkins,
or The Flying Islanders* which had been brought out on the 21st.
In the cast were Miss Cushman as Peter Wilkins, Miss DeBar as
Yourakee, and Latham as Nicodemus.

Miss Phillips had returned on February 18 and after open-
ing as Julia in *The Hunchback*, Barton replacing Forbes as
Master Walter, she appeared as Lady Teazle and as Juliana in
The Honey Moon. On the two latter occasions the afterpiece was
Selby's petite comedy, *A Day in Paris*, featuring Louisa Lane.

Thomas Cooper arrived sometime during the last week in
February and with the aid of Miss Phillips offered *Macbeth, The
Gamester, Jane Shore*, and *Othello*. In *Wives as They Were,
Much Ado about Nothing, Virginius, Rule a Wife and Have a
Wife*, and *Damon and Pythias*, the tragedian was supported by

his daughter, Priscilla Cooper. On March 12 Miss Phillips took her benefit and departed, and three nights later the Coopers made their last appearance in *The Hunchback.*

Meanwhile Caldwell had inaugurated what he hoped would become a regular feature at the St. Charles, a season of Italian Opera with performances three times a week on Sunday, Wednesday, and Friday. At the head of the troupe was Signor Montresor who had managed the disastrous opera season at the Richmond Hill Theatre in 1833.[7] The principal singers were Signoras Pedrotti and Marozzi, and Signors Ravaglia, Sapignoli, and De Rosa, all of whom had sung at Richmond Hill or at the Italian Opera House in New York. Twenty-five musicians were engaged to supplement the regular orchestra.

The first performance on March 6 was Bellini's *Il Pirata.* It was repeated on every opera night until the 18th when Rossini's *Otello* was given. Thereafter repetitions of these two operas alternated with Bellini's *Norma* and *La Straniera* and Rossini's *Zelmira.*

"The Italian Opera Company has taken the town by storm," reported the *Bee* of March 7 after the first performance. Three months later an editorial in the same paper referred to Caldwell as the opera's "sole patron and sole sufferer." It was stated that he had engaged the troupe at an expense of $20,000 and had lost $10,750 by the arrangement. The next day there appeared a contradiction of this statement. The communicant said that Montresor had told him the engagement had cost Caldwell not more than $11,000 and as nightly receipts had sometimes been from $2,000 to $3,000 such a loss was impossible.[8]

Early in the season Caldwell had declared his intention of raising the tone of the drama. Yet now he turned to equestrian plays and on March 24 revived *Timour the Tartar* with the aid of the stud of horses from Brown's circus. After frequent repetitions it made way for *El Hyder* and *The Cataract of the Ganges.* Familiar farces generally served as the curtain raisers on these nights.

Cinderella was revived on April 11, Miss Gibbs playing the title role, Finn, Pedro, Latham, Dandini, Hunt, the Prince, and Miss DeBar and Charlotte Cushman the two daughters. Once again Hunt and Charlotte Cushman were severely criticized.

---

[7] Odell, *op. cit.,* III, 642-645.
[8] *Bee,* June 8, 1836.

"We would not want to see a worse prince," commented the *Bee* on April 12. "As for the ladies who attempted to represent the daughters . . . we have scarcely seen worse attempts for some time. Miss DeBar sings ballads tolerably, but Miss Cushman can sing nothing; therefore in justice to herself and in mercy to the audience she should confine herself to acting parts in which she can perform with success."

On April 19 the management announced that *Macbeth* would be given shortly for the purpose of introducing Charlotte Cushman as Lady Macbeth "which character she has been studying under a competent teacher." The performance took place on the 23rd and at last the dramatic critic on the *Bee* was impressed. In the issue of the 25th he wrote: "To such line of character she should confine her attention, if she means to excel on the stage and then she may command approbation and applause, but as for her singing it is prodigious."

Mrs. Gibbs prepared to depart as April drew to a close. Her benefit on the 25th presented her as Countess Rosalvina to Hunt's Count Belino (*The Devil's Bridge*), as Cinderella (only the finale), and as Eudiga in the local première of Planché's *Charles XII*. On the 26th Planchè's adaptation from *The Jewess* of Scribe was introduced with Mrs. Henry Hunt, the former Louisa Lane, as Rachel.

The benefits at the St. Charles brought little in the way of novelty. The new patriotic drama, *Texas*, offered by Mrs. Bannister, seems to have been her husband's *Fall of San Antonio, or Texas Victorious*, introduced at the American Theatre earlier in the year. For his benefit Mondelli announced a translation of Victor Hugo's *Lucrece Borgia* made by F. Haynes of New Orleans. Charlotte Cushman played the name part assisted by Pearson and Barton.

The most interesting of these novelties was *The Martyr Patriots, or Louisiana in 1769* given by Pearson on May 16. The play had been written in 1834 by Thomas Warton Collens, a young lawyer of the city, and Miss Nelson had chosen it for her benefit that season at the American Theatre. Pearson, however, had refused to learn his part and the play had been laid aside.[9] Now he and Mrs. Hunt took the leads.

This poetic drama was based on an event in the colonial history of Louisiana, the uprising of the little band of loyal

---

[9] *Louisiana Advertiser*, May 7, 17, 1834.

Frenchmen against the Spanish governor, O'Reilley, in 1769. Between the fourth and fifth acts was exhibited a grand dioramic vision foretelling the independence of Louisiana and the rise and prosperity of the city of New Orleans. According to a communication in the *Bee* of May 19, this was the only feature of the play to which the management did justice. The writer said that Collens' play had been "garbled, butchered, and parodied," and "the most ridiculous and crude conception substituted in the place of the language as originally written." As representative of the careless manner in which the play had been produced, he cited the instance in the last act when the five martyr leaders of the uprising were shot by a detachment of soldiers. This consisted of only four men, we are told. "So that we must suppose them to be even greater shots than Crockett himself, for not only did they kill five men, but one of their stray balls put to death the heroine of the piece."

"By particular desire" Charlotte Cushman repeated *Macbeth* on her night (May 20), following it with Charles Selby's new interlude, *The Married Rake,* and *Blue Beard* in which she played Fatima. For Miss DeBar's benefit, Charlote Cushman enacted Rachael Heywood in *The Rent Day* assisted by Pearson as Martin. *The Wandering Boys* was revived for the occasion that the beneficiary and Mrs. Hunt might appear as Paul and Justin.

The season came to an end on May 28 when Holland's benefit presented him for the first time at the St. Charles. His bill consisted of the familiar *Whims of a Comedian, The Secret,* and *A Day after the Fair.*

This first season of the St. Charles Theatre was a disappointment to Caldwell. He had built and dedicated to the drama one of the largest theatres in the country and the public had failed to give him the support needed to maintain such an establishment. In commenting on this lack of patronage the editor of the *Bee* (May 23) suggested that contributing causes may have been the increased price of admission and public disapproval of Caldwell's having built another theatre before the expiration of Russell's lease on the American. Caldwell himself felt that a general apathy toward the legitimate drama was responsible for his failure, and accordingly he announced that next season he would concentrate on opera, melodrama, ballet, and spectacles.[10]

---

[10] *Bee,* June 7, 1836.

The St. Charles reopened on June 1 for a short summer season of comedy and farce. The opening bill featured J. M. Field, now returned after an absence of three years, as Gossamer in *Laugh When You Can* and as Jeremy Diddler in *Raising the Wind*. He played the leads in the comedies of the next few nights, enacted Carwin to Mrs. Hunt's Thérèse, and for his benefit on the 11th, essayed Sir Giles Overreach.

Mrs. Minnich of the Mobile Theatre made her bow on the 13th as Justin in *The Wandering Boys* and as Priscilla Tomboy in *The Romp*. On the 14th George Holland began a short engagement with *A Day After the Fair*.

Novelties were a feature of this summer season. The first was Charles Selby's *Frank Fix Phipps*, introduced on the 10th. The bill for the 17th consisted of the new pieces, *The King's Word* and *The Prairie Girls*, both announced as the work of "a gentleman of this city." Holland's benefit on the 22nd presented Mrs. J. R. Planché's drama, *The Sledge Driver*, and P. P. O'Callaghan's burletta, *The Married Bachelor*. James Kenney's *Not a Word* came on the 23rd a farce *Pay for Peeping* on the 27th; and on the 28th, T. J. Thackeray's comedy, *The Force of Nature*.

The season came to a close on July 4 with a first performance of J. S. Jones' *The Liberty Tree* and *Boston Boys*, patriotic songs and recitations, and *The Hole in the Wall*, Holland reappearing as Thomas. As far as the extant records show, this was the first summer season of any consequence.

CHAPTER VII

Business as Usual   1836-1837

Richard Russell and his company returned from the summer campaign in Cincinnati to a theatre which had been "newly and splendidly decorated and repainted by Joe Cowell, Jr." Noted the *Commercial Bulletin* of November 23: "The American Theatre has undergone suitable repairs . . . and the interior particularly evinces much comfort as well as taste, in the arrangements which have been made. The boxes are neatly cushioned, as also the seats in the parquette *(sic)* and an air of neatness prevails throughout which hitherto has not been so apparent."

Russell's staff consisted of F. S. Hill, stage manager; Higgins, prompter; Jones, leader of the orchestra; Graham, treasurer; Lafferty, wardrobe keeper; and Joe Cowell, Jr., chief scenic artist. In the company were Messrs. Farren, Hodges, Archer, "from the London and Park Theatres," A. W. Fenno, "from the Boston Theatre," Foster, Barclay, Fielding, Clarke, Smith, Gray, Bristow, Wallace, Sowerby, Eversul, Vancamp, Fairchild, Walton, Milot, McCoy, Phillips, Carr and Lake, Mesdames Russell, G. Rowe, Carr, Minnich, and Greene, Misses Russell, Rowe, Clarke, and Henning, and Mr. and Mrs. Bennie, the dancers. These were joined later in the season by Miss Randolph, Sam Cowell, Delmon, Burke, Kelly, and Mrs. Henry Hunt.

The theatre opened on November 21 with *The Hunchback* and *The Purse,* and on the second night came the first star, William Abbott. His Hamlet was supported by the Ophelia of Miss Clarke and the Polonius of Farren. In the afterpiece, *The Actress of All Work,* Mrs. Greene, "from the Eastern Theatre," sustained six characters. The third night saw the first appearance of Mrs. H. Lewis, the English actress, and C. B. Parsons, the American tragedian. Their performance in *Bertram* was followed by a novelty, *Tom Cringle's Log, or Mat o' the Iron Hand* by Edward Fitzball.

Abbott continued as Benedick to the Beatrice of Miss Russell, Fenno, who had been engaged as second tragedian and heavy, playing Claudio. On the 26th the star introduced *The King's Fool,* a historical drama by John Millingen, in which he had been successful in the East. Archer, the new vocalist, made his début in this as Melchior. Abott's roles were those which Caldwell had so often enacted: Don Felix in *The Wonder! A Woman Keeps a Secret,* Belcour in *The West Indian,* Duke Aranza in *The Honey Moon,* Puff in *The Critic,* etc. On December 10, he essayed Modus *(The Hunchback)* "for this night only," and on the 14th he introduced a new play, *Hofer the Tell of the Tyrol.* This melodrama of Edward Fitzball's proved so popular that he repeated it at his benefit on the 18th.

Meanwhile Mrs. Lewis and C. B. Parsons were featured on the nights when Abbott did not perform. She enacted Mariana *(The Wife)* on the 25, and Richard III on the 28th, Parsons appearing on both of these evenings in the afterpiece, *Charles II.* For the last performance prior to his departure for the Natchez theatre Parsons brought out *Caius Silius,* a new prize tragedy which N. H. Bannister had written expressly for him. After the play Bennie and Mrs. Lewis gave a dance from *La Juive.* This actress seems to have been capable of assuming any character; her Romeo was followed by personations of Bill Jones *(The Black Brig of Bermuda),* Emilia *(Othello),* and Virginius. At her benefit on December 12 she appeared in such widely diversified roles as Wiliam in *Black Eyed Susan,* Jane Shore, Sir Giles Overreach, and the Wild Boy of Bohemia in John Walker's melodrama of that name.

Mrs. Knight commenced an engagement on December 13. Miss Horton, a vocalist from Covent Garden Theatre, had been in the city for several days and on the 19th she appeared as Cinderella supported by Mrs. Knight as the Prince. In *The Marriage of Figaro,* on the 23rd, Miss Horton was Susanna, Miss Russell was Countess Almaviva, and Mrs. Knight was Cherubino the Page. Charles E. Horn, who had made his début the previous night in *Guy Mannering,* was Count Almaviva. On the second presentation of *Cinderella* Horn replaced Mrs. Knight as the Prince, the lady now appearing as the Fairy Queen. With the performance of *John of Paris* on the 31st Miss Horton and Horn departed.

The engagement of eight nights which James Wallack began on January 3 brought nothing new. It interests us, however, for during the star's visit Miss Russell appeared in many roles which had not previously been in her repertoire. She not only played opposite Wallack in *Pizarro, The Wife,* and *The Hunchback,* but she played Portia and Rachael Heywood *(The Rent Day),* as well as Mrs. General Dartmouth *(Spring and Winter)* and Nell *(The Adopted Child).* During Wallack's second engagement, which began on February 7, she appeared as Lady Macbeth, Imogiene *(Bertram),* Mary Copp *(Charles II)* and Catharine *(Catharine and Petruchio),* all new roles for her.

Hodges made his first appearance of the season on January 7 as the Prince to Mrs. Knight's Cinderella. The voice of this actress had sadly deteriorated in the last few years, but the management knew that the presence of Hodges and the popularity of the opera itself could be counted on to draw a full house. The 9th brought the local première of William Bernard's *Lucille* with Mrs. Knight in the title role. Russell showed cleverness in producing the play at this time, for the St. Charles Theatre was awaiting the arrival of Mr. and Mrs. Keeley, the English comedians for whom Bernard had written the piece. Nine days after the Keeleys had opened in T. H. Bayly's burletta, *The Swiss Cottage*, Russell brought it out at the American with Mrs. Knight as Lisette Gierstein, Hill as Natz Treck, and Archer as Corporal Max.

Charles Mason opened an engagement in *Rob Roy* on January 18. Several nights later he was joined by Mrs. Lewis and Forbes in a presentation of *Othello*, Forbes in the title role, and thereafter the three appeared together in *The Hunchback* and *Jane Shore*. The role of Alice in the former, taken earlier in the season by Miss Russell, was now played by Miss Randolph, a young actress who had made her first appearance on any stage at the St. Charles a month before. Mrs. Lewis played opposite Mason in *Macbeth* and *George Barnwell* and on her benefit night, January 30, Forbes was Alexander to her Roxana. After her departure Miss Russell again succeeded to the leads, appearing with the visiting tragedians in *Julius Caesar* and in *The Hunchback*. At Forbes' benefit on February 11 she essayed Ophelia.

Several débuts took place on February 15. Kelly, a low comedian, made his bow as Solomon Swap and afterwards Herr Cline entertained with "astonishing metamorphoses." As an added attraction during his engagement, Herr Cline was sometimes joined on the elastic cord by his grandmother, a lady who, the notices say, was able to rival him, notwithstanding her age.

Miss Nelson was welcomed back on February 23 in Barnett's opera, *The Mountain Sylph*. The piece was admirably adapted to display the actress's splendid figure and her "perilous yet beautiful descent from the clouds" had won her many admirers on her northern tour. After seven repetitions of the opera, she appeared as Hecla in *The Ice Witch*, a part which Mrs. Knight had played before her departure for Natchez, shortly after February 8. For her farewell benefit on March 10, Miss Nelson offered the cloister scene from last season's favorite, *Robert le Diable*, and appeared as Ernestine in *The Somnambulist*.

Mr. and Mrs. Lewis returned in March, bringing with them George Pitt's *The Whistler*, a new melodrama adapted from Scott's *Heart of Midlothian*. When Celeste opened at the St. Charles in *The French Spy* on March 7, Mrs. Lewis appeared in the same piece at the American. She gave it for the fourth time on the 11th when Thomas Bishop, a former member of the St. Charles company, was allowed a benefit. According to a notice in the *Daily Picayune* on April 21, Bishop had left that theatre "not wishing to hazard his reputation by singing the music of a piece at an unusually short notice."

The legitimate drama again featured in the bills when Josephine Clifton began an engagement in *Fazio* on March 23. To insure her success Russell arranged for Charles Mason to play with her. On seven consecutive nights their representations of familiar tragedies attracted "good and respectable houses." A new police officer was on hand to see that the ladies of the audience were not offended by the "rowdy set" that had frequented the theatre of late.[1]

The most popular of the season's novelties was *Lafitte,* a dramatization of Joseph Ingram's novel made by James Rees and "altered and adapted to the stage by George Farren." William Abbott reappeared in the role of the famous pirate; Farren impersonated General Andrew Jackson; and Kelly had a Yankee role, "written expressly for him." Cowell and his assistants worked hard on this piece and in one scene the audience witnessed four distinct actions occurring at the same time. In spite of the critics who pronounced it "rather dull in portions," "a ridiculous compound of 'rant, rhapsody, and rhetoric'," the play seems to have been successful and by April 14 had reached its tenth performance.

Novelty and benefits were almost daily fare in April. On the 15th Barclay introduced George Almar's melodrama, *The Fire Raiser.* The following night "the pretty little Miss Carr" offered among her entertainments the extravaganza, "The Coal Black Rose," as performed by her four year old son. Fielding's benefit on April 17 marked the first appearance this season of Mrs. Duff, who had now remarried and was living in New Orleans. The bill on this night concluded with *Hard Times in New Orleans,* a local farce written by George Harby. Hodges announced that on his night he would appear as Cinderella and sing a portion of the music "in imitation of a celebrated vocalist lately attached to this establishment." Undoubtedly he referred to Mrs. Knight who had terminated a second engagement on April 1.

---

[1] *Daily Picayune,* March 25, 1837.

There was a brief recess from novelties when Miss Clifton reappeared on the 19th. Supported by Parsons, who was more popular in New Orleans than the English actor Mason, she went through a familiar round of characters. At her benefit on April 26 Fenno was allowed to play with her in selected acts from *Fazio*.

Mrs. Duff succeeded Miss Clifton and with the aid of Parsons presented those plays which had long been associated with her name. The one role in which she had not previously appeared here was that of Victoire in *The Orphan of Paris* presented on May 2.

May was a busy month at the American. Mrs. Pritchard began an engagement on the 4th and appeared some twelve times before the end of the season. The resident members of the company continued with their benefits, introducing among the plays Bernard's melodrama, *2548, or The Farmer's Story*, and Benjamin Webster's *The Golden Farmer*. Mrs. Henry Hunt came over from the St. Charles on the 9th and, after appearing in *The Turn Out* and in *Perfection* took her "first and only benefit in New Orleans." On this evening (May 13) Hill introduced his new petite comedy, *Love and a Bunch*. The last novelty of the season was Moncrieff's seventeen-year-old melodrama, *Ivanhoe*, which had its local première on Mrs. Pritchard's benefit night.

Master Burke now appeared in *The Weathercock, The Review*, and in other familiar pieces which he had offered in April at the St. Charles. At the American the excellence of his violin concertos as well as the popularity of his supporting *artiste*, Miss Russell, may have compensated somewhat for the "peculiar tone" in his voice which had displeased the critics of the earlier engagement.

The last night of the season was given to Miss Russell for her benefit. The bill for the evening included a comedy, two farces, Fenno's recitation of his poem, "Washington and Lafayette," a dance by Miss Hennings, a trumpet solo by Gambatti, the waltz scene from *The Brigand* featuring Mrs. Pritchard and the beneficiary, and a farewell address. This was said to have been quite an occasion; a splendid gold necklace was presented to Miss Russell and wreaths and the like were showered down upon her.

The American Theatre had been well attended this season. As one critic remarked, "Dick Russell had presented the public with a variety of good things: the choicest gems of tragedy, English melodrama, new farces, and sterling comedies."[2]

The success of the past two seasons had shown Russell that he need not fear the rivalry of the new St. Charles. Often during this time the "little Camp" had not been able to accommodate the crowds that flocked there. Now, a year before his lease on the Camp expired, he issued the prospectus for a theatre to be erected by public subscription and opened in the fall of 1838.[3] In March he purchased a site on the southeast corner of Magazine Street and Delord and within a few months a company had been formed and chartered by the state legislature for the purpose of building the "New American Theatre."[4]

ST. CHARLES THEATRE, 1836-1837

The St. Charles opened for its second season on November 14, 1836. The interior which had been described as cold and cheerless on the opening night a year ago was now completely finished. "Upon it," said the *Bee* of November 25, "a liberal hand has lavished every ornament that unbounded munificence can confer." The most outstanding of the new decorations was the magnificent chandelier which had been purchased in London at a cost of $10,750. Twelve feet in height, and thirty feet in circumference, it weighed 4,500 pounds and was illuminated with one hundred and seventy-six gas lights.[5] The editor of the *Commercial Bulletin* (November 16) was eloquent in his praise of this "brilliant collection of crystals", declaring: "He who could gaze upon its magnificence as it emits its flood of mellowed light, without yielding admiration to its splendor and beauty, must be wanting much in the ingredient of taste. Such a spectacle itself should draw thousands to view it."

Many of the former company returned, among them H. G. Pearson, Barton, Finn, Latham, Hunt, Williams, DeBar, Corri, Lyons, Spencer, and Keppell, Mesdames Hunt, Bannister, and Kinlock. To these were added Mrs. Keppell, Bannister, Radcliffe, Dennison, Ruthven, Fenner, Saunders, Manley, Paret, Raylea, Tracy, and Hamilton. Later in the season came Thomas Bishop, Page, Mrs. Saunders, Mrs. H. Cramer, Miss Melton, and Mr. and Mrs. Barker, who had been engaged by Caldwell's agent on a

---

[2] *Louisiana Courier*, May 27, 1837.
[3] *Commercial Bulletin*, February 3, 1837.
[4] *Ibid.*, March 21, April 18, 1837.
[5] *The True American*, September 14, 1839.

recent visit to England. Fallon was leader of the orchestra; Barton was stage manager during the first of the season and Latham during the latter part. George Holland continued as treasurer and occasionally performed with the company.

The opening bill on the 14th consisted of the "grand spectacle", *Peter Wilkins* and *The Secret*. *Macbeth* with Charles Mason in the title role was announced for the 16th but when sudden indisposition prevented his appearance, Barton took the part. On the 18th the star made his bow in *Hamlet* assisted by Mrs. Bannister as the Queen and Mrs. Hunt as Ophelia. The next night brought the first novelty, Bannister's domestic drama, *Infidelity, or The Husband's Return*. Mrs. Hunt and Mrs. Bannister were busy these nights; they appeared as Lady Ann and Queen Elizabeth to Mason's Richard (*Richard III*), Albert and Emma to his William Tell, and Cora and Elvira to Pearson's Rolla. When Mason offered Byron's *Sardanapalus* for his benefit on November 25, Mrs. Hunt enacted the role of the Greek slave. In the afterpiece Mrs. Bannister was Catharine to the beneficiary's Petruchio.

Mrs. Shaw, "from the Theatre Royal, Drury Lane and Park Theatre," made her New Orleans début on November 24 in *The Wife*, Mason playing opposite her as St. Pierre. She continued as the Widow Cheerly, Juliet, Variella (*The Weathercock*), Lady Teazle, Christine (*The Youthful Queen*), Bianca (*Fazio*), and Cordelia (*Lear*). Barton, who was the leading man this season, appeared with her as Mercutio, Tristram Fickle, Charles Surface, Steinberg (*The Youthful Queen*), and as Lear. For her benefit, December 5, Mrs. Shaw presented a play not previously seen here, Buckstone's *Agnes de Vere*.

The next visitor was Mrs. Drake who appeared on December 3. The "tragic lioness of the West" offered nothing new, but the roles in which she appeared had long been favorite ones in this city. Barton now turned from comedy roles to assist her in *The Stranger, Rob Roy, Macbeth, The Merchant of Venice, The Gamester*, etc. On her benefit night, December 14, Pearson played opposite her in *The Tower of Nesle*.

The Italian Opera Company initiated its season with *La Cenerentola* on December 4. Included in the company were Ravaglia, Orlandi, De Rosa, Mannetti, and Signora Marozzi. On several occasions Madame Thielman and Mrs. Keppell of the

stock company sang with them. As there was still some doubt
as to whether opera would be adequately supported, the season
was a short one with performances only on Sundays. The company offered Rossini's *Il Barbier di Seviglia, L'Inganno Felica,*
and *Il Turco in Italia,* and for their last performance, on February 27, the comic opera, *Monsieur de Chiffonne.*

Mr. Balls, the light comedian, made his bow on December 12
in *Laugh When You Can* and *Three and the Deuce.* Also introduced on this night was Mrs. Saunders, "from the Theatre Royal,
Edinburgh," a new member of the company. Caldwell now announced that he would present legitimate comedy with "excep-
tional casts" which were to include Messrs. Balls, Barton, Finn,
who had rejoined the company on December 7, Holland, and Mrs.
Shaw. The first of the revivals was O'Keeffe's *Wild Oats,* Balls
enacting Rover, Mrs. Shaw, Lady Amaranthe, and Finn, Ephraim
Smooth. Other standard comedies followed but to the disappointment of many who had hoped the public taste might be elevated
by these bills, the St. Charles continued to be poorly attended.

Caldwell turned to novelties next and on December 23
brought out *Oceola, or The Death of Dade,* "an entirely new
drama never acted," written by a gentleman of Cincinnati.
Though generally the New Orleans audiences were quick to ap-
plaud native talent, *Oceola* was coolly received. Explained the
critic, "X," in the *Courier* of the 24th: "The Indian character
is not dramatic, and this subject is doubly unfortunate in being
the story of our own defeat and disgrace. The triumph of our
enemies over ourselves can never be represented with success on
any stage."

Several new recruits joined the company in December. On
the 16th Thomas Bishop made his American début as Henry
Bertram. Miss Melton, "from the Haymarket and the St. James
Theatre," made a very successful first appearance as Peggy in
The Country Girl and Ninette in *The Young Hussar.* She soon
became a favorite, appearing in such roles as Sally Scraggs in
The Englishmen in India, Ellen in *Married Yesterday,* Lady Caroline in *John Bull,* and Nannette in *The Blue Devils.* Another newcomer was Madame Thielman, a German vocalist and actress,
who made her bow on December 29 in *John of Paris.*

While waiting for the next star, Caldwell brought out the
first series of Bannister's fifteen act drama, *The Wandering Jew.*

This was the melodrama which was given in Philadelphia the following November under the title *The Destruction of Jerusalem.*[6] The New Orleans critics spoke highly of the piece and of the new scenery which had been prepared especially for it, but Caldwell did not produce the other two series.

Mrs. Pritchard opened on January 7 in *The Tower of Nesle* and *The Brigand* and performed each night until the 17th. New pieces in her repertoire were Somerset's melodrama, *The Wreck Ashore, or The Ocean Child,* George Almar's *The Rover Bride,* Isaac Harby's *Alberti Contadini, The Last of the Abruzzi,* and Selby's farce, *Hunting a Turtle.*

Mr. and Mrs. Bob Keeley, the next stars to arrive, made their début in William Bernard's *Lucille, or The Story of a Heart* and Thomas Bayly's *The Swiss Cottage, or Why Don't She Marry,* pieces which had been written expressly for them. Mrs. Shaw joined the Keeleys on January 18 in *Agnes de Verne,* and the trio continued with *The Rivals* and *Wild Oats.* The visitors featured standard comedies and farces, but for their benefit on January 30, "the largest ever witnessed here," they presented *The Yeoman's Daughter,* a domestic drama by T. J. Serle.

Balls returned on January 31 in *Englishmen in India.* The next night A. A. Adams made his New Orleans début in *Virginius.* On February 2 Mr. and Mrs. Barnes and Charlotte Barnes commenced a brief engagement and for the next few nights alternated with Adams. Mrs. Shaw assisted the tragedian and also performed with the Barneses in *A Bold Stroke for a Husband* (Donna Octavia). She appeared with Balls, on February 13, in J. Barnett's comedy, *Win Her and Woo Her,* and in *Black Eyed Susan,* and on the 15th she gave *Hamlet* as her farewell presentation. Commented a gentleman in the *Louisiana Courier* of February 13: "The usurpation of the breeches by the petticoat is not only in bad taste but deteriorates from the delicacy which we always associate with lovely women."

The night after her farewell performance Mrs. Shaw returned to assist Caldwell in the first two performances of the short engagement which he now commenced. On the 18th Mrs. H. Cramer made her American début as Lady Teazle to Caldwell's Charles Surface and on the 20th she was Juliana to his Duke

---

[6] The comparison of the casts of the two productions shows them to have been the same. It is possible, of course, that Bannister made some alterations in the play before the Philadelphia presentation.

Aranza *(The Honey Moon)*. The Barnes family assisted on the
21st when Caldwell took his farewell of the stage as Gossamer.
The afterpiece, *High Life Below Stairs,* was excellently cast with
Balls as the Lord Duke, Finn as Lovell, Latham as Sir Harry,
and Miss Melton as Mrs. Kitty.

James Wallack opened on February 22 with Jerrold's *The
Hazard of the Die* and *The Wolf and The Lamb.* He next ap-
peared as Rolla to the Elvira of Mrs. Bannister, Don Felix to the
Violante of Mrs. Shaw *(The Wonder! A Woman Keeps a Secret),*
and Shylock to the Portia of Mrs. Cramer.   At his benefit, on
March 1, William Abbott volunteered to play Romeo to his Mer-
cutio and Mrs. Cramer's Juliet, and Farren came over from the
Camp Street Theatre to assist as Prince Bianchi in *The Brigand.*

March 2 saw the première of James Rees' new melodrama,
The Unknown, or The Demon's Gift. A communication in the
Louisiana Courier of March 3 tells all that is known of the play.
"Some of the incidents are truly terrific," reported this writer,
"in fact the whole piece is a compound of horrors, such as the
superstitious gave to the character of the Germans of the four-
teenth century."

With the arrival of Celeste on March 7 melodrama and the
dance dominated the bills at the St. Charles. Celeste performed
every night but two during the month, yet not until the 21st did
she offer a new piece. This was Bishop's adaptation of Auber's
opera, *Le Dieu et La Bayadère,* and it held the stage until her
departure. On her benefit night it was preceded by *Yelva, The
Orphan of Russia,* a drama from the French of Scribe.

Mrs. Pritchard reappeared on April 1. In addition to her
familiar roles she now played Hazzi Lotzo in a new drama, *The
White Eagle;* the Widow Cheerly; Paul in *The Wandering Boys;*
and at her benefit on the 10th, Isabella in Buckstone's domestic
drama, *Isabella, or a Woman's Life,* and Mrs. G. in Morris Barnett's farce of that name. Her husband appeared with her on
this last night.

The most successful engagements of the season were in opera.
Early in April Signor Brichta's Italian Company came from
Havana for a two months' run. In the troupe were Signoras Pan-
tanelli, Marozzi, and Papanti; Signors Candi, Ceresini, Badioli,
Pantanelli, Ravaglia, Orlandi, and Fornasari. They gave Bellini's
Montrechi e Capuletti for their first performance on April 4 and

thereafter appeared regularly on Wednesdays, Fridays, and Sundays till the end of the season. Repetitions of the opening opera were frequent as were performances of the new scores: Rossini's *Semiramide* and *Il Tancredi*, Mercadante's *Donna Caritea*, and Rica's *Chiara di Rosemberg*, "first time in America."

The following critique, found in the *Bee* in April 9, is typical of many that appeared at this time.

> Last evening . . . we passed a couple of hours in a transport of delight: music, more eloquent and full of meaning than words, and voices more sweet and flexible than the carol of the nightingale, or the lute of Apollo, thrilled our soul. . . . Indeed such a feast has never been before served to the public of this city—and they will be the losers not to partake of it largely.

The Barnes family returned on the 11th in *The Belle's Stratagem* and *The Somnambulist*. On the 15th Charlotte Barnes' dramatization of Joseph Inghram's *Lafitte* was produced "in a style of unsurpassing magnificence." With the arrival of Celeste on the 18th this engagement was interrupted and the trio did not appear again until the 24th.

Master Burke made his bow on that date in the afterpiece, *The March of Intellect*. On the 27th he played Romeo to the Juliet of Miss Barnes, Barton appearing as Mercutio. For her last performance on May 1 Miss Barnes offered a novelty, *Jemmy Twitcher in France, or Mobb the Outlaw*. A few nights later Burke bade farewell including among his pieces Moncrieff's *Old Heads on Young Shoulders* which he had introduced on April 29.

Barton initiated the benefit season on May 6 with *Reuben Glenroy* and *His First Champagne* by William Rede. Mrs. Shaw, who had begun another engagement on April 3, played Rosalie Somers to his Reuben. Miss Melton's benefit on the 11th presented another novelty, Douglas Jerrold's *The Wedding Gown, or The Exiled Pole*. Bannister brought out two of his new pieces on the 13th, a tragedy, *England's Iron Days*, and a local burletta, *Life in New Orleans*. He was assisted in the latter by "Old Corn Meal", a Negro vendor whose cries had long been familiar to citizens of New Orleans. In Bannister's piece he appeared on the stage with his horse and cart and sang, so the notices say, his celebrated songs of "Fresh Corn Meal." The performance proved successful enough to warrant repetition at Radcliffe's benefit on the 16th though some objected to the introduction of a Negro on the stage.[7] An odd mixture of entertainments was featured on Williams' night. The bill, which began with *The Scottish Chief,* continued with a French vaudeville, *La Carte à Payer,* presented by M. Victorin, and a Grand War Dance by Indian chiefs and warriors in full war costume.

The last two weeks of the season brought only familiar pieces and the operas of the Italian troupe. On June 2 the theatre was turned over to the amateurs who gave a benefit for the relief of destitute widows and children. It should be noted that on this evening Caldwell reappeared as Jeremy Diddler to Mrs. Shaw's Peggy in *Raising the Wind* and that Mrs. Duff, also a volunteer, was Emily to Mrs. Shaw's Corinia and Miss Melton's Patty in the afterpiece, *Frightened to Death.* Two nights later a performance of Donizetti's *Parisina* brought the season to a close.

CHAPTER VIII

Stars and Novelties 1837-1838

AMERICAN THEATRE, 1837-1838

The American Theatre opened November 16, 1837, for what was to be the last season under the management of Richard Russell. It had been handsomely redecorated during the summer and now presented "an air of lightness and elegance well suited to its size and proportion."

The company which Russell had assembled included Messrs. Farren, F. S. Hill, Johnson, Larkin, E. Judah, Madden, George Clarke, Eversull, Kelly, Foster, and Sam Cowell, Mesdames Russell, Minnich, Foster, and Madden, and Misses Russell, Randolph, and Louisa Johnson, a dancer. F. S. Hill was stage manager; J. Cowell, Jr., chief artist; and Graham treasurer.

Information concerning the first ten weeks of the season is scarce and can be derived only from scattered editorial paragraphs and critiques in the newspapers. From these we learn that Charles B. Parsons opened an engagement as Othello on November 20, assisted by "the charming Miss Russell" as Desdemona. Apparently Mr. and Mrs. Henry Lewis arrived within the next few days, for the *Louisiana Courier* of December 1 refers to their performance in *The Black Brig of Bermuda* on the previous night. Reference is also made to an O'Connell who "nimbly danced the Sailor's Hornpipe which saved him from

---

[7] *Louisiana Courier,* May 15, 1837.

being masticated in the Pacific." According to the *Louisiana Courier* of the 13th, "O'Connell the Tattooed or Robinson Crusoe II" had been shipwrecked on an island inhabited by cannibals who, charmed by "his grace, agility, and refined method of capering on the light fantastic toe," had spared his life.

A communication in the *Louisiana Courier* of the 19th throws additional light on Russell's activities during the early part of the season. The writer was indignant that the theatre "with its exhibition of 'wonderful dogs,' many monkeys, tattooed men . . . and other buffoonery" should attract crowded houses while the sterling plays at the St. Charles were witnessed by comparatively meagre audiences. He concluded with the hope that a "most beggarly 'account of empty boxes' may grace the 'little Camp' until the manager is induced to dispense entirely with his canine and mountebank auxiliaries." This communication suggests that Messrs. Cony and Blanchard and their dogs Hector and Bruin filled an engagement at this time, appearing in the same pieces which they offered later in January, *The Cherokee Chief, or The Dogs of the Wreck,* and *The Ourang Outang and His Double.*

Parsons made his last appearance on December 18 and was succeeded by Mrs. Maeder (the former Clara Fisher). Her Letitia Hardy was not adequately supported, declared the *Bee* of the 21st, but the lady herself showed "nothing of the feebleness" which was reported to have "rendered her personations wholly unequal to their former sprightliness." Mrs. Maeder, we note, was all of twenty-six. When Miss Russell left for Natchez about this time, Mrs. Maeder assumed the leads. She introduced two new pieces: William Collier's *Kate Kearney* and Oxberry's melodrama, *Matteo Falcone, the Youthful Brigand.*

January, 1838, brought the comedian John Sefton in his celebrated role of Jemmy Twitcher in *The Golden Farmer.* The night after his arrival Mr. and Mrs. Lewis bade farewell, offering "for the second time" Henry Coleman's new nautical drama, *The Scourge of the Ocean.* Mrs. Lewis' five-year-old daughter, "La Petite Bertha," danced a sailor's hornpipe; Mrs. Lewis delivered an address written expressly for the occasion and dedicated to the firemen of New Orleans; and Sefton again enacted Jemmy Twitcher. The comedian continued after their departure, presenting in the course of his engagement several novelties, Buckstone's *John Jones,* Poole's *Uncle Sam,* Bernard's *The Man About*

Town, and Peake's melodrama, *The Climbing Boy.* At Mrs. Maeder's benefit on the 15th he acted with the beneficiary in Buckstone's new drama, *A Dream of the Future,* and in *The Barrack Room.*

The next star was "Yankee" Hill who opened on January 13 in *The Forest Rose* and *The Yankee Pedlar,* or *Old Times in Virginia,* a new piece written by Bernard. Other novelties given during this engagement of eight nights were Bernard's *Speculation, or Major Wheeler in Europe,* H. A. Buckingham's *Peaceful Pelton, the Vermonter,* and *A Day in France, or the Yankee at Calais,* a piece not yet acted in the East.

The next two weeks brought a return of Cony and Blanchard, and "the wonderful dogs", and on the 29th came the Ravel Family. On February 8 Miss Russell, now Mrs. George P. Farren, made her first appearance since her return from Natchez. She played Julia in *The Hunchback,* her husband taking the part of Master Walter.

Two popular novelties were now brought forward: *The Love Chase,* a new comedy by Sheridan Knowles, and *Life in New York, or The Major's Come,* announced as the work of George Farren. An extravaganza by this name having Major Jack Downing as the leading character had been given at the Bowery Theatre in 1834 when Farren was stage manager there, and undoubtedly this was merely an alteration of the earlier work. For this production Cowell had prepared a view of North River with steamers and as these approached the landing, national airs were introduced. The effect was said to be "thrilling."

Another visitor was Mrs. Bailey who came out on February 21 in *The Spoiled Child.* This charming young vocalist appeared in vaudeville and musical farces such as *The Swiss Cottage* and *Charles II.* A "little Miss Brittingham" was announced for the 24th in *All Is Happy,* a new piece said to have been written expressly for her. She repeated the role several times within the next month and was given a benefit on April 18.

Sefton returned on February 27 and from then until the middle of March he appeared in the roles of his earlier engagement and as Prince Prettyman in *He Is Not Amiss* and as Magnus Lobb in Buckstone's farce, *The Two Queens.*

March brought several visitors. T. D. Rice began an engagement on the 4th, introducing during his stay *Jim Crow in London, Black and White,* and *The Peacock and the Crow* by J. Parry. On the 12th Charles Parsons returned and Charles Plumer, the new recruit, made his first appearance. This vocalist had been at the St. Charles in February and had won favor with his performances in musical afterpieces. Mrs. Duff joined Parsons in *Bertram* on the 13th and their presentation of *Othello, Adelgitha,* and the standard plays, attracted large houses. "Thus evincing," commented the press, "that the legitimate drama will be patronized, notwithstanding all the slang-whagery about our perverted taste."

One of the most popular of the season's novelties was *Nick of the Woods,* a dramatization of Robert Montgomery Bird's novel by G. W. Harby. The author had given the play to Parsons in December and the actor had brought it out in Natchez sometime during the following month.[1] Its reception in New Orleans is described in a communication to the *Daily Picayune* of March 20: "To say it was successful would be too tame a praise; it was on its first presentation received with deafening applause." Noted the *Louisiana Courier* of March 19: "The alterations of Harby in plot and character produce a greater effect than is portrayed in the novel; in fact, he has taken but the germ from Dr. Bird; the tree and all its branches are the produce of his own genius and imagination."

By the last of March the visiting stars had departed and the company prepared to take their benefits. Charles Plumer offered two melodramas new to the city: Morris Barnett's *The Spirit of the Rhine* and George Pitt's *The Last Nail.* Judah's night brought *The Widow's Curse* by J. B. Phillips and *The Black Dwarf,* also a new melodrama. Foster's benefit on April 3 was not without its novelty—the exhibition of a fire escape between pieces.

On April 6 Madden brought out his own play, *The Triumph of Texas, or The Plains of San Jacinto.* The announcement of the performance stated that Colonel William H. Wharton, Envoy Extraordinary and Minister Plenipotentiary from The Republic of Texas to the United States, would attend. Mrs. Carr's offering was Thomas Wilk's drama, *The Death Token, or The Fatal Gift,* given now "for the first time in America."

---

[1] *Daily Picayune,* February 9, 1838.

The return of the Ravels on the 8th interrupted the benefits. They were resumed on the 16th when F. S. Hill offered his *Six Degrees of Crime* and his new piece, *The School of Ten Quakers*. Larkin on his night introduced *Rory O'More, or The Rebellion of 1798*, a dramatization of Samuel Lover's novel. It was reported that the officers and members of the St. Patrick Hibernian Society together with the whole Irish population of the city intended to witness the performance.

The season came to a close with Miss Russell's benefit on April 29. Miss DeBar, formerly of the St. Charles, appeared on this night as Lisette in *The Swiss Cottage* and as Catherine in *A Husband at Sight*.

SUMMER SEASON, 1838

The theatre reopened on May 5 "for a limited period of light and elegant entertainment adapted to the season." The announcement of the opening performance, *L'Auberge des Adrets, or Why Don't She Marry* and *No!*, listed several new names: Mrs. Charles Plumer, Miss DeBar, and Miss E. Randolph. Joe Cowell, Sr. apparently joined the troupe soon after this; the notice of May 11 lists him as Wormwood in *The Lottery Ticket*, "his third appearance."

An engagement with the Barnes family and Harrison brought a change in the repertoire. Musical trifles and farces were relegated to the background while the visitors presented *The School for Scandal, The Rivals,* and *Othello*. For her farewell benefit on May 19 Miss Barnes announced her own play, *Octavia Bragaldi*.

The 19th found the theatre closed, however, for early that morning Richard Russell had died.[2] Just two weeks before, on May 7, he had laid the cornerstone of the new theatre which he intended to open in the fall.[3] After his death the plans were abandoned and later the first German Theatre in New Orleans was built on the site.[4]

F. S. Hill and Graham, the treasurer, now assumed the management of the theatre as Russell's lease did not expire until June 1. The Barnes family presented *Octavia Bragaldi* when the

---

[2] *Ibid.,* May 20, 1838.
[3] *Ibid.,* May 6, 1838.
[4] *Ibid.,* November 14, 1838.

theatre opened on May 21; a repetition of the play on the 23rd was followed by *Personation* with Harrison as Lord Henry and Miss Barnes as Lady Julia. They appeared also in *A Bold Stroke for a Husband, The Love Chase,* and *The Wedding Day.* On the 30th, as Mrs. Plumer's benefit, Mrs. Duff enacted Florinda to the Pescara of Pearson in *The Apostate.* For her own benefit the following night she appeared as Mrs. Haller. This was announced as "positively the last night of the season," but when Caldwell offered Hill the use of the house for two more nights, the theatre reopened. On June 3 the company gave its last performance.

THE NEGRO THEATRE, 1838

In the winter of 1838 an attempt was made to establish a theatre for the free people of color. Unfortunately the evidence concerning the project is so limited that it is impossible to say how far the enterprise was carried.

The *Council de Ville* of the Third Municipality at its meeting on February 14 passed a resolution permitting the establishment of the theatre, and this we find printed in the *Daily Picayune* on the 24th.

> Resolved: That permission be granted E. V. Mathieu, free man of color, to establish a theatre in the Third Municipality for free people of color; that said theatre be exempt from the taxes imposed on cabarets, taverns, and ball rooms, provided the director of said theatre shall furnish a box, free of charge for the use of the Mayor, Recorder, Aldermen, and Secretary of the Council of this Municipality. . . .

On the 28th of February the *Daily Picayune* noted, in what is our last reference to the project, that the theatre was "to go ahead."

ST. CHARLES THEATRE, 1837-1838

The company for the St. Charles Theatre arrived early in October of 1837, as Caldwell planned to open "the temple" on the 9th. He had not reckoned, however, with the yellow fever epidemic which was still raging in the city and when several of his actors became seriously ill, he was forced to postpone the opening until October 16th.

The troupe had suffered many losses since last season; notable among the missing were H. J. Finn, W. H. Latham, Mr. and Mrs. Bannister, Mrs. Henry Hunt, and Miss Melton. The personnel now included Messrs. H. G. Pearson, Barton, Schinotti, Williams, Paret, Lewis, Page, DeBar, Raylea, Carr, C. W. Hunt, Alexander Pickering, Porter, William Hield, Collins, Daugherty, Archer, Huntley, Lewis, and Pacand; Mesdames Conduit, Vincent, Carr, Hield, Cramer, Pierce, and Chambers; and Misses Jones, DeBar, and Chester. The ballet leader was Mons. Barbiere; Messrs. Jackson, Davis, and Miss Hanker were solo dancers. Barton was stage manager, and John Watson, music director.

The familiar pieces of the first week served to introduce most of the newcomers. The opening bill of *No Song, No Supper* and *Perfection* featured Mrs. Conduit, the new comedy lead, as Margaretta and Kate O'Brien. Mrs. Conduit's beauty and talent won instant favor and she was pronounced "decidedly superior to the melodious automata which usually warble on our stage." Charles was played by Porter, the young son of J. G. Porter, a former manager of the Walnut Theatre in Philadelphia. Between the play and the farce the dancers gave a comic ballet entitled "L'Amour." Commented the *Bee* (October 18): "The ballet was not wretched and that is saying a great deal." This season dances rather than overtures were featured between pieces and before long critics began to speak enthusiastically of the *danseuse*, Miss Hanker.

Alexander Pickering made his bow on the second night as Darby in *The Poor Soldier*, Mrs. Conduit appearing as Patrick. These two were the chief attraction until Mr. and Mrs. Hield came out on October 23 as Julian St. Pierre and Mariana in *The Wife*. This couple had but recently recovered from an attack of yellow fever and even now Hield was said to be "yet too weak to do full justice to his powers." As supporting characters in *The Wife* Pickering and Porter continued to win favor. Reported the *Bee* on the 25th: "Porter possesses a great merit, the more conspicuous in a young man, he does not tear a 'passion to tatters', nor strut before the audience like a victorious game cock." The 25th brought the first novelty of the season, Mrs. Planché's farce, *The Pleasant Neighbor*. The following night the attraction was *King Lear* with Barton and Mrs. Hield in the leads. On the 27th Holland made the first of several appearances. His third was as Morisseau in the local première of Buckstone's drama, *The Duchess of Vaubalière*.

Comedy featuring Holland and tragedy with Barton and Mrs. Hield were now offered on alternate nights. On November 5,

Miss DeBar, a favorite of the 1836 season, returned to the scene of her American début as Yourekee in *Peter Wilkins*. H. G. Pearson made his appearance on the 7th as Shylock to the Portia of Mrs. Cramer. On the following night he was Macduff to Hield's Macbeth and on the 13th he played the lead in *The Wrecker's Daughter,* a play of Sheridan Knowles new to the city.

The first star of the season was George Barrett, the light comedian. He commenced his engagement on the 14th as Charles Surface, Mrs. Cramer enacting Lady Teazle and Miss Pierce, Mrs. Candor. Thereafter he went through a round of familiar pieces, introducing one new farce, *The Barrack Room* by Thomas Bayly. On the 21st *La Bayadère* was revived with Mons. Barbiere as Zelica and Miss Hanker as Fatima. This *danseuse* had at last overcome the timidity which had earlier displeased the critics and her performance was declared to be "little inferior to Celeste's." Mrs. Vincent (Zulma), who had been unpopular with the press since her first appearance at the beginning of the season, was again subjected to criticism. Southern chivalry seems to have been lacking where this actress was concerned. Her dancing in *La Bayadère,* however, forced a compliment from the critic of the *Daily Picayune* (November 23). "But," he added, "she is deplorably thin and dresses in very bad taste." The Hields appeared in the New Orleans première of Talfourdi's *Ion,* on the 29th, and, as usual, won praise for their just conception of the parts.

James H. Hackett opened on December 3 in *Monsieur Mallet* and *The Kentuckian.* James R. Scott, the American tragedian, was introduced on the 5th in *Richard III,* and two nights later Mrs. Sharpe began a short engagement in *Fazio.* Aided by the new arrivals Hackett presented one of the latest and most popular of his roles, that of Falstaff in *Henry IV.* This was a three act version of the play, but one which, according to the notices, "preserved the historical connection in all the scenes in which either Falstaff, the Prince (Barrett), or Hotspur (J. R. Scott) appear." The other new role in which Hackett appeared during this visit was that of Galbraith in Charles Dance's dramatization of *Horseshoe Robinson.* Mrs. Sharpe had Scott's assistance in *Macbeth* and Barrett, now announced as "re-engaged," played with her in the comedies. Her benefit night, December 18, saw the third rendition of *Henry IV* and a performance of *Lucille* with Barton as St. Cyr to her Lucille.

After Barrett's departure on the 23rd the management brought out the play which it had been unable to present in its entirety the last season, *The Jewess.* A hundred supernumeraries took part in it and the magnificence of the spectacle drew crowded houses on ten consecutive nights. It was followed by other novelties: Buckstone's domestic drama, *Ellen Warham;* Barrymore's melodrama, *Trial by Battle; The Courier of the Ocean;* and *The Battle of Austerlitz,* a drama founded on a period in the life of Napoleon.

The most important star of the season was "glorious Ellen Tree" who came for an engagement of twelve nights. She was at this time one of the greatest drawing cards in the country, and Mrs. Bailey (formerly Miss Charlotte Watson) and Plumer, vocalists who had commenced an engagement on January 9, were forced to step aside for her. The star made her début as Julia assisted by J. R. Scott as Master Walter and Barton as Sir Thomas Clifford. Of the performance the *Louisiana Courier* (January 13) spoke kindly but not enthusiastically. The first part of the play was said to have dragged and not until her reproof of Helen in the third act did the actress show her "whole powers." "We waited for this difficult passage as a criterion of her merit," acknowledged the critic, "for since the days of the lamented Jane Placide we have never before known it to be given naturally."

"Fashionable houses" witnessed her personations of Marianna *(The Wife)*, Lady Teazle, Ion (three times), Pauline *(The Ransome)*, Mrs. Haller, the youthful Queen, Marian *(The Wrecker's Daughter)*, Lady Macbeth, Letitia Hardy, Catharine, and Lady Townly *(The Provoked Husband)*. Scott won fresh laurels at her support in the tragedies, but the choice of Barton, "a gentleman declining into the vale of years," for characters unsuited to his ability caused general dissatisfaction. Public expression of this feeling may have been partly responsible for Barton's decision to retire from the stage at the conclusion of Miss Tree's engagement. He appeared at her benefit as Lord Townly and when he said farewell on January 27, she played with him in *The Jealous Wife* and *A Day After the Wedding*.

Mrs. Bailey and Plumer returned after Miss Tree's departure for five more nights of song. On the 29th Miss Josephine Clifton made her bow in N. P. Willis' *Bianca Visconti*, a tragedy written expressly for her the year before. Her engagement, like that of

Ellen Tree's, was reported to be "highly successful." Especially well received was the second tragedy which she introduced, *The Genoese* by Epes Sargent. Her chief support during this visit must have been Hield or Pearson. Scott's name is linked with hers only in the notices of *Venice Preserved* (January 31) and *Pizarro* (February 2). On February 5 the management announced his benefit and last appearance.

Ellen Tree began another engagement on February 12, but after two performances illness forced a postponement. Caldwell immediately filled in the breach with Barrett, Plumer, and Mrs. Watson, the stepmother of Mrs. Bailey. The comedies and farces of "Gentleman George" and the operatic pieces of Plumer and Mrs. Watson comprised the bills until Miss Tree reappeared two weeks later. Several of her roles were new; assisted by Barrett she enacted the heroine in *The Love Chase* of Sheridan Knowles, *Twelfth Night,* and *Court Favors.* With Hield she appeared in *Antony and Cleopatra* presented now "for the first time in America." The play attracted one of the best houses of the season and was repeated the following night. Apparently this was Hield's last performance at the St. Charles. His wife had made her last appearance on March 14 when she enacted Hamlet and Lady Margaret in *Wallace the Hero of Scotland.*

Master St. Luke, "the youthful Paganini," and his father, "the original imitator of Paganini," succeeded Miss Tree. The press described their offering, *Il Fanatico per la Musica* of Mayer, as "a most decided failure." Fortunately the St. Charles had other attractions. Mrs. Gibbs, who had been a member of the company in 1836, began an engagement on March 12, and Barrett continued to perform. Then, too, there were the Indian warriors who visited the theatre on the 14th and again on the 24th. Miss Clifton returned on the 29th for four nights of comedy with Barrett and at her benefit; Scott reappeared to play opposite her in *The Wife.*

Two new native plays were introduced at this time. Of *The Squatter* by James Rees we know nothing except that the scene was laid partly in Virignia and partly in Illinois. A critique in the *Daily Picayune,* April 3, complains of the mistreatment the piece had received at the hands of the actors. The writer thought the plot and dialogue were well written and if properly acted, the play would become popular. The second of these novelties was

The Deceived, a domestic drama by G. W. Harby.   Information concerning it is limited to the comment in the *Louisiana Courier* of April 14: "It is a sorrowing tale, well told."

The theatre remained closed on April 4 while the artists completed the preparation for *Gustavus, or The Masked Ball.* The management announced that the pit was to be floored over and a public masquerade ball would conclude the bill every evening during the run of the spectacle.   Notwithstanding a cool reception from the press the novelty drew crowded houses and was given nightly until Barrett, the Gustavus of the play, concluded his engagement on the 12th.

Mr. and Mrs. Joe Cowell now arrived and performed every night until the end of the season.   With them was their daughter, Sidney Cowell, who later became famous as Mrs. Bateman, the author of *Self.*   During this engagement she made her "first appearance on any stage", enacting Emily Worthington in *The Poor Gentleman,* Emma in *A Chip of the Old Block,* Eliza in *Paul Pry,* and Emily Tempest in *The Wheel of Fortune.*

The benefits this season brought little in the way of novelty. That for the Orphan Boys' Asylum on April 21 was signalized by the appearance of Mrs. Duff in *The Foundling of the Forest* and of Thomas Bishop in *The Turnpike Gate.* An interesting feature of C. W. Hunt's night was the presentation of the new dramatic sketch, *The Pickwickians,* with Joe Cowell as the Fat Boy. Barton returned to the stage on April 29 to play Penruddock in *The Wheel of Fortune* and with this benefit the season came to an end.

VAUXHALL GARDEN, ST. CHARLES THEATRE

The theatre reopened on June 6 under the direction of George Holland.   The advertisement in the *Louisiana Courier* of this date describes the alterations which had converted the interior of the St. Charles Theatre into Vauxhall Garden: "The Pit is covered over and formed into walks, bowers, seats, a fountain of water, grotto, saloon, etc., the whole forming a novel and pleasant appearance, calculated to pass a cool evening free from ennui or blue devils."   The entertainments were to consist of vocal and instrumental music, phantasmagoria exhibitions, and on "gala nights", light vaudevilles.

The first dramatic performance on record is *The Dumb Belle* given on June 18.   From the daily notices appearing in the *Louisiana Courier* of this week we learn that connected with the establishment were Signor Cioffi, director of music, Mrs. De-Bar (formerly Mrs. Conduit), Page, Old Cowell, Holland, and the dancers, Miss Hanker and Davis. No mention is made of other performers.

On July 12 Vauxhall Garden closed with a variety of entertainment for the benefit of George Holland. The newspapers report that the establishment had been well patronized by the most respectable citizens.

CHAPTER IX

Fashionable Houses   1838-1839

AMERICAN THEATRE, 1838-1839

The theatre on Camp Street opened on October 21, 1838, under the direction of George H. Barrett. It is not known what agreement existed between Caldwell and Barrett, but the fact that actors from the St. Charles sometimes acted at the Camp Street Theatre suggests that Barrett managed the smaller theatre for Caldwell and was not a lessee. The house had new decorations, "after the design and execution of J. Cowell," and a new drop curtain painted by the Italian artists, Ceresa and Pinoli. Barrett had secured an excellent company which included Mrs. George Barrett, Mr. and Mrs. John Greene, W. S. Fredericks, John Mills Brown, and W. F. Johnson. Among the other members were Messrs. Hodges, Thomas Fielding, William Sefton, Franklin, David, Huntley, Price, Pacaud, Austin, Kirkland, Byers, Marks, Easterman, G. Lewis, Harris, Keppell, and Gilbert, Mesdames F. Browne, Price, Hall, Anderson, Monell, and Misses McIntyre, Lewis, Wallis, Sidney Cowell, and Wray, a *danseuse*.

The leader of the orchestra was Mr. T. Jackson; J. Cowell was chief artist; Sewell, scene painter; Varden, machinist, and Huntley, prompter. Admission to the parquet was $1.00; seats in the private boxes, $1.50; and gallery $.50. During the first months of the season the doors opened at six-thirty and the curtain rose at seven.

The opening bill consisted of Bulwer's *Lady of Lyons* and Buckstone's domestic drama, *Presumptive Evidence*. Barrett could not have made a better selection in which to show the strength of his company. Bulwer's play won instant favor; it was repeated twice during the first week and before the end of the season had achieved a record run. *The Gambler's Fate,* revived on the second night, was also successful though it never attained the popularity of *The Lady of Lyons.* On the third night Mrs. Barrett appeared as Thérèse to Fredericks' Carwin, and with her husband played in *The Dumb Belle* and *33 John Street.* Mrs. Barrett was capable of enacting any role and during this season she was to play such diversified leads as Julia in *The Hunchback,* Mary Copp in *Charles II,* Kate O'Brien in *Perfection,* Morgiana in *The Forty Thieves,* and Desdemona.

W. F. Johnson made his first appearance on the 26th as Lord Priory in *Wives as They Were,* following it the next night with Captain Copp *(Charles II)* and Sir Lawrence Paragon *(Perfection).* This actor was an admirable representative of old men and had long been a favorite in Boston. *She Stoops to Conquer,* on November 3, introduced John Mills Brown, another excellent comedian from Boston. Fielding rejoined the troupe on the 11th, making his bow as Beausant in *The Lady of Lyons.* The afterpiece on this date was Thomas Bayly's burletta, *The Ladder of Love.*

Editorial comments in the *Daily Picayune* testify as to the excellence of the performances during these first weeks. From the same source we learn that the "little Camp" had now become a fashionable resort like the St. Charles. Barrett had stated in the first announcement of the season that he would maintain order and decorum at the theatre and to achieve his purpose he had secured the support of an "enlightened police under the direction of Mr. Cottam." A note in the *Daily Picayune* of November 3 tells of Barrett's success: "We dropped into this (now fashionable) Theatre last night. . . . All the private boxes were occupied by beautiful women, while the parquet shone with their charms. We cannot express our gratitude at seeing the rapid approaches of this theatre to a high and honorable place in the ranks of the drama."

Little Miss Meadows arrived on November 19 to sing, dance, and perform in familiar plays. A more important star made his début on the 25th in a revival of *Mazeppa,* which after two months of preparation was now presented with "entire new scenery, dresses, and decorations." The star was the celebrated horse Mazeppa and his chief support was furnished by Mrs. Greene and Ben DeBar of the St. Charles company. Sol Smith recalls that DeBar played Mazeppa in the St. Charles Theatre, "doing his own riding up the 'runs' and periling his life every night for $18 per week."[1] Smith must refer to these performances at the Camp; however, if the horse was as sagacious and docile as the notices proclaim, DeBar can have been in little danger.

The next visitor was Dan Marble, who opened on December 3 in *The Forest Rose* and *Black Eyed Susan*. During his stay he appeared in four pieces which had not been previously acted in New Orleans: E. H. Thompson's *Sam Patch*, N. H. Bannister's *The Bush Whacker*, C. A. Logan's *Vermont Wool Dealer*, and J. P. Adams' *The Maiden's Vow, or The Yankee in Time.*

On the 18th came Miss Nelson in *The Love Chase*. Her second, and presumably only other, role during this short engagement was that of Custace in Sheridan Knowles' drama, *Woman's Wit.*

Madame Lecompte, the dancer, and her husband, "the distinguished singer," succeeded Miss Nelson. In the announcement for *La Bayadère* on December 21 are listed Miss Turnbull, a member of their troupe, Madame Thielman of the St. Charles, and Mrs. Bennie. After a run of six nights *La Bayadère* made way for Sheridan Knowles' *Maid of Mariendorpt*, a drama which had had its American première in New York the previous night. On the 31st Mons. Martin joined the dancers and with his help they presented the grand operatic ballet, *La Sylphide*. Archer came over from the St. Charles to take the part of Hela.

The entertainment on New Year's night included a revival of Noah's *She Would Be a Soldier* with Marble as Jerry Mayflower and Mrs. Greene as Christine. Though announced "for this night only," Marble remained for three more performances of the play. On the "glorious eighth of January," the Louisiana Riflemen and the Louisiana Dragoons were special guests at a bill made up of Noah's play and Pilson's *He Would Be a Soldier.*

Barrett relied on standard plays and good acting rather than on novelties. On January 12 he offered *Macbeth* with Fredericks and Mrs. Greene as the principals. Cast as the three witches were the mainstays of his comic force, Johnson, Brown, and Greene. Another successful revival was that of *The Forty Thieves* which served as an afterpiece for four consecutive nights.

[1] Smith, *op. cit.*, 156.

A novelty was *The Water Witch, or The Skimmer of the Sea,*[2] presented on the 19th. A recent farce by Charles Mathews, Jr., *Truth, or A Glass Too Much,* served as the curtain raiser for the benefit given Thomas Williamson on the 22nd. The beneficiary himself appeared as Duke Dorgan in *Presumptive Evidence* and sang several songs. He had been a popular member of the Camp Street company in 1835 and 1836, but according to the *Daily Picayune* (December 29) he had not been able to secure an engagement this season.

Edwin Forrest began an engagement on January 28, playing Othello "to the largest house the Camp ever had." His subsequent roles, except for that of Claude Melnotte, were those in which he had often appeared. After his fourth performance a critic in the *True American* (February 4) expressed the opinion that his style of acting had greatly improved. "There is less display of his unmatched muscular talent," remarked the writer, "and more effort to produce effect by drawing upon the sympathy which nature elicits."

Josephine Clifton and J. R. Scott opened a joint engagement with *The Hunchback* on February 13. They appeared in *Macbeth* and in *Anne Boleyn,* a new tragedy of Fielding's which Miss Clifton had introduced earlier at the St. Charles. In this production Fielding played Henry VIII, Gilbert the Earl of Northumberland, Fredericks, Wolsey, and Mrs. Cowell, Selina. Young Burke joined the visiting performers on February 17, making his bow as Dennis Brulgruddery. He offered nothing new until his benefit on March 1 when he introduced Samuel Lover's *White Horse of the Peppers.*

Ellen Tree was the attraction during the last week in February. Her first appearance was *The Lady of Lyons* and *The Barrack Room,* J. R. Scott enacting Claude Melnotte and Barrett, De Crusae. The most popular of her presentations seem to have been *Twelfth Night* and *Romeo and Juliet* which she had not offered during an earlier engagement at the St. Charles. At her benefit on March 2, Barton came over from the St. Charles to play opposite her in *The Provoked Husband.*

---

[2] On the revival of this play in the fall, the *Daily Picayune,* November 20, 1839, attributed it to H. J. Finn. There are plays with the same title by R. P. Smith, C. W. Taylor, and J. S. Wallace.

Charles Eaton came on March 3 for five nights of tragedy. Scott was Othello to his Iago, Pierre to his Jaffier, and Marc Antony to his Cassius, Barton volunteering as Brutus. In the course of his last evening, March 8, Eaton delivered an address to the firemen of New Orleans and gave imitations of Forrest, Adams, Vandenhoff, Kemble, and Rice.

The Ravel Family during a two-day visit in late January had offered a pantomime in which they impersonated the Bedouin Arabs. On the night after Eaton's benefit the management introduced the "Real Bedouin Arabs." These visitors displayed their extraordinary powers in gymnastic feats and in *The Sheik of the Desert,* a grand eastern drama written expressly for them. On alternate nights Barrett featured James Porter, the Kentucky Giant, Major Stevens, the American Dwarf, and Miss Sutor, the German Dwarf, a trio that had won favor in New York several seasons before. Their repertoire consisted of David Garrick's burlesque, *Gulliver in Lilliput; Exiles in the West;* and *Nick of the Woods.* The latter was doubtless the Medina version of Robert Montgomery Bird's novel which had been introduced in New York with Porter as the original Ralph Stackpole.

The legitimate drama was not entirely neglected during these engagements. Scott and Mrs. Barrett presented *Town and Country* and *The Rent Day* at her benefit on the 12th, and after Scott's departure Fredericks and Mrs. Greene appeared in Jerrold's play. J. B. Booth commenced an engagement on the 20th, but he played to thin houses while the crowds flocked to the St. Charles to see Celeste. The press noticed Johnson's benefit bill, comprised of *Speed the Plough* and two recent farces, remarking that it was one of the most attractive of the season, but "whether it will draw a full house is another question."

The last two weeks of the season offered little of interest. Miss Nelson reappeared on the 30th for one night only. Fredericks' benefit presented Bulwer's new play, *The Dutchess de la Valliere.* On the Treasurer's night, Holland, Browne, Archer, Barton, and Scott came over from the St. Charles. Barton also appeared as Lieutenant Worthington at J. Mills Brown's benefit on April 7 and as Faulkland (*The Rivals*) at Barrett's benefit on the 8th, the last night of the season. Other volunteers from

the St. Charles were Holland who played David, J. S. Browne as
Bob Acres, and Farren as Sir Anthony Absolute. Cast in the
role of Mrs. Malaprop was Johnson, who, it was said, had played
it with decided success at the Tremont in Boston.

The theatre reopened on the 29th when Mrs. Greene was
given a complimentary benefit. The audience at her first benefit
on April 7 had been small, but at this later date she had a
"well filled and extremely fashionable house."

SUMMER SEASON, 1839

The citizens of New Orleans seemed reluctant to have the
season end and Holland, realizing this, announced that on May 9
he would open the Camp Street Theatre, "for a few nights."

He promised dramatic entertainment and a grand exhibition
imported from England at an immense expense and never before
equalled in this country in the extent and magnificent develop-
ment of its optical illusions. The price of admission to the parquet
was $1.00, to the boxes, $.75. Doors opened at seven-thirty, and
the curtain rose at eight.

The principal performers seem to have been Holland, Joe
Cowell, young Sam Cowell, and Sidney Cowell. Their names are
the only ones mentioned in the scattered advertisemnts which
appeared in the *Daily Picayune*. They offered light comedies and
farces, generally two an evening. The phantasmagoria illusions
were reported to be capital. To attract a crowd on the last night,
May 29, Holland held a lottery, the purchaser of each theatre
ticket receiving a chance. There can be no question of Holland's
shrewdness. The papers reported that the performances were
given before a house "thronged from parquet to gallery."

ST. CHARLES THEATRE, 1838-1839

The St. Charles, "thoroughly renovated and improved,"
opened for the fourth season on October 1, 1838. The whole of
the interior had been repainted and the chandelier taken to pieces
and cleaned. Improvemnts had also been effected in the orchestra
and in the company, both of which were now said to be "consid-
erably increased in number and talent." Included among the
players were Messrs. Harrison, George Farren, Charles Plumer,
Ben DeBar, H. G. Pearson, Williams, Page, Porter, Archer,
J. Cowell, Sam Cowell, Lewis, Burke, Naylor, and Paret, Mes-

dames Harrison, Farren, Plumer, DeBar, Thielman, Cioffi, Smith, and Cowell, and Misses Ravenot and Kerr, dancers. John Barton was acting manager; Pearson, stage manager; S. M. Lee, principal artist; and H. W. Jonas, leader of the orchestra.

Familiar farces and musical pieces comprised the bills of the first weeks. On the opening night Madame Thielman and Plumer were featured in *No Song, No Supper*; Mademoiselle Ravelot danced a *grand pas seul;* Cowell sang a comic song and then appeared with his wife in *The Dead Shot*. Sam Cowell made his bow on the 5th as Tom in *The Bath Road* and as Robin in *The Waterman*. Holland came out the following night in *The Secret* and appeared next in *Peter Wilkins,* assisted by Madame Thielman as Yourakee and Sam Cowell as Nondescript, a role which was turned over to DeBar when he arrived. On the 9th was presented the first novelty of the season, John Millingen's petite comedy, *Borrowed Feathers*.

Mrs. Farren and H. G. Pearson made their bows in *Thérèse* on the 10th 'and on the 12th were seen in *Town and Country,* Farren taking the part of Cosey. The operatic *John of Paris,* on the 17th, reintroduced Archer in the role of the Grand Chamberlain. On the 24th came Mr. and Mrs. Harrison, of the London and New York theatres. Harrison, it will be remembered, had supported Charlotte Barnes last season when she played at the Camp. The newcomers seem to have been equally at home in comedy, farce, melodrama, and tragedy. Early roles after their first appearance as William Tell and Albert and as Giles and Phoebe *(The Miller's Maid)* were young Heartall and Widow Cheerly, Charles II and Edward the Page *(Charles II)*, and Antonio and Juliette *(The Mountain Devils)*.

The first important novelty came on October 26, the dramatization of Bulwer's *Paul Clifford,* by Benjamin Webster. Within the next two weeks eight other new pieces were produced: Edward Fitzball's extravaganza, *Za Ze Zi Zo Zu;* Benjamin Webster's farce, *My Young Wife and My Old Umbrella;* Thomas Bayly's *Comfortable Service;* T. J. Serle's *The Ghost Story;* Charles Selby's *The Widow's Victim; Don John of Austria;* the petite comedy, *A Lesson in Love*; and Edward Fitzball's melodrama, *The Burgomaster's Daughter,* "first time in this country."

Joseph M. Field began a short engagement on November 15 with his new satirical sketch, *Victoria, or The Lion and the Kiss.*

This play and its sequel, *The White House, or All the Lions,* served as afterpieces to John Poole's *Atonement* when it had its American prmière on the 16th. Field gave his last performance on the 19th including on the bill his *Bennett in Texas* and a new satirical farce, *The Clouds, or Plato in Petticoats.*

The last of November brought another important novelty, *Esmeralda, or Quasimodo the Hunchback of Notre Dame* by Edward Fitzball. The melodrama received enthusiastic praise. According to the *Daily Picayune* (November 27), Harrison's Quasimodo was far superior to that of Henry Wallack and the Esmeralda of his wife was "an express and admirable performance."

The interest centered now in the new arrivals. Miss Meadows came out on the 28th in *The Four Mowbrays,* and on the next night the Barnes family began an engagement. On December 3, John R. Scott made his first appearance of the season opposite Charlotte Barnes in *The Wife.* As in the previous year Scott's engagement was a long one. He supported the visiting stars during their visits in December and January; later he played a short engagement at the Camp Street Theatre and then returned to the St. Charles where he remained until the end of the season. Another newcomer was James S. Browne, "from the London and New York Theatres," who made his bow as Rover in *Wild Oats* and as Jeremy Diddler in *Raising the Wind.* This actor, like Scott, seems to have been a temporary member of the company; he remained until late in April appearing nearly every night. His most popular personations were those of Robert Macaire in Charles Selby's play of that name introduced on January 6 and Sergeant Austerlitz in Mrs. Gore's *Maid of Croissy* presented later in the month.

The stately Miss Clifton was the next star, opéning on the 18th in *The Lady of Lyons.* The cast included Scott as Claude Melnotte, Farren as General Damas, DeBar as Beauseant, and Mrs. Farren as the Widow Melnotte. In the presentation of *The School for Scandal,* on the 21st, her Lady Teazle was supported by the Charles Surface of James Browne and the Sir Peter of H. J. Finn, who had made his first appearance the previous night. The most popular of Miss Clifton's offerings was the tragedy, *Anne Boleyn,* which she introduced on the 27th. The author was Thomas Fielding of the Camp Street Theatre and the play was a hit both here and in New York where it was brought out in the spring. Miss Clifton gave her last performance on January 3, appearing in *Anne Boleyn* and the farce, *The Lady and the Devil*, in which she was assisted by Browne and Finn.

In the hiatus before the arrival of the next visiting performers Browne and Finn were featured in Dance's new farces, *Naval Engagements* and *The Bengal Tiger*. These two comedians made an excellent combination and the pieces which they introduced during the two and a half months of Finn's engagement were among the most successful of the season.

The Firemen's Charitable Association was given a benefit on the 12th in grateful acknowledgment of the exertions of the Fire Department in saving the theatre from destruction on January 1. The fire had burned the gallery saloon and the ceiling of the box saloon but had not spread to the rest of the house.[3]

Miss Ellen Tree opened on January 16 in the popular *Lady of Lyons* and followed it with a range of characters made familiar by her visit of the previous season. Only her initial role and that of Meeta in *The Maid of Mariendorpt* were new. Caldwell returned to play opposite her in *Much Ado about Nothing*, *The School for Scandal*, and *The Honey Moon*. One critic was of the opinion that he played as well as he did when acting was his profession.[4]

The Ravel Family succeeded Ellen Tree, but "in consequence of Gabriel Ravel having met with some accident" they remained only two nights. Then, on February 5, came the old favorite Junius Brutus Booth, last seen here in 1829. His roles were those in which he had appeared many times at the Camp Street Theatre: Richard III, Sir Giles Overreach, Shylock, Othello, King Lear, Bertram, Hamlet, Lucius Junius Brutus, and Jerry Sneak. The *True American* of February 9 reported that he disappointed the largest audience of the season by his tame personation of Richard and not until his fourth appearance as Othello was he "himself again." From then until the end of the engagement on the 16th he was said to shine with his old lustre.

Mademoiselle Augusta, the thirteen-year-old daughter of Mrs. H. A. Williams, was the next attraction. Her dancing had created a senation in New York the previous spring and she was said to rival the most renowned *artistes* of the day. She made her

---

[3] *Daily Picayune*, January 2, 1839.
[4] *True American*, February 4, 1839.

bow as Zoloe in *La Bayadère,* assisted by Miss Kerr and Mademoiselle Ravenot as Fatima and Zelica. This and the ballet pantomime entitled *The Twelve Pages of the Duke de Vendôme* were the only pieces she offered.

The Real Bedouin Arabs came to the St. Charles on the 24th and for several nights entertained with their gymnastic feats. Finn's benefit on the 25th introduced Captain Henry Addison's *Tam O'Shanter,* and Browne's on the 27th featured another novelty, J. R. Planché's *My Schoolfellow.* These performances were among Finn's last, for on March 5 his engagement came to an end.

March brought the inimitable Celeste in melodramas and spectacles. Her opening role in W. B. Bernard's *St. Mary's Eve* introduced her in her first speaking part. She repeated the favorites of the past seasons and in addition introduced the novelties: *The Spirit Bride, The Child of the Wreck* by Planché, and *The Star of the Forest.* The newspapers reported overflowing houses on each of her twenty-four nights, and at the conclusion of the engagement the *True American* (April 1) stated that she had drawn the extraordinary sum of $30,000. Somewhat contradictory is the statement in the *Daily Picayune* of April 19 that she realized $7,000 while the management lost $900.

At Mademoiselle Ravenot's benefit on March 31 the juvenile prodigy, Miss Davenport, made her first and only appearance at the St. Charles. This young actress, "from the Theatres Royal, Drury Lane, and Haymarket," had arrived in the city ten days before and not being able to arrange an engagement at either of the American theatres had performed in the ballroom of the St. Louis Exchange. At the St. Charles she appeared in *Richard III* and in *The Manager's Daughter,* a protean comedy written for her by E. Lancaster. These were the pieces in which she had made her New Orleans début.

Edwin Forrest opened an engagement on April 1 in *Virginius,* Mrs. Barrett coming over from the Camp Street Theatre to play opposite him. Later in the engagement she appeared in *Richard III, Thérèse,* and *The Lady of Lyons* with him. He had excellent support during his stay. Mrs. Duff came out of her retirement to appear with him in *Macbeth, Lear, Metamora, Damon and Pythias, Richard III, Othello, Pizarro,* and *William Tell.* Mrs. Greene made her first appearance at the St. Charles as the Queen to his Hamlet and was Julia to his Spartacus in *The Gladiator*. John R. Scott played the second role in all of the tragedies.

The members of the company began their benefits immediately after Forrest concluded his engagement on the 15th. Scott, returning to his place as first tragedian, offered *Richard III* at the benefit given Lee, the principal artist of the theatre. He was Biron to the Isabella of Mrs. Duff when that actress made her last appearance on the 17th. On his night J. S. Browne presented *The Rivals* with Johnson, formerly of the Camp Street Theatre, as Mrs. Malaprop, and *The Old Clock, or Here She Goes, There She Goes,* a new piece written "by a gentleman of this city." The chief attraction at George Farren's benefit was the appearance of Love, the Polyphonist, who had been performing at Plough's Museum. This gentleman imitated the barking of a dog, the buzzing of a bee, and the conversation of stage coach passengers.

Celeste returned on April 22 and during a brief stay of four nights presented the last novelty of the season, Douglas Jerrold's new melodrama, *The Mother*. Mrs. Farren's farewell benefit was announced for the 26th, the night after Celeste's departure. Her name had not appeared in the daily notices since her performance in *Bertram* on February 11, nor was she listed in the cast for this night. According to the notice in the *Daily Picayune* Mrs. Harrison and Farren played the leads in *The Jewess*.

The season ended on April 28 with a benefit for stage manager Pearson. A stock company of unusual merit strengthened by engagements with popular stars and a varied repertoire mark this as one of the best seasons in the history of the St. Charles Theatre.

CHAPTER X

Caldwell in Command   1839-1840

AMERICAN THEATRE, 1839

The scarcity of money in the South may have determined Caldwell in his decision to open only one of his New Orleans theatres for the season 1839-1840. It was natural that he should inaugurate the fall season at the theatre on Camp Street, postponing the opening of the St. Charles until he was certain the larger establishment would be supported.

The company which assembled for the fall season included Messrs. Holland, DeBar, Sam Cowell, Archer, Keppell, Huntley, Schoolcraft, Boddy, Paret, Price, Naylor, and Mesdames DeBar Moore, Smith, Cioffi, Price, Jones, and Hinkie. Within a few weeks these were joined by Barrett, who acted as stage manager, Barton, J. Mills Brown, Mr. and Mrs. Williams (formerly Miss Verity), Radcliffe, Morton, and Mrs. Stuart (formerly Miss Vos).

The theatre opened on October 7 and for the first week featured musical pieces and farces, Mrs. DeBar and Sam Cowell generally taking the leads. The press reported that these were "creditably done," but as yet the theatre was not well attended. On the 15th Mrs. Stuart made her appearance in *Thérèse* and followed it the next night as Zephyrina in *The Lady and the Devil*. With the arrival of Morton to play opposite Mrs. Stuart the management turned to more serious fare, bringing out *The Hunchback* and *The Rent Day*.

Holland began an engagement on the 25th in his old favorite, *Paul Pry*. The newspapers now noted a "gradual and steady improvement in the audience" and the appearance of several ladies. On the 27th came the first novelty, Buckstone's farce, *The Irish Lion*.

When the company was further strengthened by the arrival of other members from New York, *The Lady of Lyons* was announced for November 2, Barton to appear as Claude Melnotte, Mrs. Stuart as Pauline, and Barrett in his old role as Colonel Damas. The performance elicited a comment from the *True American* of November 4. Barton and Mrs. Stuart were said to have been perceptibly nervous, but Barrett proved himself "the Colonel Damas." As usual DeBar came in for his share of unfavorable criticism. The writer regretted that he was so often compelled to speak disagreeably of this actor, but he found him "reckless to all advice or criticism." He was, "as is too often the case with him, imperfect in his part, and as is almost always the case with him very inappropriately and shabbily dressed." Just two weeks before this a critic in the *Daily Picayune* (October 23) had praised DeBar's lifelike impersonation of the drunkard in *The Rent Day*, adding, "There's a great deal in practice, that's a fact."

The management turned next to equestrain drama and with the assistance of the horse, Mazeppa, revived the play of that name. After a run of five nights it made way for *El Hyder.* The success of the spectacular *Joan of Arc* which was given for the benefit of "little Franklin," Mazeppa's owner, led to an extension of this engagement. Meanwhile Pearson had made his appearance in *The Stranger.*

The season came to an end on November 30. Within a month the theatre had been let to James Foster who soon reopened it as a Ball Room, the first in this section of the city.[1]

ST. CHARLES THEATRE, 1839-1840

The St. Charles, newly painted and decorated, opened on Sunday, December 1. Recent recruits to the company which had played in the Camp Street Theatre were Mr. and Mrs. Joseph M. Field, engaged for the leads, and Misses Melton and Melville. George Barrett continued as stage manager. Communications in the *True American* and in the *Daily Picayune* referred to this company as being better than usual and hailed Caldwell's announcement that he would try to restore the old plan of a "regular stationary company" and few stars.

The opening bill consisted of *Englishmen in India,* featuring Miss Melton as Sally Scraggs and Miss Melville as Gulnare, and *Peter Wilkins* with Mrs. DeBar in the name part. Apparently Miss Melville slipped into minor roles after this performance or left the company. Her name is not found in any other announcement and in the notice of a repetition of *Peter Wilkins* Mrs. Stuart is listed as Gulnare. On the second night *The Hunchback* reintroduced Mr. and Mrs. Field as Sir Thomas Clifford and Julia. During the first week they played Claude Melnotte and Pauline, Alonzo and Cora *(Pizarro),* and Field appeared as de Mauprat in Bulwer's new play, *Richelieu.* The press spoke favorably of the "quiet natural style" of Mrs. Field (formerly Eliza Riddle) but as yet said nothing in praise of her husband.

James Balls, the light comedian, began an engagement on December 8. Two years before he had appeared here in many of the same parts which he now offered. The recent additions to his repertoire were *The Dancing Barber* by Charles Selby; *Rafael the Libertine, The Buckle of Brilliants,* and *State Secrets,* all by T. E. Wilks; and *The Lady of Lyons.* When *The School for Scandal* was presented with Balls as Charles Surface, Barrett

---

[1] *Ibid.,* December 16, 1839.

impersonated Sir Peter Teazle, "his first appearance in that character." At Balls' benefit on December 24 Miss Melton essayed Mrs. Malaprop. Both she and Barrett undertook these roles because the company had no first old man and old woman, but only one fault could the enthusiastic critic of the *True American* (December 25) find with Miss Melton's impersonation. "Her face," commented he, "is too devilish pretty for an old woman."

Dan Marble came out before Balls concluded his engagement and on December 26 he was joined by Mrs. Lewis and La Petite Bertha. Henceforth, he offered his familiar Yankee characterizations between the plays or as afterpieces. On consecutive nights La Petite Bertha appeared as Young Norval *(Douglas),* Tom Thumb, Christine, the Youthful Queen, and Fortunato *(Matteo Falcone)* while her mother performed in *The French Spy* and *The Black Brig of Bermuda.* Marble appeared as Jerry Mayflower in the New Year's performance of *The Plains of Chippewa* and at his benefit on the 5th he took six parts, among them Long Tom Coffin and Carwin.

English opera was a popular feature of this season. With the arrival of the vocalist, John Sinclair, *Masaniello* and *Cinderella* were revived. Sinclair had lost but little of his power and sweetness reported the press, and it was still delightful to listen to him. Archer, Schoolcraft, Sam Cowell, Mrs. DeBar, and Mrs. Field furnished able assistance. The cast of *Cinderella* included Archer as Baron Pompolino, Barrett as Pedro, Field as Dandini, Mrs. DeBar as Cinderella, and Miss Melton as Clorinda. In the operatic *Spirit of Clyde,* introduced on Sinclair's last night, Miss Melton sang the feminine lead.

Mr. and Mrs. John Sloman made their first appearance in eleven years on January 23 when they opened in Sheridan Knowles' tragedy, *Love,* and F. F. Cooper's *Hercules, King of Clubs.* For five consecutive nights Mrs. Sloman appeared as the Countess of Eppenstein while Sloman enlivened the afterpieces and gave his comic songs. The couple played opposite one another in Buckstone's drama, *Henrietta the Forsaken.* During this engagement Mrs. Sloman donned trousers to play the title role in *Paul Jones,* a translation of Dumas' play made by W. Berger of this city. For her twelfth and last performance she essayed Pauline in *The Lady of Lyons* and Catharine in *Catharine and Petruchio,* Sloman appearing as Grumio in the latter piece.

Next came Mons. and Madame Lecomte and their *corps de ballet* made up of Martin, Kaiffer, Klisching, Madame Kaiffer, and Mademoiselle Desjardins. They offered the familiar *Le Dieu et la Bayadère;* a one act ballet entitled "The Masked Ball from Gustavus"; a new ballet pantomime, *Marco Bomba;* and a new extravaganza, *The Sorcerer,* in which Klisching took the part of a monkey. During a second engagement which began on February 15, the dancers appeared in the ballet pantomime, *La Somnambula,* and in the celebrated tomb scene from *Robert the Devil.*

The bills during February presented little of dramatic interest or worth. The resident company appeared only in farces and vaudevilles and, after Sinclair's return, as minor characters in operatic pieces. The new comic ballet of the dancers, Klisching's impersonation of a frog, and the farce, *Free and Easy,* by S. J. Arnold were the novelities of the month.

The management continued to feature opera and ballet in March. A trio composed of John Jones, tenor, W. F. Brough, "basso cantante," and Madame Otto, soprano, came for a series of opera. Of their nine offerings, *Amilie, or The Love Test,* with words by J. Haines and music by W. Rooke, had not previously been heard in New Orleans. *Fra Diavolo, Der Freischutz,* and *The Castle of Andalusia* had not been given before at this theatre. Madame Lecomte and her troupe returned on the 9th and for a while the vocalists and dancers alternated. Balls, who had commenced a re-engagement on February 24, remained through March.

Mr. and Mrs. Field went over to Mobile about the middle of March to shine as stars at George Chapman's theatre. When the vocalists prepared to leave, they returned and on April 5 acted in the première of Bulwer's new play, *The Sea Captain.* This, like the earlier play of W. Berger's, was an adaptation from Dumas. For a "farewell benefit" on the 9th Barton presented an evening of Shakespeare, the entertainment consisting of acts from *Lear, Much Ado about Nothing, Hamlet, Macbeth,* and a "grand procession representing tableaux from fifteen of Shakespeare's most popular plays."

Caldwell's decision to abolish the starring system seems to have been forgotten as soon as it was announced. The visitors had followed one another in rapid succession and now as the season neared its close, the Barnes family arrived. Charlotte

Barnes came out as the Countess of Eppenstein *(Love)*, and her
father gave his famous characterization of Delph *(Family Jars)*.
Charles Mason joined them on the 14th and remained to assist
Miss Barnes in oft repeated roles. Barnes with the assistance of
Miss Melton introduced John Poole's *The Scape Goat* and John
Morton's *Chaos is Come Again*. The engagement came to an end
on April 24 with a performance of Arthur Murphy's tragedy,
The Grecian Daughter.

Several of the season's most interesting plays were hastily
brought forward during these last weeks. To exhibit the talents
of his wife, Field translated and adapted Alexander Dumas'
Catharine Howard, presenting it on her benefit night. For his
own benefit he offered a translation of Dumas' *Mademoiselle de
Belle Isle,* a play which later became known in the East as
Gabrielle, or a Night's Hazard. Field was said to have expunged
the objectionable part of the French plot and to have woven a
new thread of interest into the play. The afterpiece on this evening was the beneficiary's new extravaganza entitled *Vot of It?*
He had contributed humorous poems to the *Daily Picayune* this
season under the name of "Straws" and in this "Straws" made
his appearance "for the first time in dramatic shape." The third
play on the bill was *The Lying Valet* with Sol Smith making his
first appearance in nine years as Timothy Sharp. The actor-
manager relates in his autobiography that he was passing
through the city on his way back to St. Louis when Field asked
him to appear.[2]

Mrs. Stuart's benefit introduced James Haynes' new tragedy,
Mary Stuart, Queen of Scots. On his night Radcliffe gave *The
Last Days of Pompeii* assisted by a stud of horses and two
panthers; scenes from *The Wept of Wish-ton-Wish;* and Buckstone's new farce, *Our Mary Ann.* The last novelty of the season
was N. P. Willis' *Tortesa the Usurer* presented by H. G. Pearson
on the 7th.

The benefit for George Barrett brought the season to an
end on May 10. Barrett had been an excellent manager and to
him and his company the *Daily Picayune* of May 10 offered con-
gratulations upon what it termed "a brilliant and profitable
season."

---

[2] Smith, *op. cit.,* 150.

THE CHAPMANS, 1840

George Chapman brought a branch of his "Floating Company" to New Orleans in January of 1840. They made their first appearance at the German Theatre on Magazine Street on the 16th, offering *The Fall of the Alamo, The Bully and the Dandy,* and *The Actress of All Work.* It was announced that Chapman had taken the theatre for three nights a week; yet, according to the newspaper notices, he gave only two performances there.

He went next to the Arcade Theatre, an establishment which was a large room on the floor above the *Commercial Bulletin* office, formerly occupied by the *Commercial* library.[3] Here, on February 11, he initiated a series of light comedies with *The Comet, The Two Gregories,* and *The Actress of All Work.* In the company were the manager and his wife, Mr. and Mrs. Bransom, McKibbin, Ward, Davis, Sutton, Lewis, and Harris. Burke, "recently of the St. Charles," joined them on the 19th, and two days later the *Commercial Bulletin* announced that Chapman, having made "considerable accession" to his company, could now bring out some of the sterling old plays in a suitable manner. On the same day the *Daily Picayune* carried the news that the "whole family of Chapmans with Mr. Hamilton" were about to open the Alhambra Theatre in Mobile. The last performance of which there is record took place on February 23. Apparently they left New Orleans immediately afterwards.

AMERICAN THEATRE, SUMMER SEASON, 1840

The theatre on Camp Street opened a week after the closing of the St. Charles. Foster's ballroom had not been successful and since spring the theatre had been unused. Information concerning the management and the personnel of the company which now occupied it is limited. The few extant announcements mention only the names of Mr. and Mrs. Radcliffe, Mrs. Henry, Mrs. Cioffi, L. D. Foster, Willey, Boddy, and Miss Jones, a dancer.

Comedies, melodramas, and farces generally comprised the bills offered by the little company. On the 19th, "for the benefit of an indigent family" there was a performance of *Richard III* in French. On the 22nd at the benefit for the "Natchez sufferers in the late fire", Messrs. Barton, Pearson, A. J. Roley Marks,

---

[3] *Commercial Bulletin,* Feb. 11, 1840.

Mrs. Stewart, and Miss Verity volunteered their aid. The next night a gentleman from the German theatre sang English and German songs.

Later entertainment included Negro extravaganzas by Mick Saunders of the Orleans Amphitheatre, magic and juggling by Ali Abdul Maza, and a dance recital by a horse that shuffled and cut pigeon wings. On June 10 the management featured the songs of "Old Corn Meal," the Negro who had appeared in Bannister's farce, *Life in New Orleans*. Several times during the last week of the season "Messrs. Carroll and Company" came over from the circus to entertain with still vaulting and tumbling.

The performance of June 14 was the last to be given in the "little Camp." Almost immediately carpenters began cutting away the lobbies and boxes and when next the doors opened, it was to admit merchants and customers to the Camp Street Exchange.[4]

NEW AMERICAN THEATRE, MAGAZINE STREET, 1840

Few and scattered are the records that pertain to summer theatricals in New Orleans and for 1840 there is mention of only one performance. On July 4 the *Daily Picayune* carried the announcement of an American performance at the German Theatre on Magazine Street. The bill consisted of a German farce presented by the German Company; songs by Madame Thielman, Mrs. Radcliffe, and Schoolcraft; a recital of "The Declaration of Indepenedence"; and the afterpiece, *Who's the Dupe?*, featuring Madame Thielman and Radcliffe.

That there may have been further activity in the German Theatre this summer is suggested by the wording of an advertisement in the *Daily Picayune* of September 18. This stated that the New American Theatre (late the German Theatre) on Magazine Street would reopen the following evening. The entertainment was to consist of *The Irish Tutor* and *The Rival Suitors;* named in the casts were Mr. and Mrs. Radcliffe, Mr. and Mrs. Henry, Schoolcraft, and Lloyd. This one reference to a fall season at the new American Theatre is all that has been found.

---

[4] *Daily Picayune*, June 7, 1840.

CHAPTER XI

Ludlow and Smith   1840-1841

ST. CHARLES THEATRE, 1840-1841

The theatrical monopoly which Caldwell had enjoyed for the past two years came to an end in the fall of 1840. As the St. Charles opened for its sixth season, a rival theatre erected by Messrs. Ludlow and Smith was nearing completion.

The company at the St. Charles differed little from that of the previous season. Sam Cowell, Archer, Mrs. Stuart, James M. Brown, and Miss Melton were the only serious losses. New members included Mr. and Mrs. Sloman, A. L. Pickering, a favorite of a past season, Nelson, Mr. and Mrs. Reeder, Mrs. Ennissol, and Misses Morgan and Mowbray. George Barrett continued to act as stage manager.

The theatre opened on October 9 with *Speed the Plough* and *The Loan of a Lover*. In the comedy Barrett played Bob Handy and Mrs. DeBar, Susan Ashfield; in the farce Radcliffe was Peter Spyk to Mrs. DeBar's Gertrude. Miss Mowbray was introduced in *Mischief Making*, the afterpiece on the second night, and on the 15th Miss Morgan made her debut as Eudiga in *Charles XII*, following it the next night with Margaretta in *No Song, No Supper*. Until all of the dramatic corps arrived the management continued to feature light farce such as this.

William Chapman, the first of the visiting performers, opened an engagement on the 19th. Though he was an excellent comedian, his performance in such favorites as *The Young Widow*, *The Heir at Law*, *The Turnpike Gate*, *Sweethearts and Wives*, *The Dead Shot*, and *The Hundred Pound Note* attracted few people. Commented the *Daily Picayune* on the day after his benefit (October 28) : "It is not yet fashionable to attend the theatre."

With the return of Mr. and Mrs. Field the manager turned to domestic drama bringing out *The Lady of Lyons* on November 1. The curtain raiser was Buckstone's new farce, *Shocking Events*, and the afterpiece was *His Last Legs*, a comedy by W. B. Bernard which had been introduced earlier in the week. On the 6th Barton made one of his rare appearances as Lear, Mrs. Field playing Cordelia and Pickering, Edmund. The 8th brought a novelty, Edward Stirling's dramatization of *Nicholas Nickleby*. The next night Moses S. Phillips, from the New York Theatres, made his first and only appearance in the city as Billy Lackaday in *Sweethearts and Wives*.

Ludlow and Smith opened their new theatre on November 10, and as a counterattraction the St. Charles presented Lewellen and his horse Timour in Andrew Ducrow's equestrian drama, *St. George and the Dragon,* in preparation since the commencement of the season. This ran every night during Timour's engagement and at Lewellen's benefit on November 15 was preceded by *Conanchestat, or The Indian's War Horse,* another novelty written especially for Timour.

The next visitor was the tragedian Fitzgerald Tasistro. He came out on the 19th as Othello, followed it with Beverly *(The Gamester),* and was then forced to postpone his next performance "in consequence of a recent accident." Mr. and Mrs. Sloman had now arrived and on the 22nd Sloman impersonated Jim Bags in *The Wandering Minstrel.* Tasistro reappeared on the 23rd in Sheridan Knowles' *John of Procida,* a play which had been introduced to New Orleans at the rival theatre six days before. Other roles for the tragedian were Shylock, Macbeth, Rolla, Hamlet, and Belmour *(Is He Jealous?).* The plays during Tasistro's engagement were well cast. Mr. and Mrs. Field and Mrs. Sloman gave the star excellent support; yet he played to small houses, and less than a hundred were said to have witnessed the *Merchant of Venice* in which Mrs. Sloman made her first appearance of the season. The *Bee* of November 26 said this lack of patronage was due to the inefficiency of the theatrical corps; the *Daily Picayune* of the 29th reported that the company was as good as any in the Union.

Dan Marble began an engagement on November 25 and for a while his Yankee plays and Tasistro's tragedies alternated. He appeared in two novelties during this visit, *The Gamecock of the Wilderness,* and J. H. Conway's *The Times That Tried Us,* but neither proved so successful as the familiar *Sam Patch in France, The Vermonter,* and *The Forest Rose.*

Several novelties of early December deserve mention. At the benefit for Lewellen on the conclusion of Timour's re-engagement, some of the artists from the French theatre on Orleans Street came over to present a new vaudeville entitled *Paule et Pauline, or Napoleon dans les Cent Jours.* On the 6th came a new play *Richard Savage,* translated and adapted to the English stage by Dr. M. Morton Dowler of Lafayette, Louisiana. The *Daily Picayune* of the 8th stated that the play was highly successful and so great was the interest of the audience that no one left the theatre from the rising of the curtain to the conclusion.

The middle of December brought Tyrone Power and better days for the St. Charles. The popular comedian repeated many of the roles which he had introduced in his last visit six years ago, and now for the first time in New Orleans he appeared in *The Irish Lion, His Last Legs,* and *Rory O'More.* During a second engagement which began on the 28th, he introduced W. B. Bernard's farce, *The Irish Attorney,* and Mrs. Gore's *King O'Neil.* He bade farewell on January 9 but when his steamer for Havana was detained, he returned on the 20th for another performance.

The management now brought forward Master Diamond, an Ethiopian imitator whose antics on a stage dedicated to drama were frowned upon by public and press alike. Nevertheless, his hornpipes, pigeon wings, double shuffle, and "Black Bayadère dance à la Fanny Elssler" proved the chief drawing card during the week of January 10. When both of the American theatres staged the première of Bulwer's new comedy, *Money,* on the same night, the St. Charles offered Master Diamond as an additional attraction. A match dance with someone announced as Mercer of Louisville, Kentucky, brought Diamond back on the 19th. The public, who were said to have poured $1,500 into the coffers that night, were indignant when they learned that Mercer was a supernumerary at the theatre.[1] Sol Smith says that the instigator of this "humbug match" was none other than P. T. Barnum then at the beginning of his career.[2]

This was a season of varying fortune for the St. Charles. William Ranger, the next star, played a profitless engagement "to empty boxes" though his offerings were new and his delineations of French characters were described as excellent. His repertoire consisted of *The Romantic Widow, The Artist's Wife, The Lover Husband, The Gentleman and the Upstart,* and *Le Preux Chevalier.* "Here is legitimate acting," commented the *Daily Picayune* on January 26, "pure, polished, high toned, and beautifully refined acting . . . and the St. Charles is empty."

A galaxy of stars descended on the theatre in February. John Baldwin Buckstone, the English playwright and actor, came out on the 1st. Marble returned for a short engagement, and Caldwell himself appeared on several of the "off nights." Buckstone acted in his own *Rural Felicity, A Kiss in the Dark, Single Life,* and *Weak Points.* They were all new to this city, but the actor was said to have fared no better than Ranger.

---

[1] *Ibid.,* January 26, 1841.
[2] Smith, *op. cit.,* 155.

The first of the company benefits was that of Barrett's on February 17. The chief attraction on this occasion seems to have been the theatrical début of Miss Mason. This young lady made "her first appearance on any stage" as Editha in Fitzball's melodrama, *Walter Tyrrell,* and in *Is He Jealous?* For Mrs. Field's night were announced the popular *Mademoiselle de Belle Isle* and the latest piece from the pen of her husband, "an entire new romantic antic, vocal, local sketch in verse called *G-A-G, or The Starring System.*"

The last weeks of this season belong to Fanny Elssler, the celebrated *danseuse* who had made her American début the previous May. The resident company offered little of consequence during her visit and on several nights when she did not appear, the theatre remained dark. The star made her bow on March 5 in the ballet pantomime, *La Sylphide,* assisted by the members of her troupe, Monsieur Sylvain, C. T. Parsloe, and Madame Arraline. The other ballets in which she appeared were *Nathalie, The Tarentule,* and *Le Dieu et La Bayadère.* In the latter, Riese, formerly manager of the German theatre in Philadelphia, played the Unknown. With Elssler's benefit on April 2 Barrett brought the season to a close. The press reported receipts of $3,760 on this night, all of which, except $500 for expenses of the house, went to the dancer.

Caldwell paid Elssler $1,000 for each performance; yet according to the record kept by George Holland, the engagement was a profitable one for the theatre, the receipts for the ten nights averaging $2,597.35 a night.[3] The answer as to how Caldwell succeeded where other managers had failed can be found in the admission which he charged during the engagement. Not only were the prices doubled, but on the opening night the boxes and parquet seats were sold at auction to the highest bidders.

The theatre reopened on April 7 for a complimentary benefit tendered Joseph M. Field. Though Fanny Elssler was to appear, there was no increase in price of admission. The committee had asked the dancer to name her own terms for this performance, and she, with a generosity hitherto unnoted, had declined any remuneration.[4]

---

[3] Holland Memorial, *Sketch of the Life of George Holland,* 44.
[4] *Daily Picayune,* April 7, 1841.

This season had been a disastrous one for the St. Charles. Contemporary press notices as well as the memoirs of Noah Ludlow and Sol Smith assert that only the engagements with Tyrone Power and Fanny Elssler had been profitable. A communication in the *Bee* of March 16 attributed the failure to Caldwell's reliance on others in the management of his theatre. The mediocrity of the company may be cited as another cause of failure. Caldwell had weakened his troupe at the St. Charles by sending over members as support for the stars who played in the theatre he had built in Mobile. Had Mr. and Mrs. Sloman, Mr. and Mrs. Field, Miss Morgan, and others remained in New Orleans for the entire season the St. Charles could have furnished formidable opposition to the newly erected American Theatre of Ludlow and Smith.

AMERICAN THEATRE, POYDRAS STREET, 1840-1841

Noah Ludlow and Sol Smith, the lessees of the new American Theatre, had formed a partnership in 1835 for the management of the theatres in Mobile and St. Louis. The decision to leave Mobile for New Orleans had been made suddenly when they learned that James Caldwell planned to extend his interests to the Alabama city. The town was not large enough to support two theatres and as New Orleans now had only one, they felt it wiser to compete with Caldwell in the larger and more theatrically minded city.

The site selected for the theatre was on Poydras Street, between St. Francis and Camp Street, and had originally been leased by Messrs. Dubois and Kendig who intended to erect a livery stable and circus. Smith arranged with Dubois and Kendig to build according to his specifications and to lease the establishment to him for five years at $10,000 a year.[5]

The chief feature of the new theatre was the "grand equestrian circle", forty-two feet in diameter, surrounded on three sides by a spacious pit. This was provided with a removable floor and seats which could be taken up or replaced in several hours, thus converting the circle into a parquet or the parquet into a circle as the occasion required. Two entrances led from the stables of the establishment to the circle.

The building had three tiers, each containing seventeen boxes. The interior was ornamented in a "free modern style."

[5] Smith *op. cit.*, 154.

The fluted columns supporting the boxes were purely American in style, and the four antes supporting the proscenium were modeled after "none of the ancient orders" but were of a style first used in New York. They were crowned by an elliptic arch in the center of which was an American eagle surrounded by the flags of the Union. The drop scene represented the landing of Columbus in the New World.

The stage was fifty-four feet deep and forty-four feet wide and, counting the space occupied by the scenery, the breadth was seventy feet. In addition to the usual apartments connected with the stage, dressing rooms, green room, music room, etc., there were dressing rooms for the equestrians and stabling arrangements for eighteen horses.

The architect of the theatre estimated that it could accommodate nineteen hundred persons, "allowing eighteen inches to each individual." Ludlow gives the capacity as about twelve hundred.

The company as listed in the first announcement of the season included Messrs. Ludlow, Smith, Farren, John Greene, Sankey, Baily, Johnson, Sutherland, R. Russell, Jr., F. Johnson, Maynard, C. H. Saunders, James Wright, Rose, Ross, and Lavette, Mesdames Farren, Maynard, Greene, Baily, Warren, Carroll, Wright, and Miss Crane. To these should be added the names of E. S. Conner, Beecum, Mesdames Durie and Mueller, and Miss Johnson. C. H. Mueller was leader of the orchestra, and C. L. Smith was scenic artist. The equestrian company under the direction of John Robinson numbered among its members B. W. Carroll, Foster, Harrington, Woods, W. Lake, Rogers, Jackson, Masters Hernandez and Pelby, and the clowns, George Stone and Eldred.

The theatre opened November 10, 1840 with a new national overture composed by Mueller, an address by Mrs. Farren, and *The Honey Moon*. The papers of the following day described the house as being "thronged from pit to dome." Smith recalls that the receipts for the opening were $981.25.[6] E. S. Conner came out on the second night as Cardinal Richelieu in Bulwer's play of that name and on his next appearance impersonated Angelo in *Tortesa the Usurer* and Tristram Fickle in *The Weathercock*. Jack Greene made his bow on the 14th as Murtock Delany in *Irishman in London* and on the 16th Mrs. Greene appeared

---

[6] *Ibid.*, 155.

in her favorite role of Widow Melnotte. Meanwhile *Paul Jones* was revived with Conner as Long Tom Coffin, Ludlow as Captain Broughcliffe, and Mrs. Maynard as Kate Plowden. The first of many revivals at the American this season, the play was often repeated.

An interesting novelty was Sheridan Knowles' *John of Procida* given on the 17th, "for the first time in America". The next night Conner took a benefit appearing as Huon in Knowles' earlier play, *Love,* and the American sailor in *The Star Spangled Banner,* a farce new to the city.

The equestrian troupe gave its first performance on the 19th. After the grand entrée, announced in the newspaper notices as "Greeks Preparing for Battle," Messrs. Carroll and Whitlock and Master Hernandez performed feats of horsemanship, and Foster and Luke sang comic songs. The combination of equestrian performances and dramatic entertainment on the same evening won immediate favor and though they did not appear every night, the equestrians contributed in a large measure to the success of the new theatre. On the evenings when the management featured equestrian dramas, the troupe did not perform in the circle but assisted the company. The first revival of this type was *Mazeppa* cast with Lewellen and his horse, Timour, Conner, Mrs. Farren, and Mrs. Maynard in the principal roles. It ran three nights before making way for *The Youthful Days of Harrison,* a new play founded on events in the early history of the West. On this evening the equestrians returned to the circle, offering among other entertainment, a new Chinese entrée.

Charles Eaton came out on December 1 as Richard III. Conner, now a regular member of the company, assisted as Richmond, Mrs. Farren as the Queen, and Mrs. Maynard as the Duchess of York. The visitor went through a familiar round, terminating his engagement on the 11th in *Hamlet.* His tragic characterizations had been ably supported by Mrs. Farren, Conner, Maynard, Beecom, Mrs. Maynard, Mrs. Greene, and the lesser members of the company.

The manager turned again to equestrian drama after Eaton's departure reviving *Timour the Tartar* on the 14th. The spectacle was excellently cast with Conner in the name part, Mrs. Greene as Zorilda, Mrs. Farren as Selima, and Master Hernandez as Prince Agib. Had not Charles Webb arrived at this time its run would doubtless have been longer.

On Christmas there were both day and night performances.
Though the afternoon performance consisted only of equestrian
exhibitions and tightrope dances by the visiting Sciarra family,
it attracted a good house. Henceforth the matinée became a
regular feature on holidays and often on Saturdays. The entertainment in the evening featured *George Barnwell* and the spectacular *Cherry and Fair Star* with Mrs. Greene and Mrs. Farren
in the name parts. This, like the other revivals of the season,
had many repetitions and several times served as an afterpiece to
the performances in the circle. When it was given for the sixth
time on December 30, it was coupled with Sergeant Talfourd's
new tragedy, *Glencoe*.

January, like the preceding month, was devoted largely to
revivals, *Tekeli* and *El Hyder* joining *Cherry and Fair Star* in
the bills. The equestrain company was now augmented by that
of Messrs. Fogg and Stickney. Sol Smith explains that he made
the arrangement to prevent the Fogg and Stickney troupe from
being engaged by the St. Charles Theatre. He confesses that it
was an error in management which cost the firm $9,300 and the
expense of keeping an extra stud of horses.[7] The companies made
their first joint appearance on January 10 and their last on
March 2.

One of the few novelties of this month was *Money* by Bulwer,
a comedy which was introduced at the St. Charles on the same
night. C. H. Saunders' benefit brought Master Diamond to the
theatre in a new sketch of Negro character entitled *Dark Doings*.
With Eaton's return on the 29th legitimate fare such as *A New
Way to Pay Old Debts* and *The Iron Chest* made its appearance.

Fanny Fitzwilliam, the "bright particular star of the season," arrived in February. The equestrain companies were sent
off to another section of the city; the parquet seats were replaced,
and the theatre turned over to the English comédienne. She made
her début in *The Irish Widow* and Buckstone's *Widow Wiggins*,
following it with *The Country Girl; The Soldier's Daughter*, an
alteration of Cherry's play; and *Mischief Making*. At her benefit
on the 8th she offered Moncrieff's new burletta, *The Ladies Club*.
The gentlemen of the press described the star as the "most dashing, sparkling, captivating little actress that ever visited this

---

[7] *Ibid.*

section." Sol Smith estimated that from nine hundred to a thousand people crowded the theatre each night during the engagement.[8]

Mrs. Fitzwilliam opened a second engagement on the 10th with *Foreign Airs and Native Graces,* another of Moncrieff's new burlettas. Buckstone, fresh from his engagement at the St. Charles, appeared with her in *Married Life;* his new drama, *The Banished Star;* and *Foreign Airs and Native Graces.* His benefit on the 18th presented them as Rosalind and Touchstone *(As You Like It)* and as Louisa and Timid *(The Dead Shot).*

Within the next few days Sol Smith, Mrs. Fitzwilliam, Mrs. Greene, Conner, and others of the company left for Mobile where Mrs. Fitzwilliam was to appear in Ludlow and Smith's old theatre. During their absence Signor Hervio Nano, the bat man, made an appearance in the pantomime, *Bippoo the Island Ape.* Charles Eaton reappeared on the 23rd as Carwin and Sylvester Daggerwood, and the next night brought Charles Webb as Rolla to Eaton's Pizarro. *Othello, Damon and Pythias,* and *Romeo and Juliet* now figured in the bills. Eaton left after his benefit on March 1, but Webb remained a few nights longer to play the lead in *The Forty Thieves* and *The Cataract of The Ganges.* Sol Smith may have been thinking of these performances when he recorded that Webb was the "heavy man" this season.[9]

Mrs. Fitzwilliam commenced a third engagement on March 8. While Fanny Elssler danced at the St. Charles, the star at the American caricatured her. The dancer in *Foreign Airs and Native Graces* was unmistakably patterned on Elssler and in Mark Lemon's satirical *Out of Place,* Mrs. Fitzwilliam was billed as Sophy Sollikins with songs and "La Cracovienne à la Elssler." The little comédienne was as popular as ever. Reported the *Daily Picayune* of March 14 after her benefit: "Some 300 or 400 were compelled to stand in the box lobbies . . . and what is more, the house was extremely fashionable."

Mrs. Fitzwilliam and Buckstone began another joint engagement on the 14th in *Englishmen in India* and in *Our Mary Ann.* To the roles of his previous engagement Buckstone now added those of Nicolas Dovetail in *Mischief Making,* Wormwood in *The Lottery Ticket,* Mr. Twiddy in the local première of his own drama,

---

[8] *Ibid.*
[9] *Ibid.,* 157.

The Christening, and Inkpen in *Tom Noddy's Secret.* Mrs. Fitz-william appeared for the first time in *The Barrack Room* and in *Tom Noddy's Secret.*

Signor Hervio Nano, having recovered from his indisposition, returned on the 19th, appearing now in *The Gnome Fly* and in *The Demon Dwarf.* Less spectacular were the characterizations of the next visitor, James S. Browne. He made his bow on the 26th in three of the most popular roles of his last visit and continued in familiar parts. Fanny Elssler visited the theatre on the 28th when she played Sergeant Austeriltz in the *Maid of Croissy* and Conner made his last appearance of the season in *Paul Jones.*

The equestrain corps returned the last of March after several weeks in Mobile. Commented the *Daily Picayune* on the 30th: "The taste for this amendment is by no means weary, and the skilful success of change kept up by the management is admirably in union with public feeling. Let the horses run as long as the people want them, and when business grows slack, slack the reins and trot out the drama again."

The middle of April Ludlow took some of the company to St. Louis to open the theatre there.[10] To strengthen the group that remained with Smith the manager engaged Mr. and Mrs. DeBar, formerly of the St. Charles. Mrs Fitzwilliam and Buck-stone returned on the 17th. They repeated popular roles and brought out several novelties: Edward Mayhew's *Make Your Wills,* and Buckstone's *The Snapping Turtles* and *The Dream at Sea.* The latter was introduced at the benefit given John Povey, a former actor at the Park Theatre in New York who had become the agent for Mrs. Fitzwilliam.

The season was now drawing to a close. In the ten-day interval before Mrs. Fitzwilliam and Buckstone began their final engagement, Smith featured equestrian exhibitions in the circle and spectacles with DeBar in the male lead. Two performances of this period are of more than usual interest, for they enlisted the services of the great tragic actress, Mrs. Duff. She returned to the stage on the 26th enacting Mrs. Haller to the Stranger of Beecum and the Countess of Mrs. Greene, the beneficiary. At a benefit for the Firemen's Charitable Fund the following night she appeared as Thérèse, the orphan of Geneva.

---

[10] *Ibid.,* 157.

Mrs. Fitzwilliam and Buckstone made their re-entry on May 5 when, in addition to several familiar pieces, they presented *Fashionable Friends.* The other novelty of the engagement was Bayly's farce, *My Little Adopted,* introduced on May 8 and repeated at Mrs. Fitzwilliam's farewell benefit on the 10th.

The season ended on May 11 with a benefit for Sol Smith. Two nights later the theatre was reopened for a complimentary benefit given H. G. Pearson of the St. Charles. Mrs. Fitzwilliam and Buckstone and members of Smith's company volunteered their services.

The first season of the American Theatre proved a profitable one for its managers. Said the *Daily Picayune* on the 11th: "We question whether any theatre in the Union has, during the last season, brought in such rich returns both to managers and stars." Ludlow recalls that the proceeds were $20,000.[11] Smith mentions that $12,000 of their Mobile debts were paid out of the season's profits, notwithstanding the enormous expenses involved in carrying it through.[12] Its success must be attributed not to the novelty of the equestrian performances but to the intrinsic merit of the stock company and the excellent casting of the plays.

CARROLLTON, 1841

The Carrollton House was a popular summer resort within a fifteen minute train ride of New Orleans. Since the opening of the hotel in 1837 the management had featured fireworks and concerts in the gardens. Now, the saloon of the house was "neatly and elegantly fitted up" for dramatic entertainment, and on May 30 William Chapman and Signor Cioffi began a season of vaudeville and concert. In the theatrical company were Chapman and his wife, Morton, Schoolcraft, Reeder, Mrs. Cioffi, and Miss Morgan.

The night's entertainment began with a concert "immediately after the arrival of the seven o'clock cars." Before the vaudeville there was a short intermission "for promenading and refreshment," and the performance ended in time for the spectators to catch the ten o'clock train to the city.

The season opened with the farce, *Gretna Green,* but the second performance took place at the American Exchange on Camp Street as a misunderstanding had arisen between the pro-

---

[11] Ludlow, *op. cit.,* 543.
[12] Smith, *op. cit.,* 156.

prietor of the hotel and Chapman and Cioffi.[13]   They were back at Carrollton by June 13, however, and continued to give performances each Sunday throughout July.   Scattered notices appear in the *Daily Picayune* as late as the 25th but those of the last two weeks do not name the vaudevilles which were offered.

CHAPTER XII

End of an Era   1841-1842

ST. CHARLES THEATRE, 1841-1842

The St. Charles opened for the seventh season on October 25, 1841. Caldwell had erected an "arena" on the stage, and the first two weeks were devoted to equestrian performances and pantomimes. There were "grand entrées," feats of mounting and dismounting, vaulting, ropewalking, and tumbling. The equestrian company included S. P. Stickney, Miss Rosaline Stickney, G. W. Sergeant and his two children, H. Long, Lipman, Levi, Lake, and Smith, a clown. On several evenings Monsieur Paul, the French Hercules from the Tacon Theatre, Havana, appeared with the troupe in a number of astonishing Roman and Grecian feats of strength.

The first dramatic performance was *The Secret* given on November 7 with Mrs. Sergeant, "her first appearance," and Holland as the principals. As was customary during the first six weeks of this season, the bill also included an equestrian display. Sloman and Mrs. George Rowe, a newcomer, came out the next evening in the familiar farce, *My Neighbor's Wife,* and on the 9th "Old Joe" Cowell made his first appearance in several years as Dandelion in the farce, *Hunting a Turtle.*

Chief among the recruits this season were Mr. and Mrs. Brunton who made their début on the 12th as Dermot and Sarah in *The Poor Soldier.* Besides those already mentioned the company included Mr. and Mrs. John Greene, Mr. and Mrs. Hill, Barrett, Archer, Alexander Pickering, Jewell, Pacaud, Sloman, Reeder, H. G. Pearson, William Anderson, Naylor, Mrs. Page, Mrs. Durie, and Madame de Manville. Barton was acting manager and Pearson stage manager.

Several of the lesser stars began engagements on November 14. Joe Blackburn, the famous English clown, performed in the arena. Master Wood did a Cocoa-Nut Dance, "in character," and

---

[13] *Daily Picayune,* June 6, 1841.

T. S. Cline and Wood appeared in a new drama, *The Dumb Man of Manchester*. Two nights later Cline and Wood, assisted by the wonderful dog, Bruin, introduced the nautical drama, *The Murdered Boatman and His Dog*. During this engagement Master Wood appeared with Cline in *Timour the Tartar* and with his father in the pantomime, *Philip Quarl and His Monkey*, and in E. A. Somerset's *Jack the Giant Killer*. For his benefit on December 2 Wood offered the grand oriental spectacle, *The Grateful Lion*.

Miss Blanche Kemble, a grandniece of John Kemble, starred on November 18 as Alice in *The Wreck Ashore*. On the 20th Mr. and Mrs. John Greene made their first appearance as Teague and Arabella in *The Honest Thieves*. George Barrett joined the company on the 27th, performing as O'Callaghan in the popular comedy, *His Last Legs*. The next evening brought the Swiss Family, La Petite Carline, and the dancers, Monsieur Frederic and Madame Arraline. The dancers assisted the Swiss Family in their comic ballets and pantomimes and stayed on as members of the company.

The first of the major stars was James Hackett who opened his engagement on December 6 in *Henry IV*. Assisting him were Barrett as Prince Hal and T. S. Cline as Hotspur. Hackett went through the usual round of plays offering *The Kentuckian, Mons. Mallet, Rip Van Winkle*, and *Jonathan in England*. Sol Smith says that the star drew a $600 house at his opening, played to $200 audiences for a week, and had $700 at his benefit.[1]

The "arena sports" had been discontinued during Hackett's visit but after his departure on December 13, Levi North, "the greatest equestrian rider in the world," began an engagement of six nights. When the Swiss Family took a benefit on the 18th, S. Johnson, a delineator of Negro character from New York, appeared, and J. Sandford sang some of his Negro songs accompanied by the "Virginia Paginini," Winn.

The first important dramatic presentation was Boucicault's hit of the current English season, *London Assurance*, presented on December 20 with an excellent cast led by Mr. and Mrs. Greene, Barrett, Pearson, and Mrs. Sergeant. In view of the emphasis

---

[1] Smith, *op. cit.*, 162.

this season on equestrian performances and arena sports, it is interesting to read the announcement in the *Bee* of the 20th.

> It is at all times pleasurable to the proprietor to offer the legitimate drama in the St. Charles Theatre—it was for that purpose he expended on its erection a fortune. . . . But alas! at this day he considers that he built the magnificent temple too soon, or too late, for nothing but a series of losses has followed his struggle to maintain the proudest monument to the dramatic art in this country. Should the success of this comedy be commensurate with its high merit, it being decidedly the best that has been written in a quarter of a century, and the great pains and expenses which have been devoted to it, the manager will be satisfied that his effort to restore a legitimate taste has not been unavailing.

The comedy proved highly successful and was repeated some eighteen times during the next two and a half months.

James Hackett returned on December 27 as Falstaff in *The Merry Wives of Windsor* and the next night appeared as Lear, his first representation of the role in New Orleans. Mrs. Richardson, a recent addition to the company, assisted him as Cordelia.

Those who attended the theatre on January 1, 1842, saw three new pieces: George Pitt's *Eddystone Elf,* advertised as "first time in this country," Edward Stirling's *Blue Jackets,* and *The Red Indian and His Dog.* Also featured was a "great contention" between J. Sandford and Master Diamond.

The most popular engagement of the season was that of the operatic trio, Mr. and Mrs. Edward Seguin and Manvers, who came on January 5. They opened in Bellini's *Norma* assisted by Brunton, Mrs. Richardson, and Madame Thielman. Apparently the German actress appeared only in *Norma;* her name is not included in the casts of the other operas presented by the visitors. Their seventeen performances included repetitions of *Norma, Cinderella, La Sonnambula* and *Fra Diavolo.* They also presented two operas not previously heard in New Orleans: *Zampa* by Herold, and *La Gazza Ladra* by Rossini. Commented the *Bee* of January 8 after the second presentation of *Norma:* "Our citizens have now an opportunity of exhibiting their boasted passion for fine music. We have at length at the St. Charles, the opera, the genuine opera, sung and played in a style not unworthy of the great writers of music."

Dan Marble joined the ranks of the visiting performers on January 9 and remained for two weeks, offering his Yankee characterizations on nights when the opera singers did not appear. With the exception of his opening plays, *The American Farmer* and *Ebenezer Venture,* his repertoire contained nothing new.

The arrival of J. S. Brown and Mrs. Stuart early in February strengthened the resident company. They made their first appearance in *London Assurance,* Brown taking the part of Dazzle, as he had in the American première of the comedy, and Mrs. Stuart playing Grace Harkaway. The revival was even more successful than the earlier production. Stated the announcement on the third night of its run: "The unexampled success of *London Assurance* as now cast is the only apology for the manager's continuance of this play." To this an enthusiastic critic in the *Daily Picayune* replied, "For our part we should be glad to see it run through the whole season." The popularity of the play inspired the rhymed parody, *New Orleans Assurance,* which was introduced on the 13th. The notice states that it was "written expressly by ———————— for the St. Charles."

The comédienne, Miss Rock, opened an engagement on February 11 with *The Belle's Stratagem* and *Seven's the Main.* She played opposite Barrett in the still popular *Perfection,* and in *The School for Scandal* she was supported by Barrett as Sir Peter and J. S. Browne as Joseph Surface. T. D. Rice, recently returned from Europe, came on the 16th and for six consecutive evenings he entertained with impersonations of Jim Crow, Ginger Blue, Jumbo Jim, and Zip Larkin *(Such a Gitting Up Stairs).* Of his repertoire Leman Rede's *Foreign Prince* and the farce, *Such a Gitting Up Stairs,* had been written for him since his last visit to the city.

The Italian Opera Company from Havana arrived for a series of opera near the end of February. The troupe was said to have over fifty-seven members and to exceed in number and talent all those that had preceded it. The principal singers were Albertazzi, Baliali, Ober, Perozzi, Ceconi, Rossi, and Salvatori; Signoras Marozzi, Rossi, and Albertazzi. Tuesdays, Thursdays, and Saturdays were designated as opera nights. They opened with Donizetti's *Marino Faliero* on February 22. The *Daily Picayune* reported on the following day that people had rushed to the theatre "with perfect ferocity" and before seven o'clock the pit and upper tiers were "choked up." Their ten performancs included two operas which had not previously been heard in New Orleans: Bellini's *Beatrice di Tendi* and Donizetti's *Lucia di Lammermoor*.

Miss Rock continued her engagement, appearing at Madame Arraline's benefit (February 23) in the farce, *The Barrack Room*, and at Pearson's in *Seven's the Main*. On the latter occasion *The Lady of Lyons* was revived for the first time this season, the beneficiary playing Claude Melnotte to the Pauline of Mrs. Stuart. Samuel Butler, "late from Drury Lane," came on the 28th and for the next few nights appeared in Shakespearian roles. He played opposite Mrs. Stuart in *Macbeth* when she took a benefit on March 2 and assisted Miss Rock in her benefit performance of *Hamlet*.

The eleventh presentation of the Italian Opera Company was advertised for Sunday, March 13, but the performance did not take place. That evening, about half-past six, a coffin factory behind the theatre caught fire. The flames spread to the windows of the St. Charles and soon the entire building was burning. The editor of the *Bee*, who had been present at the fire, wrote feelingly of the event the following day:

> . . . We gazed in mute amazement of the terrific sight until the colossal statue of Tragedy, which adorned the front of the building caught on fire, and the mask of her dramatic sister, Comedy, was likewise in flames. . . . From the extended arms of Tragedy the fire glowed with surprising effect. When the blaze died away, after having consumed the outer painting, her hands were a coal of fire, red as Lady Macbeth's after dipping hers in the blood of Duncan; whilst the face of Comedy was as Lady Teazle when discovered in the apartments of Joseph Surface. They were the last mementos of the exquisite and sublime representations we had witnessed in the Temple, and when they fell from their pedestals, we turned with a moist eye and heaving bosom; we had witnessed the last scene of the St. Charles. The curtain had fallen to rise no more, and the glory of the drama has vanished forever.

The American Theatre on Poydras Street opened for its second season on November 20, 1841. The dress circle had been improved and the managers now stated that "ALL who purchase tickets for that part of the house will be certain of being accommodated with good seats."

The dramatic company included Managers Ludlow and Smith, Farren, Sankey, Bailey, Johnson, Sutherland, Maynard, Saunders, James Wright, Rose, Ross, De Gentzen, Cook, Reid, DeBar, Thorne, Leicester, Germon, Lavette, a dancer, Mesdames Farren, Johnson, Wright, Mueller, Foster, Germon, Warren, Russell, and Misses Eliza Petrie and Louisa Johnson, the dancer. Joseph Foster came in February to direct and act in melodramatic spectacles, and later in the season Morris, Samuel Jones, and A. J. Marks joined the company. C. H. Mueller was leader of the seventeen-piece orchestra, C. L. Smith, scenic artist, and Cranner, machinist. In the equestrian troupe again headed by J. Robinson were Whitlock, Clarke, D. Stone, E. Stone, Master Hernandez, and the clowns, G. Stone and G. Eldred.

The comedy of the opening night was *The Heir at Law* featuring Jemmy Thorne and Mrs. Richard Russell, favorite performers who had been absent from the city for several years. This was followed by Benjamin Webster's new farce, *Swiss Swains*, with music by Mueller. "The performances were very fair indeed," stated the *Bee* on the 22nd. "We have seen some of the characters better played; but it has rarely been our lot to witness a better general performance. There were no blunders; no stage waiting; no prompting." In *Rob Roy* on the second night Germon, the new singing actor, made his début as Frank Osbaldistone, Eliza Petrie appearing as Julia Mannering. This young actress had played in Mobile and St. Louis since she left the "Little Camp" in 1835 and was to prove a valuable addition to the company at the American. "Though she is not exactly 'the tallest girl in the cotton patch'," asserted the *Daily Picayune* of November 24, "she can sing 'The Banks of the Blue Moselle' and 'Liberty for Me' and play a wide range of business, too, with remarkable excellence."

The equestrian troupe made its first appearance on November 23 and henceforth until December 7, performances in the circle comprised part of the nightly bills. Sol Smith recalls incorrectly

that the American, "finding the St. Charles going it so strong on
the horses," played nothing but the legitimate during the first
month.[2]

Master Diamond began an engagement on November 25 and
on the 28th Davenport, "from New York," entertained with imitations of Fanny Elssler in "La Cracovienne." The last night of
the month saw a performance of *Town and Country*, Ludlow
enacting his favorite role of Kit Cosey and Leicester, a newcomer,
as Reuben Glenroy. Though rain kept many from witnessing the
performance, the enthusiasm of those who attended induced the
managers to bring out other "sterling plays." For the 7th they
announced *Henry IV*, cast with Thorne as Falstaff, Ludlow as
Hotspur, Farren as King Henry, Mrs. Farren as Lady Percy, and
Mrs. Russell as Dame Quickly. The *Daily Picayune* of December
9 informs us that Thorne had been able to spend only three days
on the part, yet the attempt was good. Ludlow's spirited impersonation of Hotspur was applauded throughout the evening.

Novelties were plentiful during mid-December. On the 8th
came T. E. Wilks' burletta, *The Railroad Station;* on the 11th, *My
Sister Kate* by Mark Lemon. The most ambitious of the new
plays was Dion Boucicault's recent comedy, *London Assurance*,
which, presented on December 12, antedated the St. Charles production by eight days. The advertisement stated that it was
produced "with a strict regard to stage appointments" and from
the *Daily Picayune* of the 14th, we learn that these included car-
peted floors and expensive furniture "to an extent . . . as far as
the patronage of the times will warrant." A week later the managers introduced Sheridan Knowles' *Old Maids*, a comedy which
was less successful than his other plays.

The equestrian troupe made its seventh appearance of the
month at a benefit for Master Hernandez on the 20th and returned
on Christmas for a day performance. The Lapland Dwarfs
opened on the latter date and they and the Ravel Family proved
an "immense attraction" during the holiday season. They were
succeeded by Herr Otto Motty, "the unapproachable Equestrian
Gymnast," who juggled cannon balls on his shoulders as he
galloped around the ring at full speed. These performances were
hailed by all who saw them, and his engagement was extended
to fifteen nights.

---

[2] *Ibid.*, 162.

The matinée on New Year's featured Otto Motty, Christian the Tyrolese singer, and the equestrians; the bill in the evening was made up of Charles Dance's new farce, *Alive and Merry*, and the popular *Paul Jones* of W. H. Wallack. A feature of the bill on January 2 was the appearance of the clown, George Stone, as Baptiste in *The Death Token.*

Levi North came on January 12 and thereafter appeared nightly with the equestrian troupe until their departure for Havana on the 24th.

The bills for January list several new plays. These were Charles Selby's melodrama, *Jacques Strop*, a sequel to the popular *Robert Macaire*, and A'Beckett's *Roof Scrambler*, a burlesque parody of the opera *La Somnambula*. In this Thorne made his first appearance as a prima donna, enacting the role of Molly Brown. Less than a week later came M. C. Field's *Schinder Eller*, "a highly concentrated burlesque opera founded on events which occurred (or might have occurred) in and about New Orleans during the 19th century." This travesty was a decided hit and was repeated nightly until the end of the month. At the benefit given Field on the 24th the program included another of his pieces, *Schaggs Family, or Stage Mad.*

This season was notable for its dramatic fare rather than for its stars. When James Hackett came to the American after his return from Mobile, he offered nothing that had not been played during an earlier engagement at the St. Charles. Herr Cline, the Swiss Brothers, and La Petite Carline began a five night engagement on February 2.

The most splendid of the season's productions was *The Naiad Queen*, a spectacle produced on February 12 under the direction of Joseph Foster. He had brought dresses, banners, and props with him from Philadelphia and in order to insure complete success the theatre remained closed while the cast rehearsed for two nights previous to the opening performance. The press had only praise for the acting and the scenery. The *Daily Picayune* (November 14) urged everyone to see it, assuring its readers that this was "no catch penny, no humbug brought out to suck in a credulous public." The spectacle saw ten nights and on February 22 was presented at a day performance "for the accommodation of children and families."

This was a winter of spectacles. The popular *Last Days of Pompeii* had a tenth performance on the 25th, and on the following night *Cherry and Fair Star* was revived. *The Naiad Queen* had its thirteenth presentation on the 28th when it was given for the benefit of Charles Smith, the scenic artist. Earlier in the evening Smith appeared in *Bombastes Furioso* as General Bombastes, "for the first and last time."

The equestrians were welcomed back from Havana on March 1 and for several nights thereafter they shared the stage with the popular *Naiad Queen*. Then on the 5th came *Rookwood*, another of Joseph Foster's productions, in which both the dramatic and equestrian companies participated.

The brightest of the stars was Mrs. Fitzwilliam who opened her engagement on March 9 with *Grandfather's Will* and *The Widow Wiggins*. J. B. Buckstone joined her the following evening in *My Old Woman* and *The Snapping Turtles*, and during the rest of the engagement the two continued in familiar roles.

The company benefits began after the stars left for Mobile on the 17th. Foster offered an interesting bill which included the first act of *Mazeppa*, the third act of *Rookwood*, and T. J. Dibdin's pantomime, *Mother Goose*.

The audiences at the American these last nights in March saw many new plays. On the 24th Eliza Petrie introduced *The Sentinel*, a musical farce by T. Mildenhall. Saunders' presentations were J. H. Payne's *The Fall of Algiers* and a burlesque, *The Lady of Irons*. As part of her bill Mrs. Farren featured Benjamin Webster's *Alpine Maid*. At the benefit tendered J. S. Browne on April 1, George Pitt's domestic drama, *The Last Man*, had its local première.

The lengths to which managers were forced to go to attract the public is shown in the program for March 27. The city was crowded with visitors who had come for the racing season and on this evening the American Theatre Plate was presented to the winner of the principal race of the day. The horse was led on the stage by its jockey to receive the award.

Visiting performers at this time were Mr. and Mrs. Bannister, last here in 1837 when they were members of the St. Charles company. Originally announced "for one night only," they remained for five. They opened in Bannister's *Robert Emmett* and during their brief visit introduced his recent plays: *The Syracusan Brothers, The Gentleman of Lyons,* and *The Maine Question.*

Mrs. Fitzwilliam and Buckstone commenced their farewell engagement on April 3 with *The Pet of the Petticoats* and *Foreign Airs and Native Graces.* To the plays which they had enacted on previous visits were now added Buckstone's new monopolylogue, *The Belle of the Hotel,* and the old favorite, *Roxalana.* Mrs. Fitzwilliam sustained seven characters in the new piece, among them being that of an American Fire Boy. Commented the *Daily Picayune* on April 9: "We think Fanny will yet find a better study for her Fire Boy."

On April 12, after the departure of the stars, the theatre was turned over to H. G. Pearson, for a complimentary benefit tendered by "some of the gentlemen of New Orleans." His portrayal of Reuben Glenroy *(Town and Country)* and King Charles *(Charles XII)* were witnessed by an audience which included the Honorable Martin Van Buren and his friend James Kirk Paulding. It may have been the presence of the noted strangers and not the popularity of this former member of the St. Charles company that filled the theatre and brought receipts estimated at eleven or twelve hundred dollars.

The last of the spectacular novelties was M. R. Lacy's *Napoleon Bonaparte* produced by Foster on April 13. The notices proclaimed this drama "the most intricate and difficult ever attempted on the Southern stage." The equestrian troupe was increased and a hundred supernumeraries were engaged for the production. It ran through the 23rd when Foster took a benefit. He and Robinson, the equestrian leader, had decided to join forces for a summer campaign and the following night the equestrians bade farewell.[3]

The remaining few weeks of the season were devoted to revivals of popular comedies, farces, and melodramas. The old favorite, *Animal Magnetism,* "altered and adapted to suit the present time," was presented on May 13. During the play several interesting and convincing experiments in mesmerism were given by two professors who were said to have studied the science "especially with the intention of operating on this occasion." Doubt-

---

[3] *Daily Picayune,* April 23, 1842.

less the theatre was crowded on this night and on many others during the first weeks in May for, "in consideration of the pressure of the time," the managers had reduced the price of admission, boxes and parquet now being fifty cents, gallery and parterre, twenty-five. The regular prices were resumed on the 19th but were again cut on the night of Sol Smith's benefit.

This performance on May 24, 1842, brought the season to a close. The members of the company participated in a free benefit for the Orphan Boys on the 25th, and the next day they left for St. Louis. On July 30 the American Theatre was fired by an incendiary and burned to the ground.

CONCLUSION

The destruction of the American Theatre on July 30, 1842, left the English drama without a regular home in New Orleans. However, the city was not without theatrical entertainment. While James Caldwell and Ludlow and Smith made preparations for the reconstruction of their houses, a small company managed by H. Corri and Roley Marks offered music and vaudevilles in a theatre which they had fitted up in Tivoli Garden, "formerly known as Hubert's Garden." In the fall the troupe moved into the Athenaeum on Camp Street and performed here until December 5, when the opening of Caldwell's new theatre apparently brought about its disbanding.

After the burning of the St. Charles in March, James Caldwell announced various plans for its rebuilding and throughout the summer the newspapers carried references to the opera house which he intended to erect on the site of his old theatre.[4] The fall, however, brought news of his having rented the theatre which Dubois and Kendig were building on Poydras Street,[5] and on December 5, the New American opened under his management. On hearing of this, Ludlow and Smith, who had understood that the theatre was to be theirs, immediately arranged for the reconstruction and the leasing of the St. Charles, negotiating with the Gas Bank, which owned the lot.[6]

The New St. Charles opened on January 18, 1843. A few days before this Caldwell had withdrawn from the management of the New American, thus leaving Ludlow and Smith to dominate the theatrical scene.[7] Their rise to power marks the beginning of a new era in the history of the English theatre at New Orleans.

[4] *Ibid.*, June 17, August 16, 24, 1842.
[5] *Commercial Bulletin*, September 24, 1842.
[6] Smith, *op. cit.*, 168; Ludlow, *op. cit.*, 554.
[7] *Daily Picayune*, January 8, 14, 1843.

Selected Bibliography
BOOKS AND SPECIAL ARTICLES

Alger, William. *Life of Edwin Forrest, the Tragedian.* 2 vols. Philadelphia: J. B. Lippincott & Co., 1877.

Ashe, Thomas. *Travels in America, Performed in 1806.* 3 vols. London: Richard Phillips, 1808.

Baroncelli, Joseph G. De. *Le Théâtre Français à la Nouvelle Orleans.* New Orleans: G. Muller, 1906.

Brown, T. Allston. *History of the American Stage . . . , 1733 to 1870.* New York: Dick & Fitzgerald, 1870.

Cowell, Joe. *Thirty Years Passed Among the Actors and Actresses of England and America.* New York: Harper & Bros., 1845.

Dunlap, William. *A History of the American Theatre.* New York: J. & J. Harper, 1832.

Fortier, Alcée. *History of Louisiana.* 4 vols. New York: Manzi, Joyant & Co., 1904.

Gaisford, John. *The Drama in New Orleans.* New Orleans, 1849.

Gates, William B. "The Theatre in Natchez," *Journal of Mississippi History.* Vol. III, No. 2 (April, 1941).

Gafford, Lucile. *"Material Conditions in the New Orleans Theatres before the Civil War."* Unpublished Master's thesis, University of Chicago, 1925.

—————. "A History of the St. Charles Theatre in New Orleans, 1835-1842." Unpublished Ph. D. dissertation, University of Chicago, 1930.

Gibson's Guide and Directory of the State of Louisiana and the Cities of New Orleans and Lafayette. New Orleans, 1838.

Holland Memorial. *Sketch of the Life of George Holland.* New York: T. H. Morrell, 1871.

Ireland, Joseph N. *Records of the New York Stage from 1750 to 1860.* 2 vols. New York: T. H. Morrell, 1866.

Ludlow, Noah M. *Dramatic Life as I Found It.* St. Louis: G. I. Jones & Co., 1880.

McCutcheon, R. P. "The First English Plays in New Orleans," *American Literature,* Vol. XI (May, 1939).

Nicoll, Allardyce. *A History of Early Nineteenth Century Drama, 1800-1850.* 2 vols. Cambridge: University Press, 1930.

Odell, George C. D. *Annals of the New York Stage.* 5 vols. New York: Columbia University Press, 1927-28.

Paxton, John A. *New Orleans Directory and Register.* New Orleans, 1822.

Phelps, H. P., *Players of a Century: A Record of the Albany Stage.* Albany, Joseph McDonough, 1880.

Post, Karl. *The Americans as They Are.* London: Hurst, Chance & Co., 1828.

194   *Selected Bibliography*

Price, Nellie Warner, "Le Spectacle de la Rue St. Pierre,"
    Louisiana Historical Quarterly, Vol. I (January, 1918).
Quinn, Arthur Hobson. *A History of the American Drama from
    the Beginnings to the Civil War*. New York: Harper & Bros.,
    1923.
Rees, James. *Dramatic Authors of America*. Philadelphia: G. B.
    Zieber & Co., 1845.
Rourke, Constance. *American Humor*. New York: Harcourt,
    Brace & Co., 1931.
Smith, Sol. *Theatrical Management in the West and South for
    Thirty Years*. New York: Harper & Bros., 1868.

NEWSPAPERS

Louisiana Gazette, July 31, 1804 - October 25, 1808; 1810-1826.
    City Hall Archïves, New Orleans.
Moniteur de la Louisiane, October 22, 1806 - April 12, 1809; April
    15, 1809 - January 1, 1811. City Hall Archives.
Louisiana Courier, 1813; 1816 - 1833; 1836 - 1839. City Hall
    Archives.
L'Ami des Lois, 1816-1824. City Hall Archives.
Louisiana Advertiser, November 18, 1820 - May 12, 1821; October
    6, 1826 - October 1, 1828. Wisconsin State Historical Society,
    Madison, Wisconsin.
    —————, 1826; 1828-1835. City Hall Archives.
Argus, 1826-1827; 1830. City Hall Archives.
The Bee, 1835-1842. Library, Louisiana Historical Society, New
    Orleans.
Daily Picayune, January 25, 1837-1842. Library, Times-Picayune
    Bldg., New Orleans.
New Orleans Commercial Bulletin, 1837-1842. City Hall Archives.
The True American, January-June, 1839, City Hall Archives.

MANUSCRIPTS, ETC.

Documents, records, in City Hall Archives, New Orleans.
Documents, New Orleans playbills, in Louisiana Historical So-
    ciety, New Orleans.
Letters, notarial acts, in Court House, New Orleans.
Letters, New Orleans playbills, Harvard Theatre Collection.

ANNUAL CHRONOLOGICAL RECORDS

The following pages give the day-by-day record of the English plays in the New Orleans theatres from 1806 to 1842. The title of the play is starred with an asterisk (*) whenever it appears in the record for the first time and with two asterisks (**) whenever it is the first American production of the play. Whenever available, the cast for a first-night performance is listed in brackets [] after the title of the play.

The several pieces played at a theatre in one evening are separated by semicolons. Commas serve to separate the names of the players in a first performance.

The following abbreviations for the theatres have been used:

S.P.—St. Philip Street Theatre.
O.—Orleans Street Theatre.
A.—American or Camp Street Theatre.
S.C.—St. Charles Theatre.
Am.—New American or American Theatre, Poydras Street.
O.C.—Olympic Circus.
G.—German Theatre.
V.—Vauxhall Garden in the St. Charles Theatre.

The following abbreviations for the halls and rooms temporarily serving as theatres have been used:

M.B.—Moore's Building.
Con.—Conde Ball Room.
B.—Bienville Street Hall.
E.—English Opera House.
Ar.—Arcade Theatre.
M.—Marine Ball Room.
C.—Carrollton House.
Or.—Orleans Ball Room.
S.L.—St. Louis Exchange.
A.E.—American Exchange.

April, 1806

29. Tuesday:
    M.B.—Doctor's Courtship*; Don Juan*.

May

7. Wednesday:
    M.B.—New Way to Pay Old Debts*; Unfortunate Gentle-
    man*.
16. Friday:
    M.B.—Battle of the Nile*.

April, 1811

26. Friday:
    S.P.—Unfortunate Gentleman; Doctor's Courtship.

June

29. Saturday:
    Con.—Slaves in Barbary*.

August

7. Wednesday:
    Con.—Two Quakers*; Two Hunters*.

January, 1812

24. Friday:
    S.P.—John Bull*.

April

3. Friday:
    S.P.—Heir at Law*; Raising the Wind*.

May

21. Thursday:
    B.—Two Blind Fiddlers*.

January, 1813

23. Saturday:
    S.P.—The Poor Gentleman*.

February

23. Saturday:
    S.P.—The Poor Gentleman; The Weathercock*.

November

13.   S.P.—A Cure for the Heartache*.

February, 1816

17.   S.P.—A Cure for the Heartache.

March

28. Thursday:
    S.P.—Who Wants a Guinea?*; Taste*.

April

27. Saturday:
    S.P.—The Somnambula* [Somno—Robinson].

November

21. Thursday:
    S.P.—The Point of Honor*; 'Tis All a Farce*.

February, 1817

12. Wednesday:
    S.P.—Abaellino*.

March

11. Tuesday:
    S.P.—The Honey Moon*; The Father Out-Witted*.
22. S.P.—Entertainment consisting of Moral, Patriotic, and Humorous Recitations and Songs.
28. Friday:
    S.P.—The Honey Moon; All the World's a Stage*.

April

8. Tuesday:
    S.P.—The Magpie and the Maid*; All the World's a Stage.

May

23. Friday:
    S.P.—The Miller and His Men* [Grundoff—Keen, Lothair —Cargill, Karl—Robinson]; The Weathercock.

June

2. Monday:
    S.P.—Othello* [Othello—Jones, Iago—Cargill, Roderigo— Robinson]; The Village Lawyer* [Scout—Jones, Snarl —Cargill, Sheepface—Robinson].
5. O.C.—The Battle of Bunker Hill*.

November

4. Tuesday:
    S.P.—How to Die for Love*; Intrigue*; The Toothache*.

December

15. Monday:
    S.P.—Henry IV* [Hotspur—Vos, Henry IV—Cargill, Prince of Wales—Robinson, Falstaff—Jones]; The Toothache.
18. O.C.—Henry IV.
26. Friday:
    O.C.—How to Die for Love; The Toothache.

January, 1818

5. Monday:
    S.P.—Othello.
9.   O.C.—The Duel*; The Toothache.
13. Tuesday:
    S.P.—The Honey Moon; The Midnight Hour* [Marquis—
        Hanna, Mathias—H. Vaughan, Nicholas—Morgan,
        Sebastian—Ludlow, Julia—Mrs. Ludlow, Flora—Mrs.
        Morgan].
16.   S.P.—The Foundling of the Forest* [Count De Valmont—
        Vaughan, Florian—Ludlow, Unknown Female—Mrs.
        Cummins, Rosabelle—Mrs. Morgan]; The Weather-
        cock.
21. Wednesday:
    S.P.—The Castle Spectre* [Osmond—Vaughan, Percy—
        Ludlow, Angela—Mrs. Cummins, Alice—Mrs. Mor-
        gan]; The Purse* [Will Steady—Morgan, Theodore—
        Hanna, Page—Mrs. Ludlow, Sally—Mrs. Morgan].
22.   O.C.—The Toothache.
25. Sunday:
    O.C.—The Watchword*.
30.   S.P.—She Stoops to Conquer* [Young Marlow—Vaughan,
        Tony Lumpkins—Morgan, Hastings—Ludlow, Miss
        Hardcastle—Mrs. Cummins]; The Father Outwitted.

February

4. Wednesday:
    S.P.—Douglas* [Lord Randolph—H a n n a, Glenalvon—
        Vaughan, Old Norval—Lucas, Young Norval—Morgan,
        Lady Randolph—Mrs. Cummins]; Plot and Counter-
        plot* [Pedrillo—Ludlow, Donna Lorenza—Mrs. Lud-
        low, Juana—Mrs. Cummins, Don Gaspard de Rosellas—
        H. Vaughan, Fabio—Morgan].
7.   S.P.—The Farm House*; The Rival Soldiers*.
21. Saturday:
    S.P.—The Merchant of Venice*; Fortune's Frolic*.
24. Tuesday:
    S.P.—The Curfew*; Turn Out*.
26.   O.C.—Timour the Tartar*.
27.   S.P.—Speed the Plough*; Of Age Tomorrow*.

March

4. Wednesday:
    S.P.—The Stranger*; Darkness Visible*.
6.   S.P.—John Bull; Catharine and Petruchio*.
10. Tuesday:
    S.P.—Romeo and Juliet*; Miss in Her Teens*.
14.   S.P.—King Richard III* [Richmond—Vaughan, Duke of
        Gloucester—Vos, King Henry—Lucas, Queen Eliza-
        beth—Mrs. Cummins, Lady Ann—Mrs. Morgan];
        Budget of Blunders*.

17. Tuesday:
    S.P.—George Barnwell*; Fashions*; Turn Out.
21.   S.P.—Tekeli*; The Irishman in London*.
24. Tuesday:
    S.P.—The Way to Get Married*; The Purse.
27.   S.P.—The Mountaineers*; The Hotel*.

April

2. Thursday:
    S.P.—Venice Preserved*; Darkness Visible.
4.   S.P.—The Foundling of the Forest; The Day after the
    Wedding* [Lady Elizabeth—Mrs. Savage].
8. Wednesday:
    S.P.—Ella Rosenberg*; The Romp*.
11.   S.P.—The Blind Boy*; The Poor Soldier.
15. Wednesday:
    S.P.—Laugh When You Can*; The Waterman*.
18.   S.P.—The Blind Boy; The Village Lawyer.
21. Tuesday:
    S.P.—The Doubtful Son* [Barachio—Jones]; Raising the
    Wind.
23.   S.P.—The Birthday*; Don Juan.
25.   S.P.—Lovers' Vows*; Plot and Counterplot.
29. Wednesday:
    S.P.—The Honey Moon; The Poor Soldier.

May

1. Friday:
    S.P.—The Castle Spectre; Miss in Her Teens.

March, 1819

8. Monday:
    S.P.—Three Weeks after Marriage*, principal scenes.
10.   Or.—Histrionic Divertissement.
13.   S.P.—Bertram*; Matrimony*.
15. Monday:
    S.P.—Histrionic Divertissment.
17.   S.P.—Douglas; The Prize.
20.   S.P.—The Man of Fortitude*; The Purse.
24. Wednesday:
    S.P.—The Revenge* [Zanga—Phillips].
27.   S.P.—Venice Preserved; The Day after the Wedding.
30. Tuesday:
    S.P.—Adelgitha* [M i c h a e l—Phillips, Adelgitha—Mrs.
    Turner, Imma—Mrs. Fitzallan, Lothair—Hanna]:
    Intrigue.

April

7. Wednesday:
    S.P.—Barbarossa*; The Prize.
10.   S.P.—The Sultan*; Bombastes Furioso*; The Bee Hive*.

14. Tuesday:
    S.P.—Lovers' Vows; The Weathercock.
17.   S.P.—The Tale of Mystery* [Francisco—Douvillier]; Tom
    Thumb* [Tom Thumb—Master Turner].
28. Wednesday:
    S.P.—She Stoops to Conquer; The Hunter of the Alps*.

May

 4. Tuesday:
    S.P.—Pizarro*; Tom Thumb.
 8.   S.P.—Isabella*; The Sleep Walker.
17. Monday:
    S.P.—The Busy Body*; Frightened to Death*. Last night
    of the season.

November

22.   E.—The Vampire*.

January, 1820

 7. Friday:
    S.P.—Honey Moon; Three and the Deuce* [Pertinax, Pere-
    grine, and Percival Single—Caldwell, Mrs. Milford—
    Mrs. Williams, Taffline—Mrs. Russell].
 8.   S.P.—Laugh When You Can; Rosina* [Rosina—Mrs.
    Gray, Belville—Jones, Phoebe—Mrs. Russell].
    O.—Turnpike Gate* [Crack—Entwistle].
10. Monday:
    S.P.—Bertram; Turn Out.
11.   S.P.—Soldier's Daughter* [Frank Heartall—Caldwell];
    Of Age Tomorrow.
    O.—Douglas; The Review* [Looney M'Twolter—Entwistle,
    Caleb Quotem—Hunter, Grace Gaylove—Mrs. Yates,
    Lucy—Mrs. Monier].
12.   S.P.—Richard III; Irishman in London.
13.   S.P.—Belle's Stratagem* [Doricourt—Caldwell, Letitia
    Hardy—Mrs. Anderson, Mrs. Racket—Mrs. Williams,
    Sir George Touchwood—Hutton]; Three and the
    Deuce.
14.   S.P.—Devil's Bridge* [Count Belino—Keene, Rosalvina—
    Mrs. Gray]; Village Lawyer.
15.   S.P.—West Indian*; No Song, No Supper*.
17. Monday:
    S.P.—Hamlet*; Love à la Mode*.
18.   S.P.—She Stoops to Conquer; Rosina.
19.   S.P.—Mountaineers; The Liar*.
20.   S.P.—Devil's Bridge; Spoiled Child*.
21.   S.P.—Romeo and Juliet; Devil to Pay*.
22.   S.P.—School of Reform*; Raising the Wind.

24. Monday:
    S.P.—Brutus*; The Purse.
25.   S.P.—Green Man*; The Liar.
26.   S.P.—Hamlet; Day after the Wedding.
27.   S.P.—Guy Mannering*; [Guy Mannering—Hutton, Henry Bertram—Keene, Dandie Dinmont—Entwistle, Julia Mannering—Mrs. Gray, Lucy Bertram—Mrs. Russell, Meg Merriless—Mrs. Williams]; Turnpike Gate.
28.   S.P.—John Bull; Poor Soldier.
29.   S.P.—Douglas; Catharine and Petruchio.
31. Monday:
    S.P.—Pizarro; Blue Devils*.

February

1. Tuesday:
    S.P.—Stranger; Forty Thieves*; [Ali Baba—Entwistle, Hassarac—Hutton, Morgiana—Mrs. Gray].
2.   S.P.—Road to Ruin*; Maid and Magpie*.
3.   S.P.—Lodoiska*; Matrimony.
4.   S.P.—Poor Gentleman; The Romp.
5.   S.P.—Paul and Virginia*; [Paul—Keene, Virginia—Mrs. Gray]; Forty Thieves.
7. Monday:
    S.P.—Othello; Rendezvous*; [Simon—Entwistle].
8.   S.P.—Guy Mannering; Children in the Wood*; [Walter—Entwistle, Josephine—Mrs. Russell].
9.   S.P.—Speed the Plough; Paul and Virginia.
10.   S.P.—Forty Thieves; Rendezvous.
11.   S.P.—Point of Honor; Lady of the Lake*.
12.   S.P.—School for Scandal* [Charles Surface—Caldwell]; Rosina.
14. Monday:
    O.—Honey Moon; Three and the Deuce.
16.   O.—Hamlet; The Purse.
18.   O.—Mountaineers; Turn Out.
19.   O.—School for Scandal; Poor Soldier.
21. Monday:
    O.—Macbeth* [Macbeth—Caldwell, Lady Macbeth—Mrs. Williams].
22.   S.P.—Glory of Columbia, Her Yeomanry*; Feast of Apollo.
23.   O.—Soldier's Daughter; Padlock* [Mungo—Entwistle].
25.   O.—Love in a Village* [Young Meadows—Keene, Rosetta —Mrs. Gray]; Sleep Walker.
26.   O.—Green Man; Of Age Tomorrow.
28. Monday:
    O.—Romeo and Juliet; Boarding House* [Simon Spatterdash—Entwistle].
29.   S.P.—Lodoiska; Padlock.

March

1. Wednesday:
    O.—Belle's Stratagem; Highland Reel* [Maggy McGil-
    pin—Mrs. Anderson].
2.   S.P.—Love in a Village.
3.   O.—Foundling of the Forest; Turnpike Gate.
4.   O.—Cure for the Heartache; No Song, No Supper.
6. Monday:
    O.—Pizarro; The House that Jack Built*.
8.   O.—Suspicious Husband* [Ranger—Caldwell]; The House
    that Jack Built.
9.   S.P.—Love in a Village; The House that Jack Built.
10.   O.—She Would be a Soldier* [Captain Pendragon—Cald-
    well, Adela—Mrs. Russell, Christine—Mrs. Williams,
    Jerry—Entwistle]; The Liar.
11.   O.—She Would be a Soldier; Magpie and the Maid.
13. Monday:
    O.—Suspicious Husband; Tale of Mystery.
15.   O.—Rivals*; Honest Thieves*.
17.   O.—Wild Oats*; The Critic.
18.   O.—Heir at Law; The Romp.
20. Monday:
    O.—She Would be a Soldier; High Life below Stairs*
    [Lovel—Caldwell, Kitty—Mrs. Williams].
22.   O.—The Wonder!*; Sylvester Daggerwood*; Lock and
    Key*.
24.   O.—Much Ado about Nothing* [Beatrice—Mrs. Ander-
    son, Benedick—Caldwell]; Ella Rosenberg.
25.   O.—Devil's Bridge; Hunter of the Alps.
27. Monday:
    O.—Apostate* [Malec—Caldwell]; Don Giovanni*.
29.   O.—Merchant of Venice; Love Laughs at Locksmiths*.
30.   S.P.—Town and Country*; Fortune's Frolic.

April

5. Wednesday:
    O.—Henry IV; Children in the Wood.
7.   O.—Castle Spectre; Honest Thieves.
8.   O.—School for Scandal; Forest of Bondy*.
10. Monday:
    O.—Wives as They Were*; Rosina.
11.   S.P.—Foundling of the Forest; Bluebeard*.
12.   O.—Marmèon*; Married Yesterday.
13.   S.P.—Timour the Tartar; Bluebeard.
14.   O.—As You Like It*; Raising the Wind.
15.   O.—Gamester*; Forest of Bondy.
17. Monday:
    O.—She Would be a Soldier; Rendezvous.
18.   S.P.—Laugh When You Can; Forty Thieves.
19.   O.—Hunter of the Alps.

June

10. Saturday:
    S.P.—Gamester; Sylvester Daggerwood.

January, 1821

31. Wednesday:
    O.—Soldier's Daughter; The Liar.

February

3. Saturday:
    O.—Honey Moon; Sydney and His Dog*.
5. Monday:
    O.—Devil's Bridge; Spoiled Child.
7.   O.—Much Ado about Nothing; Sydney and His Dog.
9.   O.—Guy Mannering; Weathercock.
10. O.—Rule a Wife and Have a Wife* [Leon—Caldwell,
     Estifania—Mrs. Entwistle]; Three Weeks after Mar-
     riage.
12. Monday:
    O.—Brother and Sister* [Don Sylvio—Keene, Donna Isi-
    dora—Mrs. Burke, Donna Camilda—Mrs. Legg].
14. O.—Love in a Village; Of Age Tomorrow.
16. O.—School for Scandal; Ways and Means* [Sir David
     Dunder—Burke].
17. O.—Mountaineers; Rosina.
19. Monday:
    O.—No Song, No Supper.
21. O.—Pizarro; Animal Magnetism* [Doctor—Burke, Con-
     stance—Mrs. Legg, Lisette—Mrs. Russell].
23. O.—Young Quaker* [Sadboy—Caldwell, Araminta—Mrs.
     Burke]; Spoiled Child.
24. O.—Jealous Wife* [Lord Trinket—Caldwell]; Three and
     the Deuce.
26. Monday:
    O.—Virginius* [Virginius — Caldwell, Virginia — Mrs.
    Williams]; Beaux Without Belles* [Scapegrace—
    Keene, Maxwell—Hutton, Charles Safety—Jefferson].

March

2. Friday:
    O.—Lear*; The Review.
3.   O.—Road to Ruin; Paul and Virginia.
5. Monday:
    O.—Marmion; Highland Reel.
7.   O.—The Inconstant* [Young Mirabell—Caldwell, Biz-
     arre—Mrs. Entwistle]; American Tar.
9.   O.—Henri Quatre* [Henri Quatre—Hutton, Crillon—
     Keene, Clothilde de Biron—Mrs. Legg]; Rendezvous.
10. O.—The Aethiop* [Aethiop—Caldwell]; The Romp.

14. Wednesday:
    O.—West Indian; The Citizen*.
16.   O.—The Stranger; Forest of Bondy.
17.   O.—The Aethiop; Fortune's Frolic.
19. Monday:
    O.—John of Paris* [Princess of Navarre—Mrs. Burke];
    Budget of Blunders.
23.   O.—Macbeth; The Review.
26. Monday:
    O.—Rule a Wife and Have a Wife; Love Laughs at Lock-
    smiths.
28.   O.—Venice Preserved; Who's the Dupe?* [Old Doiley—
    Burke].
30.   O.—Hamlet; Blue Devils.

April

4. Wednesday:
    O.—Othello; Modern Antiques*.
6.   O.—Virginius; Turnpike Gate.
9. Monday:
    O.—Bertram; Of Age Tomorrow.
11.   O.—Julius Caesar*.
14.   O.—Gamester; Forty Thieves.
16. Monday:
    O.—The Robbers* [Robert—Cooper].
27. Friday:
    O.—Critic; Brother and Sister; The Liar.

May

2. Wednesday:
    O.—Provoked Husband* [Lord Townly—Caldwell, Lady
    Townly—Mrs. Entwistle].
4.   O.—The Birthday.
12. Saturday:
    O.—Laugh When You Can; Lady of the Lake.

December

10. Monday:
    O.—Honey Moon; Three and the Deuce.
12.   O.—Fazio*.
19. Wednesday:
    O.—School of Reform; Sleep Walker.

January, 1822

11. Friday:
    O.—Richard III.

February

6. Wednesday:
   O.—Richard III.
8.   O.—Othello.
9.   O.—Virginius.
11. Monday:
   O.—Virginius.

March

15. Friday:
   O.—Timour the Tartar; Irishman in London.
16.   O.—Timour the Tartar; Laugh When You Can.
18. Monday:
   O.—Lodoiska; Turn Out.
20.   O.—Timour the Tartar; Lodoiska.
23.   O.—Alexander the Great*.
27. Wednesday:
   O.—Zaire* [Orosmane—Cooper].

April

6. Saturday:
   O.—Bluebeard.
24. Wednesday:
   S.P.—Adelgitha; Bombastes Furioso.

January, 1823

4. Saturday:
   O.—Road to Ruin; The Reapers.
6. Monday:
   O.—She Stoops to Conquer; Poor Soldier.
8.   O.—She Would be a Soldier.
10.   O.—Folly as It Flies* [Tom Tick—Caldwell, Lady Melmoth—Jane Placide, Georgianna—Miss Seymour]; Paul and Virginia.
11.   O.—School for Scandal.
13. Monday:
   O.—Exiles of Siberia* [Empress Elizabeth—Mrs. Baker, Catharine—Miss Seymour, Alexina—Miss Placide]; The Liar.
15.   O.—Laugh When You Can; John of Paris.
17.   O.—Macbeth; Rendezvous.
18.   O.—Wandering Boys* [Count de Croissy—Ludlow, Justin—Miss Seymour, Paul—Miss Placide]; Lady and the Devil* [Wildlove—Ludlow, Zephyrina—Miss Placide, Negombo—Miss Seymour].
20. Monday:
   O.—Warlock of the Glen* [Matthew—William Forrest, Adela—Miss Placide, Marian—Miss Seymour]; Town and Country.

22.   O.—Dramatist* [Vapid—Caldwell, Louisa Courtney—Mrs. Baker, Marianne—Miss Seymour] ; Forty Thieves.
24.   O.—Hamlet; Warlock of the Glen.
25.   O.—Wandering Boys; Three and the Deuce.
27. Monday:
       O.—Abaellino; Spoiled Child.
29.   O.—Wandering Boys; My Aunt* [Dashall—Caldwell, Emma—Miss Seymour] ; John of Paris.
31.   O.—Damon and Pythias; Agreeable Surprise* [Lingo—Williams, Laura—Miss Seymour, Cowslip—Miss Placide].

February

 1. Saturday:
       O.—Dramatist; Forty Thieves.
 5. Wednesday:
       O.—Know Your Own Mind* [Dashwood—Caldwell, Lady Jane—Miss Seymour, Madame La Rouge—Miss Placide] ; Warlock of the Glen.
 7. O.—Lionel and Clarissa* [Lionel—Garner, Clarissa—Miss Seymour, Jenny—Miss Placide] ; Hunter of the Alps.
 8.   O.—Soldier's Daughter; Turnpike Gate.
10. Monday:
       O.—Rob Roy* [Rob Roy—Caldwell, Helen M'Gregor—Mrs. Baker, Diana Vernon—Miss Placide, Francis Osbaldistone—Garner] ; Promissory Note* [Scamper—Ludlow, Mrs. Markam—Miss Seymour, Caroline—Mrs. Ludlow, Cicely—Mrs. Russell].
12.   O.—Merchant of Venice; Three Weeks after Marriage.
14.   O.—Foundling of the Forest; The Lying Valet* [Sharp—Alexander Drake, Miss Gadabout—Miss Seymour, Melissa—Mrs. Baker, Kitty Pry—Mrs. Russell].
17. Monday:
       O.—Know Your Own Mind; For Freedom Ho!* [Sir Francis Faddle—Ludlow, Michael—Miss Seymour, Miss Eliza Arundel—Mrs. Baker, Lisette—Miss Placide].
19.   O.—Gamester; Wandering Boys.
21.   O.—Rob Roy; Agreeable Surprise.
22.   O.—Columbus* [Columbus—Ludlow, Alonzo—Forest, Nelti—Mrs. Drake, Cora—Miss Placide] ; For Freedom Ho!
24. Monday:
       O.—Stranger; Lady of the Lake.
26.   O.—Lovers' Vows; The Review.
28.   O.—Romeo and Juliet; Honest Thieves.

March

1. Saturday:
   > O.—Mountaineers; Miss in Her Teens.
3. Monday:
   > O.—Rob Roy; Agreeable Surprise.
5. O.—Richard III; Raising the Wind.
7. O.—Barbarossa; Matrimony.
8. O.—Richard III; Of Age Tomorrow.
10. Monday:
    > O.—Douglas; Poor Soldier.
12. O.—Hamlet; Miss in Her Teens.
14. O.—The Way to Keep Him; Blind Boy.
15. O.—Pizarro; Poor Soldier.
17. Monday:
    > O.—Sons of Erin* [FitzEdward—Caldwell, Captain Rivers —Ludlow, Lady Ann Lovel—Mrs. Drake, Mrs. Rivers —Miss Placide]; St. Patrick's Day* [Lieutenant O'Conner—Ludlow, Doctor Rosy—Drake, Lauretta— Mrs. Rowe].
19. O.—Laugh When You Can; Wandering Boys.
21. O.—Macbeth; Lovers' Quarrels.
22. O.—Virginius; The Liar.
24. Monday:
    > O.—Venice Preserved; No Song, No Supper.
26. O.—Julius Caesar; Rendezvous.
29. O.—Damon and Pythias; The Day after the Wedding.

April

4. Friday:
   > O.—King John* [King John—Cooper, Falconbridge— Caldwell, Prince Henry—Mrs. Rowe, Constance— Mrs. Drake]; Who's the Dupe?
5. O.—Bertram; Catharine and Petruchio.
7. Monday:
   > O.—Othello; Love Laughs at Locksmiths.
9. O.—Virginius; Manager in Distress*; St .Patrick's Day.
11. O.—Fair Penitent* [Lothario—Cooper, Horatio—Caldwell, Calistra—Mis Placide, Lavinia—Mrs. Baker]; Manager in Distress; Miss in Her Teens.
12. O.—West Indian; Of Age Tomorrow.
14. Monday:
    > O.—Devil's Bridge; The Day after the Wedding.
16. Devil's Bridge; Valentine and Orson*.
18. O.—Fontainbleau* [Henry—Phillips, Lackland—Caldwell, Rosa—Miss Placide, Celia—Mrs. Rowe]; Lock and Key.

21. Monday:
      O.—Richard III; Blue Devils.
23.   O.—School for Scandal; Valentine and Orson.
25.   O.—Barber of Seville* [Count Almaviva—Phillips, Rosina
         —Miss Placide]; Spoiled Child.
26.   O.—M.P.*.
30. Wednesday:
      O.—Cure for the Heartache; Ruse contre Ruse.

May

 3. Saturday:
      O.—Tancred and Sigismunda* [Tancred—Master Smith,
         Sigismunda—Miss Smith, Laura—Mrs. Rowe]; Three
         and the Deuce.
 5. Monday:
      O.—The Wonder; The Romp.
 7.   O.—Pizarro; Sprigs of Laurel.
 9.   O.—The Way to Get Married; Turn Out.
14. Wednesday:
      A.—Dramatist; The Romp.
16.   A.—Honey Moon; Rosina.
17.   A.—Iron Chest; Love Among the Roses* [Sharpsett—Rus-
         sell, Hollyhock—Drake, Rose—Mrs. Russell].
19. Monday:
      A.—Bold Stroke for a Wife* [Col. Fainwell—Caldwell,
         Ann Lovely—Mrs. Rowe]; Animal Magnetism.
21.   A.—Mountaineers; Village Lawyer.
23.   A.—Wheel of Fortune* [Penruddock—Caldwell, Emily
         Tempest—Miss Placide]; Highland Reel.
24.   A.—Rule a Wife and Have a Wife; Turnpike Gate.
28. Wednesday:
      A.—Lovers' Vows; No Song, No Supper. Last night of the
         season.

January, 1824

 1. Thursday:
      A.—Town and Country; Of Age Tomorrow.
 3.   A.—School of Reform; Turnpike Gate.
 5. Monday:
      A.—Rule a Wife and Have a Wife; Two Strings to Your
         Bow.
 8.   A.—Marion* [Marion—Caldwell, Emma—Miss Placide,
         Miss FitzHenry—Mrs. Baker]; American Tar.
10.   A.—Heir at Law; Monsieur Tonson*.
12. Monday:
      A.—Deserted Daughter* [Cheveril—Ludlow, Donald—
         Page, Lady Ann Mordent—Miss Placide, Joanna—
         Mrs. Baker]; Sprigs of Laurel.

14. A.—Rob Roy; Rendezvous.
16. A.—Macbeth; Lock and Key.
17. A.—Virginius; Poor Soldier.
19. Monday:
        A.—Hamlet; Lovers' Quarrels.
21. A.—Julius Caesar; Honest Thieves.
23. A.—Damon and Pythias; Three and the Deuce.
24. A.—Rob Roy; Catharine and Petruchio.
26. Monday:
        A.—Fall of Tarquin; The Liar.
28. A.—Pizarro; Hunter of the Alps.
30. A.—Abaellino; No Song, No Supper.
31. A.—Guy Mannering; Spoiled Child.

February

2. Monday:
        A.—Soldier's Daughter; Highland Reel.
4. A.—Venice Preserved; Simpson and Company* [Mr. Simpson—Ludlow, Mr. Bromly—Russell, Mrs. Bromly —Mrs. Baker].
6. A.—Adeline* [Dorlin—E. Forest, Count Wilhelm—Ludlow, Adeline—Miss Placide]; Bold Stroke for a Wife.
7. A.—Rob Roy; Simpson and Company.
9. Monday:
        A.—Forest of Rosenwald* [Raymond—E. Forrest, Robert—Ludlow, Agnes—Mrs. Rowe, Margarette—Miss Placide, Bleeding Nun—Mrs. Baker]; Dramatist.
11. A.—She Would be a Soldier; Forest of Rosenwald.
12. A.—Robbers; Raising the Wind.
13. A.—Foundling of the Forest; Love Laughs at Locksmiths.
14. A.—Durazzo* [Durazzo — Pelby, Alonzo — E. Forrest, Zelinda—Miss Placide, Lenora—Mrs. Rowe].
16. Monday:
        A.—Forest of Rosenwald; She Would be a Soldier.
18. A.—John Bull; Wandering Boys.
20. A.—Falls of Clyde* [Malcolm—Caldwell, Edward Enfield—E. Forrest, Ellen Enfield—Miss Placide]; Of Age Tomorrow.
21. A.—Falls of Clyde; Simpson and Company.
23. Monday:
        A.—Columbus; Day after the Wedding.
24. A.—Durazzo; Mr. H.—* [Mr. H.—Ludlow, Melerinda— Miss Placide].
25. A.—Pizarro; Too Late for Dinner* [Frank Poppleton— Ludlow, Miss E. Somerton—Miss Placide, Letty— Mrs. Russell].

26.   A.—Riches* [Luke—Pelby, Edward Lacy—E. Forest, Eliza—Mrs. Rowe, Maria—Mrs. Baker]; Forest of Rosenwald.
27.   A.—John Bull; Simpson and Company.
28.   A.—Honey Moon; Falls of Clyde.

March

 1. Monday:
        A.—Dolly and the Rat* [Tom Brisket—Page, Gregory Rook—Ludlow, Dolly—Mrs. Russell]; West Indian.
 3.   A.—Devil's Bridge; Three and the Deuce.
 5.   A.—Aethiop; Blue Devils.
 6.   A.—Bertram; Monsieur Tonson.
 8. Monday:
        A.—Aethiop; Love Among the Roses.
 9.   A.—Iron Chest; Turn Out.
10.   A.—Road to Ruin; Dolly and the Rat.
11.   A.—Cure for the Heartache; Wandering Boys.
12.   A.—Rob Roy—Hit or Miss* [Dick Cypher—Caldwell, James Jumble—Ludlow, Clara Sterling—Miss Placide, Dolly O'Daisy—Mrs. Russell].
13.   A.—Warlock of the Glen; Hit or Miss.
15. Monday:
        A.—Alexander the Great; Promissory Note.
17.   A.—St. Patrick's Day; Poor Soldier; Love in a Camp* [Father Luke—Gray, Captain Patrick—Garner, Darby—Russell, Flora—Mrs. Rowe].
19.   A.—Richard III; Three Weeks after Marriage.
20.   A.—Who Wants a Guinea?; Forty Thieves.
22. Monday:
        A.—Othello; Rendezvous.
24.   A.—Forty Thieves; Adeline.
26.   A.—Richard III; Matrimony.
27.   A.—Forest of Rosenwald; Falls of Clyde.
29. Monday:
        A.—Poor Gentleman; Rosina.
30.   A.—Forest of Rosenwald; Falls of Clyde.
31.   A.—She Stoops to Conquer; Love, Law and Physics* [Dr. Camphor—Gray, Flexible — Ludlow, Laura — Mrs. Rowe, Mrs. Hilary—Mrs. Higgins].

April

 2. Friday:
        A.—Cato* [Cato—Caldwell, Juba—E. Forrest, Marcia—Mrs. Rowe, Lucia—Mrs. Baker]; Love, Law and Physics.
 3.   A.—The Stranger; Lady of the Lake.

5. Monday:
   A.—Marmion; Simpson and Company.
7.   A.—Zembuca* [Rorac — Caldwell, Zembuca — Ludlow, Selim—E. Forrest, Almazaide—Miss Placide, Ebra—Mrs. Russell]; Too Late for Dinner.
8.   A.—Zembuca; Monsieur Tonson.
9.   A.—Irishman in London; Zembuca.
10.   A.—Honest Thieves; Zembuca.
12. Monday:
   A.—Lady and the Devil; Zembuca.
14.   A.—Zembuca; The Purse.
15.   A.—Castle Spectre; Tekeli.
17.   A.—The Stranger; La Fille Malgarde.
19. Monday:
   A.—Rob Roy; La Fille Malgarde.
20.   A.—Wanted a Wife* [Frank Cleverly—Caldwell, Arthur Wildfire—Ludlow, Lillian Eden—Mrs. Rowe, Catharine Arragon—Mrs. Russell]; Paul and Virginia.
21.   A.—Rivals; Annette and Lubin.
22.   A.—Wanted a Wife; Lady of the Lake.
23.   A.—Annette and Lubin; School for Scandal.
24.   A.—The Birthday; La Fille Malgarde.
26. Monday:
   A.—The Prize; Zembuca.
28.   A.—Speed the Plough; Turnpike Gate.
29.   A.—She Would be a Soldier; Adeline.

May

1. Saturday:
   A.—Zembuca; Devil to Pay.
3. Monday:
   A.—Belle's Stratagem; Little Red Riding Hood; Rendezvous.
5.   A.—The Will* [George Howard—Caldwell, Veritas—Ludlow, Albina Mandeville—Miss Placide, Sir Solomon Cynic—Gray]; Tale of Mystery.
7.   A.—Life in London* [Tom—Caldwell, Jerry Hawthorn—Russell, Logic—Ludlow, Primefit—E. Forrest, Sue—Mrs. Russell]; The Liar.
8.   A.—Tom and Jerry; Turn Out.
10. Monday:
   A.—Tom and Jerry; Budget of Blunders.
12.   A.—Wallace* [Wallace—E. Forrest, Douglas—Ludlow, Helen—Miss Placide, Earl of Gloster—Garner]; Ways and Means.
14.   A.—Speed the Plough; The Birthday.
15.   A.—The Will; Tom Thumb.

17. Monday:
    A.—Wild Oats; Boarding House.
19.   A.—Town and Country; Spoiled Child.
21.   A.—Rivals; The Critic.
22.   A.—Richard III; Don Juan.
24. Monday:
    A.—Battle of New Orleans* [Sir E. Packenham—Forrest, General Jackson—Ludlow, Theodore—E. Forrest, Louisa—Mrs. Rowe, Charlotte—Miss Placide]; No Song, No Supper.
26.   A.—Miller and His Men; Three and the Deuce.
28.   A.—Rob Roy; The Purse.

June

2. Wednesday:
    A.—Solitary of Mount Savage* [The Unknown—Caldwell, Elodia—Miss Placide, Mary—Mrs. Mongin]; Hunter of the Alps.
4.   A.—Solitary of Mount Savage; The Review.
5.   A.—Bluebeard; Miller and His Men.
7. Monday:
    A.—Honey Moon; Miss in Her Teens.
9.   A.—Laugh When You Can; Poor Soldier. Last Night of the season.

January, 1825

3. Monday:
    A.—Soldier's Daughter; No Song, No Supper.
18. Tuesday:
    A.—Tom and Jerry.
19.   A.—Tom and Jerry.
20.   A.—Tom and Jerry.
21.   A.—Tom and Jerry.

March

2. Wednesday:
    A.—Othello; Village Lawyer.
5.   A.—Provoked Husband; Of Age Tomorrow.
8. Tuesday:
    A.—Rule a Wife and Have a Wife; Rosina.
9.   A.—Virginius; The Liar.
11.   A.—Virginius; Hunter of the Alps.
12.   A.—Orphan* [Castali—Conway, Chamont—Caldwell]; Forest of Rosenwald.
14. Monday:
    A.—Apostate; Turnpike Gate.

April
4. Monday:
    A.—Tom Thumb; Timour the Tartar.
11. Monday:
    A.—Lafayette*; Three and the Deuce.
18. Monday:
    A.—Percy* [Percy—Wilson, Ontario—E. Forrest, Matilda Mrs. Rowe]; Tom and Jerry.
23.   A.—Cure for the Heartache; Spoiled Child.
30. Saturday:
    A.—Cataract of the Ganges* [Mokarra—Caldwell, Mordaunt—E. Forrest, Princess Dessa—Mrs. Rowe, Ubra—Miss Russell, Zamine—Miss Placide].

May
2. Monday:
    A.—Cataract of the Ganges.
3.   A.—Cataract of the Ganges.
4.   A.—Cataract of the Ganges.
16. Monday:
    A.—Peveril of the Peak*.

January, 1826
24. Tuesday:
    A.—Honey Moon; Three and the Deuce.
25.   A.—William Tell* [Tell—Caldwell, Albert—Miss Russell, Emma—Mrs. Russell]; The Review.
26.   A.—Henry IV; Nature and Philosophy* [Colin—Miss Placide, Eliza—Mrs. Rowe].
27.   A.—Wives as They Were; Don Juan.
28.   A.—Tom and Jerry; The Secret* [Mr. Dearlove—Drummond, Mrs. Dearlove—Mrs. Russell, Eliza—Mrs. Higgins].
30. Monday:
    A.—Merry Wives of Windsor* [Master Abraham Slender—Caldwell, Mrs. Ford—Mrs. Russell, Mrs. Page—Mrs. Rowe, Falstaff—Gray]; Nature and Philosophy.
31.   A.—William Tell; The Romp.

February
1. Wednesday:
    A.—Zembuca; The Purse.
2.   A.—Dramatist; Magpie and the Maid.
3.   A.—Foundling of the Forest; Falls of Clyde.
4.   A.—Rob Roy; Matrimony.
6. Monday:
    A.—Rosina; Cataract of the Ganges.
7.   A.—Hamlet; Lovers' Quarrels.
8.   A.—Guy Mannering; Miller and His Men.

9.   A.—Poor Soldier; Tom and Jerry.
10.   A.—Monsieur Tonson; Forty Thieves.
11.   A.—No Song, No Supper; Cataract of the Ganges.
13. Monday:
      A.—Mountaineers; Forest of Rosenwald.
14.   A.—Aethiop; Blue Devils.
15.   A.—Venice Preserved; Rendezvous.
16.   A.—School for Scandal; The Young Widow* [Mandeville
      —Gray, Splash—Russell, Amelia—Mrs. Russell].
17.   A.—The Hypocrite* [Doctor Cantwell—Caldwell, Maw-
      worm—Russell, Col. Lambert—Drummond, Old Lady
      Lambert—Higgins, Young Lady Lambert—Mrs.
      Rowe, Charlotte—Mrs. Russell]; The Secret.
18.   A.—She Would be a Soldier; Fortune's Frolic.
20. Monday:
      A.—Devil's Bridge; The Weathercock.
21.   A.—The Hypocrite; Spoiled Child.
22.   A.—Montgomery* [General Montgomery—Caldwell, Nina
      —Miss Placide, Altamah—Mrs. Rowe, Col. O'Sham-
      rock—Russell]; American Tar.
23.   A.—School of Reform; Village Lawyer.
24.   A.—Road to Ruin; Sponge in Town* [Sponge—Russell,
      Mr. Grumpy—Gray, Mrs. Grumpy—Mrs. Higgins,
      Dorothy Grumpy—Mrs. Rowe].
25.   A.—Rob Roy; Spectre Bridegroom* [Squire—Oldwinkle
      —Gray, Dickory—Russell, Miss Georgiana Oldwinkle
      —Mrs. Rowe, Lavinia—Mrs. Russell].
27. Monday:
      A.—Hunter of the Alps; Thérèse* [Carwin—Wilson, Fon-
      taine—Kelsey, Thérèse—Miss Placide, Countess—Mrs.
      Bloxton].

March

1. Wednesday:
      A.—Hypocrite; Spectre Bridegroom.
3.   A.—Montgomery; Forest of Rosenwald.
4.   A.—Battle of New Orleans; Thérèse.
6. Monday:
      A.—Barbarossa; Highland Reel.
8.   A.—Castle Spectre; Spoiled Child.
9   A.—Merchant of Venice; Miller and His Men.
10.   A.—Hypocrite; Paul and Virginia.
13. Monday:
      A.—Tom and Jerry; Death of Life in London* [Logic—
      Gray, Ghost of Corinthian Tom—Drummond, Ghost
      of Jerry—Russell].
14.   A.—Helpless Animals* [Mulberry—Gray, Letitia Mul-
      berry—Mrs. Rowe].
15.   A.—Exile of Siberia; The Day after the Wedding.

16.   A.—Simpson and Company; Forest of Bondy.
17.   A.—She Would be a Soldier; St. Patrick's Day.
18.   A.—Spectre Bridegroom; Der Freischutz* [Casper—Cald-
        well, Wilhelm—Still, The Black Huntsman of Bohemia
        —Forest, Bertha—Miss Placide, Linda—Mrs. Rowe].
20. Monday:
        A.—The Wedding Day; Der Freischutz.
21.   A.—Belle's Stratagem; Forest of Bondy.
22.   A.—The Hypocrite; Tom Thumb.
23.   A.—Devil to Pay; Cataract of the Ganges.
25.   A.—Sweethearts and Wives* [Admiral Franklin—Gray,
        Charles Franklin—Drummond, Billy Lackaday—Rus-
        sell, Eugenia—Miss Placide, Laura—Mrs. Rowe, Su-
        san—Mrs. Russell]; Der Freischutz.
27. Monday:
        A.—Sweethearts and Wives; Helpless Animals.
28.   A.—William Tell; The Sultan.
29.   A.—The Stranger; The Secret.
30.   A.—Laugh When You Can; La Perouse* [La Perouse—
        Caldwell, Kariko—Drummond, Madame Perouse—
        Mrs. Russell, Umba—Mrs. Rowe].
31.   A.—Cure for the Heartache; The Day after the Wedding.

April

1. Saturday:
        A.—The Critic; Monsieur Tonson.
3. Monday:
        A.—Der Freischutz.
4.   A.—Sweethearts and Wives; La Perouse.
5.   A.—Virginius; Don Juan.
6.   A.—Geroge Barnwell; Frederick the Great* [Frederick—
        Caldwell, Theodore—Miss Placide, Augustus—Mrs.
        Rowe, Caroline—Mrs. Johns, Madame Phelps—Mrs.
        Russell].
7.   A.—The Talisman* [Kenneth the Leopard—Caldwell,
        Richard Coeur de Lion—Wilson, Saladin—Drummond,
        Queen Berengaria—Mrs. Rowe, Edith Plantagenant—
        Mrs. Johns]; Nature and Philosophy.
8.   A.—Robinson Crusoe* [Robinson Crusoe—Gray, Friday—
        Murray, Pariboo—Drummond, Inis—Mrs. Russell];
        Of Age Tomorrow.
10. Monday:
        A.—The Talisman.
11.   A.—Damon and Pythias; Turn Out.
12.   A.—Rule a Wife and Have a Wife; Wandering Boys.
13.   A.—Speed the Plough; Forty Thieves.
14.   A.—Merchant of Venice; Hamlet; Romeo and Juliet; Julius
        Caesar; Richard III (acts from each); Children in
        the Wood.
15.   A.—Lady and the Devil; The Talisman.

17. Monday:
    A.—King Charles II* [Charles—Wilson, Rochester—
    Drummond, Edward—Still, Captain Copp—Gray,
    Mary—Miss Placide]; Falls of Clyde.
18.   A.—Pizarro; Spectre Bridegroom.
19.   A.—Frederick the Great; Simpson and Company.
20.   A.—Wandering Boys; Der Freischutz.
22.   A.—King Charles II; Tom and Jerry Revived.
24. Monday:
    A.—Cherry and Fair Star* [Cherry—Miss Placide, San-
    guinbeck—Wilson, Hassanbad—Gray, Fair Star—
    Mrs. Rowe, Papillo—Mrs. Johns, Fairy Queen—Mrs.
    Russell]; The Weathercock.
25.   A.—The Liar.
26.   A.—Cherry and Fair Star.
27.   A.—Wedding Day; Cherry and Fair Star.
28.   A.—Raising the Wind; Cherry and Fair Star.
29.   A.—Catharine and Petruchio; Cherry and Fair Star.

May

1. Monday:
   A.—Spoiled Child; Cherry and Fair Star.
2.   A.—Soldier's Daughter; King Charles II.
3.   A.—Cure for the Heartache; Poor Soldier.
4.   A.—The Hypocrite; The Sleep Walker.
5.   A.—Brutus; Hunter of the Alps.
6.   A.—Day after the Wedding; Cherry and Fair Star.
8. Monday:
   A.—Cherry and Fair Star; Three and the Deuce.
9.   A.—Guy Mannering; The Romp.
10.   A.—The Will; Magpie and the Maid.
11.   A.—Honey Moon; The Purse.
12.   A.—Heir at Law; Lock and Key.
13.   A.—She Stoops to Conquer; Warlock of the Glen.
15. Monday:
    A.—Marmion; Don Giovanni.
16.   A.—Rob Roy; Irishman in London.
17.   A.—She Would be a Soldier; Is He Jealous?* [Mr. Bel-
    mour—Drummond, Mrs. Belmour—Miss Placide, Har
    riet—Mrs. Rowe, Rose—Mrs. Russell].
18.   A.—Sweethearts and Wives; Promissory Note.
19.   A.—Town and Country; Rendezvous.
20.   A.—Love in a Village; Tale of Mystery.
22. Monday:
    A.—Everyone Has His Faults; Turnpike Gate.
23.   A.—Pizarro; Is He Jealous?
24.   A.—Iron Chest; Spectre Bridegroom.
26.   A.—Speed the Plough; Sprigs of Laurel.
27.   A.—Point of Honor; Highland Reel.

29. Monday:
    A.—The Vampire; Cherry and Fair Star. Last night of the season.

February, 1827

2. Friday:
    A.—Paul Pry* [Sir Spangle Rainbow—Caldwell, Paul Pry—Russell, Crimp—Mrs. Russell, Laura—Mrs. Johns]; Of Age To-morrow; Spoiled Child.
3.   A.—Foundling of the Forest; Lock and Key.
5. Monday:
    A.—Paul Pry; Vampire.
6.   A.—Rob Roy; Boarding School*.
7.   A.—Belle's Stratagem; Benevolent Tar.
8.   A.—The Aethiop; Blue Devils.
9.   A.—Much Ado about Nothing; Rosina.
10.   A.—The Wonder; The Prize.
12. Monday:
    A.—Much Ado about Nothing; Rosina.
13.   A.—Exile of Siberia; Sprigs of Laurel.
14.   A.—School for Scandal; Turn Out.
15.   A.—Gamester; Paul Pry.
16.   A.—As You Like It; Tale of Mystery.
17.   A.—Honey Moon; Of Age To-morrow.
19. Monday:
    A.—The Stranger; Rendezvous.
20.   A.—Speed the Plough; Love Laughs at Locksmiths.
21.   A.—Wives as They Were; The Day after the Wedding.
22.   A.—Plains of Chippewa; Spectre Bridegroom.
23.   A.—She Stoops to Conquer; Turn Out.
24.   A.—Belle's Stratagem; Children in the Wood.
26. Monday:
    A.—Jealous Wife; Midnight Hour.
28.   A.—Wives as They Were; Rosina.

March

1. Thursday:
    A.—Thérèse; 'Tis All a Farce.
2.   A.—The Will; No Song, No Supper.
3.   A.—Guy Mannering; Paul Pry.
5. Monday:
    A.—Der Freischutz; Simpson and Company.
6.   A.—The Birthday; Turnpike Gate.
8.   A.—Venice Preserved; Devil to Pay.
9.   A.—Soldier's Daughter; No Song, No Supper.
10.   A.—Der Freischutz; Know Your Own Mind.
12. Monday:
    A.—She Stoops to Conquer; Three Weeks after Marriage.
13.   A.—Apostate; Spoiled Child.
16.   A.—Cherry and Fair Star; Hunter of the Alps.

19. Monday:
    A.—Sons of Erin; Cherry and Fair Star.
20.   A.—Rob Roy; The Romp.
21.   A.—Road to Ruin; Timour the Tartar.
22.   A.—Laugh When You Can.
23.   A.—Tekeli; Spoiled Child.
24.   A.—Timour the Tartar; Magpie and the Maid.
26. Monday:
    A.—Adelgitha; La Perouse.
27.   A.—Fish Out of Water* [Sam Savoury—Russell]; Cherry
        and Fair Star.
28.   A.—Macbeth; Fortune's Frolic.
29.   A.—Forty Thieves; Fish Out of Water.
30.   A.—Hamlet; American Tar.

April

2. Monday:
    A.—Virginius; Tom Thumb.
3.   A.—Pizarro; Fish Out of Water.
4.   A.—Damon and Pythias; Irishman in London.
5.   A.—Miller and His Men; Irish Widow* [Widow Brady—
        Mrs. Tatnall].
6.   A.—Venice Preserved; Forest of Rosenwald.
7.   A.—Richard III; Cherry and Fair Star.
10. Tuesday:
    A.—Tom and Jerry; Irish Widow.
11.   A.—Bertram; Lady and the Devil.
14.   A.—Gamester; Forest of Bondy.
16. Monday:
    A.—Virginius; Malvina* [Conlath—Caldwell, Morna—
        Mrs. Tatnall, Malvina—Miss Placide].
17.   A.—Damon and Pythias; Zembuca.
18.   A.—Othello; The Duel.
19.   A.—Malvina; Boarding House.
20.   A.—William Tell; Catharine and Petruchio.
23. Monday:
    A.—Honest Thieves; Timour the Tartar.
25.   A.—Monsieur Tonson; Timour the Tartar.
27.   A.—Dramatist; Blue Beard.
28.   A.—Blue Beard; Timour the Tartar.
30. Monday:
    A.—Cataract of the Ganges; The Review.

May

1. Tuesday:
    A.—Cataract of the Ganges; Mogul Tale* [Johnny Atkins
        —Russell, Fanny—Mrs. Russell].
4.   A.—Sweethearts and Wives; Forty Thieves.
5.   A.—Tekeli; Cataract of the Ganges.

7. Monday:
    A.—Timour the Tartar; Cataract of the Ganges.
8.   A.—Lodoiska; Spoiled Child.
10.   A.—Sweethearts and Wives; Mogul Tale.
11.   A.—Plains of Chippewa; Broken Sword* [Count Rigolio—
      Caldwell, Myrtillo—Tatnall].
12.   A.—Sweethearts and Wives; Valentine and Orson.

14. Monday:
    A.—Honey Moon; Lock and Key.
16.   A.—Three and the Deuce.
18.   A.—Broken Sword.
19.   A.—The Critic.

21. Monday:
    A.—Raising the Wind.
23.   A.—Town and Country; Turnpike Gate.
25.   A.—West Indian; Valentine and Orson.
26.   A.—Merry Days of Charles II; Broken Sword.

28. Monday:
    A.—Wild Oats; Highland Reel.
30.   A.—Soldier's Daughter; Children in the Wood.
31.   A.—Hypocrite; Irish Widow.

June

1. Friday:
    A.—Mountaineers; Of Age To-morrow.
2.   A.—Rivals; Rendezvous.
6. Wednesday:
    A.—Everyone Has His Faults; Agreeable Surprise.
8.   A.—Not at Home* [Celestial Calfcling—Caldwell, Dix-
      ory—Russell, Jessamine—Mrs. Russell]; Wood Dae-
      mon* [Levlyn—Mrs. Russell, Una—Mrs. Tatnall].
      Last night of the season.

December

21. Friday:
    A.—Man and Wife* [Charles Austencourt—Caldwell,
      Doctor Cornelius O'Dedimus — Crampton; Abel
      Growse — Anderson, Helen Worrett — Mrs. Rowe,
      Fanny—Mrs. Crampton]; X.Y.Z.* [Captain Gal-
      liard—L. Smith, Neddy Bray—Russell].
22.   A.—Rob Roy; Sweethearts and Wives.

24. Monday:
    A.—Montgomery; Lock and Key.
25.   A.—Bertram; X.Y.Z.
26.   A.—Douglas; Paul Pry.
27.   A.—Abaellino; Irish Tutor* [Jerry O'Rourke—Cramp-
      ton].

28.   A.—Marion; Family Jars* [Delph—S. Smith, Diggory—
       McCafferty, Lyddy—Mrs. S. Smith].
29.   A.—Chip of the Old Block* [Andrew—S. Smith, Chip—
       Russell, Rose—Mrs. Russell, Emma—Mrs. Rowe];
       Cherry and Fair Star.

January, 1828

1. Tuesday:
       A.—Glory of Columbia, Her Yeomanry; Irish Tutor.
2.   A.—Wood Daemon; Douglas.
3.   A.—Chip of the Old Block; Warlock of the Glen; Family
       Jars.
4.   A.—Way to Get Married; I n n Keeper's Daughter*
       [Richard—Caldwell, Mary—Mrs. Hartwig].
5.   A.—Cherry and Fair Star; Wood Daemon.
7. Monday:
       A.—John Bull; Love in Humble Life* [Ronstaus—Cramp-
       ton, Christine—Mrs. Russell].
8.   A.—Plains of Chippewa; Nature and Philosophy.
10.   A.—School for Scandal; No Song, No Supper.
11.   A.—Mountaineers; Raising the Wind.
12.   A.—Wanderer* [Sigismond—Caldwell, Countess Valdes-
       tein—Mrs. Hartwig]; Cherry and Fair Star.
14. Monday:
       A.—Richard III; Three Weeks after Marriage.
15.   A.—Castle Spectre; The Lying Valet.
16.   A.—Hamlet; The Liar.
17.   A.—The Birthday; Paul and Virginia.
18.   A.—New Way to Pay Old Debts; Day after the Wedding.
19.   A.—Othello; Irish Tutor.
21. Monday:
       A.—Distressed Mother* [Orestes—Booth, Hermione—
       Mrs. Hartwig, Andromache—Mrs. Rowe]; Three and
       the Deuce.
23.   A.—King Lear; Family Jars.
25.   A.—Town and Country; Matrimony.
26.   A.—New Way to Pay Old Debts; Inn Keeper's Daughter.
28. Monday:
       A.—Sylla* [Sylla—Booth, Claudius—Caldwell, Valeria—
       Mrs. Hartwig]; Of Age To-morrow.
30.   A.—Merchant of Venice; Mayor of Garratt.

February

1. Friday:
       A.—Iron Chest.
2.   A.—Richard III; The Review.
4. Monday:
       A.—Bertram; Catharine and Petruchio.
6.   A.—Brutus; Broken Sword.
8.   A.—Apostate; 'Tis All a Farce.

12. Tuesday:
    A.—Rob Roy; Chip of the Old Block.
13.   A.—Iron Chest; King Lear, third, fourth, and fifth acts; Simpson and Company.
14.   A.—Guy Mannering; Spoiled Child.
15.   A.—Love and Reason* [General Dorlon—Gray, Captain Albert—Lear, Mr. Dingle—Russell, Alice—Mrs. Rowe, Mrs. Dingle—Mrs. Russell]; Wandering Boys.
16.   A.—Exile of Siberia; Love and Reason.
18. Monday:
    A.—Irish Tutor; Bride of Abydos* [Selim—Caldwell, Giaffer—Anderson].
19.   A.—Romp; Bride of Abydos.
20.   A.—Family Jars; Bride of Abydos.
21.   A.—Fortune's Frolic; Bride of Abydos.
22.   A.—Battle of New Orleans; Snow Storm*.
23.   A.—School of Reform; Lock and Key.
25. Monday:
    A.—Love and Reason; Snow Storm.
26.   A.—Exile of Siberia; Fortune's Frolic.
27.   A.—Agreeable Surprise; Bride of Abydos.
28.   A.—Boarding House; Tom and Jerry.
29.   A.—Henry IV; Sleep Walker.

March

1. Saturday:
    A.—The Way to Get Married; Monsieur Tonson.
3.   A.—Devil to Pay; Woodman's Hut*.
4.   A.—Devil's Bridge; Maid and Magpie.
5.   A.—Poor Soldier; Woodman's Hut.
6.   A.—Falls of Clyde; Forty Thieves.
7.   A.—Turn Out; Woodman's Hut.
8.   A.—All the World's a Stage; Forest of Rosenwald; Paul Pry.
10. Monday:
    A.—Everyone Has His Faults; Sprigs of Laurel.
11.   A.—Cherry and Fair Star; All the World's a Stage.
13.   A.—Woodman's Hut.
14.   A.—El Hyder* [El Hyder—Lear, Abensellah—McCafferty, Harry Clinton—Mrs. Hartwig].
15.   A.—El Hyder.
17. Monday:
    A.—Jealous Wife; La Perouse.
18.   A.—El Hyder; Woodman's Hut.
19.   A.—Road to Ruin; All the World's a Stage.
20.   A.—Love and Reason; Love in Humble Life.
21.   A.—The Aethiop; High Life below Stairs.
22.   A.—Tom and Jerry; Woodman's Hut.

24. Monday:
    A.—West Indian; Highland Reel.
29.   A.—Timour the Tartar; Nature and Philosophy; Budget of Blunders.
31. Monday:
    A.—Comedy of Errors* [Antipholus of Ephesus—Lear, Dromio of Syracuse—Russell, Dromio of Ephesus—Gray]; Spoiled Child. Last night till Easter Monday.

April

7. Monday:
    A.—Belle's Stratagem; Winning a Husband*.
8.   A.—Honey Moon; Blue Devils.
9.   A.—Rule a Wife and Have a Wife; Animal Magnetism.
10.   A.—Dramatist; Winning a Husband.
12.   A.—Spoiled Child; Tom and Jerry; Tom Thumb.
14. Monday:
    A.—Soldier's Daughter; Blind Boy.
15.   A.—Paul Pry; The Purse.
16.   A.—Winning a Husband; Of Age To-morrow; Wandering Boys.
17.   A.—Honey Moon; Poor Soldier.
18.   A.—Speed the Plough; The Critic.
19.   A.—Hundred Pound Note* [Billy Black—Russell, Miss Arlington—Mrs. Rowe]. Last night of the season.

December

17. Wednesday:
    A.—Soldier's Daughter; Of Age To-morrow.
18.   A.—Honey Moon; No Song, No Supper.
19.   A.—Much Ado about Nothing; Poor Soldier.
20.   A.—Douglas; Spoiled Child.
22. Monday:
    A.—Town and Country; All on the Wing* [Tantalus Twist—Crooke].
23.   A.—Pizarro; Family Jars.
24.   A.—Guy Mannering; Rendezvous.
25.   A.—George Barnwell; Paul Pry.
26.   A.—Lovers' Vows; Fortune's Frolic.
27.   A.—Rob Roy; 'Twas I* [Delorme—Crooke, Georgette—Mrs. Russell].
29. Monday:
    A.—School for Scandal; 'Twas I.
30.   A.—Douglas; 'Twas I.
31.   A.—Adelgitha; Hunter of the Alps.

January, 1829

1. Thursday:
   A.—Lafayette; Hundred Pound Note.
2. A.—Hamlet.
3. A.—'Twas I; Gambler's Fate* [Albert Germaine—Crooke, Malcour—Barry, Julia—Mrs. Crooke].

5. Monday:
   A.—The Liar; Gambler's Fate.
6. A.—Hundred Pound Note; Gambler's Fate.
7. A.—Richard III; Lock and Key.
8. A.—Glory of Columbia, Her Yeomanry; Gambler's Fate.
9. A.—Hamlet; Young Widow.
10. A.—New Way to Pay Old Debts; Three Deep.

12. Monday:
    A.—Merchant of Venice; Poachers* [Count Elberfelt— Williams, Countess de Lisle—Mrs. Russell].
13. A.—West Indian; Poachers.
14. A.—Macbeth; Tom Thumb.
15. A.—Children in the Wood; Gambler's Fate.
16. A.—Stranger; All the World's a Stage.
17. A.—King Lear; 'Twas I.

19. Monday:
    A.—Othello; Sprigs of Laurel.
20. A.—Town and Country; Spoiled Child.
21. A.—Sweethearts and Wives; Day after the Fair*.
24. A.—Mountaineers; Raising the Wind.

26. Monday:
    A.—The Secret* [Mr. Dupuis—Still, Nalere—Pearson, Thomas—Holland, Cecile—Mrs. Russell, Angelica— Mrs. Kenny]; Turnpike Gate; Whims of a Comedian*.
27. A.—Haunted Tower* [Adela—Mrs. Knight]; Three and the Deuce.
28. A.—Whims of a Comedian; Hunter of the Alps; Deaf as a Post* [Tristram Sappy—Holland].
29. A.—Love in a Village; Catharine and Petruchio.
30. A.—Paul Pry* [Paul Pry—Holland, Colonel Hardy— Clarke, Phoebe—Mrs. Russell]; The Secret.
31. A.—She Stoops to Conquer; Deaf as a Post.

February

2. Monday:
   A.—Soldier's Daughter; Day after the Fair.
3. A.—Dramatist; No Song, No Supper.
4. A.—Whims of a Comedian; Paul Pry.
5. A.—Guy Mannering; Turn Out.
6. A.—The Will; Somnambulist* [Ernestine—Mrs. Rowe].
7. A.—Rob Roy; The Romp.

9. Monday:
   A.—Brother and Sister; Secret; Gretna Green* [Betty Finiken—Mrs. Knight].
10.   A.—Love and Reason; Somnambulist.
11.   A.—Brother and Sister; Rosina.
12.   A.—Fontainbleau; Tom and Jerry.
13.   A.—Frederick the Great; Somnambulist.
14.   A.—Laugh When You Can; Invincible* [Victoire—Mrs. Knight, Juliette—Mrs. Russell, Sophie—Mrs. Kenny, Elise—Mrs. Higgins, Victorim—Mrs. Carr, Therese—Mrs. LaCombe, Desire—Mrs. Rowe].
16. .Monday:
   A.—Rosina; Invincibles.
17.   A.—The Hypocrite; The Prize.
18.   A.—Paul and Virginia; Invincibles.
19.   A.—Richard III; The Prize.
20.   A.—Lord of the Manor* [Annette—Mrs. Knight]; Invincibles.
21.   A.—Iron Chest.
23. Monday:
   A.—Brutus; Wool Gathering* [Wander—Caldwell].
24.   A.—Love and Reason; Somnambulist.
25.   A.—Bertram; Wool Gathering.
26.   A.—Fortune's Frolic; Gambler's Fate.
27.   A.—Wool Gathering; Gambler's Fate.
28.   A.—Gambler's Fate; Agreeable Surprise.

March

2. Monday:
   A.—Virginius; Lock and Key.
3.   A.—Distressed Mother; Mayor of Garratt.
4.   A.—Damon and Pythias; Invincibles.
5.   A.—Isabella; Fish Out of Water.
6.   A.—Othello; Turnpike Gate.
7.   A.—Stranger; Family Jars.
9. Monday:
   A.—Venice Preserved.
10.   A. Foundling of the Forest—Deaf as a Post.
11.   A.—The Wonder; Animal Magnetism.
12.   A.—Pizarro; Haunted Inn*.
13.   A.—The Critic; Invincibles.
14.   A.—Othello; Blue Devils.
18. Wednesday:
   A.—Jane Shore; Catharine and Petruchio.
19.   A.—Macbeth; Rendezvous.
20.   A.—School for Scandal; Lottery Ticket.
21.   A.—Jealous Wife; Lottery Ticket.

23. Monday:
    A.—Wives as They Were; Modern Antiques.
24. A.—Provoked Husband; Old and Young*; [Four Mowbrays
    —Miss Russell].
25. A.—Jane Shore; Intrigue.
26. A.—Douglas; Wool Gathering.
27. A.—Gamester; Gambler's Fate.
28. A.—Romeo and Juliet; Actress of All Work*.
30. Monday:
    A.—Julius Caesar; Twelve Precisely*.
31. A.—Heir at Law; Old and Young.

April

1. Wednesday:
   A.—The Rivals; Sergeant's Wife* [Lisette—Mrs. Sloman,
   Rubin—Sloman].
2. A.—Actress of All Work; Paris and London* [Frizac—
   Caldwell, Lord Volatile—Pearson].
3. A.—Spoiled Child; Paris and London.
4. A.—Evadne* [Evadne—Mrs. Sloman, Ludovico—Booth];
   Intrigue.
6. Monday:
   A.—Modern Antiques; Paris and London.
7. A.—Thérèse; Richard III, fourth and fifth acts; Twelve
   Precisely.
9. A.—Village Lawyer; Paris and London.
10. A.—Damon and Pythias; Children in the Wood.
11. A.—Thérèse; Haunted Inn.
13. Monday:
    A.—Virginius; Day after the Wedding.
14. A.—Iron Chest; Paris and London.
15. A.—Othello; Matrimony.
16. A.—Stranger; Blue Devils.
18. A.—William Tell; Touch and Take*.
20. Monday:
    A.—King Lear; Touch and Take.
21. A.—Sergeant's Wife; Touch and Take.
22. A.—William Tell; Hunter of the Alps.
23. A.—Much Ado about Nothing; Highland Reel.
24. A.—Brutus; High Life below Stairs.
25. A.—Paris and London; Broken Sword.
27. Monday:
    A.—Pizarro; Touch and Take.
28. A.—Magpie and the Maid; Dumb Girl of Genoa* [Julietta
    —Celeste].
29. A.—Hamlet; Half an Hour's Courtship* [Duke de Riche-
    lieu—Caldwell, Madame de Guise—Mrs. Rowe].
30. A.—Half an Hour's Courtship; Dumb Girl of Genoa.

May

1. Friday:
   A.—Venice Preserved; Half an Hour's Courtship.
2.   A.—Deaf and Dumb*; Broken Sword.
4. Monday:
   A.—Richard III; The Purse.
5.   A.—Gambler's Fate.
6.   A.—Rienzi* [Rienzi—Edwin Forrest]; Wandering Boys.
7.   A.—Deaf and Dumb.
8.   A.—Damon and Pythias; Raising the Wind.
9.   A.—Bertram; Valentine and Orson.
11. Monday:
    A.—School of Reform; Lovers' Quarrels.
12.   A.—Wheel of Fortune; Broken Sword.
13.   A.—Winning a Husband; Of Age To-morrow.
14.   A.—Dumb Girl of Genoa; Valentine and Orson.
15.   A.—The Spy* [Harvey Birch—Caldwell, Henry Wharton
    —Pearson, Frances Wharton—Mrs. Rowe, B e t t y
    Flanagan—Mrs. Russell]; Monsieur Tonson.
16.   A.—She Stoops to Conquer; Is It a Lie?* [Chatterton—
    Caldwell].
18. Monday:
    A.—School for Scandal; Tom and Jerry.
19.   A.—Belle's Stratagem; Falls of Clyde.
22.   A.—West Indian; Is It a Lie? Last night of the season.

December

9. Wednesday:
   A.—Luke the Labourer* [Squire Chase—Gilbert]; School
   of Reform; Hundred Pound Note.
10.   A.—Speed the Plough; The Romp.
11.   A.—Clari* [Clari—Miss Placide]; Invincibles.
12.   A.—Charles XII*; Luke the Labourer.
14. Monday:
    A.—Ambrose Gwinette* [Ambrose Gwinette—Pearson];
    Warlock of the Glen.
16.   A.—Guy Mannering; The Lancers*.
17.   A.—Paul Pry; Clari.
18.   A.—Rob Roy; Actress of All Work.
19.   A.—Devil's Bridge; Young Widow.
21. Monday:
    A.—Virginius; Spoiled Child.
22.   A.—Brother and Sister; Rosina.
24.   A.—Love in a Village; Young Widow.
25.   A.—George Barnwell; Gambler's Fate.
28. Monday:
    A.—Macbeth; Actress of All Work.
29.   A.—Sweethearts and Wives; Poor Soldier.
30.   A.—Revenge; Love in Wrinkles*.
31.   A.—John of Paris; Paris and London.

January, 1830

1. Friday:
   A.—George Barnwell; Of Age To-morrow.
2. A.—Blue Beard; John of Paris.
4. Monday:
   A.—William Tell; Turnpike Gate.
5. A.—Paul Pry; Lock and Key.
6. A.—Belle's Stratagem; Husbands and Wives*.
7. A.—The Cabinet* [Prince Orlando—Howard, Floretta— Miss Kelly, Whimsicolo—Cowell]; Turnpike Gate.
8. A.—Eighth of January*; Much Ado about Nothing.
9. A.—Tom and Jerry.
11. Monday:
    A.—Damon and Pythias.
12. A.—The Hypocrite; Agreeable Surprise.
13. A.—The Stranger; Turnpike Gate.
14. A.—Ambrose Gwinette; Agreeable Surprise.
15. A.—Merchant of Venice; The Hotel.
16. A.—May Queen* [Caleb Pipkin—Cowell]; Chip of the Old Block.
19. Tuesday:
    A.—Thérèse; Turn Out.
20. A.—Fatal Dowry* [Romont—Hamblin]; Husbands and Wives.
21. A.—West Indian; Chip of the Old Block.
22. A.—Virginius; Poor Soldier.
23. A.—Richard III; The Review.
25. Monday:
    A.—Belle's Stratagem; Spoiled Child.
26. A.—Black Eyed Susan* [Blue Peter—Howard]; Devil to Pay.
27. A.—The Will; Four Mowbrays.
28. A.—Black Eyed Susan; Brother and Sister.
29. A.—Much Ado About Nothing; Actress of All Work.
30. A.—She Would and She Would Not* [Hypolita—Clara Fisher]; Invincibles.

February

1. Monday:
   A.—School for Scandal; Dead Shot* [Mr. Timid—Cowell, Louisa—Clara Fisher].
2. A.—Black Eyed Susan; May Queen; Paul and Virginia.
3. A.—Man and Wife; Dead Shot.
4. A.—Hypocrite; Dolly and the Rat.
5. A.—Lovers' Vows; Youth, Love and Folly* [Arinette— Clara Fisher].
6. A.—Country Girl* [Miss Peggy—Clara Fisher]; Wandering Boys.

8. Monday:
   A.—Wives as They Were; Actress of All Work.
9.   A.—The Hypocrite; Maid or Wife*.
10.   A.—Romeo and Juliet; Tom Thumb.
11.   A.—Adrian and Orilla* [Madame Clermont—Miss Placide]; Maid or Wife.
12.   A.—Clari; Youth, Love and Folly.
13.   A.—As You Like It; Highland Reel.
15. Monday:
    A.—The Wonder.
16.   A.—Guy Mannering; How to Die for Love.
17.   A.—Spoiled Child; Turnpike Gate; Dead Shot.
18.   A.—School for Scandal; How to Die for Love.
19.   A.—Birthday; Maid or Wife.
20.   A.—Fish Out of Water; Lottery Ticket.
23. Tuesday:
    A.—Honey Moon; Falls of Clyde.
24.   A.—Town and Country; Black Eyed Susan.
25.   A.—She Would Be a Soldier; My Master's Rival.*
26.   A.—Ambrose Gwinette; My Master's Rival.
27.   A.—Foundling of the Forest; Broken Sword.

March

1. Monday:
   A.—Rule a Wife and Have a Wife; Blue Devils.
2.   A.—Maid and Magpie; Haunted Inn.
3.   A.—Barber of Seville; Of Age To-morrow.
5.   A.—Cure for the Heartache; Lancers.
6.   A.—Mountaineers; Osman and Arsana*.
8. Monday:
   A.—The Cabinet; The Prize.
9.   A.—Raising the Wind; All the World's a Stage.
10.   A.—Rob Roy; Village Lawyer.
11.   A.—The Way to Get Married; Osman and Arsana.
12.   A.—Love in a Village; Hunter of the Alps.
13.   A.—Wandering Boys; Jocko*; Chip of the Old Block.
15. Monday:
    A.—The Libertine* [Masetto—Howard, Zerlina—Madame Feron]; May Queen.
16.   A.—Comedy of Errors; The Day after the Wedding; Honest Thieves.
17.   A.—John of Paris; Poor Soldier; St. Patrick's Day.
18.   A.—Lear of Private Life*; Paul Pry at Dover*.
19.   A.—Rob Roy; The Libertine.
20.   A.—Comedy of Errors; Twelve Precisely; The Review.
22. Monday:
    A.—Marriage of Figaro* [Susannah—Madame Feron]; Three Weeks After Marriage; Napoleon*.
23.   A.—Lear of Private Life; Monsieur Tonson.

24.   A.—The Sultan; Napoleon; No Song, No Supper.
25.   A.—Road to Ruin; Simpson and Company.
26.   A.—Young Hussar* [Carolina—Madame Feron]; The Liar; Gretna Green.
27.   A.—Marriage of Figaro; Father and Daughter.
29. Monday:
    A.—Young Hussar; Seven's the Main; Rosina.
30.   A.—Lady of the Lake; Tekeli.
31.   A.—The Exile; Gretna Green.

April

1. Thursday:
    A.—Folly as It Flies; Promissory Note.
2.   A.—Broken Sword; Haunted Inn.
3.   A.—Castle of Andalusia*; Of Age To-morrow.
5. Monday:
    A.—Miller and His Men; How to Die for Love.
6.   A.—Irma** [Remington—Caldwell, Irma—Miss Placide, Willoughby—Gilbert, Harold—Field, Ashton—Pearson, Hinda—Mrs. McClure, Clara—Miss Clarke, Ruth—Mrs. Carr]; Hundred Pound Note. Last night until Easter Monday.
12. Monday:
    A.—Irma; Children in the Wood.
13.   A.—Lady of the Lake; Valentine and Orson.
14.   A.—Antonio Cirenza; Miller and His Men.
15.   A.—Irma; Lovers' Quarrels.
16.   A.—Black Eyed Susan; Touch and Take.
17.   A.—Masaniello* [Fenella—Celeste, Masaniello—Pearson].
19. Monday:
    A.—Masaniello; Lear of Private Life.
20.   A.—Irma; Married Yesterday.
21.   A.—Paul and Virginia; Masaniello.
22.   A.—Nature and Philosophy; Masaniello.
23.   A.—Masaniello; Lady and the Devil.
24.   A.—Paul and Peter Shack; Masaniello, last act.
26. Monday:
    A.—Last of the Mohicans* [Magua—Pearson, Hawkeye—Gray, Cora—Mrs. Rowe]; Three and the Deuce.
27.   A.—Last of the Mohicans.
28.   A.—The Jew* [Sheva—Russell, Jabel—Master Russell].
29.   A.—Last of the Mohicans; Paul and Peter Shack.
30.   A.—Last of the Mohicans; Masaniello; Jonathan Postfree* [Jonathan—Gray].

May

1. Saturday:
    A.—Caliph of Bagdad; Masaniello.
3. Monday:
    A.—She Would be a Soldier; Ladies at Home*.

4.   A.—Love and Reason; Honest Yankee.
5.   A.—Pizarro; The Liar.
6.   A.—Husbands and Wives; Highland Reel.
7.   A.—Last of the Mohicans; Brother and Sister.
8.   A.—Speed the Plough; Sea Serpent* [Oceanus—Miss M. E.
        Clarke]; 102*.
10. Monday:
        A.—Soldier's Daughter; Alonzo the Brave and the Fair
        Imogine* [Marcella—Miss Placide].
12.   A.—She Stoops to Conquer; The Disguises*.
13.   A.—102; Alonzo the Brave and the Fair Imogine.
14.   A.—Sea Serpent; Alonzo the Brave and the Fair Imogine.
15.   A.—William Tell; The Day after the Wedding.
17. Monday:
        A.—Green Eyed Monster* [Baron Speyenhausen—Clarke,
        Lady Speyenhausen—Mrs. Rowe, Amelia Rosenthal—
        Mrs. McClure]; Sea Serpent; 102.
18.   A.—Honey Moon; Benevolent Tar.
19.   A.—El Hyder; Is He Jealous?
20.   A.—Green Eyed Monster; American Tar.
21.   A.—The Jew.
22.   A.—Bold Stroke for a Wife; Brian Boroihme*.
        Last night of the season.

December

15. Wednesday:
        A.—Much Ado about Nothing; Two Gregories*.
16.   A.—Paul Pry; Day after the Fair.
17.   A.—The Wonder; A Roland for an Oliver*.
18.   A.—Sweethearts and Wives; The Secret.
20. Monday:
        A.—School for Scandal; Turnpike Gate.
21.   A.—Of Age To-morrow; Whims of a Comedian; Chip of
        the Old Block.
22.   A.—William Tell; The Bath Road.
23.   A.—She Stoops to Conquer; Promissory Note.
24.   A.—The Robbers; Honest Thieves.
25.   A.—George Barnwell; Bombastes Furioso.
27. Monday:
        A.—Damon and Pythias; Haunted Inn.
28.   A.—Foundling of the Forest; Deaf as a Post.
29.   A.—Othello; Rendezvous.
30.   A.—Town and Country; Day After the Fair.
31.   A.—Virginius; May Queen.

January, 1831

1. Saturday:
        A.—Pizarro; Whims of a Comedian.
3. Monday:
        A.—Hamlet; Irish Tutor.

4.   A.—Rienzi.
5.   A.—Henry IV; Deaf as a Post.
6.   A.—Brutus; The Romp.
7.   A.—Gamester; Gambler's Fate.
8.   A.—Wine Does Wonders; Bold Dragoons*.
10. Monday:
    A.—Jane Shore; Turnpike Gate.
11.   A.—Honey Moon; Day After the Fair.
12.   A.—Julius Caesar, second and third acts; Merchant of Venice, fourth act; Bold Dragoons.
13.   A.—Paul Pry; Masaniello.
14.   A.—Venice Preserved; We Fly by Night* [Gaby Grim—Holland, Ferret—Cowell].
15.   A.—Henry IV; Masaniello.
17. Monday:
    A.—Henry VIII* [Cardinal Wolsey—Cooper, Henry VIII—Scott, Duke of Buckingham—Raymond, Cromwell—Ludlow, Queen Catharine—Miss Placide, Anne Bullen—Mrs. Rowe]; Two Gregories.
18.   A.—Honest Thieves; Falls of Clyde.
19.   A.—Much Ado About Nothing; Actress of All Work.
20.   A.—Frederick the Great; Whims of a Comedian; Cherry Bounce* [Gregory—Holland].
21.   A.—The Will; Four Mowbrays.
22.   A.—John Bull; Cherry Bounce.
24. Monday:
    A.—She Would and She Would Not; Spoiled Child.
25.   A.—Poor Gentleman; Alonzo the Brave and the Fair Imogine.
26.   A.—Wives as They Were; Perfection* [Charles Paragon—Caldwell, Kate O'Brien—Clara Fisher].
27.   A.—Chip of the Old Block; Whims of a Comedian.
28.   A.—School for Scandal; Miller's Maid* [Phoebe—Clara Fisher].
29.   A.—Paul Jones* [Long Tom Coffin—Scott]; The Bath Road.
31. Monday:
    A.—Belle's Stratagem; Perfection.

February

1. Tuesday:
    A.—Paul Jones; Day After the Fair.
2.   A.—As You Like It; Perfection.
3.   A.—Paul Jones; Rendezvous.
4.   A.—Invincibles; Youth, Love and Folly; Dead Shot.
5.   A.—Miantonimoh* [Metacom—Author of the Play]; Cherry Bounce.
7. Monday:
    A.—Lovers' Vows; Hundred Pound Note.

8.   A.—Miantonimoh; Paul Jones.
9.   A.—All in the Wrong* [Sir John Restless—Caldwell, Lady
       Restless—Clara Fisher].
10.   A.—School of Reform; Hamlet Travestie* [Hamlet—
       Young Cowell, Ophelia—Holland].
11.   A.—Clari; Husband at Sight* [Catherine—Clara Fisher];
       Is He Jealous?
12.   A.—The Avenger* [Avenger—Scott, Stella—Miss Pla-
       cide]; Paul Jones.
15. Tuesday:
       A.—Irma; Lock and Key.
16.   A.—Romeo and Juliet.
17.   A.—The Miller's Maid; Gretna Green; Perfection.
18.   A.—Devil's Bridge; Winning a Husband.
19.   A.—Love in a Village; Turn Out.
21. Monday:
       A.—Rob Roy; Of Age To-morrow.
22.   A.—The Avenger; Lock and Key.
23.   A.—The Cabinet; Scape Grace* [Charles Darlington—
       (Mrs.) C. Plumer].
24.   A.—Lady of the Lake; The Hotel.
25.   A.—The Soldier's Daughter; Rosina.
26.   A.—The Smoked Miser*; Paul Jones.
28. Monday:
       A.—Richard III; Lottery Ticket.

March

1. Tuesday:
       A.—Belle's Stratagem; Brother and Sister.
2.   A.—New Way to Pay Old Debts; Chip of the Old Block.
3.   A.—School for Scandal; Poor Soldier.
4.   A.—Merchant of Venice; Turnpike Gate.
5.   A.—Rob Roy; Hundred Pound Note.
7. Monday:
       A.—Iron Chest; Lady of the Lake.
8.   A.—Guy Mannering; Clari.
9.   A.—New Way to Pay Old Debts; Lady and the Devil.
10.   A.—Honey Moon; Paul Jones.
11.   A.—Town and Country; 'Twas I.
12.   A.—Rencontre*; Giovanni in London* [Don Giovanni—
       Mrs. C. Plumer].
14. Monday:
       A.—The Stranger; Raising the Wind.
15.   A.—Last of the Mohicans; Lottery Ticket.
17.   A.—Rencontre; St. Patrick's Day; Poor Soldier.
18.   A.—Brutus; Hunter of the Alps.
19.   A.—Giovanni in London; Last of the Mohicans.

21. Monday:
   A.—Marriage of Figaro; Love and Mercy.
22.   A.—Othello; Lady and the Devil.
23.   A.—All in the Wrong; Dead Shot.
24.   A.—Rake Hellies* [Ralph—Raymond, Major Lincoln—Field, Nat—Miss Placide]; Hotel.
25.   A.—Town and Country; Perfection.
26.   A.—Revenge; Rake Hellies.
28. Monday:
   A.—Love and Reason; Wandering Boys; Husband at Sight.
29.   A.—Pizarro; Agreeable Surprise.
30.   A.—The Rivals; Simpson and Company.
31.   A.—Venice Preserved; Pop! Sparrow Shooting* [Old Fizzlegig—Gray, Old Quizley—Anderson, Hoaxley—Field, Miss Dolly Fizzlegig—Mrs. Gray, Miss Fizzlegig—Miss Voss].

April

2. Saturday:
   A.—Man and Wife; Highland Reel.
4. Monday:
   A.—Wine Does Wonders; Thérèse.
5.   A.—The Brigand* [Allessandro Massaroni—Caldwell, Maria—Miss Placide]; Lovers' Quarrels.
7.   A.—The Wonder; Actress of All Work.
8.   A.—Husband at Sight; Gretna Green; The Day after the Wedding.
9.   A.—The Brigand; Bombastes Furioso.
11. Monday:
   A.—Twelfth Night* [Duke Orsino—Raymond, Sir Toby Belch—Page, Sir Andrew Aguecheek—Gray, Viola—Clara Fisher, Olivia—Mrs. Rowe]; Hundred Pound Note.
12.   A.—The Brigand; Chip of the Old Block. Theatre closed until April 16.
16.   A.—The Brigand; Teddy the Tiler*.
18. Monday:
   A.—Romeo and Juliet; Teddy the Tiler.
19.   A.—Rencontre; Poor Soldier.
20.   A.—Point of Honor; Highland Reel.
21.   A.—Marriage of Figaro; Love and Mercy.
22.   A.—Iron Chest; Four Mowbrays.
23.   A.—Barber of Seville; The Brigand.
25. Monday:
   A.—Hamlet; Pop! Sparrow Shooting.
26.   A.—Beggar's Opera* [Captain Macheath—C. Plumer, Polly—Mrs. C. Plumer]; Fortune's Frolic.

27.   A.—Town and Country; Thérèse.
28.   A.—The Cabinet; Love à la Mode.
29.   A.—Honey Moon; Actress of all Work.
30.   A.—Heir at Law; Peasant Boy* [Julian—Mrs. C. Plumer, Hypolito—C. Plumer, Ludovico—Cowell, Fabian—Gray].

May

2.   Monday:
      A.—Romeo and Juliet; Winning a Husband.
3.   A.—Beggar's Opera; Brigand.
4.   A.—New Way to Pay Old Debts; Warlock of the Glen.
5.   A.—Peasant Boy; No Song, No Supper.
6.   A.—Happiest Day of My Life* [Mr. Gilman—Cowell, Sophia—Mrs. Cowell]; Perfection; Rip Van Winkle* [Rip—Cowell, Alice—Mrs. Cowell].
7.   A.—Rob Roy; Rosina.
9.   Monday:
      A.—Henri Quatre; The Critic.
10.   A.—Happiest Day of My Life; Rip Van Winkle.
11.   A.—Wheel of Fortune; Paul and Virginia.
12.   A.—Henri Quatre; No Song, No Supper.
13.   A.—John of Paris; Brother and Sister; Tale of Mystery.
14.   A.—Barber of Seville; Raising the Wind.
16.   Monday:
      A.—Wild Oats; Maid or Wife.
17.   A.—Marriage of Figaro; Maid or Wife.
18.   A.—Road to Ruin; Winning a Husband.
19.   A.—The Gambler's Fate; Elbow Shakers*.
20.   A.—Guy Mannering; Effect of Endorsing.
21.   A.—John of Paris; Of Age To-morrow.
24.   Tuesday:
      A.—Catharine and Petruchio; The Tragedians** [George Clifford, Mons. Jean Jacques Claude Jose Marie Phillippi Alexander Charlemagne D'Argenta, and Michael Murphy—Rawlinson, Jumble—Hernizen, Sam Fry—Page, Thompson—Anderson]; Forty Thieves.
25.   A.—Bohemian Mother* [Count Manheim—Raymond, Matilde — Miss Placide]; Aladdin* [Aladdin — Miss Placide].
26.   A.—Speed the Plough; Monsieur Tonson.
27.   A.—Cure for the Heartache; Aladdin.
28.   A.—Bohemian Mother; Three and the Deuce.
30.   Monday:
      A.—West Indian; Highland Widow** [Elspat M'Tavish—Miss Placide]. Last night of the season.

November

23. Wednesday:
    A.—Wild Oats; No Song, No Supper.
24. A.—Paul Pry; Maid or Wife.
25. A.—Pizarro; Dead Shot.
26. A.—Perfection; The Brigand.
28. Monday:
    A.—Cure for the Heartache; True Use of Riches.
29. A.—Gambler's Fate; Popping the Question* [Mr. Primrose—Cowell, Bobbin—Mrs. Cowell].
30. A.—Snakes in the Grass* [Mr. Janus—Cowell, Mrs. Janus—Mrs. Cowell]; Thérèse.

December

2. Friday:
   A.—William Tell; Chip of the Old Block.
3. A.—Drunkard's Fate* [Vernon—Field, Granville—Raymond, Alicia—Miss Placide]; Snakes in the Grass.
5. Monday:
   A.—Speed the Plough; Animal Magnetism.
6. A.—Lear of Private Life; Popping the Question.
7. A.—Soldier's Daughter; Ways and Means.
8. A.—Drunkard's Fate; Bombastes Furioso.
9. A.—Poor Gentleman; Monsieur Tonson.
10. A.—Aladdin; Bold Dragoons.
12. Monday:
    A.—John Bull; Turn Out.
13. A.—Courier of Naples* [Ferdinand—Field, Sanelza—Raymond, Georgetta—Miss Petrie]; Popping the Question.
14. A.—Town and Country; Lock and Key.
15. A.—Bohemian Mother; The Jew and the Doctor*.
16. A.—Laugh When You Can; Courier of Naples.
17. A.—Brigand; Aladdin.
19. Monday:
    A.—School for Scandal; Hurrah for the Boys of the West*.
20. A.—Will Watch* [Will Watch—Raymond, Mary—Miss Placide]; Review.
21. A.—Melmoth* [Melmoth—Muzzy, Popo—Cowell, Immalee—Miss Placide]; Happiest Day of My Life.
22. A.—The Rivals; The Hotel.
23. A.—Marion; Bold Dragoons.
24. A.—The Will; Poor Soldier.
25. Sunday:
    A.—George Barnwell; Gambler's Fate.
26. A.—Rob Roy; Will Watch.
27. A.—School for Scandal; Courier of Naples.

28.   A.—Two Gentlemen of Verona** [Proteus—Raymond,
       Thurio—Field, Launce—Cowell, Julia—Mrs. Rowe,
       Sylvia—Mrs. Cowell, Lucetta—Miss Petrie] ; Happiest
       Day of My Life.
29.   A.—The Rivals; Ambrose Gwinette.
30.   A.—Melmoth; Hunter of the Alps.
31.   A.—Way to Get Married; Wedding Day; The Day after
       the Wedding.

January, 1832

1. Sunday:
       A.—She Would be a Soldier; Miller's Maid.
2.   A.—George Barnwell; Gambler's Fate.
4.   A.—Cherry and Fair Star.
5.   A.—Much Ado about Nothing; Cherry and Fair Star.
6.   A.—Paul and Peter Shack; Cherry and Fair Star.
7.   A.—Snakes in the Grass; Husband at Sight; Popping the
       Question.
8. Sunday:
       A.—Glory of Columbia; Dead Shot.
9.   A.—William Thompson* [Wm. Thompson—Cowell, Wm.
       Thompson—Field] ; Cherry and Fair Star.
10.   A.—Drunkard's Fate; Wine Does Wonders.
11.   A.—Perfection; Paul Jones.
12.   A.—The Liar; Paul Jones.
13.   A.—Town and Country; High Ways and By Ways*.
14.   A.—Tom and Jerry; Highland Widow.
16. Monday:
       A.—Cradle of Liberty* [Capt. Noodle—Caldwell, Mike
       Mainsail—Raymond, Seth Page—Gray, Cecile—Mrs.
       Rowe, Nat—Miss Placide] ; Effects of Endorsing.
20.   A.—Rob Roy; Hundred Pound Note.
21.   A.—Cradle of Liberty; Wm. Thompson.
23. Monday:
       A.—Married and Single* [Beaux Shatterly—Finn] ; Prize.
24.   A.—New Way to Pay Old Debts; Teddy the Tiler.
25.   A.—Legion of Honor; The Hypocrite.
26.   A.—William Tell; Husband at Sight.
27.   A.—School for Scandal; Sleep Walker.
28.   A.—Sweethearts and Wives; Falls of Clyde.
30. Monday:
       A.—Poor Gentleman; Hundred Pound Note.
31.   A.—Macbeth; Green Eyed Monster.

February

1. Wednesday:
       A.—Clandestine Marriage* [Lord Oglesby—Finn] ; Prize.
2.   A.—Damon and Pythias; Spectre Bridegroom.
3.   A.—Married and Single; Cherry and Fair Star.
4.   A.—Hamlet; Gretna Green.

6. Monday:
   A.—102; The Hypocrite.
7. A.—Richard III; Bombastes Furioso.
8. A.—Heir at Law; Tom and Jerry.
9. A.—Much Ado about Nothing; Lottery Ticket.
10. A.—She Stoops to Conquer; Paul and Peter Shack.
11. A.—Romeo and Juliet; Rendezvous.
13. Monday:
   A.—Iron Chest; Of Age To-morrow.
14. A.—Hamlet; Two Thompsons.
15. A.—Wild Oats; Killing No Murder* [Buskin—Finn].
17. A.—Richard III; Rendezvous.
18. A.—Macbeth; Legion of Honor.
20. Monday:
   A.—Romeo and Juliet; Catharine and Petruchio.
21. A.—May Queen; Brigand.
22. A.—Last of the Mohicans; Raising the Wind.
23. A.—Joan of Arc* [Joan of Arc—Miss Placide].
24. A.—Douglas; Irish Tutor.
25. A.—Speed the Plough; The Review.
27. Monday:
   A.—Merchant of Venice; Whirligig Hall.
28. A.—Douglas; Irish Tutor.
29. A.—Heir at Law; Whirligig Hall.

March

1. Thursday:
   A.—Richard III; Irishman in London.
2. A.—Poor Gentleman; High Life below Stairs.
3. A.—Romeo and Juliet; Agreeable Surprise.
5. Monday:
   A.—John Bull; March of Intellect* [All characters—
   Master Burke].
6. A.—Richard III; The Weathercock.
7. A.—West Indian; March of Intellect.
8. A.—Paul Pry; The Review.
9. A.—Hamlet; Death's Head*; March of Intellect.
10. A.—Poor Soldier; Irish Tutor; High Life below Stairs.
12. Monday:
   A.—Young Napoleon, Duke of Reichstadt*; The Prize.
13. A.—John Bull; Bombastes Furioso.
14. A.—Speed the Plough; March of Intellect.
15. A.—Hamlet, first and third acts; Turnpike Gate.
16. A.—Man and Wife; Devil to Pay.
17. A.—March of Intellect; St. Patrick's Day; Barney Brallaghan* [Barney Brallaghan—Master Burke].
19. Monday:
   A.—Lion of the West* [Col. Wildfire—James Hackett];
   Lady and the Devil.
20. A.—Lion of the West; Popping the Question.

21.   A.—Jonathan in England* [Solomon Swap—Hackett];
      Lock and Key.
22.   A.—Rip Van Winkle; Down East, scene* [Major Joe
      Bunker—Hackett]; Monsieur Tonson.
23.   A.—Jonathan in England; Sylvester Daggerwood; Married
      Yesterday.
24.   A.—The Times* [Industrious Doolittle—Hackett]; Mon-
      sieur Tonson.

26. Monday:
      A.—Rip Van Winkle; Down East, scene; Lion of the West.
27.   A.—Poor Gentleman; Raising the Wind.
28.   A.—Virginius; Fortune's Frolic.
29.   A.—Rule a Wife and Have a Wife; Two Thompsons.
30.   A.—Hamlet; Whims of a Comedian.
31.   A.—Snakes in the Grass; Perfection; Turnpike Gate.

April

2. Monday:
      A.—Bertram; The Secret.
3.   A.—Sweethearts and Wives; Joan of Arc.
4.   A.—Damon and Pythias; Joan of Arc.
5.   A.—Gamester; Day after the Fair.
6.   A.—Henry IV; Whims of a Comedian.
7.   A.—Joan of Arc; Honest Thieves.

9. Monday:
      A.—Damon and Pythias; School for Scandal, a detached
      portion; Two Gregories.
10.   A.—Joan of Arc; Day after the Fair.
11.   A.—The Critic; P. S. Come to Dinner* [Peter Pickwell—
      Holland]; The Secret.
12.   A.—Merchant of Venice; March of Intellect.
13.   A.—John Bull; Irish Tutor.
14.   A.—Agreeable Surprise; Irishman in London; The Re-
      view.

16. Monday:
      A.—Hamlet, third act; Richard III, fifth act; Love à la
      Mode.
17.   A.—Man and Wife; March of Intellect.

23. Monday:
      A.—Rochester* [Rochester—Cowell, Countess of Love-
      laugh—Mrs. Cowell]; 33 John Street* [Mr. Thomas
      Tomkins—Cowell, Lady Crazy—Mrs. Cowell].
24.   A.—Joan of Arc; Three and the Deuce.
25.   A.—Lear; Fortune's Frolic.
26.   A.—Charles the Terrible* [Charles—Houpt, Leontine—
      Mrs. Rowe]; The Day After the Wedding.

27.   A.—Macbeth; First of April* [Sir P. Pedigree—Page,
       Mrs. Belford—Mrs. Muzzy].
28.   A.—Laugh When You Can; Zembuca.
30. Monday:
       A.—The Revenge; Two Gregories.

May

1. Tuesday:
       A.—Charles the Terrible; First of April.
2.   A.—Lear; A Roland for an Oliver.
3.   A.—The Aethiop; Rendezvous.
4.   A.—Virginius; Animal Magnetism.
5.   A.—Management* [Mist, the Manager—Gray, Juliana—
       Mrs. Rowe]; Mischief Making* [Annette — Mrs.
       Rowe].
7. Monday:
       A.—Werner* [Werner—Barton]; Mischief Making.
8.   A.—Provoked Husband; Thérèse.
10.   A.—Pizarro; Mischief Making.
11.   A.—Jealous Wife; The Romp.
12.   A.—Venice Preserved; The Roman Actor, sketch* [Paris—
       Barton]; Catharine and Petruchio.
14. Monday:
       A.—Innkeeper's Daughter; Haunted Inn.
15.   A.—Werner.
16.   A.—Belle's Stratagem; Three Weeks after Marriage.
17.   A.—Honey Moon; Cherry and Fair Star.
18.   A.—Rob Roy; Irishman in London.
19.   A.—Maurice the Wood Cutter*; Dramatist. Last night of
       the season.

November

21. Wednesday:
       A.—Soldier's Daughter; Victorine* [Victorine — Miss
       Placide].
22.   A.—William Tell; American Tar.
23.   A.—Foundling of the Forest; Adopted Child.
24.   A.—Venice Preserved; The Review.
26. Monday:
       A.—School of Reform; Sleep Walker.
27.   A.—Isabella; Teddy the Tiler.
28.   A.—School for Scandal; Clari.
29.   A.—The Stranger; Victorine.
30.   A.—Paul Pry; Inn Keeper's Daughter.

December

1. Saturday:
       A.—Gamester; Auld Robin Gray* [Auld Robin Gray—
       Scott, Jamie—Russell, Jenny—Miss Placide].

3. Monday:
   A.—Rent Day* [Martin Heywood—Hilson, Rachel Heywood—Mrs. Hilson] ; Sprigs of Laurel; Young Widow.
4.   A.—Adelgitha; Lock and Key.
5.   A.—Rent Day; Charles XII.
6.   A.—Macbeth; The Purse.
7.   A.—Fraternal Discord* [Capt. Bertram—Hilson, Jack Bowline — Scott, Charlotte — Mrs. Hilson] ; Sleep Walker.
8.   A.—Robber's Wife* [Larry O'Gig—Thorne, Mr. Briarly—Muzzy, Rose Redland—Mrs. Duffy] ; Barber of Seville.
10. Monday:
   A.—Much Ado About Nothing; Paul the Poacher* [Paul —Hilson, Margaret—Mrs. Muzzy].
11.   A.—Jane Shore; Robber's Wife.
12.   A.—Francis the First of France* [Gonzales—Scott, Queen Mother—Miss Placide, Francois—Mrs. Hilson, Margaret—Mrs. Muzzy] ; Ladies! Do Not Stay at Home; 'Tis All a Farce.
13.   A.—Pizarro; Old Maid* [Miss Harlow—Mrs. Ludlow].
14.   A.—School for Scandal; Auld Robin Gray.
15.   A.—Lear; Happiest Day of My Life.
17. Monday:
   A.—John Bull; Agreeable Surprise.
18.   A.—Apostate; Young Widow.
19.   A.—Merry Wives of Windsor; Ladies! Do Not Stay at Home.
20.   A.—Francis the First; Old Maid.
21.   A.—Bertram; Children in the Wood.
22.   A.—Simpson and Company; Tom and Jerry.
24. Monday:
   A.—Bohemian Mother; Joan of Arc.
25.   A.—George Barnwell; Paul Jones.
27.   A.—Evadne; Young Widow.
28.   A.—She Stoops to Conquer; Invincibles.
29.   A.—Adrian and Orilla; Thérèse.
31. Monday:
   A.—Dramatist; Invincibles.

January, 1833

1. Tuesday:
   A.—Lamorah* [Ozemba — Scott, St. Francis — Muzzy, Lamorah—Placide, Virginia—Mrs. Rowe] ; Day After the Fair.
2.   A.—Marriage of Figaro; Perfection.
3.   A.—Popping the Question; Jocko* [Jocko—Gouffe] ; The Secret.
4.   A.—Rob Roy; Rosina.
5.   A.—Laugh When You Can; Jocko.

7. Monday:
    A.—Hamlet; National Guard* [Pauline—Mrs. Knight].
8.   A.—He Would Be a Soldier* [Col. Talbot—Scott, Capt. Crevelt—Field, Charlotte—Mrs. Russell, Harriett—Mrs. Rowe]; Hundred Pound Note.
9.   A.—Marriage of Figaro; Invincibles.
10. A.—Iron Chest; Jack Robinson and His Monkey* [Mashagug—Gouffe, Jack Robinson—Fletcher].
11. A.—Town and Country; Grenadier*; Hole in the Wall.
12. A.—Virginius; Island Ape*.
14. Monday:
    A.—Cradle of Liberty; Pitcairn's Island* [Monkey—Gouffe, John Adams—Fletcher].
15. A.—Eugene Aram* [Eugene Aram—Forbes, Madeline—Miss Placide]; Two Gregories.
16. A.—Rule a Wife and Have a Wife; La Perouse.
17. A.—Sweet Home* [Chevalier Charles Vancour—Thorne, Nantz—Russell, Lisette—Mrs. Russell, Madame Gernadee—Mrs. Knight]; Turn Out.
18. A.—Wild Oats; Jocko.
19. A.—Merchant of Venice; No Song, No Supper.
21. Monday:
    A.—Thérèse; Paul and Virginia; Jack Robinson and His Monkey.
22. A.—Paul Pry; Ladies at Home.
24. A.—Cure for the Heartache; Jocko.
25. A.—Ambrose Gwinette; Sweet Home.
26. A.—Idiot Witness* [LeSeur Arnaud—Scott, Paul Tugscull—Russell, Walter Arlington—Mrs. Russell, Gilbert—Holland]; Abon Hassan* [Zulima—Mrs. Knight]; Ramfylde Moore Carew* [Tom Mittimus—Holland].
28. A.—Hunchback* [Master Walter—Hilson, Sir Thomas Clifford—Forbes, Modus—Thorne, Julia—Miss Placide, Helen—Mrs. Hilson]; John of Paris.
29. A.—Hunchback; Gambler's Fate.
30. A.—The Will; Apotheosis to the Memory of Napoleon*; Husband at Sight.
31. A.—Hunchback; Will Watch.

February

1. A.—Adopted Child; Timour the Tartar.
2. A.—Of Age To-morrow; Timour the Tartar.
4. Monday:
    A.—Romeo and Juliet; Timour the Tartar.
5. A.—Adrian and Orilla; El Hyder.
6. A.—Othello; Devil to Pay.
7. A.—Children in the Wood; Cataract of the Ganges.
8. A.—Hunchback; Sprigs of Laurel.
9. A.—Gamester; Cataract of the Ganges.

11. Monday:
    A.—Hunchback; Blue Beard.
12. A.—Lady and the Devil; Forty Thieves.
13. A.—The Stranger; Mazeppa** [Mazeppa—J. M. Field, Olinska—Mrs. Rowe].
14. A.—El Hyder; Mazeppa.
15. A.—Lady of the Lake; Timour the Tartar.
18. Monday:
    A.—Lady and the Devil; Cinderella* [Felix—Field, Baron Pompolino—Thorne, Dandini—Caldwell, Pedro—Russell, Cinderella—Miss Placide, Clorinda—Mrs. Russell, Thisbe—Mrs. Rowe].
19. A.—Lottery Ticket; Cinderella.
20. A.—Rendezvous; Cinderella.
21. A.—The Day After the Wedding; Cinderella.
22. A.—Cinderella.
25. Monday:
    A.—Lovers' Quarrels; Cinderella.
26. A.—Douglas; Tom and Jerry.
27. A.—Blue Devils; Cinderella.
28. A.—Cinderella; Mischief Making.

March

1. Friday:
   A.—Cinderella; Fire and Water*.
2. A.—Cinderella; Old Maid.
4. Monday:
   A.—Washington at Valley Forge** [General Washington —Gilbert, Robert Doane—Scott, Old Herbert Gray— Field, Epsesh—Miss Placide, Alice—Mrs. Rowe].
5. A.—Hunchback; Animal Magnetism.
6. A.—Cinderella; Fortune's Frolic.
7. A.—Washington at Valley Forge; Animal Magnetism.
8. A.—Hunchback; My Wife or My Place*
9. A.—Everyone Has His Faults; Merchant of Venice, fourth act; Robber's Wife.
11. Monday:
    A.—Shakespeare's Early Days* [Wm. Shakespeare—Caldwell, Doctor Orthodox—Gray, Richard Burbage— Thorne, Queen Elizabeth—Mrs. Rowe]; Washington at Valley Forge.
12. A.—Cinderella; My Wife or My Place.
13. A.—Road to Ruin; Honest Thieves; Jocko.
14. A.—Shakespeare's Early Days; My Wife or My Place.
15. A.—Young Widow.
16. A.—Dramatist; Washington at Valley Forge.
18. Monday:
    A.—Pizarro; My Aunt.
19. A.—Mischief Making; Cinderella.
20. A.—Pizarro; My Aunt.

21.   A.—The Wonder; Adopted Child.
22.   A.—Hamlet; American Tar.
23.   A.—Rent Day; My Aunt.
25. Monday:
    A.—Rent Day; Spring and Autumn* [Rattle—Wallack].
26.   A.—Richard III; Husband at Sight.
27.   A.—Brigand; Children in the Wood.
28.   A.—Brigand; Spring and Autumn.
29.   A.—Pizarro; My Aunt.
30.   A.—Rent Day; Wolf and the Lamb* [Bob Honeycomb—
    Wallack, Mary—Mrs. Russell]; Adopted Child.

April

1. Monday:
    A.—Much Ado About Nothing; Sylvester Daggerwood;
    Children in the Wood.
2.   A.—Blue Devils; Cinderella.
3.   A.—Abon Hassan; Heart of Midlothian* [Staunton—
    Scott, Madge Wildfire—Miss Placide].
4.   A.—Dead Shot; Cinderella.
5.   A.—The Tempest* [Prospero—Scott, Caliban—Thorne,
    Hypolita—Mrs. Russell, Aeriel—Mrs. Knight]; My
    Wife or My Place.
8. Monday:
    A.—Hunchback; My Wife or My Place.
9.   A.—Cinderella; Three Hunchbacks* [Badekin—Thorne,
    Syahink—Hernizen, Ibaid—Russell, Nohomoa—Mrs.
    Russell].
10.   A.—Macbeth; Wolf and the Lamb.
11.   A.—Husband at Sight; Cinderella.
12.   A.—Hunchback; Three Hunchbacks.
13.   A.—My Own Lover*; John of Paris.
15. Monday:
    A.—Rent Day; Three and the Deuce.
16.   A.—Lamorah; The Pilot, one act; Presumptive Evidence.
17.   A.—Timour the Tartar; Bell's Stratagem.
18.   A.—Mountaineers; My Own Lover.
19.   A.—Honey Moon; Invincibles.
20.   A.—Pizarro; Lady and the Devil.
22. Monday:
    A.—Cradle of Liberty; Perfection; My Aunt.
23.   A.—Flying Dutchman*; [Vanderdecker—Caldwell, Peter
    Von Rummel—Russell, Toby Varnish—Thorne, Les-
    telle—Mrs. Rowe, Lucy—Mrs. Russell].
24.   A.—Mischief Making; Flying Dutchman.
25.   A.—Rendezvous; Flying Dutchman.
26.   A.—Flying Dutchman; Old Maid.
27.   A.—Cinderella.

29. Monday:
>   A.—Banished Provincial** [Joe Mizen—Scott, Clifford—
>   Field, Sir Dickey Doughead—Hernizen, Altorf—
>   Gilbert, Nicholas Van Dunberdum—Gray, **Terry**
>   **O'Rourke**—Thorne, Emily Stanton—Miss Coleman];
>   Matrimony.

30. A.—Catharine and Petruchio; Haunted Inn; Richard III,
>   fifth act.

May

1. Wednesday:
>   A.—Metamora* [Metamora—Edwin Forrest, Lord Fitz-
>   Arnold—Scott, Oceana—Mrs. Rowe, Kaneshine—
>   Allen]; Irishman in London.

2.   A.—Metamora; Animal Magnetism.
3.   A.—Metamora; True Use of Riches.
4.   A.—Damon and Pythias; The Jew and the Doctor.
6. Monday:
>   A.—The Gladiator* [Spartacus—Edwin Forrest, Cras-
>   sus—Scott, Phasarius—Field, Senora—Mrs. Russell];
>   Young Widow.

7.   A.—Valley Forge, two acts; Iron Chest, one act; Tourists
>   in America* [Miss Lucretia Fitzblue—Miss Petrie,
>   Phoebe, Piety Hopkins, Philomela Dismal and Hecate
>   Melpomone Scraggs—Mrs. Rowe, Master Diogenes—
>   Hernizen, Tristram Doggrel—Field]; John Overy*.

8.   A.—William Tell; No Song, No Supper.
9.   A.—White Phantom; The Lying Valet; Tourists in
>   America.

10. A.—Virginius; Rosina.
11. A.—Othello; Tourists in America.
13. Monday.
>   A.—The Gladiators; Hunter of the Alps.

14. A.—Cinderella; Rendezvous.
15. A.—Brutus; Lock and Key.
16. A.—Barber of Seville; Jew and the Doctor.
17. A.—Irishman in London.
18. A.—Cinderella; Matrimony.
20. Monday:
>   A.—Simpson and Company.

21. A.—Lottery Ticket; The Prize.
22. A.—Lock and Key.
23. A.—Husband at Sight.
24. A.—The Pilot; Coming Out* [Romeo Moonshine Esq.—
>   Field, Old Moonshine—Page, Omenia Pod—Gray].

25. A.—Speed the Plough; Monsieur Tonson.
27. Monday:
>   A.—Laugh When You Can.

28. A.—West Indian. Last night of the season.

November

28. Thursday:
    A.—Belle's Stratagem; Irishman in London.
29. A.—Clari; Perfection.
30. A.—She Stoops to Conquer; No Song, No Supper.

December

2. Monday:
    A.—Wives as They Were; Simpson and Company.
3. A.—Soldier's Daughter; Abon Hassan.
4. A.—Marriage of Figaro; The Tempest.
5. A.—School for Scandal; Actress of All Work.
6. A.—Honey Moon; Spoiled Child.
7. A.—The Will; The Romp.
9. Monday:
    A.—As You Like It; Dead Shot.
10. A.—Dramatist; Raising the Wind.
11. A.—Much Ado About Nothing; Day After the Wedding.
12. A.—Hunchback; Dumb Belle* [Vivian—Barrett, Eliza—Mrs. Barrett].
13. A.—Belle's Stratagem; Wandering Boys.
14. A.—The Wonder; Actress of All Work.
16. Monday:
    A.—Guy Mannering; The Review.
17. A.—The Wife* [Julian St. Pierre—Barrett, Mariana—Mrs. Barrett]; Dumb Belle.
18. A.—The Cabinet; No!* [Frederick—Sinclair, Maria—Mrs. Russell].
19. A.—Hunchback; Free and Easy* [Sir Charles Freeman—Barrett].
20. A.—Rob Roy; Is He Jealous?
21. A.—Two Friends* [Ambrose—Barrett, Elinor—Mrs. Barrett]; Dumb Belle; Tom and Jerry.
23. Monday:
    A.—Englishmen in India* [Capt. Tancred—Sinclair, Sally Scraggs—Fisher, Gilmore—Knight]; Four Sisters*.
24. A.—Two Friends; Perfection; The Critic.
25. A.—She Would be a Soldier; High Ways and By Ways.
26. A.—The Wife.
27. A.—Englishmen.in India; Rosina.
28. A.—School for Scandal; High Ways and By Ways.
30. Monday:
    A.—Love in a Village; Dead Shot; Midas* [Apollo—Sinclair].
31. A.—The Tempest; Spoiled Child.

January, 1834

1. Wednesday:
    A.—Marriage of Figaro; Hundred Pound Note.
2. A.—Cinderella.
4. A.—Wine Does Wonders; Damon and Pythias.

6. Monday:
    A.—Englishmen in India; Midas.
7.   A.—She Stoops to Conquer; Thérèse.
10.   A.—Cinderella; Is He Jealous?
11.   A.—Hunchback; Turnpike Gate.
13. Monday:
    A.—The Tempest; My Wife's Mother* [Felix Bud—Field,
    Ned Waverly—Thorne, Uncle Foozle—Gilbert, Thomas
    —Hunt, Ellen—Mrs. Rowe, Mrs. Fitzosborne—Miss
    Petrie, Mrs. Quickfidget—Mrs. Crooke].
14.   A.—Bold Stroke for a Husband; Thérèse.
15.   A.—The Tempest; Husband at Sight.
16.   A.—Cinderella; Perfection.
17.   A.—Barber of Seville; Sleep Walker.
18.   A.—Marriage of Figaro; No Song, No Supper.
20. Monday:
    A.—Cinderella; Irish Tutor.
21.   A.—Jonathan in England; Housekeeper** [Felecia—Pla-
    cide, Sophy Hawes, Mrs. Russell, Window Duckling—
    Mrs. Crooke].
22.   A.—Cinderella; No!
23.   A.—Jonathan in England; Housekeeper.
24.   A.—Cinderella; Tempest, fifth act.
25.   A.—Green Mountain Boy* [Jedediah Homebred—Hill];
    Thérèse.
27. Monday:
    A.—Beggar's Opera; Actress of All Work.
28.   A.—Green Mountain Boy; The Hypocrite, second and fifth
    acts.
29.   A.—Guy Mannering; Rosina.
30.   A.—East and West* [Joshua Horsereddish—Hill]; Falls
    of Clyde.
31.   A.—Cinderella; Spoiled Child.

February

1. Saturday:
    A.—Beggar's Opera; Jonathan Bradford* [Jonathan Brad-
    ford—H. G. Pearson].
3. Monday:
    A.—Rob Roy; John of Paris.
4.   A.—Forest Rose* [Jonathan Ploughboy—Hill]; Jonathan
    Bradford; Jocko.
5.   A.—Jonathan Bradford; Beggar's Opera; The Tempest,
    fifth act.
6.   A.—The Foundling of the Sea* [Zachariah Dickerwell—
    Hill]; Housekeeper; Jocko.
7.   A.—East and West; Is He Jealous?; Forest Rose; The
    Hypocrite, fifth act.
8.   A.—Jonathan in England, second and third acts; Jocko,
    last act; Green Mountain Boy.

10. Monday:
    A.—Blue Devils; Masaniello.
11.   A.—My Aunt; Masaniello.
12.   A.—True Use of Riches; Masaniello.
13.   A.—Lovers' Quarrels; Masaniello.
14.   A.—The Lord of the Manor; Abon Hassan.
15.   A.—Man and Wife; Four Sisters.
17. Monday:
    A.—Laugh When You Can; Of Age To-morrow.
18.   A.—Honey Moon; My Neighbor's Wife*.
19.   A.—Masaniello; The Tempest, second and third acts.
20.   A.—Jonathan Bradford; My Neighbor's Wife.
21.   A.—Cinderella; Day after the Wedding.
22.   A.—Washington**; Invincibles.
24. Monday:
    A.—Artaxerxes* [Arbaces—Sinclair, Artabanes—Thorne, Artaxerxes—Clara Fisher, Princess Mandane—Mrs. Austin]; My Neighbor's Wife; No!
25.   A.—School for Scandal; The Mummy* [Toby Tramp—Caldwell].
26.   A.—Masaniello; My Neighbor's Wife.
27.   A.—The Wreck Ashore* [Miles Bertram—H. G. Pearson, Alice—Placide]; Perfection; Housekeeper.
28.   A.—Young Widow; Artaxerxes; No Song, No Supper.

March

1. Saturday:
    A.—Hamlet; Actress of All Work.
3. Monday:
    A.—Cinderella; Lock and Key; The Tempest, second act.
4.   A.—Timour the Tartar.
5.   A.—A Roland for an Oliver; Timour the Tartar.
6.   A.—Englishmen in India; Victorine.
7.   A.—Paul Pry; Paul Jones.
8.   A.—Manager in Distress; Dramatist; The Wreck Ashore.
10. Monday:
    A.—The Devil's Bridge; El Hyder.
11.   A.—As You Like It; Sprigs of Laurel.
14.   A.—Siege of Belgrade* [Seraskier—Sinclair, Colonel Cohenberg—Scott, Leopold—Hilson, Lilia—Knight, Katherine—Rowe]; Agreeable Surprise.
15.   A.—Country Girl; Masaniello.
17. Monday:
    A.—Englishmen in India; St. Patrick's Day.
18.   A.—Henry IV; Rendezvous.
19.   A.—The Gladiator; Devil to Pay.
20.   A.—Fontainbleau; Rent Day.
21.   A.—Metamora; Dumb Belle.
22.   A.—Hamlet; Four Sisters.

24. Monday:
    A.—The Gladiator; Dumb Belle.
25.   A.—Broken Sword; Sleep Walker.
26.   A.—Metamora; Three Weeks After Marriage.
27.   A.—School for Scandal; Marriage of Figaro.
28.   A.—Pizarro; Happiest Day of My Life.
29.   A.—Damon and Pythias.
31. Monday:
    A.—Broker of Bogota* [Baptisa Febro—Forrest, Juana —Mrs. Barrett]; Is He Jealous?

April

1. Tuesday:
    A.—Love in a Village; Two Friends.
2.   A.—Broker of Bogota; Young Widow.
3.   A.—Masaniello; Sprigs of Laurel.
4.   A.—The Gladiator; Wandering Boys.
5.   A.—My Aunt; Fra Diavolo* [Fra Diavolo—Sinclair, Zerlina—Mrs. Knight].

7. Monday:
    A.—Broker of Bogota; Dumb Belle.
8.   A.—Virginius; Englishmen in India.
9.   A.—Oralloossa* [Oralloossa — Forrest, Ocallie — M r s. Rowe]; Simpson and Company.
10.   A.—Fra Diavolo; Three Weeks After Marriage; Highland Reel.
11.   A.—William Tell; Chimney Piece*.
12.   A.—The Liar; Raising the Wind; Tom and Jerry.
14. Monday:
    A.—Blue Devils; Othello, third act; Hunter of the Alps; Virginius, fourth act; Dumb Belle.
15.   A.—The Tempest; Highland Reel.
16.   A.—Oralloossa; Chimney Piece.
17.   A.—Metamora; The Weathercock.
18.   A.—Damon and Pythias; Turnpike Gate.
19.   A.—Othello; The Review.
21. Monday:
    A.—Julius Caesar; My Aunt.
22.   A.—Venice Preserved; Young Widow.
23.   A.—Broker of Bogota; Catharine and Petruchio.
24.   A.—Virginius; Thérèse.
25.   A.—Wild Oats; Barber of Seville.
26.   A.—Brutus; Midas.
28. Monday:
    A.—West Indian; Turn Out.
29.   A.—Guy Mannering; Rent Day.
30.   A.—Masaniello; Country Girl.

May

1. Thursday:
   A.—Englishmen in India; Rosina.
2. A.—Fra Diavolo; Wandering Boys.
3. A.—Abon Hassan; Invincibles; Music and Prejudice*
   [Count Creomora—Thorne; Alfred—Mrs. Austin].
5. Monday:
   A.—Cinderella; No!
6. A.—Brian Boroihme; Paul Jones.
7. A.—Beggar's Opera; Clari.
8. A.—Richard III; My Neighbor's Wife.
9. A.—The Weathercock; Caliph of Bagdad* [Haroun Alra-
   shid—Hodges].
10. A.—Cure for the Heartache; The Miniature** [Diaper
    Garrett—Gilbert, Mrs. Lucy Garrett—Mrs. Russell].
12. Monday:
    A.—The Aethiop; The Cabinet.
13. A.—Hamlet; Sylvester Daggerwood.
14. A.—Hunchback; 'Tis All a Farce.
15. A.—Brian Boroihme; Midas.
16. A.—She Stoops to Conquer; Giovanni in London.
17. A.—The Headsman** [Headsman—Scott]; Nature and
    Philosophy.
19. Monday:
    A.—Belle's Stratagem; Giovanni in London.
20. A.—Mazeppa; Nature and Philosophy.
21. A.—Music and Prejudice; Mazeppa.
23. A.—The Review; Mazeppa.
24. A.—As You Like It; Of Age To-morrow.
26. Monday:
    A.—Nature and Philosophy; Mazeppa.
27. A.—School of Reform; Mazeppa. List night of the season.

November

24. Monday:
    A.—Love in a Village; Young Widow.
25. A.—Lovers' Quarrels; Fazio; The Secret.
26. A.—Belle's Stratagem; Adopted Child.
27. A.—Hunchback; No!
28. A.—As You Like It; Is He Jealous?
29. A.—Evadne; Dead Shot.

December

1. Monday:
   A.—The Wife; Ladies at Home.
2. A.—Guy Mannering; Green Eyed Monster.
3. A.—Apostate; Illustrious Stranger*.
4. A.—Love in a Village; Thérèse.
5. A.—Adelgitha; Green Eyed Monster.
6. A.—Englishmen in India; Ghost or No Ghost.

8. Monday:
   A.—Isabella; Lady and the Devil.
9.   A.—Clari; Perfection; Poor Soldier.
10. A.—My Neighbor's Wife; Fazio; Ladies at Home.
11. A.—Pizarro; Spoiled Child.
12. A.—Green Eyed Monster; Cinderella.
13. A.—Rob Roy; Brigand.
15. Monday:
   A.—Devil's Bridge; A Roland for an Oliver.
16. A.—Mischief Making; Brigand; Poor Soldier.
17. A.—The Stranger; Sprigs of Laurel.
18. A.—Brigand; Sprigs of Laurel; Happiest Day of My Life.
19. A.—Cinderella; Mischief Making.
20. A.—Jane Shore; Forty Thieves.
21. Sunday:
   A.—Brigand; Heart of Midlothian.
22. A.—Jonathan in England; How to Die for Love.
23. A.—She Would be a Soldier; My Daughter, Sir!* [Francis
       Vivid—Williamson, Sam—Thorne, Mr. Dobbs—Far-
       ren, Mary—Mrs. Knight].
24. A.—Green Mountain Boys; Brigand.
25. A.—George Barnwell; Paul Jones.
27. A.—Cinderella; The Romp.
29. Monday:
   A.—Knight of the Golden Fleese* [Sy Saco—Hill, Orsorio
       de Luna—H. G. Pearson, Vittoria—Mrs. Rowe, Bene-
       dicta—Mrs. Russell]; Poor Soldier.
30. A.—I'll be Your Second* [Placid—Thorne, George Lovell—
       Williamson].
31. A.—Yankee in Spain; Cinderella.

January, 1835

2. Friday:
   A.—Fazio.
5. Monday:
   A.—Jonathan in England, second and third acts; Brother
       and Sister; Yankee Pedlar, second act; Green Moun-
       tain Boy, first and second acts.
7.   A.—John Bull; Teddy the Tiler; I'll be Your Second.
10. A.—Born to Good Luck* [Paudeen O'Rafferty—Power];
       Teddy the Tiler; Perfection.
13. Tuesday:
   A.—Irish Ambassador* [Sir Patrick O'Plenipo—Power,
       Prince Rodolph—Williamson, Lady Emily—Mrs. Hil-
       son]; Irishman in London; Spoiled Child.
14. A.—As You Like It; Married Yesterday.
15. A.—Nervous Man and the Man of Nerve* [McShane—
       Power, Aspin—Farren, Leech—Mrs. Hilson]; Irish
       Tutor; Nature and Philosophy.

16.   A.—School for Scandal; Rendezvous.

18.   A.—The Stranger; Cinderella, first act.

20. Tuesday:

      A.—Nervous Man and Man of Nerve; Monsieur Tonson; Lady and the Devil.

22.   A.—Irish Ambassador; The Review; Nature and Philosophy.

24.   A.—Etiquette Run Mad* [Captain Dennis O'More—Power, Sir Peregrine Langley—Farren, Bob—Thorne, Louisa Forester—Mrs. Hilson, Belle—Mrs. Russell]; I'll be Your Second.

26. Monday:

      A.—Poor Gentleman.

27.   A.—Nervous Man and Man of Nerve; Teddy the Tiler; Promissory Note.

28.   A.—Thérèse; Wandering Boys.

29.   A.—Etiquette Run Mad; Monsieur Tonson; The Day after the Wedding.

31.   A.—The Rivals; Irish Valet* [Larry—Power].

February

3. Tuesday:

      A.—Jonathan in England; Monsieur Tonson; My Neighbor's Wife.

4.   A.—Thérèse; The Citizen.

5.   A.—Intrigue; Promissory Note.

7.   A.—Job Fox, the Yankee Valet* [Job Fox—Hackett, Betty—Miss Nelson] The Citizen.

10. Tuesday:

      A.—Rip Van Winkle, Job Fox; Rendezvous.

12.   A.—Two Sisters*; Dog of Montargis.

13.   A.—Barber of Seville; Wandering Boys.

14.   A.—Paul Pry; Yankee in Spain.

16. Monday:

      A.—Rob Roy.

17.   A.—Yankee Pedlar; Veteran of 102; The Hypocrite, principal scenes.

21.   A.—Tutoona** [General Gates—Scott, Col Thomas—Williamson, Capt. Davis—Hernizen, Major Scott—Reynoldson, Doyle—Thorne, Mary Scott—Mrs. Rowe, Copper Snake—H. G. Pearson, Mantogo—Bannister, Tutoona—Mrs. Russell].

23. Monday:

      A.—Sweethearts and Wives; Ovid and Obid* [Obid Bigelow—Hill, Ovid Daggerell—Thorne, Ellen—Mrs. Hubbard]; A Grand Masquerade* [Doorkeeper—Hill]; Prize.

25.   A.—Kasper Hauser** [Dr. Lott Whittle—Hill, Baron
       Rhenfelt—H. G. Pearson, Kasper Hauser—Miss Nel-
       son]; Removing the Deposits** [Mr. Paul Popp—
       Finn, Mrs. Lucy Popp—Mrs. Rowe]; Love Laughs at
       Locksmiths.
28.   A.—Tutoona; Jonathan Doubikins* [Doubikins—Hill].

March

2. Monday:
       A.—Barber of Seville; Monsieur Mallet* [Mons. Mallet—
       Hackett].
3.   A.—Jonathan in England, second and third acts; Clari;
       Kentuckian.
4.   A.—Beggar's Opera; Paul Pry.
5.   A.—Monsieur Mallet; Sylvester Daggerwood; Kentuckian,
       first act.
7.   A.—Rob Roy; Monsieur Mallet.
9.   Monday:
       A.—Irish Ambassador; Irish Tutor; Fortune's Frolic.
10.   A.—The Rivals; Teddy the Tiler.
11.   A.—Born to Good Luck; Irishman in London; A Roland
       for an Oliver.
12.   A.—Nervous Man and the Man of Nerve; The River; The
       Secret.
13.   A.—The Day After the Wedding; St. Patrick's Eve*;
       Nature and Philosophy.
14.   A.—St. Patrick's Eve; The Citizen; Adventures of a
       Sailor*.
16. Monday:
       A.—St. Patrick's Eve; Paddy Carey*; Is He Jealous?
17.   A.—Bertram; Mistletoe Bough** [Lord Lovel—William-
       son].
18.   A.—Thérèse; More Blunders Than One; King Charles II.
19.   A.—Macbeth; Mistletoe Bough.
20.   A.—Hamlet; Lady and the Devil.
23. Monday:
       A.—The Wife; Catharine and Petruchio.
24.   A.—New Way to Pay Old Debts; Adventures of a Sailor.
27.   A.—Mistletoe Bough; Life in Philadelphia* [Hector Tom
       Skere Debil—Rice]; Lady and the Devil.
30. Monday:
       A.—Robert le Diable* [Robert — Hodges, Rimbaut—
       Thorne, Alberti—Williamson, Alice—Mrs. Knight,
       Helena—Miss Nelson].
31S.   A.—Oh! Hush!* [Gumbo Cuff—Rice, Sam Johnson Esq.—
       S. Pearson]; Robert le Diable.

April

1. Wednesday:
       A.—Robert le Diable; Jim Crow; Lottery Ticket.

2.   A.—Robert le Diable; Jim Crow.
3.   A.—Robert le Diable; Jim Crow; Nature and Philosophy.
4.   A.—Heir at Law; Jim Crow; Love Laughs at Locksmiths.
6. Monday:
      A.—Hamlet; Jim Crow; Lottery Ticket.
7.   A.—Robert le Diable; Removing the Deposits.
8.   A.—Kasper Hauser; Is He Jealous?; Gretna Green.
9.   A.—Tutoona; Sleep Walker.
10.   A.—Cinderella, first act; My Master's Rival; Miller and
      His Men.
11.   A.—Robert le Diable; Legion of Honor.
13. Monday:
      A.—School for Scandal; Forest of Bondy.
14.   A.—Robert le Diable; May Queen.
15.   A.—Iron Chest; Beggar's Opera.
16.   A.—Married and Single; The Hypocrite, principal scenes
      comprised in one act; Family Jars.
17.   A.—Cinderella; Paul and Peter Shack.
20. Monday:
      A.—Isabella; Forest of Bondy.
21.   A.—Soldier's Daughter; Family Jars.
22.   A.—Romeo and Juliet.
24.   A.—Rathenemus the Roman**; Black Eyed Susan.
25.   A.—Cinderella; Invincibles.
27. Monday:
      A.—Francis the First; Comedy of Errors.
28.   A.—Pizarro; Jim Crow; Spectre Bridegroom.
29.   A.—School for Scandal; Forest of Bondy.
30.   A.—The Apostate; Botheration*.

May

1. Friday:
      A.—Castle Spectre; Jim Crow; Oh! Hush!; Turnpike Gate.
2.   A.—Hunchback; Jim Crow; Comedy of Errors.
5. Tuesday:
      A.—Wives as They Were; Oh! Hush!; Jim Crow; Cockney
      Fishmonger.
6.   A.—Alexander the Great; The Pilot.
7.   A.—Last Days of Pompeii* [Soria—Barnes, Nydia—Miss
      Barnes, Saga—Mrs. Barnes]; Jim Crow; Family Jars.
8.   A.—Belle's Stratagem; Jim Crow; Turn Out.
11. Monday:
      A.—Honey Moon; Jim Crow in French and English; Vir-
      ginia Mummy* [Ginger Blue—Rice].
12.   A.—Othello; Brigand.
14.   A.—Washington; A Day in New Orleans** [Capt. Wilson
      —Fielding, Paterino—Bannister, Bob—Bristow, Mrs.
      Dixon—Mrs. Stone, Lucy—Miss Petrie].
16.   A.—Midnight Murder** [Felix—Bannister]; Venice Pre-
      served; Old Ironsides** [Tom Splinter—Scott, Wil-
      liam—Master Russell].

20. Wednesday:
    A.—Masaniello; Idiot Witness; Robert le Diable, cloister scene.
21. A.—Lady and the Devil; Valentine and Orson.
22. A.—La Tour de Nesle*; Blue Beard.
23. A.—The Sublime and Beautiful*; Robert le Diable, third act; Blind Boy.
25. Monday:
    A.—Cinderella.
26. A.—Damon and Pythias; Brigand.
27. A.—Masaniello; Magpie and the Maid.
28. A.—Tour de Nesle; Young Widow; Robert le Diable, cloister scene. Last night of the season.

November

19. Thursday:
    A.—Soldier's Daughter.
20. A.—Richard III; Gretna Green.
21. A.—Hunchback; Crossing the Line* [Woulter Van Broom —Thorne, Wouverman Van Broom—Hill, Pomona Vindertriller—Miss Crampton].
23. Monday:
    A.—The Wife; Nature and Philosophy.
24. A.—Hunchback; Crossing the Line.
25. A.—The Stranger; Lady and the Devil.
26. A.—Merchant of Venice; Unfinished Gentleman* [Lord Tatterly—Farren, Billy Downey — Russell, James Miller—Thorne, Louisa Bloomfield—Miss C. Crampton, Mary Chintz—Mrs. Russell].
27. A.—Tour de Nesle; Unfinished Gentleman.
28. A.—Tour de Nesle; Victorine.
30. Monday:
    S.C.—School for Scandal; Spoiled Child.

December

1. Tuesday:
    S.C.—Marriage of Figaro; Unfinished Gentleman.
    A.—Evadne; Spoiled Child.
2. S.C.—Hamlet.
    A.—Hamlet; Crossing the Line.
3. S.C.—Marriage of Figaro.
    A.—Iron Chest; Victorine.
4. S.C.—Honey Moon; Unfinished Gentleman.
    A.—The Secret; Shoemaker of Toulouse* [Jacob Odel— Scott, Pajot—Farren, Henry Pajot—Hill, Adelaide —Miss Nelson, Margaret—Mrs. Russell] ; Rendezvous.
5. S.C.—John of Paris; Charles II.
    A.—Shoemaker of Toulouse; Unfinished Gentleman.

7. Monday:
    S.C.—Hunchback; Dead Shot.
    A.—Shoemaker of Toulouse; Simpson and Company.
8.   S.C.—Venice Preserved; Legion of Honor.
    A.—Murrell, the Western Land Pirate* [Murrell—Bannister, Virgil A. Stewart—Fielding, Jedediah—Master Russell, Bob Stetborn—Scott, Mary—Mrs. Wallack]; Sweethearts and Wives.
9.   S.C.—Fazio; Personation* [Lord Henry—Ternan; Julia—Mrs. Ternan].
    A.—Murrell; Devil's Bridge.
10.   S.C.—Gamester; Marriage of Figaro.
    A.—Rob Roy; Murrell.
11.   S.C.—All in the Wrong; Monsieur Tonson.
12.   S.C.—As You Like It; Personation.
    A.—Englishman in India; Irish Tutor.
14. Monday:
    S.C.—Blue Devils; French Spy; Ballet of La Bayadere.
    A.—Barber of Seville; Luke the Laborer.
15.   S.C.—No Song, No Supper; French Spy; Actress of All Work; Ballet of La Bayadere.
    A.—Schinderhannes* [Schinderhannes—Scott, Sir Griffin —Thorne, Jacob Jenkins—Master Russell, Leise—Miss C. Crampton, Hag of the Troop—Mrs. Wallack]; Englishmen in India.
16.   S.C.—Poor Soldier; French Spy; Ballet of La Bayadere.
    A.—Barber of Seville; My Master's Rival.
17.   S.C.—Weathercock; French Spy; Ballet of La Bayadere.
    A.—Simpson and Company; Shoemaker of Toulouse; Promissory Note.
18.   S.C.—French Spy; Perfection; Ballet of La Bayadere.
    A.—Poor Gentleman; Schinderhannes.
19.   S.C.—Charles the Second; French Spy; Ballet of La Bayadere.
    A.—Marriage Contract** [Marldy—Scott, Woodbury—Hill, Sir Peter Petulent—Farren, Bouton—Bannister, Hon. A. Tasty—Williamson, Edmond—Meynard, Gibby—Thorne, Spendthrift—Bristow, Miss Osmond —Mrs. Russell, Eliza—Miss C. Crampton,ʼ Amelia—Miss Rae, Dorethea—Mrs. Horne]; Paul Jones.
21. Monday:
    S.C.—Wizard Skiff* [Alexa, Alexis, Agata—Celeste].
    A.—Spectre Bridegroom; Cinderella.
22.   S.C.—Wizard Skiff; Poor Soldier.
    A.—Marriage Contract; Shoemaker of Toulouse.
23.   A.—She Would Be a Soldier; Lottery Ticket; Black Eyed Susan.
24.   S.C.—The Wept of Wish-ton-Wish* [Nanamatah—Celeste]; Spoiled Child.
    A.—Adventurers of a Sailor; Cinderella.

25.   S.C.—George Barnwell; Old King Cole*; Wept of Wish-
        Ton-Wish.
        A.—Unfinished Gentleman; Mistletoe Bough; Harlequin
        and Mother Goose* [Clown—Parsloe, Harlequin—
        Bennie, Columbine—Mrs. Bennie].
26.   S.C.—John of Paris; Wept of Wish-Ton-Wish.
28. Monday:
        S.C.—Wept of Wish-Ton-Wish; Raising the Wind.
        A.—Cinderella; Unfinished Gentleman.
29.   S.C.—Wept of Wish-Ton-Wish; Wizard Skiff.
        A.—Married Life* [Mr. Samuel Coddle—Farren, Mrs.
        Lyon Lynox—Miss Rae, Mr. Henry Dow—Thorne,
        Mrs. Henry Dow—Mrs. Wallack, Mr. George Dismal—
        Fielding]; Nature and Philosophy; Charles II.
30.   S.C.—Dumb Brigand* [Alp, Enrico, Manuel—Celeste]:
        Monsieur Tonson.
        A.—Robert Le Diable; The Secret.
31.   S.C.--Dumb Brigand; No Song, No Supper.
        A.—Hamlet; Lottery Ticket.

January, 1836
1. Friday:
        S.C.—Wizard Skiff; Cradle of Liberty.
        A.—Fall of San Antonio**; Invincibles.
2.   S.C.—Wept of Wish-Ton-Wish; Marriage of Figaro.
3. Sunday:
        S.C.—The Moorish Page* [Adhel—Celeste, Red Robert—
        DeBar, Lady Blanche—Miss Lane, Clotilde—Miss De-
        Bar].
4.   S.C.—Guy Mannering; Moorish Bride*:
        A.—Guy Mannering; Fall of San Antonio.
5.   S.C.—Guy Mannering; Moorish Bride.
6.   S.C.—Devil's Daughter* [Miranda and Heart—Celeste,
        Sunbeam—Miss Lane, Astoroth—Pearson, Zamine—
        Miss DeBar, Hannibal—Cowell]; William Thompson.
        A.—Evadne; Capers and Coronets* [Marquis de Granvillo
        —Farren, Hon. Frank Rivers—Miss C. Crampton,
        Mille. Flore—Miss Rae].
7.   S.C.—Devil's Daughter; Unfinished Gentleman.
        A.—William Tell; My Master's Rival.
8.   S.C.—Devil's Daughter.
        A.—Soldier's Daughter; Washington Preserved** [Gen.
        Washington—Scott, British Officer—Bannister]; The
        Hypocrite, last act.
9.   S.C.—Devil's Daughter; The Weathercock.
11. Monday:
        S.C.—Romeo and Juliet; Bold Dragoons.
12.   S.C.—Hunchback; Dead Shot.
        A.—Fazio; Opera Mad*.

13. S.C.—Merchant of Venice; Perfection.
  A.—The Wife.
14. S.C.—Gamester; Four Mowbrays.
  A.—Tour deNesle; A Roland for an Oliver.
15. S.C.—The Stranger; Wm. Thompson.
  A.—Macbeth; Crossing the Line.
16. S.C.—Soldier's Daughter; Poor Soldier.
  A.—Man in the Iron Mask*; Teddy the Tiler.
18. Monday:
  S.C.—Macbeth; Married Rake*.
  A.—Pizarro; Promissory Note.
19. S.C.—The Wife; My Master's Rival.
  A.—Rob Roy; Napoleon* [Napoleon—Mason].
20. S.C.—Jealous Wife; Spoiled Child.
  A.—Venice Preserved; Green Eyed Monster.
21. S.C.—Othello; Married Rake.
  A.—Othello; Golden Farmer* [Golden Farmer—Walton, Jimmy Twitcher—Thorne, Elizabeth—Miss Rae].
22. A.—Adrian and Orilla; Catharine and Petruchio.
23. S.C.—Provoked Husband; Four Mowbrays.
  A.—School for Scandal; Golden Farmer.
25. Monday:
  S.C.—Venice Preserved; Michel Perrin* [Michel Perrin—Finn].
  A.—Robert le Diable; Three Hunchbacks.
26. S.C.—My Native Land* [Aurelio—Hunt, Guiseppo—Decamp, Perigrino—Latham, Tancredi—DeBar, Clymante—Miss Cushman, Coelia—Mrs. Maeder, Zamira—Miss DeBar]; The Married Rake.
  A.—Virginius; Golden Farmer.
27. S.C.—Jonathan in England; Michel Perrin.
  A.—Macbeth; Promissory Note.
28. S.C.—Knight of the Golden Fleece; My Aunt.
  A.—Cinderella; Bath Road.
29. S.C.—Native Land; Forest Rose; Four Mowbrays.
  A.—Oranaska* [Oranaska—Parsons]; A Roland for an Oliver.
30. S.C.—Jonathan in England; Knight of the Golden Fleece.
  A.—Gilderoy* [Gilderoy—Parsons]; Barber of Seville.

February

1. Monday:
  S.C.—Blue Devils; Kasper Hauser; Spoiled Child.
  A.—Oranaska; My Fellow Clerk* [Tactic—F. S. Hill]; Gilderoy.
2. S.C.—Kasper Hauser; Brother and Sister.
  A.—Tour de Nesle; Merchant of Venice, Trial scene; My Fellow Clerk.

3.   S.C.—Green Mountain Boy; Brother and Sister.
      A.—Iron Chest; Soldier's Daughter.
4.   S.C.—Jonathan Doubikins; Kasper Hauser.
      A.—New Way to Pay Old Debts; Three Hunchbacks.
5.   S.C.—The Adventure*; Knight of the Golden Fleece, sec-
      ond and third acts.
      A.—Julius Caesar; Pig and Whistle* [Lamplighter—
      Eaton]; The Review.
6.   S.C.—Julius Caesar; Jonathan Doubikins.
      A.—Robert le Diable; My Fellow Clerk.
7. Sunday:
      S.C.—Rob Roy; Dead Shot.
8.   S.C.—Fazio; Personation.
      A.—Songstress and Semptress; Unfinished Gentleman;
      Idiot Witness.
9.   S.C.—Pizarro; Actress of All Work.
      A.—Cinderella; My Fellow Clerk.
10.   S.C.—All in the Wrong; Michel Perrin.
11.   S.C.—Wept of Wish-Ton-Wish; Brother and Sister.
      A.—Shoemaker of Toulouse; Paul Jones, first act; The
      Hypocrite, last act.
12.   S.C.—She Stoops to Conquer; Moorish Page.
      A.—Robert Le Diable; The Review.
13.   S.C.—Wept of Wish-Ton-Wish; Moorish Page.
      A.—Barber of Seville; Black Eyed Susan.
14. Sunday:
      S.C.—Brother and Sister; Poor Soldier.
15.   S.C.—The Wife; Turning the Tables* [Jack Humphries—
      Finn, Jeremiah Bumps—Latham].
16.   S.C.—Shadow on the Wall* [Luke Eveline—Tiernan,
      Cicily—Mrs. Tiernan]; Personation; Turning the
      Tables.
      A.—Speed the Plough; Unfinished Gentleman.
17.   S.C.—Belle's Stratagem; Shadow on the Wall.
      A.—Wives as They Were; Virginia Mummy.
18.   S.C.—Hunchback; Turning the Tables.
      A.—Belle's Stratagem; Loan of a Lover* [Peter Spyk—
      Thorne, Gertrude—Mrs. Knight].
19.   S.C.—School for Scandal; Day in Paris*.
      A.—Barber of Seville; Virginia Mummy; Oh! Hush!
20.   S.C.—Honey Moon; Day in Paris.
      A.—Englishmen in India; Loan of a Lover.
21. Sunday:
      S.C.—Peter Wilkins* [Peter Wilkins—Miss Cushman,
      Nicodemus—Latham, Phelim—Burke, Narde—DeBar,
      Yourakee—Miss DeBar].
22.   S.C.—Beggar of Bethnal Green*; Loan of a Lover.
      A.—Bold Stroke for a Husband; Virginia Mummy.

23. S.C.—The Gamester; Loan of a Lover.
    A.—The Tempest; Bone Squash Diavolo* [Bone Squash—Rice].
24. S.C.—Turning the Tables; Peter Wilkins.
    A.—Bold Stroke for a Husband; Bone Squash Diavolo.
25. S.C.—Macbeth; Day in Paris.
    A.—Cinderella; Oh! Hush!
26. S. C.—Wives as They Were; Michel Perrin.
    A.—The Tempest; Sweethearts and Wives.
27. S.C.—Gamester; Loan of a Lover.
    A.—Loan of a Lover; Bone Squash Diavolo; My Fellow Clerk.
28. Sunday:
    S.C.—Turnpike Gate; Peter Wilkins.
29. S.C.—Much Ado About Nothing; The Quaker* [Lubin—Larkin, Steady—Hunt, Solomon—Latham, Gillini—Miss Cushman, Floretta—Miss DeBar].
    A.—Cinderella; Sweethearts and Wives; Robert le Diable, cloister scene.

March

1. Tuesday:
    S.C.—Jealous Wife; Peter Wilkins.
    A.—Bath Road; Dumb Belle; Bone Squash Diavolo.
2. S.C.—Virginius; The Quaker.
    A.—Beggar's Opera; Virginny Cupids.
3. S.C.—Jane Shore; Catharine and Petruchio.
    A.—Ice Witch* [Harold—Scott, Magnus Snoro—Thorne, Sweno—Fielding, Gath—Ratcliffe, Freyr—F. S. Hill, Ulla—Mrs. Katz, Minna—Mrs. Knight, Heda—Miss Nelson, Norna—Mrs. Cowell, Urfred—Mrs. Bennie].
4. S.C.—Much Ado About Nothing; Peter Wilkins.
    A.—Dumb Belle; Ice Witch.
5. S.C.—Provoked Husband; Peter Wilkins.
    A.—Loan of a Lover; Ice Witch.
6. Sunday:
    S.C.—Il Pirata.
7. S.C.—Turning the Tables; Rule a Wife and Have a Wife; Loan of a Lover.
    A.—Exiles of Siberia; Ice Witch.
8. S.C.—Damon and Pythias; Unfinished Gentleman.
    A.—Hunchback; My Fellow Clerk.
9. S.C.—Il Pirata
    A.—The Wife; No Song, No Supper.
10. S.C.—Othello; Rendezvous.
    A.—Bertram; Happiest Day of My Life.
11. S.C.—Il Pirata.
    A.—School for Scandal; Black Eyed Susan.

12.   S.C.—The Stranger; Wedding Day.
       A.—Romeo and Juliet; Napoleon; Mutiny at the Nore*
       [Richard—C. Mason, Mary Parker—Miss Mason].
13. Sunday:
       S.C.—Il Pirata.
14.   S.C.—Wives as They Were; The Quaker.
15.   S.C.—Catharine and Petruchio; Bottle Imp*.
       A.—Bold Stroke for a Husband; Ice Witch.
16.   S.C.—Peter Wilkins; Day in Paris.
       A.—Lock and Key; Ice Witch; Perfection.
17.   S.C.—Hunchback; Turning the Tables.
       A.—Black Eyed Susan; Ice Witch; St. Patrick's Day.
18.   S.C.—Otello.
       A.—Loan of a Lover; Ice Witch; Perfection.
19.   S.C.—Bottle Imp; Peter Wilkins.
       A.—Ice Witch; Bone Squash Diavolo.
20. Sunday:
       S.C.—Otello.
21.   S.C.—The Hypocrite; Bottle Imp.
       A.—Nature and Philosophy; Six Degrees of Crime* [Julin
       —Hill, Robert—Williamson, Charles—Radcliffe, Mi-
       chael—Scott, Ferdinand—Thorne, Francis—Bannis-
       ter, Eugene Herbert—Maynard, Col. Firefly—Field-
       ing, Louise—Mrs. Knight].
22.   S.C.—Blind Beggar; Turnpike Gate.
23.   S.C.—Otello.
       A.—Six Degrees of Crime.
24.   S.C.—Married and Single; Timour the Tartar.
            A.—Six Degrees of Crime.
25.   S.C.—Il Pirata.
       A.—Six Degrees of Crime.
26.   S.C.—Loan of a Lover; Timour the Tartar.
       A.—Cinderella; Christening*.
27. Sunday:
       S.C.—Otello; Il Pirata, second act.
       A.—Masaniello, scenes; Tom and Jerry, scenes; Ice Witch,
       scenes; Golden Farmer.
28.   S.C.—Spoiled Child; Timour the Tartar.
       A.—Brian Boroihme; The Pilot; Black Eyed Susan.
29.   S.C.—Kill or Cure* [Mr. Brown—Finn]; Timour the
       Tartar.
       A.—Six Degrees of Crime; Ice Witch.
30.   S.C.—Kill or Cure; Timour the Tartar.
       A.—My Daughter, Sir; Dumb Belle; Pet of the Petticoats*
       [Paul—Mrs. Knight].
31.   S.C.—Happiest Day of My Life; Timour the Tartar.
       A.—Christening; Wags of Windsor; Gaulantus the Gaul**
       [Gaulantus—Bannister].

April

1. Friday:
    S.C.—Norma.
    A.—Ice Witch; Pet of the Petticoats.
2.   S.C.—Kill or Cure; El Hyder.
3. Sunday:
    S.C.—Norma.
4.   S.C.—Happiest Day of My Life; El Hyder.
    A.—The Rake's Progress* [Sam—Thorne, Harry—Hill, Fred—Hodges, Fanny—Miss Nelson]; Four Mowbrays; Deep, Deep Sea* [Great American Sea Serpent —Thorne].
5.   S.C.—Timour the Tartar; El Hyder.
    A.—Ice Witch; Poor Soldier.
6.   S.C.—Norma.
    A.—My Fellow Clerk; Perfection; Weathercock.
7.   S.C.—Cataract of the Ganges; Married and Single.
    A.—Honey Moon; Oh! Hush!; Richard III, third act.
8.   S.C.—Norma.
    A.—Four Mowbrays; Ice Witch; My Fellow Clerk.
9.   S.C.—Paul Pry; Bottle Imp.
    A.—Harcanlack**; Lovers' Quarrels; Spoiled Child.
10. Sunday:
    S.C.—Norma.
11.   S.C.—Cinderella; Day in Paris.
    A.—Youthful Queen* [Christine—Miss Russell]; Will Watch; Catharine and Petruchio.
12.   S.C.—Cinderella; Happiest Day of My Life.
13.   S.C.—Il Pirata.
14.   S.C.—Cinderella; Simpson and Company.
    A.—Will Watch; Christening; Youthful Queen.
15.   S.C.—Norma.
    A.—John Bull; Youthful Queen.
16.   S.C.—Cinderella.
17. Sunday:
    S.C.—Otello.
18.   S.C.—Rob Roy; Married Yesterday.
    A.—La Sonnambula; My Fellow Clerk.
19.   S.C.—Cinderella; Perfection.
    A.—La Sonnambula; Love Alone Can Fix Him.
20.   S.C.—Norma.
    A.—La Sonnambula, principal scenes; Four Mowbrays.
21.   S.C.—Guy Mannering; Is He Jealous?
    A.—La Sonnambula; Unfinished Gentleman.
22.   S.C.—Rob Roy MacGregor; Married Yesterday.
    A.—La Sonnambula; No Song, No Supper.
23.   S.C.—Macbeth; Married Yesterday.
    A.—Laugh When You Can; Sam Patch, Jr.*; Roman Nose*.

24. Sunday:
    S.C.—Zelmira.
25. S.C.—Devil's Bridge; Cinderella; Charles XII.
    A.—Perfection; Charlotte Temple** [Charlotte—Miss Russell]; Youthful Queen.
26. S.C.—The Jewess* [Mordecai—Barton, Haman—Pearson, Queen Vashti—Mrs. Bannister, Esther—Mrs. Hunt]; Simpson and Company.
    A.—Christening; Charlotte Temple; Roman Nose.
27. S.C.—Zelmira; Married Yesterday.
    A.—Fortune's Frolic; La Sonnambula.
28. S.C.—The Jewess; Married Yesterday.
    A.—Birthday; Charlotte Temple.
29. S.C.—Morina; Is He Jealous?
    A.—Unfinished Gentleman; Will Watch; Roman Nose.
30. S.C.—Rob Roy MacGregor; Peasant Boy.
    A.—Skeleton Witness* [Jeremy Jernincham—Wills]; Honest Thieves; My Fellow Clerk.

May

1. Sunday:
   S.C.—Il Pirata.
2. S.C.—Rienzi; Two Gregories; Perfection.
   A.—Skeleton Witness; Unfinished Gentleman.
3. S.C.—Everyone Has His Faults; American Sea Serpent.
   A.—Young Widow; The Jewess.
4. S.C.—Norma; Two Gregories.
   A.—Irish Tutor; The Jewess.
5. S.C.—William Tell; Thérèse.
6. S.C.—Norma.
   A.—The Jewess.
7. S.C.—Texas; Two Friends; Lady and the Devil.
   A.—The Jewess.

8. Sunday:
   S.C.—Il Pirata.
   A.—The Jewess.
9. S.C.—National Guard; Pet of the Petticoats.
   A.—My Fellow Clerk; The Jewess.
10. S.C.—National Guard; Texas.
    A.—Roman Nose; The Jewess.
11. S.C.—La Straniera.
    A.—The Jewess.
12. S.C.—The Tempest; Loan of a Lover.
    A.—The Jewess.
13. S.C.—Pet of the Petticoats; Peasant Boy.
    A.—The Jewess.
14. S.C.—Lucrece Borgia**; Forty Thieves.
    A.—The Jewess.

16. Monday:
    S.C.—Martyr Patriots** [Lapraniere—Pearson, Adelaide
       —Mrs. Hunt]; Happiest Day of My Life.
    A.—The Jewess.
17.   S.C.—Martyr Patriots; Forty Thieves.
    A.—Will Watch; Fortune's Frolic.
18.   S.C.—La Straniera.
    A.—Ice Witch, first act; Robert le Diable, cloister scene.
19.   S.C.—Robber's Wife; Blue Beard.
    A.—The Jewess.
20.   S.C.—Macbeth; Married Rake; Blue Beard.
    A.—The Jewess.
21.   S.C.—Rent Day; Spoiled Child; Wandering Boys.
    A.—The Jewess; Honest Thieves.
23. Monday:
    S.C.—Norma.
    A.—Youthful Queen; Victorine.
24.   S.C.—Blue Beard; Forty Thieves.
    A.—Rendezvous; The Jewess.
25.   A.—Victorine; Unfinished Gentleman; Perfection. **Last
      night of the season.**
26.   S.C.—Clari; Deep Deep Sea.
27.   S.C.—Zelmira.
28.   S.C.—Whims of a Comedian; The Secret.
    A.—Day After the Fair. Last night of the season.
29.   S.C.—Barbiere di Seviglia*.
    A.—Christine of Sweden; Perfection.
31.   S.C.—Barbiere di Seviglia.

June

1. Wednesday:
    S.C.—Laugh When You Can; Raising the Wind.
2.   S.C.—Charles II; My Aunt.
3.   S.C.—Simpson and Company; No Song, No Supper.
4.   S.C.—Lady and the Devil; Children in the Wood.
6. Monday:
    S.C.—Laugh When You Can.
7.   S.C.—Charles II; Raising the Wind.
8.   S.C.—Orphan of Geneva; Children in the Wood.
9.   S.C.—A Roland for an Oliver; Day in Paris.
10.   S.C.—A Roland for an Oliver; Frank Fix Phipps* [Frank
      Fix Phipps—Field, Peter Popkins—Decamp].
11.   S.C.—New Way to Pay Old Debts; Tourists in America.
13. Monday:
    S.C.—Wandering Boys; The Romp.
14.   S.C.—My Friend the Governor* [Governor—Keppell, Per-
      quitto—DeCamp, Julian—DeBar]; Day After the
      Fair.
15.   S.C.—Day in Paris; My Friend the Governor.
16.   S.C.—No Song, No Supper; The Secret.

17. S.C.—The King's Word* [King Charles—Hunt, Martin—
     Keppell, Johnson—DeBar, William—DeCamp, Kate—
     Mrs. Hunt] ; The Prairie Girls** [Col. Davy Crock-
     ett—DeCamp, Ella Marallo—Mrs. Minnich, Nell
     Gwynn—Mrs. Hunt].
18. S.C.—The Secret; Day After the Fair.
20. Monday:
     S. C.—The King's Word; Lottery Ticket.
21. S.C.—The Sledge Driver* [Ivan—Hunt, Paul—DeCamp,
     Catherine—Mrs. Hunt, Theodore—Mrs. Minnich] ;
     Nature and Philosophy.
22. S.C.—Whims of a Comedian; The Sledge Driver; Married
     Bachelor* [Sharp—Holland].
23. S.C.—Not a Word* [Count Sambunc—Keppell, DeCourcy
     —DeBar, Louisa—Mrs. Minnich] ; Nature and Phil-
     osophy.
24. S.C.—Not a Word; The King's Word.
25. S.C.—Animal Magnetism.
27. Monday:
     S.C.—Sledge Driver; Pay for Peeping*.
28. S.C.—Force of Nature*; Family Jars.
29. S.C.—Young Widow; Hamlet; Animal Magnetism.
30. S.C.—Dumb Girl of Genoa; Pay for Peeping.

July

 1. Friday:
     S.C.—Dumb Girl of Genoa; Not a Word.
 2. S.C.—My Friend the Governor; No!; Pay for Peeping.
 4. Monday:
     S.C.—The Liberty Tree*; Hole in the Wall. Last night of
     the summer season.

November

14. Monday:
     S.C.—Peter Wilkins; The Secret.
15. S.C.—Peter Wilkins; Nature and Philosophy.
16. S.C.—Macbeth; Two Gregories.
17. S.C.—Peter Wilkins; Day in Paris.
18. S.C.—Hamlet; Rendezvous.
19. S.C.—Infidelity** [Valerio—Bannister, Bertha—Mrs. Ban-
     nister] ; Sledge Driver.
21. Monday:
     S.C.—Richard III; Pay for Peeping.
     A.—Hunchback; The Purse.
22. S.C.—William Tell; Peter Wilkins.
     A.—Hamlet; Actress of All Work.
23. S.C.—Pizarro; Infidelity.
     A.—Bertram; Tom Cringle's Log* [Tom Cringle—Par-
     sons, Elizabeth—Miss Russell, Fan Fanglove—Mrs.
     Rowe].

24.   S.C.—The Wife; No Song, No Supper.
      A.—Much Ado About Nothing; The Critic.
25.   S.C.—Sardanapalus* [Sardanapalus—Mason, Salemenes —Pearson, Myrrha—Mrs. Hunt]; Catharine and Petruchio.
      A.—The Wife; Charles II.
26.   S.C.—Soldier's Daughter; Charles II.
      A.—King's Fool* [Friboulet—Abbott, Francis—Foster, Melchior—Archer, Blanche—Mrs. Greene]; Youthful Queen.
28. Monday:
      S.C.—Provost of Bruges* [Berthulpe—Barton, Bouchard —Pearson, Constance—Mrs. Hunt]; Sledge Driver.
      A.—Richard III; Charles II.
29.   S.C.—Romeo and Juliet; The Weathercock.
      A.—King's Fool; Youthful Queen.
30.   S.C.—School for Scandal; Youthful Queen.
      A.—Caius Silius** [Caius Silius—Parsons, Florena—Miss Russell]; Paul Jones.

December

1. Thursday:
      S.C.—Fazio; Petticoat Government*.
      A.—The Wonder; Hunter of the Alps; Actress of All Work.
2.   S.C.—King Lear.
      A.—Romeo and Juliet; Catching an Heiress.
3.   S.C.—Hunchback; Petticoat Government.
      A.—West Indian; The Weathercock.
4. Sunday:
      S.C.—La Cenerentola.
5.   S.C.—Agnes de Vere* [Agnes—Mrs. Shaw]; Youthful Queen.
      A.—Last Words of Bill Jones* [Bill Jones—Lewis]; Catching an Heiress.
6.   S.C.—The Stranger.
      A.—Othello; Day After the Wedding.
7.   S.C.—Rob Roy; My Master's Rival.
      A.—Last Words of Bill Jones; Perfection.
8.   S.C.—Macbeth.
      A.—Honey Moon; Victorine.
9.   S.C.—Agnes de Vere; Merchant of Venice, scenes; Wm. Thompson.
      A.—Virginius; All in the Dark.
10.   S.C.—Gamester; Legion of Honor.
      A.—Hunchback; Sylvester Daggerwood.
11. Sunday:
      S.C.—Barbiere di Seviglia.
12.   S.C.—Laugh When You Can; Three and the Deuce.
      A.—Black Eyed Susan, first act; Jane Shore, fifth act; New Way to Pay Old Debts, fifth act; Wild Boy of Bohemia.

13.   S.C.—Wild Oats; Agnes de Vere.
        A.—Soldier's Daughter; Dumb Belle.
14.   S.C.—Tour de Nesle; Roman Actor, sketch; Forty Thieves.
        A.—Blue Devils; Hofer, the Tell of the Tyrol* [Andreas
            Hofer—Abbott, Marie—Miss Russell]; One Hour*
            [Julia—Miss Russell].
15.   S.C.—Way to Get Married; Three and the Deuce.
        A.—Hofer; The Critic.
16.   S.C.—Guy Mannering; Youthful Queen.
        A.—Hofer; Maid or Wife; the Weathercock.
17.   S.C.—The Dramatist; The Weathercock.
        A.—Belle's Stratagem; Unfinished Gentleman.

18. Sunday:
        S.C.—Barbiere di Seviglia.
        A.—Hofer; Tom and Jerry.
19.   S.C.—Poor Gentleman; Young Widow.
        A.—Married Yesterday; Cinderella.
20.   S.C.—Rob Roy; My Master's Rival.
        A.—One Hour, Cinderella.
21.   S.C.—Barbiere di Seviglia.
        A.—Perfection; Cinderella.
22.   S.C.—All in the wrong; Too Late for Dinner.
        A.—Guy Mannering; One Hour.
23.   S.C.—Oceola** [Oceola—Pearson, Major Dade—Bannis-
            ter, Emma—Mrs. Bannister]; Guy Mannering.
        A.—Marriage of Figaro; Hofer.
24.   S.C.—Cure for the Heartache; 33 John Street.
        A.—Devil's Bridge; Victorine.

25. Sunday:
        S.C.—George Barnwell; Le Cenerentola.
        A.—The Jewess.
26.   S.C.—Much Ado about Nothing; Raising the Wind.
27.   S.C.—Country Girl; Young Hussar.
        A.—Cinderella; Review.
28.   S.C.—Way to Get Married; P P* [Mr. Splasher—Balls,
            Bob Buckskin—Latham].
        A.—The Jewess; Innkeeper's Bride.
29.   S.C.—The Wonder; John of Paris.
        A.—Marriage of Figaro; Youthful Queen.
30.   S.C.—Of Age To-morrow; Young Hussar; Young Widow.
        A.—Cinderella; Turn Out.
31.   S.C.—Englishmen in India; John of Paris.
        A.—John of Paris; The Jewess.

January, 1837

 1. Sunday:
        S.C.—Belle's Stratagem; L'Inganno Felice.
 2.   S.C.—Fontainbleau; Maid or Wife; 33 John Street.

3.   S.C.—Wandering Jew** [Jewantus—Pearson, Judas Is-
     cariot—Bannister, Satan—DeBar]; Englishmen in
     India.
     A.—Pizarro; My Aunt.
4.   S.C.—Wandering Jew; John of Paris.
     A.—The Wife; The Weathercock.
5.   S.C.—Wandering Jew; Monsieur Jacques* [Monsieur
     Jacques—Finn]; Married Yesterday.
     A.—Hamlet; Loan of a Lover.
6.   S.C.—John Bull; Young Hussar.
     A.—Pizarro; My Aunt.
7.   S.C.—Tour de Nesle; The Brigand.
     A.—Cinderella; One Hour; Dumb Belle.
8.   Sunday:
     S.C.—The Glorious Eighth of January.
9.   A.—Lucille* [St. Cyr—Hill, Lucille—Knight].
10. S.C.—Heart of Midlothian; Mons. Jacques; Mischief
     Making.
     A.—Merchant of Venice; My Aunt.
11. S.C.—Wandering Jew; The Wreck* [Hary Helm—Mrs.
     Pritchard, Parry Helm—Pearson, Peter Pankin—
     Latham].
     A.—Lucille; Guy Mannering.
12. S.C.—The Wreck; Is He Jealous?
     A.—The Wonder; Children in the Wood.
13. S.C.—Hunting a Turtle* [Mrs. Turtle—Mrs. Pritchard];
     The Wreck; Blue Devils.
     A.—Hunchback; Children in the Wood.
14. S.C.—Pizarro; The Wreck.
     A.—Unfinished Gentleman; Lucille; Loan of a Lover.
15. Sunday:
     S.C.—Il Turco in Italia.
16. S.C.—Rover's Bride* [Marmaduke Magog—Pritchard,
     Alice—Mrs. Pritchard]; Two Gregories; Alberti Con-
     tadini* [Alberti—Mrs. Pritchard].
     A.—Richard III; Perfection.
17. S.C.—Bath Road; Lucille; Swiss Cottage* [Lisette Gier-
     stein—Mrs. Keeley, Natz Treck—Keeley].
18. S.C.—Agnes de Vere; Swiss Cottage; Is He Jealous?
     A.—Rob Roy; Loan of a Lover.
19. S.C.—She Stoops to Conquer; Loan of a Lover.
     A.—Adopted Child; Spring and Autumn; Rent Day.
20. S.C.—Lucille; Swiss Cottage.
     A.—Venice Preserved; Wild Boy of Bohemia.
21. S.C.—The Rivals; Loan of a Lover.
     A.—Othello; Dumb Belle.
22. Sunday:
     S.C.—Lucille; Swiss Cottage.

23.   S.C.—Hide and Seek* [Moses—Keeley, Mrs. Mordaunt—
      Mrs. Keeley]; Clari, last act; Twice Killed* [Facile—
      Keeley, Fanny Pepper—Miss Melton]; No Song, No
      Supper.
      A.—Hunchback; Black Brig of Bermuda.
24.   S.C.—The Rivals; My Husband's Ghost* [Drummer Gilkes
      —Keeley].
      A.—Charlotte Temple; Black Brig of Bermuda; One Hour.
25.   S.C.—Charles II; Twice Killed; Rosina.
      A.—Cinderella, first act; Purse; Don Juan.
26.   S.C.—Wild Oats; Loan of A Lover.
      A.—Jane Shore; Swiss Cottage.
27.   S.C.—Charles II; Poor Soldier; My Master's Rival.
      A.—Macbeth; Don Juan.
28.   S.C.—Heir at Law; An Affair of Honor* [Capt. Carnage—
      Keeley].
      A.—Richard III; Swiss Cottage.
29. Sunday:
      S.C.—L'Inganno Felice; Hide and Seek; Swiss Cottage.
      A.—George Barnwell; Black Brig of Bermuda.
30.   S.C.—Yeoman's Daughter* [Jemmy—Keeley, Arthur—
      Pearson]; Review; Loan of a Lover.
      A.—Alexander the Great; Swiss Cottage; Winning a Hus-
      band.
31.   S.C.—Englishman in India; Hunter of the Alps.
      A.—The Jewess; Loan of a Lover.

February

1. Wednesday:
      S.C.—Virginius; My Master's Rival.
      A.—Cinderella; Charlotte Temple.
2.   S.C.—School for Scandal; Raising the Wind.
      A.—Julius Caesar; Turnpike Gate.
3.   S.C.—Othello; Young Hussar.
      A.—Hunchback; Swiss Cottage.
4.   S.C.—Bold Stroke for a Husband; Mons. Jacques.
      A.—Bold Stroke for a Husband; Rendezvous.
5. Sunday:
      S.C.—Macbeth; Innkeeper's Bride.
      A.—Blue Devils; Ice Witch; Swiss Cottage.
6.   S.C.—Honey Moon; 33 John Street.
      A.—Ice Witch; The Jewess.
7.   S.C.—Damon and Pythias; Turning the Tables.
      A.—Pizarro; My Aunt.
8.   S.C.—Wives as They Were; Young Widow; Family Jars.
      A.—Charlotte Temple; Ice Witch.
9.   S.C.—Hamlet; Three and the Deuce.
      A.—Pizarro; My Aunt.

10.   S.C.—Three Weeks After Marriage; Fazio; Personation.
        A.—Blue Devils; Rent Day; Spring and Autumn.
11.   S.C.—William Tell; 33 John Street.
        A.—Hamlet; Tom Cringle's Log.
12. Sunday:
        S.C.—Richard III; Orphan of Geneva.
        A.—Macbeth; One Hour.
13.   S.C.—Win Her and Wear Her; [Col. Feignwell—Balls,
        Obadiah Prim—Finn, Sir Philip Modelove—Barton,
        Ann Lovely—Mrs. Shaw]; Gretna Green; Black Eyed
        Susan.
        A.—Much Ado about Nothing; Adopted Child.
14.   S.C.—School for Reform; Removing the Deposits; Tekeli.
        A.—Richard III; Christine of Sweden.
15.   S.C.—Hamlet; High Life below Stairs.
        A.—Jonathan in England; Turnpike Gate.
16.   S.C.—West Indian; The Waterman.
        A.—Bertram; Ice Witch.
17.   S.C.—Much Ado about Nothing; Charles XII of Sweden.
        A.—Belle's Stratagem; Charles II.
18.   S.C.—School for Scandal; The Waterman.
        A.—Tour de Nesle, first and second acts; Catharine and
        Petruchio; Young Widow; Venice Preserved, fourth
        act.
19. Sunday:
        S.C.—Monsieur De Chiffonne; Lady and the Devil; Bar-
        biere di Seviglia, second act.
        A.—Robbers; Napoleon.
20.   S.C.—Honey Moon; Turn Out.
        A.—Ice Witch; The Review.
21.   S.C.—Laugh When You Can; High Life below Stairs.
        A.—Bold Stroke for a Husband; Victorine.
22.   S.C.—Rendezvous; Hazard of the Die* [David Durigne—
        Wallack, Cato—Latham]; Wolf and the Lamb* [Rob
        Honeycomb—Wallack, Col. Bronze—Barton, Elvira—
        Mrs. Shaw, Mary—Miss Melton].
        A.—The Jewess; Roman Nose.
23.   S.C.—Pizarro; Wolf and the Lamb.
        A.—Mountain Sylph* [Christie—Hill, Hela—Farren, Eolia
        —Miss Nelson]; Innkeeper's Bride; Roman Nose.
24.   S.C.—The Wonder; Hazard of the Die.
        A.—Charlotte Temple; Mountain Sylph.
25.   S.C.—Is He Jealous?; Brigand; Spring and Autumn.
        A.—Christine of Sweden; Mountain Sylph.
26. Sunday.
        S.C.—Spring and Autumn; Cinderella.
        A.—Six Degrees of Crime; Roman Nose.

27.   S.C.—Monsieur De Chiffonne; Youthful Queen.
      A.—Innkeeper's Bride; Ice Witch; One Hour.
28.   S.C.—Merchant of Venice; My Aunt.
      A.—All in the Dark; Dumb Belle; Mountain Sylph.

March

1. Wednesday:
      S.C.—Romeo and Juliet, first, second and third acts;
         Adopted Child; Brigand.
      A.—Mountain Sylph; Black Brig of Bermuda.
2.   S.C.—The Unknown** [The Unknown—Pearson, Rodolph
         —Bannister, Marcelline—Mrs. Bannister, Rosa—Mrs.
         Hunt]; Rendezvous.
      A.—Six Degrees of Crime; My Fellow Clerk.
3.   S.C.—The Unknown; Turn Out.
      A.—Black Brig of Bermuda; Mountain Sylph; Don Juan.
4.   S.C.—John of Paris; Peter Wilkins.
      A.—The Whistler* [The Whistler—Mrs. Lewis, Donacha
         Dhu—Fielding, Lady Staunton—Mrs. Russell, Mrs.
         Butler—Miss Randolph]; Mountain Sylph.
5. Sunday:
      S.C.—Infidelity; Day After the Wedding; No Song, No
         Supper.
      A.—The Whistler; Purse; Ice Witch.
6.   S.C.—The Unknown; Young Reefer* [Julian—Mrs. Pritch-
         ard, Simon Perry—Pritchard].
      A.—Ice Witch; One Hour; Mountain Sylph.
7.   S.C.—French Spy; John of Paris.
      A.—French Spy; Christine of Sweden.
8.   S.C.—French Spy; Catharine and Petruchio.
      A.—Ice Witch; French Spy.
9.   S.C.—French Spy; Turn Out.
      A.—Mountain Sylph; French Spy.
10.   S.C.—Wept of Wish-ton-Wish; Charles II.
      A.—Mountain Sylph; Robert le Diable, cloister scene; Som-
         nambulist.
11.   S.C.—Wept of Wish-ton-Wish; Charles II.
      A.—Guy Mannering; French Spy.
12. Sunday:
      S.C.—French Spy; The Waterman.
      A.—French Spy; Husband at Sight.
13.   S.C.—Wept of Wish-ton-Wish; Matrimony.
      A.—Cinderella, first act; Swiss Cottage.
14.   S.C.—Infidelity.
      A.—Bold Stroke for a Husband; Robert le Diable, cloister
         scene; Roman Nose.
15.   S.C.—Heir at Law; Irish Tutor.
      A.—Charlotte Temple; Swiss Cottage.
16.   S.C.—Wizard Skiff; Charles XII.
      A.—The Whistler; Four Sisters; One Hour.

17.　S.C.—Wizard Skiff; John of Paris.
　　　A.—Husband at Sight; Wild Boy of Bohemia.
18.　S.C.—Wizard Skiff; Day After the Wedding; Day in Paris.
　　　A.—Purse; Four Sisters; The Whistler.
19.　Sunday:
　　　S.C.—French Spy; Lady and the Devil.
　　　A.—Cinderella, first act; Don Juan.
20.　S.C.—Moorish Prince; Wizard Skiff.
　　　A.—Black Brig of Bermuda; French Spy.
21.　S.C.—Le Dieu et la Bayadere* [Zelica—Mlle. Celeste, Un-
　　　known—Hunt, Olifour—Page, Leila—Mad. Thielman,
　　　Fatima—Signora Manette, Zulma—Mrs. Hunt]; Lady
　　　and the Devil.
　　　A.—Jonathan in England; Dumb Belle.
22.　S.C.—Matrimony; Le Dieu et la Bayadere.
　　　A.—My Fellow Clerk; Handsome Husband*; Ice Witch.
23.　S.C.—Day After the Wedding; Le Dieu et la Bayadere.
　　　A.—Fazio; Roman Nose.
24.　S.C.—Infidelity; Le Dieu et la Bayadere.
　　　A.—The Wife; The Weathercock.
25.　S.C.—Le Dieu et la Bayadere; Is He Jealous?
　　　A.—Hunchback.
26.　Sunday:
　　　S.C.—Moorish Page; Charles XII.
　　　A.—The Stranger; Christine of Sweden.
27.　S.C.—Le Dieu et la Bayadere; Day after the Wedding.
　　　A.—Macbeth; My Fellow Clerk.
28.　S.C.—Le Dieu et la Bayadere; Happiest Day of My Life.
　　　A.—Hunchback; Swiss Cottage.
29.　S.C.—Lady and the Devil; Le Dieu et la Bayadere.
　　　A.—Venice Preserved; Catharine and Petruchio.
30.　S.C.—Green Eyed Monster; Le Dieu et la Bayadere.
　　　A.—The Wife; Napoleon; Mutiny at the Nore.
31.　S.C.—Yelva* [Yelva—Celeste]; Le Dieu et la Bayadere.
　　　A.—Victorine; Purse; Husband at Sight.

April

1.　Saturday:
　　　S.C.—Tour de Nesle; Ocean Child.
　　　A.—Speed the Plough; Husband at Sight.
2.　Sunday:
　　　S.C.—Brigand; Married Yesterday; Dead Shot.
　　　A.—Cinderella, first act; Robert le Diable, cloister scene;
　　　Handsome Husband.
3.　S.C.—Hunting a Turtle; Youthful Queen; The White
　　　Eagle*.
　　　A.—Lafitte the Pirate of the Gulf** [Lafitte—Abbott, An-
　　　drew Jackson—Farren, Ben Ratlin—Kelly, Theo-
　　　dore—Mrs. Russell, Constanza—Miss Russell].

4. S.C.—Montrechi e Capuletti.
    A.—Rendezvous; Lafitte.
5. S.C.—Mischief Making; Happiest Day of My Life; The White Eagle.
    A.—My Fellow Clerk; Lafitte.
6. S.C.—Montrechi e Capuletti.
    A.—Innkeeper's Bride; Lafitte.
7. S.C.—Soldier's Daughter; The White Eagle.
    A.—Rose D'Amour; Youthful Queen.
8. S.C.—Wandering Boys; The White Eagle.
    A.—The Jewess; The Weathercock.
9. Sunday:
    S.C.—Montrechi e Capuletti.
    A.—Who Wins?*; Lafitte.
10. S.C.—Woman's Life* [Apollo—Pritchard, Isabelle—Mrs. Pritchard, Madame Sophie—Miss Melton]; Mrs. G.* [Sergeant Bellerose—Pritchard, Mrs. G—Mrs. Pritchard, Marietta—Mrs. Hunt].
    A.—Roman Nose; Lafitte.
11. S.C.—Belle's Stratagem; Somnambulist.
    A.—Lovers' Quarrels; Lafitte.
12. S.C.—Semiramide; Montrechi e Capuletti, third act.
    A.—Lafitte.
13. S.C.—Jane Shore; Somnambulist.
    A.—Mountain Sylph; Lafitte.
14. S.C.—Montrechi e Capuletti.
    A.—Lafitte; How To Die For Love.
15. S.C.—Family Jars; Lafitte* [Lafitte—Pearson, Marlingspike—Barnes, Theodore—Miss C. Barnes, Constanza—Mrs. Barnes].
    A.—Fire Raiser* [Elkanah White—Farren, Ralph Gayton—Barclay, Crazy Ruth—Miss Russell, Catherine Grey—Mrs. Carr]; Village Lawyer.
16. Sunday:
    S.C.—Agnes de Vere; Swiss Cottage; Three Weeks after Marriage.
    A.—Cottager's Daughter; Ice Witch, first act; Two Galley Slaves* [Brant—Kelly, Louise—Mrs. Carr].
17. S.C.—Lafitte.
    A.—Fatal Marriage; Hard Times in New Orleans** [McGoslin—Fielding, Cash—Delmon, First City Guard—Archer].
18. S.C.—La Bayadere; Young Widow.
    A.—Mountain Sylph, first act; Brutus; Cinderella, first act.
19. S.C.—Norma.
    A.—Apostate; Husband at Sight.
20. S.C.—Gentleman in Difficulties* [Sedley—Latham, Piminey—Miss Melton]; La Bayadere.
    A.—Bertram; One Hour.

21.   S.C.—Norma; La Bayadere.
     A.—Gamester; Village Lawyer.
22.   S.C.—La Bayadere.
     A.—Hunchback; Fire Raiser.
23. Sunday:
     S.C.—Norma.
24.   S.C.—Lafitte; March of Intellect.
     A.—Much Ado About Nothing; Christine of Sweden.
25.   S.C.—Lafitte; March of Intellect.
     A.—Caius Silius; Village Lawyer.
26.   S.C.—Donna Caritea.
     A.—Macbeth; Fazio, third, fourth and fifth acts; Is He Jealous?
27.   S.C.—Romeo and Juliet; Mogul Tale.
     A.—The Stranger; Fire Raiser.
28.   S.C.—Norma.
     A.—Bertram; Fire Raiser.
29.   S.C.—Hunchback; Old Heads Upon Young Shoulders*.
     A.—Macbeth; One Hour.
30. Sunday:
     S.C.—Donna Caritea; Swiss Cottage.
     A.—Oronaska; Paul Jones.

May

1. Monday:
     S.C.—Lafitte; Mobb the Outlaw*.
     A.—Isabella; My Fellow Clerk.
2.   S.C.—Gentleman in Difficulties; Old Heads Upon Young Shoulders; More Blunders than One.
     A.—Charlotte Temple; Victorine; Husband at Sight.
3.   S.C.—Chiara de Rosenberg**; Charles II.
     A.—Merchant of Venice, trial scene; Venice Preserved, fourth and fifth acts; Jane Shore, last act; How To Die for Love.
4.   S.C.—Irish Ambassador; Old Heads Upon Young Shoulders; Barney Brallaghan.
     A.—Tour de Nesle; Wreck Ashore.
5.   S.C.—Montrechi e Capuletti.
     A.—Gretna Green; Timour the Tartar; The Romp.
6.   S.C.—Town and Country; His First Champagne*.
     A.—Golden Farmer; Irishman in London; Blue Devils.
7. Sunday:
     S.C.—Norma.
     A.—2548!* [Bustle—F. S. Hill, Stephen Lockwood—Farren, Mary Lockwood—Miss Russell]; Mischief Making; Timour the Tartar.
8.   S.C.—Lear of Private Life; Rent Day.
     A.—Young Reefer; Farmer's Story.
9.   S.C.—His First Champagne.
     A.—Charlotte Temple; Mrs. G.; Turn Out.

10.   S.C.—Lear of Private Life; His First Champagne.
       A.—Pedlar's Acre* [Margaret—Mrs. Pritchard]; Perfec-
          tion; Farmer's Story.
11.   S.C.—Wedding Gown*; Four Sisters; Dumb Girl of Genoa.
       A.—Jonathan in England; Brigand; Richard III.
12.   S.C.—Il Tancredi.
       A.—Tour de Nesle; Is He Jealous?; Young Reefer.
13.   S.C.—England's Iron Days** [Wilfred—Bannister, El-
          gira—Mrs. Bannister]; Life in New Orleans**
          Homo—Bannister, Corn Meal—Corn Meal, Mrs.
          Homo—Mrs. Bannister, Gentleman in Black—Wil-
          liams, Dashaway—Page].
       A.—Maid and Magpie; Love and a Bunch* [Henry Hurri-
          cane—F. S. Hill, Mrs. Blithesome—Mrs. Hunt];
          Crossing the Line.
14. Sunday:
       S.C.—Il Tancredi.
       A.—Ivanhoe* [Ivanhoe—Mrs. Pritchard, Isaac—Farren,
          Prince John of England—F. S. Hill, Richard Coeur
          de Lion—Fenno, Rebecca—Miss Russell]; Married
          Rake.
15.   S.C.—Sweethearts and Wives; Loan of a Lover.
       A.—The Jewess; How to Die for Love.
16.   S.C.—Brian Boroihme; Life in New Orleans.
       A.—Brigand, second act; Murrell, the Western Land
          Pirate; Perfection.
17.   S.C.—Il Tancredi.
       A.—2548!; The Weathercock; The Review.
18.   S.C.—The Stranger; Loan of a Lover.
       A.—Timour the Tartar; Ivanhoe, second act; Twelve
          Precisely.
19.   S.C.—Semiramide.
       A.—Speed the Plough; Irishman in London.
20.   S.C.—The Scottish Chief; My Fellow Clerk.
       A.—Whirligig Hall; Merchant of Venice, trial scene; Irish
          Tutor.
21. Sunday.
       S.C.—Semiramide.
       A.—Hamlet, first, third and fifth acts; Honest Thieves.
22.   S.C.—Semiramide.
       A.—Romeo and Juliet, second, third, and fifth acts;
          Whirligig Hall; Twelve Precisely.
23.   S.C.—Rent Day; Warlock of the Glen.
       A.—Richard III, fourth and fifth acts; Old Heads on
          Young Shoulders; Omnibus* [Pat Rooney—Master
          Burke].
24.   S.C.—Semiramide.
       A.—Timour the Tartar; Mischief Making; Perfection.

25.   S.C.—Laugh When You Can; An Uncle Too Many*.
      A.—The Jewess, fourth and fifth acts; Twelve Precisely;
      Innkeeper's Bride.
26.   S.C.—Norma.
      A.—Murrell.
27.   S.C.—Turn Out; The Waterman.
      A.—The Soldier's Daughter; French Washerwoman; One
      Hour.
28. Sunday:
      S.C.—Barbiere di Seviglia.
      A.—Farmer's Story; Omnibus; Husband at Sight. Last
      night of the season.
29.   S.C.—Barbiere di Seviglia.
30.   S.C.—Warlock of the Glen; The Jewess, exhibition of the
      first and second scenes.
31.   S.C.—Barbiere di Seviglia.

June

1. Thursday:
      S.C.—Swiss Cottage; The Jewess, exhibition of the first
      and second scenes.
2.   S.C.—Barbiere di Seviglia.
3.   S.C.—Raising the Wind; Frightened to Death.
4.   S.C.—Parisina. Last night of the season.

October

16. Monday:
      S.C.—No Song, No Supper; Perfection.
17.   S.C.—Poor Soldier; Turn Out.
18.   S.C.—Bath Road; Rendezvous.
19.   S.C.—Hunter of the Alps; A Roland for an Oliver.
20.   S.C.—Poor Soldier; Perfection.
21.   S.C.—No Song, No Supper; Nature and Philosophy.
22. Sunday:
      S.C.—Hunter of the Alps; Swiss Cottage.
23.   S.C.—The Wife; Why Don't She Marry?
24.   S.C.—The Wonder; Why Don't She Marry?
25.   S.C.—Rob Roy; Pleasant Neighbor* [Christopher Strap—
      Pickering, Nancy Strap—Mrs. Conduit].
26.   S.C.—Lear; Pleasant Neighbor.
27.   S.C.—Soldier's Daughter; The Secret.
28.   S.C.—Honey Moon; The Secret.
29. Sunday:
      S.C.—Duchess de la Vaubaliere* [Regent of France—
      Porter, Duke — Pickering, Morisseau — Holland,
      Adrian—Hield, Julia—Mrs. Hield]; Perfection.
30.   S.C.—Duchess de la Vaubaliere; A Roland for an Oliver.
31.   S.C.—Hunchback; Hide and Seek.

November

1. Wednesday:
   S.C.—The Stranger; Luke the Laborer.
2.   S.C.—Paul Pry; Raising the Wind.
3.   S.C.—Hamlet; Is He Jealous?
4.   S.C.—Englishmen in India; Spoiled Child.
5. Sunday:
   S.C.—Peter Wilkins.
6.   S.C.—Bride of Lammermoor* [Edgar Ravenswood—Barton, Sir William Ashton—Collins, Col. Ashton—Porter, Lucy—Mrs. Hield].
7.   S.C.—Merchant of Venice; Peter Wilkins.
8.   S.C.—Macbeth; Pleasant Neighbor.
9.   S.C.—Poor Soldier; Peter Wilkins.
10.   S.C.—Wild Oats; Two Gregories.
11.   S.C.—Pizarro; Unfinished Gentleman.
12. Sunday:
   S.C.—Day After the Fair; Peter Wilkins.
13.   S.C.—The Wrecker's Daughter*.
14.   S.C.—School for Scandal.
15.   S.C.—Richard III; Lady and the Devil.
16.   S.C.—Wild Oats; The Mummy.
17.   S.C.—Belle's Stratagem; 33 John Street
18.   S.C.—Duchess de la Vaubaliere; The Mummy; The Secret.
19. Sunday:
   S.C.—Unfinished Gentleman; Day After the Fair.
20.   S.C.—Cure for the Heartache; Barrack Room*.
   A.—Othello.
21.   S.C.—Luke the Laborer.
22.   S.C.—Two Friends; Barrack Room; Married Rake.
23.   S.C.—Spoiled Child; La Bayadere.
   A.—Rienzi.
24.   S.C.—Wives as They Were; My Fellow Clerk.
25.   S.C.—Mountain Devil; Le Dieu et la Bayadere.
26. Sunday:
   S.C.—La Bayadere; The Mummy.
27.   S.C.—Road to Ruin; Peter Wilkins.
28.   S.C.—La Bayadere; Dumb Girl of Genoa.
29.   S.C.—Ion* [Adrastus—Hield, Ion—Mrs. Hield, Clemanthe —Mrs. Pierce].
30.   S.C.—Peter Wilkins; La Bayadere.
   A.—Mohawk Chief; Black Brig of Bermuda.

December

1. Friday:
   S.C.—Ion; Mountain Devil.
2.   S.C.—Monsieur Mallet; Kentuckian.
3. Sunday:
   S.C.—Agnes de Vere; La Bayadere.
4.   S.C.—Rip Van Winkle; Kentuckian.

5.   S.C.—Richard III; Blue Devils.
7.   S.C.—Fazio.
8.   S.C.—Henry IV.
9.   S.C.—Horse Shoe Robinson*; Monsieur Tonson.
11. Monday:
    S.C.—Rip Van Winkle; Down East, scene; Perfection; Kentuckian, second act.
13.   S.C.—Macbeth.
14.   S.C.—Henry IV; Ransom* [Pauline—Mrs. Sharp].
15.   S.C.—Wives as They Were; Perfection.
    A.—Knight of the Golden Cross; Baboon.
16.   S.C.—The Woman; Ransom.
18. Monday:
    S.C.—Henry IV; Lucille; Kentuckian, first act.
    A.—Wallace.
20.   S.C.—Damon and Pythias.
21.   A.—Bold Stroke for a Husband.
22.   S.C.—Cure for the Heartache; Deep, Deep Sea.
23.   S.C.—Children in the Wood; The Critic; A Day after the Fair.
24. Sunday:
    S.C.—The Jewess.
25.   S.C.—The Jewess.
    A.—The Travelling Painter
26.   S.C.—The Jewess.
27.   S.C.—The Jewess.
    A.—Kate Kearney* [Kate Kearney—Mrs. Maeder, Lanty O'Loghin—Larkin]; Matteo Falcone, the Youthful Brigand*.
28.   S.C.—The Jewess.
29.   S.C.—The Jewess.
30.   S.C.—The Jewess.
31. Sunday:
    S.C.—The Jewess.

January, 1838

1. Monday:
    S.C.—The Jewess.
    A.—Golden Farmer; Kate Kearney.
2.   S.C.—Ellen Warham*; Trial by Battle*.
    A.—Scourge of the Ocean*; Golden Farmer.
3.   S.C.—Damon and Pythias; Courier of the Ocean*.
    A.—Golden Farmer; Kate Kearney.
4.   S.C.—Old Gentleman*; Le Dieu et la Bayadere.
    A.—Golden Farmer; L'Amant Prete; Catching an Heiress.
5.   S.C.—Virginius; Trial by Battle.
    A.—Catching an Heiress; Kate Kearney; John Jones* [Guy Goodluck—John Sefton].

6.   S.C.—Thérèse; La Bayadere.
       A.—Climbing Boy* [Jack Ragg—Sefton]; Actress of All
       Work; John Jones.
7. Sunday:
       S.C.—Old Gentleman; The Jewess.
8.   S.C.—Battle of Austerlitz*; Adopted Child.
9.   S.C.—Guy Mannering; Swiss Cottage.
       A.—Jemmy Twitcher in France; Swiss Cottage.
10.   S.C.—John of Paris.
       A.—Uncle Sam* [Shirts—Sefton, Lady Aubry—Mrs. Fos-
       ter]; Kate Kearney; Man about Town*.
11.   S.C.—The Hunchback; Poor Soldier.
       A.—John Jones; Jemmy Twitcher in France; Man about
       Town.
12 .   S.C.—The Wife; Loan of a Lover.
       A.—L'Amant Prete; Kate Kearney; Catching an Heiress.
13.   S.C.—School for Scandal; No Song, No Supper.
       A.—Forest Rose; Old Times in Virginia* [Hiram Dodge—
       Hill].
14. Sunday:
       S.C.—The Jewess.
15.   S.C.—Ioh; Everybody's Husband*.
       A.—Dream of the Future* [Capt. Valentine—Hill, Pere-
       grine Mildway—Sefton, Honoria—Mrs. Maeder, Geor-
       gianna—Mrs. Russell]; John Jones; Barrack Room;
       Lurline* [Lurline—Miss Johnson].
16.   S.C.—Ion; Rosina.
       A.—Green Mountain Boy; Yankee Pedlar.
17.   S.C.—The Hunchback; Loan of a Lover.
       A.—Forest Rose; Speculation* [Major Wheeler—Hill];
       Lurline.
18.   S.C.—As You Like It; Ransom.
       A.—Knight of the Golden Fleece; Speculation; How to Die
       for Love.
19.   S.C.—Stranger; Youthful Queen.
       A.—Green Mountain Boy; Jonathan Doubikins.
20.   S.C.—Much Ado About Nothing; Wrecker's Daughter.
       A.—Knight of the Golden Fleece; Hypocrite, second and
       fifth acts; Nature and Philosophy.
21. Sunday:
       S.C.—Skeleton Robber.
       A.—Kasper Hauser; Forest Rose, first act; Jonathan Dou-
       bikins, fifth act; Hypocrite, fifth act.
22.   S.C.—Ion; Poor Soldier.
       A.—Kasper Hausar; Peaceful Pelton, the Vermonter*.
23.   S.C.—Macbeth; Blue Devils.
       A.—Lurline; Seven Clerks* [Claude Darnaud—Judah, Vic-
       torine—Mrs. Russell].
24.   S.C.—Belle's Stratagem; Catharine and Petruchio.
       A.—Seven Clerks; Lurline.

25.   S.C.—Ion; Swiss Cottage.
      A.—Seven Clerks; Kabri* [Kabri—Maeder, Nichol—F. S. Hill, Fairy Blanche—Miss Johnson].
26.   S.C.—Provoked Husband; Barrack Room.
      A.—Two Gregories; Seven Clerks; Kabri.
27.   S.C.—Jealous Wife; A Day After the Wedding; Deaf as a Post.
      A.—Cherokee Chief* [Capt. Moreton—Blanchard, Cherokee Chief—Cony, Matilda—Mrs. Minnich]; Ourang Ourang; Seven Clerks.
28. Sunday:
      S.C.—La Sonnambula; Trial by Battle.
      A.—Forest of Bondy; Don Juan.
29.   S.C.—Bianca Visconti* [Bianca Visconti—Miss Clifton, Sporza—Hield].
      A.—Seven Clerks.
30.   S.C.—La Sonnambula.
      A.—My Husband's Ghost.
31.   S.C.—Venice Preserved; Charles II.
      A.—Kabri.

February

1. Thursday:
      S.C.—Everybody's Husband; Cinderella.
      A.—My Husband's Ghost; Purse.
2.   S.C.—Pizarro; Loan of a Lover.
      A.—Midnight Hour.
3.   S.C.—Fazio; Cinderella.
      A.—My Husband's Ghost; Kabri.
4. Sunday:
      A.—My Fellow Clerk.
5.   S.C.—Thérèse; La Sonnambula.
      A.—Nature and Philosophy; Purse.
6.   S.C.—The Genoese* [Montaldo—Miss Clifton]; Thérèse.
      A.—Three Faced Frenchman*; Lottery Ticket.
7.   S.C.—Walden, the Avenger* [Walden—J. R. Scott]; The Review.
      A.—Kasper Hauser; Green Mountain Boy; A Day in France* [Joshiah Higgins—Hill].
8.   S.C.—Macbeth; The Old Gentleman.
      A.—Hunchback; One Hour.
9.   S.C.—Gamester; Dead Shot.
      A.—Jonathan Doubikins; Yankee Pedlar.
10.   S.C.—The Genoese; Perfection.
      A.—Who Wants a Guinea?; Speculation.
11. Sunday:
      S.C.—The Old Oak Chest**; Forty Thieves.
      A.—Kasper Hauser; Husband at Sight; Forest Rose.
12.   S.C.—Ion; No Song, No Supper.
      A.—Knight of the Golden Fleece; Perfection; Jonathan Doubikins.

13.   S.C.—As You Like It; Youthful Queen.
       A.—The Love Chase* [Sir Wm. Fondlove—Farren, Wild-
          rake—F. S. Hill, Constance—Mrs. Farren]; One Hour.
14.   S.C.—The Secret; Le Dieu et la Bayadere.
       A.—Love Chase; Family Jars.
15.   S.C.—Wild Oats; Children of the Wood.
       A.—Love Chase; Roman Nose.
16.   S.C.—Damon and Pythias; Married Rake.
       A.—Love Chase; Seven Clerks.
17.   S.C.—Marriage of Figaro; Raising the Wind.
       A.—Family Jars; Life in New York* [Major Jack Down-
          ing—Kelly, Capt. Basil Hall, R. N.—Farren, Rose—
          Mrs. Russell].
18. Sunday:
       S.C.—Old Gentleman; Cinderella.
       A.—Life in New York; One Hour.
19.   S.C.—La Sonnambula; Mummy.
       A.—My Husband's Ghost; Life in New York.
20.   S.C.—Cinderella; Pleasant Neighbor.
       A.—Life in New York; Dumb Belle.
21.   S.C.—Marriage of Figaro; Blue Devils.
       A.—Spoiled Child; Life in New York.
22.   S.C.—John of Paris; 33 John Street.
       A.—Purse; Swiss Cottage; Life in New York.
23.   S.C.—Cinderella; Loan of a Lover.
       A.—Charles II; Life in New York.
24.   S.C.—La Sonnambula; Mummy.
       A.—Farmer's Story; Swiss Cottage; All Is Happy*.
25. Sunday:
       S.C.—Rob Roy; Three Weeks After Marriage.
       A.—Opera Mad; One Hour; Life in New York.
26.   S.C.—Barber of Seville; No!
       A.—All Is Happy; No!; Opera Mad.
27.   S.C.—Clari; Black Eyed Susan.
       A.—Golden Farmer; Venus in Arms* [Arabella—Mrs.
          Maeder]; Old and Young.
28.   S.C.—Love Chase; Loan of a Lover.
       A.—Kate Kearney; John Jones.

March

1. Thursday:
       S.C.—Love Chase; Swiss Cottage.
       A.—Catching an Heiress; Perfection; Life in New York.
2.   S.C.—Love Chase; Perfection.
       A.—The Jewess; Loan of a Lover.
3.   S.C.—Twelfth Night; Married Rake.
       A.—The Jewess; Barrack Room.
4. Sunday:
       S.C.—Hamlet; Wallace, the Hero of Scotland.
       A.—All is Happy; Virginia Sarcophagus.

5.   A.—Dream of the Future; Virginia Sarcophagus; Une Heure de la Vie d'un Soldat*.
6.   S.C.—Ion; 33 John Street.
      A.—Dream of the Future; Jim Crow in London*; My Husband's Ghost.
7.   S.C.—Twelfth Night; Youthful Queen.
      A.—Venus in Arms; Jim Crow in London; Family Jars.
8.   S.C.—Antony and Cleopatra** [Cleopatra—Miss Tree, Antony—Hield]; Handsome Husband.
      A.—He's Not A-Miss; Virginia Sarcophagus.
9.   S.C.—Antony and Cleopatra; Mummy.
      A.—Golden Farmer; Black and White* [Sambo—Rice]; My Husband's Ghost.
10.   S.C.—Love Chase; Court Favour* [Lucy—Miss Tree, David Brown—Barrett].
      A.—A Dream of the Future; Black and White; Intrigue.
11. Sunday:
      S.C.—Il Fanatico per la Musica*; Trial by Battle.
      A.—Peacock and the Crow* [Jim Crow—Rice]; Lottery Ticket; Purse.
12.   S.C.—Guy Mannering; Handsome Husband.
      A.—Oranaska; The Waterman; The Two Queens*.
13.   S.C.—Il Fanatico per la Musica; Raising the Wind.
      A.—Bertram; A Husband at Sight; He's Not A-Miss.
14.   S.C.—La Sonnambula; Il Fanatico per la Musica.
      A.—Simpson and Company; Two Queens; The Waterman.
15.   S.C.—Rob Roy; Pleasant Neighbor.
      A.—King Lear; Two Queens.
16.   S.C.—Peter Wilkins; The Mummy.
      A.—Caius Silius; Life in New York.
17.   S.C.—Charles XII; Handsome Husband.
      A.—Adelgitha; The Waterman; Venus in Arms.
18. Sunday:
      S.C.—The Review; La Bayadere.
      A.—Nick of the Woods* [Ralph Stackpole—Parsons, Nathan Slaughter—Farren, Edith—Mrs. Farren]; Perfection; Purse.
19.   S.C.—Englishmen in India; Rent Day.
      A.—Nick of the Woods; Opera Mad.
20.   S.C.—Clari; La Savoyard.
      A.—Oranaska; The Waterman.
21.   S.C.—La Sonnambula; Love at All Corners*.
      A.—Apostate; Pay to My Order* [Thibeaut—Sefton].
22.   S.C.—Wool Gathering; La Savoyard; The Secret.
      A.—Macbeth; Venus in Arms.
23.   S.C.—Charles XII; No Song, No Supper.
      A.—Nick of the Woods; Merchant of Venice, trial scene; No!

24.   S.C.—Wool Gathering; Wild Boy of Bohemia.
        A.—Foundling of the Forest; Jane Shore, last act; The
        Waterman.
25. Sunday:
        S.C.—Charles XII.
        A.—Gaulantus; My Fellow Clerk; Paul Jones.
26.   S.C.—The Cherry Tree* [Georgette—Mrs. Gibbs]; La
        Savoyard; The Olympic Devils* [Orpheus—Mrs.
        Gibbs, Euridice—Mrs. Conduit].
        A.—The Welsh Girls* [Julia—Mrs. Maeder]; Le Baiser
        d'Amitie; Valentine and Orson.
27.   S.C.—Wool Gathering; Le Dieu et la Bayadere.
        A.—Soldier's Daughter; Venus in Arms; One Hour.
28.   S.C.—Turn Out; 33 John Street; Swiss Cottage.
        A.—Brian Boroihme; Dumb Girl of Genoa.
29.   S.C.—Much Ado About Nothing; Pleasant Neighbor.
        A.—Spirit of the Rhine* [Arthur Huntley—Plumer];
        Welsh Girl; The Last Nail* [Sigismund—Plumer].
30.   S.C.—The Wonder; Perfection.
        A.—Gustavus III* [Gustavus III—Judah]; Last Nail.
31.   S.C.—Romeo and Juliet; The Squatter**.
        A.—Kate Kearney; Spirit of the Rhine; Swiss Cottage.

April

1. Sunday:
        S.C.—The Deceived**; Peter Wilkins.
        A.—The Widow's Curse* [Mark Ringold—J u d a h];
        Lovers' Quarrels; The Black Dwarf* [Eskie—Judah].
2.   S.C.—School for Scandal; Why Don't She Marry?
        A.—Broken Sword; Young Widow; Wandering Boys.
3.   S.C.—The Wife; Dumb Belle.
        A.—Lady of the Lake; Spirit of the Rhine.
4.   A.—Richard III; The Glorious Minority.
5.   S.C.—Gustavus.
        A.—Liberty Tree; The Weathercock.
6.   S.C.——Gustavus.
        A.—Huzza for Ballyraiget* [Charles—Plumer]; Triumph
        of Texas* [Santa Anna—Judah].
7.   S.C.—Gustavus.
        A.—The Death Token** [Mariette—Mrs. Farren, Lauretta
        —Mrs. Carr, Belair—Judah]; Widow's Curse.
8. Sunday:
        S.C.—Gustavus.
        A.—Family Jars.
9.   S.C.—Gustavus.
        A.—The Waterman.
10.   S.C.—Gustavus.
        A.—Lottery Ticket.
11.   S.C.—Gustavus; Old Gentleman.
        A.—The Glorious Minority.

12.   S.C.—Gustavus; Dumb Belle.
      A.—Le Garcon a Trois Visages; Bath Road.
13.   S.C.—The Deceived; The Squatter.
      A.—Love Chase; Death Token.
14.   S.C.—Unfinished Gentleman; Swiss Cottage; Peter Wilkins.
      A.—Perfection.
15. Sunday:
      S.C.—Black Eyed Susan; Turnpike Gate.
      A.—The Weathercock.
16.   S.C.—Town and Country; Lottery Ticket.
      A.—Six Degrees of Crime; School of Ten Quakers*.
17.   S.C.—Poor Gentleman; Dead Shot.
      A.—Fire Raiser; Widow's Curse.
18.   S.C.—She Would Be a Soldier; Husband at Sight; Valentine and Orson.
      A.—Kabri; All is Happy; Black Dwarf.
19.   S.C.—Rent Day; Dead Shot.
      A.—Rory O'More* [Rory O'More—Larkin, Kathleen—Mrs. Farren].
20.   S.C.—Intrigue; Poor Soldier.
      A.—Swiss Cottage; Romeo and Juliet, one act; Four Mowbrays.
21.   S.C.—Foundling of the Forest; Rendezvous; Turnpike Gate.
      A.—Widow's Curse; The Glorious Minority.
22. Sunday:
      S.C.—La Bayadere, first act; The Review; Trial by Battle.
      A.—Rory O'More; Purse.
23.   S.C.—The Pickwickians* [Fat Boy—Cowell, Sam Weller—Hunt]; Unfinished Gentleman.
      A.—Lottery Ticket; Rory O'More.
24.   S.C.—Miller's Maid; Irishman in London.
      A.—Triumph of Texas; Kabri.
25.   S.C.—Rent Day; Mountain Devil.
      A.—Farmer's Story.
26.   S.C.—The Pickwickians; The Secret; Chip of the Old Block.
27.   S.C.—Guy Mannering; Why Don't She Marry?
28.   S.C.—Paul Pry; Peter Wilkins.
      A.—Dumb Belle; Spoiled Child.
29. Sunday:
      S.C.—Wheel of Fortune; Deaf as a Post. Last night of the season.
      A.—Purse; Swiss Cottage; Husband at Sight. Last night of the season.

May

4. Friday:
   A.—The Swiss Cottage; No!; Old and Young.
5.   A.—The Curfew; How to Die for Love.
6. Sunday:
   A.—Loan of a Lover; The Waterman; Twelve Precisely.
8.   A.—Loan of a Lover; Dead Shot.
9.   A.—No Song, No Supper; Monsieur Tonson; Twelve Pre-
      cisely.
10.   A.—Charlotte Temple; Turn Out; A Husband at Sight.
11.   A.—Lottery Ticket; Crossing the Line; Seven's the Main.
12.   A.—My Wife and I; No!; My Fellow Clerk.
14. Monday:
   A.—Englishmen in India; Midas; Highland Reel.
15.   A.—School for Scandal; Swiss Cottage.
16.   A.—Rivals; Lucille.
17.   A.—Apostate; Lady and the Devil.
18.   A.—Othello; Family Jars.
21. Monday:
   A.—Octavia Bragaldi* [Octavia Bragaldi—Miss Barnes,
      Francesco Bragaldi — Harrison, Alberto — M r s .
      Barnes]; Sprigs of Laurel.
22.   A.—Octavia Bragaldi; Sprigs of Laurel.
23.   A.—Octavia Bragaldi; Personation.
24.   A.—Bold Stroke for a Husband; Spoiled Child.
25.   A.—Simpson and Company; Dumb Belle; Winning a
      Husband.
26.   A.—The Love Chase; Personation; Devil to Pay.
27. Sunday:
   A.—How Do You Manage?; My Neighbor's Wife; Turn-
      pike Gate.
28.   A.—Monsieur Tonson; Wedding Day; Young Reefer.
29.   A.—Black Eyed Susan; Dumb Belle; Charles II.
30.   A.—Apostate; A Roland for an Oliver.
31.   A.—The Stranger; Charles II. Last night of the season.

June

2. Saturday:
   A.—The Waterman; Dumb Belle; Dutch Brothers.
3. Sunday:
   A.—The Regatta*; Two Cracks; My Fellow Clerk.
18. Monday:
   V.—Dumb Belle.
19.   V.—The Secret.
20.   V.—How Do You Manage?
21.   V.—King Charles II.
22.   V.—Comfortable Service*.
23.   V.—Love in Humble Life.

25. Monday:
  V.—Dumb Belle.
26. V.—The Secret.
27. V.—How Do You Manage?
28. V.—King Charles II.
29. V.—Comfortable Service.
30. V.—Love in Humble Life.

July

1. Sunday:
  V.—Love in Humble Life.
8. V.—A Day After the Fair.
10. Tuesday:
  V.—Whims of a Comedian.
12. V.—Last night of the season.

October

1. Monday:
  S.C.—No Song, No Supper; Dead Shot.
2. S.C.—Poor Soldier; Family Jars.
3. S.C.—Lottery Ticket; The Waterman.
4. S.C.—Turnpike Gate; Rendezvous.
5. S.C.—Bath Road; No!; The Waterman.
6. S.C.—Lottery Ticket; The Secret; Turnpike Gate.
7. Sunday:
  S.C.—No!; Peter Wilkins.
8. S.C.—Borrowed Feathers* [Sir Fred May Weather—Burke, Tom May—S. Cowell, Frank Millbank—Page, Rosamond—Madame Thielman, Lucy—Mrs. Plumer]; Crossing the Line.
9. S.C.—Borrowed Feathers; No!; Crossing the Line.
10. S.C.—Thérèse; Loan of a Lover.
11. S.C.—Englishmen in India; Charles XII.
12. S.C.—Town and Country; Turn Out.
13. S.C.—Guy Mannering; Crossing the Line.
14. Sunday:
  S.C.—Forty Thieves; Peter Wilkins.
15. S.C.—Rent Day; Forty and Fifty* [Mr. Lillywhite—Farren, Altamonte Lillywhite—DeBar, Mrs. Lillywhite—Mrs. Smith].
16. S.C.—Paul Pry; One Hour.
17. S.C.—John of Paris; Robber's Wife.
18. S.C.—Sweethearts and Wives; How Do You Manage?
19. S.C.—Borrowed Feathers; Brother and Sister; Forty and Fifty.
20. S.C.—The Jewess; Crossing the Line.
21. Sunday:
  S.C.—Le Dernier du Comtes Egmont; Crossing the Line.
  A.—Lady of Lyons* [Claude Melmotte—Fredericks, General Damas—Barrett, Beauseant—Sefton, Pauline—Mrs. Barrett]; Presumptive Evidence.

22.   S.C.—Lottery Ticket; The Jewess.
23.   S.C.—Devil's Bridge; Hole in the Wall.
       A.—Lady of Lyons; Raising the Wind.
24.   S.C.—William Tell; Miller's Maid.
       A.—Thérèse; Dumb Belle; 33 John Street.
25.   S.C.—Soldier's Daughter; Spoiled Child.
       A.—Lady of Lyons; 33 John Street.
26.   S.C.—Paul Clifford* [Paul Clifford—Plumer, Dr. Shop-
           perton—Farren, Dominie Dunnaker—Cowell, Scarlet
           Jack—Page, Loud Ned—DeBar, Sir Wm. Brandon—
           Williams, Lord Mauleverer—S. Cowell, Miss Terpsi-
           chord—Shopperton—Mrs. Farren, Lucy Brandon—
           Mrs. DeBar]; One Hour.
       A.—Wives as They Were; The Mummy.
27.   S.C.—Charles II; Za Ze Zi Zo Zu* [Za Ze Zi Zo Zu—Har-
           rison, Grozbec—Cowell, Li Li—Mrs. Harrison, Queen
           of Hearts—Mrs. Farren, Tant-a-Tant—Mrs. Cowell].
       A.—Charles II; Perfection; The Mummy.
28. Sunday:
       S.C.—Paul Clifford; Za Ze Zi Zo Zu.
       A.—Gambler's Fate; Three Weeks After Marriage.
29.   S.C.—Miller's Maid; Peter Wilkins.
30.   S.C.—Mountain Devil; Za Ze Zi Zo Zu.
       A.—Gambler's Fate; Perfection.
31.   S.C.—Turnpike Gate; Poor Soldier; My Young Wife and
           My Old Umbrella* [Gregory—Cowell, Dinah—Mrs.
           Plumer].
       A.—Lady of Lyons; Dumb Belle.

November

 1. Thursday:
       S.C.—Don Juan of Austria* [Charles V—Pearson, Philip
           of France—DeBar, Don Juan of Austria—Harrison,
           Donna Florinda—Mrs. Farren]; Za Ze Zi Zo Zu.
       A.—Gambler's Fate; My Fellow Clerk.
 2.   S.C.—Paul Pry; Comfortable Service.
       A.—Lady of Lyons; Gambler's Fate.
 3.   S.C.—Gambler's Fate; My Young Wife and My Old Um-
           brella.
       A.—She Stoops to Conquer; Thérèse.
 4. Sunday:
       S.C.—Cinderella; A Ghost Story*.
       A.—Gambler's Fate; Lady of Lyons.
 5.   S.C.—Macbeth; Forty and Fifty.
       A.—The Carmelites*; Victorine.
 6.   S.C.—My Young Wife and My Old Umbrella; Cinderella.
       A.—The Carmelites; Victorine.
 7.   S.C.—Don Juan of Austria; Loan of a Lover.
       A.—School for Scandal; Raising the Wind.

8. S.C.—Crossing the Line; Cinderella.
   A.—The Review; Lady of Lyons.
9. S.C.—A Lesson in Love* [John Grantly—Harrison, Lady Grantly—Mrs. Farren, Fanny—Mrs. Harrison]; Comfortable Service; Za Ze Zi Zo Zu.
   A.—Gambler's Fate; The Carmelites.
10. S.C.—Pizarro; The Widow's Victim*.
    A.—She Stoops to Conquer; Victorine.
11. Sunday:
    S.C.—A Lesson in Love; The Burgomaster's Daughter**.
    A.—Lady of Lyons; Ladder of Love* [Chevalier—Barrett, Francois—Brown, Marchioness—Mrs. Greene, Susannah—Mrs. Barrett].
12. S.C.—Burgomaster's Daughter; Widow's Victim.
13. S.C.—A Lesson in Love; Burgomaster's Daughter.
    A.—Hunchback; Ladder of Love.
14. S.C.—Burgomaster's Daughter; Widow's Victim.
    A.—Lady of Lyons; Ladder of Love.
15. S.C.—Brugomaster's Daughter; Victoria* [Bennett—Field, Prince John—DeBar, Wellington—Paret, Melbourne—Burke, Queen Victoria—Mrs. Farren].
    A.—John Bull; Barrack Room.
16. S.C.—Atonement*; Victoria; The White House* [Mr. Bennett—Field, Mr. Kinderhook—Farren, Prince John—DeBar, Mr. Blazon—Williams, Queen Victoria—Mrs. Farren, Mrs. Royal—Mrs. Harrison].
    A.—Rivals; Ladder of Love.
17. S.C.—Burgomaster's Daughter; Victoria; The White House.
    A.—The Way to Get Married; The Review.
18. Sunday:
    S.C.—Gustavus; Bennett in Texas* [Bennett—Field].
    A.—Wedding Day; Tom and Jerry.
19. S.C.—My Young Wife and My Old Umbrella; My Aunt; Bennett in Texas; The Clouds*.
20. S.C.—Atonement; Trial by Battle.
    A.—Spoiled Child; Tom and Jerry.
21. S.C.—Gustavus; Widow's Victim.
    A.—Lady of Lyons; One Hour.
22. S.C.—Green Eyed Monster; Illustrious Stranger.
    A.—One Hour; The Review; Swiss Cottage.
23. S.C.—A Bridegroom from the Sea; A Ghost Story.
    A.—Lady of Lyons; The Weathercock.
24. S.C.—Dutch Brothers; Green Eyed Monster.
    A.—Lady of Lyons; Four Mowbrays.
25. Sunday:
    S.C.—Esmeralda* [Quasimodo—Harrison, Esmeralda—Mrs. Harrison, C l a u d e — Pearson]; Illustrious Stranger.
    A.—Wedding Day; Mazeppa.

26.   S.C.—Esmeralda; Dead Shot.
    A.—Mazeppa.
27.   S.C.—Esmeralda; Comfortable Service.
    A.—Lottery Ticket; Mazeppa.
28.   S.C.—Esmeralda; Four Mowbrays.
    A.—Lottery Ticket; Mazeppa.
29.   S.C.—Two Thompsons; Fazio; Swiss Cottage.
    A.—Wandering Minstrels*; Mazeppa.
30.   S.C.—School for Scandal; Spoiled Child.
    A.—Lady of Lyons; Irishman in London.

December

1. Saturday:
    S.C.—Youthful Queen; Lafitte.
    A.—Irishman in London; Mazeppa.
2. Sunday:
    S.C.—Mountain Sylph; Confounded Foreigners*.
    A.—Lady of Lyons; Mazeppa.
3.   S.C.—The Wife; Family Jars.
    A.—Forest Rose; Black Eyed Susan.
4.   S.C.—Wild Oats; Raising the Wind.
    A.—Lady of Lyons; Mazeppa.
5.   S.C.—Damon and Pythias; Lucille.
    A.—Solomon Swap; Luke the Laborer.
6.   S.C.—The Rivals; Robert Macaire* [Robert Macaire—
    Browne].
    A.—Lady of Lyons; Mazeppa.
7.   S.C.—The Stranger; Robert Macaire.
    A.—Forest Rose; Sam Patch* [Sam Patch—Marble];
    Black Eyed Susan.
8.   S.C.—Octavia Bragaldi; Lafitte.
    A.—The Maiden's Vow* [Jacob Jewsharp — Marble,
    Peggy—Miss Sydney Cowell, Emily—Mrs. Greene];
    Sam Patch; Luke the Laborer.
9. Sunday:
    S.C.—Mountain Sylph; Illustrious Stranger.
    A.—Lady of Lyons; Mazeppa.
10.   S.C.—Octavia Bragaldi; Robert Macaire.
    A.—Sam Patch.
11.   S.C.—Mountain Sylph; Robert Macaire.
    A.—Wedding Day; Bush Whacker*; Sam Patch.
12.   S.C.—Merchant of Venice; Robert Macaire.
    A.—Vermont Wool Dealer*; Sam Patch; Tom Cringle.
13.   S.C.—The Way to Get Married; Youthful Queen.
    A.—Lady of Lyons; Isabelle.
14.   S.C.—Mountain Sylph; Robert Macaire.
    A.—Lady of Lyons; Isabelle.
15.   S.C.—Love Chase; Rent Day.
    A.—Irishman in London; Isabelle; Wandering Minstrel.

16. Sunday:
    S.C.—Esmeralda; Mountain Sylph.
    A.—Lady of Lyons; Mazeppa.
17.   S.C.—Peter Wilkins; Flying Dutchman.
18.   S.C.—Lady of Lyons; High Life below Stairs.
    A.—Love Chase; Isabelle.
19.   S.C.—Love Chase; Frightened to Death.
    A.—Love Chase; Mazeppa.
20.   S.C.—Lady of Lyons; Monsieur Jacques.
    A.—Woman's Wit* [Custace—Miss Nelson, Sir Wm. Fond-love—Johnson, Walsingham—Fredericks]; Isabelle.
21.   S.C.—School for Scandal; High Life below Stairs.
    A.—Three Weeks after Marriage; La Bayadere.
22.   S.C.—Lady of Lyons; Maid of Croissy* [Sergeant Auster-litz—J. S. Browne, Theresa—Mrs. Farren].
    A.—Woman's Wit; Irishman in London.
23. Sunday:
    S.C.—Flying Dutchman; Confounded Foreigners.
    A.—Lady of Lyons; Cradle of Liberty.
24.   S.C.—Much Ado about Nothing; Monsieur Jacques.
    A.—La Bayadere.
25.   S.C.—George Barnwell; Flying Dutchman.
    A.—George Barnwell; Cradle of Liberty.
26.   S.C.—Lady of Lyons; Maid of Croissy.
    A.—Dumb Belle; La Bayadere.
27.   S.C.—Anne Boleyn** [Anne Boleyn—Miss Clifton, Earl Percy—J. R. Scott, Henry VIII—Harrison, Cardinal Wolsey—Pearson]; Country Squire*.
    A.—Lottery Ticket; La Bayadere.
28.   S.C.—Anne Boleyn; Old English Gentleman* [Squire Broadlands—Finn, Horace—J. S. Browne].
    A.—Dumb Belle; La Bayadere.
29.   S.C.—Anne Boleyn; Maid of Croissy.
    A.—Maid of Mariendorpt* [Metta—Mrs. Barrett, Gen. Kleiner — W. F. Johnson, Esther — Mrs. Greene, Hans—Browne]; Lady of Lyons.
30. Sunday:
    S.C.—Green Eyed Monster; Flying Dutchman.
    A.—Maid of Mariendorpt; Cradle of Liberty.
31.   S.C.—Maid of Mariendorpt; Old English Gentleman.

January, 1839

1. Tuesday:
    S.C.—Phantom Ship.
    A.—She Would Be a Soldier; Irishman in London; Sam Patch.
2.   S.C.—Maid of Mariendorpt.
    A.—Maid of Mariendorpt; Lottery Ticket.

3.   S.C.—Anne Boleyn; Lady and the Devil.
      A.—She Would Be a Soldier; Irishman in London; Sam
      Patch.
4.   S.C.—Rory O'More; Old English Gentleman.
      A.—Forest Rose; Cradle of Liberty; Black Eyed Susan.
5.   S.C.—Poor Gentleman; Adopted Child.
      A.—She Would Be a Soldier; Tom Cringle.
6. Sunday:
      S.C.—Rory O'More; Flying Dutchman.
      A.—Gambler's Fate; Vermont Wool Dealer.
7.   S.C.—New Way to Pay Old Debts; Naval Engagements*
      [Admiral Kingston—Finn, Lieutenant Kingston—
      Browne, Short—Cowell, Miss Mortimer—Mrs. Plu-
      mer].
      A.—Barrack Room; La Sylphide* [The Sylph—Madame
      Lecompte, Donald—Lecompte, Hela—Archer].
8.   S.C.—Battle of Bunker Hill; Robert Macaire.
      A.—He Would Be a Soldier; She Would Be a Soldier.
9.   S.C.—Old English Gentleman; Esmeralda.
      A.—Wedding Day; La Sylphide.
10.   S.C.—Rory O'More; Turning the Tables.
      A.—Born to Good Luck, first act; Perfection; Jonathan in
      England, second act; Thérèse, third act; Pizarro, last
      act; Adopted Child; Black Eyed Susan, last act; Ver-
      mont Wool Dealer.
11.   S.C.—Rob Roy; Maid of Croissy.
      A.—My Fellow Clerk; La Sylphide.
12.   S.C.—Laugh When You Can; Naval Engagements.
      A.—Macbeth; Irishman in London.
13. Sunday:
      S.C.—Virginius; The Bengal Tiger*.
      A.—Lady of Lyons; Forty Thieves.
14.   S.C.—Clandestine Marriage; Frightened to Death.
      A.—Gambler's Fate; Forty Thieves.
15.   S.C.—Guy Mannering; Maid of Croissy.
      A.—Lady of Lyons; Forty Thieves.
16.   S.C.—Lady of Lyons; Swiss Cottage.
      A.—Maid of Mariendorpt; Forty Thieves.
17.   S.C.—Love Chase; Monsieur Jacques.
      A.—Lady of Lyons; Naval Engagements.
18.   S.C.—The Wife; Frightened to Death
      A.—Belle's Stratagem; Naval Engagements.
19.   S.C.—Lady of Lyons; Turning the Tables.
      A.—Naval Engagements; Water Witch* [Alderman—
      Johnson, Tom Tiller—Barrett, Seadrift—Mrs. Barrett,
      Alida—Mrs. Greene].
20. Sunday:
      S.C.—Ion.
21.   S.C.—Ion; Old English Gentleman.
      A.—Naval Engagements; Water Witch.

22.   S.C.—Ion; Turning the Tables.
     A.—Truth* [Nina—Mrs. Barrett; Albert—Fredericks];
      Dumb Belle; Presumptive Evidence.
23.   S.C.—As You Like It; Maid of Croissy.
     A.—Cradle of Liberty; Isabelle.
24.   S.C.—Maid of Mariendorpt; Youthful Queen.
     A.—Truth; Water Witch.
25.   S.C.—Hunchback; Frightened to Death.
     A.—Truth; Forty Thieves.
26.   S.C.—The Stranger; Perfection.
     A.—George Barnwell; Isabelle.
27. Sunday:
     S.C.—Richard III; Crossing the Line.
     A.—Belle's Stratagem.
28.   S.C.—Love Chase; Youthful Queen.
     A.—Othello; Truth.
29.   S.C.—Much Ado About Nothing; Maid of Croissy.
     A.—Six pieces by the Ravels.
30.   S.C.—Maid of Mariendorpt; Robert Macaire.
     A.—Damon and Pythias; The Critic.
31.   S.C.—School for Scandal; Bombastes Furioso.
     A.—The Review.

February

1. Friday:
     S.C.—Mountain Sylph; Trial by Battle.
     A.—Lady of Lyons; Three Weeks After Marriage.
2.   S.C.—Honey Moon; Simpson and Company.
     A.—Lady of Lyons; Naval Engagements.
3. Sunday:
     S.C.—Green Eyed Monster.
     A.—Virginius.
4.   S.C.—The Waterman; My Young Wife and My Old Um-
     brella.
     A.—King Lear; Wags of Windsor.
5.   S.C.—Richard III; Bombastes Furioso.
     A.—Virginius; Truth.
6.   S.C.—New Way to Pay Old Debts; Turning the Tables.
     A.—Gladiator; The Day After the Wedding.
7.   S.C.—Merchant of Venice; Naval Engagements.
     A.—Metamora; Dumb Belle.
8.   S.C.—Othello; My Young Wife and My Old Umbrella.
     A.—Macbeth; Irishman in London.
9.   S.C.—Richard III; Turning the Tables.
     A.—King Lear; Dumb Belle.
10. Sunday:
     S.C.—King Lear.
     A.—Metamore; Dumb Belle.
11.   S.C.—Bertram; Naval Engagements.
     A.—Hamlet; Is He Jealous?

12. S.C.—Hamlet; My Young Wife and My Old Umbrella.
     A.—Lady of Lyons; El Hyder.
13. S.C.—Turning the Tables; La Bayadere.
     A.—Hunchback; Lottery Ticket.
14. S.C.—Richard III; High Life Below Stairs.
     A.—Macbeth; Wandering Minstrels.
15. S.C.—Raising the Wind; La Bayadere
     A.—Fazio; Adopted Child.
16. S.C.—Brutus; Mayor of Garratt.
     A.—Anne Boleyn; The Mummy.
17. Sunday:
     S.C.—Forty and Fifty; La Bayadere.
         A.—John Bull; El Hyder.
18. S.C.—Peculiar Position* [Champignon—Finn, Countess—
         Mrs. Farren]; The Pages of the Duke de Vendome*
         [Duke—DeBar, Count de Manet—Burke, Pedrillo—
         Mrs. Russell, Victor—Mlle. Augusta]; Frightened to
         Death.
     A.—Anne Boleyn; Irish Tutor.
19. S.C.—Naval Engagements; Pages of the Duke de Ven-
         dome; Peculiar Position.
     A.—Anne Boleyn; The Review.
20. S.C.—La Bayadere; Turning the Tables.
     A.—Irish Ambassador; Wives as They Were; Mummy.
21. S.C.—La Bayadere; Monsieur Jacques.
     A.—Lady of Lyons; Barrack Room.
22. S.C.—La Bayadere; Pages of the Duke de Vendome.
     A.—Love Chase; Youthful Queen.
23. S.C.—Old English Gentleman; A Day after the Wedding;
         Frightened to Death.
     A.—Twelfth Night; Omnibus.
24. Sunday:
     S.C.—Green Eyed Monster; Bengal Tiger.
     A.—Virginius; Irish Ambassador.
25. S.C.—Tam O'Shanter* [Tam O'Shanter—Finn, Souter
         Jonnie—Farren]; Hundred Pound Note; Tom and
         Jerry.
     A.—Ion; Irish Tutor.
26. S.C.—Charles II; My Young Wife and My Old Umbrella.
     A.—Twelfth Night; Perfection.
27. S.C.—Busy Body; My Schoolfellow* [Mr. Cool—Browne,
         Shrub—Finn]; Robert Macaire.
     A.—Romeo and Juliet; More Blunders Than One.
28. S.C.—Maid of Croissy; Peculiar Position.
     A.—Romeo and Juliet; Omnibus.

March

1. Friday:
   S.C.—Hundred Pound Note; The Secret; Removing the Deposits; Bombastes Furioso.
   A.—White Horse of the Peppers* [Gerald Pepper—Young Burke]; More Blunders Than One; Irish Ambassador.
2. S.C.—Turning the Tables; Naval Engagements.
   A.—Provoked Husband; Simpson and Company.
3. Sunday:
   S.C.—A Lesson in Love; Swiss Cottage.
   A.—Othello; Fortune's Frolic.
4. S.C.—St. Mary's Eve* [Madeline—Celeste, Major Wentworth—DeBar, Tom Bags—Cowell]; Removing the Deposits.
   A.—Damon and Pythias; Lottery Ticket.
5. S.C.—Monsieur Jacques; St. Mary's Eve; My Schoolfellow.
   A.—Venice Preserved; Irishman in London.
6. S.C.—Forty and Fifty; La Bayadere.
   A.—Richard III; Fortune's Frolic.
7. S.C.—My Schoolfellow; La Bayadere.
   A.—Shiek of the Desert* [The Shiek—Fielding, Col. Paragraph—Johnson, Twitter—Mrs. Greene, Hassan, Hossun, Ali—Three Arabs].
8. S.C.—French Spy; My Young Wife and My Old Umbrella.
   A.—Julius Caesar; Irishman in London.
9. S.C.—French Spy; Nabob for an Hour.
   A.—Sheik of the Desert; Fortune's Frolic.
10. Sunday:
    S.C.—Peter Wilkins; Poor Soldier.
    A.—Lady of Lyons; Gulliver in Lilliput* [Gulliver—Porter, Lord Flimnaap—Stevens, Lady Flimnaap—Miss Sutor].
11. S.C.—Wept of Wish-ton-Wish; La Bayadere.
    A.—Gambler's Fate; Sheik of the Desert.
12. S.C.—Wept of Wish-ton-Wish; La Bayadere
    A.—Town and Country; Rent Day.
13. S.C.—St Mary's Eve; Nabob for an Hour
    A.—Cradle of Liberty; Gulliver in Lilliput.
14. S.C.—French Spy; Robert Macaire
    A.—Rent Day; Sheik of the Desert.
15. S.C.—Nabob for an Hour; Spirit Bride and the Magi's Daughter* [Zela (Magi's daughter) assuming the characters of Alcares (a Greek Warrior), Tofak (a Tartar Chief)—Celeste].
    A.—Gulliver in Lilliput; George Barnwell; Exiles in the West* [Nathan Small—Porter, Lord Magno—Stevens, Lady Magno—Miss Sutor].
16. S.C.—Frightened to Death; Spirit Bride.
    A.—Macbeth; Sheik of the Desert.

17. Sunday:
    S.C.—One Hour; Cinderella.
    A.—Gulliver in Lilliput; Exiles in the West.
18.   S.C.—Child of the Wreck* [Maurice—Celeste]; La Baya-
        dere.
    A.—Rent Day; Irish Tutor.
19.   S.C.—Child of the Wreck; Maid of Cashmere.
    A.—Town and Country; Gulliver in Lilliput; Exiles in the
        West.
20.   S.C.—Wept of Wish-ton-Wish; French Spy.
    A.—Richard III; Lottery Ticket.
21.   S.C.—Wizard Skiff; Robert Macaire.
    A.—Englishmen in India; Gulliver in Lilliput; Exiles in
        the West.
22.   S.C.—Child of the Wreck; Wizard Skiff.
    A.—New Way to Pay Old Debts; Irishman in London.
23.   S.C.—Child of the Wreck; French Spy.
    A.—Nick of the Woods; Gulliver in Lilliput; Exiles in the
        West.
24. Sunday:
    S.C.—Cinderella; Oliver Twist*.
    A.—Speed the Plough; Does Your Mother Know You're
        Out?* [Bolt—Barrett, Mizzle—Johnson]; Tom Nod-
        dy's Secret* [Tom—Johnson, Ormond—Barrett, Ga-
        brielle—Mrs. Barrett].
25.   S.C.—Moorish Page; Wizard Skiff.
    A.—Lear.
26.   S.C.—Moorish Page; Wizard Skiff.
    A.—Nick of the Woods; Gulliver in Lilliput; Exiles in the
        West.
    S.L.—Richard III, principal scenes; Manager's Daughter*
        [Mr. Davenport—Davenport, Mrs. Davenport—Mrs.
        Davenport, Miss Davenport in six characters besides
        her own].
27.   S.C.—Star of the Forest* [Wyandhee—Celeste]; French
        Spy.
    A.—Richard III.
    S.L.—School for Scandal; Manager's Daughter.
28.   S.C.—Child of the Wreck; Star of the Forest.
    A.—Apostate; Amateurs and Actors* [Geoffrey Muffincap
        —Booth].
    S.L.—Merchant of Venice; Spoiled Child.
29.   S.C.—Maid of Cashmere; Robert Macaire.
    A.—Speed the Plough; Tom Noddy's Secret.
30.   S.C.—Wept of Wish-ton-Wish; Maid of Cashmere.
        A.—Hunchback; Fortune's Frolic.
    S.L.—Douglas; Actress of All Work.
31. Sunday:
    S.C.—Richard III, first, fourth, and fifth acts; Manager's
        Daughter.
    A.—Lady of Lyons; Tom Noddy's Secret.

April

1. Monday:
    S.C.—Virginius; Nabob for an Hour.
    A.—Rent Day; Irish Tutor.
2. S.C.——Macbeth; My Young Wife and My Old Umbrella.
    A.—Speed the Plough; Tom Noddy's Secret.
3. S.C.—King Lear; Bombastes Furioso.
    A.—Duchess de la Valliere* [Duchess—Mrs. Barrett, De Bragelone—Fredericks]; Lady of Lyons.
4. S.C.—Metamora; Swiss Cottage.
    A.—Venice Preserved, fourth act; School for Scandal, fourth act; The Secret; Raising the Wind; Irish Tutor.
5. S.C.—Damon and Pythias; Robert Macaire.
    A.—Wrecker's Daughter; Matrimony; Honest Thieves.
6. S.C.—Othello; My Young Wife and My Old Umbrella.
    A.—Duchess de la Valliere; Joan of Arc.
7. Sunday:
    S.C.—Hamlet; Spoiled Child.
    A.—Poor Gentleman; Tom Noddy's Secret.
8. S.C.—Brutus; Frightened to Death.
    A.—Rivals. Last night of the season.
9. S.C.—Damon and Pythias; Maid of Croissy.
10. S.C.—Gladiator; My Schoolfellow.
11. S.C.—Richard III; Dumb Belle.
12. S.C.—Gladiator; Naval Engagements.
13. S.C.—Pizarro; Thérèse.
14. Sunday:
    S.C.—Richard III; Tom Noddy's Secret.
15. S.C.—Lady of Lyons; William Tell.
16. S.C.—Richard III; Joan of Arc.
17. S.C.—Isabelle; Tom Noddy's Secret.
18. S.C.—Rivals; The Old Clock*; The Review.
19. S.C.—Every One Has His Faults; Tom Cringle's Log.
20. S.C.—Belle's Stratagem; Clari.
21. Sunday:
    S.C.—Burgomaster's Daughter; Tom and Jerry, first and second acts.
22. S.C.—Child of the Wreck; Maid of Cashmere.
23. S.C.—Wept of Wish-ton-Wish; Wizard Skiff.
24. S.C.—Moorish Page; French Spy.
25. S.C.—The Mother* [Mother—Celeste, Capt. Devenant—DeBar, Foxglove — Harrison, Larceny — S. Cowell, Fringella—Mrs. Plumer]; Maid of Cashmere.
26. S.C.—The Jewess.
27. S.C.—School for Scandal; Irish Tutor.
28. Sunday:
    S.C.—Englishmen in India; Paul Jones. Last night of the season.
29. A.—School for Reform.

May

28. Tuesday:
    A.—Borrowed Feathers; My Neighbor's Wife.

June

19. Wednesday:
    M.—Perfection; Four Mowbrays.
21.   M.—Swiss Cottage; No!

October

 8. Tuesday:
    A.—Perfection; Swiss Cottage.
 9.   A.—My Neighbor's Wife; No Song, No Supper.
10.   A.—Poor Soldier; Two Gregories.
12.   A.—Miller's Maid; Lottery Ticket.
13. Sunday:
    A.—Turn Out; Forty Thieves.
15.   A.—My Neighbor's Wife; Thérèse.
16.   A.—No!; Lady and the Devil.
17.   A.—Unfinished Gentleman; Youthful Queen.
18.   A.—Comfortable Service; Thérèse.
19.   A.—A Roland for an Oliver; Forty Thieves.
20. Sunday:
    A.—Hunchback; Dumb Girl of Genoa.
21.   A.—Paul Pry.
22.   A.—Rent Day; The Secret.
23.   A.—Soldier's Daughter; Maid of Munster.
24.   A.—Hunchback; No!
25.   A.—Thérèse; Mountain Devil.
26.   A.—Sledge Driver; Forty Thieves.
27. Sunday:
    A.—Rob Roy; Irish Lion* [Tom Moore—Radcliffe, Mrs.
        Cernlea Fizgig—Mrs. Stuart].
29.   A.—Rob Roy; Irish Lion.
30.   A.—Sweethearts and Wives; Mischief Making.
31.   A.—Robber's Wife; Dead Shot.

November

 1. Friday:
    A.—Sledge Driver; Irish Lion.
 2.   A.—Lady of Lyons; Raising the Wind.
 3. Sunday:
    A.—Irish Lion; Gambler's Fate.
 4.   A.—Rory O'More; Charles II.
 5.   A.—Gambler's Fate; Rory O'More.
 6.   A.—Lady of Lyons; Irish Lion.
 7.   A.—Rob Roy; Charles II.
 8.   A.—Lady of Lyons; Swiss Cottage.
 9.   A.—Sledge Driver; Raising the Wind; Frightened to
        Death.

10. Sunday:
     A.—Irish Lion; Mazeppa.
11.   A.—Mazeppa.
12.   A.—Frightened to Death; Mazeppa.
13.   A.—Irish Lion; Mazeppa.
14.   A.—Raising the Wind; Mazeppa.
15.   A.—Charles II; El Hyder.
16.   A.—Paul Pry; Forty Thieves.
17. Sunday:
     A.—El Hyder; Mazeppa.
18.   A.—The Stranger; Dumb Girl of Genoa.
19.   A.—Mazeppa, first act; Joan of Arc.
20.   A.—Irish Lion; Water Witch.
21.   A.—Water Witch; Joan of Arc.
22.   A.—Water Witch; El Hyder.
23.   A.—Joan of Arc; El Hyder.
24. Sunday:
     A.—Frightened to Death; Naomie* [Margrave—Brown,
     Naomie—Mrs. Stuart]; The Mummy.
26.   A.—Sledge Driver; Naomie; Black Phantom.
27.   A.—Much Ado about Nothing; Dead Shot.
28.   A.—Naomie; The Mummy; Black Phantom.
29.   A.—Rob Roy; Forty Thieves.
30.   A.—Duchess de la Vaubaliere; Frightened to Death. Last
     night of the season.

December

1. Sunday:
     S.C.—Englishmen in India; Peter Wilkins.
2.   S.C.—Hunchback; Peter Wilkins.
3.   S.C.—Lady of Lyons; Peter Wilkins.
4.   S.C.—Pizarro; The Mummy.
5.   S.C.—Rob Roy; Irish Lion.
6.   S.C.—Englishmen in India; Gambler's Fate.
7.   S.C.—Richelieu* [Cardinal de Richelieu—Barton, Chevalier de Mauprat—Field, Julie—Mrs. Stuart]; Swiss Cottage.
8. Sunday:
     S.C.—Dramatist; Dancing Barber* [Narcissus Fitzfruzzle —Balls].
9.   S.C.—Laugh When You Can; Rafael the Libertine* [Rafael—Balls, Alfonso—Field, Marie—Mrs. Stuart].
10.   S.C.—Belle's Stratagem; Dancing Barber.
11.   S.C.—She Stoops to Conquer; Rafael the Libertine.
12.   S.C.—Lady of Lyons; Buckle of Brilliants* [Fredericks— Balls, Albert—Field, Katharine—Miss Melton].
13.   S.C.—The Way to Get Married; Dancing Barber.
14.   S.C.—Lady of Lyons; Buckle of Brilliants.

15. Sunday:
      S.C.—School for Scandal; Duchess de la Vaubaliere.
16.   S.C.—Who Wants a Guinea?; Sam Patch.
17.   S.C.—Poor Gentleman; 33 John Street.
18.   S.C.—Forest Rose; Sam Patch.
19.   S.C.—Rafael the Libertine; Buckle of Brilliants; Dancing
              Barber.
21.   S.C.—Win Her and Wear Her; Buckle of Brilliants.
22. Sunday:
      S.C.—Sam Patch in France* [Sam—Marble, Bridget—
              Miss Melton]; sketch founded on Joe Miller* [Timo-
              theus Tactum—Balls, Kitty—Miss Verity]; Sam
              Patch.
23.   Lady of Lyons; Flying Dutchman.
24.   S.C.—Rivals; Vermonter; State Secrets* [Gregory Thim-
              blewell—Balls, Hugh Neville—Morton, Humphrey
              Hedghog—Boddy, Maud—Miss Verity].
25.   S.C.—George Barnwell; Peter Wilkins.
26.   S.C.—Douglas; French Spy.
27.   S.C.—French Spy; Sam Patch in France; Tom Thumb.
28.   S.C.—Youthful Queen; Sam Patch in France; Black Brig
              of Bermuda.
29. Sunday:
      S.C.—Black Brig of Bermuda; Yankee in Time; **Matteo
              Falcone**.
30.   S.C.—Yankee in Time; Forest Rose; Douglas.
31.   S.C.—French Spy; Vermonter; Lottery Ticket.

January, 1840

 1. Wednesday:
      S.C.—Plains of Chippewa; Flying Dutchman.
 2.   S.C.—Tour de Nesle; Vermonter; Black Eyed Susan.
 3.   S.C.—Yankee in Time; Sam Patch in France; Don Juan.
 4.   S.C.—Plains of Chippewa; Forest Rose; Don Juan.
 5. Sunday:
      S.C.—Jonathan in England, first act; Sam Patch; The
              Pilot, second and third acts; Thérèse, fourth act;
              Born to Good Luck; Black Eyed Susan.
 7.   S.C.—Timour the Tartar; Youthful Brigand; French Spy.
 8.   S.C.—Laugh When You Can; Peter Wilkins.
 9.   S.C.—Irish Lion; Masaniello.
10.   S.C.—Dead Shot; Masaniello.
11.   S.C.—The Mummy; Masaniello.
12. Sunday:
      S.C.—Masaniello; Timour the Tartar.
13.   S.C.—Masaniello; Timour the Tartar.
14.   S.C.—Irish Lion; Cinderella.
15.   S.C.—Cinderella; No!

16. S.C.—Cinderella; El Hyder.
     G.—Fall of the Alamo* [Col. Crockett—G. Chapman,
       Patty Snow—Mrs. G. Chapman]; Bully and the
       Dandy; Actress of All Work.
17. S.C.—Masaniello; El Hyder.
18. S.C.—Masaniello; Spirit of the Clyde* [Kenneth—Sin-
       clair, Alice—Miss Melton].

19. Sunday:
     S.C.—El Hyder; Irish Tutor; Joan of Arc.
20. S.C.—Richelieu.
21. S.C.—Guy Mannering, second act; Masaniello, second act;
       Sam Patch in France; Spirit of the Clyde.
22. S.C.—Vermonter; Yankee in Time; Black Eyed Susan.
23. S.C.—Love* [Hiron—J. M. Field, Sir Rupert—Pearson,
       Countess—Mrs. Sloman, Catharine—Mrs. J. M.
       Field]; Hercules, King of Clubs* [Tim—Sloman].
24. S.C.—Love; Married Yesterday.
25. S.C.—Love; Hercules.
     G.—Fall of the Alamo; Pleasant Neighbor; Dead Shot.

26. Sunday:
     S.C.—Peter Wilkins; Flying Dutchman.
27. S.C.—Love; Wandering Minstrel.
28. S.C.—Love; Hercules, King of Clubs.
29. S.C.—School for Scandal; Wandering Minstrel.
30. S.C.—Henrietta the Forsaken* [Pierre Gigot—Sloman,
       Henrietta—Mrs. Sloman]; Lovers' Quarrels; Fish out
       of Water.
31. S.C.—Paul Jones* [Paul Jones—Mrs. Sloman, Marquis
       d'Auray—Barton, Count Emanuel—J. M. Field,
       Marchioness d'Auray — Mrs. S t u a r t, Margaret
       d'Auray—Mrs. J. M. Field]; The Day after the
       Wedding.

February

1. Saturday:
    S.C.—Paul Jones; Naomie.
2. Sunday:
    S.C.—Love; Fish Out of Water.
3. S.C.—Henrietta the Forsaken; Lovers' Quarrels; Wander-
      ing Minstrel.
4. S.C.—Married Yesterday; Lady of Lyons; Catharine and
      Petruchio.
5. S.C.—Lady and the Devil; Le Dieu et la Bayadere.
6. S.C.—Dead Shot; Masked Ball from Gustavus; 33 John
      Street.
7. S.C.—Irish Tutor; Le Dieu et la Bayadere.
8. S.C.—Sledge Driver; Masked Ball from Gustavus; Irish
      Lion.

9. Sunday:
      S.C.—Le Dieu et la Bayadere.
11.   S.C.—Sorcerer* [Mammon the Monkey—Mons. Klisch-
      ing]; The Weathercock; Masked Ball from Gustavus.
      Ar.—The Comet* [Sir Credulous Testy—McKibbere,
      Plotwell—G. Chapman, Belmont—Ward, Emily—Mrs.
      G. Chapman]; Two Gregories; Actress of All Work.
12.   S.C.—Irish Lion; Fra Diavolo.
13.   S.C.—Le Dieu et la Bayadere; The Weathercock.
14.   S.C.—Masaniello; Spirit of the Clyde.
      Ar.—Bully and the Dandy; Pleasant Neighbor; A Trip to
      Scotland.
15.   S.C.—Dead Shot; Sorcerer.
      Ar.—Eccentric Lover; Enraged Politician; Actress of All
      Work.

16. Sunday:
      S.C.—Le Dieu et la Bayadere; The Mummy.
17.   S.C.—The Sorcerer.
      Ar.—The Denouncer; Old Maid.
18.   S.C.—Sorcerer; The Day After the Wedding.
      Ar.—The Comet; Pleasant Neighbor.
19.   S.C.—Rob Roy; Guy Mannering, last two acts.
      Ar.—Animal Magnetism; Turn Out.
20.   S.C.—Le Dieu et la Bayadere; Lady and the Devil.
      Ar.—Thérèse; Where Did the Money Come From?
21.   S.C.—Fra Diavolo; Spirit of the Clyde.
      Ar.—Idiot Witness; Old Maid.
22.   S.C.—Free and Easy; Dumb Belle.
      Ar.—Fall of the Alamo; Soldier's Return; The Review.

23. Sunday:
      S.C.—Lovers' Quarrels; Nature and Philosophy.
      Ar.—Iron Chest.
25.   S.C.—Nature and Philosophy; Irish Tutor; Le Dieu et la
      Bayadere.
26.   S.C.—Fontainbleau; Buckle of Brilliants; Spirit of the
      Clyde.
27.   S.C.—Married Yesterday; Robert the Devil, tomb scene;
      Free and Easy.
28.   S.C.—Fra Diavolo; Dancing Barber; No!
29.   S.C.—Irish Tutor; Nature and Philosophy; La Bayadere.

March

1. Sunday:
      S.C.—Lord of the Isles* [Ronald—Sinclair, Lord of Lorn—
      Archer, Robert Bruce—Pearson, Lady Isabel—Mrs.
      DeBar]; Buckle of Brilliants; Sorcerer.
3.   S.C.—West Indian; Dancing Barber.

4.   S.C.—Soldier's Courtship* [Col. Grayton—J. M. Field, Lady Melford—Mrs. J. M. Field, Fanny—Miss Melton]; Robert the Devil, tomb scene; Lady of Lyons, fourth and fifth acts; Masaniello, second act.

5.   S.C.—Laugh When You Can; Children in the Wood.

6.   S.C.—My Aunt; La Sonnambula.

7.   S.C.—The Way to Get Married; Dancing Barber.

8. Sunday:
    S.C.—Soldier's Courtship; Cinderella.

10.   S.C.—Dead Shot; La Sonnambula.

11.   S.C.—Dramatist; Le Dieu et la Bayadere.

12.   S.C.—Loan of a Lover; Cinderella.

13.   S.C.—Laugh When You Can; Robert the Devil, tomb scene; Buckle of Brilliants.

14.   S.C.—My Aunt; Fra Diavolo.

15. Sunday:
    S.C.—Three and the Deuce; La Sylphide.

16.   S.C.—Barber of Seville.

17.   S.C.—Love Alone Can Fix Him; La Sylphide; 33 John Street.

18.   S.C.—Dead Shot; Cinderella.

19.   S.C.—Irish Tutor; La Sylphide; Masaniello, first and second acts.

20.   S.C.—Three and the Deuce; Amilie* [Von der Teimer—Brough, Jose—Jones, Paul—Archer, Amilie—Madame Otto].

21.   S.C.—Nature and Philosophy; Amilie.

22. Sunday:
    S.C.—Dumb Belle; Amilie.

24.   S.C.—Rafael the Libertine; Fra Diavolo, second act; Robert Macaire.

25.   S.C.—Gambler's Fate; Peter Wilkins.

26.   S.C.—Der Freischutz, second act; Cinderella, first act; Barber of Seville, second act.

27.   S.C.—Sledge Driver; Amilie.

28.   S.C.—Cinderella; Der Freischutz, second act.

29. Sunday:
    S.C.—Robert Macaire; Masaniello.

31.   S.C.—Fra Diavolo; Mountain Sylph, third act; Masaniello, second act.

April

1. Wednesday:
    S.C.—Barber of Seville; Robert Macaire.

2.   S.C.—La Sonnambula; Robert Macaire.

3.   S.C.—Castle of Andalusia; No Song, No Supper.

4.   S.C.—Lady of Lyons; Swiss Cottage.

5 Sunday:
    S.C.—Sea Captain*; Peter Wilkins.

6.   S.C.—Sea Captain.

7. S.C.—Charles XII of Sweden; Spirit of the Clyde; Flying Dutchman.
8. S.C.—Sea Captain; Loan of a Lover.
9. S.C.—Lear, first act; Much Ado About Nothing, second act; Hamlet, third act; Macbeth, second act; Frightened to Death.
10. S.C.—Love; Family Jars.
11. S.C.—Paul Jones; Masaniello, second act; Hole in the Wall** [Ranger—J. M. Field].
12. Sunday:
S.C.—Lady of Lyons; Charles XII of Sweden.
13. S.C.—Macbeth.
14. S.C.—The Wonder; Lafitte.
15. S.C.—School for Scandal; Catharine and Petruchio.
16. S.C.—The Wife; Exchange No Robbery* [Sam Swypes—Barnes, Mrs. Swypes—Mrs. Durie].
17. S.C.—Richelieu; Exchange No Robbery.
18. S.C.—Merchant of Venice; Scape Goat* [Ignatius Polyglot—Barnes, Molly Moggs—Miss Melton].

19. Sunday:
S.C.—Richard III; Napoleon.
21. S.C.—Love; Chaos Is Come Again* [Col. Chaos—Barnes, Jack Bruce—Barrett].
22. S.C.—Octavia Bragaldi; Lafitte.
23. S.C.—Octavia Bragaldi; Chaos Is Come Again; Scape Goat.
24. S.C.—The Grecian Daughter* [Evander—Barton, Dionysius — Pearson, Phocion — Field, Euphrasia — C. Barnes]; Chaos Is Come Again; Lafitte.
25. S.C.—Dumb Belle; Is He Jealous?; Charles XII.
26. Sunday:
S.C.—Robert Macaire; Peter Wilkins.
27. S.C.—Mountain Sylph, act; Marriage of Figaro, act; Cinderella, act.
28. S.C.—La Sonnambula, first act; Deep, Deep Sea; Valentine and Orson.
29. S.C.—Catharine Howard** [Henry VIII—Pearson, Earl of Ethelwood—J. M. Field, Catharine Howard—Mrs. J. M. Field]; Barrack Room.

May

1. Friday:
S.C.—Last Days of Pompeii; Wept of Wish-ton-Wish, two scenes; Our Mary Anne* [Jonathan Tunks—Radcliffe, Mary Anne—Mrs. Radcliffe, Ernestine—Mrs. J. M. Field].
2. S.C.—The Mummy; Invincibles.
3. Sunday:
S.C.—Irish Lion; Last Days of Pompeii.

5.   S.C.—Mary Stuart, Queen of Scots* [David Rizzio—J. M. Field, Earl of Ruthven—Barton, Darnley—Morton, Mary Stuart—Mrs. Stuart, Lady Catharine—Mrs. Field]; The Secret.
6.   S.C.—Mademoiselle de Belle Isle* [Marquis—Barrett, D'Aubigny—J. M. Field, Mlle de Belle Isle—Mrs. Field]; Lying Valet; Vot of It?** [Straws—Himself].
7.   S.C.—Tortesa the Usurer* [Tortesa—Pearson, Angelo— J. M. Field, Tomaso—Holland, Isabella—Mrs. Field]; Plains of Chippewa.
8.   S.C.—Whims of a Comedian; Tortesa the Usurer; Day after the Fair.
9.   S.C.—Gamester; Rival Valets.
10. Sunday:
      S.C.—Mademoiselle de Belle Isle; Irish Lion; Soldier's Courtship; Tom and Jerry. Last night of the season.
17. Sunday:
      A.—Golden Farmer; Review.
19.   A.—Richard III; Tour de Nesle, prison scene.
20.   A.—Ins and Outs*; Our Mary Anne; Hunter of the Alps.
22.   A.—Soldier's Daughter; Thérèse.
23.   A.—Honest Thieves; Family Jars.
26. Tuesday:
      A.—The Denouncer; Ins and Outs.
27.   A.—The Denouncer; Tom Cringle's Log.
29.   A.—Iron Chest.
31. Sunday:
      A.—Ice Witch; Family Jars.

June

3.   Wednesday:
      A.—A Ghost in Spite of Himself; Timour the Tartar.
4.   A.—Timour the Tartar; Comfortable Service.
5.   A.—Forty Thieves; Ice Witch.
7.   Sunday:
      A.—Forty Thieves; Timour the Tartar.
9.   A.—Cure for Jealousy* [Thomas—Radcliffe]; Ice Witch.
11.   A.—Mischief Making; Spectre Bridegroom.
12.   A.—Jonathan in Difficulty; Mischief Making.
13.   A.—Tale of Blood.
14.   A.—Manager in Distress; Sprigs of Laurel; Fortune's Frolic. Last night of the season.

July

4.   Saturday:
      G.—Who's the Dupe?

September

19. Friday:
      G.—Irish Tutor; Rival Suitors.

October

9. Friday:
   S.C.—Speed the Plough; Loan of a Lover.
10.   S.C.—Laugh When You Can; Mischief Making.
11. Sunday:
   S.C.—Loan of a Lover; The Mummy; Robert Macaire.
12.   S.C.—Dumb Girl of Genoa; The Secret; Irish Tutor.
13.   S.C.—Robert Macaire; Perfection; No!
14.   S.C.—Paul Pry; Unfinished Gentleman.
15.   S.C.—Charles XII; Forty Thieves.
16.   S.C.—Comfortable Service; The Mummy; No Song, No
        Supper.
17.   S.C.—Robert Macaire; Forty Thieves.
18. Sunday:
   S.C.—Rory O'More; Peter Wilkins.
19.   S.C.—Mountain Devil; The Review; Young Widow.
20.   S.C.—Heir at Law; Turnpike Gate.
21.   S.C.—Sweethearts and Wives; Young Widow.
22.   S.C.—Rory O'More; Dead Shot; Fish Out of Water.
23.   S.C.—Robert Macaire; Peter Wilkins.
24.   S.C.—Sweethearts and Wives; Hundred Pound Note.
25. Sunday:
   S.C.—His Last Legs* [O'Callaghan—Barrett, Charles—
        DeBar]; Flying Dutchman.
26.   S.C.—Hundred Pound Note; Crossing the Line; Lottery
        Ticket.
27.   S.C.—His Last Legs; Flying Dutchman.
28.   S.C.—Rip Van Winkle; Luck in a Name; Amateurs and
        Actors.
29.   S.C.—Paul Pry; Robert Macaire.
30.   S.C.—Rory O'More; Flying Dutchman.
31.   S.C.—Town and Country; Swiss Cottage.

November

1. Sunday:
   S.C.—Shocking Events* [Puggs—Holland]; Lady of
        Lyons; His Last Legs.
2.   S.C.—Thérèse; His Last Legs; Loan of a Lover.
3.   S.C.—Charles XII; Irish Tutor; Mischief Making.
4.   S.C.—Dumb Girl of Genoa; Shocking Events; Flying
        Dutchman.
5.   S.C.—Lady of Lyons; His Last Legs.
6.   S.C.—King Lear; Shocking Events.
7.   S.C.—Lady of Lyons; Robert Macaire.
8.   S.C.—Nicholas Nickleby* [Nicholas—Field, Smike—Mrs.
        Field, Kate Nickleby—Mrs. Williams, Miss Squeers—
        Miss Morgan]; His Last Legs; Peter Wilkins.
9.   S.C.—Sweethearts and Wives; Nicholas Nickleby; Family
        Jars.

10. S.C.—Lady of Lyons; Nicholas Nickleby.
     Am.—Honey Moon.
11. S.C.—His Last Legs; St. George and the Dragon*
     [George—Lewellen, The Dragon Fiend—Signor Car-
     robalana, Kate—Mrs. DeBar, Sabia—Mrs. Williams].
     Am.—Richelieu; Three and the Deuce.
12. S.C.—Nicholas Nickleby; St. George and the Dragon.
     Am.—Reform; Of Age To-morrow.
13. S.C.—Nicholas Nickleby; St. George and the Dragon.
     Am.—Tortesa the Usurer; Weathercock.
14. S.C.—His Last Legs; St. George and the Dragon.
     Am.—Richelieu; Irishman in London.
15. Sunday:
     S.C.—Conanchestat* [Conanchestat — Lewellen, Addal-
     letta—Mrs. Williams]; St. George and the Dragon.
     Am.—Alice; Paul Jones.
16. S.C.—Nicholas Nickleby; You Can't Marry Your Grand-
     mother*; The Fortunes of Smike*.
     Am.—Lady of Lyons; Paul Jones.
17. S.C.—Lady of Lyons; Peter Wilkins.
     Am.—John of Procida** [John of Procida—Conner, Fer-
     nando — Maynard, Governor—Beecum, Guiscardo—
     Johnson, Isoline—Mrs. Farren]; Honest Thieves.
18. S.C.—Gambler's Fate; The Fortunes of Smike.
     Am.—Love; The Star Spangled Banner* [Tom—Conner,
     Rose—Mrs. Maynard].
19. S.C.—Othello; Shocking Events.
     Am.—The Liar.
20. S.C.—Gamester; His Last Legs.
     Am.—Charles II.
21. S.C.—Lady of Lyons; Charles XII.
     Am.—Dramatist.
22. Sunday:
     S.C.—George Barnwell; Wandering Minstrel.
     Am.—Gambler's Fate; Paul Jones.
23. S.C.—John of Procida; Hercules, King of Clubs.
     Am.—Isabelle.
24. S.C.—Merchant of Venice; Fish Out of Water.
     Am.—Laugh When You Can.
25. S.C.—Sam Patch in France; Wandering Minstrel; Black
     Eyed Susan.
     Am.—The Conquering Game; Mazeppa.
26. S.C.—Macbeth; Printer's Devil* [Pierra Pica—Holland,
     Duke—Pickering, Count—Field, Cecile—Mrs. Wil-
     liams].
     Am.—Mrs. White* [Mr. Peter White—Saunders, Col.
     Pepper — Farren, Widow White — Mrs. Farren];
     Mazeppa.

27.   S.C.—Who Wants a Guinea?; Hercules, King of Clubs;
       The Vermonter.
       Am.—Hunting a Turtle; Mazeppa.
28.   S.C.—Pizarro; Printer's Devil.
       Am.—Mazeppa; A Day in Paris.
29. Sunday:
       S.C.—Game Cock of the Wilderness* [Sampson Hard-
       head—Marble]; Tom and Jerry.
       Am.—The Youthful Days of Harrison* [Capt. Wm. Henry
       Harrison—Conner, Gen. Wayne—Beecum, Gen. Carle-
       ton — Farren, Jane — Mrs. Farren, Ruth — Mrs.
       Greene].
30.   S.C.—John of Procida; Luck in a Name.
       Am.—Mazeppa; The Weathercock.

December

1. Tuesday:
       S.C.—Game Cock of the Wilderness; Yankee in Time.
       Am.—Richard III; Nature and Philosophy.
2.   S.C.—Vermonter; Poor Soldier; Luke the Laborer.
       Am.—New Way to Pay Old Debts; The Youthful Days
       of Harrison.
3.   S.C.—Hamlet; Is He Jealous?
       Am.—Married Life.
4.   S.C.—Sam Patch in France; Timour the Tartar.
       Am.—Merchant of Venice; Promissory Note.
5.   S.C.—Timour the Tartar, first act; Two Friends; Paule et
       et Pauline*.
       Am.—Apostate; Sprigs of Laurel.
6. Sunday:
       S.C.—Richard Savage** [Richard Savage—Pearson, Sir
       Richard Steele—Field, Lord Rivers—Pickering, Mar-
       quis of Lushington—Radcliffe, Daniel Page—DeBar,
       Nancy—Mrs. Sloman, Mary—Mrs. Williams]; Timour
       the Tartar.
       Am.—Paul Jones.
7.   S.C.—The Times That Tried Us*; Fortune's Frolic; Black
       Eyed Susan.
       Am.—Othello; The Day after the Wedding.
8.   S.C.—Richard Savage; Sam Patch in France.
       Am.—Maidens Beware* [Rose Boquet—Mrs. Maynard];
       Lying Valet.
9.   S.C.—Road to Ruin; Wandering Minstrel.
       Am.—Ambrose Gwinett.
10.   S.C.—Rob Roy; The Times That Tried Us.
       Am.—Iron Chest; The Critic.
11.   S.C.—She Stoops to Conquer; Yankee in Time.
       Am.—Hamlet; Nature and Philosophy.
12.   S.C.—Richard Savage; Forest Rose.
       Am.—Irishman in London.

13. Sunday:
    S.C.—Tom and Jerry; Bottle Imp.
    Am.—Paul Jones.
14.   S.C.—Flying Dutchman; Forest Rose; Bottle Imp.
    Am.—The Conquering Game; Timour the Tartar.
15.   S.C.—Shocking Events; Born to Good Luck; Swiss Cottage.
    Am.—Mrs. White; Timour the Tartar.
16.   S.C.—Lady of Lyons; Bottle Imp.
    Am.—The Liar; Timour the Tartar.
17.   S.C.—Born to Good Luck; Irish Lion.
    Am.—Victorine; Timour the Tartar.
18.   S.C.—Irish Ambassador; Loan of a Lover.
    Am.—Damon and Pythias.
19.   S.C.—His Last Legs; Irish Tutor; You Can't Marry Your
    Grandmother.
    Am.—Timour the Tartar; Sprigs of Laurel.

20. Sunday:
    S.C.—Vermonter; Hercules, King of Clubs.
    Am.—Timour the Tartar.
21.   S.C.—John Bull; His Last Legs.
    Am.—Siamese Twins* [Siamese Twins — Greene and
    Saunders].
22.   S.C.—Rory O'More; Raising the Wind.
    Am.—Tortesa the Usurer.
23.   S.C.—Born to Good Luck; Irish Lion.
    Am.—Pizzaro; Turn Out.
24.   S.C.—Rory O'More; The Day After the Wedding.
    Am.—Timour the Tartar.
25.   S.C.—Rory O'More; Sam Patch in France.
    Am.—George Barnwell; Cherry and Fair Star.
26.   S.C.—Irish Ambassador; Irish Lion.
    Am.—Dumb Belle; Cherry and Fair Star.

27. Sunday:
    S.C.—Married Life; Jonathan in England, second act;
    Thérèse, last act; Yankee in Time, scenes.
    Am.—Cherry and Fair Star.
28.   S.C.—Irish Attorney* [Pierce O'Hara—Power]; Irish
    Tutor; Two Friends.
    Am.—Dead Shot; Cherry and Fair Star.
29.   S.C.—Irish Attorney; Omnibus; Married Life.
    Am.—Cherry and Fair Star.
30.   S.C.—Irish Ambassador; Teddy the Tiler; You Can't
    Marry Your Grandmother.
    Am.—Glencoe* [Halbert MacDonald—Conner, Melan—
    Farren, Lady MacDonald—Mrs. Greene, Helen Camp-
    bell—Mrs. Farren]; Cherry and Fair Star.
31   S.C.—Irish Attorney; Irish Lion.
    Am.—Cherry and Fair Star.

January, 1841

1. Friday:
   S.C.—White Horse of the Peppers; Peter Wilkins.
   Am.—Tour de Nesle; Cherry and Fair Star.
2. S.C.—White Horse of the Peppers; Omnibus; Swiss Cottage.
   Am.—Cherry and Fair Star; Timour the Tartar.
3. Sunday:
   S.C.—Married Life; The Spitfire* [Toby—Sloman].
   Am.—Tekeli.
4. S.C.—Irish Attorney; His Last Legs; Shocking Events.
5. S.C.—King O'Neil* [Capt. O'Neil—Power, Louis XV—
   Pearson, Richelieu—Field, Count Dillon—Barrett,
   Marchioness de Clermont—Mrs. Field]; The Mummy.
   Am.—Tekeli.
6. S.C.—King O'Neil; Irish Lion; Lottery Ticket.
   Am.—El Hyder; Cherry and Fair Star.
7. S.C.—Nervous Man and the Man of Nerve; Omnibus;
   Crossing the Line.
   Am.—Timour the Tartar; Turn Out.
8. S.C.—King O'Neil; Plains of Chippewa.
   Am.—The Conscript*; Paul Jones.
9. S.C.—Nervous Man and the Man of Nerve; His Last Legs;
   Swiss Cottage.
   Am.—Sprigs of Laurel.
10. Sunday:
    S.C.—Plains of Chippewa; Aladdin.
    Am.—Of Age To-morrow.
11. S.C.—Mischief Making; Hunting the Turtle; Aladdin.
    Am.—Conscript.
12. S.C.—Two Friends; Soldier's Courtship; Aladdin.
    Am.—Timour the Tartar.
13. S.C.—Dead Shot; 33 John Street; Aladdin.
    Am.—Richard III.
14. S.C.—Aladdin; Robert Macaire.
    Am.—Tour de Nesle.
15. S.C.—Aladdin; Two Friends.
    Am.—Timour the Tartar.
16. S.C.—Shocking Events; 33 John Street; Comfortable Service; No!
    Am.—Paul Jones.
17. Sunday:
    S.C.—Money* [Capt. Dudley Smith—Barrett, Evelyn—
    Field, Clara—Mrs. Field]; Aladdin.
    Am.—Money* [Evelyn—Conner, Sir John—Farren, Lady
    Franklin—Mrs. Greene, Sir Frederick—Maynard,
    Clara—Mrs. Farren].
18. S.C.—Romantic Widow* [Marquis de St. Croix—Ranger,
    Ernestine—Mrs. Field]; Money.
    Am.—Black Eyed Susan; Dark Doings*; Idiot Witness.

19.   S.C.—Money; Hunting a Turtle.
         Am.—Laugh When You Can.
20.   S.C.—King O'Neil; Omnibus.
         Am.—Mrs. White; Brian Boroihme.
21.   S.C.—The Artist's Wife* [Clermont—Ranger, Lady Charlotte—Mrs. Field]; Romantic Widow; Unfinished Gentleman.
         Am.—Brian Boroihme.
22.   S.C.—The Artist's Wife; Forest Rose; Loan of a Lover.
         Am.—Brian Boroihme.
23.   S.C.—Romantic Widow; Money.
         Am.—Brian Boroihme.
24. Sunday:
         S.C.—Romantic Widow; The Artist's Wife; Aladdin.
         Am.—Brian Boroihme; Paul Jones.
25.   S.C.—The Lover Husband* [Lord Sensitive—Ranger, Jack Jovial—Barrett, Lady Flora—Mrs. Field]; Aladdin.
         Am.—Money; Mazeppa.
26.   S.C.—The Lover Husband; Aladdin.
         Am.—Mazeppa.
27.   S.C.—Esmeralda; Aladdin.
         Am.—Charcoal Sketches*; Nicholas Nickleby.
28.   S.C.—The Artist's Wife; Aladdin.
         Am.—Mazeppa.
29.   S.C.—Gentleman and the Upstart* [Chuck—Ranger].
         Am.—A New Way to Pay Old Debts; Mad Actor.
30.   S.C.—Le Preux Chevalier* [Chevalier—Ranger]; The Artist's Wife; Aladdin.
         Am.—Iron Chest; Paul Jones.
31. Sunday:
         Am.—William Tell; Aethiop.

February

1. Monday:
         S.C.—Rural Felicity* [Simon Sly—Buckstone]; A Kiss in the Dark* [Mr. S. Pettibone—Buckstone].
2.   S.C.—Dramatist; The Secret.
         Am.—Richard III.
3.   S.C.—Rural Felicity; Vermonter.
         Am.—Promissory Note; Irish Widow; Widow Wiggins* [Widow Wiggins—Mrs. Fitzwilliam]; Mrs. White.
4.   S.C.—Forest Rose; Kiss in the Dark; Black Eyed Susan.
         Am.—Country Girl; Widow Wiggins; 'Tis All a Farce.
5.   S.C.—Esmeralda; Irish Lion.
         Am.—Promissory Note; Irish Widow; Widow Wiggins; Mrs. White.
6.   S.C.—Laugh When You Can; Printer's Devil.
         Am.—Soldier's Daughter; Mischief Making; Rendezvous.

7. Sunday:
    S.C.—Single Life* [Mr. Peter Pickney—Buckstone]; Vermonter; Flying Dutchman.
    Am.—Country Girl; Nature and Philosophy.
8.   S.C.—School for Scandal; No!
    Am.—Blue Devils; Ladies Club* [Mrs. Fitzsmyth—Mrs. Fitzwilliam]; Widow Wiggins; Rendezvous.
9.   S.C.—Single Life; Kiss in the Dark.
    Am.—Two Gregories; Timour the Tartar.
10.   S.C.—Single Life; Rural Felicity.
    Am.—Ladies Club; Foreign Airs and Native Graces* [Emily Staples—Mrs. Fitzwilliam].
11.   S.C.—West Indian; Irish Lion.
    Am.—Soldier's Daughter; Foreign Airs and Native Graces.
12.   S.C.—Weak Points* [Jemmy Wheedle—Buckstone]; Kiss in the Dark; Dumb Girl of Genoa.
    Am.—Bold Stroke for a Husband; Foreign Airs and Native Graces; Irish Tutor.
13.   S.C.—Money; Aladdin.
    Am.—Marired Life; Widow Wiggins; Married Yesterday.
14. Sunday:
    S.C.—Esmeralda; Robert Macaire.
    Am.—Banished Star* [Charley—Buckstone, Mlle. Fanny Nonpareil—Mrs. Fitzwilliam]; Paul Jones.
15.   S.C.—His Last Legs; Virginia Mummy; H B*; Masquerade.
    Am.—Banished Star; Widow Wiggins; Irish Tutor.
16.   S.C.—Dramatist; Single Life.
    Am.—Banished Star; Foreign Air and Native Graces.
17.   S.C.—Walter Tyrrell* [William II—Pearson, Walter Tyrrell—Field, Editha—Miss Mason]; Is He Jealous?; His Last Legs.
    Am.—Married Life; Timour the Tartar.
18.   S.C.—Le Preux Chevalier; The Artist's Wife; Dumb Girl of Genoa.
    Am.—As You Like It; Dead Shot.
19.   S.C.—El Hyder; Zembuca.
    Am.—Tour de Nesle.
20.   S.C.—Mademoiselle de Belle Isle; G-A-G** [Manager—Field, True-taste — Pearson, Shakespeare — DeBar, Stuffy—Boddy, Puffy—Radcliffe, Small parts—Reeder, All-to-say—Schoolcraft].
    Am.—Bippo, the Island Ape.
21. Sunday:
    S.C.—Nicholas Nickleby; A Day After the Fair.
    Am.—Bippo, the Island Ape.
22.   S.C.—Tutoona; Zembuca.
    Am.—The Hypocondriac; Bippo, the Island Ape.
23.   S.C.—Walter Tyrrell; Aladdin.
    Am.—Thérèse.

24. S.C.—Mademoiselle de Belle Isle; G-A-G; Irish Lion.
    Am.—Pizarro.
25. S.C.—Tutoona; Esmeralda.
    Am.—Othello.
26. S.C.—West Indian; Aladdin.
    Am.—Damon and Pythias.
27. S.C.—H.B.; G-A-G; Zembuca.
    Am.—Romeo and Juliet.
28. Sunday:
    S.C.—Weak Points; El Hyder.
    Am.—Richelieu, first act; The Wife, fourth act.

March

1. Monday:
   S.C.—Othello; Which is Which?
   Am.—Merchant of Venice.
2. S.C.—Romantic Widow; Cataract of the Ganges.
   Am.—Forty Thieves.
3. S.C.—Gamester; Cataract of the Ganges.
   Am.—Virginius.
4. S.C.—Hamlet; H.B.
   Am.—Forty Thieves.
5. Am.—Cataract of the Ganges.
6. S.C.—Perfection; La Sylphide; Handsome Husband.
   Am.—Cataract of the Ganges.
7. Sunday:
   Am.—Cataract of the Ganges.
8. S.C.—The Weathercock; La Sylphide; Three Weeks after
   Marriage.
   Am.—Young Widow; Widow Wiggins; Two Gregories.
9. Am.—Mrs. White; Irish Widow; Foreign Airs and Native
   Graces; Lovers' Quarrels.
10. S.C.—Dumb Belle; La Sylphide; The Day after the
    Wedding.
    Am.—Blue Devils; Out of Place* [Sophy Sollikins—Mrs.
    Fitzwilliam]; The Middy Ashore** [Harry Halcyon—
    Mrs. Fitzwilliam]; Rendezvous.
11. Am.—Married Yesterday; Wedding Day; Out of Place;
    Lottery Ticket.
12. S.C.—Three Weeks after Marriage; Nathalie*; Soldier's
    Courtship.
    Am.—Dumb Belle; Foreign Airs and Native Graces; The
    Middy Ashore; Where Did the Money Come From?
13. S.C.—Nathalie.
    Am.—Spectre Bridegroom; Out of Place; Widow Wiggins.
14. Sunday:
    S.C.—Handsome Husband; Nathalie; The Day After the
    Wedding.
    Am.—Englishman in India; Out of Place; Our Mary Anne.

15.   Am.—Banished Star; The Weathercock.
16.   S.C.—His Last Legs; Nathalie; The Weathercock.
       Am.—Married Life; Foreign Airs and Native Graces;
           Mischief Making.
17.   Am.—Our Mary Anne; Irish Widow; Widow Wiggins;
           St. Patrick's Day.
18.   S.C.—My Aunt; La Tarentule; Swiss Cottage.
       Am.—Lottery Ticket; Barrack Room; Out of Place; The
           Christening.
19.   Am.—The Conquering Game; Gnome Fly*.
20.   Am.—Napoleon; Tom Noddy's Secret; Out of Place; The
           Christening.
21. Sunday:
       Am.—Irishman in London; Gnome Fly; Family Jars;
           Napoleon.
22.   S.C.—Money; Flying Dutchman.
       Am.—Gnome Fly; No Song, No Supper; Bippo.
23.   S.C.—Honey Moon; Dumb Girl of Genoa.
       Am.—Ambrose Gwinett; Blue Beard, first act; Irishman
           in London.
24. S.C.—Lady of Lyons; Zembuca.
       Am.—Aethiop; Bippo.
25.   S.C.—Three Weeks after Marriage; La Tarentule; Swiss
           Cottage.
       Am.—Richelieu; The Birthday, first act; Death Token.
26.   S.C.—Esmeralda; Robert Macaire.
       Am.—Maid of Croissy; My Young Wife and My Old
           Umbrella; Raising the Wind.
27.   S.C.—Crossing the Line; La Tarentule; Loan of a Lover.
       Am.—Too Late for Dinner; Robert Macaire.
28. Sunday:
       S.C.—Town and Country; El Hyder.
       Am.—Blue Beard, first act; Maid of Croissy; Paul Jones.
29.   S.C.—Unfinished Gentleman; Nathalie; No!
30.   Am.—St. Patrick's Day.
31.   S.C.—Shocking Events; Le Dieu et la Bayadere, ballet**
           [Zoloe—Elssler, The Unknown—Riese].
       Am.—Isabelle.

April

1. Thursday:
       Am.—Irish Tutor; Cataract of the Ganges.
2.   S.C.—Unfinished Gentleman; La Sylphide; Shocking
           Events. Last night of the season.
       Am.—Cataract of the Ganges.
3.   Am.—Cataract of the Ganges.
4. Sunday:
       Am.—Cataract of the Ganges.
5.   Am.—Cataract of the Ganges; Magic Box*.

6.   Am.—Forest of Bondy; Timour the Tartar.
7.   S.C.—Mademoiselle de Belle Isle; Robert Macaire.
     Am.—Cobbler's Frolic*; Forest of Bondy.
8.   Am.—Maid of Croissy; Cataract of the Ganges.
9.   Am.—Shoemaker of Toulouse.
10. Am.—Hunting a Turtle; Masked Ball.
11. Sunday:
     Am.—Family Jars; Cataract of the Ganges.
12. Am.—Green Man; Green Eyed Monster.
13. Am.—Cataract of the Ganges.
15. Am.—Robert Macaire.
18. Sunday:
     Am.—A Kiss in the Dark; Out of Place; Make Your Wills*
     [Joseph Brag—Buckstone].
19. Am.—Is He Jealous?; Foreign Airs and Native Graces;
     A Kiss in the Dark.
20. Am.—Swiss Cottage; Snapping Turtles**; Tom Noddy's
     Secret.
21. Am.—Perfection; Snapping Turtles; Out of Place.
22. Am.—Married Yesterday; Irish Widow; A Kiss in the
     Dark.
23. Am.—A Kiss in the Dark; Snapping Turtles; Widow
     Wiggins.
24. Am.—Is He Jealous?; Tom Noddy's Secret; Mischief
     Making.
25. Sunday:
     Am.—Dream at Sea* [Tim Tinkle—Buckstone, Biddy—
     Mrs. Fitzwilliam]; Foreign Airs and Native Graces.
26. Am.—The Stranger; Lady and the Devil.
27. Am.—Orphan of Geneva; Dumb Belle.
28. Am.—Rob Roy.
29. Am.—Idiot Witness.
30. Am.—Charles II; Two Gregories.

May

1. Saturday:
     Am.—Lady of the Lake, first and second acts.
2. Sunday:
     Am.—Last Days of Pompeii; Perfection.
3.   Am.—Last Days of Pompeii.
4.   Am.—Last Days of Pompeii.
5.   Am.—Fashionable Friends* [Simmons—Buckstone];
     Snapping Turtles; Rendezvous.
6.   Am.—Dream at Sea; Widow Wiggins; Bath Road.
7.   Am.—Barrack Room; Foreign Airs and Native Graces;
     Fashionable Friends.
8.   Am.—Perfection; My Little Adopted* [Lauretta Seymour
     —Mrs. Fitzwilliam]; Snapping Turtles.

9. Sunday:
    Am.—Dream at Sea; Out of Place.
10.   Am.—Irish Widow, first act; Foreign Airs and Native
    Graces, prima donna scene; My Little Adopted; Widow
    Wiggins, last scene; Out of Place, scene; Married
    Yesterday.
11.   Am.—Last Days of Pompeii; Three and the Deuce. Last
    night of the season.
13.   Am.—As You Like It; Widow Wiggins, scene; Three and
    the Deuce.
30. Sunday:
    C.—Gretna Green.

June

6. Sunday:
    A.E.—Sketch from Matthews Mail Coach Adventures;
    Dialogue between a lisping lady, Frenchman, and a
    Critic in Black.
13.   C.—Industry Must Prosper.
20.   C.—Swiss Cottage.
27.   C.—Young Widow.

July

4 Sunday:
    C.—Uncle Sam.

October

25. Monday:
    S.C.—Jeremiah Blackstitch* [Sir Wm. Cabbage—H. Long,
    Jeremiah Blackstitch—Levi, Mr. Calandar—Smith].
26.   S.C.—Jeremiah Blackstitch.
27.   S.C.—Merry Market Men*.
28.   S.C.—Merry Market Men.
29.   S.C.—Clown Turned Dentist*.
30.   S.C.—Clown Turned Dentist.
31. Sunday:
    S.C.—Don Quixote.

November

1. Monday:
    S.C.—Don Quixote.
2.   S.C.—Harlequin Frolics*.
3.   S.C.—Harlequin Frolics.
4.   S.C.—Jeremiah Blackstitch.
5.   S.C.—Jeremiah Blackstitch.
7. Sunday:
    S.C.—The Secret.
8.   S.C.—My Neighbor's Wife.
9.   S.C.—Hunting a Turtle.
10.   S.C.—Dead Shot.

11.   S.C.—Hercules, King of Clubs.
12.   S.C.—Poor Soldier.
13.   S.C.—No!; How Do You Manage?
14. Sunday:
       S.C.—Wandering Minstrel; Dumb Man of Manchester*
       [Tom—Wood, Edward Wilten—T. S. Cline].
15.   S.C.—How Do You Manage?; Dumb Man of Manchester.
16.   S.C.—Loan of a Lover; The Murdered Boatman and His
       Dog* [Dick—Wood, Will Wherry—T. S. Cline].
17.   S.C.—The Murdered Boatman and His Dog.
18.   S.C.—Wreck Ashore; Dumb Man of Manchester.
19.   S.C.—The Evening Star*; The Wreck Ashore; The Mur-
       dered Boatman and His Dog.
20.   S.C.—Honest Thieves; Forest of Bondy.
       Am.—Heir at Law; Swiss Swains* [Swig—Sol Smith,
       Walter—DeBar,   Burgomaster—Sankey,   Rosette—
       Mrs. Farren, Mrs. Glib—Mrs. Russell].
21. Sunday:
       S.C.—Timour the Tartar; Philip Quarll and His Monkey**
       [Philip Quarll—Wood, Monkey—Master Wood].
       Am.—Rob Roy; Don Juan.
22.   S.C.—Turnpike Gate; Philip Quarll and His Monkey; Tim-
       our the Tartar.
       Am.—Guy Mannering; Swiss Cottage.
23.   S.C.—Philip Quarll and His Monkey; Review; Timour the
       Tartar.
       Am.—Simpson and Company.
24.   S.C.—The Stranger; Timour the Tartar.
       Am.—Loan of a Lover.
25.   S.C.—Jack the Giant Killer* [Kinderfresser—Wood, Little
       Jack—Master Wood]; Wandering Minstrel; Hunting
       a Turtle; El Hyder.
       Am.—Ladder of Love.
26.   S.C.—Jack the Giant Killer; Husband at Sight; El Hyder.
       Am.—Robert Macaire.
27.   S.C.—His Last Legs; Forty Thieves.
       Am.—Introduce Me*; Ladder of Love.
28. Sunday:
       S.C.—Raising the Wind; Mad as a March Hare; Blue
       Beard.
       Am.—Swiss Swains; Don Giovanni.
29.   S.C.—Dumb Belle; Mad as a March Hare; Blue Beard.
       Am.—The Stranger.
30.   S.C.—Married Rake; Mad as a March Hare; Blue Beard.
       Am.—Black Eyed Susan.

December

 1. Wednesday:
       S.C.—Blue Beard; Timour the Tartar.
       Am.—Town and Country.

2.   S.C.—The Grateful Lion* [Androcles—Wood]; El Hyder.
      Am.—Dumb Girl of Genoa; Masked Ball.
3.   S.C.—Perfection.
      Am.—Forest of Rosenwald; Bombastes Furioso.
4.   S.C.—Is He Jealous?
      Am.—Sweethearts and Wives; Don Giovanni.
5. Sunday:
      S.C.—The Mummy; Harlequin's Olio*.
      Am.—Paul Jones; Ladder of Love.
6.   S.C.—King Henry IV, Part I; Harlequin's Olio.
      Am.—Town and Country; John Jones.
7.   S.C.—The Kentuckian; Monsieur Mallet; Harlequin's Olio.
      Am.—Henry the IV; Mrs. White.
8.   S.C.—Rip Van Winkle; Harlequin's Olio.
      Am.—Brigand; Rail Road Station* [Mr. Sampson Jones—
          Thorne].
9.   S.C.—Henry IV, Part I; Mad as a March Hare.
      Am.—Henry IV.
10.   S.C.—Jonathan in England; Monsieur Mallet.
      Am.—Old English Gentleman; Rail Road Station; Forest
          of Rosenwald.
11.   S.C.—Henry IV; Review.
      Am.—My Sister Kate* [Kate—Mrs. Farren]; Dumb Girl
          of Genoa.
12. Sunday:
      S.C.—Peter Wilkins; Wreck of Punchinello, ballet.
      Am.—London Assurance* [Sir Harcourt Courtly—Farren,
          Meddle—Thorne, Max Harkaway—Sankey, Charles
          Courtly—Maynard, Mr. Spanker—Ludlow, Dazzle—
          DeBar, Lady Gay Spanker—Mrs. Farren, Grace Hark-
          away—Miss Petrie]; Dead Alive*.
13.   S.C.—Merry Wives of Windsor; Monsieur Mallet; Har-
          lequin's Olio.
      Am.—London Assurance.
14.   S.C.—33 John Street; Turnpike Gate.
      Am.—London Assurance.
15.   S.C.—Wreck of Punchinello.
      Am.—London Assurance; Pleasant Neighbor.
16.   S.C.—The Pride of the Navy*; Middy Ashore; **Poor**
          Soldier.
      Am.—Robert Macaire; Barber of Seville.
17.   S.C.—Perfection.
      Am.—Lady of Lyons; Barber of Seville.
18.   S.C.—Middy Ashore; Virginia Mummy.
      Am.—Tour de Nesle; Barber of Seville.
19. Sunday:
      S.C.—Handsome Husband; Whirlwind, ballet.
      Am.—Old Maids* [Sir Philip Brilliant—DeBar, Master
          Blunt—Sankey, Thomas Blunt—Maynard, J o h n
          Blunt—Saunders, Lady Ann—Mrs. Farren, Lady
          Blanche—Miss Petrie]; Paul Jones.

20. S.C.—London Assurance; Rendezvous.
    Am.—My Friend the Governor; Frightened to Death.
21. S.C.—London Assurance; Woman's the Devil*.
    Am.—Old Maids; Rail Road Station.
22. S.C.—London Assurance; Woman's the Devil; Middy Ashore.
    Am.—My Friend the Governor; Hortense*.
23. S.C.—London Assurance; Nonpareil* [Jack Nonpareil—Barrett].
    Am.—My Sister Kate.
24. S.C.—London Assurance; Woman's the Devil.
    Am.—Is He Jealous?; Three Faced Frenchman.
25. S.C.—George Barnwell; Aladdin.
    Am.—La Pension de Ma Soeur*.
26. Sunday:
    S.C.—Aladdin.
    Am.—Ladder of Love; Monsieur Duguigon.
27. S.C.—Merry Wives of Windsor; Philip Quarll and His Monkey.
    Am.—Fer et Poison*; Four Lovers.
28. S.C.—King Lear; Loan of a Lover.
29. S.C.—Merry Wives of Windsor; Swiss Cottage.
    Am.—'Tis She!
30. S.C.—Rip Van Winkle; Monsieur Mallet.
31. S.C.—Henry IV, Part I; The Kentuckian.
    Am.—Simpson and Company; Brigand.

January, 1842

1. Saturday:
    S.C.—Eddystone Elf**; Blue Jackets*; Red Indian and His Dog*.
    Am.—Alive and Merry*; Paul Jones.
2. Sunday:
    S.C.—Gambler's Fate; Blue Jackets; Masquerade.
    Am.—Alive and Merry; Death Token.
3. S.C.—London Assurance; Loan of a Lover.
    Am.—Rob Roy; My Friend the Governor.
4. S.C.—London Assurance; Blue Jackets.
    Am.—Alive and Merry; The Murder and the Orphan.
5. S.C.—Married Rake; Norma.
    Am.—Conscript; Valet de Sham* [Wigler—Thorne, Miss Marchmont—Mrs. Farren, Clipper—Miss Petrie].
6. S.C.—London Assurance; Red Indian and His Dog.
    Am.—Guy Mannering; Valet de Sham.
7. S.C.—The Mummy; Norma.
    Am.—School for Scandal.
8. S.C.—She Would Be a Soldier; Station House* [Valentine Quill—Barrett]; Wild Boy of Bohemia.
    Am.—She Would Be a Soldier.

9. Sunday:
   S.C.—American Farmer; All the World's a Stage; Harlequin's Olio.
   Am.—Last Days of Pompeii; Paul Jones.
10.   S.C.—Station House; Norma.
   Am.—Reform; Last Days of Pompeii.
11.   S.C.—Yankee in Time; Luke the Laborer.
   Am.—Englishmen in India; Turning the Tables.
12.   S.C.—Handsome Husband; Norma.
   Am.—Bold Dragoons.
13.   S.C.—Sam Patch in France; Vermonter; Black Eyed Susan.
   Am.—Last Days of Pompeii.
14.   S.C.—Pleasant Neighbors; La Sonnambula.
   Am.—Valet de Sham.
15.   S.C.—Game Cock of the Wilderness; All the World's a Stage; Yankee in Time.
   Am.—Jacques Strop* [Robert Macaire—DeBar, Jacques Strop—Saunders].
16. Sunday:
   S.C.—The Gambler's Fate; La Sonnambula.
   Am.—Cherry and Fair Star.
17.   S.C.—American Farmer; Sam Patch in France; Floating Beacon* [Jack Junk—Marble, Mariette—Mrs. Richardson].
   Am.—Roof Scrambler* [Swelvino—Rose, Rodolpho—DeBar, Bobby—Saunders, Notary—Lake, Molly Brown—Thorne, Lizzy—Mrs. Farren, Therese—Mrs. Russell].
18.   S.C.—Loan of a Lover; Norma.
   Am.—Cherry and Fair Star.
19.   S.C.—The Times That Tried Us; Game Cock of the Wilderness; Vermonter.
   Am.—Roof Scrambler.
20.   S.C.—Jealous Husband; Zampa* [Zampa — Manvers, Bruno—Sequin, Alphonso—Brunton, Camilla—Mrs. Sequin, Ritta—Mrs. Richardson].
   Am.—Last Days of Pompeii.
21.   S.C.—Ebenezer Venture* [Ebenezer Venture—Marble, Emma—Mrs. Sergeant]; Luke the Laborer.
   Am.—Bombastes Furioso.
22.   S.C.—Lottery Ticket; Zampa.
   Am.—Valet de Sham; Schinder Eller* [Doctor Truman Stillman—DeBar, Col. Umbrella—Thorne, Ricardo—Farren, Schinder Eller—Mrs. Farren, Miss Martineau — Mrs. Russell, Lady Blessington — Mrs. Wright]; Frightened to Death.
23 Sunday:
   S.C.—Aladdin; Wandering Minstrel.
   Am.—Jacques Strop; Schinder Eller.

24.   S.C.—My Husband's Ghost; La Sonnambula.
        Am.—Sckaggs Family*; Schinder Eller.
25.   S.C.—A Dazzle by the Great Western*; American Farmer;
        Sam Patch in France; Born to Good Luck; Who Wants
        a Guinea?; The Wife; Thérèse; Black Eyed Susan.
        Portrayal of one role from each.
        Am.—Ladder of Love; Schinder Eller; Turning the Tables.
26.   S.C.—Young Widow; Norma.
        Am.—Henry IV; Schinder Eller.
27.   S.C.—Crossing the Line; Cinderella.
        Am.—King Lear; Schinder Eller.
28.   S.C.—My Husband's Ghost; Cinderella.
        Am.—Merry Wives of Windsor; Schinder Eller.
29.   S.C.—Cinderella; Promissory Note.
        Am.—Rip Van Winkle; Kentuckian, first act; Monsieur
        Mallet; Schinder Eller.
30. Sunday:
        S.C.—Cinderella, first act; La Sonnambula, first act;
        Zampa, third act.
        Am.—Lady of the Lake; Tom and Jerry.
31.   S.C.—The Will; Nicholas Nickleby.
        Am.—Heir at Law; Schinder Eller.

February

1. Tuesday:
        S.C.—La Sonnambula, first act; La Gazza Ladra* [LaRoche
        —Archer, Gianetto—Manvers, Fernando—Seguin,
        Peppo—Mrs. Richardson, Ninetta—Mrs. Seguin].
        Am.—Rifle Brigade*; Last Days of Pompeii.
2.   S.C.—A Lesson for Ladies* [St. Val—Pearson, Made-
        moiselle Debreur—Mrs. Richardson]; Nicholas
        Nickleby.
        Am.—Rifle Brigade; Harlequin and the Magic Sword.
3.   S.C.—Fra Diavolo; The Waterman.
        Am.—Turning the Tables; Rifle Brigade.
4.   S.C.—A Lesson for Ladies; Aladdin.
        Am.—My Neighbor's Wife; Harlequin.
5.   S.C.—Norma, first act; La Gazza Ladra; Pleasant
        Neighbor.
        Am.—Speed the Plough; Mischief Making.
6. Sunday:
        S.C.—Pizarro; Miller and His Men.
        Am.—Swiss Cottage; Rail Road Station; Harlequin's Olio.
7.   S.C.—London Assurance; Nabob for an Hour.
8.   S.C.—London Assurance; His Last Legs.
        Am.—Old Maids; Introduce Me.
9.   S.C.—London Assurance; My Young Wife and My Old
        Umbrella.
        Am.—Cure for the Heartache; Orphan and the Murderer.

10.   S.C.—London Assurance; Robert Macaire.
11.   S.C.—Belle's Stratagem; Seven's the Main.
12.   S.C.—London Assurance; Seven's the Main; Fish Out of
        Water.
        Am.—Naiad Queen* [Schnapp—DeBar, Carraline—Mrs.
        Farren, Queen—Miss Petrie].
13.   Sunday:
        S.C.—My Husband's Ghost; New Orleans Assurance**
        [Mrs. Shabbycoat Shortly—Barrett, Pat Barkaway—
        Greene, Hardly Shortly—Pearson, Mr. Banker—Slo-
        man, Ph. G. Dazzle Still Esq.—Hill, Park Peddle—
        Cowell, Warm—Reeder, Mrs. Guy Banker—Mrs.
        Greene, Grease Barkaway—Mrs. Sergeant]; Per-
        fection.
        Am.—Naiad Queen.
14.   S.C.—School for Scandal; Maid of Croissy.
        Am.—Naiad Queen.
15.   S.C.--London Assurance; Maid of Croissy.
        Am.—Naiad Queen.
16.   S.C.—The Foreign Prince* [Jim Crow—Rice, Barney—
        Cowell, Emily—Mrs. Hill, Letty—Mrs. Sergeant];
        Handsome Husband; Sarcophagus.
        Am.—Naiad Queen.
17.   S.C.—London Assurance; Jumbo Jim* [Jumbo Jim—
        Rice].
        Am.—Naiad Queen.
18.   S.C.—Jim Crow in London; Extravaganza of Jim Crow;
        Four Sisters; The Foreign Prince.
        Am.—Naiad Queen.
19.   S.C.—Peacock and Crow; Nabob for an Hour; Jumbo Jim.
        Am.—Naiad Queen.
20.   Sunday:
        S.C.—Jumbo Jim; Robert Macaire; Sarcophagus.
        Am.—Naiad Queen.
21.   S.C.—Sarcophagus; Such a Gitting up Stairs* [Zip Larkin
        —Rice]; Perfection; The Foreign Prince.
        Am.—Naiad Queen.
22.   S.C.—Marino Faliero*.
        Am.—Rifle Brigade; Naiad Queen.
23.   S.C.—London Assurance; Barrack Room.
        Am.—What Will the World Say?* [Lord Norwald—Sankey,
        Hon. Charles Norwald—Maynard, Mr. Warner—Far-
        ren, Lady Norwald—Miss Petrie, Marian—Mrs. Far-
        ren]; Valet de Sham.
24.   S.C.—London Assurance; Four Sisters.
        Am.—What Will the World Say?; My Fellow Clerk.
25.   S.C.—Lady of Lyons; Seven's the Main; My Young Wife
        and My Old Umbrella.
        Am.—Last Days of Pompeii; Wedding Ring*.

26.   S.C.—Marino Faliero.
        Am.—Alive and Merry; Cherry and Fair Star.
27. Sunday:
        S.C.—Lucia di Lammermoor*.
        Am.—Lovers' Quarrels; Naiad Queen.
28.   S.C.—Hamlet; Welsh Girl.
        Am.—Bombastes Furioso; Naiad Queen.

March

1. Tuesday:
        S.C.—Lucia di Lammermoor.
        Am.—Naiad Queen.
2.   S.C.—Macbeth; Simpson and Company.
        Am.—Naiad Queen.
3.   S.C.—Marino Faliero.
        Am.—Three and the Deuce.
4.   S.C.—London Assurance; The Secret.
        Am.—What Will the World Say?
5.   S.C.—Beatrice di Tenda*.
        Am.—Rookwood*.
6. Sunday:
        S.C.—Beatrice di Tenda.
        Am.—Rookwood.
7.   S.C.—London Assurance; My Friend the Captain* [Mr.
        T. D. Brown—Barrett, Gabriel Snoxell—Sloman].
        Am.—Rookwood.
8.   S.C.—Beatrice di Tenda.
        Am.—The Wedding Day; Rookwood.
9.   S.C.—Hamlet; Four Sisters.
        Am.—My Grandfather's Will; Widow Wiggins; Bombastes
        Furioso.
10.   S.C.—Chiari di Rosenberg.
        Am.—My Old Woman; Snapping Turtles; Loan of a Lover.
11.   S.C.—Merchant of Venice; Sleep Walker.
        Am.—Fashionable Friends; Irish Widow; Foreign Airs
        and Native Graces.
12.   S.C.—Lucia di Lammermoor.
        Am.—My Little Adopted; Widow Wiggins; Make Your
        Wills.
13. Sunday:
        S.C.—Theatre destroyed by fire.
14.   Am.—Irish Widow; Kiss in the Dark.
15.   Am.—My Old Woman; Out of Place; Joseph Brag.
16.   Am.—Pet of the Petticoats; Out of Place; Kiss in the Dark.
17.   Am.—Mazeppa, first act; Rookwood, third act; Rival
        Pages; Mother Goose*.
18.   Am.—Damon and Pythias, fourth and fifth acts; Mazeppa.
19.   Am.—John Bull; The Widow's Victim; Mother Goose.

20. Sunday:
     Am.—The Denouncer; Widow's Victim; Mother Goose.
21.   Am.—Fire Raiser; Lafitte, second scene; The Captive*; Mother Goose.
22.   Am.—My Friend the Governor; Two Friends; My Young Wife and My Old Umbrella; His Last Legs.
23.   Am.—Sweethearts and Wives; Timour the Tartar.
24.   Am.—Rookwood; The Sentinel* [King—Farren, Schroppsen—DeBar, Linda—Miss Petrie].
25.   Am.—Fall of Algiers* [Harry Helm—DeBar, Peter Pounce Saunders, Emeline—Mrs. Farren, Jannette—Miss Petrie]; Lady of Irons** [Clawed Fitz-Henry Wilkins —Saunders, Polly Ann—Mrs. Farren].
26.   Am.—Clari; The Captive; Alpine Maid*.
27. Sunday:
     Am.—The Sentinel; Timour the Tartar.
28.   Am.—Robert Emmett* [Robert Emmett—Bannister, O'Deary—Farren, Patrick—DeBar, Miss Carran— Mrs. Bannister, Kathleen—Mrs. Farren]; Lady of Irons.
29.   Am.—Alice; Robert Emmett.
30.   Am.—Syracusan Brothers* [Lucinius—Bannister, Clothinia—Mrs. Farren]; The Sentinel.
31.   Am.—Gentleman of Lyons** [Julian—Bannister, Dorval— DeBar, Count de Valcour—Farren, Duke de Valcour— Leicester, Ernestine—Mrs. Bannister, Adeliade—Mrs. Farren, Bridget—Miss Petrie]; The Maine Question* [Bob Buckeye—Bannister, Sally—Mrs. Bannister].

April

1. Friday:
     Am.—The Last Man* [Jeffrey Dale—J. S. Browne, Major Battergale—Farren, Jacob Codling—Saunders, Barbara Gay—Miss Petrie]; My Little Adopted; Robert Macaire.
2.   Am.—Gentleman of Lyons; Robert Emmett.
3. Sunday:
     Am.—Pet of the Petticoats; Foreign Airs and Native Graces.
4.   Am.—Banished Star; Dead Shot.
5.   Am.—Irish Widow; Widow Wiggins; Make Your Wills.
6.   Am.—Belle of the Hotel**.
7.   Am.—My little Adopted; Belle of the Hotel; Our Mary Anne.
8.   Am.—Tom Noddy's Secret; Belle of the Hotel; The Christening.
9.   Am.—Roxalana; Belle of the Hotel; Joseph Brag.
10. Sunday:
     Am.—Valet de Sham; Belle of the Hotel; Kiss in the Dark.

11.   Am.—The Ladies Club; Belle of the Hotel; Kiss in the Dark.
12.   Am.—Town and Country; Charles XII.
13.   Am.—Closed for night rehearsal of Napoleon.
14.   Am.—Napoleon Bonaparte* [Napoleon—J. Foster, Molly —Thorne].
15.   Am.—Napoleon Bonaparte.
16.   Am.—Napoleon Bonaparte.
17. Sunday:
        Am.—Napoleon Bonaparte.
19.   Am.—Napoleon Bonaparte.
20.   Am.—Napoleon Bonaparte.
21.   Am.—Napoleon Bonaparte.
22.   Am.—Napoleon Bonaparte.
23.   Am.—Napoleon Bonaparte.
24. Sunday:
        Am.—Widow's Victim.
25.   Am.—Foundling of the Forest; Turnpike Gate.
26.   Am.—Mrs. White; Paul Jones.
27.   Am.—Alice; Of Age To-morrow.
28.   Am.—Wedding Day; No Song, No Supper.
29.   Am.—Youthful Queen; My Friend the Governor.
30.   Am.—Green Eyed Monster; Two Gregories.

May

1. Sunday:
        Am.—Charles II; Of Age To-morrow.
2.   Am.—Alive and Merry; Warlock of the Glen.
3.   Am.—Sweethearts and Wives; Post of Honor.
4.   Am.—Charles XII; Pleasant Neighbor.
5.   Am.—Simpson and Company; Loan of a Lover.
6.   Am.—Blind Boy; Sprigs of Laurel.
7.   Am.—Ways and Means; Bleeding Nun.
8. Sunday:
        Am.—She Stoops to Conquer; Warlock of the Glen.
9.   Am.—Blind Boy; Review.
10.   Am.—Catharine and Petruchio; The Captive; My Neighbor's Wife.
11.   Am.—Old English Gentleman; Irish Tutor.
12.   Am.—Heir at Law; Sentinel.
13.   Am.—The Bleeding Nun; Animal Magnetism.
14.   Am.—Charles XII; Lying Valet.
15. Sunday:
        Am.—Promissory Note; Forty Thieves.
16.   Am.—Rivals; Animal Magnetism.
17.   Am.—Youthful Queen; A Roland for an Oliver.
18.   Am.—Green Eyed Monster; My Neighbor's Wife.
19.   Am.—Woodcutter of Bagdad; Pleasant Neighbor.
20.   Am.—A Roland for an Oliver; Married Rake.
21.   Am.—Simpson and Company; No Song, No Supper.

23. Monday:
    Am.—A Wife's First Lesson; Blind Boy.
24. Am.—The Hypocrite; Swiss Cottage. Last night of the season.
25. Am.—She Stoops to Conquer; No Song, No Supper. Benefit for the Orphan Boys.

The Play List

The following list presents in compact form the record of the plays given on the English stage at New Orleans from 1806 to 1842.

In this list numerals enclosed in parentheses signify the year the play was performed, (21) thus representing 1821. Parentheses are used also to enclose the name of the playwright when the authorship of the play is uncertain. Quotation marks are used to enclose statements of authorship made by the newspaper announcements of the play.

Numerals representing the days and the months of the year are separated by commas and semi-colons, respectively; years are also separated by semi-colons.

The following entry will serve to explain this use of abbreviation and punctuation.

Catching an Heiress; farce by Charles Selby: (36) A.-12.2,5; (38) A.-1.4,5,12; 3.1.

The record means that *Catching an Heiress* appeared for the first time in New Orleans at the American Theatre, December 2, 1836, remaining for December 5. In 1838, the farce appeared at the American Theatre, January 4, remaining for January 5 and 12, and returning on March 1.

Abaellino, the Great Bandit; by William Dunlap: (17) S.P.-2.12; (23) O.-1.27; (24) A.-1.30; (27) A.-12.27.

Abon Hassan; comic opera by William Dimond: (33) A.-1.26; 4.3; (33) A.-12.3; (34) A.-2.14; 5.3.

Actress of All Work; farce by W. H. Oxberry: (29) A.-3.28; 4.2; 12.18,28; (30) A.-1.29; 2.8; (31) A.-1.19; 4.7,29; (33) A.-12.5,14; (34) A.-1.27; 3.1; (35) S.C.-12.15; (36) S.C.-2.9; A.-11.22; 12.1; (38) A.-1.6; (39) S.L.-3.30; (40) G.-1.16; Ar.-2.11,15.

Adelgitha; tragedy by M. G. Lewis: (19) S.P.-3.30; (22) S.P.-4.24; (27) A.-3.26; (28) A.-12.31; (32) A.-12.4; (34) A.-12.5; (38) A.-3.17.

Adeline; melodrama by J. H. Payne: (24) A.-2.6; 3.24; 4.29.

The Adopted Child; musical farce by Samuel Birch: (32) A.-11.23; (33) A.-2.1; 3.21,30; (34) A.-11.26; (37) A.-1.19; 2.13; S.C.-3.1; (38) S.C.-1.8; (39) S.C.-1.5; A.-1.10; 2.15.

Adrian and Orilla; by William Dimond: (30) A.-2.11; (32) A.-12.29; (33) A.-2.5; (36) A.-1.22.

The Adventures of a Sailor; by N. H. Bannister: (35) A.-3.14,24; 12.24.

The Adventure; by J. S. Jones: (36) S.C.-2.5.

The Aethiop; melodrama by Dimond: (21) O.-3.10,17; (24) A.-3.5,8; (26) A.-2.14; (27) A.-2.8; (28) A.-3.21; (32) A.-5.3; (34) A.-5.12; (41) Am.-1.31; 3.24.

Affair of Honor; farce by W. L. Rede: (37) S.C.-1.28.

Agnes de Vere; drama by J. B. Buckstone: (36) S.C.-12.5,9,13; (37) S.C.-1.18; 4.16; 12.3.

The Agreeable Surprise; comic opera by John O'Keeffe: (23) O.-1.31; 2.21; 3.3; (27) A.-6.6; (28) A.-2.27; (29) A.-2.28; (30) A.-1.12,14; (31) A.-3.29; (32) A.-3.3; 4.14; 12.17; (34) A.-3.14.

Aladdin; operatic play by (George Soane): (31) A.-5.25,27; (31) A.-12.10,17; (41) S.C.-1.10, 11, 12, 13, 14, 15, 17, 24, 25, 26, 27, 28, 30; 2.13, 23, 26; 12.25, 26; (42) S.C.-1.23; 2.4.

Alberti Contadini, the last of the Abruzzi; tragedy by Isaac Harby: (37) S.C.-1.16.

Alexander the Great; tragedy by Nathaniel Lee: (22) O.-3.23; (24) A.-3.15; (35) A.-5.6; (37) A.-1.30.

Alice; see *Love and Reason.*

Alive and Merry; farce by Charles Dance: (42) Am.-1.1, 2, 4; 2.26; 5.2.

All in the Dark; see *Rendezvous.*

All on the Wing; farce by Joseph Lunn: (28) A.-12.22; (29) A.-1.10.

All in the Wrong; farce by Arthur Murphy: (31) A.-2.9; 3.23; (35) S.C.-12.11; (36) S.C.-2.10; 12.22.

All is Happy; "new piece written expressly for little Miss Brittingham": (38) A.-2.24,26; 3.4; 4.18.

All the World's a Stage; farce by Isaac Jackman: (17) S.P.-3.28; 4.8; (28) A.-3.8, 11, 19; (29) A.-1.16; (30) A.-3.9; (42) S.C.-1.9, 15.

Alonzo the Brave and the Fair Imogine; melodrama by T. J. Dibdin: (30) A.-5.10, 13, 14; (31) A.-1.25.

The Alpine Maid; by Benjamin Webster: (42) Am.-3.26.

L'Amant Prete; see *Loan of a Lover.*

Amateurs and Actors; by R. B. Peake: (39) A.-3.28; (40) S.C.-10.28.

Ambrose Gwinette; melodrama by Douglas Jerrold: (29) A.-12.14; (30) A.-1.14; 2.26; (31) A.-12.29; (33) A.-1.25; (40) Am.-12.9; (41) Am.-3.23.

The American Captive; see *The Sultan.*

The American Farmer; see *Forest Rose.*

The American Sea Serpent; see *Deep, Deep Sea.*

The American Tar; see *The Purse.*

Amilie; opera by J. T. Haines: (40) S.C.-3.20,21,22,27.

Animal Magnetism; farce by Mrs. Inchbald: (21) O.-2.21; (23)
A.-5.19; (28) A.-4.9; (29) A.-3.11; (31) A.-12.5; (32) A.-
5.4; (33) A.-3.5,7; 5.2; (36) S.C.-6.25,29; (40) Ar.-2.19;
(42) Am.-5.13,16.

Anne Boleyn; drama by Thomas Fielding: (38) S.C.-12.27,28,29;
(39) S.C.-1.3; A.-2.16,18,19.

Annette and Lubin; ballet: (24) A.-4.21,23.

Antonio Cirenza, the Mountain Robber; see *Dumb Girl of Genoa.*

Antony and Cleopatra; by William Shakespeare: (38) S.C.-3.8,9.

The Apostate; tragedy by R. S. Shiel: (20) O.-3.27; (25) A.-3.14;
(27) A.-3.13; (28) A.-2.8; (32) A.-12.18; (34) A.-12.3; (35)
A.-4.30; (37) A.-4.19; (38) A.-3.21; 5.17,30; (39) A.-3.28;
(40) Am.-12.5.

An Apotheosis to the Memory of Napoleon: (33) A.-1.30.

Artaxerxes; opera by T. A. Arne: (34) A.-2.24,28.

The Artist's Wife; farce by Gilbert A. Beckett: (41) S.C.-1.21,
22,24,28,30; 2.18.

As You Like It; by William Shakespeare: (20) O.-4.14; (27) A.-
2.16; (30) A.-2.13; (31) A.-2.2; (33) A.-12.9; (34) A.-3.11;
5.24; 11.28; (35) A.-1.14; S.C.-12.12; (38) S.C.-1.18; 2.13;
(39) S.C.-1.23; (41) Am.-2.18; 5.13.

The Atonement; by John Poole: (38) S.C.-11.16,20.

Auld Robin Gray; by George Macfarren: (32) A.-12.1,14.

The Avenger; by G. W. Lovell: (31) A.-2.12,22.

The Baboon, or Ourang Ourang: (37) A.-12.15; (38) A.-1.27.

Le Baiser d'Amitie; see *Pay to My Order.*

The Banished Star; comedy by J. B. Buckstone: (41) Am.-2.14,
15,16; 3.15; (42) Am.-4.4.

The Banished Provincial; by S. E. Glover: (33) A.-4.29.

Barbarossa; tragedy by John Brown: (19) S.P.-4.7; (23) O.-3.7;
(26) A.-3.6.

The Barber of Seville; opera by Rossini: (30) A.-3.3; (31) A.-
4.23; 5.14; (32) A.-12.8; (33) A.-5.16; (34) A.-1.17; 4.25;
(35) A.-2.13; 3.2; 12.14,16; (36) A.-1.30; 2.13,19; (38) S.C.-
2.26; (40) S.C.-3.16,26; 4.1; (41) Am.-12.16,17,18.

Il Barbiere di Seviglia; opera by Rossini: (36) S.C.-5.29,31; 12.11,
18,21; (37) S.C.-2.19; 5.28,29,31,; 6.2.

Barney Brallaghan; farce: (32) A.-3.17; (37) S.C.-5.4.

The Barrack Room; farce by Thomas Bayly: (37) S.C.-11.20,22;
(38) A.-1.15; S.C.-1.26; A.-3.3; 11.15; (39) A.-1.17; 2.21;
(40) S.C.-4.29; (41) Am.-3.18; 5.7; (42) S.C.-2.23.

The Bath Road; see *Intrigue.*

The Battle of Austerlitz; melodrama: (38) S.C.-1.8.

The Battle of Bunker Hill; pantomime: (17) O.C.-6.5.

The Battle of Bunker Hill; national drama (by J. D. Burk): (39)
S.C.-1.8.

The Battle of New Orleans; by C. E. Grice: (24) A.-5.24; (26)
A.-3.4; (28) A.-2.22.

The Battle of the Nile; (06) M.B.-5.16. This may be T. J. Dibdin's interlude, *The Mouth of the Nile.*

La Bayadere; ballet: (35) S.C.-12.14,15,16,17,18,19.

La Bayadere; see *Le Dieu et la Bayadere.*

Beatrice di Tenda; opera by Bellini: (42) S.C.-3.5,6,8.

Beaux without Belles; farce by David Darling: (21) O.-2.26.

The Bee Hive, or Industry Must Prosper; musical farce by J. G. Millingen: (19) S.P.-4.10; (41) C.-6.13.

The Beggar of Bethnal Green, or The Blind Beggar; by J. S. Knowles: (36) S.C.-2.22; 3.22.

The Beggar's Opera; by John Gay: (31) A.-4.26; 5.3; (34) A.-1.27; 2.1,5; 5.7; (35) A.-3.4; 4.15; (36) A.-3.2.

The Belle of the Hotel; comedy by J. B. Buckstone: (42) Am.-4.6, 7,8,9,10,11.

The Belle's Stratagem; comedy by Mrs. Cowley: (20) S.P.-1.13; O-.3.1; (24) A.-5.3; (26) A.-3.21; (27) A.-2.7,24; (28) A.-4.7; (29) A.-5.19; (30) A.-1.6,25; (31) A.-1.31; 3.1; (32) A.-5.16; (33) A.-4.17; 11.28; 12.13; (34) A.-5.19; 11.26; (35) A.-5.8; (36) S.C.-2.17; A.-2.18; 12.17; (37) S.C.-1.1; A.-2.17; S.C.-4.11; 11.17; (38) S.C.-1-24; (39) A.-1.18,27; S.C.-4.20; 12.10; (42) S.C.-2.11.

The Benevolent Tar; see *The Purse.*

The Bengal Tiger; farce by Charles Dance: (39) S.C.-1.13; 2.24.

Bennett in Texas; farce by J. M. Field: (38) S.C.-11.18,19.

Bertram; tragedy by Charles R. Maturin: (19) S.P.-3.13; (20) S.P.-1.10; (21) O.-4.9; (23) O.-4.5; (24) A.-3.6; (27) A.-4.11; 12.25; (28) A.-2.4; (29) A.-2.25; 5.9; (32) A.-4.2; 12.21; (35) A.-3.17; (36) A.-3.10; 11.23; (37) A.-2.16; 4.20, 28; (38) A.-3.13; (39) S.C.-2.11.

Bianca Visconti; tragedy by N. P. Willis: (38) S.C.-1.29.

Bippo; see *The Island Ape.*

The Birthday; (by T. Dibdin or Wm. Dunlap): (18) S.P.-4.23; (21) O.-5.4; (24) A.-4.24; 5.14; (27) A.-3.6; (28) A.-1.17; (30) A.-2.19; (36) A.-4.28; (41) Am.-3.25.

Black Brig of Bermuda; see *The Last Words of Bill Jones.*

The Black Dwarf: (38) A.-4.1, 18.

Black Eyed Susan; melodrama by Douglas Jerrold: (30) A.-1.26, 28; 2.2, 24; 4.16; (35) A.-4.24; 12.23; (36) A.-2.13; 3.11, 17, 28; 12.12; (37) S.C.-2.13; (38) S.C. 2.27; 4.15; A.-5.29; 12.3, 7; (39) A.-1.4, 10; (40) S.C.-1.2, 5, 22; 11.25; 12.7; (41) Am.-1.18; S.C.-2.4; Am.-11.30; (42) S.C.-1.13,25.

The Black Phantom; see *Will Watch.*

Black and White; farce: (38) A.-3.9, 10.

The Bleeding Nun; see *The Forest of Rosenwald.*

The Blind Beggar, see *The Beggar of Bethnal Green.*

The Blind Boy; by Wm. Dunlap: (18) S.P.-4.11, 18; (23) O.-3.14; (28) A.-4.14; (35) A.-5.23; (42) Am.-5.9, 23.

Blue Beard; melodrama by (George Colman the Younger): (20)
S.P.-4.11, 13; (22) O.-4.6; (24) A.-6.5; (27) A.-4.27, 28;
(30) A.-1.2; (33) A.-2.11; (35) A.-5.22; (36) S.C.-5.19,20,
24; (41) Am.-3.23, 28; S.C.-11.28, 29, 30; 12.1.

The Blue Devils; farce by Colman the Younger: (20) S.P.-1.31;
(21) O.-3.30; (23) O.-4.21; (24) A.-3.5; (26) A.-2.14; (27)
A.-2.8; (28) A.-4.8; (29) A.-3.14; 4.16; (30) A.-3.1; (33)
A.-2.27; 4.2; (34) A.-2.10; 4.14; (35) S.C.-12.14; (36) S.C.-
2.1; A.-12.14; (37) S.C.-1.13; A.-2.5, 10; 5.6; S.C.-12.5;
(38) S.C.-1.23; 2.21; (41) Am.-2.8, 22; 3.10.

Blue Jackets; farce by Edward Stirling: (42) S.C.-1.1, 2, 4.

The Boarding House; farce by Beasley: (20) O.-2.28; (24) A.-
5.17; (27) A.-4.19; (28) A.-2.28.

The Boarding School; farce by W. B. Bernard: (27) A.-2.6.

The Bohemian Mother, or Presumptive Evidence; melodrama:
(31) A.-5.25,28; (31) A.-12.15; (32) A.-12.24; (33) A.-4.16.

The Bold Dragoons; farce by Morris Bennett: (31) A.-1.8, 12;
12.10, 23; (36) S.C.-1.11; (42) Am.-1.12.

A Bold Stroke for a Husband; comedy by Mrs. Cowley: (36)
A.-2.22, 24; 3.15; (37) S.C.-2.4, 21; A.-2.4; 3.14; 12.21; (38)
A.-5.24; (41) Am.-2.12.

A Bold Stroke for a Wife; comedy by Mrs. Centlivre: (23) A.-
5.19; (24) A.-2.6; (30) A.-5.22; (34) A.-1.14; (37) S.C.-
12.21.

Bombastes Furioso; burletta by William Rhodes: (19) S.P.-4.10;
(22) S.P.-4.24; (30) A.-12.25; (31) A.-4.9; 12.8; (32) A.-
2.7; 3.13; (39) S.C.-1.31; 2.5; 3.1; 4.3; (41) Am.-12.3;
(42) Am.-1.21; 2.28; 3.9;

Bone Squash Diavolo; comic opera by T. D. Rice: (36) A.-2.23,
24,27; 3.1,19.

Born to Good Luck; farce by Tyrone Power: (35) A.-1.10; 3.11;
(39) A.-1.10; (40) S.C.-1.5; 12.15, 17, 23; (42) S. C.-1.25.

Borrowed Feathers; burletta by Millingen: (38) S.C.-10.8,9,19;
(39) A.-5.28.

Botheration; farce by W. C. Oulton: (35) A.-4.30.

The Bottle Imp; musical piece by R. B. Peake: (36) S.C.-3.15, 19,
21; 4.9; (40) S. C.-12.13,14,16.

Brian Boroihme; drama by J. S. Knowles: (30) A.-5.22; (34)
A.-5.6,15; (36) A.-3.28; (37) S.C.-5.16; (38) A.-3.28; (41)
Am.-1.20,21,22,23,24.

The Bride of Abydos; melodrama by William Dimond: (28)
A.-2.18,19,20,21,27.

The Bride of Lammermoor; melodrama by T. J. Dibdin: (27)
S.C.-11.6.

A Bridegroom from the Sea; see *The Wreck Ashore.*

The Brigand; drama by J. R. Planché: (31) A.-4.5,9,12,16,23;
5.3; 11.26; 12.17; (32) A.-2.21; (33) A.-3.27,28; (34) A.-
12.13,16,18,21,24; (35) A.-5.12,26; (37) S.C.-1.7; 2.25; 3.1;
4.2; A.-5.11, 16; (41) Am.-12.8,31.

The Broken Sword, or The Murder and the Orphan; melodrama
by William Dimond: (27) A.-5.11,18,26; (28) A.-2.6; (29)
A.-4.25; 5.2,12; (30) A.-2.27; 4.2; (34) A.-3.25; (38) A.-4.2;
(42) Am.-1.4; 2.9.
The Broker of Bogota; tragedy by R. M. Bird: (34) A.-3.31; 4.2,
7,23.
Brother and Sister; comic opera by William Dimond: (21) O.-
2.12; 4.27; (29) A.-2.9,10; 12.22; (30) A.-1.28; 5.7; (31)
A.-3.1; 5.13; (36) S.C.-2.2,3,11,14; (38) S.C.-10.19.
Brutus, or The Fall of Tarquin; tragedy by J. H. Payne: (20)
S.P.-1.24; (24) A.-1.26; (26) A.-5.5; (28) A.-2.6; (29)
A.-2.23; 4.24; (31) A.-1.6; 3.18; (33) A.-5.15; (34) A.-4.26;
(37) A.-4.18; (39) S.C.-2.16; 4.8.
The Buckle of Brilliants; farce by T. E. Wilks: (39) S.C.-12.12,
14,19,21; (40) S.C.-2.26; 3.1,13.
Budget of Blunders; farce by Greffulke: (18) S.P.-3.14; (21)
O.-3.19; (24) A.-5.10; (28) A.-3.29.
The Bully and the Dandy; see *Miss in Her Teens.*
The Burgomaster's Daughter; melodrama by Edward Fitzball;
(38) S.C.- 11.11,12,13,14,15,17; (39) S.C.-4.21.
Bushwhacker; by N. H. Bannister: (38) A.-12.11.
The Busy Body; comedy by Mrs. Centlivre: (19) S.P.-5.17; (39)
S.C.-2.27.
The Cabinet; opera by T. J. Dibdin; (30) A.-1.7; 3.8; (31) A.-
2.23; 4.28; (33) A.-12.18; (34) A.-5.12.
Caius Silius; tragedy by N. H. Bannister: (36) A.-11.30; (37)
A.-4.25; (38) A.-3.16.
Caliph of Bagdad; ballet: (30) A.-5.1.
The Caliph of Bagdad; opera by Boieldieu: (34) A.-5.9.
Capers and Coronets: comedy by Joseph Lunn: (36) A.-1.6.
The Captive; "acting poem" by M. G. Lewis: (42) Am.-3.21,26;
5.10.
The Carmelites; drama by Edward Fitzball: (38) A.-11.5,6,9.
Castle of Andalusia; comic opera by John O'Keeffe: (30) A.-4.3;
(40) S.C.-4.3.
The Castle Spectre; melodrama by M. G. Lewis: (18) S.P.-1.21;
5.1; (20) O.-4.7; (24) A.-4.15; (26) A.-3.8; (28) A.-1.15.
The Cataract of the Ganges; melodrama by W. T. Moncrieff:
(25) A.-4.30; 5.2,3,4; (26) A.-2.6,11; 3.23; (27) A.-4.30;
5.1,5,7; (33) A.-2.7, 9; (36) S.C.-4.7; (41) S.C.-3.2,3; Am.-
3.5,6,7; 4.1,2,3,4,5,8,11,13.
Catching an Heiress; farce by Charles Selby: (36) A.-12.2,5;
(38) A.-1.4, 5,12; 3.1.
Catharine Howard; "translated from the French of Dumas and
adapted to the English Stage by J. M. Field": (40) S.C.-4.29.
Catharine and Petruchio, farce by David Garrick after Shakespeare: (18) S.P.-3.6; (20) S.P.-1.29; (23) O.-4.5; (24) A.-
1.24; (26) A.-4.29; (27) A.-4.20; (28) A.-2.4; (29) A.-1.29;
3.18; (31) A.-5.24; (32) A.-2.20; 5.12; (33) A-4.30; (34)

A.-4.23; (35) A.-3.23; (36) A.-1.22; S.C.-3.3,15; A.-4.11;
S.C.-11.25; (37) A.-2.18; S.C.-3.8; A.-3.29; (38) S.C.-1.24;
(40) S.C.-2.4; 4.15; (42) Am.-5.10.

Cato; tragedy by Joseph Addison: (24) A.-4.2.

La Cenerentola; opera by Rossini: (36) S.C.-12.4,25.

Chaos is Come Again; farce by John Morton: (40) S.C.-4.21,23,24.

Charcoal Sketches: (41) Am.-1.27.

Charles the Second, or The Merry Days of Charles the Second;
comedy by J. H. Payne and Washington Irving: (26) A.-
4.17,22; 5.2; (27) A.-5.26; (35) A.-3.18; S.C.-12.5,19; A.-
12.29; (36) S.C.-6.2,7; A.-11.25,28; S.C.-11.26; (37) S.C.-
1.25,27; 3.10,11; 5.3; (38) S.C.-131; A.-2.23; 5.29,31; V.G.-
6.21,28; S.C.-10.27; A.-10.27; (39) SC.-2.26; A.-11.4,7,15;
(40) Am.-11.20; (41) Am.-4.30; (42) Am.-5.1.

Charles of Sweden; see *Charles XII.*

Charles the Terrible; melodrama: (32) A.-4.26; 5.1.

Charles XII, or Charles of Sweden; drama by J. R. Planché: (29)
A.-12.12; (32) A.-12.5; (36) S.C.-4.25; (37) S.C.-2.17;
3.16,26; (38) S.C.-3.17,23,25; 10.11; (40) S.C.-4.7,12,25;
10.15; 11.3,21; (42) Am.-4.12; 5.4,14.

Charlotte Temple; by Jamse Rees: (36) A.-4.25,26,28; (37) A.-
1.24; 2.1,8,24; 3.15; 5.2; (38) A.-5.10.

The Cherokee Chief: (38) A.-1.27.

Cherry and Fair Star: (26) A.-4.24,26,27,28,29; 5.1,6,8,29; (27)
A.-3.16,19,27; 4.7; 12.29; (28) A.-1.5,12; 3.11; (32) A.-1.4,5,
6,7; 2.3; 5.17; (40) Am.-12.25,26,27,28,29,30,31; (41) Am.-
1.1,2,6; (42) Am.-1.16,18; 2.26.

Cherry Bounce; farcetta by R. J. Raymond: (31) A.-1.20,22;
2.5.

The Cherry Tree; comedy: (38) S.C.-3.26.

Chiara de Resemberg; opera by Rica: (37) S.C.-5.3; (42) S.C.-
3.10.

The Child of the Wreck; melodrama by J. R. Planché: (39) S.C.-
3.18,19.22,23,28; 4.22.

The Children in the Wood; musical interlude by Thomas Morton: (20) S.P.-2.8; O.-4.5; (26) A.-4.14; (27) A.-2.24; 5.30;
(29) A.-1.15; 4.10; (30) A.-4.12; (32) A.-12.21; (33) A.-2.7;
3.27; 4.1; (36) S.C.-6.4,8; (37) S.C.-1.12; A.-1.13; S.C.-
12.23; (38) S.C.-2.15; (40) S.C.-3.5.

The Chimney Piece; farce by G. H. Rodwell: (34) A.-4.11,16.

A Chip of the Old Block; farce by E. P. Knight: (27) A.-12.29;
(28) A.-1.3; 2.12; (30) A.-1.16,21; 3.13; 12.21; (31) A.-1.27;
3.2; 4.12; 12.2; (38) S.C.-4.26.

Christine of Sweden; see *The Youthful Queen.*

The Christening; farce by J. B. Buckstone: (36) A.-3.26,31; 4.14,
26; (41) Am.-3.18,20; (42) Am.-4.8.

Cinderella; adaptation of Rossini's opera by Rophino Lacy: (33)
A.-2.18,19,20,21,22,25,27,28; 3.1,2,6,12,19; 4.2,4,9,11,27; 5.14,
18; (34) A.-1.2,10,16,20,22,24,31; 2.21; 3.3; 5.5; 12.12,19,27,

31; (35) A.-1.18; 4.10,17,25; 5.25; 12.21,24,28; (36) A.-1.28;
2.9,25,29; 3.26; S.C.-4.11,12,14,16,19,25; A.-12.19,20,21,27,30;
(37) A.-1.7,25; 2.1; S.C.-2.26; A.-3.13,19; 4.2,18; (38); S.C.-
2.1,3,18,20,23; 11.4,6,8,; (39) S.C.-3.17,24; (40) S.C.-1.14,15,
16; 3.8,12,18,26,28; 4.27; (42) S.C.-1.27,28,29,30.

The Citizen; comedy by Arthur Murphy: (21) O.-3.14; (35) A.-
2.4,7; 3.14.

The Clandestine Marriage; comedy by Colman the Elder and David
Garrick: (32) A.-2.1; (39) S.C.-1.14.

Clari, the Maid of Milan; musical piece by J. H. Payne: (29) A.-
12.11,17; (30) A.-2.12; (31) A.-2.11; 3.8; (32) A.-11.28;
(33) A.-11.29; (34) A.-5.7; 12.9; (35) A.-3.3; (36) S.C.-5.26;
(37) S.C.-1.23; (38) S.C.-2.27; 3.20; (39) S.C.-4.20; (42)
Am.-3.26.

The Climbing Boy; comedy by R. B. Peake: (38) A.-1.6.

The Clouds; farce by (J. M. Field): (38) S.C.-11.19.

The Clown turned Dentist; pantomime: (41) S.C.-10.29,30.

The Cobbler's Frolic; pantomime: (41) Am.-4.7.

The Cockney Fishmongers; see *The Two Thompsons.*

Columbus; melodrama by Thomas Morton: (23) O.-2.22; (24)
A.-2.23.

Comedy of Errors; by William Shakespeare: (28) A.-3.31; (30)
A.-3.16,20; (35) A.-4.27; 5.2.

The Comet; comedy: (40) Ar.-2.11,18.

Comfortable Service; farce by Thomas Bayly: (38) V.G.-6.22,29;
S.C.-11.2,9,27; (39) A.-10.18; (40) A.-6.4; S.C.-10.16; (41)
S.C.-1.16.

Coming Out; farce by J. M. Field: (33) A.-5.24.

Conanchestat; equestrian drama written for Lewellen: (40) S.C.-
11.15.

Confounded Foreigners; farce by John Hamilton Reynolds: (38)
S.C.-12.2,23.

The Conquering Game; farce by W. B. Bernard: (40) Am.-11.25;
12.14; (41) Am.-3.19.

The Conscript; farce by W. H. Oxberry: (41) Am.-1.8,11; (42)
Am.-1.5.

The Cottager's Daughter; see *Lovers' Vows.*

The Country Girl; comedy by David Garrick: (30) A.-2.6; (34)
A.-3.15; 4.30; (36) S.C.-12.27; (41) Am.-2.4,7.

The Country Squire; comedy by Charles Dance: (38) S.C.-12.27.

The Courier of Naples: (31) A.-12.13,16,27.

The Courier of the Ocean: (38) S.C.-1.3.

Court Favour; burletta by J. R. Planché: (38) S.C.-3.10.

The Cradle of Liberty; national drama by S. E. Glover: (32) A.-
1.16,21; (33) A.-1.14; 4.22; (36) S.C.-1.1; (38) A.-12.23,25,
30; (39) A.-1.4,23; 3.13. This may be an adaptation of the
author's *Rake Hellies.*

The Critic; farce by R. B. Sheridan: (20) O.-3.17; (21) O.-4.27;
(24) A.-5.21; (26) A.-4.1; (27) A.-5.19; (28) A.-4.18; (29)

A.-3.13; (31) A.-5.9; (32) A.-4.11; (33) A.-12.24; (36) A.-11.24; 12.15; (37) S.C.-12.23; (39) A.-1.30; (40) Am.-12.10.

Crossing the Line, or The Dutch Brothers; farce by George Almar: (35) A.-11.21,24; 12.2; (36) A.-1.15; (37) A.-5.13; (38) A.-5.11; 6.2; S.C.-10.8,9,13,20,21; 11.8,24; (39) S.C.-1.27; (40) S.C.-10.26; (41) S.C.-1.7; 3.27; (42) S.C.-1.27.

A Cure for the Heartache; comedy by Thomas Morton: (13) S.P.-11.13; (16) S.P.-2.17; (20) O.-3.4; (23) O.-4.30; (24) A.-3.11; (25) A.-4.23; (26) A.-3.31; 5.3; (30) A.-3.5; (31) A.-5.27; (32) A.-11.27; (33) A.-1.24; (34) A.-5.10; (36) S.C.-12.24; (37) S.C.-11.20; 12.22; (42) Am.-2.9.

A Cure for Jealousy; comedy by John Corey: (40) A.-6.9.

The Curfew; comedy by John Tobin: (18) S.P.-2.24; (38) A.-5.5.

Damon and Pythias; tragedy by John Banim: (23) O.-1.29; (24) A.-1.23; (26) A.-4.11; (27) A.-4.4,17; (29) A.-3.4; 4.10; 5.8; (30) A.-1.11; 12.27; (32) A.-2.2; 4.4,9; (33) A.-5.4; (34) A.-1.4; 3.29; 4.18; (35) A.-5.26; (36) S.C.-3.8; (37) S.C.-2.7; 12.20; (38) S.C.-1.3; 2.16; 12.5; 4.5,9; A.-1.30; 3.4; (40) Am.-12.18; (41) Am.-2.26; (42) Am.-3.18.

The Dancing Barber; farce by Charles Selby: (39) S.C.-12.8,10, 13,19; (40) S.C.-2.28; 3.3,7.

Dark Doings; sketch: (41) Am.-1.18.

Darkness Visible; farce by Theodore Hook: (18) S.P.-3.4; 4.2.

A Day after the Fair, or Whirligig Hall; farce by C. A. Somerset: (29) A.-1.21; 2.2; (30) A.-12.16,30; (31) A.-1.11; 2.1; (32) A.-2.27,29; 4.5,10; (36) S.C.-5.28; 6.14; (37) A.-5.20,22; S.C.-11.12,19; 12.23; (38) V.G.-7.8; (40) S.C.-5.8; (41) S.C.-2.21.

The Day after the Wedding, or A Wife's First Lesson; comedy by Marie Therese Kemble: (18) S.P.-4.4; (19) S.P.-3.27; (20) S.P.-1.26; (23) O.-3.29; 4.14; (24) A.-2.23; (26) A.-3.15,31; 5.6; (27) A.-2.21; (28) A.-1.18; (29) A.-4.13; (30) A.-3.16; 5.15; (31) A.-4.8; 12.31; (32) A.-4.26; (33) A.-2.21; 12.11; (34) A.-2.21; (35) A.-1.29; 3.13; (36) A.-12.6; (37) S.C.-3.5,18,23,27; (38) S.C.-1.27; (39) A.-2.6; S.C.-2.23; (40) S.C.-1.31; 2.18; Am.-12.7; S.C.-12.24; (41) S.C.-3.10,14; (42) Am.-5.23.

A Day in France: (38) A.-2.7.

A Day in New Orleans; farce by John R. Dumont: (35) A.-5.14.

A Day in Paris; comedy by Charles Selby: (36) S.C.-2.19,20,25; 3.16; 4.11; 6.9,15,18; 11.17; (37) S.C.-3.18; (40) Am.-11.28.

A Dazzle by the Great Western: (42) S.C.-1.25.

The Dead Alive; farce by John O'Keeffe: (41) Am.-12.12.

The Dead Shot; farce by J. B. Buckstone: (30) A.-2.1,3,17; (31) A.-2.4,9; 3.23; 11.25; (32) A.-1.8; (33) A.-4.4; 12.9,30; (34) A.-11.29; (35) S.C.-12.7; (36) S.C.-1.12; 2.7; (37) S.C.-4.2; (38) S.C.-2.9; 4.17,19; A.-5.8; S.C.-10.1; 11.26; (39) A.-10.31; 11.27; (40) S.C.-1.10; G.-1.25; S.C.-2.6,15; 3.10,18; 10.22; Am.-12.28; (41) S.C.-1.13; Am.-2.18; S.C.-11.10; (42) Am.-4.4.

Deaf and Dumb; melodrama by Holcroft: (29) A.-5.2,7.

Deaf as a Post; farce by John Poole: (29) A.-1.28,31; 3.10; (30) A.-12.28; (31) A.-1.5; (38) S.C.-1.27; 4.29.

Death of Life in London; burlesque by T. Greenwood: (26) A.-3.13.

The Death Token; drama by T. E. Wilks: (38) A.-4.7,13; (41) Am.-3.25; (42) Am.-1.2.

Death's Head; farce: (32) A.-3.9.

The Deceived; domestic drama by George Washington Harby: (38) S.C.-4.1,13.

The Deep, Deep Sea, or The American Sea Serpent; burletta by Charles Dance: (36) A.-4.4; S.C.-5.3,26; (37) S.C.-12.22; (40) S.C.-4.28.

The Denouncer; see *Seven Clerks.*

Der Freischutz; music by C. M. von Weber; altered by J. R. Planché: (26) A.-3.18,20,25; 4.3,20; (27) A.-3.5,10; (40) S.C.-3.26,28.

The Deserted Daughter; comedy by Holcroft: (24) A.-1.12.

The Devil to Pay; farce by Charles Coffey: (20) S.P.-1.21; (24) A.-5.1; (26) A.-3.23; (27) A.-3.8; (28) A.-3.3; (30) A.-1.26; (32) A.-3.16; (33) A.-2.6; (34) A.-3.19; (38) A.-5.26.

The Devil's Bridge; opera by S. J. Arnold: (20) S.P.-1.14,20; O.-3.25; (21) O.-2.5; (23) O.-4.14,16; (24) A.-3.3; (26) A.-2.20; (28) A.-3.4; (29) A.-12.19; (31) A.-2.18; (34) A.-3.10; 12.15; (35) A.-12.9; (36) S.C.-4.25; A.-12.24; (38) S.C.-10.23.

The Devil's Daughter; melodrama by George Almar: (36) S.C.-1.6,7,8,9.

Le Dieu et la Bayadere, or The Maid of Cashmere, "operatic ballet" by Auber: (37) S.C.-3.21,22,23,24,25,27,28,29,30,31; 4.18,20,21,22; 11.23,25,26,28,30; 12.3; (38) S.C.-1.4,6; 2.14; 3.18,27; 4.22; A.-12.21,24,26,27,28; (39) S.C.-2.13,15,17,20, 21,22; 3.6,7,11,12,18,19,29,30; 4.22,25; (40) S.C.-2.5,7,9,13,16, 20,25,29; 3.11.

Le Dieu and la Bayadere; "grand ballet": (41) S.C.-3.31.

Disguises; farce by R. Haworth: (30) A.-5.12.

The Distressed Mother; tragedy by Ambrose Philips: (28) A.-1.21; (29) A.-3.3.

The Doctor's Courtship; comedy: (06) M.B.-4.29; (11) S.P.-4.26.

Does Your Mother Know You're Out?; farce by Oxenford: (39) A.-3.24.

The Dog of Montargis; see *The Forest of Bondy.*

Dolly and the Rat; burlesque by Douglas Jerrold: (24) A.-3.1,10; (30) A.-2.4.

Don Giovanni; burlesque by Thomas Dibdin: (20) O.-3.27; (26) A.-5.15; (41) Am.-11.28; 12.4.

Don Juan; pantomime by Delphini: (06) M.B.-4.29; (18) S.P.-
4.23; (24) A.-5.22; (26) A.-1.27; 4.5; (37) A.-1.25,27; 3.3,19;
(38) A.-1.28; (40) S.C.-1.3,4; (41) Am.-11.21.

Don Juan; ballet: (30) A.-4.24.

Don Juan of Austria; opera by Wolfgang Mozart: (38) S.C.-
11.1,7.

Don Quixote; pantomime: (41) S.C.-10.31.

Donna Caritea; opera by Mercadante: (37) S.C.-4.26,30.

The Doubtful Son; melodrama by William Dimond: (18) S.P.-
4.21.

Douglas; tragedy by John Home: (18) S.P.-2.4; (19) S.P.-
3.17; (20) O.-1.11; S.P.-1.29; (23) O.-3.10; (27) A.-12.26;
(28) A.-1.2; 12.20,30; (29) A.-3.26; (32) A.-2.24,28; (33)
A.-2.26; (39) S.L.-3.30; S.C.-12.26,30.

Down East; farce: (32) A.-3.22,26; (37) S.C.-12.11.

The Dramatist; comedy by Frederick Reynolds: (23) O.-1.22;
2.1; A.-5.14; (24) A.-2.9; (26) A.-2.2; (27) A.-4.27; (28)
A.-4.10; (29) A.-2.3; (32) A.-5.19; 12.31; (33) A.-3.16;
12.10; (34) A.-3.8; (39) S.C.-12.8; (40) S.C.-3.11; Am.-
11.21; (41) S.C.-2.2,16.

The Dream at Sea; drama by Buckstone: (41) Am.-4.25; 5.6,9.

A Dream of the Future; comedy by Charles Dance: (38) A.-1.15;
3.5,6,10.

The Drunkard's Fate; melodrama by Jerrold: (31) A.-12.3,8;
1.10.

Duchess de la Valliere; drama by Edward Bulwer Lytton: (39)
A.-4.3,6.

Duchess de la Vaubaliere; drama by Buckstone: (37) S.C.—10.29,
30; 11.18; (39) A.-11.30; S.C.-12.15.

The Duel, or My Two Nephews; farce by R. B. Peake: (27) A.-
4.18.

The Duel, or The Way to Win Her; operatic comedy: (18)
O.C.-1.9.

The Dumb Belle; farce by J. R. Planché: (33) A-12.12,17,21;
(34) A.-3.21,24; 4.7,14; (36) A.-3.1,4,30; 12.13; (37) A.-
1.7,21; 2.28; 3.21; (38) A.-2.20; S.C.-4.3,12; A.-4.28; 5.25,29;
6.2; V.G.—6.18,25; A.-10.24,31; 12.26,28; (39) A.-1.22; 2.7,
9,10; S.C.-4.11; (40) Ar.2.5; S.C.-2.22; 3.22; 4.25; Am.-12.26;
(41) Am.-3.12; 4.27; S.C.-3.10; 11.29.

The Dumb Brigand; melodramatic spectacle: (35) S.C.-12.30,31.

*The Dumb Girl of Genoa, or The Bandit Merchant, or The Moun-
tain Devil;* melodrama by John Farrell: (29) A.-4.28,30;
5.14; (30) A.-4.14; (36) S.C.-6.30; 7.1; (37) S.C.-5.11;
11.25,28; 12.1; (38) A.-3.27; S.C.-4.25; 10.30; (39) A.-10.20,
25; 11.18; (40) S.C.-10.12,19; 11.4; (41) S.C.-2.12,18; 3.23;
Am.-12.2,11.

The Dumb Man of Manchester; melodrama by B. F. Rayner:
(41) S.C.-11.14,15,18.

Durazzo; tragedy by James Haynes: (24) A.-2.14,24.

The Dutch Brothers; see *Crossing the Line.*

East and West; farce: (34) A.-1.30; 2.7.

Ebenezer Venture; (by Lawrence LeBree) : (42) S.C.-1.21.

The Eccentric Lover; see *The Dumb Belle.*

The Eddystone Elf; melodrama by George Pitt: (42) S.C.-1.1.

The Effect of Endorsing; see *The Promissory Note.*

The Eighth of January; by R. P. Smith: (30) A.-1.8; (37) S.C.-1.8.

The Elbow Shakers; burletta by F. F. Cooper: (31) A.-5.19.

El Hyder; melodramatic spectacle by William Barrymore: (28) A.-3.14,15,18; (30) A.-5.19; (33) A.-2.5,14; (34) A.-3.10; (36) S.C.-4.2,4,5; (39) A.-2.12,17; 11.15,17,22,23; (40) S.C.-1.16,17,19; (41) Am.-1.16; S.C.-2.19,28; 3.28; 11.25,26; 12.2.

Ella Rosenberg; melodrama by James Kenney: (18) S.P.-4.8; (20) O.-3.24.

Ellen Warham; domestic drama by Buckstone: (38) S.C.-1.2.

England's Iron Days; tragedy by N. H. Bannister: (37) S.C.-5.13.

Englishmen in India; comic opera by William Dimond: (33) A.-12.23,27; (34) A.-1.6; 3.6,17; 4.8; 5.1; 12.6; (35) A.-12.12,15; (36) A.-2.20; S.C.-12.31; (37) S.C.-1.3,31; 11.4; (38) S.C.-3.19; A.-5.14; S.C.-10.11; (39) A.-3.21; S.C.-4.28; 12.1,6; (41) Am.-3.14; (42) Am.-1.11.

The Enraged Politician, see *Turn Out.*

Esmeralda; melodrama by Fitzball: (38) S.C.-11.25,26,27,28; 12.16; (39) S.C.-1.9; (41) S.C.-1.27; 2.5,14,25; 3.26.

Etiquette Run Mad; comedy by Tyrone Power: (35) A.-1.24,29.

Eugene Aram; "dramatized from Lytton" by J. H. Caldwell: (33) A.-1.15.

Evadne; tragedy by R. L. Sheil: (29) A.-4.4; (32) A.-12.27; (34) A.-11.29; (35) A.-12.1; (36) A.-1.6.

The Evening Star; equestrian drama: (41) S.C.-11.19.

Everybody's Husband; farce by Richard Ryan: (38) S.C.-1.15; 2.1.

Everyone Has His Fault; comedy by Mrs. Inchbald: (26) A.-5.22; (27) A.-6.6; (28) A.-3.10; (33) A.-3.9; (36) S.C.-5.3; (39) S.C.-4.19.

Exchange No Robbery; comedy by T. E. Hook, adapted from *He Would be a Soldier:* (40) S.C.-4.16,17.

The Exile; see *The Exiles of Siberia.*

The Exiles of Siberia; melodrama by Frederick Reynolds: (23) O.-1.13; (26) A.-3.15; (27) A.-2.13; (28) A.-2.16,26; (30) A.-3.31; (36) A.-3.7.

The Exiles in the West: (39) A.-3.15,17,19,21,23,26.

The Fair Penitent; tragedy by Nicholas Rowe: (23) O.-4.11.

The Fall of the Alamo: (40) G.-1.16,25; Ar.-2.22.

The Fall of Algiers; by J. H. Payne: (42) Am.-3.25.

The Fall of San Antonio, or Texas; by N. H. Bannister: (36)
 A.-1.1,4; S.C.-5.7,10.
The Fall of Tarquin; see Brutus.
The Falls of Clyde; melodrama by George Soane: (24) A.-2.20,
 21,28; 3.27,30; (26) A.-2.3; 4.17; (28) A.-3.6; (29) A.-5.19;
 (30) A.-2.23; (31) A.-1.18; (32) A.-1.28; (34) A.-1.30.
Family Jars; farce by Joseph Lunn: (27) A.-12.28; (28) A.-1.3,
 23; 2.20; 12.23; (29) A.-3.7; (35) A.-4.16,21; 5.7; (36)
 S.C.-6.28; (37) S.C.-2.8; 4.15; (38) A.-2.14,17; 3.7; 4.8; 5.18;
 S.C.-10.2; 12.3; (40) S.C.-4.10; A.-5.23,31; S.C.-11.9; (41)
 Am.-3.21; 4.11.
Il Fanatico per la Musica; opera by Mayer: (38) S.C.-3.11,13,14.
The Farm House; altered from *The Country Lassies* by Charles
 Johnson: (18) S.P.-2.7.
The Farmer's Story; see 2548.
Fashions; pantomime: (18) S.P.-3.17.
Fashionable Friends; farce: (41) Am.-5.5,7; (42) Am.-3.11.
The Fatal Dowry; tragedy by Philip Massinger; (30) A.-1.20.
The Fatal Marriage; see Isabella.
Father and Daughter; see The Lear of Private Life.
The Father Outwitted; farce: (17) S.P.-3.11; (18) S.P.-1.30.
Fazio; tragedy by H. M. Milman: (21) O.-12.12; (34) A.-11.25;
 12.10; (35) A.-1.2; S.C.-12.9; (36) A.-1.12; S.C.-2.8; 12.1;
 (37) S.C.-2.10; A.-3.23; 4.26; S.C.-12.7; (38) S.C.-2.3; 11.29;
 (39) A.-2.15.
The Feast of Apollo; (20) S.P.-2.22.
Fer et Poison; vaudeville: (41) Am.-12.27.
La Fille Malgardé; ballet: (24) A.-4.17,19,24.
Fire and Water; operetta by Beazley: (33) A.-3.1.
The Fire Raiser; melodrama by George Almar: (37) A.-4.15, 22,
 27; (38) A.-4.17; (42) Am.-3.21.
The First of April; farce by Caroline Boaden: (32) A.-4.27; 5.1.
Fish Out of Water; farce by Joseph Lunn: (27) A.-3.27, 29; 4.3;
 (29) A.-3.5; (30) A.-2.20; (40) S.C.-1.30; 2.2; 10.22; 11.24;
 (42) S.C.-2.12.
The Floating Beacon; melodrama by Edward Fitzball: (42)
 S.C.-1.17.
The Flying Dutchman, or The Phantom Ship; melodrama by
 Edward Fitzball: (33) A.-4.23,24,25,26; (38) S.C.-12.17,23,
 25,30; (39) S.C.-1.1,6; 12.23; (40) S.C.-1.1,26; 4.7; 10.25,
 27,30; 11.4; 12.14; (41) S.C.-2.7; 3.22.
Folly as It Flies; comedy by Frederick Reynolds: (23) O.-1.10;
 (30) A.-4.1.
Fontainbleau; comic opera by O'Keeffe: (23) O.-4.18; (29) A.-
 2.12; (34) A.-3.20; (37) S.C.-1.2; (40) S.C.-2.26.
The Force of Nature, or The Secret Marriage; comedy by Thomas
 James Thackeray: (36) S.C.-6.28.
Foreign Airs and Native Graces; burletta by Moncrieff: (41)
 Am.-2.10,11,12,16; 3.9,12,16; 4.19,25; 5.7,10; (42) Am.-3.11;
 4.3.

The Foreign Prince; by W. L. Rede: (42) S.C.-3.16,18,21.

The Forest of Bondy, or the Dog of Montargis; melodrama by
T. J. Dibdin: (20) O.-4.8,15; (21) O.-3.16; (26) A.-3.16,21;
(27) A.-4.14; (35) A.-2.12; 4.13,20,29; (38) A.-1.28; (41)
Am.-4.6,7; S.C.-11.20.

The Forest of Rosenwald, or The Bleeding Nun; melodrama by
J. Stokes: (24) A.-2.9,11,16,26; 3.27,30; (25) A.-3.12; (26)
A.-2.13; 3.3; (27) A.-4.6; (28) A.-3.8; (41) Am.-12.3,10;
(42) Am.-5.13.

The Forest Rose, or The American Farmer; comedy by Samuel
Woodworth: (34) A.-2.4,7; (36) S.C.-1.29; (38) A.-1.13,17,
21; 2.11; 12.3,7; (39) A.-1.4; S.C.-12.18,30; (40) S.C.-1.4;
12.12,14; (41) S.C.-1.22; 2.4; (42) S.C.-1.9,17,25.

For Freedom Ho!; opera by Pocock: (23) O.-2.17,22.

Fortune's Frolic, or The True Use of Riches; farce by J. T. Allingham: (18) S.P.-2.21; (20) S.P.-3.30; (21) O.-3.17; (26)
A.-2.18; (27) A.-3.28; (28) A.-2.21,26; 12.26; (29) A.-2.26;
(31) A.-4.26; 11.28; (32) A.-3.28; 4.25; (33) A.-3.6; 5.3;
(34) A.-2.12; (35) A.-3.9; (36) A.-4.27; 5.17; (39) A.-3.3,
6,9,30; (40) A.-6.14; S.C.-12.7.

The Fortunes of Smike; drama by Edward Stirling: (40) S.C.-
11.16,18.

Forty and Fifty; farce by Thomas Bayly: (38) S.C.-10.15,19;
11.5; (39) S.C.-2.17; 3.6.

The Forty Thieves, or The Woodcutter of Bagdad; melodrama:
(20) S.P.-2.1,5,10; 4.18; (21) O.-4.14; (23) O.-1.22; 2.1;
(24) A.-3.20,24; (26) A.-2.10; 4.13; (27) A.-3.29; 5.4; (28)
A.-3.6; (31) A.-5.24; (33) A.-2.12; (34) A.-12.20; (36)
S.C.-5.14,17,24; 12.14; (38) S.C.-2.11; 10.14; (39) A.-1.13,
14,15,16,25; 10.13,19,26; 11.16,29; (40) A.-6.5,7; S.C.-10.15,
17; (41) Am.-3.2,4; S.C.-11.27; (42) Am.-5.15,19.

The Foundling of the Forest; melodrama by William Dimond:
(18) S.P.-1.16; 4.4; (20) O.-3.3; S.P.-4.11; (23) O.-2.14;
(24) A.-2.13; (26) A.-2.3; (27) A.-2.3; (29) A.-3.10; (30)
A.-2.27; 12.28; (32) A.-11.23; (38) A.-3.24; S.C.-4.21; (42)
Am.-4.25.

The Foundling of the Sea, or The Yankee Pedlar; melodrama by
Samuel Woodworth: (34) A.-2.6; (35) A.-1.5; 2.17; (38)
A.-1.16; 2.9.

The Four Lovers; ballet pantomime: (41) Am.-12.27.

The Four Mowbrays; see *Old and Young.*

The Four Sisters; farce by W. B. Bernard: (33) A.-12.23; (34)
A.-2.15; 3.22; (37) A.-3.16,18; S.C.-5.11; (42) S.C.-2.18,24;
3.9.

Fra Diavolo; opera by Lacy: (34) A.-4.5,10; 5.2; (40) S.C.-2.12,
21,28; 3.14,24,31; (42) S.C.-2.3.

Francis the First of France; tragedy by Fanny Kemble: (32)
A.-12.12,20; (35) A.-4.27.

Frank Fox Phipps; farce by Charles Selby: (36) S.C.-6.10.

Fraternal Discord; comedy by William Dunlap: (32) A.-12.7.
Frederick the Great; farce by John Poole: (26) A.-4.6,19; (29)
    A.-2.13; (31) A.-1.20.
Free and Easy; farce by S. J. Arnold: (33) A.-12.19; (40) S.C.-
    2.22,27.
The French Spy; by J. T. Haines: (35) S.C.-12.14,15,16,17,18,19;
    (37) S.C.-3.7,8,9,12,19; A.-3.7,8,9,11,12,20; (39) S.C.-3.8,9,
    14,20,23,27; 4.24; 12.26,27,31; (40) S.C.-1.7.
The French Washerwoman; see *Mischief Making.*
Frightened to Death; farce by Oulton: (19) S.P.-5.17; (37)
    S.C.-6.3; (38) S.C.-12.19; (39) S.C.-1.14,18,25; 2.18,23; 3.16;
    4.8; A.-11.9,12,24,30; (40) A.-4.9; (41) Am.-12.20; (42)
    Am.-1.22.
G-A-G; by J. M. Field: (41) S.C.-2.20,24,27.
The Gambler's Fate; melodrama (by H. M. Milner): (29) A.-1.3,
    5,6,8,15; 2.26,27,28; 5.5; 12.25; (31) A.-1.7; 5.19; 11.29;
    12.25; (32) A.-1.2; (33) A.-1.29; (38) A.-10.28,30; 11.1,2,
    4,9; S.C.-11.3; (39) A.-1.6,14; 3.11; 11.3,5; S.C.-12.6; (40)
    S.C.-3.25; 11.18; Am.-11.22; (42) S.C.-12.16.
The Game Cock of the Wilderness; drama by W. L. Rede: (40)
    S.C.-11.29; 12.1; (42) S.C.-1.15,19.
The Gamester; tragedy by Edward Moore: (20) O.-4.15; S.P.-
    6.10; (21) O.-4.14; (23) O.2.19; (27) A.-2.16; 4.14; (29)
    A.-3.27; (31) A.-1.7; (32) A.-4.5; 12.1; (33) A.-2.9; (35)
    S.C.-12.10; (36) S.C.-1.14; 2.23,27; 12.10; (37) A.-4.21;
    (38) S.C.-2.9; (40) S.C.-5.9; 11.20; (41) S.C.-3.2.
Le Garcon à Trois Visages; see *The Three Faced Frenchman.*
Gaulantus the Gaul; tragedy by N. H. Bannister: (36) A.-3.31;
    (38) A.-3.25.
La Gazza Ladra; opera by Rossini: (42) S.C.-3.1,5.
The Genoese; tragedy by Epes Sargent: (38) S.C.-2.6,10.
The Gentleman and the Upstart; comedy by E. W. Ranger: (41)
    S.C.-1.29.
A Gentleman in Difficulties; by T. H. Bayly: (37) S.C.-4.20; 5.2.
The Gentleman of Lyons; by N. H. Bannister: (42) Am.-3.31; 4.2.
George Barnwell; tragedy by George Lillo: (18) S.P.-3.17; (26)
    A.-4.6; (28) A.-12.25; (29) A.-12.25; (30) A.-1.1; 12.25;
    (31) A.-12.25; (32) A.-1.2; 12.25; (34) A.-12.25; (35) S.C.-
    12.25; (36) S.C.-12.25; (37) A.-1.29; (38) S.C.-12.25; A.-
    12.25; (39) A.-1.26; 3.15; S.C.-12.25; (40) S.C.-11.22; Am.-
    12.25; (41) S.C.-12.25.
Ghost or No Ghost; see *The Spectre Bridegroom.*
A Ghost in Spite of Himself; see *The Spectre Bridegroom.*
A Ghost Story; farce by T. J. Serle: (38) S.C.-11.4,23.
Gilderoy; melodrama by William Barrymore: (36) A.-1.30; 2.1.
Giovanni in London; operatic extravaganza by Moncrieff: (31)
    A.-3.12,19; (34) A.-5.16,19.
The Gladiator; tragedy by R. M. Bird: (33) A.-5.6,13; (34) A.-
    3.19,24; 4.4; (39) A.-2.6; S.C.-4.10,12.

Glencoe; tragedy by Sergeant Talfourd: (40) Am.-12.30.
The Glorious Minority; see *No!*
The Glory of Columbia, Her Yeomanry; by William Dunlap: (20)
    S.P.-2.22; (28) A.-1.1; (29) A.-1.8; (32) A.-1.8.
The Gnome Fly; (41) Am.-3.19,21,22.
The Golden Farmer; melodrama by Benjamin Webster: (36) A.-
    1.21,23,26; 3.27; (37) A.-5.6; (38) A.-1.1,2,3,4; 2.27; 3.9;
    (40) A.-5.17.
A Grand Masquerade, or The Masked Ball, or The Negro Door
    Keeper; extravaganza: (35) A.-2.23; 5.6; (41) S.C.-2.15;
    Am.-4.10; 12.2; (42) S.C.-1.2.
The Grateful Lion; oriental spectacle, music by Cooke: (41) S.C.-
    12.2.
The Grecian Daughter; tragedy by Arthur Murphy: (40) S.C.-
    4.24.
The Green Eyed Monster; comic opera by J. R. Planché: (30)
    A.-5.17,20; (32) A.-1.31; (34) A.-12.2,5,12; (36) A.-1.20;
    (37) S.C.-3.30; (38) S.C.-11.22,24; 12.30; (39) S.C.-2.3,24;
    (41) Am.-4.12; (42) Am.-4.30; 5.18.
The Green Man; comedy by Richard Jones: (20) S.P.-1.25; O.-
    2.26; (41) Am.-4.12.
The Green Mountain Boy; comedy by J. S. Jones: (34) A.-1.25,28;
    2.8; A.-12.24; (35) A.-1.5; (35) S.C.-2.3; (38) A.-1.16,19;
    2.7.
The Grenadier, or The Savoyard; musical burletta by O'Keeffe:
    (33) A.-1.11; (38) S.C.-3.20,22,26.
Gretna Green, or A Trip to Scotland; farce by Beazley: (29) A.-
    2.9; (30) A.-3.26,31; (31) A.-2.7; 4.8; (32) A.-2.4; (35) A.-
    4.8; 11.20; (37) S.C.-2.13; A.-5.5; (40) Ar.-2.14; (41) S.C.-
    5.30.
Gulliver in Lilliput; farce by David Garrick: (39) A.-3.10,13,15,
    17,19,21,23,26.
Gustavus III; (by H. M. Milner or J. R. Planché) : (38) A.-3.30;
    S.C.-4.5,6,7,8,9,10,11,12; 11.18,21.
Guy Mannering; melodrama (by Daniel Terry) : (20) S.P.-1.27;
    2.8; (21) O.-2.9; (24) A.-1.31; (26) A.-2.8; 5.9; (27) A.-3.3;
    (28) A.-2.14; 12.24; (29) A.-2.5; 12.16; (30) A.-2.16; (31)
    A.-3.8; 5.20; (33) A.-12.16; (34) A.-1.29; 4.29; 12.2; (36)
    A.-1.4; S.C.-1.4,5; 4.21; 12.16,23; A.-12.22; (37) A.-1.11;
    3.11; (38) S.C.-1.9; 3.12; 4.27; 10.13; (39) S.C.-1.15; (40)
    S.C.-1.21; 2.19; (41) Am.-11.22; (42) Am.-1.6.
Half an Hour's Courtship; burletta by J. R. Planché: (29) A.-
    4.29,30; 5.1.
Hamlet; by William Shakespeare: (20) S.P.-1.17,26; O.-2.16; (21)
    O.-3.30; (23) O.-1.24; 3.12; (24) A.-1.19; (26) A.-2.7; 4.14;
    (27) A.-3.30; (28) A.-1.16; (29) A.-1.2,9; 4.29; (31) A.-1.3;
    4.25; (32) A.-2.2; 3.9,15,30; 4.16; (33) A.-1.5; 3.22; (34)
    A.-3.1,22; 5.13; (35) A.-3.20; 4.6; 12.2,31; S.C.-12.2; (36)
    S.C.-6.29; 11.18; A.-11.22; (37) A.-1.5; S.C.-2.9,15; A.-2.11;

5.21; S.C.-11.3; (38) S.C.-3.4; (39) A.-2.11; S.C.-2.12; 4.7;
(40) S.C.-4.9; 12.3; Am.-12.11; (41) S.C.-3.4; (42) S.C.-
2.28; 3.9.

Hamlet Travestie: (31) A.-2.10.

A Handsome Husband; farce by Mrs. J. R. Planché: (37) A.-3.22;
4.2; (38) S.C.-3.8,12,17; (41) S.C.-3.6,14; 12.19; (42) S.C.-
1.12; 2.16.

The Happiest Day of My Life; comedy by J. B. Buckstone: (31)
A.-5.6,10; 12.21,28; (32) A.-12.15; (34) A.-3.28; 12.18; (36)
A.-3.10; S.C.-3.31; 4.4,12; 5.16; (37) S.C.-3.28; 4.5.

Harcanlack; melodrama by N. H. Bannister: (36) A.-4.9.

Hard Times in New Orleans; by George Washington Harby: (37)
A.-4.17.

The Harlequin and the Golden Egg; see *Harlequin and Mother
Goose.*

*Harlequin and Mother Goose, or The Harlequin and the Golden
Egg;* pantomime by J. T. Dibdin: (35) A.-12.25; (42) Am.-
3.17,19,20,21.

Harlequin and the Magic Sword; pantomime: (42) Am.-2.2.

Harlequin; pantomime: (42) Am.-2.4.

Harlequin Frolics; farce: (41) S.C.-11.2,3.

Harlequin's Olio: (41) S.C.-12.5,6,7,8,13; (42) S.C.-1.9; Am.-2.6.

The Haunted Inn; farce by R. B. Peake: (29) A.-3.12; 4.11; (30)
A.-3.2; 4.2; 12.27; (32) A.-5.14; (33) A.-4.30.

The Haunted Tower; opera by J. Cobb: (29) A.-1.27.

The Hazard of the Die; tragedy by Douglas Jerrold: (37) S.C.-
2.22,24.

H. B.; farce by R. B. Peake: (41) S.C.-2.15,27; 3.1,4.

He's Not A-Miss, or Une Heure de la Vie d'un Soldat; musical
farce by T. E. Wilks: (38) A.-3.5,8,13.

He Would Be a Soldier; comedy by Pilson: (33) A.-1.8; (39)
A.-1.8.

The Headsman; by James Rees: (34) A.-5.17.

The Heart of Midlothian; melodrama by Thomas Dibdin: (33)
A.-4.3; (34) A.-12.21; (37) S.C.-1.10.

The Heir at Law; comedy by Colman the Younger: (12) S.P.-
4.3; (20) O.-3.18; (24) A.-1.10; (26) A.-5.12; (29) A.-3.31;
(31) A.-4.30; (32) A.-2.8,29; (35) A.-4.4; (37) S.C.-1.28;
3.15; (40) S.C.-10.20; (41) Am.-11.20; (42) Am.-1.31; 5.12.

Helpless Animals; farce by Thomas Parry: (26) A.-3.14,27.

Henri Quatre; opera by Thomas Morton: (21) O.-3.9; (31) A.-
5.9,12.

Henrietta the Forsaken; drama by Buckstone: (40) S.C.-1.30; 2.3.

Henry IV; by William Shakespeare: (17) S.P.-12.15; O.-12.18;
(20) O.-4.5; (26) A.-1.26; (28) A.-2.29; (31) A.-1.5; (32)
A.-4.6; (34) A.-3.18; (37) S.C.-12.8,14,18; (41) S.C.-12.6,9,
11,31; Am.-12.7,9; (42) Am.-1.26.

Henry VIII; by William Shakespeare: (31) A.-1.17.

Hercules, King of Clubs; farce by F. F. Cooper: (40) S.C.-1.23, 25,28; 11.23,27; 12.20; (41) S.C.-11.11.

Une Heure de la Vie d'un Soldat; see *He's Not A-Miss.*

Hide and Seek; musical interlude by Joseph Lunn: (37) S.C.-1.23, 29; 10.31.

The Highland Reel; farce by O'Keeffe: (20) O.-3.1; (21) O.-3.5; (23) A.-5.23; (24) A.-2.2; (26) A.-3.6; 5.27; (27) A.-5.28; (28) A.-3.24; (29) A.-4.23; (30) A.-2.13; 5.6; (31) A.-4.2,20; (34) A.-4.10,15; (38) A.-5.14.

The Highland Widow: (31) A.-5.30.

High Life Below Stairs; farce by David Garrick: (20) O.-3.20; (28) A.-3.21; (29) A.-4.24; (32) A.-3.2,10; (37) S.C.-2.15, 21; (38) S.C.-12,18,21; (39) S.C.-2.14.

High Ways and By Ways; farce by Benjamin Webster: (32) A.-1.13; (33) A.-12.25,28.

His First Champagne; farce by W. L. Rede: (37) S.C.-5.6,10.

His Last Legs; farce by W. B. Bernard: (40) S.C.-10.25,27; 11.1,2,5,8,11,14,20; 12.19,21; (41) S.C.-1.4,9; 2.15,17; 3.16; 11.27; (42) S.C.-2.8; Am.-3.22.

Hit or Miss; musical farce by Pocock: (24) A.-3.12,13.

Hofer, the Tell of the Tyrol; melodrama by Edward Fitzball; (36) A.-12.14,15,16,18,23.

The Hole in the Wall; see *The Secret.*

The Hole in the Wall, or A Dangerous Neighbor; translated from Kotzebue by W. Berger: (40) S.C.-4.11.

The Honest Thieves; by Thomas Knight: (20) O.-3.15; 4.7; (23) O.-2.28; (24) A.-1.21; 4.10; (27) A.-4.22; (30) A.-3.16; 12.24; (31) A.-1.18; (32) A.-4.7; (33) A.-3.13; (36) A.-4.30; 5.21; (37) A.-5.21; (39) A.-4.5; (40) A.-5.23; Am.-11.17; (41) S.C.-11.20.

The Honest Yankee; see *Jonathan Postfree.*

The Honey Moon; comedy by John Tobin: (17) S.P.-3.11,28; (18) S.P.-1.13; 4.29; (20) S.P.-1.7; O.-2.14; (21) O.-2.3; (23) A.-5.16; (24) A.-2.28; 6.7; (26) A.-1.24; 5.11; (27) A.-2.17; 5.14; (28) A.-4.8,17; 12.18; (30) A.-2.23; 5.18; (31) A.-1.11; 3.10; 4.29; (32) A.-5.17; (33) A.-4.19; 12.6; (34) A.-2.18; (35) A.-5.11; S.C.-12.4; (36) S.C.-2.20; A.-4.7; 12.8; (37) S.C.-2.6,20; 10.28; (39) S.C.-2.2; (40) Am.-11.10; (41) S.C.-3.23.

Horse Shoe Robinson; by Charles Dance: (37) S.C.-12.9.

Hortense: (41) Am.-12.22.

The Hotel, or Two Strings to Your Bow; farce by Andrew Cheery: (18) S.P.-3.27; (24) A.-1.5; (30) A.-1.15; (31) A.-2.24; 3.24; 12.22.

The House that Jack Built; ballet: (20) O.-3.6,8,9.

The Housekeeper; comedy by Jerrold: (34) A.-1.21,23; 2.6,27.

How Do You Manage?; farce by T. H. Bayly: (38) A.-5.27; V.G.-6.20,27; S.C.-10.18; (41) S.C.-11.13,15.

How to Die for Love; farce: (17) S.P.-11.4,26; (30) A.-2.16,18;
    4.5; (34) A.-12.22; (37) A.-4.14; 5.3,15; (38) A.-1.18; 5.5.
The Hunchback; drama by J. S. Knowles: (33) A.-1.28,29,31;
    2.8,11; 3.5,8; 4.8,12; 12.12,19; (34) A.-1.11; 5.14; 11.27;
    (35) A.-5.2; 11.21,24; S.C.-12.7; (36) S.C.-1.12; 2.18; 3.17;
    A.-3.8; 11.21; S.C.-12.3; A.-12.10; (37) A.-1.13,23; 2.3;
    3.25,28; 4.22,29; S.C.-10.31; (38) S.C.-1.11,17; A.-2.8; 11.13;
    (39) S.C.-1.25; A.-2.13; 3.30; 10.20,24; S.C.-12.2.
Hundred Pound Note; farce by R. B. Peake: (28) A.-4.19; (29)
    A.-1.1,6; 12.9; (30) A.-4.6; (31) A.-2.7; 3.5; 4.11; (32)
    A.-1.30; (33) A.-1.8; (34) A.-1.1; (39) S.C.-2.25; 3.1; (40)
    S.C.-10.24,26.
The Hunter of the Alps; melodrama by William Dimond: (19)
    S.P.-4.28; (20) O.-3.25; 4.19; (23) O.-2.7; (24) A.-1.28; 6.2;
    (25) A.-3.11; (26) A.-2.27; 5.5; (27) A.-3.16; (28) A.-12.31;
    (29) A.-1.28; 4.22; (30) A.-3.12; (31) A.-3.18; 12.30; (33)
    A.-5.13; (34) A.-4.14; (36) A.-12.1; (37) S.C.-1.31; 10.19,
    22; (40) A.-5.20.
Hunting a Turtle; farce by Charles Selby: (37) S.C.-1.13; 4.3;
    (40) Am.-11.27; (41) S.C.-1.11,19; Am.-4.10; S.C.-11.9,25.
Hurrah for the Boys of the West; by G. W. P. Curtis: (31)
    A.-12.19.
A Husband at Sight; farce by J. B. Buckstone: (31) A.-2.11;
    3.28; 4.8; (32) A.-1.7,26; (33) A.-3.26; 4.11; 5.23; (34)
    A.-1.15; (37) A.-3.12,17,31; 4.1,19; 5.2,28; (38) A.-2.11;
    3.13; S.C.-4.18; A.-4.29; 5.10; (41) S.C.-11.26.
Husbands and Wives; comedy by Pocock: (30) A.-1.6,20; 5.6.
Huzza for Ballyragget; (38) A.-4.6.
The Hypocondriac; see *The Blue Devils.*
The Hypocrite; comedy by Isaac Bickerstaff: (26) A.-2.17,21;
    3.1,10,22; 5.4; (27) A.-5.31; (29) A.-2.17; (30) A.-1.12;
    2.4,9; (32) A.-1.25; 2.6; (34) A.-1.28; 2.7; (35) A.-2.17;
    4.16; (36) A.-1.8; 2.11; S.C.-3.21; (38) A.-1.20,21; (42)
    Am.-5.24.
The Ice Witch; romantic drama by Buckstone: (36) A.-3.3,4,5,7,
    15,16,17,18,19,27,29; 4.1,5,8; 5.18 (37) A.-2.5,6,8,16,20,27;
    3.5,6,8,22; 4.16; (40) A.-5.31; 6.5,9.
The Idiot Witness, or a Tale of Blood; melodrama by J. T. Haines:
    (33) A.-1.26; (35) A.-5.20; (36) A.-2.8; (40) Ar.-2.21;
    A.-6.13; (41) Am.-1.18; 4.29.
I'll Be Your Second; farce by G. H. Rodwell: (34) A.-12.30; (35)
    A.-1.7,24.
The Illustrious Stranger; farce by James Kenney and Millingen:
    (34) A.-12.3; (38) S.C.-11.22,25; 12.9.
The Inconstant, or Wine Does Wonders, or The Way to Keep Him;
    comedy by George Farquhar: (21) O.-3.7; (23) O.-3.14;
    (31) A.-1.8; 4.4; (32) A.-1.10; (34) A.-1.4.
Industry Must Prosper; see *The Bee Hive.*

Infidelity; farce by N. H. Bannister: (36) S.C.-11.19, 23; (37) S.C.-3.5,14,24.

L'Inganno Felice; opera by Rossini: (37) S.C.-1.1,29.

The Innkeeper's Bride; see *Intrigue.*

The Innkeeper's Daughter; melodrama by George Soane: (28) A.-1.4,26; (32) A.-5.14; (32) A.-11.30; (36) A.-12.28.

Ins and Outs; farce by Mark Lemon: (40) A.-5.20,26.

Intrigue, or Married Yesterday, or The Bath Road, or My Wife and I, or The Innkeeper's Bride, or The Rival Suitors, or The Jealous Husband; farce by John Poole: (17) S.P.-11.4; (19) S.P.-3.30; (20) O.-4.12; (29) A.-3.25; 4.4; (30) A.-4.20; 12.22; (31) A.-1.29; (32) A.-3.23; (35) A.-1.14; 2.5; (36) A.-1.28; 3.1; S.C.-4.18,22,23,27,28; A.-12.19; (37) S.C.-1.5, 17; 2.5; A.-2.23,27; S.C.-4.2; A.-4.6; 5.25; S.C.-10.18; (38) S.C.-4.12; A.-5.12; S.C.-10.5; (40) S.C.-1.24; 2.4,27; G.-9.19; (41) Am.-2.13; 3.11; 4.22; 5.6,10; (42) S.C.-1.20.

Introduce Me; farce by T. Wilks: (41) Am.-11.27; (42) Am.-2.8.

The Invincibles; musical farce by Thomas Morton: (29) A.-2.14, 16,18,20; 3.4,13; 12.11; (30) A.-1.30; (31) A.-2.4; (32) A.-12.28,31; (33) A.-1.9; 4.19; (34) A.-2.22; 5.3; (35) A.-4.25; (36) A.-1.1; (40) S.C.-5.2.

The Invisible Harlequin; pantomime: (41) Am.-12.24.

Ion; tragedy by Sergeant Talfourd: (37) S.C.-11.29; 12.1; (38) S.C.-1.15,16,22,25; 2.12; 3.6; (39) S.C.-1.20,21,22; A.-2.25.

The Irish Ambassador; farce by James Kenney: (35) A.-1.13,22; 3.9; (37) S.C.-5.4; (39) A.-2.20,24; 3.1; (40) S.C.-12.18,26, 30.

The Irish Attorney; farce by W. B. Bernard: (40) S.C.-12.28, 29, 31; (41) S.C.-1.4.

The Irish Lion; farce by Buckstone: (39) A.-10.27,29; 11.1,3,6, 10,13,20; S.C.-12.5; (40) S.C.-1.9,14; 2.8,12; 5.3,10; 12.17, 23,26,31; (41) S.C.-1.6; 2.5,11,24.

The Irishman in London; farce by William Macready: (18) S.P.-3.21; (20) S.P.-1.12; (22) O.-3.15; (24) A.-4.9; (26) A.-5.16; (27) A.-4.4; (32) A.-3.1; 4.14; 5.18; (33) A.-5.1,17; 11.28; (34) A.-5.22; (35) A.-1.13; 3.11; (37) A.-5.6,19; (38) S.C.-4.24; A.-11.30; 12.1,15,22; (39) A.-1.1,3,12; 2.8; 3.5,8, 22; (40) Am.-11.14; 12.12; (41) Am.-3.21,23.

The Irish Tutor; farce by R. Butler: (27) A.-12.27; (28) A.-1.1,19; 2.18; (31) A.-1.3; (32) A.-2.24,28; 3.10; 4.13; (34) A.-1.20; (35) A.-1.15; 3.9; (35) A.-12.12; (36) A.-5.4; (37) S.C.-3.15; A.-5.20; (39) A.-2.18,25; 3.18; 4.1,4; S.C.-4.27; (40) S.C.-1.19; 2.7,25,29; 3.19; G.-9.19:; S.C.-10.12; 11.3; 12.9,28; (41) Am.-2.12,15; 4.1.

The Irish Valet, or More Blunders than One; farce by G. H. Rodwell: (35) A.-1.31; 3.18; (37) S.C.-5.2; (39) A.-2.27; 3.1.

The Irish Widow; farce by David Garrick: (27) A.-4.5,10; 5.31; (41) Am. 2.3,5; 3.9,17; 4.22; 5.10; (42) Am.-3.11,14; 4.5.

Irma; by James H. Kennicott: (30) A.-4.6,12,15,20; (31) A.-2.15.

The Iron Chest; melodrama by Colman the Younger: (23)
    A.-5.17; (24) A.-3.9; (26) A.-5.24; (28) A.-2.1,13; (29)
    A.-2.21; 4.14; (31) A.-3.7; 4.22; (32) A.-2.13; (33) A-1.10;
    5.7; (35) A.-4.15; 12.3; (36) A.-2.3; (40) Ar.-2.23; A.-5.29;
    Am.-12.10; (41) Am.-1.30.
Isabella, or The Fatal Marriage; tragedy by Thomas Southerne:
    (19) S.P.-5.8; (29) A.-3.5; (32) A.-11.27; (34) A.-12.8;
    (35) A.-4.20; (37) A.-4.17; 5.1; (39) S.C.-4.17.
Isabelle; see *A Woman's Life.*
Is He Jealous?; operetta by Beazley: (26) A.-5.17,23; (30) A.-
    5.19; (31) A.-2.11; (33) A.-12.20; (34) A.-1.10; 2.7; 3.31;
    11.28; (35) A.-3.16; 4.8; (36) S.C.-4.21,29; (37) S.C.-1.12,
    18; 2.25; 3.25; A.-4.26; 5.12; S.C.-11.3; (39) A.-2.11; (40)
    S.C.-4.25; 12.3; (41) S.C.-2.17; Am.-4.19,24; S.C.-12.4; Am.-
    12.24.
Is It a Lie?; farce: (29) A.-5.16,22.
The Island Ape, or Bippo: (33) A.-1.12; (41) Am.-2.20,21,22;
    3.22,24.
Ivanhoe; melodrama (by Moncrieff) : (37) A.-5.14,18.
Jack the Giant Killer; "petit drama of enchantment written es-
    pecially for Master Wood by C. A. Somerset": (41) S.C.-
    11.25,26.
Jack Robinson and His Monkey; entertainment by William Barry-
    more: (33) A.-10.21.
Jacques Strop; melodrama by Charles Selby: (42) Am.-1.15,23.
Jane Shore; tragedy by Nicholas Rowe: (29) A.-3.18,25; (31)
    A.-1.10; (32) A.-12.11; (34) A.-12.20; (36) S.C.-3.3; A.-
    12.12; (37) A.-1.26; S.C.-4.13; A.-5.3; (38) A.-3.24.
The Jealous Husband; see *Intrigue.*
The Jealous Wife; comedy by Colman the Elder: (21) O.-2.24;
    (27) A.-2.26; (28) A.-3.17; (29) A.-3.21; (32) A.-5.11; (36)
    S.C.-1.20; 3.1; (37) A.-5.25; (38) S.C.-1.27.
Jemmy Twitcher in France; see *Mobb, the Outlaw.*
Jeremiah Blackstitch: (41) S.C.-10.25,26; (42) S.C.-2.4,5.
The Jew and the Doctor; farce by T. J. Dibdin: (31) A.-12.15;
    (33) A.-5.4,16.
The Jew; comedy by Richard Cumberland: (30) A.-4.28.
The Jewess, or The Fate of Haman: (36) S.C.-4.26,28.
The Jewess, or The Council of Constance; historical drama (by
    J. R. Planché or W. T. Moncrieff) : (36) A.-5.3,4,6,7,8,9.10,11,
    12,13,14,16,19,20,21,24; 12.25,28,31; (37) A.-2.6,22; 4.8; 5.15;
    S.C.—5.30; 12.24,25,26,27,28,29,30,31; (38) S.C.-1.1,7,14; A.-
    3.2,3; S.C.-10.20,22; (39) S.C.-4.26.
Jim Crow; extravaganza: (35) A.-4.1,2,3,4,5,6,28; 5.1,2,5,7,8,11;
    (42) S.C.-2.18.
Jim Crow in London; extravaganza by T. D. Rice: (38) A.-3.6,7;
    (42) S.C.-2.18.

Joan of Arc; melodrama by Edward Fitzball: (32) A.-2.23; 4.3, 4,7,10,24; 12.24; (39) A.-4.6; S.C.-4.16; A.-11.19,21,23; (40) S.C.-1.19.

Job Fox, the Yankee Valet; by W. B. Bernard: (35) A.-2.7,10.

Jocko, or The Brazilian Ape; burletta by T. J. Dibdin: (33) A.-1.3, 5,18,24; 3.13; (34) A.-2.4,6,8.

Jocko; ballet: (30) A.-3.13.

Joe Miller; sketch: (39) S.C.-12.22.

John Bull; comedy by Colman the Younger: (12) S.P.-1.24; (18) S.P.-3.6; (20) S.P.-1.28; (24) A.-2.18,27; (28) A.-1.7; (31) A.-1.22; 12.12; (32) A.-3.5,13; 4.13; 12.17; (35) A.-1.7; (36) A.-4.15; (37) S.C.-1.6; (38) A.-11.15; (39) A.-2.17; (40) S.C.-12.21; (42) Am.-3.19.

John Jones; farce by Buckstone: (37) A.-1.5,6,11,15; (38) A.-2.28; (41) Am.-12.6.

John Overy; melodrama by Douglas Jerrold: (33) A.-5.7.

John of Paris; opera by Pocock: (21) O.-3.19; (23) O.-1.15,29; (29) A.-12.31; (30) A.-1.2; 3.17; (31) A.-5.13,21; (33) A.-1.28; 4.13; (34) A.-2.3; (35) S.C.-12.5,26; (36) S.C.-12.29,31; A.-12.31; (37) S.C.-1.4; 3.4,7,17; (38) S.C.-1.10; 2.22; 10.17.

John of Procida; tragedy by J. S. Knowles: (40) Am.-11.17; S.C.-11.23,30.

Jonathan Bradford; melodrama by Edward Fitzball: (34) A.-2.1, 4,5,20.

Jonathan Doubikins; farce: (35) A.-2.28; (36) S.C.-2.4,6; (38) A.-1.19, 21; 2.9,12.

Jonathan Postfree, the Honest Yankee; national drama by L. Beach: (30) A.-4.30; 5.4.

Jonathan in Difficulty: (40) A.-6.12.

Jonathan in England; comedy altered by J. H. Hackett from Colman's *Who Wants a Guinea?:* (32) A.-3.21,23; (34) A.-1.21,23; 2.8; 12.22; (35) A.-1.5; 2.3; 3.3; (36) S.C.-1.27,30; (37) A.-2.15; 3.21; 5.11; (38) A.-12.5; (39) A.-1.10; (40) S.C.-1.5; 12.27; (41) S.C.-12.10.

Joseph Bragg; see *Make Your Wills.*

Julius Caesar; by William Shakespeare; (21) O.-4.11; (23) O.-3.26; (24) A.-1.21; (26) A.-4.14; (29) A.-3.30; (31) A.-1.12; (34) A.-4.21; (36) A.-2.5; S.C.-2.6; (37) A.-2.1; (39) A.-3.8.

Jumbo Jim; farce by T. D. Rice: (42) S.C.-2.17,19,20.

Kabri: (38) A.-1.25,26,31; 2.3; 4.18,24.

Kasper Hauser; by H. J. Finn: (35) A.-2.25; 4.8; (36) S.C.-2.1, 2,4; (38) A.-1.21,22; 2.7,11.

Kate Kearney; romantic drama by William Collier: (37) A.-12.27; (38) A.-1.1,3,5,10,12; 2.28; 3.31.

The Kentuckian; revision of *The Lion of the West:* (35) A.-2.5; 3.3,5; (37) S.C.-12.2,4,11,18; (41) S.C.-12.7,31; (42) Am.-1.29.

Kill or Cure; farce by Charles Dance: (36) S.C.-3.29,30; 4.2.

Killing No Murder; musical farce by T. E. Hook: (32) A.-2.15.

King John; by William Shakespeare: (23) O.-4.4.
King Lear; by William Shakespeare: (21) O.-3.2; (28) A.-1.23;
      2.13; (29) A.-1.17; 4.20; (32) A.-4.25; 5.2; 12.15; (36) S.C.-
      12.2; (37) S.C.-10.26; (38) A.-3.15; (39) A.-2.4,9; S.C.-2.10;
      A.-3.25; S.C.-4.3; (40) S.C.-4.9; 11.6; (41) S.C.-12.28; (42)
      Am.-1.27.
King O'Neil; melodrama by Mrs. Gore: (41) S.C.-1.5,6,8,20.
The King's Fool; by John Millingen: (36) A.-11.26,29.
The King's Word; interlude by Captain H. R. Addison: (36) S.C.-
      6.17,20,24.
A Kiss in the Dark; farce by Buckstone: (41) S.C.-2.1,4,9,12; Am.-
      4.18,19,22,23; (42) Am.-3.14,16,; 4.10,11.
The Knight of the Golden Fleece, or The Yankee in Spain; comedy
      by J. A. Stone: (34) A.-12.29,31; (35) A.-2.14; (36) S.C.-
      1.28,30; 2.5; (37) A.-12.15; (38) A.-1.18,20; 2.12.
Know Your Own Mind; comedy by Arthur Murphy: (23) O.-
      2.5,17; (27) A.-3.10.
La Perouse; pantomime by John Fawcett: (26) A.-3.30; 4.4;
      (27) A.-3.26; (28) A.-3.17; (33) A.-1.16.
The Ladder of Love; comedy by T. H. Bayly: (38) A.-11.11,13,
      14,16; (41) Am.-11.25,27; 12.5,26; (42) Am.-1.25.
Ladies at Home, or Ladies! Do Not Stay at Home: (30) A.-5.3;
      (32) A.-12.12,19; (33) A.-1.22; (34) A.-12.1,10.
Ladies! Do Not Stay at Home; see *Ladies at Home.*
The Ladies' Club; burletta by Mark Lemon: (41) Am.-2.8,10;
      (42) Am.-4.11.
The Lady and the Devil; farce by Wm. Dimond: (23) O.-1.18;
      (24) A.-4.12; (26) A.-4.15; (27) A.-4.11; (30) A.-4.23; (31)
      A.-3.9,22; (32) A.-3.19; (33) A.-2.12,18; 4.20; (34) A.-12.8;
      (35) A.-1.20; 3.20,27; 5.21; 11.25; (36) S.C.-5.7; 6.4; (37)
      S.C.-2.19; 3.19,21,29; 11.15; (38) A.-5.17; (39) S.C.-1.3;
      A.-10.16; (40) S.C.-2.5,20; (41) Am.-4.26.
The Lady of Irons; burlesque: (42) Am.-3.25,28.
Lady of the Lake; melodrama by T. J. Dibdin: (20) S.P.-2.11;
      (21) O.-5.12; (23) O.-2.24; (24) A.-4.3,22; (30) A.-3.30;
      4.13; (31) A.-2.24; 3.7; (33) A.-2.15; (38) A.-4.3; (41)
      Am.-5.1; (42) Am.-1.30.
The Lady of Lyons; romantic drama by Edward Bulwer Lytton:
      (38) A.-10.21,23,25,31; 11.2,4,8,11,14,21,23,24,30; 12.2,4,6,9,
      13,14,16,23,29; S.C.-12.18,20,22,26; (39) A.-1.13,15,17; S.C.-
      1.16,19; A.-2.1,2,12,21; 3.10; 4.3; S.C.-4.15; A.-11.2,6,8; S.C.-
      12.3,12,14,23; (40) S.C.-2.4; 3.4; 4.4,12; 11.1,5,7,10,17,21;
      Am.-11.16; S.C.-12.16; (41) S.C.-3.24; Am.-12.17; (42)
      S.C.-2.25.
Lafayette; by Samuel Woodworth: (25) A.-4.11; (29) A.-1.1.
Lafitte, the Pirate of the Gulf; by James Rees: (37) A.-4.3,4,5,6,
      9,10,11,12,13,14; (42) Am.-3.21.
Lafitte; by Charlotte Barnes: (37) S.C.-4.15,17,24,25; 5.1; (38)
      S.C.-12.1,8; (40) S.C.-4.14,22,24.

Lamorah!; by Mrs. Hentz: (38) A.-1.1; 4.16.
The Lancers; farce by J. H. Payne: (29) A.-12.16; (30) A.-3.5.
The Last Days of Pompeii; by Charlotte Barnes: (35) A.-5.7.
The Last Days of Pompeii; melodrama by Edward Fitzball: (40)
    S.C.-5.1,3; (41) Am.-5.2,3,4,11; (42) Am.-1.9,10,13,20; 2.1,25.
The Last Man; domestic drama by Pitt: (42) Am.-4.1.
The Last of the Mohicans; by S. E. Glover: (30) A.-4.26,27,29,
    30; 5.7; (31) A.-3.15,19; (32) A.-2.22.
The Last Nail; melodrama by G. Pitt: (38) A.-3.29,30.
Last Words of Bill Jones, or The Black Brig of Bermuda; melo-
    drama by J. H. Amherst: (36) A.-12.5,7; (37) A.-1.23,24,29;
    3.1,3,20; 11.30; (39) S.C.-12.28,29.
Laugh When You Can; comedy by Frederick Reynolds: (18)
    S.P.-4.15; (20) S.P.-1.8; 4.18; (21) O.-5.12; (22) O.-3.16;
    (23) O.-1.15; 3.19; (24) A.-6.9; (26) A.-3.30; (27) A.-3.22;
    (29) A.-2.14; (31) A.-12.16; (32) A.-4.28; (33) A.-1.5; 3.4;
    5.27; (34) A.-2.17; (36) A.-4.23; (39) S.C.-12.9; (40) S.C.-
    1.8; 3.5,13; 10.10; Am.-11.24; (41) Am.-1.19; S.C.-2.6.
The Lear of Private Life; drama by Moncrieff: (30) A.-3.18,23,
    27; 4.19; (31) A.-12.6; (37) S.C.-5.10.
The Legion of Honor; see *One Hundred and Two.*
A Lesson for Ladies; comedy by Buckstone: (42) S.C.-2.2,4.
A Lesson in Love; comedy: (38) S.C.-11.9,11; (39) S.C.-3.3.
The Liar; farce by Samuel Foote: (20) S.P.-1.19,25; O.-3.10;
    (21) O.-1.31; 4.27; (23) O.-1.13; 3.22; (24) A.-1.26; 5.7;
    (25) A.-3.9; (26) A.-4.25; (28) A.-1.16; (29) A.-1.5; (30)
    A.-3.26; 5.5; (34) A.-4.12; (40) Am.-11.19; 12.16.
The Libertine; "a literal translation of Mozart's celebrated opera
    of *Il Don Giovanni* with original music as selected and ar-
    ranged by H. R. Bishop": (30) A.-3.15,19.
The Liberty Tree; comedy by J. S. Jones: (36) S.C.-7.4; (38)
    A.-4.5.
Life in London, or Tom and Jerry; burletta by Moncrieff: (24)
    A.-5.7,8,10; (25) A.-1.18,19,20,21; 4.18; (26) A.-1.28; 2.9;
    3.13; 4.22; (27) A.-4.10; (28) A.-2.28; 3.22; 4.12,19; (29)
    A.-2.12; 5.18; (30) A.-1.9; (32) A.-2.8; 12.22; (33) A.-2.26;
    12.21; (34) A.-4.12; (36) A.-3.27; 12.18; (38) A.-11.18,20;
    (39) S.C.-2.25; 4.21; (40) S.C.-5.10; 11.29; 12.13; (42)
    Am.-1.30.
Life in New Orleans; burletta by N. H. Bannister: (37) S.C.-5.13,
    16.
Life in New York; an adaptation of the anonymous play of this
    name by George Farren: (38) A.-2.17,18,19,20,21,22,23,25;
    3.1,16.
Life in Philadelphia: (35) A.-3.27.
Like Master Like Man; see *Lovers' Quarrels.*
Lion of the West; comedy by J. A. Stone: (32) A.-3.19,20,26.
Lionel and Clarissa; comic opera by Bickerstaff: (23) O.-2.7.
Little Red Riding Hood; ballet: (24) A.-5.3.

The Loan of a Lover; vaudeville by J. R. Planché: (36) A.-2.18,
    20,27; S.C.-2.22,23,27; A.-3.5,18; S.C.-3.7,26; 5.12; (37)
    A.-1.5,14,18,31; S.C.-1.19,21,26,30; 5.15,18; (38) A.-1.4,12;
    S.C.-1.12,17; 2.2,23; A.-2.28; 3.2; 5.6,8; S.C.-10.10; 11.7;
    (40) S.C.-3.12; 4.8; 10.9,11; 11.2; 12.18; (41) S.C.-1.22;
    3.27; 11.16; Am.-11.24; S.C.-12.28; (42) S.C.-1.3,18; Am.-
    3.10; 5.5.
Lock and Key; farce by Prince Hoare: (20) O.-3.22; (23) O.-4.18;
    (24) 1.16; (26) A.-5.12; (27) A.-2.3; 5.14; 12.24; (28) A.-
    2.23; (29) A.-1.7; 3.2; (30) A.-1.5; 4.28; (31) A.-2.15,22;
    12.14; (32) A.-3.21; 12.4; (33) A.-5.15,22; (34) A.-3.3; (36)
    A.-3.16.
Lodoiska; opera by T. J. Dibdin: (20) S.P.-2.3; O.-2.29; (22)
    O.-3.18,20; (27) A.-5.8.
London Assurance; comedy by D. Boucicault: (41) Am.-12.12,13,
    14,15; S.C.-12.20,21,22,23,24; (42) S.C.-1.3,4,6; 2.7,8,9,10,
    12,15,17,23,24; 3.4,7.
The Lord of the Isles; comic opera by Edward Fitzball: (40)
    S.C.-3.1.
The Lord of the Manor; comic opera by Charles Dibdin, Jr.: (29)
    A.-2.20; (34) A.-2.14.
The Lottery Ticket; French musical piece: (17) O.-6.5.
The Lottery Ticket; farce by Beazley: (29) A.-3.20,21; (30)
    A.-2.20; (31) A.-2.28; 3.15; (32) A.-2.9; (33) A.-2.19; 5.21;
    (35) A.-4.1,6; 12.23,31; (36) S.C.-6.20; (38) A.-2.6; 3.11;
    4.10,23; S.C.-4.16; A.-5.11; S.C.-10.3,6,22; A.-11.27,28; 12.27;
    (39) A.-1.2; 2.13; 3.4,20; 10.12; S.C.-12.31; (40) S.C.-10.26;
    (41) S.C.-1.6; Am.-3.11,18; (42) S.C.-1.22.
Love; drama by J. S. Knowles: (40) S. C.-1.23,24,25,27,28; 2.2;
    4.10,21; Am.-11.18.
Love à la Mode; farce by Charles Macklin: (20) S.P.-1.17; (31)
    A.-4.28; (32) A.-4.16.
Love Among the Roses; farce, music by Dr. Kitchiner: (23) A.-
    5.17; (24) A.-3.8.
Love and Mercy; see *The Young Hussar.*
Love and a Bunch; comedy by F. S. Hill: (37) A.-5.13.
Love and Reason, or Alice; comedy by Lacy: (28) A.-2.15,16,25;
    3.20; (29) A.-2.10,24; (30) A.-5.4; (31) A.-3.28; (40) Am.-
    11.15; (42) Am.-3.29; 4.27.
Love at All Corners; farce by Frank Dumont: (38) S.C.-3.21.
The Love Chase; comedy by J. S. Knowles: (38) A.-2.13,14,15,16;
    S.C.-2.28; 3.1,2,10; A.-4.13; 5.26; S.C.-12.15,19; A.-12.18,19;
    (39) S.C.-1.17,28; A.-2.22.
Love in a Camp; farce by O'Keeffe: (24) A.-3.17.
Love in Humble Life; dramatic sketch by J. H. Payne: (28) A.-
    1.7; 3.20; (38) V.G.-6.23,30; 7.1.
Love in a Village; comic opera by Bickerstaff: (20) O.-2.25;
    S.P.-3.2,9; (21) O.-2.14; (26) A.-5.20; (29) A.-1.29; 12.24;
    (30) A.-3.12; (31) A.-2.19; (33) A.-12.30; (34) A.-4.1;
    11.24; 12.4.

Love in Wrinkles or My Old Woman; comic opera by Lacy: (29) A.-12.30; (42) Am.-3.10,15.

Love Alone Can Fix Him; see *The Weathercock.*

Love Laughs at Locksmiths; musical farce by Colman the Younger: (20) O.-3.29; (21) O.-3.26; (23) O.-4.7; (24) A.-2.13; (27) A.-2.20; (35) A.-2.25; 4.4.

The Lover Husband; comedy (by E. Ranger): (41) S.C.-1.25,26.

Lovers' Quarrels; by T. King: (23) O.-3.21; (24) A.-1.19; (26) A.-2.7; (29) A.-5.11; (30) A.-4.15; (31) A.-4.5; (33) A.-2.25; (34) A.-2.13; 11.25; (36) A.-4.9; (37) A.-4.11; (40) S.C.-1.30; 2.3,23; (41) Am.-3.9; (42) Am.-2.27.

Lovers' Vows, or The Cottager's Daughter; by Mrs. Inchbald: (18) S.P.-4.25; (19) S.P.-4.14; (23) O.-2.26; A.-5.28; (28) A.-12.26; (30) A.-2.5; (31) A.-2.7; (37) A.-4.16.

Lucia di Lammermoor; opera by Donizetti: (42) S.C.-2.27; 3.1,12.

Lucille; domestic drama by W. B. Bernard: (37) A.-1.9,11,14; S.C.-1.17,20,22; 12.18; (38) A.-5.16; S.C.-12.5.

Luck in a Name; see *The Two Gregories.*

Lucrece Borgia; "translated from the French by F. Haynes of this city": (36) S.C.-5.14.

Luke the Labourer; melodrama by J. B. Buckstone: (29) A.-12.9, 12; (35) A.-12.14; (37) S.C.-11.1,21; (38) A.-12.5,8; (40) S.C.-12.2; (42) S.C.-1.11,21.

Lurline; melodrama by Pitt: (38) A.-1.15,17,23,24.

The Lying Valet; farce by David Garrick: (23) O.-2.14; (28) A.-1.15; (33) A.-5.9; (40) S.C.-5.6; Am.-12.8; (42) Am.-5.14.

Macbeth; by William Shakespeare: (20) O.-2.21; (21) O.-3.23; (23) O.-1.17; 3.21; (24) A.-1.16; (27) A.-3.28; (29) A.-1.14; 3.19; (29) A.-12.28; (32) A.-1.31; 2.18; 4.27; 12.6; (33) A.-4.10; (35) A.-3.19; (36) A.-1.15,27; S.C.-1.18; 2.25; 4.23; 5.20; 11.16; 12.8; (37) A.-1.27; S.C.-2.5; A.-2.12; 3.27; 4.26, 29; S.C.-11.8; 12.13; (38) S.C.-1.23; 2.8; A.-3.22; S.C.-11.5; (39) A.-1.12; 2.8,14; 3.16; S.C.-4.2; (40) S.C.-4.9,13; 11.26; (42) S.C.-3.2.

The Mad Actor; see *Sylvester Daggerwood.*

Mad as a March Hare; comic pastoral pantomime: (41) S.C.-12.9.

Mademoiselle de Belle Isle; translated from Dumas by J. M. Field: (40) S.C.-5.6,10; (41) S.C.-2.20,24; 4.7.

The Magic Box; pantomime: (41) Am.-4.5.

The Magpie and the Maid; melodrama by Pocock: (17) S.P.-4.8; (20) S.P.-2.2; O.-3.11; (26) A.-2.2; 5.10; (27) A.-3.24; (28) A.-3.4; (29) A.-4.28; (30) A.-3.2; (35) A.-5.27; (37) A.-5.13.

The Maid and the Magpie; see *The Magpie and the Maid.*

The Maid of Cashmere; see *La Bayadere.*

The Maid of Croissy; drama by Mrs. Gore: (38) S.C.-12.22,26,29; (39) S.C.-1.11,15,23,29; 2.28; 4.9; (41) Am.-3.26,28; 4.8; (42) S.C.-2.14,15.

The Maid of Mariendorpt; drama by J. S. Knowles: (38) A.-
  12.29,30; S.C.-12.31; (39) A.-1.2,16; S.C.-1.2,24,30.

The Maid of Munster; see *Perfection.*

Maid or Wife; farce by Barham Livius: (30) A.-2.9,11,19; (31)
  A.-5.16,17; 11.24; (36) A.-12.16; (37) S.C.-1.2.

Maidens Beware; farce by J. T. Haines: (40) Am.-12.8.

The Maiden's Vow, or The Yankee in Time; (by J. P. Addams):
  (38) A.-12.8; (39) S.C.-12.29,30; (40) S.C.-1.3,22; 12.1,11,27;
  (42) S.C.-1.11,15.

Mail Coach Adventures; sketch by Charles Mathews: (41)
  A.E.-6.6.

The Maine Question; drama by N. H. Bannister: (42) Am.-3.31.

Make Your Wills, or Joseph Bragg; farce by Edward Mayhew and
  G. Smith: (41) Am. 4.18; (42) Am.-3.12,15; 4.5,9.

Malvina; dramatic opera by George Macfarren: (27) A.-4.16,19.

Man and Wife; comedy by S. J. Arnold: (27) A.-12.21; (30) A.-
  2.3; (31) A.-4.2; (32) A.-3.16; 4.17; (34) A.-2.15.

The Man about Town; farce by W. B. Bernard: (38) A.-1.10,11.

The Man in the Iron Mask; melodrama by James Haynes: (36)
  A.-1.16.

The Man of Fortitude; by Hodgkinson: (19) S.P.-3.20.

Management; comedy by Frederick Reynolds: (32) A.-5.5.

The Manager in Distress; farce by Colman the Elder: (23) O.-
  4.9,11; (34) A.-3.8; (40) A.-6.14.

The Manager's Daughter; by Edward Lancaster: (39) S.L.-3.26,
  27; S.C.-3.31.

The March of Intellect; by G. Macfarren: (32) A.-3.5,7,9,14,17;
  4.12,17; (37) S.C.-4.24,25.

Marino Faliero; opera by Donizetti: (42) S.C.-2.22,26; 3.3.

Marion; national drama by M. M. Noah: (24) A.-1.8; (27) A.-
  12.28; (31) A.-12.23.

Marmion; by J. N. Barker: (20) O.-4.12; (21) O.-3.5; (24) A.-
  4.5; (26) A.-5.15.

The Marriage of Figaro; opera by Mozart: (30) A.-3.22,27; (31)
  A.-3.21; 4.21; 5.17; (33) A.-1.2,9; 12.4; (34) A.-1.1,18; 3.27;
  (35) S.C.-12.1,3,10; (36) S.C.-1.2; A.-12.23,29; (38) S.C.-
  2.17; (40) S.C.-4.27.

The Marriage Contract; by N. H. Bannister: (35) A.-12.19,22.

Married and Single; comedy by Poole: (32) A.-1.23; 2.3; (35)
  A.-4.16. (36) S.C.-3.24; 4.7.

The Married Bachelor; burletta by P. P. O'Callaghan: (36) S.C.-
  6.22.

Married Life; comedy by J. B. Buckstone: (35) A.-12.29; (40)
  Am.-12.3; S.C.-12.27,29; (41) S.C.-1.3; Am.2.13,17; 3.16.

The Married Rake; comedy by Charles Selby: (36) S.C.-1.18,21,
  26; 5.20; (37) A.-5.14; S.C.-11.22; (38) S.C.-2.16; 3.3; (41)
  S.C.-11.30; (42) S.C.-1.5; Am.-5.20.

Married Yesterday; see *Intrigue.*

The Martyr Patriots; by Thomas Wharton Collens: (36) S.C.-5.16,17.

Mary Stuart, Queen of Scots; tragedy by James Haynes: (40) S.C.-5.5.

Masaniello; opera by Auber: (30) A.-4.17,19,21,22,23,24,30; 5.1; (31) A.-1.13,15; (34) A.-2.10,11,12,13,19,26; 3.15; 4.3,30; (35) A.-5.20,27; (36) A.-3.27; (40) S.C.-1.9,10,11,12,13,17, 18,21; 2.14; 3.4,19,29,31; 4.11.

The Masked Ball; see *A Grand Masquerade.*

Masked Ball from Gustavus; ballet pantomime in one act: (40) S.C.-2.6,8,11.

The Masquerade; see *A Grand Masquerade.*

Matteo Falcone, or The Youthful Brigand; melodrama by Oxberry: (37) S.C.-12.27; (39) S.C.-12.29; (40) S.C.-1.7.

Matrimony; comic opera by James Kenney: (19) S.P.-3.13; (20) S.P.-2.3; (23) O.-3.7; (24) A.-3.26; (26) A.-2.4; (28) A.-1.25; (29) A.-4.15; (33) A.-4.29; 5.18; (37) S.C.-3.13,22; (39) A.-4.5.

Maurice, the Wood Cutter; melodrama by C. A. Somerset: (32) A.-5.19.

The Mayor of Garratt; farce by Samuel Foote: (28) A.-1.30; (29) A.-3.3; (39) S.C.-2.16.

The May Queen; melodrama by J. B. Buckstone: (30) A.-1.16; 2.2; 3.15; 12.3; (32) A.-2.21; (35) A.-4.14.

Mazeppa; romantic drama by H. M. Milner: (33) A.-2.13,14; (34) A.-5.20,21,22,23,26,27; (38) A.-11.25,26,27,28,29; 12.1,2,4,6, 9,16,19; (39) A.-11.10,11,12,13,14,17,19; (40) Am.-11.25,26, 27,28,30; (41) Am.-1.25,26,28; (42) Am.-3.17,18.

Melmoth; melodrama; (31) A.-12.21,30.

The Merchant of Venice; by William Shakespeare: (18) S.P.-2.21; (20) O.-3.29; (23) O.-2.12; (26) A.-3.9; 4.14; (28) A.-1.30; (29) A.-1.12; (30) A.-1.15; (31) A.-1.12; 3.4; (32) A.-2.27; 4.12; (33) A.-1.19; 3.9; (35) A.-11.26; (36) S.C.-1.13; A.-2.2; S.C.-12.9; (37) A.-1.10; S.C.-2.28; A.-5.3,20; S.C.-11.7; (38) A.-3.23; S.C.-12.12; (39) S.C.-2.7; S.L.-3.28; (40) S.C.-4.18; 11.24; Am.-12.4; (41) Am.-3.1; (42) S.C.-3.11.

The Merry Days of Charles II; see *Charles II.*

The Merry Market Men; (41) S.C.-10.27,28.

The Merry Wives of Windsor; by William Shakespeare: (26) A.-1.30; (32) A.-12.19; (41) S.C.-12.13,27,29; (42) Am.-1.28.

Metamora; tragedy by J. A. Stone: (33) A.-5.1,2,3; (34) A.-3.21, 26; 4.17; (39) A.-2.7,10; S.C.-4.4.

Miantonimoh; (31) A.-2.5,8.

Michel Perrin; comedy by J. R. Planché: (36) S.C.-1.25,27; 2.10,26.

Midas, burletta by Kane O'Hara: (33) A.-12.30; (34) A.-1.6; 4.26; 5.15; (38) A.-5.14.

The Middy Ashore; farce by W. B. Bernard: (41) Am.-3.10,12;
    S.C.-12.16,18,22.
The Midnight Hour, or Ruse Contra Ruse; comedy by Mrs. Inch-
    bald: (18) S.P.-1.13; (23) O.-4.30; (27) A.-2.26; (38)
    A.-2.2.
The Midnight Murder; by N. H. Bannister: (35) A.-5.16.
The Miller and His Men; melodrama by Pocock: (17) S.P.-5.23;
    (24) A.-5.26; 6.5; (26) A.-2.8; 3.9; (27) A.-4.5; (30) A.-4.5,
    14; (35) A.-4.10; (42) S.C.-2.6.
The Miller's Maid; melodrama by John Faucit: (31) A.-1.28;
    2.17; (32) A.-1.1; (38) S.C.-4.24; 10.24,29; (39) A.-10.12.
The Miniature; farce by James Rees: (34) A.-5.10.
Mischief Making, or The French Washerwoman; farce by J. B.
    Buckstone: (32) A.-5.5,7,10; (33) A.-2.28; 3.19; 4.24; (34)
    A.-12.16,19; (37) S.C.-1.10; 4.5; A.-5.7,24,27; (39) A.-10.30;
    (40) A.-6.11,12; S.C.-10.10; 11.3; (41) S.C.-1.11; Am.-2.6;
    3.16; 4.24; (42) Am.-2.5.
Miss in Her Teens; farce by Andrew Cheery: (18) S.P.-3.10; 5.1;
    (23) O.-3.1,12; 4.11; (24) A.-6.7; (40) G.-1.16; Ar.-2.14.
The Mistletoe Bough; by James Rees: (35) A.-3.17,19,27; 12.25.
Mobb the Outlaw, or Jemmy Twitcher in France; (37) S.C.-5.1;
    (38) A.-1.9,11.
Modern Antiques; farce by O'Keeffe: (21) O.-4.4; (29) A.-3.23;
    4.6.
The Mogul Tale; farce by Mrs. Inchbald: (27) A.-5.1,10; (37)
    S.C.-4.27.
The Mohawk Chief; see *Oranaska.*
Money; comedy by Edward Bulwer Lytton: (41) S.C.-1.17,18,19,
    23; Am.-1.17,25; S.C.-2.13; 3.22.
Monsieur de Chiffonne; comic opera: (37) S.C.-2.19,27.
Monsieur Duguigon; ballet pantomime: (41) Am.-12.26.
Monsieur Jacques; farce by Morris Barnett: (37) S.C.-1.5,10;
    2.4; (38) S.C.-12.20,24; (39) S.C.-1.17; 2.21; 3.5.
Monsieur Mallet; comedy by Moncrieff: (35) A.-3.2,5,7; (37)
    S.C.-12.2; (41) S.C.-12.7,10,13,30; (42) Am.-1.29.
Monsieur Tonson; farce by Moncrieff: (24) A.-1.10; 2.14; 3.6;
    4.8; (26) A.-2.10; 4.1; (27) A.-4.25; (28) A.-3.1; (29) A.-
    5.15; (30) A.-3.23; (31) A.-5.26; 12.9; (32) A.-3.22,24; (33)
    A.-5.25; (35) A.-1.29; 2.3; S.C.-12.11,30; (37) S.C.-12.9;
    (38) A.-5.9,28.
Montgomery; by H. J. Finn: (26) A.-2.22; 3.3; (27) A.-12.24.
Montrechi e Capuletti; opera by Bellini: (37) S.C.-4.4,6,9,12,14;
    5.5.
The Moorish Bride; tragedy by Caroline L. Hentz: (36) S.C.-
    1.4,5.
The Moorish Page, or The Moorish Prince; by H. M. Milner:
    (36) S.C.-1.3; 2.12,13; (37) S.C.-3.20,26; (39) S.C.-3.25,26;
    4.24.
The Moorish Prince; see *The Moorish Page.*

More Blunders than One; see *The Irish Valet.*
Morina; opera: (36) S.C.-4.29.
The Mother; melodrama by Jerrold: (39) S.C.-4.25.
Mother Goose; see *Harlequin and Mother Goose.*
The Mountain Devil; see *The Dumb Girl of Genoa.*
The Mountain Sylph; opera by T. J. Thackeray, music by J. Bar-
    nett: (37) A.-2.23,24,25,28; 3.1,3,4,6,9,10; 4.13,18; (38)
    S.C.-12.2,9,11,14,16; (39) S.C.-2.1; (40) S.C.-3.31; 4.27.
The Mountaineers; melodrama by Colman the Younger: (18)
    S.P.-3.27; (20) S.P.-1.19; O.-2.18; (21) O.-2.17; (23) O.-3.1;
    A.-5.21; (26) A.-2.13; (27) A.-6.1; (28) A.-1.11; (29) A.-
    1.24; (30) A.-3.6; (33) A.-4.18.
M.P.; comic opera by Thomas Moore: (23) O.-4.26.
Mr. H.; farce by Charles Lamb: (24) A.-2.24.
Mrs. G.; farce by Morris Barnett: (37) S.C.-4.10.
Mrs. White; farce by Richard Raymond: (40) Am.-11.26; 12.15;
    (41) Am.-1.20; 2.3,5; 3.9; 12.7; (42) Am.-4.26.
Much Ado about Nothing; by William Shakespeare: (20) O.-3.24;
    (21) O.-2.7; (27) A.-2.9,11; (28) A.-12.19; (29) A.-4.23;
    (30) A.-1.8,29; 12.15; (31) A.-1.19; (32) A.-1.5; 2.9; (33)
    A.-4.1; 12.11; (36) S.C.-2.29; 3.4; A.-11.24; S.C.-12.26; (37)
    A.-2.13; S.C.-2.17; A.-4.24; (38) S.C.-1.20; 3.29; 12.24; (39)
    S.C.-1.29; A.-11.27; (40) S.C.-4.9.
The Mummy; farce by W. B. Bernard: (34) A.-2.25; (37) S.C.-
    11.16,18,26; (38) S.C.-2.19,24; 3.9,16; A.-10.26,27; (39) A.-
    2.16,20; 11.24,28; S.C.-12.4; (40) S.C.-1.11; 2.16; 5.2; 10.11,
    16; (41) S.C.-1.5; 12.5; (42) S.C.-1.7.
The Murder and the Orphan; see *The Broken Sword.*
The Murdered Boatman and His Dog; melodrama: (41) S.C.-
    11.16,17,19.
Murrell, the Western Land Pirate; by N. H. Bannister: (35)
    A.-12.8,9,10; (37) A.-5.16,26.
Music and Prejudice; operetta: (34) A.-5.3,21.
The Mutiny at the Nore; melodrama by Jerrold: (36) A.-3.12;
    (37) A.-3.30.
My Aunt; (by J. Galt): (23) O.-1.29; (33) A.-3.18,20,23,29; 4.22;
    (34) A.-2.11; 4.5,21; (36) S.C.-1.28; 6.2; (37) A.-1.3,6,10;
    2.7,9; S.C.-2.28; (38) S.C.-11.19; (40) S.C.-3.6,14; (41)
    S.C.-3.18.
My Daughter, Sir; farce by J. R. Planché: (34) A.-12.23; (36)
    A.-3.30.
My Fellow Clerk; farce by J. Oxenford: (36) A.-2.1,2,6,9; 2.27;
    3.8; 4.6,8,18,30; 5.9; (37) A.-3.2,22,27; 4.5; 5.1; S.C.-5.20;
    11.24; (38) A.-2.4; 3.25; 5.12; 6.3; 11.1; (39) A.-1.11; (42)
    Am.-2.24.
My Friend the Captain; farce by John Sterling Coyne: (42)
    S.C.-3.7.
My Friend the Governor; burletta by J. R. Planché: (36) S.C.-
    6.14,15; 7.2; (41) Am.-12.20,22; (42) Am.-1.3; 3.22; 4.29.

My Grandfather's Will; see *The Will.*

My Husband's Ghost; farce by John Morton: (37) S.C.-1.24; (38) A.-1.30; 2.1,3,19; 3.6,9; (42) S.C.-1.24,28; 2.13.

My Little Adopted; farce by T. H. Bayly: (41) Am.-5.8,10; (42) Am.-3.12; 4.1,7.

My Master's Rival, or Paul and Peter Shack; farce by R. B. Peake: (30) A.-2.25,26; 4.24,29; (32) A.-1.6; 2.10; (35) A.-4.10,17; 12.16; (36) A.-1.7; S.C.-1.19; 12.7,20; (37) S.C.-1.27; 2.1.

My Native Land; dramatic opera by William Dimond: (36) S.C.-1.26,29.

My Neighbor's Wife; farce by Alfred Bunn: (34) A.-2.18,20,24, 26; 5.8; 12.10; (35) A.-2.3; (38) A.-5.27; (39) A.-5.28; 10.9, 15; (41) S.C.-11.8; (42) Am.-2.4; 5.10,18.

My Old Woman; see *Love in Wrinkles.*

My Own Lover; comedy by G. H. Rodwell: (33) A-.4.13.18.

My Schoolfellow; interlude by J. R. Planché: (39) S.C.-2.27; 3.5,7; 4.10.

My Sister Kate; farce by Mark Lemon: (41) Am.-12.11,23.

My Wife and I; see *Intrigue.*

My Wife or My Place; farce by Charles Shannon: (33) A.-3.8,12, 14; 4.5,8.

My Wife's Mother; comedy by Charles James Mathews: (34) A.-1.13.

My Young Wife and My Old Umbrella; farce by Benjamin Webster: (38) S.C.-10.31; 11.3,6,19; 2.4,8,12,26; 3.8; 4.2,6; (41) Am.-3.26; (42) S.C.-2.9,25; Am.-3.22.

A Nabob for an Hour; see *Uncle Sam.*

The Naiad Queen: (42) Am.-2.12,13,14,15,16,17,18,19,20,21,22, 27,28; 3.1,2.

Naomi; melodrama: (39) A.-11.24,26,28; (40) S.C.-2.1.

Napoleon, or The Emperor and the Robber; farce: (36) A.-1.19; 3.12; (37) A.-2.19; 3.30; (40) S.C.-4.19.

Napoleon, or the The Emperor and the Soldier; drama by John Walker: (30) A.-3.22,24; (41) Am.-3.20,21.

Napoleon Bonaparte; dramatic spectacle by M. R. Lacy: (42) Am.-4.14,15,16,17,18,19,20,21,22,23.

Nathalie; ballet pantomime: (41) S.C.-3.12,13,14,16,29.

The National Guard; opera by Auber: (33) A.-1.7; (36) S.C.-5.9,10.

Nature and Philosophy: (26) A.-1.26,30; 4.7; (28) A.-1.8; 3.29; (30) A.-4.22; (34) A.-5.17,20,26; (35) A.-1.15,22; 3.13; 4.3; 11.23; 12.29; (36) A.-3.21; S.C.-6.21,23; 11.15; (37) S.C.-10.21; (38) A.-1.20; 2.5; (40) S.C.-2.23,25,29; 3.21; Am.-12.1,11; (41) Am.-2.7.

Naval Engagements; burletta by Charles Dance: (39) S.C.-1.7. 12; A.-1.17,18,19,21; S.C.-2.7,11,19; 3.2; 4.12.

The Negro Door Keeper; see *A Grand Masquerade.*

The Nervous Man and the Man of Nerve; comedy by W. B. Bernard: (35) A.-1.15,20,27; 3.12; (41) S.C.-1.7,9.

New Orleans Assurance: (42) S.C.-2.13.

A New Way to Pay Old Debts; comedy by Philip Massinger: (06) M.B.-5.7;(28)A.-1.18,26;(29)A.-1.10;(31) A.-3.2,9; 5.4; (32) A.-1.24; (35) A.-3.24; (36) A.-2.4; S.C.-6.11; A.-12.12; (39) S.C.-1.7; 2.6; A.-3.22; (40) Am.-12.2; (41) Am.-1.29.

Nicholas Nickleby; burletta by Edward Stirling: (40) S.C.-11.8, 9,10,12,13,16; (41) Am.-1.27; S.C.-2.21; (42) S.C.-1.31; 2.2.

Nick of the Woods; by George Washington Harby: (38) A.-3.18, 19,23.

Nick of the Woods; melodrama by L. H. Medina: (39) A.-3.23,26.

No!, or The Glorious Minority; operatic farce by William Henry Murray: (33) A.-12.18; (34) A.-1.22; 2.24; 5.5; 11.27; (36) S.C.-7.2; (38) S.C.-2.26; A.-2.26; 3.23; 4.4,11,21; 5.4,12; S.C.-10.5,7,9; (39) M.-6.21; A.-10.16,24; (40) S.C.-1.15; 2.28; 10.13; (41) S.C.-1.16; 2.8; 3.29; 11.13.

Nonpareil; farce: (41) S.C.-12.23.

Norma; opera by Bellini: (36) S.C.-4.1,3,6,8,10,15,20; 5.4,6,23; (37) S.C.-4.19,21,23,28; 5.7,26; (42) S.C.-1.5,7,10,12,18,26; 2.5.

No Song, No Supper; farce by Prince Hoare: (20) S.P.-1.15; O.-3.4; (21) O.-2.19; (23) O.3.24; A.-5.28; (24) A.-1.30; 5.24; (25) A.-1.3; (26) A.-2.11; (27) A.-3.2,9; (28) A.-1.10; 12.18; (29) A.-2.3; (30) A.-3.24; (31) A.-5.5,12; 11.23; (33) A.-1.19; 5.8; 11.30; (34) A.-1.18; 2.28; (35) S.C.-12.15,31; (36) A.-3.9; 4.22; S.C.-6.3,16; 11.24; (37) S.C.-1.23; 3.5; 10.16,21; (38) S.C.-1.13; 2.12; 3.23; A.-5.9; S.C.-10.1; (39) A.-10.9; (40) S.C.-4.3; 10.16; (41) Am.-3.22; (42) Am.-4.28; 5.21,25.

Not at Home; farce "by a gentleman of New Orleans": (27) A.-6.8.

Not a Word; burletta by James Kenney: (36) S.C.-6.23,24; 7.1.

The Ocean Child; see *The Wreck.*

Oceola; (by J. H. Sherburne): (36) S.C.-12.23.

Octavia Bragaldi; tragedy by Charlotte Barnes: (38) A.-5.21,22, 23; S.C.-12.8,10,11; (40) S.C.-4.22,23.

Of Age To-morrow; musical farce by Thomas J. Dibdin: (18) S.P.-2.27; (20) S.P.-1.10; O.-2.26; (21) O.-2.14; 4.9; (23) O.-3.8; 4.12; (24) A.-1.1; 2.20; (25) A.-3.5; (26) A.-4.8; (27) A.-2.2,17; 6.1; (28) A.-1.28; 4.16; 12.17; (29) A.-5.13; (30) A.-1.1; 3.3; 4.3; 12.21; (31) A.-2.21; 5.21; (32) A.-2.13; (33) A.-2.2; (34) A.-2.17; 5.24; (36) S.C.-12.30; (40) Am.-11.12; (41) Am.-1.10; (42) Am.-4.27; 5.1.

Oh! Hush! or The Virginny Cupids; "Ethiopian opera" by Rice: (35) A.-3.31; 5.1,5; (36) A.-2.19,25; 3.2; 4.7.

Old and Young, or The Four Mowbrays; farce by J. Poole: (29) A.-3.24,31; (30) A.-1.27; (31) A.-1.21; 4.22; (36) S.C.-1.14, 23,29; A.-4.4,8,20; (38) A.-2.27; 4.20; 5.4; 11.24; S.C.-11.28; (39) M.-6.19.

The Old Clock; farce "by a gentleman of this city" : (39) S.C.-4.18.

The Old English Gentleman; comedy by Charles Dance: (38)
S.C.-12.28,31; (39) S.C.-1.4,9,21; 2.23; (41) Am.-12.10;
(42) Am.-5.11.

The Old Gentleman; farce by Benjamin Webster: (38) S.C.-
1.4,7; 2.8,18; 4.11.

Old Heads upon Young Shoulders; melodrama by Moncrieff: (37)
S.C.-4.29; 5.2,4,23.

Old Ironsides; by N. H. Bannister: (35) A.-5.16.

Old King Cole: (35) S.C.-12.25.

Old Maid; farce by A. Murphy: (32) A.-12.13,20; (33) A.-3.2;
4.26; (40) Ar.-2.17,21.

The Old Maids; comedy by J. S. Knowles: (41) Am.- 12.19,21;
(42) Am.-2.8.

The Old Oak Chest; melodrama by Miss Scott: (38) S.C.-2.11.

Old Times in Virginia, or The Yankee Pedlar; farce by W. B.
Bernard: (38) A.-1.13,16; 2.9.

Oliver Twist; by James Rees: (39) S.C.-3.24.

Olympic Devils; burletta by J. R. Planché: (38) S.C.-3.26.

The Omnibus; an alteration of R. J. Raymond's *Cherry Bounce,*
by Isaac Pocock: (37) A.-5.23,28; (39) A.-2.23,28; (40) S.C.-
12.29; (41) S.C.-1.2,7,20.

One Hour; by T. H. Bayly: (36) A.-12.14,20,22; (37) A.-1.7,24;
2.12,27; 3.6,16; 4.20,29; (38) A.-2.8,13,18,25; 3.27; S.C.-10.6,
26; 11.21,22; (39) S.C.-3.17.

One Hundred and Two, or The Legion of Honor; comedy by H. M.
Milner: (30) A.-5.8,13,17; (32) A.-1.25; 2.6,18; (35) A.-2.17;
4.11; S.C.-12.8; (36) S.C.-12.10.

Opera Mad; comedy by F. S. Hill: (36) A.-1.12; 2.8; (38) A.-2.25,
26; 3.19.

Oralloossa, Last of the Incas; tragedy by Bird: (34) A.-4.9,16.

Oranaska, or The Chief of the Mohawks; tragedy by Jonas B.
Phillips: (36) A.-1.29; 2.1; (37) A.-4.30; 11.30; (38) A.-
3.12,20.

The Orphan; tragedy by Otway: (25) A.-3.12.

The Orphan of Geneva; see *Thérèse.*

The Orphan and the Murderer; see *The Broken Sword.*

Osman and Arsana; ballet: (30) A.-3.6,11.

Otello, opera by Rossini: (36) S.C.-3.18,20,23,27; 4.17.

Othello; by William Shakespeare: (17) S.P.-6.2; (18) S.P.-1.5;
(20) S.P.-2.7; (21) O.-4.4; (22) O.-2.8; (23) O.-4.7; (24)
A.-3.22; (25) A.-3.2; (27) A.-4.18; (28) A.-1.19; (29) A.-
1.19; 3.6,14; 4.15; (30) A.-12.29; (31) A.-3.22; (33) A.-2.6;
5.11; (34) A.-4.14,19; (35) A.-5.12; (36) A.-1.21; S.C.-1.21;
3.10; A.-12.6; (37) A.-1.21; S.C.-2.3; A.-11.20; (38) A.-5.18;
(39) A.-1.28; S.C.-2.8; A.-3.3; S.C.-4.6; (40) S.C.-11.19;
Am.-12.7; (41) Am.-2.25; S.C.-3.1.

Ourang Ourang; see *The Baboon.*

Our Mary Anne; farce by J. B. Buckstone: (40) S.C.-5.1,20; (41) Am.-3.14,17; (42) Am.-4.7.

Out of Place; farce by Mark Lemon: (41) Am.-3.10,11,13,14,18, 20; 4.18,21; 5.9,10; (42) Am.-3.15,16.

Ovid and Obid: (35) A.-2.23.

Paddy Carey; interlude by Tyrone Power: (35) A.-3.16.

The Padlock; opera by Bickerstaff: (20) O.-2.23; S.P.-2.29.

The Pages of the Duke de Vendome; ballet: (39) S.C.-2.18,19,22.

Parisina; opera by Donizetti: (37) S.C.-6.4.

Paris and London; comedy by Moncrieff: (29) A.-4.2,3,6,9,14,25; 12.31.

Paul and Peter Shack; see *My Master's Rival.*

Paul and Virginia; opera by Cobb: (20) S.P.-2.5,9; (21) O.-3.3; (23) O.1.10; (24) A.-4.20; (26) A.-3.10; (28) A.-1.17; (29) A.-2.18; (30) A.-2.2; 4.21; (31) A.-5.11; (33) A.-1.21.

Paul Clifford; drama by Benjamin Webster: (38) S.C.-10.26,28.

Paul Jones, the Pilot of the German Ocean; melodrama by W. H. Wallack: (31) A.-1.29; 2.1,3,8,12,26; 3.10; (32) A.-12.25; (33) A.-4.16; 5.24; (34) A.-3.7; 5.6; 12.25; (35) A.-5.6; 12.19; (36) A.-2.11; 3.28; 11.30; (37) A.-4.30; (38) A.-3.25; (39) S.C.-4.28; (40) S.C.-1.5; Am.-11.15,16,22; 12.6,13; (41) Am.-1.8,16,24,30; 2.14; 3.28; 12.5,19; (42) Am.-1.19; 4.26.

Paul Jones; translated from Dumas by W. Berger: (40) S.C.-1.31; 2.1; 4.11.

Paule et Pauline: (40) S.C.-12.5.

Paul Pry; comedy by Charles Dibdin, Jr.: (27) A.-2.2,5,16; 3.3; 12.26; (28) A.-3.8; 4.15; 12.25.

Paul Pry; comedy by John Poole: (29) A.-1.30; 2.4; 12.17; (30) A.-1.5; 12.16; (31) A.-1.13; 11.24; (32) A.-3.8; 11.30; (33) A.-1.22; (34) A.-3.7; (35) A.-2.14; 3.4; (36) S.C.-4.9; (37) S.C.-11.2; (38) S.C.-4.28; 10.16; 11.2; (39) A.-10.21; 11.16; (40) S.C.-10.14,29.

Paul Pry at Dover; farce: (30) A.-3.18.

Paul, the Poacher: (32) A.12.10.

Pay to My Order, or Le Baiser d'Amitie; vaudeville by J. R. Planché: (38) A.-3.21,26.

Pay for Peeping; farce: (36) S.C.-6.27,30; 7.2; 11.21.

Peaceful Pelton; by H. A. Buckingham: (38) A.-1.22.

The Peacock and the Crow; farce by Parry: (38) A.-3.11; (42) S.C.-2.19.

The Peasant Boy; melodrama by William Dimond: (31) A.-4.30; 5.5; (36) S.C.-4.30; 5.13.

A Peculiar Position; farce by J. R. Planché: (39) S.C.-2.18,19,28.

Pedlar's Acre; drama by George Almar: (37) A.-5.10.

La Pension de Ma Soeur; vaudeville: (41) Am.-12.25.

Percy; "new American drama written by an American Gentleman": (25) A.-4.18.

Perfection, or the Maid of Munster; comedy by T. H. Bayly: (31)
    A.-1.26,31; 2.2,17; 3.25; 5.6; 11.26; (32) A.-3.31; (33) A.-
    1.2; 4.22; 11.29; 12.24; (34) A.-1.16; 2.27; 12.9; (35) A.-
    1.10; S.C.-12.18; (36) S.C.-1.13; A.-3.16,18; 4.6,25; S.C.-4.19;
    5.2; A.-5.25,29; 12.7,21; (37) A.-1.16; 5.10,16,24; S.C.- 10.16,
    20,29; 12.11,15; (38) S.C.-2.10; A.-2.12; 3.1,18; S.C.-3.2,30;
    A.-4.14; 10.27,30; (39) A.-1.10; S.C.-1.26; A.-2.26; M.-6.19;
    A.-10.8,23; (40) S.C.-10.13; (41) S.C.-3.6; Am.-4.21; 5.2,8;
    S.C.-12.3,17; (42) S.C.-2.13,21.

Personation; farce by Marie Therese Kemble: (35) S.C.-12.9,12;
    (36) S.C.-2.8,16; (37) S.C.-2.10; (38) A.-5.23,26.

The Pet of the Petticoats; operetta by Buckstone: (36) A.-3.30;
    4.1; S.C.-5.9,13; (42) Am. 3.16; 4.3.

Peter Wilkins; spectacle: (36) S.C.-2.21,24,28; 3.1,4,5,16,19;
    11.4,15,17,22; (37) S.C.-3.4; 11.5,7,9,12,27,30; (38) S.C.-
    3.16; 4.1,14,28; 10.7,14,29; 12.17; (39) S.C.-3.10; 12.1,2,3,
    25; (40) S.C.-1.8,26; 3.25; 4.5,26; 10.18.23; 11.8,17; (41)
    S.C.-1.1; 12.12.

Petticoat Government; farce by Charles Dance: (36) S.C.-12.1,3.

The Phantom Ship; see *The Flying Dutchman.*

Philip Quarle and His Monkey; pantomime: (41) S.C.-11.21,22,
    23; 12.27.

The Pickwickians; burletta by Moncrieff: (38) S.C.-4.23,26.

Pig and Whistle; burletta: (36) A.-2.5.

The Pilot; see *Paul Jones.*

Il Pirata; opera by Bellini: (36) S.C.-3.6,9,11,13,25,27; 4.13;
    5.1,8.

Pitcarin's Island; ballet spectacle by T. J. Dibdin: (33) A.-1.14.

Pizarro; tragedy by R. B. Sheridan: (19) S.P.-5.4; (20) S.P.-
    1.31; O.-3.6; (21) O.-2.21; (23) O.-3.15; 5.7; (24) A.-1.28;
    2.25; (26) A.-4.18; 5.23; (27) A.-4.3; (28) A.-12.23; (29)
    A.-3.12; 4.27; (30) A.-5.5; (31) A.-1.1; 3.29; 11.25; (32)
    A.-5.10; 12.13; (33) A.-3.18,20,29; 4.20; (34) A.-3.28; 12.11;
    (35) A.-4.28; (36) A.-1.18; S.C.-2.9; 11.23; (37) A.-1.3,6;
    S.C.-1.14; A.-2.7,9; S.C.-2.23; 11.11; (38) S.C.-2.2,10; (39)
    A.1.-10; S.C.-4.13; 12.4; (40) S.C.-11.28; Am.-12.23; (41)
    Am.-2.24; (42) S.C.-2.6.

Plains of Chippewa; see *She Would Be a Soldier.*

A Pleasant Neighbor; farce by Mrs. J. R. Planché: (37) S.C.-
    10.25,26; 11.8; (38) S.C.-2.20; 3.15,29; (40) G.-1.25; Ar.-
    2.14,18; (41) Am.-12.15; 5.4,19; (42) S.C.-1.14; 2.5.

Plot and Counterplot; farce by Charles Kemble: (18) S.P.-2.4;
    4.25.

The Poachers; farce by R. B. Peake: (29) A.-1.12,13.

The Point of Honor; comedy by Charles Kemble: (16) S.P.-11.21;
    (20) S.P.-2.11; (26) A.-5.27; (31) A.-4.20.

The Poor Gentleman; comedy by Colman the Younger: (13) S.P.-
1.23; 2.23; (20) S.P.-2.4; (24) A.-3.29; (31) A.-1.25; 12.9;
(32) A.-1.30; 3.2,27; (35) A.-1.26; 12.18; (36) S.C.-12.19;
(38) S.C.-4.17; (39) A.-4.7; S.C.-12.17.

The Poor Soldier; comedy by O'Keeffe: (18) S.P.-4.11,29; (20)
S.P.-1.28; O.-2.19; (23) O.1.6; 3.10,15; (24) A.-1.17; 3.17;
6.9; (26) A.-2.9; 5.3; (28) A.-3.5; 4.17; 12.19; (29) A.-
12.29; (30) A.-1.22; 3.17; (31) A.-3.3,17; 4.19; 12.24; (32)
A.-3.10; (34) A.-12.9,16,29; (35) S.C.-12.16,22; (36) S.C.-
1.16,27; 2.14; A.-4.5; (37) S.C.-10.17,20; 11.9; (38) S.C.-
1.11,22; 4.20; 10.2,31; (39) S.C.-3.10; A.-10.10; (40) S.C.-
12.2; (41) S.C.-11.12; 12.16.

Pop! Sparrow Shooting; (31) A.-3.31; 4.25.

Popping the Question; farce by J. B. Buckstone: (31) A.-11.29;
12.6,13; (32) A.-1.7; 3.20; (33) A.-1.3.

The Post of Honor; see *The Sentinel.*

P.P.; farce by Thomas Parry: (36) S.C.-12.28.

The Prairie Girls; by (James Rees) : (36) S.C.-6.17.

Presumptive Evidence; see *The Bohemian Mother.*

Presumptive Evidence; domestic drama by J. B. Buckstone: (38)
A.-10.21; (39) A.-1.22.

Le Preux Chevalier; comedy: (41) S.C.-1.30; 2.18.

The Pride of the Navy; equestrian drama: (41) S.C.-12.16.

The Printer's Devil; farce by J. R. Planché: (40) S.C.-11.26,28;
(41) S.C.-2.6.

The Prize; musical farce by Prince Hoare: (19) S.P.-3.17; 4.7;
(24) A.-4.26; (27) A.-2.11; (29) A.-2.17,19; (30) A.-3.8;
(32) A.-1.23; 2.1; 3.12; (33) A.-5.21; (35) A.-2.23.

The Promissory Note, or The Effect of Endorsing; farce: (23)
O.-2.10; (24) A.-3.15; (26) A.-5.18; (30) A.-4.1; 12.23; (31)
A.-5.20; (35) A.-1.27; 2.5; 12.17; (36) A.-1.18,27; (40)
Am.-12.4; (41) Am.-2.3,5; (42) S.C.-1.29; Am.-5.15.

The Provoked Husband; comedy by Colley Cibber: (21) O.-5.2;
(25) A.-3.5; (29) A.-3.24; (32) A.-5.9; (36) S.C.-1.23; 3.5;
(38) S.C.-1.26; (39) A.-3.2.

The Provost of Bruges; tragedy by George Lovell: (36) S.C.-11.28.

P.S. Come to Dinner; farce by R. J. Raymond: (32) A.-4.11.

The Purse, or The American Tar, or The Benevolent Tar; musical
farce by James C. Cross: (18) S.P.-1.21; 3.24; (19) S.P.-
3.20; (20) S.P.-1.24; O.-2.16; (21) O.-3.7; 5.2; (24) A.-1.8;
4.14; 5.28; (26) A.-2.1,22; 5.11; (27) A.-2.7; 3.30; (28)
A.-4.15; (29) A.-5.4; (30) A.-5.18,20; (32) A.-11.22; 12.6;
(33) A.-3.22; (36) A.-11.21; (37) A.-1.25; 3.5,18,31; (38)
A.-2.1,5,22; 3.11,18; 4.22,29.

The Quaker; musical farce by Charles Dibdin: (36) S.C.-2.29;
3.2,14.

Rafael the Libertine; melodrama: (39) S.C.-12.9,11,19; (40)
S.C.-3.24. This is probably T. E. Wilks' drama, *Raffaelle the
Reprobate.*

The Rail Road Station; burletta by T. E. Wilks: (41) Am.-12.8,10, 21; (42) Am.-2.6.

Raising the Wind; farce by James Kenney: (12) S.P.-4.3; (18) S.P.-4.21; (20) S.P.-1.22; O.-4.14; (23) O.-3.5; (24) A.-2.12; (26) A.-4.28; (27) A.-5.21; (28) A.-1.11; (29) A.-1.24; 5.8; (30) A.-3.9; (31) A.-3.14; 5.14; (32) A.-2.22; 3.27; (33) A.-12.10; (34) A.-4.12; (35) S.C.-12.28; (36) S.C.-6.1,7; 12.26; (37) S.C.-2.1; 6.3; 11.2; (38) S.C.-2.17; 3.13; A.-10.23; 11.7; S.C.-12.4; (39) S.C.-2.15; A.-4.4; 11.2,9,14; (40) S.C.-12.22; (41) Am.-3.26; S.C.-11.28.

Rake Hellies; by Stephen E. Glover: (31) A.-3.24,26.

The Rake's Progress; melodrama by W. L. Rede: (36) A.-4.4.

Ramfylde Moore Carew; pantomime: (33) A.-1.26.

The Ransom; farce by Mrs. J. R. Planché: (37) S.C.-12.14,16; (38) S.C.-1.18.

Rathenemus the Roman; by N. H. Bannister: (35) A.-4.24.

The Reapers; see *Rosina.*

The Red Indian and His Dog; melodrama: (42) S.C.-1.1,6.

Reform; see *The School of Reform.*

The Regatta: (38) A.-6.3.

Removing the Deposits; comedy by H. J. Finn: (35) A.-2.25; 4.7; (37) S.C.-2.14; (39) S.C.-3.1,4.

Rencontre; farce by J. R. Planché: (31) A.-3.12,17; 4.19.

The Rendezvous, or *All in the Dark;* farce by Ayton: (20) S.P.-2.7,10; O.-4.17; (21) O.-3.9; (23) O.-1.17; 3.26; (24) A.-1.14; 3.22; 5.3; (26) A.-2.15; 5.19; (27) A.-2.19; 6.2; (28) A.-12.24; (29) A.-3.19; (30) A.-12.29; (31) A.-2.3; (32) A.-2.11,17; 5.3; (33) A.-2.20; 4.25; 5.14; (34) A.-3.18; (35) A.-1.16; 2.10; 12.4; (36) S.C.-3.10; A.-5.24; S.C.-11.18; A.-12.9; (37) A.-2.4,28; S.C.-2.22; 3.2; A.-4.4; S.C.-10.18; (38) S.C.-4.21; 10.4; (41) Am.-2.6,8; 3.10; 5.5; S.C.-12.20.

The Rent Day; melodrama by D. W. Jerrold: (32) A.-12.3,5; (33) A.-3.23,25,30; 4.15; (34) A.-3.20; 4.29; (36) S.C.-5.21; (37) A.-1.19; 2.10; S.C.-5.23; (38) S.C.-3.19; 4.19,25; 10.15; 12.15; (39) A.-3.12,14,18; 4.1; 10.22.

The Revenge; tragedy by Edward Young: (19) S.P.-3.24; (29) A.-12.30; (31) A.-3.26; (32) A.-4.30.

The Review, or *The Wags of Windsor;* farce by Colman the Younger: (20) O.-1.11; (21) O.-3.2,23; (23) O.-2.26; (24) A.-6.4; (26) A.-1.25; (27) A.-4.30; (28) A.-2.2; (30) A.-1.23; 3.20; (31) A.-12.20; (32) A.-2.25; 3.8; 4.14; 11.24; (33) A.-12.16; (34) A.-4.19; 5.23; (35) A.-1.22; 3.12; (36) A.-2.5; 3.31; 12.27; (37) A.-1.30; 2.20; 5.17; (38) S.C.-2.7; 3.18; 4.22; A.-11.8,17,22; (39) A.-1.31; 2.4,19; S.C.-4.18; (40) Ar.-2.22; A.-5.17; S.C.-10.19; (41) S.C.-11.23; 12.11; (42) Am.-5.9.

Richard Savage; "translated and adapted to the English stage by M. Morton Dowler": (40) S.C.-12.6,8,12.

Rihard III; by Wiliam Shakespeare: (18) S.P.-3.14; (20) S.P.-
1.12; (22) O.-1.11; 2.6; (23) O.-3.5,8; 4.21; (24) A.-3.19,26;
5.22; (26) A.-4.14; (27) A.-4.7; (28) A.-1.14; 2.2; (29)
A.-1.7; 2.19; 4.7; 5.4; (30) A.-1.23; (31) A.-2.28; (32)
A.-2.7,17; 3.1,6; 4.16; (33) A.-3.26; 4.30; (34) A.-5.8; (35)
A.-11.20; 4.7; (36) S.C.-11.21; A.-11.28; (37) A.-1.16,28;
S.C.-2.12; A.-2.14; 5.11,23; S.C.-11.15; 12.5; (38) S.C.-1.27;
A.-4.4; (39) S.C.-2.5,9,14; A.-3.6,20,27; S.L.-3.26; S.C.-3.31;
4.11,14,16; (40) S.C.-4.19; A.-5.19; Am.-12.1; (41) Am.-
1.13; 2.2.
Richelieu; drama by Edward Bulwer Lytton: (39) S.C.-12.7;
(40) S.C.-1.20; 4.17; Am.-11.11,14; (41) Am.-2.28; 3.25.
Riches; an adaptation of Massinger's *City Madame,* by Sir James
Bland Burges: (24) A.-2.26.
Rienzi; tragedy by Mrs. Mitford: (29) A.-5.6; (31) A.-1.4; (36)
S.C.-5.2; (37) A.-11.23.
The Rifle Brigade: (42) Am.-2.1,2,3,22.
Rip Van Winkle; (by John Kerr): (31) A.-5.6,10; (32) A,-3.22,
26; (35) A.-2.10; (37) S.C.-12.4,11; (40) S.C.-10.28; (41)
S.C.-12.8,30; (42) Am.-1.29.
The Rival Lovers; see *Intrigue.*
The Rival Pages; farce by Charles Selby: (42) Am.-3.17.
The Rival Soldiers, or Sprigs of Laurel; farce by O'Keeffe: (18)
S.P.-2.7; (23) O.-5.5; (24) A.-1.12; (26) A.-5.26; (27) A.-
2.13; (28) A.-3.10; (29) A.-1.19; (32) A.-12.3; (33) A.-2.8;
(34) A.-3.11; 4.3; 12.17,18; (38) A.-5.21,22; (40) A.-6.14;
Am.-12.5,19; (41) Am.-1.9; (42) Am.-5.6.
The Rivals; comedy by R. B. Sheridan: (20) O.-3.15; (24) A.-4.21;
5.21; (27) A.-6.2; (29) A.-4.1; (31) A.-3.30; 12.22,29; (35)
A.-1.31; 3.10; (37) S.C.-1.21,24; (38) A.-5.16; 11.16; S.C.-
12.6; (39) A.-4.8; S.C.-4.18; 12.24; (42) Am.-5.16.
The Rival Suitors; see *Intrigue.*
The Rival Valets; farce by Joseph Ebsworth: (40) S.C.-5.9.
The Road to Ruin; comedy by Thomas Holcroft: (20) S.P.-2.2;
(21) O.-3.3; (23) O.-1.4; (24) A.-3.10; (26) A.-2.24; (27)
A.-3.21; (28) A.-3.19; (30) A.-3.25; (31) A.-5.18; (33) A.-
3.13; (37) S.C.-11.27; (40) S.C.-12.9.
The Robbers; tragedy from Schiller: (21) O.-4.16; (24) A.-2.12;
(30) A.-12.24; (37) A.-2.19.
The Robber's Wife; melodrama by Pocock: (32) A.-12.8,11; (33)
A.-3.9; (36) S.C.-5.19; (38) S.C.-10.17; (39) A.-10.31.
Robert Emmett; by N. H. Bannister: (42) Am.-3.28,29; 4.2.
Robert le Diable; opera by Meyerbeer; (35) A.-3.30,31; 4.1,2,3,7,
11,14; 5.20,23,28; 12.30; (36) A.-1.25; 2.6,29; 5.18; (37) A.-
3.10,14; 4.2; (40) S.C.-2.27; 3.4,13.
Robert Macaire; burletta by Charles Selby: (38) S.C.-12.6,7,10,
12,14; (39) S.C.-1.8,30; 2.27; 3.14,21,29; 4.5; (40) S.C.-3.24,
29; 4.1,2,26; 10.11,13,17,23,29; 11.7; (41) S.C.-1.14; 2.14;
3.26; Am.-3.27; S.C.-4.7; Am.-4.15; 11.26; 12.16; (42) S.C.-
2.10,20; Am.-4.1.

Robinson Crusoe; melodrama by Pocock: (26) A.-4.8.
Rob Roy Macgregor; musical drama by Pocock: (23) O.-2.10,21;
    3.3; (24) A.-1.14,24; 2.7; 3.12; 4.19; 5.28; (26) A.-2.4,25;
    3.14; 5.16; (27) A.-2.6; 3.20; 12.22; (28) A.-2.12; 12.27;
    (29) A.-2.7; 12.18; (30) A.-3.10,19; (31) A.-2.21; 3.5; 5.7;
    12.26; (32) A.-5.18; (33) A.-1.4; 12.20; (34) A.-2.3; 12.13;
    (35) A.-2.16; 3.7; 12.10; (36) A.-1.19; S.C.-2.7; 4.18,22,30;
    12.7,20; (37) A.-1.18; S.C.-10.25; (38) S.C.-2.25; 3.15; (39)
    S.C.-1.11; A.-10.27,29; 11.7,29; S.C.- 12.5; (40) S.C.-2.19;
    12.10; (41) Am.-4.28; 11.21; (42) Am.-1.3.
Rochester; comedy by Moncrieff: (32) A.-4.23.
A Roland for an Oliver; farce by Thomas Morton: (30) A.-12.17;
    (32) A.-5.2; (34) A.-3.5; 12.15; (35) A.-3.11; (36) A.-1.14,
    29; 6.9,10; (37) S.C.-10.19,30; (38) A.-5.30; (39) A.-10.19;
    (42) Am.-5.17,20.
The Roman Actor; by Philip Massinger: (32) A.-5.12; (36) S.C.-
    12.14.
The Roman Nose; farce by George Almar: (36) A.-4.23,26,29;
    5.10; (37) A.-2.22,23,26; 3.14,23; 4.10; (38) 2.15.
The Romantic Widow; comedy by Ranger: (41) S.C.-1.18,21,23,
    24; 3.2.
Romeo and Juliet; by William Shakespeare: (18) S.P.-3.10; (20)
    S.P.-1.21; O.-2.28; (23) O.-2.28; (26) A.-4.14; (29) A.-3.28;
    (30) A.-2.10; (31) A.-2.16; 4.18; 5.2; (32) A.-2.11,20; 3.3;
    (33) A.-2.4; (35) A.-4.22; (36) S.C.-1.11; A.-3.12; S.C.-
    11.29.31; A.-12.2; (37) S.C.-3.1; 4.27; A.-5.22; (38) S.C.-
    3.31; A.-4.20; (39) A.-2.27,28; (41) Am.-2.27.
The Romp; farce by Bickerstaff: (18) S.P.-4.8; (20) S.P.-2.4;
    O.-3.18; (21) O.-2.12; 3.10; (23) O.-5.5; A.-5.14; (26) A.-
    1.31; 5.9; (27) A.-3.20; (28) A.-2.19; (29) A.-2.7; 12.10;
    (31) A.-1.6; (32) A.-5.11; (33) A.-12.7; (34) A.-12.27; (36)
    S.C.-6.13; (37) A.-5.5.
The Roof Scrambler; burlesque opera by À Beckett: (42) Am.
    1.17,19.
Rookwood; melodrama by George Pitt: (42) Am.-3.5,6,7,8,17,24.
Rory O'More; burletta by Samuel Lover: (38) A.-4.19,22,23; (39)
    S.C.-1.4,6,10; A.-11.4,5; (40) S.C.-10.18,22,30; 12.22,24,25.
Rose D'Amour: (37) A.-4.7.
Rosina, or The Reapers; comic opera by Mrs. Brooke: (20) S.P.-
    1.8,18; 2.12; O.-4.10; (21) O.-2.17; (23) O.-1-4; A.-5.16;
    (24) A.13.29; (25) A.-3.8; (26) A.-2.6; (27) A.-2.9,11,28;
    (29) A.-2.11,16; 12.22; (30) A.-3.29; (31) A.-2.25; 5.7; (33)
    A.-1.4; 5.10; 12.27; (34) A.-1.29; 5.1; (37) S.C.-1.25; (38)
    S.C.-1.16.
The Rover's Bride; melodrama by George Almar: (37) S.C.-1.16.
Roxalana; see *The Sultan.*
Rule a Wife and Have a Wife; comedy by Beaumont and Fletcher:
    (21) O.-2.10; 3.26; (23) A.-5.24; (24) A.-1.5; (25) A.-3.8;
    (26) A.-4.12; (28) A.-4.9; (30) A.-3.1; (32) A.-3.29; (33)
    A.-1.16; (36) S.C.-3.7.

Rural Felicity; comedy by J. B. Buckstone: (41) S.C.-2.1,3,10.

Ruse contre Ruse; see The Midnight Hour.

St. George and the Dragon; spectacle by Andrew Ducrow: (40) S.C.-11.11,12,13,14,15.

St. Mary's Eve; burletta by W. B. Bernard: (39) S.C.-3.4,5,13.

Saint Patrick's Day; farce by R. B. Sheridan: (23) O.-3.17; 4.9; (24) A.-3.17; (26) A.-2.23; 3.17; (30) A.-3.17; (31) A.-3.17; (32) A.-3.17; (34) A.-3.17; (36) A.-3.17; (41) Am.-3.17,30.

Saint Patrick's Eve; drama by Tyrone Power: (35) A.-3.13,14,16.

Sam Patch; by E. H. Tompson: (38) A.-12.7,8,10,11,12; (39) A.-1.1,3; S.C.-12.16,18,22; (40) S.C.-1.5.

Sam Patch in France; comedy by J. P. Addams: (39) S.C.-12.22, 27,28; (40) S.C.-1.3,21; 11.25; 12.4,8,25; (42) S.C.-1.13,17.25.

Sam Patch, Jr.; (36) A.-4.23.

Sardanapalus; an adaptation of Lord Byron's tragedy: (36) S.C.-11.25.

La Savoyard; see The Grenadier.

The Scape Goat; farce by Poole: (40) S.C.-4.18,23.

The Scape Grace; farce by Beazley: (31) A.-2.23.

Schinder Eller; burlesque opera by M. C. Field: (42) Am.-1.22,23, 24,25,26,27,28,29,31.

Schinderhannes; melodrama by George Almar: (35) A.-12.15,18.

The School for Scandal; comedy by R. B. Sheridan: (20) S.P.-2.12; O.-2.19; 4.8; (21) O.-2.16; (23) O.-1.11; 4.23; (24) A.-4.23; (26) A.-2.16; (27) A.-2.14; (28) A.1.10; 12.29; (29) A.-3.20; 5.18; (30) A.-2.1,18; 12.20; (31) A.-1.28; 3.3; 12.19,27; (32) A.-1.27; 4.9; 11.28; 12.14; (33) A.-12.5,28; (34) A.-2.25; 3.27; (35) A.-1.16; 4.13,29; S.C.-11.30; (36) A.-1.23; S.C.-2.19; A.-3.11; S.C.-11.30; (37) S.C.-2.1,18; 11.14; (38) S.C.-1.13; 4.2; A.-5.14; 11.7; S.C.-11.30; 12.21; (39) S.C.-1.31; S.L.-3.27; A.-4.4; S.C.-4.27; 12.15; (40) S.C.-1.29; 4.15; (41) S.C.-2.8; (42) Am.-1.7; S.C.-2.14.

The School of Reform, or Reform; comedy by Thomas Morton: (20) S.P.-1.22; (21) O.-12.19; (24) A.-1.3; (28) A.-2.23; (29) A.-5.11; 12.9; (31) A.-2.10; (32) A.-11.26; (34) A.-5.27; (37) S.C.-2.14; (39) S.C.-4.29; (40) Am.-11.12; (42) Am.-1.10.

The School of Ten Quakers; comedy by F. S. Hill: (38) A.-4.16,25.

Sckaggs Family; by J. M. Field: (42) Am.-1.24.

The Scottish Chief; see Wallace.

Scourge of the Ocean; melodrama (by Henry Coleman): (38) A.-1.2.

The Sea Captain; by Edward Bulwer Lytton: (40) S.C.-4.5,6,8.

The Sea Serpent; (by T. J. Dibdin): (30) A.-5.8,14,17.

The Secret, or The Hole in the Wall; comedy by John Poole: (29) A.-1.26,30; 2.9; (30) A.-12.18; (32) A.-4.2,11; (33) A.-1.3,11; (34) A.-11.25; (35) A.-3.12; 12.4,30; (36) S.C.-5,28; 6.16,18; 7.4; 11.14; (37) S.C.-10.27,28; 11.18; (38)

S.C.-2.14; 3.22; 4.26; V.G.-6.19,26; (38) S.C.-10.6,23; (39) S.C.-3.1; A.-4.4; 10.22; (40) S.C.-5.5; 10.12; (41) S.C.-2.2; 11.7; (42) S.C.-3.4.

The Secret, or Natural Magic; farce by Moncrieff: (26) A.-1.28; 2.17; 3.29.

Semiramide; opera by Rossini: (37) S.-C.-4.12; 5.19,21,22,24.

The Sentinel, or the Post of Honor; musical farce by T. Mildenhall: (42) Am.-3.24,27,30; 5.3,12.

The Sergeant's Wife; drama by John Banim: (29) A.-4.1,21.

Seven Clerks, or The Denouncer; drama by T. E. Wilks: (38) A.-1.23,24,25,26,27,29; 2.16; (40) Ar.-2.17; A.-5.26,27; (42) Am.-3.20.

Seven's the Main; see *Winning a Husband.*

The Shadow on the Wall; melodrama by T. J. Serle, music by J. Thompson: (36) S.C.-2.16,17.

Shakespeare's Early Days; burletta by C. A. Somerset: (33) A.-3.11,14.

The Sheik of the Desert; melodrama: (39) A.-3.7,9,11,14,16.

She Stoops to Conquer; comedy by Oliver Goldsmith: (18) S.P.-1.30; (19) S.P.-4.28; (20) S.P.-1.17; (23) O.-1.6; (24) A.-3.31; (26) A.-5.13; (27) A.-2.23; 3.12; (29) A.-1.31; 5.16; (30) A.-5.12; 12.23; (32) A.-2.10; 12.28; (33) A.-11.30; (34) A.-1.7; 5.16; (36) S.C.-2.12; (38) A.-11.3,10; (39) S.C.-12.11; (40) S.C.-12.11; (42) Am.-5.25.

She Would and She Would Not; comedy by Colley Cibber: (30) A.-1.30; (31) A.-1.24.

She Would Be a Soldier, or The Plains of Chippewa; comedy by M. M. Noah: (20) O.-3.10,11,20; 4.17; (23) O.-1.8; (24) A.-1.11; 2.16; 4.29; (26) A.-2.18; 3.17; 5.17; (27) A.-2.22; 5.11; (28) A.-1.8; (30) A.-2.25; (32) A.-1.1; (33) A.-12.25; (34) A.-12.23; (35) A.-12.23; (38) S.C.-4.18; (39) A.-1.1, 3,5,8; (40) S.C.-1.1,4; 5.7; (41) S.C.-1.8,10; (42) S.C.-1.8; Am.-1.8.

Shocking Events; farce by J. B. Buckstone: (40) S.C.-11.1,4,6, 19; 12.15; (41) S.C.-1.4,16; 3.31; 4.2.

The Shoemaker of Toulouse; by F. S. Hill: (35) A.-12.4,5,7,17, 22; (36) A.-2.11; (41) Am.-4.9.

The Siamese Twins; farce by A. Beckett: (40) Am.-12.21.

The Siege of Belgrade; opera by Cobb: (34) A.-3.14.

Simpson and Company; farce by Poole: (24) A.-2.4,7,21,27; 4.5; (26) A.-3.16; 4.19; (27) A.-3.5; (30) A.-3.25; (31) A.-3.30; (32) A.-12.22; (33) A.-5.20; 12.2; (34) A.-4.9; (35) A.-12.7, 17; (36) S.C.-4.14,26; 6.3; (38) A.-3.14; 5.25; (39) S.C.-2.2; A.-3.2; (41) Am.-11.23; 12.31; (42) S.C.-3.2; Am.-5.5,21.

Single Life; comedy by J. B. Buckstone: (41) S.C.-2.7,9,10,16.

Six Degrees of Crime; by F. S. Hill: (36) A.-3.21,23,24,25,29; (37) A.-2.26; 3.2; (38) A.-4.16.

The Skeleton Robber; by Stevens: (38) S.C.-1.21.

The Skeleton Witness; drama by W. L. Rede: (36) A.-4.30; 5.2.

The Slaves in Barbary; spectacle by T. J. Dibdin: (11) Con.-6.29.

The Sledge Driver; drama by Mrs. J. R. Planché: (36) S.C.-6.21, 22,27; 11.19,28; (39) A.-10.26; 11.1,9,26; (40) S.C.-2.8; 3.27.

The Sleep Walker; see *The Somnambula.*

The Smoked Miser; interlude by Douglas Jerroll: (31) A.-2.26.

Snakes in the Grass; farce by J. B. Buckstone: (31) A.-11.30; 12.3; (32) A.-1.7; 3.31.

The Snapping Turtles; farce by J. B. Buckstone: (41) Am.-4.20,21,23; 5.5,8; (42) Am.-3.10.

The Snow Storm: (28) A.-2.22,25.

The Soldier's Courtship; comedy by Poole: (40) S.C.-3.4,8; 5.10; (41) S.C.-1.12; 3.12.

The Soldier's Daughter; comedy by Cheery: (20) S.P.-1.11; O.-2.23; (21) O.-1.31; (23) O.-2.8; (24) A.-2.2; (25) A.-1.3; (26) A.-5.2; (27) A.-3.9; 5.30; (28) A.-4.14; 12.17; (29) A.-2.2; (30) A.-5.10; (31) A.-2.25; 12.7; (32) A.-11.21; (33) A.-12.3; (35) A.-4.21; 11.19; (36) A.-1.8,16; 2.3; S.C.-11.26; A.-12.13; (37) S.C.-4.7; A.-5.27; S.C.-10.27; (38) A.-3.27; S.C.-10.25; (39) A.-10.23; (40) A.-5.22; (41) Am.-2.6,11.

The Soldier's Return; comic opera by T. E. Hook: (40) Ar.-2.22.

The Solitary of Mount Savage; "translated by a gentleman of this city": (24) A.-6.2,4.

Solomon Swap; see *Jonathan in England.*

The Somnambula; or The Sleep Walker; farce by Oulton: (16) S.P.-4.27; (19) S.P.-5.8; (20) O.-2.25; (21) O.-12.19; (26) A.-5.4; (28) A.-2.29; (32) A.-12.27; (33) A.-11.26; 12.7; (34) A.-1.17; 3.25; (35) A.-4.9; (42) S.C.-3.11.

The Somnambulist, or The White Phantom; drama by Moncrieff: (29) A.-2.6,10,13,24; (33) A.-5.9; (37) A.-3.10; S.C.-4.11,13.

Songstress and Semptress; see *Opera Mad.*

La Sonnambula; opera by Bellini: (36) A.-4.18,19,20,21,22,27; (38) S.C.-1.28,30; 2.5,19,24; 3.14,21; (40) S.C.-3.6,10; 4.2, 28; (42) S.C.-1.14,16,24,30; 2.1.

The Sons of Erin; comedy by Mrs. Lanfau: (23) O.-3.17; (27) A.-3.19.

The Sorcerer; extravaganza: (40) S.C.-2.11,15,17,18; 3.1.

The Spectre Bridegroom, or Ghost or No Ghost, or A Ghost in Spite of Himself; farce by Moncrieff: (26) A.-2.25; 3.1,18; 4.18; 5.24; (27) A.-2.22; (32) A.-2.2; (34) A.-12.6; 4.28; 12.21; (40) A.-6.3,11; (41) Am.-3.13.

Speculation farce by W. B. Bernard: (38) A.-1.17,18; 2.10.

Speed the Plough; comedy by Thomas Morton: (18) S.P.-2.27; (20) S.P.-2.9; (24) A.-4.28; 5.14; (26) A.-4.13; 5.26; (27) A.-2.20; (28) A.-4.18; (29) A.-12.10; (30) A.-5.8; (31) A.-5.26; 12.5; (32) A.-2.25; 3.14; (33) A.-5.25; (36) A.-2.16; (37) A.-4.1; 5.19; (39) A.-3.24,29; 4.2; (40) S.C.-10.9; (42) Am.-2.5.

The Spirit Bride and the Magi's Daughter: (39) S.C.-3.15,16.

The Spirit of the Clyde: (40) S.C.-1.18,21; 2.14,21,26; 4.7.
The Spirit of the Rhine; melodrama by Morris Barnett: (38)
  A.-3.29,31; 4.3.
The Spitfire; farce by John Morton: (41) S.C.-1.3.
The Spoiled Child; farce by Bickerstaff: (20) S.P.-1.20; (21)
  O.-2.5,23; (23) O.-1.27; 4.25; (24) A.-1.31; 5.19; (25) A.-
  4.23; (26) A.-2.21; 3.8; 5.1; (27) A.-2.2,3,13; 3.23; 5.8;
  (28) A.-2.14; 3.31; 4.12; 12.20; (29) A.-1.20; 4.3; 12.21;
  (30) A.-1.25; 2.17; (31) A.-1.24; (33) A.-12.6,31;
  (34) A.-1.31; 12.11; (35) A.-1.13; S.C.-11.30; A.-12.1; S.C.-
  12.24; (36) S.C.-1.20; 2.1; 3.28; A.-4.9; S.C.-5.21; (37)
  S.C.-11.4,23; (38) A.-2.21; 4.28; 5.24; S.C.-10.25; A.-11.20;
  S.C.-11.20; (39) S.L.-3.28; S.C.-4.7.
Sponge in Town: (26) A.-2.24.
The Sprigs of Laurel; see *The Rival Soldiers.*
Spring and Autumn; farce by James Kenney: (33) A.-3.25,28;
  (37) A.-1.19; 2.10; S.C.-2.25,26.
The Spy; by C. P. Clinch: (29) A.-5.15.
The Squatter; domestic drama by James Rees; (38) S.C.-3.31;
  4.13.
The Star of the Forest: (39) S.C.-3.27,28.
The Star Spangled Banner: (40) Am.-11.18.
State Secrets; burletta by T. E. Wilks: (39) S.C.-12.24.
The Station House; interlude by Charles Dance: (42) S.C.-1.8,10.
The Stranger; domestic drama by William Dunlap: (18) S.P.-3.4;
  (20) S.P.-2.1; (21) O.-3.16; (23) O.-2.24; (24) A.-4.3,17;
  (26) A.-3.29; (27) A.-2.19; (29) A.-1.16; 3.7; 4.16; (30)
  A.-1.13; (31) A.-3.14; (32) A.-11.29; (33) A.-2.13; (34)
  A.-12.17; (35) A.-1.18; 11.25; (36) S.C.-1.15; 3.12; 12.6;
  (37) A.-3.26; 4.27,28; S.C.-5.18; 11.1; (38) S.C.-1.19; A.-
  5.31; S.C.-12.7; (39) S.C.-1.26; A.-11.18; (41) Am.-4.26;
  S.C.-11.24; Am.-11.29.
La Straniera; opera by Bellini: (36) S.C.-5.11,18.
The Sublime and Beautiful; opera by Thomas Morton: (35)
  A.-5.23.
Such a Gitting up Stairs; farce by T. D. Rice: (42) S.C.-2.21.
The Sultan, or Roxalana; by Bickerstaff: (19) S.P.-4.10; (21)
  O.-5.2; (26) A.-3.28; (30) A.-3.24; (42) Am.-4.9.
The Suspicious Husband, or The Rival Lovers; comedy by Hoad-
  ley: (20) O.-3.8,13.
Sweethearts and Wives; comedy by James Kenney: (26) A.-3.25,
  27; 4.4; 5.18; (27) A.-5.4,10,12; 12.22; (29) A.-1.21; 12.29;
  (30) A.-12.18; (32) A.-1.28; 4.3; (35) A.-2.23; 12.8; (36)
  A.-2.26,29; (37) S.C.-5.15; (38) S.C.-10.18; (39) A.-10.30;
  (40) S.C.-10.21,24; 11.9; (41) Am.-12.4; (42) Am.-3.23; 5.3.
Sweet Home!; musical drama by Pocock: (33) A.-1.17,25.
The Swiss Cottage, or Why Don't She Marry?; burletta by T. H.
  Bayly: (37) S.C.-1.17,18,20,22; A.-1.26,28,29,30; 2.3,5; 3.13,
  15,28; S.C.-4.16,30; 6.1; 10.22,23,24; (38) S.C.-1.9,25; A.-1.9;

2.22,24,31; S.C.-3.1,28; 4.2,14,27; A.-4.20,29; 5.4,14; 11.22;
S.C.-11.29; (39) S.C.-1.16; 3.3; 4.4; M.-6.21; A.-10.8; 11.8;
S.C.-12.7; (40) S.C.-4.4; 10.31; 12.15; (41) S.C.-1.2,9; 3.18,
25; Am.-4.20; C.-6.20; Am.-11.22; S.C.-12.29; (42) Am.-
2.6; 5.24.

The Swiss Swains; vaudeville by Benjamin Walker: (41) Am.-
11.20,28.

Sydney and His Dog; melodrama: (21) O.-2.3,7.

Sylla; tragedy "by a gentleman of New York": (28) A.-1.28.

Sylvester Daggerwood, or The Mad Actor; interlude made from
Colman the Younger's *New Hay at the Old Market:* (20)
O.-3.22; S.P.-6.10; (32) A.-3.23; (33) A.-4.1; (34) A.-5.13;
(35) A.-3.5; (36) A.-12.10; (41) Am.-1.29.

La Sylphide; ballet pantomime by Scribe and Taglioni: (39)
A.-1.7,9,11; (40) S.C.-3.15,17,19; (41) S.C.-3.6,8,10. 4.2.

The Syracusan Brothers; tragedy by N. H. Bannister: (42) Am.-
3.30.

A Tale of Blood; see *The Idiot Witness.*

The Tale of Mystery; melodrama by Thomas Holcroft: (19) S.P.-
4.17; (20) O.-3.13; (24) A.-5.5; (27) A.-2.16; (31) A.-5.13.

The Talisman; "by a gentleman of this city"; (26) A.-4.7,10,15.

Tam O'Shanter; farce by Captain Addison: (39) S.C.-2.25.

Tancred and Sigismunda; tragedy by James Thomson: (23)
O.-5.3.

Il Tancredi; opera by Rossini: (37) S.C.-5.12,14,17.

La Tarentule; comic ballet: (41) S.C.-3.18,25,27.

Taste; interlude by Samuel Foote: (16) S.P.-3.28.

Teddy the Tiler; farce by G. H. Rodwell: (31) A.-4.16,18; (32)
A.-1.24; 11.27; (35) A.-1.7,10,27; 3.10; (36) A.-1.16; (40)
S.C.-12.30.

Tekeli; melodrama by T. E. Hook: (18) S.P.-3.21; (24) A.-4.15;
(27) A.-3.23; 5.1; (30) A.-3.30; (37) S.C.-2.14; (41) Am.-
1.3,5.

The Tempest; an adaptation of Shakespeare's play, by Davenant
and Dryden: (33) A.-4.5; 12.4,31; (34) A.-1.13,15,24; 2.5,19;
3.3; 4.15; (36) A.-2.23,26; S.C.-5.12.

Texas; see *The Fall of San Antonio.*

Thérèse, or The Orphan of Geneva; melodrama by J. H. Payne:
(26) A.-2.27; 3.4; (27) A.-3.1; (29) A.-4.7,11; (30) A.-1.19;
(31) A.-4.4,27; 11.30; (32) A.-5.9; 12.29; (33) A.-1.21; (34)
A.-1.7,14,15,25; 4.24; 12.4; (35) A.-1.28; 2.4; 3.18; (36)
S.C.-5.5; 6.8; (37) S.C.-2.12; (38) S.C.-1.6; 2.5,6; 10.10;
A.-10.24; 11.3; (39) A.-1.10; S.C.-4.13; A.-10.15,18,25; (40)
S.C.-1.5; Ar.-2.20; A.-5.22; S.C.-11.2; 12.27; (41) Am.-2.23;
4.27; (42) S.C.-1.25.

33 John Street; burletta by Buckstone: (32) A.-4.23; (36) S.C.-
12.24; (37) S.C.-1.2; 2.6,11; 11.17; (38) S.C.-2.22; 3.6,28;
A.-10.24,25; (39) S.C.-12.17; (40) S.C.-2.6; 3.17; (41) S.C.-
1.13,16; 12.14.

Three and the Deuce; farce by Prince Hoare: (20) S.P.-1.7,13;
    O.-2.14; (21) O.-2.24; (23) O.-1.25; 5.3; (24) A.-1.23; 3.3;
    5.26; (25) A.-4.11; (26) A.-1.24; 5.8; (27) A.-5.16; (28)
    A.-1.21; (29) A.-1.27; (30) A.-4.26; (31) A.-5.28; (32)
    A.-4.24; (33) A.-4.15; (36) S.C.-12.12,15; (37) S.C.-2.9;
    (40) S.C.-3.15,20; Am.-11.11; (41) Am.-5.11,13; (42) Am.-
    3.3.
Three Deep; see *All on the Wing.*
Three Faced Frenchman; comic vaudeville: (38) A.-2.6; 4.12;
    (41) Am.-12.24.
The Three Hunchbacks; melodrama by Edward Fitzball: (33)
    A.-4.9,12; (36) A.-1.25; 2.4.
Three Weeks after Marriage; comedy by A. Murphy: (19) S.P.-
    3.8; (21) O.-2.10; (23) O.-2.12; (24) A.-3.19; (27) A.-3.12;
    (28) A.-1.14; (30) A.-3.22; (32) A.-5.16; (34) A.-3.26; 4.10;
    (37) S.C.-2.10; 4.16; (38) S.C.-2.25; A.-10.28; 12.21; (39)
    A.-2.1; (41) S.C.-3.8,12,25.
The Times; "dramatic satire in two acts partly founded on *John
    Bull in America,* written expressly for Hackett": (32)
    A.-3.24.
The Times That Tried Us; By H. J. Conway: (40) S.C.-12.7,10;
    (42) S.C.--1.19.
Timour the Tartar; melodrama by M. G. Lewis: (18) S.P.-2.26;
    (20) S.P.-4.13; (22) O.-3.15,16,20; (25) A.-4.4; (27) A.-
    3.21,24; 4.23,25,28; 5.7; (28) A.-3.29; (33) A.-2.1,2,4,15;
    4.17; (34) A.-3.4,5; (36) S.C.-3.24,26,28,29,30,31; 4.5; (37)
    A.-5.5,7,18,24; (40) S.C.-1.7,12,13; A.-6.3,4,7; S.C.-12.4,5,6;
    Am.-12.14,15,16,17,19,20,24; (41) Am.-1.2,7,12,15; 2.9,17;
    4.6; S.C.-11.21,22,23,24; 12.1; (42) Am.-3.23,27.
'Tis All a Farce; farce by J. T. Allingham: (16) S.P.-11.21; (27)
    A.-3.1; (28) A.-2.8; (32) A.-12.12; (34) A.-5.14; (41)
    Am.-2.4.
'Tis She; farce by Poole: (41) Am.-12.29.
Tom Cringle; see *Tom Cringle's Log.*
Tom Cringle's Log; drama by Edward Fitzball: (36) A.-11.23;
    (37) A.-2.11; (38) A.-12.12; (39) A.-1.5; S.C.-4.19; (40)
    A.-5.27.
Tom and Jerry; see *Life in London.*
Tom and Jerry Revived; see *Life in London.*
Tom Noddy's Secret; farce by T. H. Bayly: (39) A.-3.24,29,31;
    4.2,7; S.C.-4.14,17; (41) Am.-3.20; 4.20,24; (42) Am.-4.8.
Tom Thumb; adaptation of Henry Fielding's burletta, by O'Hara:
    (19) S.P.-4.17; 5.4; (24) A.-5.15; (25) A.-4.4; (26) A.-3.22;
    (27) A.-4.2; (28) A.-4.12; (29) A.-1.14; (30) A.-2.10; (39)
    S.C.-12.27.
The Toothache; farce by John Bray: (17) S.P.-11.4,15,26; (18)
    O.C.-1.9,22.
Too Late for Dinner; farce by Richard Jones: (24) A.-2.25; 4.7;
    (36) S.C.-12.22; (41) Am.-3.27.

Tortesa, the Usurer; tragedy by N. P. Willis: (40) S.C.-5.7,8; Am.-11.13; 12.22.

Touch and Take: (29) A.-4.18,20,21,27; (30) A.-4.16.

La Tour de Nesle; "George Almar's historical drama from the French of Victor Hugo with alterations by B. Parsons": (35) A.-11.27,28; (36) A.-1.14; 2.2; S.C.-12.14; (37) S.C.-1.7; 4.1; (40) S.C.-1.2; A.-5.19.

La Tour de Nesle; see *The Tower de Nesle.*

Tourists in America; farce by J. M. Field: (33) A.-5.7,9,11; (36) S.C.-6.11.

The Tower of Nesle, or La Tour de Nesle; adapted by George Farren from Frank Haynes' translation of Victor Hugo: (35) A.-5.22,28; (37) A.-2.18; 5.4,12; (41) Am.-1,1,14; 2.19; 12.18.

Town and Country; comedy by Thomas Morton: (20) S.P.-3.30; (23) O.-1.20; (24) A.-1.1; 5.19; (26) A.-5.19; (27) A.-5.23; (28) A.-1.25; 12.22; (29) A.-1.20; (30) A.-2.24; 12.30; (31) A.-3.11,25; 4.27; 12.14; (33) A.-1.11; (37) S.C.-5.6; (38) S.C.-4.16; 10.12; (39) A.-3.12,19; (40) S.C.-10.31; (41) S.C.-3.28; Am.-12.1,6; (42) Am.-4.12.

The Tragedians; farce by Rawlinson, "a gentleman of this city": (31) A.-5.24.

The Traveling Painter: (37) A.-12.25. This may be Douglas Jerrold's *Painter of Ghent.*

Trial by Battle; melodrama by W. Barrymore: (38) S.C.-1.2,5,28; 3.11; 4.22; 11.20; (39) S.C.-2.1.

A Trip to Scotland; see *Gretna Green.*

The Triumph of Texas; by Madden: (38) A.-4.6,24.

The True Use of Riches; see *Fortune's Frolic.*

Truth; comedy by Charles Mathews, Jr.: (39) A.-1.22,24,25,28; 2.5.

Il Turco in Italia; opera by Rossini: (37) S.C.-1.15.

Turning the Tables; comedy by John Poole; (36) S.C.-2.15,16,18, 24; 3.7,17; (37) S.C.-2.7; (39) S.C.-1,10,19,22; 2.6,9,13,20; 3.2; (42) Am.-1.11,25; 2.3.

Turn Out, or The Enraged Politician; farce by James Kenney: (18) S.P.-2.24; 3.17; (20) S.P.-1.10; O.-2.18; (21) O.-5.4; (22) O.-3.18; (23) O.-5.9; (24) A.-3.9; 5.8; (26) A.-4.11; (27) A.-2.14,23; (28) A.-3.7; (29) A.-2.5; (30) A.-1.19; (31) A.-2.19; 12.12; (33) A.-1.17; (34) A.-4.28; (35) A.-5.8; (36) A.-12.30; (37) S.C.-2.20; 3.3; 5.27; 10.17; (38) S.C.-3.28; A.-5.10; S.C.-10.12; (39) A.-10.13; (40) Ar.-2.15,19; Am.-12.23; (41) Am.-1.7.

The Turnpike Gate, or The Two Cracks; farce by T. Knight: (20) O.-1.8; S.P.-1.27; O.-3.3; (21) O.-4.6; (23) O.-2.8; A.-5.24; (24) A.-1.3; 4.28; (25) A.-3.14; 5.22; (27) A.-3.6; 5.23; (28) A.-3.14; (29) A.-1.26; 3.6; (30) A.-1.4,7,13; 2.17; 12.20; (31) A.-1.10; 3.4; (32) A.-3.15,31; (34) A.1.11; 4.18; (35)

A.-5.1; (36) S.C.-2.28; 3.22; (37) A.-2.1,15; (38) S.C.-4.15,
21; A.-5.27; 6.3; S.C.-10.4,6,30; (40) S.C.-10.20; (41) S.C.-
11.22; 12.14; (42) Am.-4.25.
Tutoona; by George Washington Harby: (35) A.-2.21,28; 4.9;
(41) S.C.-2.22,25.
'Twas I; farce by J. H. Payne: (28) A.-12.27,29,30; (29) A.-1.3,
17; (31) A.-3.11.
Twelfth Night; by William Shakespeare: (31) A.-4.11; (38) S.C.-
3.3,7; (39) A.-2.23,26.
Twelve Precisely; burletta by H. M. Milner: (29) A.-3.30; 4.7;
(30) A.-3.20; (37) A.-5.18,22,25; (38) A.-5,6,9.
Twice Killed; farce by John Oxenford: (37) S.C.-1.23,25.
Two Blind Fiddlers: (12) B.-5.21.
The Two Cracks; see *The Turnpike Gate.*
2548! or The Farmer's Story; melodrama by W. B. Bernard: (37)
A.-5.7,10,17,28; (38) A.-2.24; 4.25.
The Two Friends; comedy by M. R. Lacy: (33) A.-12.21,24; (34)
A.-4.1; (36) S.C.-5.7; (37) S.C.-11.22; (40) S.C.-12.5,28;
(41) S.C.-1.12,15; (42) Am.-3.22.
The Two Galley Slaves; melodrama by Payne: (37) A.-4.16.
*The Two Gregories, or Luck in a Name, or Where Did the Money
Come From?;* musical farce by T. J. Dibdin: (30) A.-12.15,
17; (32) A.-4.9,30; (33) A.-1.15; (36) S.C.-5.2,4; 11.16;
(37) S.C.-1.16; 11.10; (38) A.-1.26; (39) A.-10.10; (40)
Ar.-2.11,20; S.C.-10.28; 11.30; (41) Am.-2.9; 3.8,12; 4.30;
(42) Am.-4.30.
Two Gentlemen of Verona; by William Shakespeare: (31) A.-
12.28.
Two Hunters; pantomime; (11) Con.-8.7.
Two Quakers; pantomime; (11) Con.-8.7.
The Two Queens; burletta by Buckstone: (38) A.-3.12,14,15.
The Two Sisters; by E. H. Keating: (35) A.-2.12.
Two Strings to Your Bow; see *The Hotel.*
The Two Thompsons; see *William Thompson.*
An Uncle Too Many; musical farce by C. P. Thompson: (37)
S.C.-5.25.
Uncle Sam, or a Nabob for an Hour; farce by Poole: (38) A.-1.10;
(39) S.C.-3.9,13,15; 4.1; (41) C.-7.4; (42) S.C.-2.7,19.
The Unfinished Gentleman; farce by Charles Selby: (35) A.-11.26,
27; S.C.-12.1,4; A.-12.5,25,28; (36) S.C.-1.7; A.-2.8,16; S.C.-
3.8; A.-4.21,29; 5.2,25; 12.17; (37) A.-1.14; S.C.-11.11,19;
(38) S.C.-4.14,23; (39) A.-10.17; (40) S.C.-10.14; (41) S.C.-
1.21; 3.29; 4.2.
The Unfortunate Gentleman; (06) M.B.-5.7; (11) S.P.-4.26.
The Unknown; melodrama by James Rees: (37) S.C.-3.2,3,6.
Valentine and Orson; melodrama by T. J. Dibdin: (23) O.-4.16,23;
(27) A.-5.12,25; (29) A.-5.9,14; (30) A.-4.13; (35) A.-5.21;
(38) A.-3.26; S.C.-4.18; (40) S.C.-4.28.
Valet de Sham; farce by Charles Selby: (42) Am.-1.5,6,13,22;
2.23; 4.10.

The Vampire; melodrama: (19) E.-11.22; (26) A.-5.29; (27)
  A.-2.5.
Venice Preserved; tragedy by Otway: (18) S.P.-4.2; (19) S.P.-
  3.27; (21) O.-3.28; (23) O.-3.24; (24) A.-1.4; (26) A.-2.15;
  (27) A.-3.8; 4.6; (29) A.-3.9; 5.1; (31) A.-1.14; 3.31; (32)
  A.-5.12; 11.24; (34) A.-4.22; (35) S.C.-12.8; (36) A.-1.20;
  S.C.-1.25; (37) A.-1.20; 2.18; 3.29; 5.3; (38) S.C.-1.31; (39)
  A.-3.5; 4.4.
Venus in Arms: (38) A.-2.27; 3.7,17,22,27.
The Vermonter; see *The Vermont Wool Dealer.*
The Vermont Wool Dealer, or The Vermonter; comedy by C. A.
  Logan: (38) A.-12.12; (39) A.-1.6,10; S.C.-12.24,31; (40)
  S.C.-1.2,22; 11.27; 12.2,20; (41) S.C.-2.3; (42) S.C.-1.13,19.
The Veteran of 102; see *One Hundred and Two.*
Victoria; satirical farce by J. M. Field: (38) S.C.-11.15,16,17.
Victorine; drama by J. B. Buckstone: (32) A.-11.21,29; (34)
  A.-3.6; (35) A.-11.28; 12.3; (36) A.-5.23,25; 12.8,24; (37)
  A.-2.21; 3.31; 5.2; (38) A.-11.5,6,10; (40) Am.-12.17.
The Village Lawyer; farce by William Macready: (17) S.P.-6.2;
  (18) S.P.-4.18; (20) S.P.-1.14; (23) A.-5.21; (25) A.-3.2;
  (26) A.-2.23; (29) A.-4.9; (30) A.-3.10; (37) A.-4.15,21,25.
Virginia Mummy, or The Virginia Sarcophagus; farce by T. D.
  Rice: (35) A.-5.11; (36) A.-2.17,19,22; (38) A.-3.4,5,8; (41)
  S.C.-2.16; 12.18; (42) S.C.-2.16,20,21.
Virginia Sarcophagus; see *The Virginia Mummy.*
Virginius; tragedy by J. S. Knowles: (21) O.-2.26; 4.6; (22)
  O.-2.9,11; (23) O.-3.22; 4.9; (24) A.-1.17; (25) A.-3.9,11;
  (26) A.-4.5; (27) A.-4.2,16; (29) A.-3.2; 4.13; 12.21; (30)
  A.-1.22; 12.31; (32) A.-3.28; 5.4; (33) A.-1.12; 5.10; (34)
  A.-4.8,14,24; (36) A.-1.26; S.C.-3.2; A.-12.9; (37) S.C.-2.1;
  (38) S.C.-1.5; (39) S.C.-1.13; A.-2.3,5,24; S.C.-4.1; (41)
  Am.-3.3.
Virginny Cupids; see *Oh! Hush!*
Vot of It?; extravaganza by J. M. Field: (40) S.C.-5.6.
The Wags of Windsor; see *The Review.*
Walden, the Avenger; tragedy by Mark Lemon: (38) S.C.-2.7.
Wallace, or The Scottish Chief; tragedy by C. E. Walker: (24)
  A.-5.12; (37) S.C.-5.20; A.-12.18; (38) S.C.-3.4.
Walter Tyrrell; tragedy by Edward Fitzball: (41) S.C.-2.17,23.
The Wanderer; drama by Charles Kemble: (28) A.-1.12.
The Wandering Boys; melodrama by M. M. Noah: (23) O.-1.18,
  25,27; 2.19; 3.19; (24) A.-2.18; 3.11; (26) A.-4.12,20; (28)
  A.-2.15; 4.16; (29) A.-5.6; (30) A.-2.6; 3.13; (31) A.-3.28;
  (33) A.-12.13; (34) A.-4.4; 5.2; (35) A.-1.28; 2.13; (36)
  S.C.-5.21; 6.13; (37) S.C.-4.8; (38) A.-4.2.
The Wandering Jew; by N. H. Bannister: (37) S.C.-1.3,4,5,11.
The Wandering Minstrel; farce by Henry Mayhew: (38) A.-
  11.29; 12.15; (39) A.-2.14; (40) S.C.-1.27,29; 2.3; 11.22,25;
  12.9; (41) S.C.-11.14,25; (42) S.C.-1.23.

Wanted a Wife; comedy by Moncrieff: (24) A.-4.20,22.

The Warlock of the Glen; melodrama by C. E. Walker: (23) O.-1.20,24; 2.5; (24) A.-3.13; (26) A.-5.13; (28) A.-1.3; (29) A.-12.14; (31) A.-5.4; (37) S.C.-5.23,30; (42) Am.-5.2.

Washington; by John Dumont: (34) A.-2.22; (35) A.-5.14.

Washington at Valley Forge; "historical drama written by two gentlemen of New Orleans": (33) A.-3.4,7,11,16; 5.7. James Rees claims the authorship of the play.

Washington Preserved; by James Rees: (36) A.-1.8.

The Watchword; spectacle by Robert Bell: (18) O.C.-1.25.

The Waterman; operatic farce by C. Dibdin: (18) S.P.-4.15; (37) S.C.-2.16,18; 3.12; 5.27; (38) A.-3.12,14,17,20,24; 4.9; 5.6; 6.2; S.C.-10.3,5; (39) S.C.-2.4; (42) S.C.-2.3.

The Water Witch; (by H. J. Finn): (39) A.-1.19,21,24; 11.20, 21,22.

The Way to Get Married; comedy by Thomas Morton: (18) S.P.-3.24; (23) O.-5.9; (28) A.-1.4; 3.1; (30) A.-3.11; (31) A.-12.31; (36) S.C.-12.15,28; (38) A.-11.17; S.C.-12.13; (39) S.C.-12.13; (40) S.C.-3.7.

The Way to Keep Him; see *The Inconstant.*

Ways and Means; farce by Colman the Younger: (21) O.-2.16; (24) A.-5.12; (31) A.-12.7.

Weak Points; comedy by J. B. Buckstone: (41) S.C.-2.12,28.

The Weathercock, or Love Alone Can Fix Him; farce by J. T. Allingham: (17) S.P.-5.23; (18) S.P.-1.16; (19) S.P.-4.14; (21) O.-2.9; (26) A.-2.20; 4.24; (32) A.-3.6; (34) A.-4.17; 5.9; (35) S.C.-12.17; (36) S.C.-1.9; A.-4.6,19; S.C.-11.29; A.-12.3,16; S.C.-12.17; (37) A.-1.4; 3.24; 4.8; 5.17; (38) A.-4.5,15; 11.23; (40) S.C.-2.11,13; 3.17; Am.-11.13,30; (41) S.C.-3.8,16; Am.-3.15.

The Wedding Day; comedy by Mrs. Inchbald: (26) A.-3.20; 4.27; (31) A.-12.31; (36) S.C.-3.12; (38) A.-5.28; 11.18,25; 12.11; (39) A.-1.9; (41) Am.-3.11; (42) Am.-3.8; 4.28.

The Wedding Gown; comedy by Jerrold: (37) S.C.-5.11.

The Wedding Ring; farce by C. D. Dibdin: (42) Am.-2.25.

We Fly by Night; interlude by Colman the Younger: (31) A.-1.14.

The Welsh Girl; farce by Mrs. J. R. Planché: (38) A.-3.26,29; (42) S.C.-2.28.

The Wept of Wish-ton-Wish; burletta by W. B. Bernard: (35) S.C.-12.24,25,26,28,29; (36) S.C.-1.2; 2.11,13; (37) S.C.-3.10, 11,13; (39) S.C.-3.11,12,20,30; 4.23; (40) S.C.-5.1.

Werner; tragedy adapted by William Macready from Byron's poem: (32) A.-5.7,15.

The West Indian; comedy by Richard Cumberland: (20) S.P.-1.15; (21) O.-3.14; (23) O.-4.12; (24) A.-3.1; (27) A.-5.25; (28) A.-3.24; (29) A.-5.22; (30) A.-1.21; (31) A.-5.30; (32) A.-3.7; (33) A.-5.28; (34) A.-4.28; (36) A.-12.3; (37) S.C.-2.16; (40) S.C.-3.3; (41) S.C.-2.11,26.

What Will the World Say?; comedy: (42) Am.-2.23,24; 3.4.

The Wheel of Fortune; comedy by Richard Cumberland: (23) A.-5.23; (29) A.-5.12; (31) A.-5.11; (38) S.C.-4.29.

Where Did the Money Come From?; see *The Two Gregories.*

Which is Which?; see *H. B.*

Whims of a Comedian; medley by G. H. Holland: (29) A.-1.26,28; 2.4; (30) A.-12.21; (31) A.-1.1,20,27; (32) A.-3.30; 4.6; (36) S.C.-5.28; 6.22; (38) V.G.-7.10; (40) S.C.-5.8.

Whirligig Hall; see *A Day after the Fair.*

The Whirlwind; ballet: (41) S.C.-12.19.

The Whistler; drama by George Pitt: (37) A.-3.4,5,16,18.

The White Eagle; melodrama: (37) S.C.-4.3,5,7,8.

The White Horse of the Peppers; comedy by Samuel Lover: (39) A.-3.1; (41) S.C.-1.1,2.

The White House; satirical farce by J. M. Field: (38) S.C.-11.16, 17.

The White Phantom; see *The Somnambulist.*

Who's the Dupe?; farce by Mrs. Cowley: (21) O.-3.28; (23) O.-4.4; (40) G.-7.4.

Who Wants a Guinea?; comedy by Colman the Younger: (16) S.P.-3.28; (24) A.-3.20; (38) A.-2.10; (39) S.C.-12.16; (40) S.C.-11.27; (42) S.C.-1.25.

Who Wins?; farce by J. T. Allingham: (37) A.-4.9.

Why Don't She Marry?; see *The Swiss Cottage.*

Widow Wiggins; monologue by Buckstone: (41) Am.-2.3,4,5,8, 13,15; 3.8,13,17; 4.23; 5.6,10,13; (42) Am-3.9,12; 4.5.

The Widow's Curse; by J. B. Phillips: (38) A.-4.1,7,17,21.

The Widow's Victim; farce by Charles Selby: (38) S.C.-11.10,12, 14,21; (42) Am.-3.19,20; 4.24.

The Wife; tragedy by J. S. Knowles: (33) A.-12.17,26; (34) A.-12.1; (35) A.-3.23; 11.23; (36) A.-1.13; S.C.-1.19; 2.15; A.-3.9; S.C.-11.24; A.-11.25; (37) A.-1.4; 3.24,30; S.C.-10.23; (38) S.C.-1.12; 4.3; 12.3; (39) S.C.-1.18; (40) S.C.-4.16; (41) Am.-2.28; (42) S.C.-1.25.

A Wife's First Lesson; see *The Day after the Wedding.*

The Wild Boy of Bohemia; melodrama by John Walker: (36) A.-12.12; (37) A.-1.20; 3.17; (38) S.C.-3.24; (42) S.C.-1.8.

Wild Oats; comedy by O'Keeffe: (20) O.-3.17; (24) A.-5.17; (27) A.-5.28; (31) A.-5.16; 11.23; (32) A.-2.15; (33) A.-1.18; (34) A.-4.25; (36) S.C.-12.13; (37) S.C.-1.26; 11.10,16; (38) S.C.-2.15; 12.4.

The Will, or My Grandfather's Will; comedy by Frederic Reynolds: (24) A.-5.5,15; (26) A.-5.10; (27) A.-3.2; (29) A.-2.6; (30) A.-1.27; (31) A.-1.21; 12.24; (33) A.-1.30; 12.7; (42) S.C.-1.31; Am.-3.9.

Will Watch, or The Black Phantom; melodrama: (31) A.-12.20, 26; (33) A.-1.31; (36) A.-4.11,14,29; 5.17; (39) A.-11.26,28.

William Tell; drama by J. S. Knowles: (26) A.-1.25,31; 3.28;
(27) A.-4.20; (29) A.-4.18,22; (30) A.-1.4; 5.15; 12.22;
(31) A.-12.2; (32) A.-1.26; 11.22; (33) A.-5.8; (34) A.-4.11;
(36) A.-1.7; S.C.-5.5; 11.22; (37) S.C.-2.11; (38) S.C.-10.24;
(39) S.C.-4.15; (41) Am.-1.31.

William Thompson, or The Two Thompsons; farce by Caroline
Boaden: (32) A.-1.9; 2.14; 3.29; (35) A.-5.5; (36) S.C.-1.6,
15; 12.9; (38) S.C.-11.29.

Win Her and Wear Her; adaptation of Mrs. Centilivre's *A Bold
Stroke for a Wife,* by J. Barnett: (37) S.C.-2.13; (39) S.C.-
12.21.

Wine Does Wonders; see *The Inconstant.*

Winning a Husband, or Seven's the Main; interlude by George
Macfarren: (28) A.-4.7,10,16; (29) A.-5.13; (30) A.-3.29;
(31) A.-2.18; 5.2,18; (37) A.-1.30; (38) A.-5.11,25; (42)
S.C.-2.11,12,25.

Wives as They Were and Maids as They Are; comedy by Mrs.
Inchbald: (20) O.-4.10; (26) A.-1.27; (27) A.-2.21,28; (29)
A.-3.23; (30) A.-2.8; (31) A.-1.26; (33) A.-12.2; (35) A.-
5.5; (36) A.-2.17; S.C.-2.26; 3.14; (37) S.C.-2.8; 11.24;
12.15; (38) A.-10.26; (39) A.-2.20.

The Wizard Skiff; melodrama by J. T. Haines: (35) S.C.-12.21,
22,29; (36) S.C.-1.1; (37) S.C.-3.16,17,18,20; (39) S.C.-3.21,
22,25,26; 4.23.

The Wolf and the Lamb; farce by T. E. Wilks: (33) A.-3.30; 4.10;
(37) S.C.-2.23.

The Woman: (37) S.C.-12.16.

A Woman's Life, or Isabelle; drama by Buckstone: (37) S.C.-
4.10; (38) A.-12.13,14,15,18,20; (39) A.-1.23,26; (40) Am.-
11.23; (41) Am.-3.31.

Woman's the Devil; farce: (42) S.C.-12.21,22,24.

Woman's Wit; drama by J. S. Knowles: (38) A.-12.20,22.

The Wonder! A Woman Keeps a Secret; comedy by Mrs. Centilivre: (20) O.-3.22; (23) O.-5.5; (27) A.-2.11; (29) A.-3.11;
(30) A.-2.15; 12.17; (31) A.-4.7; (33) A.-3.21; 12.14; (36)
A.-12.1; S.C.-12.29; (37) A.-1.12; S.C.-2.24; 10.24; (38)
S.C.-3.30; (40) S.C.-4.14.

The Wood Cutter of Bagdad; see *The Forty Thieves.*

The Wood Daemon; melodrama by M. G. Lewis: (27) A.-6.8;
(28) A.-1.2,5.

The Woodman's Hut; melodrama by S. J. Arnold: (28) A.-3.3,5,
7,13,18,22.

Wool Gathering; farce by Brayley: (29) A.-2.23,25,27; 3.26;
(38) S.C.-3.22,24,27.

The Wreck, or The Ocean Child; nautical drama by C. A. Somerset: (37) S.C.-1.11,12,13,14; 4.1.

The Wreck Ashore, or A Bridegroom from the Sea; domestic drama by J. B. Buckstone:: (34) A.-2.27; 3.8; (37) A.-5.4; (38) S.C.-11.23; (41) S.C.-11.18,19.

The Wreck of Punchinello; comic ballet: (42) S.C.-12.12,15.

The Wrecker's Daughter; tragedy by J. S. Knowles: (37) S.C.-11.13; (38) S.C.-1.20; (39) A.-4.5.

X Y Z; farce by Colman the Younger: (27) A.-12.21,25.

The Yankee Pedlar; see *Old Times in Virginia.*

The Yankee Pedlar; see *The Foundling of the Sea.*

The Yankee in Spain; see *The Knight of the Golden Fleece.*

The Yankee in Time; see *The Maiden's Vow.*

Yelva; melodrama by Sir Henry Rowley Bishop: (37) S.C.-3.31.

The Yeoman's Daughter; domestic drama by T. J. Serle: (37) S.C.-1.30.

You Can't Marry Your Grandmother; farce by T. H. Bayly: (40) S.C.-11.16; 12.19,30.

The Young Hussar, or Love and Mercy; operetta by Dimond: (30) A.-3.26,29; (31) A.-3.21; 4.21; (36) S.C.-12.27,30; (37) S.C.-1.6.

Young Napoleon, Duke of Reichstadt; "new drama never acted in any theatre, written expressly for Master Burke": (32) A.-3.12.

The Young Quaker; comedy by O'Keeffe: (21) O.-2.23.

The Young Reefer; farce by George Soane: (37) S.C.-3.6; A.-5.12; (38) A.-5.28.

The Young Widow; farce by J. T. C. Rodwell: (26) A.-2.16; (29) A.-1.9; 12.19,24; (32) A.-12.3,18,27; (33) A.-3.15; 5.6; (34) A.-2.28; 4.2,22; 11.24; (35) A.-5.28; (36) A.-5.3; 6.29; S.C.-12.19,30; (37) S.C.-2.8; A.-2.18; S.C.--4.18; (38) A.-4.2; (40) S.C.-10.19,21; (41) Am.-3.8; C.-6.27; (42) S.C.-1.26.

The Youthful Brigand; see *Matteo Falcone.*

The Youthful Days of Harrison: (40) Am.-11.29; 12.2.

The Youthful Queen, or Christine of Sweden; comedy by Charles Shannon: (36) A.-4.11,14,15; 5.23,29; 11.26,29; S.C.-11.30; 12.5,16; A.-12.29; (37) A.-2.14,25; S.C.-2.27; A.-3.7,26; S.C.-4.3; A.-4.7,24; (38) S.C.-1.19; 2.13. 3.7; 12.1,13; (39) S.C.-1.24,28; A.-2.22; 10.17; S.C.-12.28; (42) Am.-4.29; 5.17.

Youth, Love, and Folly; music drama by Dimond: (30) A.-2.5,12; (31) A.-2.4.

Zairi; "translated from Voltaire by H. Hill": (22) O.-3.27.

Zampa, the Red Corsair; opera by Herold: (42) S.C.-1.20,22,30.

Za Ze Zi Zo Zu; extravaganza by Edward Fitzball: (38) S.C.-10.27,28,30; 11.1,9.

Zelmira; opera by Rossini: (36) S.C.-4.24,27; 5.27.

Zembuca; melodrama by Pocock: (24) A.-4.7,8,9,10,12,14,26; 5.1; (26) A.-2.1; (27) A.-4.17; (32) A.-4.28; (41) S.C.-2.19,22,27; 3.24.

The Player List includes the names of all the actors, actresses, dancers, and special artists who appeared in the New Orleans theatres between 1806 and 1842.

The name of the actor is followed by the year or years of his appearance, the name of the theatre in which he played, and the abbreviation, reg., if he was a regular member of the resident company. For illustration take the entry: (36-7) A.-reg.; (38-9) S.C.-10.17 reg. This means that during the season of 1836-1837 the actor was a regular member of the company at the American Theatre; during the season of 1838-1839 he was a member of the company at the St. Charles Theatre, making his first appearance on the seventeenth day of the tenth month.

The notation which follows the name of a visiting player includes, whenever possible, the date of his first appearance and the length of his engagement. As an illustration take the name of Mrs. Austin. The record is as follows: (34) A.-1.13-7,27-14; 4.15-15. This means that Mrs. Austin appeared in 1834 at the American Theatre, beginning on the thirteenth day of the first month, for an engagement of seven nights; on the twenty-seventh of that month she returned for a second engagement; and on the fifteenth day of the fourth month she began a third engagement of fifteen nights.

When a record is incomplete, the fact is indicated. For example take the name of Clara Fisher for 1837. The notation, (37) A.-(record incomplete), means that she appeared in 1837 at the American Theatre, but the date of her initial appearance and the length of her engagement cannot be determined.

Two abbreviations which have not been used elsewhere appear in this list: E.H.—Elkin's Hotel and T.R.—Tessier's Room.

Abbott, William: (36) A.-11.22-14.
Abercrombie: (19) S.P.-4.14-reg.
Adams: (19) S.P.-reg.
Adams, A. A., tragedian: (37) S.C.-2.1-7.
Adams, J. J.: (35) A.-4.28; 5.6,12.
Albertazzi, Signor, with Italian Opera Company from Havana: (42) S.C.-2.22-10.
Albertazzi, Signora M., with Italian Opera Company from Havana: (42) S.C.-2.22-10.
Ali Abdul Maza, magician and juggler: (40) S.C.-3.4; Am.-5.26-6.
Allen, Andrew Jackson: (33) A.-5.1,2,3; (34) A.-4.12.

Anderson, William: (20) S.P. and O.-reg; (27-8) A.-reg.; (28-9) A.-reg.; (30-1) A.-reg.

Anderson, Mrs. William: (20) S.P. and O.-reg.; (22) O.-reg.

Anderson: (41-2) S.C.-reg.

Anderson, Mrs.: (38-9) A.-reg.; M.-6.19,21.

Andrews: (32-33) A.-reg.

Archer, singing actor: (36-7) A.-reg.; (37-8) S.C.-reg.; (38-9) S.C.-10.17-reg.; A.-1.7-3; 4.4; (39-40) A. and S.C.-reg.; (41-2) S.C.-reg.

Arraline, Madame, dancer: (41) S.C.-3.6-11; 4.7; (41-2) S.C.-11.28-reg.

Augusta, Mlle., ballet danseuse: (39) S.C.-2.13-8.

Auguste: (32-3) A.-reg.

Austin: (38-9) A.-reg.

Austin, Mrs. singing actress: (34) A.-1.13-7,27-14; 4.15-15.

Badiali, Signor F., with the Italian Opera Company from Havana: (37) S.C.-4.4-27; (42) S.C.-2.22-10.

Bail(e)y: (40-1) Am.-reg.; (41-2) Am.-reg.

Bail(e)y: (40-1) Am.-reg.

Bailey, Mrs. W. H., singing actress: (38) S.C.-1.9-7; A.-2.21-6.

Baker, Mrs.: (23) O.-reg.; (24) A.-reg.

Baldwin: (18) S.P.-1.13-reg.

Baldwin, Mrs.: (28) A.-1.28-reg.

Balls, J. S., light comedian: (36) S.C.-12.12-11; (37) S.C.-1.31-11; A.-2.17; (39) S.C.-12.8-14; (40) S.C.2.24-15.

Bannister, N. H., playwight and actor: (34-5) A.-reg.; (35-6) A.-reg.; (36-7) S.C.-reg.; (42) Am.-3.28-5.

Bannister, Mrs. N. H.; see Mrs. Legg.

Barbiere, Mons., dancer: (37-8) S.C.-reg.

Barclay: (36-7) A.-reg.

Barker: (37) S.C.-2.8-reg.

Barker, Mrs.: (37) S.C.-2.13-reg.

Barnes, Charlotte, heroine: (35) A.-4.22-9; (37) S.C.-2.2-6; 4.11-10; (38) A.-5.15-8; S.C.-11.29-9; 12.10-4; (40) S.C.-4.10-10.

Barnes, John, comedian: (35) A.-4.21-10; (37) S.C.-2.2-6; 4.11-11; (38) A.-5.15-8; S.C.-11.29-7; 12.12-2; (40) S.C.-4.10-10.

Barnes, Mrs. John: (35) A.-4.20-6; (37) S.C.-2.2-5; 4.11-10; (38) A.-5.15-7; S.C.-11.30-4; 12.15; (40) S.C.-4.14-4.

Barnett: (25) A.-reg.

Barrett, Mrs. George: (33) A.-12.12-7; (34) A.-3.21-12; (38-9) A.-reg.; S.C.-4.1,9-reg.

Barrett, George, light comedian: (33) A.-12.10-9; (34) A.-1.2-7; 3.20-12; (37) S.C.-11.14-6; 12.11-6; (38) S.C.-2.15-41; (38-9) A.-reg.; S.C.-4.11-reg.; (39-40) A.-11.2-reg.; S.C.-reg.; (40-1) S.C.-reg.; (41-2) S.C.-11.27-reg.; Am.-3.22.

Barry: (28-9) A.-reg.

Barton, John H.: (32) A.-4.25-11; 11.22-8; (33) A.2.6; (35-6) S.C.-reg.; (36-7) S.C.-reg.; (37-8) S.C.-reg.; (38-9) S.C.-acting manager; A.-3.2-3; 4.4-3; (39-40) S.C.-reg.; A.-11.2-3; 5.22; (40-1) S.C.-occasional performances.

Bartow: (20) S.P.-1.26-3.

Battersby, Mrs., heroine: (25) A.-reg.

Bedouin Arabs: (39) S.C.-2.24-5; A.-3.7-6.

Beecum: (40-1) Am.-reg.

Benedict: (35-6) S.C.-reg.

Bennie, dancer: (35-6) A.-11.30-reg.; (36-7) A.-reg.

Bennie, Mrs., dancer: (35-6) A.-11.30-reg.; (36-7) A.-reg.; (38-9) S.C.-reg.; A.-12.21-5.

Benoni, Mons., dancer: (30) A.-3.2-5.

Benoni, Virginia, dancer: (30) A.-3.2-5.

Benton, W. H.: (20) S.P. and O.-reg.; (21) O.-reg.; (22) O.-reg.; (23) O.-reg.

Bishop, Thomas, singing actor: (36-7) S.C.-12.16-reg.; A.-3.11; (38) S.C.-4.21.

Blackburn, Joe, clown; (36) A.-4.7; (41) S.C.-11.14-4.

Blanchard, appearing with Cony: (38) A.-1.27-2.

Blisse, Carl Von, Tyrolese minstrel: (31) A.-11.28-2.

Bloxton: (23) O.-reg.; (24) A.-reg.; (25) A.-reg.; (26) A.-reg.; (27) A.-reg.

Bloxton, Mrs.: (23) O.-reg.; (24) A.-reg.; (25) A.-reg.; (26) A.-reg.; (27) A.-reg.

Boddy: (36-7) A.-12.27-reg.; (39-40) A. and S.C.-reg.; A.-summer; (40-1) S.C.-reg.

Bolton: (20) S.P.-6.10.

Booth, Junius Brutus, tragedian: (22) O.-1.11 (record incomplete); (28) A.-1.14-11; 2.2-7; O.-2.19,21; (29) A.-1.7-9; 2.19-8; 3.6-13; 4.10-14;·(39) S.C.-2.5-10; A.-3.20-5.

Bowman: (18) S.P.-reg.

Boyle: (20) S.P. and O.-reg.; (22) O.-3.18-reg.

Brace: (34-5) A.-reg.; (35-6) S.C.-reg.

Brady, amateur: (28) A.-1.11.

Brainbridge, R. C.: (18) S.P.-reg.

Branson: (40) G.-1.25; Ar.-reg.

Branson, Mrs., (40) G.-1.25; Ar.-reg.

Brennan, singing actor: (21) O.-reg.

Brichta, Madame, singer: (33) A.-5.14-4.

Briley: (11) Con.-6.29.

Bristow: (34-5) A.-reg.; (35-6) A.-reg.; (36-7) A.-reg.

Brittingham, Miss: (38) A.-2.24-4.

Brough, singing actor: (40) S.C.-3.6-19.

Brown: (32-3) A.-reg.

Brown, "professor of the Grecian Exercises": (30) A.-12.25-8.

Brown, John Mills, comedian: (38-9) A.-11.3-reg.; (39-40) A.-11.2-reg.; S.C.-reg.

Brown(e), Mrs. Frederick: (35-6) S.C.-reg.; (38-9) A.-11.16-reg.

Browne, James S., comedian: (38) S.C.-12.4-62; (39) S.C.-3.5-25; 4.4,8; (41) Am.-3.26-4; 4.8; S.C.-4.7; (42) S.C.-2.7-reg.; Am.-3.19,22; 4.1.

Brunton: (41-2) S.C.-reg.

Brunton, Mrs.: (41-2) S.C.-reg.

Buckstone, John Baldwin, playwright and comedian: (41) S.C.-2.1-7; Am.-2.13-6; 3.14-6; 4.17-9; 5.5-7; (42) Am.-3.10-6; 4.1,3-9.

Burke, Master: (32) A.-2.24-14; 3.12-6; 4.12-5; (37) S.C.-3.14-2; 4.24-6; A.-5.6-8; (39) A.-2.17-9.

Burke, Thomas, comedian: (21) O.-reg.

Burke, Mrs. Thomas: (21) O.-2.5-reg.

Burke: (35-6) S.C.-reg.; (37) A.-2.15-reg.; (38-9) S.C.-reg.; M.-6.19,21; (39-40) S.C.-(record incomplete); Ar.-2.19-reg.

Burke, Mrs.: (35-6) S.C.-reg.

Butler, Samuel, tragedian: (42) S.C.-2.28-4.

Byers: (38-9) A.-reg.

Caines, Mrs.: (32-3) A.-reg.

Caldwell, Edward: (23) O.-reg.; (24) A.-reg.

Caldwell, James H., theatre owner, manager, and actor: (20) S.P. and O.-reg.; (21) O.-reg.; (22) O.-reg.; (23) O.-reg.; (24) A.-reg.; (25) A.-reg.; (26) A.-reg.; (27) A.-reg.; (27-8) A.-reg.; (28-9) A.-reg.; (29-30) A.-reg.; (30-1) A.-reg.; (31-2) A.-reg.; (32-3) A.-reg.; (34) A.-2.17-8; (37) S.C.-2.16-5; (39) S.C.-1.12,29-4; (41) S.C.-2.2-5.

Caldwell, Thomas: (22) O.-reg.

Cambridge, H. N.: (28) A.-1.11-reg.

Campion: (29-30) A.-reg.

Candi, Pietro, with the Italian Opera Company from Havana: (37) S.C.-4.4-27.

Cargill, A.: (17) S.P.-3.22; 5.23; 6.2; O.C.-6.5; S.P.-11.4; 12.15-3; (18) O.C.-1.9-3; 2.26; (19) S.P.-3.8-reg.

Carlos: (36) A.-2.5-reg.

Carpender: (20) O.-1.10; 3.25.

Carpenter, Miss, dancer: (27) A.-2.27-reg.

Carr: (20) S.P. and O.-reg.

Carr, singing actor: (28-9) A.-reg.; (29-30) A.-reg.; (30-1) A.-reg.; (31-2) A.-reg.; (32-3) A.-reg.; (33-4) A.-reg.; (34-5) A.-reg.; (35-6) A.-reg.; (36-7) A.-reg.; (37-8) S.C.-reg.

Carr, Mrs.: (28-9) A.-reg.; (29-30) A.-reg.; (30-1) A.-reg.; (31-2) A.-reg.; (34-5) A.-reg.; (35-6) A.-reg.; (36-7) A.-reg.; (37-8) S.C. and A.-reg.

Carr, Master: (35-6) A.-occasional performances; (37) A.-1.6.

Carroll, acrobat: (40) A.-6.12-3.

Carroll, B. W., equestrian: (40-1) Am.-reg.

Carroll, Mrs.: (40-1) Am.-reg.

Carter: (11) Con.-6.29.

Carter: (25) A.-reg.

Carter, Mrs.: (25) A.-reg.

Ceconi, with Italian Opera Company from Havana: (42) S.C.-
2.22-10.

Celeste, Mlle.: (29) A-4.16-15; (30) A.-4.2-9,19-10; (35) S.C.-
12.14-20; (36) S.C.-2.11-3; (37) S.C.-3.-7-23; 4.18-4; (39)
S.C.-3.4-24; 4.22-4.

Ceressini, with Italian Opera Company from Havana: (37) S.C.-
4.4-27.

Chambers, Mrs.: (37-8) S.C.-reg.

Chapman, George, comedian: (40) G.-1.16,25; Ar.-reg.

Chapman, Mrs. George: (40) G.-1.16,25; Ar.-reg.

Chapman, William, low comedian: (40) S.C.-10.19-7; (41) C.-
reg.

Chapman, Mrs. William: (41) C.-reg.

Charnock: (31) A.-5.26-reg.; (31-2) A.-reg.; (32-3) A.-reg.

Charnock, Miss: (33) A.-3.27.

Chester, Miss: (37-8) S.C.-reg.; (38-9) S.C.-reg.

Chipp(s): (36) S.C.-4.28.

Chipp(s), Mrs.: (36) S.C.-4.28.

Christian, Tyrolean Singer: (42) Am.-1.1-4.

Cioffi, Mrs.: (38-9) S.C.-reg.; (39-40) A. and S.C.-reg.; A.-sum-
mer; (41) C.-reg.

Clarke, equestrian: (41-2) Am.-reg.

Clarke, George: (28-9) A.-reg.; (29-30) A.-reg.; (36-7) A.-reg.;
(37-8) A.-reg.

Clarke, Miss: (29-30) A.-reg.; (36-7) A.-reg.

Clarke, Miss M. E.: (30) A.-5.8.

Clifton, Miss Josephine: (37) A.-3.23-8; 4.19-8; (38) S.C.-1.29-
8; 3.29-5; 12.18-12; (39) A.-2.13.6.

Cline, Herr: (30) A.-2.19-5; (35) A.-1.12-9; (37) A.-2.15-8;
3.2-10; (41) S.C.-11.7-11; 12.5-9; (42) Am.-2.2-5.

Cline, T. S.: (41) S.C.-11.14-17.

Coleman, Miss: (33) A.-2.12-reg.

Collins: (37-8) S.C.-reg.

Conduit, Mrs., later Mrs. Ben DeBar: (37-8) S.C.-reg.; V.-reg.;
(38-9) S.C.-reg.; (39-40) A. and S.C.-reg.; (40-1) S.C.-reg.

Coney: (32-3) A.-reg.

Conner, E. S.; (30-1) A.-12.31-reg.; (40) Am.-11.11-7,21-reg.

Conner, Master: (31) A.-12.30.

Conner, Miss: (31) A.-12.30.

Constance, dancer: (29) A.-4.16-15; (30) A.-4.2-9,19-10.

Conway, William, tragedian: (25) A.-3.2-8.

Cony and his dogs, Hector and Bruin: (38) A.-1.27-2.

Cook: (41-2) Am.-reg.

Cooper, Miss P. E.: (34) A.-4.12,24; (36) S.C.-2.29-10.

Cooper, Thomas A., tragedian: (21) O.-3.23-10; 4.11-6 (22) O.-2.6-(record incomplete); (23) O.-3.21-12; (27) A.-3.28-14; (29) A.-3.2-9,23-5; (30) A.-12.27-10; (32) A.-3.28-8; (34) A.-4.12,18-6; (36) S.C.-2.25-13.

Copeland, Miss: (35-6) S.C.-reg.

Corri: (33-4) A.-reg.; (34-5) A.-reg.; (35-6) S.C.-reg.; (36-7) S.C.-reg.

Cowell, Joe, comedian: (30) A.-1.4-10; 2.1-16; (30-1) A.12.20-reg.; (31-2) A.-reg.; (35-6) S.C.-reg.; (38) S.C.-4.15-13; A.-(record incomplete); V.-reg.; (38-9) S.C.-reg.; A.-5.9-reg.; (41-2) S.C.-reg.; Am.-3.19.

Cowell, Mrs. Joe: (30-1) A.-12.20-reg.; (31-2) A.-reg.; (36) S.C.-reg.; A.-2.18-reg.; (38) S.C.-4.15-13; (38-9) S.C.-reg.; A.-5.9-reg.

Cowell, Sam (Young): (30) A.-1.13-7; (30-1) A.-reg.; (31-2) A.-reg.; (36-7) A.-reg.; (37-8) A.-reg.; (38-9) S.C.-reg.; A.-5.9-reg.; (39-40) A. and S.C.-reg.

Cowell, Miss Sydney: (38) S.C.-4.-17-4; (38-9) A.-reg.

Cramer, Mrs. H.; (37) S.C.-2.16-reg.; (37-8) S.C.-reg.

Crampton, H.: (27-8) A.-reg.; (28-9) A.-reg.

Crampton, Mrs. H.: (27-8) A.-reg.

Crampton, Miss Charlotte: (28) A.-3.24: (35-6) A.-reg.

Crane, Miss: (40-1) Am.-reg.

Crooke, Robert: (28-9) A.-reg.

Crooke, Mrs. Robert; see Mrs. Entwis(t)le.

Cummins: (18) S.P.-reg.

Cummins, Mrs.: (18) S.P.-reg.

Cushman, Charlotte: (35-6) S.C.-reg.

Dalton, John, comedian: (23) O.-4.30; A.-5.24; (24) A.-reg.

Daugherty: (37-8) S.C.-reg.

Davis, Mrs.: (20) S.P.-6.10.

Davenport: (41) Am.-11.28.

Davenport: (39) S.L.-3.26-4; S.C.-3.31.

Davenport, Miss Jean Margaret: (39) S.L.-3.26-4; S.C.-3.31.

Davenport, Mrs.: (39) S.L.-3.26-4; S.C.-3.31.

David: (38-9) A.-reg.

Davis, dancer: (37-8) S.C.-reg.; V.-reg.

Davis: (40) Ar.-reg.

Davis, Mrs.: (20) S.P.-6.10.

DeBar, Ben: (35-6) S.C.-reg.; (36-7) S.C.-reg.; (37-8) S.C.-reg.; (38-9) S.C.-reg.; A.-11.25-12; (39-40) A.-reg.; S.C.-reg.; (40-1) S.C.-reg.; (41-2) Am.-reg.

DeBar, Miss: (35-6) S.C.-reg.; (37-8) S.C.-11.5-reg.; A.-4.29; 5.5-reg.

DeBar, Mrs. Ben. See Mrs Conduit.

DeCamp, Vincent: (35-6) S.C.-reg.

DeGentzen: (41-2) Am.-reg.

DeGrove: (26) A.-reg.

DeGrush, Mrs. See Mrs. Thomas Morgan.

Delman: (34-5) A.-reg.; (37) A.-1.23-reg.
DeManville, Madame: (41-2) S.C.-11.24-reg.
Dennison: (35-6) S.C.-reg.; (36-7) S.C.-reg.
DeRosa, with Italian Opera Company: (36) S.C.-3.6-32; 12.4-11.
Desjardin, Mlle. Pauline, dancer: (40) S.C.-2.5-7,15-10; 3.9-6.
Diamond, Master, negro dancer: (41) S.C.-1.10-8; 2.10-4; Am.-
    4.7-4; 11.25-7; 12.8-4; S.C.-12.29-6.
Douvillier: (19) S.P.-4.17.
Douvillier, Mme.: (11) Con.-7.7.
Drake, Alexander, comedian: (23) O.-2.14-reg.
Drake, Mrs. Alexander: (23) O.-2.12-reg.; (28) A.-12.20-8; (29)
    A.-3.3-6; (34) A.-11.25-8; (35) A.-11.21-8; (36) A.-1.6-11;
    S.C.-12.3-7.
Drummond: (20) O.-reg; (26) A.-1.24-reg.; (34-5) A.-reg.
Duff, William: (11) S.P.-4.26; Con.-6.29; 7.7; (12) B.-5.21,25,30.
Duff, Mrs.: (11) S.P.-4.26.
Duff, Mrs.: (32) A.-11.27-14; (33) A.-1.23-9; (37) A.-4.17,27-6;
    (38) A.-3.13-7; S.C.-4.21; A.-5.17,30,31; (39) S.C.-4.2-12.
Duffy, William: (26) A.-reg.; (27) A.-reg.
Durie, Mrs.: (40) S.C.-4.10-reg.; (40-1) Am.-reg.; (41-2) S.C.-
    reg.
Dwyer, John: (23) O.-3.19; 4.12-3.

Easterman: (38-9) A.-reg.
Eaton, Charles: (35) A.-11.20-9; (36) A.-1.6-7; (39) A.-3.3-5;
    (40) Am.-12.1-7,23; (41) Am.-1.29-5; 2.23-8.
Edouard, Mme., dancer: (31) A.-1.6-reg.; (31-2) A.-reg.
Edstram, Mrs.: (28-9) A.-reg.
Eldred, George, clown with the equestrian company: (40-1) Am.-
    reg.; (41-2) Am.-reg.
Elssler, Fanny, dancer: (41) S.C.-3.6-11; 4.7.
Emberton, Samuel: (20) S.P.-reg.; O.-reg; (27) A.-reg.
Ennissol, Mrs.: (40-1) S.C.-reg.
Entwis(t)le, comedian: (20) O.-1.8, 11-reg.; S.P.-1.22-reg.; (21)
    O.-reg.
Entwis(t)le, Mrs., later Mrs. Crooke: (21) O.-reg.; (28-9) A.-reg.
Everard: (38-9) S.C.-reg.
Eversull: (32-3) A.-reg.; (33-4) A.-reg.; (35-6) A.-reg.; (36-7)
    A.-reg.; (37-8) A.-reg.

Fairchild: (34-5) A.-reg.; (36-7) A.-reg.
Farren, George P.: (34-5) A.-reg.; (35-6) A.-reg.; (36-7) A.-
    reg.; (37-8) A.-reg.; (38-9) S.C.-reg.; A.-4.8; (40-1) Am.-
    reg.; (41-2) Am.-reg.
Farren, Mrs. George P. See Miss Mary Ann Russell.
Farren, Miss: (42) Am.-3.21,26.
Feltman, dancer: (30) A.-3.2-5.
Feltman, Mme., dancer: (30) A.-3.2-5.
Fenner: (36-7) S.C.-reg.

Fenno, A. W.: (28-9) A.-reg.; (29-30) A.-reg.; (30-1) A.-reg.;
(36-7) A.-reg.

Feron, Mme., vocalist: (30) A.-3.3-14.

Field, J.M.: (29-30) A.-reg.; (30-1) A. reg.; (31-2) A.-reg.;
(32-3) A.-reg.; (33-4) A.-reg.; (36) S.C.-6.1-10;
(38) S.C.-11.15-5; (39-40) S.C.-reg.; (40-1) S.C.-11.1-reg.

Field, Mrs. J. M.: (39-40) S.C.-reg.; (40-1) S.C.-11.1-reg.

Fielding, Thomas: (20) S.P.-reg.; O.-reg.; (21) O.-reg.; (34-5)
A.-reg.; (35-6) A.-reg.; (36-7) A.-reg.; (38-9) A.-11.11-reg.

Finn, H. J., comedian: (32) A.-(record incomplete, 16 performances); (35) A.-2.14-5; 3.18; 4.10; (35-6) S.C.-reg.; (36-7)
S.C.-reg.; (38-9) S.C.-12-20-38.

Fisher, Clara, later Mrs. James Maeder: (30) A.-1.25-13; (31)
A.-1.19-13; 3.23-9; 4.18-8; (33) A.-12.5-18; (34) A.-1.27-12;
2.18-11; (35-6) S.C.-reg.; (37) A.-(record incomplete).

Fitzallan, Mrs.: (19) S.P.-reg.

Fitzwilliam, Mrs., comedienne: (41) Am.-2.3-6; 10-8; 3.8-6; 14-6;
4.17-9; 5.5-7; (42) Am.-3.9-7; 4-1; 3.9.

Fletcher, "Venetian Statues": (33) A.-1.4-7.

Forbes, J. W.: (32) A.-(record incomplete); (33) A.-1.7-11;
(35-6) S.C.-reg. until 2.7; (37) A.-1.21-7.

Ford: (35-6) S.C.-reg.

Fornasari, with the Italian Opera Company of Havana: (37)
S.C.-5.19-10.

Forrest: (32-3) A.-12.27-reg.

Forrest, Edwin: (24) A.-2.4-reg.; (25) A.-reg.; (29) A.-4.10-13;
(33) A.-5.1-10; (34) A.-3.19-9; 4.7-14; (39) A.-1.28-12; S.C.-
4.1-15.

Forrest, William: (23) O.-reg.; (24) A.-reg.; (25) A.-reg.; (26)
A.-reg.

Foster, Joseph, director of melodrama: (42) Am-2.12-reg.

Foster, Young: (42) Am.-2.12; 4.14.

Foster, equestrian: (40-1) Am.-reg.

Foster, L. D.: (40) A.-summer.

Foster, "from the Western theatres": (35-6) A.-reg.; (36-7)
A.-reg.; (37-8) A.-reg.; (41-2) Am.-reg.

Foster, Mrs.: (37-8) A.-reg.; (41-2) Am.-reg.

Franklin: (38-9) A.-reg.; M.-6.19,21.

Frederic(k), Mons., dancer: (41-2) S.C.-11.28-reg.

Fredericks: (31) A.-1.22-reg.; (31-2) A.-reg.

Fredricks, W. S.: (38-9) A.-reg.

Frethy, George: (24) A.-reg.

Garner, singing actor: (23) O.-reg.; (24) A.-reg.; (25) A.-reg.

Gaskill: (32-3) A.-reg.

Gay, dancer: (33-4) A.-reg.

Gay, Mrs., dancer: (33-4) A.-reg.

Germon: (41-2) Am.-reg.

Germon, Mrs.: (41-2) Am.-reg.

Gibbs, Mrs.: (35-6) S.C.-reg. until 4.18; (38) S.C.-3.12-10.
Gilbert: (38-9) A.-reg.
Gilbert, John: (29-30) A.-reg.; (30-1) A.-reg.; (33) A.-1.3-reg.; (33-4) A.-reg.
Goll, ballet master and dancer: (20) S.P.-1.21-reg.; O.-reg.
Gouffe, Mons., the man monkey: (33) A.-1.3-8; (34) A.-2.4-5.
Graham, Miss: (35-6) S.C.-reg.
Gray, Jackson: (20) S.P.-reg.; O.-reg.; (21) O.-reg.; (22) O.-reg.; (23) O.-reg.; (24) A.-reg.; (25) A.-reg.; (26) A.-reg.; (27) A.-2.13-reg.; (27-8) A.-reg.; (28-9) A.-reg.; (29-30) A.-reg.; (30-1) A.-reg.; (31-2) A.-reg.; (32-3) A.-reg.; (33-4) A.12.16-reg.; (34-5) A.-reg.; (35-6) A.-reg.; (36-7) A.-reg.
Gray, Mrs. Jackson: (20) S.P.-reg.; O.-reg.
Gray, Mrs.: (29) A.-3.19-reg.; (29-30) A.-reg.; (30-1) A.-reg.; (31-2) A.-reg.; (32-3) A.-reg.
Greek Brothers, strong men: (36) S.C.-12.2-4.
Green, Mrs.: (36-7) A.-reg.
Greene, John, comedian: (25) A.-reg.; (38-9) A.-reg.; S.C.-4.11-reg.; (40-1) Am.-reg.; (41-2) S.C.-11.20-reg.; Am.-3.19.
Greene, Mrs. John: (25) A.-reg.; (38-9) A.-reg.; S.C.-4.7,10-reg.; (40-1) Am.-reg.; (41-2) S.C.-11.20-reg.

Hackett, James: (32) A.-3.19-7; (35) A.-2.3-10; (37) S.C.-12.2-7; (41) S.C.-12.6-7, 27.5; (42) Am.-1.26-4.
Hall, Mrs.: (38-9) A.-reg.
Hamblin, Thomas S., tragedian: (29) A.12.21-7; (30) A.-1.11-7.
Hamilton: (11) Con.-6.29.
Hamilton: (36-7) S.C.-reg.
Hanker, Miss, dancer: (37-8) S.C.-reg.; V.-reg.
Hanna: (18) S.P.-reg.; (19) S.P.-reg.; (21) O.-3.16-reg.
Harrington, equestrian: (40-1) Am.-reg.
Harris: (35-6) S.C.-reg.; (38-9) A.-reg.; M.-6.19,21; (40) Ar.-2.19-reg.
Harrison: (38) A.-5.15-8; (38-9) S.C.-10.24-reg.
Harrison, Mrs.: (38-9) S.C.-10.24-reg.
Hartwig: (27) A.-2.27-reg.; (27-8) A.-reg.
Hartwig, Mrs. See Mrs. Tatnall.
Harvey: (38-9) S.C.-reg.
Hays: (23) O.-2.28-reg.
Henderson: (28-9) A.-reg.
Hendricks, equestrian: (41-2) Am.-reg.
Henning, Miss, dancer: (35-6) S.C.-reg.; (36-7) A.-reg.
Henry: (40) G.-9.19.
Henry, Mrs.: (39-40) S.C.-reg.; A.-summer; G.-9.19; (40-1) S.C.-reg.
Herbert, John: (31) A.12.5-12; (36) A.-3.1-reg.
Herbert, Mrs. John: (36) A.-3.1-reg.
Hernandez, Master, equestrian: (40-1) Am.-reg.; (41-2) Am.-reg.

Hernizen, George: (28-9) A.-reg.; (29-30) A.-reg.; (30-1) A.-reg.; (31-2) A.-reg.; (32-3) A.-reg.; (33-4) A.-reg.
Hield, William: (37-8) S.C.-10.23-reg.
Hield, Mrs. William: (37-8) S.C.-10.23-reg.
Higgins, John, prompter: (20) S.P.-reg.; O.-reg.; (21) O.-reg. (22) O.-reg.; (23) O.-reg.; (24) A.-reg.; (25) A.-reg.; (26) A.-reg.; (27) A.-reg.; (27-8) A.-reg.; (28-9) A.-reg.; (31-2) A.-reg.; (32-3) A.-reg.; (33-4) A.-reg.; (35-6) A.-reg.; (36-7) A.-reg.
Higgins, Mrs.: (23) O.-reg.; (24) A.-reg.; (25) A.-reg.; (26) A.-reg.; (27) A.-reg.; (27-8) A.-reg.; (28-9) A.-reg.; (30-1) A.-5.26; (31-2) A.-reg.; (32-3) A.-reg.; (33-4) A.-reg.; (34-5) A.-reg.; (35-6) A.-reg.
Hill: (41-2) S.C.-reg.
Hill, Mrs.: (41-2) S.C.-reg.
Hill, Frederic S.: (35-6) A.-reg.; (36-7) A.-reg.; (37-8) A.-reg.
Hill, George H.: (34) A.-1.21-9; 12.22-6; (35) A.-2.14-6; (36) S.C.-1.27-9; (38) A.-1.13-9; 2.9-4.
Hilson, Thomas, low comedian: (21) O.-12.19 (record incomplete); (32) A.-11.26-12; (33) A.-1.22-7; (34) A.-3.7-reg.
Hilson, Mrs. Thomas: (32) A.-11.28-9; (33) A.-1.22-9; (34) A.-5.14; (34-5) A.-reg.
Hinkie, Mrs.; (39-40) A. and S.C.-reg.
Hodges, Charles: (34) A.-3.10-reg.; (34-5) A.-reg.; (35-6) A.-12.9-reg.; (37) A.-1.7-reg.; (38-9) A.-reg.; S.C.-3.17.
Holland, George, comedian: (29) A.-1.21-7; 2.4-6; (30) A.-12.16-9; (31) A.-1.1-13, 22-8; (32) A.-3.30-9; (33) A.-1.1-8; 5.28; (35-6) S.C.-5.28; 6.14-5; (36-7) S.C.-reg.; (37-8) S.C.-reg.; V.-reg.; (38-9) S.C.-reg.; A.-4.4,8; 5.9-reg.; (39-40) A.10.21-reg.; S.C.-reg.; (40-1) S.C.-reg.; (41-2) S.C.-reg.
Honey, Mrs., dancer: (30-1) A.-12.18-reg.
Home, Mrs.: (34-5) A.-reg.; (35-6) A.-reg.
Horn, C. E.: (36) A.-12.22-7.
Horton, Miss: (36) A.12.19-8.
Hosack, H.: (29) A.-5.15,19.
Houpt: (32) A.-3.28-reg.; (32-3) A.-reg.
Hoyt, Negro impersonator and banjo player: (32) Am.-1.12.5.
Howard, James, singing actor: (29-30) A.-12.16-reg.
Hubbard: (34-5) A.-reg.; (35-6) A.-reg.
Hubbard, Mrs.: (34-5) A.-reg.; (35-6) A.-reg.
Hughes: (22) O.-reg.
Hughes, Mrs.: (22) O.-reg.
Hughes: (31-2) A.-12.20-reg.
Hungarian Singers: (40) S.C.-4.25-4; (42) Am.-4.28-3.
Hunt: (33-4) A.-reg.
Hunt, C. W., low comedian: (37-8) S.C.-11.11-reg.
Hunt, Henry, singing actor: (35-6) S.C.-reg.; (36-7) S.C.-reg.
Hunt, Mrs. Henry. See Louisa Lane.
Hunter: (20) O.-1.10.
Huntington: (26) A.-12.10.

Huntley: (37-8) S.C.-reg.; (38-9) A.-reg.; (39-40) A. and S.C.-
  reg.
Hutton, Joseph: (20) S.P.-reg.; O.-reg.; (21) O.-reg.
Hutton, Mrs. Joseph: (20) S.P.-reg.; O.-reg.; (21) O.-reg.
Hutton, Miss: (20) S.P.-reg.; O.-reg.; (21) O.-reg.

Jackson: (27) A.-2.22-reg.; (27-8) A.-reg.; (28-9) A.-reg.
Jackson, Mrs.: (27) A.-3.6-reg.
Jackson, equestrian: (40-1) Am.-reg.
Jackson, dancer: (37-8) S.C.-reg.
Jefferson, singer: (36) A.-12.1,6.
Jefferson, Thomas: (21) O.-reg.; (22) O.-reg.
Jewell: (40) S.C.-4.25; (41.2) S.C.-reg.
Johns, Mrs.: (26) A.-3.8-reg.; (27) A.-reg.; (27-8) A.-reg.;
  (28-9) A.-reg.
Johnson: (32-3) A.-reg.
Johnson: (37-8) A.-reg.
Johnson, equestrian: (40-1) Am.-reg.
Johnson, Mrs.: (41-2) Am.-reg.
Johnson, F.: (40-1) Am.-reg.; (41-2) Am.-reg.
Johnson, Louisa, dancer and actress: (37-8) A.-reg.; (40-1) Am.-
  reg.; (41-2) Am.-reg.
Johnson, S., delineator of Negro character: (41) S.C.-12.18.
Johnson, W. F.: (38-9) A.-reg.; S.C.-4.12-reg.
Jones: (20) S.P.-reg.; O.-reg.
Jones, J.: (40) S.C.-3.6-19.
Jones: (39-40) S.C.-reg.
Jones, Miss, dancer and actress: (37-8) S.C.-reg.; (38-9) S.C.-
  reg.; (39-40) A. and S.C.-reg.; A.-summer.
Jones, (Richard): (17) S.P.-5.23; 6.2; O.C.-6.5; S.P.-12.15,18,26;
  (18) O.C.-1.9,22; S.P.-4.21.
Jones, Samuel P., comedian: (24) A.-reg.; (26) A.-5.2-reg.; (27)
  A.-reg.; (28) A.-reg.; (28-9) A.-reg.; (42) Am.-5.11-reg.
Judah, E.: (21) O.-reg.; (22) O.-reg.; (34-5) A.-reg.; (37-8)
  A.-reg.

Kaiffer, Mons., dancer: (40) S.C.-2.6-5, 15-10; 3.9-6.
Kaiffer, Mme., dancer: (40) S.C.-2.6-5, 15-10: 3.9-6.
Kean, Charles: (31) A.-2.28-11; 4.18-7.
Keeley, Robert, comedian: (37) S.C.-1.17-13.
Keeley, Mrs. Robert, comedienne: (37) S.C.-1.17-13.
Keen(e), Arthur, singing actor: (20) S.P.-reg.; O.-reg.; (21)
  O.-reg.; (34) A.-12.2-6, 16-6; (35) A.-2.13-6.
Kelly, comedian: (37) A.-2.15-reg.; (37-8) A.-reg.
Kelly, Lydia: (27) A.-2.7-13; 3.5—(record incomplete); (30) A.-
  1.6-3.
Kelsey: (25) A.-reg.; (26) A.-reg.; (27) A.-2.16-reg.
Kemble, Blanche: (41-2) S.C.-11.18-reg.
Kenny: (20) S.P.-6.10.
Kenny: (28-9) A.-reg.; (29-30) A.-reg.

Kenny, Mrs.: (28-9) A.-reg.; (29-30) A.-reg.
Keppell, William H.: (32) A.-2.7-6; (34-5) A.-reg.; (35-6) S.C.-reg.; (36-7) S.C.-reg.; (38-9) A.-reg.; M.-6.19,21; (39-40) A.-reg.; S.C.-reg.
Keppell, Mrs.: (36) A.-3.9-reg.; S.C.-6.3-reg.; (36-7) S.C.-reg.; (39) M.-6.19,21.
Kerr, Miss, dancer: (38-9) S.C.-reg.
Keyl, equestrian: (31) A.-5.24.
Kidd: (29) A.-1.30-reg.
King: (17) S.P.-5.23,26; (18) O.C.-1.9,22; S.P.-3.14.
Kinlock, Mrs.: (35-6) S.C.-reg.; (36-7) S.C.-reg.
Kirkland: (38-9) A.-reg.
Klisching, Mons.: (40) S.C.-2.6-5, 15-10.
Knight, Mrs. Edward: (29) A.-1.27-9; 2.13-5; (32) A.-12.28-7; (33) A.-1.17-8; 4.2-10; 11.27-7; 12.16-10; (34) A.-3.6-19; 11.24-8; 12.13-6; (35) A.-2.13-11; (36) A.-2.18-25; 12.13-12; (37) A.-1.3-14; 3.13-8.
Ku(a)tz, Mrs.: (35-6) A.-reg.

Lacomb(e), Mrs.: (28-9) A.-reg.: (29-30) A.-reg.
Lake: (36-7) A.-reg.
Lake, W., equestrian: (40-1) Am.-reg.; (41-2) S.C.-reg.
Lane, Louisa, in 1836 became Mrs. Henry Hunt: (29) A.-3.28-6; (35-6) S.C.-reg.; (36-7) S.C.-reg., until 5.9; A.-5.9,10,12,13.
Langton: (30) A.-5.10-reg.; (30-1) A.-reg.
La Petite Bertha: (38) A.-1.2; (39) S.C.-12.26-10.
La Petite Caroline, dancer: (41) S.C.-11.28-13; (42) Am.-2.2-5.
Lapland Dwarfs: (41) Am.-12.22-3.
Larkin: (35-6) S.C.-reg.; (37-8) A.-reg.
Latham, W. H.: (35-6) S.C.-reg.; (36-7) S.C.-reg.
Lavette, dancer: (40-1) Am.-reg.; (41-2) Am.-reg.
Lear: (27) A.-reg.; (28) A.-reg.; (28-9) A.-reg.
Lecom(p)te, Mme., dancer: (38) A.-12.21-9; (40) S.C.-2.5-7, 15-10; 3.9-6.
Lecom(p)te, Mons., singer and dancer: (38) A.-12.21-7; (40) S.C.-2.5-7, 15-10; 3.9-6.
Leicester: (41-2) Am.-11.30-reg.
Legg, Mrs., later Mrs. Stone and Mrs. Bannister: (21) O.-reg.; (35) A.-3.17-reg.; (36-6) S.C.-reg.; (36-7) S.C.-reg.; (42) Am.-3.28-5.
Len(n)ox: (35-6) S.C.-reg.
Levi, equestrian: (41-2) S.C.-reg.
Lewellen, G.: (40) S.C.-11.11-5; 12.4-3, Am.-11.25-6.
Lewellen, Mrs.: (40) S.C.-12.5.
Lewis: (40) Ar.-reg.
Lewis, G.: (38-9) A.-reg.
Lewis: (37-8) S.C.-reg.; (38-9) S.C.-reg.; (39-40) A. and S.C.-reg.
Lewis, (J. or H.): (23) O.-reg.; (29-30) A.-reg.; (30-1) A.-reg.

Lewis, Henry: (36) A.-12.2-3; (37) A.-1.23-5; 3.1-9; (record in-
    complete for third engagement) ; (39) S.C.-12.26-9.
Lewis, Mrs. Henry: (36) A.-11.23-10; (37) A.-1.21-9; 3.-1-14;
    (record incomplete for third engagement) ; (38) S.C.-1.4;
    (39) S.C.-12.26-9.
Lewis, Miss: (38-9) A.-reg.
Lipman, equestrian: (41-2) S.C.-reg.
Lloyd: (40) G.-9.19.
Logan, Cornelius A., comedian: (35) A.-12.23-4.
Loomis: (35-6) S.C.-reg.
Love: (12) B.-5.25,30.
Love, the Polphonist: (39) S.C.-4.21,22,26.
Love, H., equestrian: (41-2) S.C.-reg.
Lowry: (26) A.-reg.
Lucas: (18) S.P.-reg.
Lucas: (26) A.-reg.
Ludlow, Noah M., actor and manager: (18) S.P.-reg.; (21) O.-
    4.27-reg.; (22) O.-reg.; (23) O.-reg.; (24) A.-reg.; (30-1)
    A.-12.23-reg.; (33) A.-5.9; (40-1) Am.-reg.; (41-2) Am.-reg.
Ludlow, Mrs. Noah M.: (18) S.P.-reg.; (23) O.-reg.; (24) A.-
    reg.; (30-1) A.-12.23-reg.; (32-3) A.-12.13-reg.
Lynde: (41-2) S.C.-reg.; Am.-3.19.
Lyne: (32-3) A.-reg.
Lyons: (35-6) S.C.-reg.; (36-7) S.C.-reg.

Machado, Juan, dancer from the Spanish Theatre: (42) Am.-2.5.
Madden: (32) A.-1.31-reg.; (37-8) A.-reg.
Madden, Mrs.: (37-8) A.-reg.; (38-9) S.C.-reg.
Maeder, Mrs. J. G. See Clara Fisher.
Manl(e)y: (34-5) A.-reg.; (35-6) A.-reg.; (36-7) S.C.-reg.
Mannetti, with Italian Opera Company: (36) S.C.-12.4-11.
Manvers, in opera: (42) S.C.-15-17.
Marble, Dan: (38) A.-12.3-7; (39) A.-1.1-7; S.C.-12.16-16; (40)
    S.C.-11.2-9; 12.11-6; (41) S.C.-1.22; 2.1-4; (42) S.C.-1.9-8.
Markham: (35-6) S.C.-reg.
Marks, A. J. "Rowley", comedian: (26) A.-5.13-reg.; (29-30)
    A.-reg.; (30-1) A.-reg.; (33-4) A.-reg.; (34-5) A.-reg.; (37)
    A.-3.16; (38) A.-4.1; 5.28; (40) S.C.-4.27; A.-5.22; (41)
    C.-5.30; (42) Am.-2.5-3; 4.28; 5.2-reg.
Marks: (38-9) A.-reg.
Marozzi, Signora Lorenza, with Italian Opera Company: (36)
    S.C.-3.6-32; 12.4-11; (37) S.C.-4.4-27; (42) S.C.-2.22-10.
Martin, Mons., dancer: (38) A.-12.31-4; (40) S.C.-2.6-5, 15.10.
Mason, Charles: (35) A.-3.19-6; (36) A.-1.15-7; 3.8-5; S.C.-11.18-
    5; 12.29; (37) A.-1.18-9; 3.23-8; (40) S.C.-4.13-7.
Mason, Miss: (36) A.-3.8-5.
Mason, Miss, amateur: (41) S.C.-2.17.
Mathis, posture master: (26) A.-2.27-6; (27) A.-3.22.
Ma(e)ynard: (35-6) A.-reg.; (40-1) Am.-reg.; (41-2) **Am.-reg.**

Maynard, Mrs.: (40-1) Am.-reg.
M(c) Cafferty, William: (20) S.P.-reg.; O.-reg.; (21) O.-reg.;
    (22) O.-reg.; (23) O.--reg.; (24) A.-reg.; (25) A.-reg.; (26)
    A.-reg.; (27) A.-reg.; (27-8) A.-reg.
M(c) Clure: (29-30) A.-12.19-reg.
M(c) Clure, Mrs.: (29-30) A.-12.19-reg.; (30-1) A.-reg.
McCoy: (36-7) A.-reg.
McIntyre, Miss: (38-9) A.-reg.
McKibbin: (40) G.-1.16; Ar.-reg.
Meadows, Miss: (35) S.C.-12.24-5; (36) A.-4.4-8; (38) A.-11.19-
    6; S.C.-11.28-3.
Melton, Miss: (36-7) S.C.-12.27-reg.; (39-40) S.C.-reg.
Melville: (19) S.P.-reg.
Melville, Miss: (39) S.C.-12.1.
Mercer, equestrian: (41-2) Am.reg.
Millis, the American Fire King: (31) A.-12.6-3.
Milot: (36-7) A.-reg.
Minnich, Mrs.: (36) S.C.-6.13-reg.; (36-7) A.-12.1-reg.; (37-8)
    A.-reg.
Monell, Mrs.: (38-9) A.-reg.; M.-6.19,21.
Mongin, Mrs.: (24) A.-reg.
Mongin, Miss: (24) A.-occasional performances.
Monier: (20) O.-1.10; 3.25-reg.
Monier, Mrs.: (20) O.-1.10; 3.25-reg.
Montegin, with Italian Opera Company from Havana: (42) S.C.-
    2.22-10.
Montresor, director of Italian Opera Company: (36) S.C.-3.6-32.
Moore, American Hercules: (41) Am.-12.14.
Moore, John: (25) A.-reg.; (26) A.-reg.; (27) A.-reg.
Moore, Mrs.: (39-40) A. and S.C.-reg.
Morgan, Thomas: (18) S.P.-reg.
Morgan, Mrs. Thomas, later Mrs. DeGrush: (18) S.P.-reg.; (22)
    S.P.-4.24.
Morgan, negro imitator from Mexico: (42) Am.-1.20.
Morgan, Miss: (40) S.C.-3.12; (40-1) S.C.-reg.; C.-reg.
Morris: (42) Am.-3.20-reg.
Morton: (28-9) A.-reg.; (29-30) A.-reg.; (30-1) A.-reg.; (31-2)
    A.-reg.; (32-3) A.-reg.; (39-40) A.-10.20-reg.; (41) C.-reg.
Motty, Herr Otto, strong man: (41) Am.-12.30-7; (42) Am.-1.8-8.
Mowbray, Miss: (40-1) S.C.-reg.
Mueller, Mrs. C. H.; (40-1) Am.-reg.; (41-2) Am.-reg.
Mulhollon: (27) A.-reg.
Murdoch, James: (35-6) S.C.-12.17-reg.
Murray: (25) A.-reg.; (26) A.-reg.; (27) A.-reg.
Muzzy, Charles: (31-2) A.-reg.; (32-3) A.-reg.; (34-5) A.-reg.
Muzzy, Mrs. Charles: (31-2) A.-reg.; (32-3) A.-reg.; (34-5)
    A.-reg.

Nano, Signor Hervio: (41) Am.-2.20-7.
Naylor: (36-7) S.C.-reg.; (37-8) S.C.-reg.; (38-9) S.C.-reg.;
    (39-40) A. and S.C.-reg.; (40-1) S.C.-reg.; (41-2) S.C.-reg.
Nelson: (38-9) S.C.-reg.; (40-1) S.C.-10.26-reg.
Nelson, Miss: (34) A.-3.11-reg.; (35) A.-1.14-reg.; (35-6) A.-
    reg.; (37) A.-2.23-15; (38) A.-12.18-4; (39) A.-3.30.
Noke, Mrs. (23) O.-reg.; (24) A.-reg.
North, Levi, equestrian: (41) S.C.-12.14-6; (42) Am.-1.12-8.

Ober, with Italian Opera Company from Havana: (42) S.C.-
    2.22-10.
O'Connell, James F., tattooed man: (37) A.-(record incomplete).
Olympic Brothers (Laraux), in pantomime: (33) A.-12.10-(record
    incomplete).
Orlandi, with Italian Opera Company: (36) S.C.-12.4-11.
O'Rourke, Sam, pugilist: (32) A.-12.22; (33) A.-2.16.
Otto, Mme., in opera: (40) S.C.-3.6-19.

Pacaud: (37-8) S.C.-reg.; (38-9) A.-reg.; (40-1) S.C.-reg.;
    (41-2) S.C.-reg.
Page, Joseph, singing actor: (24) A.-1.12-reg.; (25) A.-reg.; (31)
    A.-1.3-reg.; (31-2) A.-reg.; (32-3) A.-reg.
Page, "vocalist of Theatres Royal, London and Dublin": (37)
    S.C.-2.16-reg.; (37-8) S.C.-reg.; V.-reg.; (38-9) S.C.-reg.
Page, Mrs.: (41-2) S.C.-reg.
Palmer: (27) A.-reg.; (27-8) A.-reg.
Pantanelli, Signora, with Italian Opera Company, Havana: (37)
    S.C.-4.4-27.
Papanti, Signora, with Italian Opera Company, Havana: (37)
    S.C.-4.9-25.
Pa(e)ret: (36-7) S.C.-reg.; (37-8) S.C.-reg.; (38-9) S.C.-reg.;
    (39-40) A. and S.C.-reg.
Parker: (25) A.-reg.; (26) A.-reg.
Parker, Mrs.: (25) A.-reg.; (26) A.-reg.
Parker: (36) A.-12.28-reg.
Parsloe, Charles, pantomimist: (35) A.-12.25; (36) A.-1.1; (41)
    S.C.- 3.6-11; 4.7.
Parsons, Charles B.: (36) A.-1.26-6; 11.23-5; (37) A.-4.19-8;
    11.20-(record incomplete); (38) A.-3.12-13.
Paul, Mons., acrobat: (41) S.C.-10.31; Am.-12.9.
Pearman, vocalist: (31) A.-5.13-4.
Pearman, Mrs., vocalist: (31) A.-5.13-4.
Pearson, Henry G.: (28-9) A.-reg.; (29-30) A.-reg.; (33-4) A.-
    reg.; (34-5) A.-reg.; (35-6) S.C.-reg.; (36-7) S.C.-reg.;
    (37-8) S.C.-11.7-reg.; (38-9) S.C.-10.10-reg.; (39-40) A.-
    11.18-reg.; S.C.-reg.; A.-5.22; (40-1) S.C.-reg.; (41-2) S.C.-
    reg.; Am.-3.22; 4.12.
Pearson, Sidney: (33-4) A.-reg.; (34-5) A.-reg.
Pearson, T.: (33-4) A.-reg.
Pedrotti, Signor, with Italian Opera Company: (36) S.C.-3.6-32.

Pelby, William, tragedian: (23) O.-5.7; (24) A.-1.15-8; 2.12-6; (30) A.-12.28-4; (31) A.-1.14-2.
Pelby, Master, equestrian: (40-1) Am.-reg.
Pelham, Miss: (35-6) S.C.-reg.
Pemberton, Mrs.: (39-40) S.C.-reg.
Perozzi, Luigi; with Italian Opera Company from Havana: (42) S.C.-2.22-10.
Peters, the antipodean: (31) A.-12.13-3.
Petrie: (20) S.P.-1.28-reg.; O.-reg.; (23) O.-reg.
Petrie, Mrs.: (28-9) A.-reg.
Petrie, Eliza: (31-2) A.-reg.; (32-3) A.-reg.; (33-4) A.-reg.; (34-5) A.-reg.; (41-2) Am.-reg.
Phelan, pugilist: (39) S.C.-4.21.
Phillips, Aaron J.: (19) O.-3.10,15; S.P.-3.24-3; (20) O.-1.10; S.P.-1.21.
Phil(l)ips: (34-5) A.-reg.; (36-7) A.-reg.
Phillips, Miss, tragedian: (36) S.C.-1.11-10; 2.18-9.
Phillips, Moses S., comedian: (40) S.C.-11.9.
Phillips, T., vocalist: (23) O.-4.14-4, 25-2.
Pickering, Alexander: (37-8) S.C.-reg.; (40-1) S.C.-11.6-reg.; (41-2) S.C.- 12.6-reg.
Pierce, Mrs.: (37-8) S.C.-reg.
Placide, Eliza: (21) O.-reg.; (22) O.-reg.
Placide, Jane: (23) O.-reg.; (24) A.-reg.; (25) A.-reg.; (26) A.-reg.; (27) A.-reg.; (29) A.-3.12-6; 4.10-14; (29-30) A.-reg.; (30-1) A.-reg.; (31-2) A.-reg.; (32-3) A.-reg.; (34) A.-1.11-9; (35) A.-3.18.
Placide, Thomas: (26) A.-1.24,25,26,27.
Plumer, Charles, vocalist: (38) S.C.-1.9-7; 2.17-11; A.-3.12-reg.; (38-9) S.C.-reg.
Plumer, Mrs. Charles: (38) A.-5.5-reg.; (38-9) S.C.-reg.
Plumer, Cramer: (31) A.-2.18-14; 4.19-17.
Plumer, Mrs. Cramer: (31) A.-2.18-14; 4.19-17.
Porter: (37-8) S.C.-reg.; (38-9) S.C.-reg.
Porter, James, the Kentucky giant: (39) A.-3.10-8.
Powell: (32-3) A.-reg.
Power, Tyrone, Irish comedian: (35) A.-1.6-14; 3.9-7; (40) S.C.-12.15-10, 28-11; (41) S.C.-1.20.
Price: (20) S.P.-reg.; O.-reg.; (38-9) A.-reg.; (39-40) A. and S.C.-reg.
Price, Mrs.: (20) S.P.-reg.; O.-reg.; (38-9) A.-reg.; (39-40) A. and S.C.-reg.
Pritchard: (37) S.C.-1.16; 3.6; 4.10; A.-5.4-3.
Pritchard, Mrs. See Mrs. Tatnall.

Radcliffe, Thomas: (34-5) A.-reg.; (35-6) A.-reg.; (36-7) S.C.-reg.; (39-40) A. and S.C.-reg.; A.-summer; G.-7.4; 9.19; (40-1) S.C.-reg.
Radcliffe, Mrs. Thomas: (40) S.C.-5.1; A.-summer; G.-7.4; 9.19.

Rae, Alexander: (35) A.-5.21.
Rae, Miss: (35) A.-4.4-reg.; (35-6) A.-reg.
Randolph, Miss: (36) S.C.-12.2; (37) A.-1.25-reg. (37-8) A.-reg.
Randolph, Miss E.: (37) A.-4.18; (38) A.-4.20; 5.5-reg.
Ranger, E. W., light comedian: (41) S.C.-1.18-10; 2.18; 3.2.
Rannie, ventriloquist and actor: (06) T.R.-3.14; M.B.-4.17,29; 5.7,16.
Rannie, Mrs.: (06) M.B.-5.7.
Ravaglia, with Italian Opera Company: (36) S.C.-3.6-32; 12.4-11.
Ravel Family: (33) A.-5.17-6; (38) A.-1.29-9; 4.8-7; (39) A.-1.27-2; S.C.-2.3-2; (41) Am.-12.22-8.
Ravenot, Miss, dancer: (38-9) S.C.-reg.
Rawlinson: (31) A.-5.24.
Raylea: (36-7) S.C.-reg.; (37-8) S.C.-reg.
Raymond, Edward: (31) A.-.1.1-reg.; (31-2) A.-reg. until March.
Reeder: (40-1) S.C.-10.26-reg.; C.-reg.; (41-2) S.C.-reg.
Reid: (41-2) Am.-reg.
Reynolds: (20) S.P.-6.10.
Reynoldson, J. T., musical director and singing actor: (34-5) A.-12.27-reg.; (35-6) A.-reg.
Rhodes, Miss: (35-6) S.C.-reg.
Rice: (34) A.-3.7-reg.
Rice, T. D.: (35) A.-3.27-8; 4.28; 5.1-7; (36) A.-2.17-10; (38) A.-3.4-8; (42) S.C.-2.16-6.
Richards: (20) S.P.-6.10.
Richardson, Mrs.: (41-2) S.C.-12.28-reg.
Richings: (32-3) A.-reg.
Riese: (41) S.C.-3.31.
Roberts, Mrs.: (32-3) A.-reg.
Robertson, Eugene: (27) A.-5.16-5.
Robinson (Robertson): (16) S.P.-3.28; 4.27; 11.21; (17) S.P.-5.23; 6.2; 12.15,18,26; (18) O.C.-1.9,22,25; S.P.-3.14.
Robinson, John, director of the equestrian company: (40-1) Am.-reg.; (41-2) Am.-reg.
Rock, Miss, comedienne: (42) S.C.-2.11-10.
Rogers, equestrian: (40-1) Am.-reg.
Roper, "celebrated master of self-defense": (34) A.-4.12.
Rose, J., prompter: (40-1) Am.-reg.; (41-2) Am.-reg.
Ross: (40-1) Am.-reg.; (41-2) Am.-reg.
Rossi, Signora, with Italian Opera Company from Havana: (37) S.C.-4.4-27; (42) S.C.-2.22-10.
Rossi, Signora, with Italian Opera Company for Havana: (42) S.C.-2.22-10.
Rousset, Mons., dancer: (24) A.-4.16-6.
Rousset, Mme., dancer: (24) A.-4.16-6.
Rowe, Mrs. James. See Miss Seymour.
Rowe, Mrs. George: (34-5) A.-reg.; (36-7) A.-reg.; (41-2) S.C.-reg.
Rowe, Miss Josephine: (36-7) A.-reg.

Russell, Richard, stage manager and low comedian: (20) S.P.-reg.; O.-reg.; (21) O.-reg.; (22) O.-reg.; (23) O.-2.8-reg. (24) A.-reg.; (25) A.-reg.; (26) A.-reg.; (27) A.-reg.; (27-8) A.-reg.; (28-9) A.-reg.; (29-30) A.-reg.; (32-3) A.-reg.; (33-4) A.-reg.; (34-5) A.-reg.; (35-6) A.-reg.; (36-7) A.-reg.; (37-8) A.-reg.

Russell, Mrs. Richard: (20) S.P.-reg. O.-reg.; (21) O.-reg.; (22) O.-reg.; (23) O.-2.8-reg.; (24) A.-reg.; (25) A.-reg.; (26) A.-reg.; (27) A.-reg.; (27-8) A.-reg.; (28-9) A.-reg.; (29-30) A.-reg.; (32-3) A.-reg.; (33-4) A.-reg.; (34-5) A.-reg.; (35-6) A.-reg.; (36-7) A.-reg.; (37-8) A.-reg.; (41-2) Am.-reg.

Russell, Miss Mary Ann, in 1838 became Mrs. George Farren; (25) A.-reg.; (26) A.-reg.; (27) A.-reg.; (28) A.-reg.; (28-9) A.-reg.; (29-30) A.-reg.; (35-6) A.-12,14-reg.; (36-7) A.-reg.; (37-8) A.-reg.; (38-9) S.C.-10.10-reg.; (40-1) Am.-reg.; (41-2) Am.-reg.

Russell, Master: (30) A.-4.28; 5.21; (32-3) A.-occasional performances; (33-4) A.-occasional performances; (34-5) A.-occasional performances; (35-6) A.-occasional performances; (40-1) Am.-reg. Am.-reg.

Russell, Richard, Jr. See Master Russell.

Ruthven: (36-7) S.C.-reg.

St. Aman, French actor: (37) S.C.-5.20.

St. Luke, Master: (38) S.C.-3.11-8.

St. Luke: (38) S.C.-3.11-8.

Sakoski: (27) A.-5.12-3.

Salvatori, with Italian Opera Company from Havana: (42) S.C.-2.22-10.

Salzman, Mrs.: (33-4) A.-reg.; (35-6) A.-reg.

Sanders: (11) Com.-6.29.

Sandford: (27) A.-reg.

San(d)ford, J.: (41) S.C.-12.18-7; (42) Am.-2.1-2.

Sankey: (40-1) Am.-reg.; (41-2) Am.-reg.

Sapignoli, with Italian Opera Company: (36) S.C.-3.6-32.

Saunders, C. H.: (40-1) Am.-reg.; (41-2) Am.-reg.

Saunders, Mick, Negro impersonator: (40) A.-5.24-(record incomplete).

Saunders: (36-7) S.C.-reg.

Saunders, Mrs.: (36-7) S.C.-12.12-reg.

Savage, John: (18) S.P.-4.2-5.

Savage, Mrs. John: (18) S.P.-4.4-4.

Schinotti: (37-8) S.C.-reg.

Scholes, James: (20) S.P.-reg.; O.-reg.; (21) O.-reg.; (22) O.-reg.; (23) O.-reg.; (24) A.-reg.

Schoolcraft, singing actor: (32-3) A.-reg.; (39-40) A. and S.C.-reg.; G.-9.19; (40-1) S.C.-reg.; C.-reg.

Scott, James M.: (22) O.-reg.; (30-1) A.-12.22-reg.; (32-3) A.-
    reg.; (34) A.-3.7-reg.; (34-5) A.-reg.; (35-6) A.-reg.
Scott, John R.: (37) S.C.-12.5-22; (38) S.C.-2.13-3; 12.3-27;
    (39) A.-2.13-6, 20-9; 4.4; S.C.-4.2-11.
Scott, Moses Y.: (24) A.-reg.; (25) A.-reg.; (26) A.-reg.
Scrivener: (20) S.P.-6.10.
Sefton, John, comedian; (38) A.-1.1-8.9.-5; 2.27-18.
Sefton, William: (38) A.-10.21,23,25,31; 11.2.
Seiltanzar, Herr Jose Campos, artist on the Elatsic cord: (31)
    A.-1.27.
Sequin, Edward, in opera: (42) S.C.-1.5-17.
Sequin, Mrs., in opera: (42) S.C.-1.5-17.
Sergeant, G. W., equestrian: (41-2) S.C.-reg.
Sergeant, Mrs. G. W.; (31) A.-5.24; (41-2) S.C.-reg.; Am.-3.19.
Sergeant, Master, equestrian: (41-2) S.C.-reg.
Sergeant, Miss, equestrian: (41-2) S.C.-reg.
Seymour, Rosina, in March 1823 became Mrs. James Rowe: (23)
    O.-reg.; (24) A.-1.31-reg.; (25) A.-reg.; (26) A.-reg.; (27)
    A.-reg.; (27-8) A.-reg.; (29) A.-2.6-reg.; (29-30) A.-reg.;
    (30-1) A.-reg.; (31-2) A.-reg.; (32-3) A.-reg.; (33-4) A.-
    reg.; (34-5) A.-reg.
Sharpe, Mrs.: (35) A.-1.2-5; (37) S.C.-12.7-7.
Shaw, Mrs.: (36) S.C.-11.24-8; 12.13-13; (37) S.C.-1.18-15;
    2.23-4; 4.3-10.
Siggismundi, acrobat: (12) B.-5.21,25,30.
Simonds: (33-4) A.-reg.
Sinclair, in opera: (33) A.-12.16-9; (34) A.-1.20-11; 2.12-22;
    (40) S.C.-1.9-11; 2.10-11.
Sloman: (29) A.-3.5-8,24-6; (40) S.C.-1.23-13; (40-1) S.C.-11.22-
    reg.; (41-2) S.C.-reg.
Sloman, Mrs.: (29) A.-3.5-9,20-8; (40) S.C.-1.23-12; (40-1) S.C.-
    11.24-reg.
Smelzer: (38-9) S.C.-reg.
Smith: (35-6) A.-reg.; (36-7) A.-reg.
Smith, clown with the equestrian company: (41-2) S.C.-reg.
Smith, Mrs.: (20) O.-1.10.
Smith, Mrs.: (38-9) S.C.-reg.; (39-40) A.-reg.; S.C.-reg.; (40-1)
    S.C.-reg.
Smith, Master C. F.: (23) O.-2.26-9; 4.11,21-3.
Smith, Miss: (23) O.-2.28-5; 5.3-2.
Smith, Lemuel: (25) A.-reg.; (27-8) A.-reg.; (28-9) A.-reg.
Smith, Mrs. Lemuel: (27-8) A.-reg.
Smith, Sol, actor and manager: (27-8) A.-reg.; (28-9) A.-reg.;
    (30-1) A.-reg.; (40) S.C.-5.6; (40-1) Am.-reg.; (41-2) Am.-
    reg.
Smith, Mrs. Sol: (27-8) A.-reg.; (29) A.-2.5-reg.; (30-1) A.-
    reg.
Soloman: (35-6) S.C.-reg.
Sophie, Mlle., dancer: (24) A.-4.16-6.

Sowerby: (36-7) A.-reg.

Spencer: (11) Con.-6.29.

Spencer: (34) A.-3.7-reg.; (35-6) S.C.-reg.; (36-7) S.C.-reg.

Stanley: (35-6) S.C.-reg.

Stevens, Major, the American dwarf: (39) A.-3.10-8.

Stickney, equestrian: (41) Am.-1.10-(record incomplete); (41-2) S.C.-reg.; Am.-4.24.

Stickney, Rosalie, equestrian: (41-2) S.C.-reg.; Am.-4.24.

Still, J. A., singing actor: (26) A.-2.4-reg.; (27) A.-reg.; (27-8) A.-reg.

Stith: (34-5) A.-reg.

Stone, Mrs. See Miss Legg.

Stone, D., equestrian: (41-2) Am.-reg.

Stone, E., equestrian: (41-2) Am.-reg.

Stone, George, clown with the equestrian company: (40-1) Am.-reg.; (41-2) Am.-reg. until middle of January.

Stuart (Stewart), Mrs. See Miss Mary Vos(s).

Sutherland: (40-1) Am.-reg.; (41-2) Am.-reg.

Sutor, Miss, the German dwarf: (39) A.-3.10-8.

Sutton: (40) Ar.-reg.

Sutton, with Italian Opera Company from Havana: (42) S.C.-2.22-10.

Sutton, Mrs., with Italian Opera Company from Havana: (42) S.C.-2.22-10.

Swiss Family, pantomimists: (41) S.C.-11.28-18; (42) S.C.-1.9-3; Am.-2.2-5.

Sylvain, Mons., dancer: (41) S.C..-3.6-11; 4.7.

Tasistro, Fitzgerald, tragedian: (40) S.C.-11.19-8; (41) S.C.-3.1-3.

Tatem: (28-9) A.-reg.

Tatnall, Mrs., later Mrs. Hartwig and Mrs. Pritchard: (27) A.-3.8-6; 4.4-reg.; (27-8) A.-reg.; (34) A.-12.11-11; (35) A.-5.22,26,27; (37) S.C.-1.7-8; 3.6; 4.1-10; A.-5.4-12; (41) S.C.-1.8-4.

Taylor: (11) Con.-6.29.

Taylor: (21) O.-reg.; (23) O.-reg.

T(i)ernan: (35) S.C.-12.7-6; (36) S.C.-2.8-7.

T(i)ernan, Mrs.: (35) S.C.-12.7-6; (36) S.C.-2.8-7.

Tessier: (11) Con.-7.7.

Thielman, Madame: (36-7) S.C.-12.29-reg.; (38-9) S.C.-reg.; A.-12.21-5; (40) G.-7.4; (42) S.C.-1.5-5.

Thompson: (11) S.P.-4.26; Con.-6.29.

Thorne, James, singing actor: (32-3) A.-reg.; (33-4) A.-reg.; (34-5) A.-reg.; (35-6) A.-reg.; (41-2) Am.-reg.

Thorne, Mrs.: (35-6) S.C.-reg.

Tilden, Miss: (22) O.-reg.

Tracy: (36-7) S.C.-reg.

Tree, Ellen: (38) S.C.-1.11-14; 2.12-11; (39) S.C.-1.16-16; A.-
    2.21-8.
Turnbull, dancer: (38) A.-12.21-9.
Turner, Emma: (19) S.P.-reg.
Turner, Master: (19) S.P.-reg.
Turner, William A., manager: (19) S.P.-reg.
Turner, Mrs. William A.: (19) S.P.-reg.
Tyron: (29) A.-1.14-reg; (30-1) A.-reg.

Vancamp:(36-7) A.-reg.
Vaughan, Henry: (18) S.P.-reg.; (21) E.H.-11.17; (22) O.-reg.
Vaughan, John: (18) S.P.-reg.
Vaughan, Mrs. Henry: (18) S.P.-2.24-reg.
Verity, Miss, later Mrs. Williams: (35-6) S.C.-reg.; (39-40)
    A.-11.4-reg.; 5.22; S.C.-reg.; (40-1) S.C.-10.28-reg.
Victorin, French actor: (37) S.C.-5.20.
Vincent, Mrs.: (37-8) S.C.-reg.
Vos, John H.: (17) S.P.-12.15,18,26; (18) O.C.-1.9,22,25;
    S.P.-3.14.
Vos(s), Mary, later Mrs. Stuart: (31) A.-2.3-reg.; (39-40)
    A.-10.15-reg.; 5.22; S.C.-reg.; (42) S.C.-2.6-reg.

Waldron: (33-4) A.-reg.
Wallace: (36-7) A.-reg.; (38-9) S.C.-reg.
Wallack, James: (33) A.-3.18-12; 4.8-9; (37) A.-1.3-9; 2.7-9;
    S.C.-2.22-7.
Wallack, Mrs.: (35-6) A.-reg.
Wallis, Miss (38-9) A.-reg.
Walters: (20) S.P.-6.10.
Walton: (34-5) A.-reg.; (36-7) A.-reg.
Walton (Thomas), tragedian: (35) A.-12.31-7.
Ward: (40) Ar.-reg.
Warrell, J.: (34-5) A.-reg.; (36) A.-3.16.
Warren, Mrs.: (40-1) Am.-reg.; (41-2) Am.-reg.
Watson: (26) A.-5.5,19,24; (29) A.-3.19-reg.
Watson, Mrs.: (38) S.C.-2.17-10.
Webb, Charles, tragedian: (33) A.-2.15; (40) Am.-12.18-2;
    (41) Am.-2.24-11.
Weil: (39-40) S.C.-reg.
Wells, equestrian: (31) A.-5.24.
Wells, Master, dancer: (41) Am.-12.23-4.
Wells, Miss H., dancer: (41) Am.-12.23-4.
Wheeler: (20) S.P.-2.1.
Wheeler, Mrs.: (20) S.P.-2.1.
Whitlock, equestrian: (41-2) Am.-reg.
Wilcox: (11) S.P.-4.26; Con.-6.29.
Wiles: (11) Con.-6.29.
Wilkie: (20) O.-1.10; S.P.-6.10.
Wilkie, Mrs.: (20) S.P.-6.10.
Willey: (40) A.-summer.

Williams: (35-6) S.C.-reg.; (36-7) S.C.-reg.; (37-8) S.C.-reg.;
    (38-9) S.C.-reg.; (39-40) A. and S.C.-reg.; (40-1) S.C.-reg.
Williams, Mrs. See Miss Verity.
Williams, H. A.: (21) O.-reg.; (28-9) A.-reg.; (29-30) A.-reg.;
    (31-2) A.-reg.
Williams, Mrs. H. A.: (20) S.P.-reg. O.-reg.; (21) O.-reg.; (28-9)
    A.-reg.; (31-2) A.-reg.
Williams: (23) O.-reg.
Williamson, T.: (34-5) A.-reg.; (35-6) A.-reg.; (38) A.-12.29.
Wills, James: (36) A.-2.5- (record incomplete).
Wilson, Alexander: (24) A.-3.6-6; (25) A.-reg.; (26) A.-2.13-reg.
Wood, J.: (11) S.P.-4.26; Con.-6.29.
Wood, Master: (41) S.C.-11.14-15.
Wood, W.: (41) S.C.-11.14-16.
Woods, equestrian: (40-1) Am.-reg.
Wray, Miss, dancer: (38-9) A.-reg.; M.-6.19,21.
Wright, James: (40-1) Am.-reg.; (41-2) Am.-reg.
Wright, Mrs.: (40-1) Am.-reg.; (41-2) Am.-reg.

Yates, Mrs.: (20) O.-1.10.

THE PLAYWRIGHT LIST

The following list includes the known authors of the recorded plays presented in New Orleans between 1806 and 1842, listing the plays of each author under his name. Parentheses enclose play-titles whenever there is any doubt as to the authorship.
A Beckett, Gilbert: The Artist's Wife; The Roof Scrambler; The
    Siamese Twins.
Addams, J. P.: (The Maiden's Vow) ; Sam Patch in France.
Addison, Henry Robert: The King's Word; Tam O'Shanter.
Addison, Joseph: Cato.
Allingham, John Till: Fortune's Frolic; 'Tis All a Farce; The
    Weathercock; Who Wins?
Almar, George: Crossing the Line; The Devil's Daughter; The
    Fire Raiser; Pedlar's Acre; The Roman Nose; The Rover's
    Bride; Schinderhannes; La. Tour de Nesle.
Amherst, J. H.: Last Words of Bill Jones.
Arne, T. A.: Artaxerxes.
Arnold, Samuel James: The Devil's Bridge; Free and Easy;
    Man and Wife; The Woodman's Hut.
Auber, Francois: Le Dieu et la Bayadere; Masaniello; The National Guard.
Ayton, Richard: The Rendezvous.

Banim, John: Damon and Pythias; The Sergeant's Wife.
Bannister, N. H.: The Adventures of a Sailor; Bushwhacker;
    Caius Silius; England's Iron Days; The Fall of San Antonio; Gaulantus the Gaul; The Gentleman of Lyons; Har-

canlack; Infidelity; Life in New Orleans; The Maine Question; The Marriage Contract; The Midnight Murder; Murrell, the Western Land Pirate; Old Ironsides; Rathenemus
the Roman; Robert Emmett; The Syracusan Brothers; The
Wandering Jew.

Barker, James N.: Marmion.

Barnes, Charlotte: Lafitte; The Last Days of Pompeii; Octavia
Bragaldi.

Barnett, J.: Win Her and Wear Her.

Barnett, Morris: The Bold Dragoons; Monsieur Jacques; Mrs.
G.; The Spirit of the Rhine.

Barrymore, William: El Hyder; Gilderoy; Jack Robinson and
His Monkey; Trial by Battle.

Bayly, Thomas H.: The Barrack Room; Comfortable Service;
Forty and Fifty; A Gentleman in Difficulties; How Do You
Manage?; The Ladder of Love; My Little Adopted; One
Hour; Perfection; The Swiss Cottage; Tom Noddy's Secret;
You Can't Marry Your Grandmother.

Beach, L.: Jonathan Postfree, the Honest Yankee.

Beazley, Samuel: The Boarding House; Fire and Water; Gretna
Green; Is He Jealous?; The Lottery Ticket; The Scape Grace.

Beaumont and Fletcher: Rule a Wife and Have a Wife.

Bell, Robert: The Watchword.

Bellini, Vicenzo: Beatric di Tenda; Montrechi e Capuletti;
Norma; Il Pirata; La Sonnambula; La Straniera.

Berger, W.: The Hole in the Wall; Paul Jones.

Bernard, William Bayle: The Boarding School; The Conquering
Game; The Four Sisters; His Last Legs; The Irish Attorney;
Job Fox, the Yankee Valet; Lucille; The Man about Town;
The Middy Ashore; The Mummy; The Nervous Man and the
Man of Nevre; Old Times in Virginia; St. Mary's Eve; Spec-
ulation; 2548!; The Wept of Wish-ton-Wish.

Bickerstaff, Isaac: The Hypocrite; Lionel and Clarissa; Love in
a Village; The Padlock; The Romp; The Spoiled Child; The
Sultan.

Birch, Samuel: The Adopted Child.

Bird, Robert Montgomery: The Broker of Bogota; The Gladiator;
Oralloossa, Last of the Incas.

Bishop, Henry Rowley: Yelva.

Boaden, Caroline: The First of April; William Thompson.

Boieldieu: The Caliph of Bagdad.

Boucicault, Dion; London Assurance.

Bray, John: The Toothache.

Brayley: Wool Gathering

Brooke, Mrs. Frances: Rosina.

Brown, John: Barbarossa.

Buckingham, H. A.: Peaceful Pelton.

Buckstone, John Baldwin: Agnes de Vere; The Banished Star;
The Belle of the Hotel; The Christening; The Dead Shot;
The Dream at Sea; Duchess de la Vaubaliere; Ellen War-

ham; The Happiest Day of My Life; Henrietta the Forsaken; A Husband at Sight; The Ice Witch; The Irish Lion; John Jones; A Kiss in the Dark; A Lesson for Ladies; Luke the Labourer; Married Life; The May Queen; Mischief Making; Our Mary Ann; The Pet of the Petticoats; Popping the Question; Presumptive Evidence; Rural Felicity; Shocking Events; Single Life; Snakes in the Grass; The Snapping Turtles; 33 John Street; The Two Queens; Victorine; Weak Points; Widow Wiggins; A Woman's Life; The Wreck Ashore.

Bunn, Alfred: My Neighbor's Wife.

Burges, James Bland: Riches.

Burk, J. D.: (The Battle of Bunker Hill).

Butler, R.: The Irish Tutor.

Byron, Lord George Gordon: Sardanapalus.

Caldwell, James H.: Eugene Aram.

Centlivre, Mrs. Susannah: A Bold Stroke for a Wife; The Busy Body; The Wonder! A Woman Keeps a Secret.

Cherry, Andrew: The Hotel; Miss in Her Teens; The Soldier's Daughter.

Cibber, Colley: The Provoked Husband; She Would and She Would Not.

Clinch, C. P.: The Spy.

Cobb, James: The Haunted Tower; Paul and Virginia; The Siege of Belgrade.

Coffey, Charles: The Devil to Pay.

Coleman, Henry: (Scourge of the Ocean).

Collier, William: Kate Kearney.

Collens, Thomas Wharton: The Martyr Patriots.

Colman, George, the Elder: The Clandestine Marriage; The Jealous Wife; The Manager in Distress.

Colman, George, the Younger: (Blue Beard); The Blue Devils; The Heir at Law; The Iron Chest; John Bull; Love Laughs at Locksmiths; The Mountaineers; The Poor Gentleman; The Review; Sylvester Daggerwood; Ways and Means; We Fly by Night; Who Wants a Guinea?; X. Y. Z.

Conway, H. J.: The Times that Tried Us.

Cooper, F. F.: The Elbow Shakers; Hercules, King of Clubs.

Corey, John: A cure for Jealousy.

Cowley, Mrs. Hannah: The Belle's Stratagem; A Bold Stroke for a Husband; Who's the Dupe?

Coyne, John Sterling: My Friend the Captain.

Cross, James C.: The Purse.

Cumberland, Richard: The Jew; The West Indian; The Wheel of Fortune.

Curtis, G.W.P.: Hurrah for the Boys of the West.

Dance, Charles: Alive and Merry; The Bengel Tiger; The Country Squire; The Deep, Deep Sea; A Dream of the Future; Horse Shoe Robinson; Kill or Cure; Naval Engagements; The Old English Gentleman; Petticoat Government; The Station House.

Darling, David: Beaux Without Belles.

Davenant and Dryden: The Tempest, an adaptation of Sheakespeare's play.

Delphini, Carlo: Don Juan.

Dibdin, Charles: The Quaker; The Waterman; The Wedding Ring.

Dibdin, Charles, Jr.: The Lord and the Manor; Paul Pry; Peter Wilkins.

Dibdin, Thomas John: Alonzo the Brave and the Fair Imogine; (The Battle of the Nile); The Bride of Lammermoor; The Cabinet; The Forest of Bondy; Don Giovanni; Harlequin and Mother Goose; The Heart of Midlothian; The Jew and the Doctor; Jocko, the Brazilian Ape; Lady of the Lake; Lodoiska; Of Age To-morrow; Pitcairn's Island; (The Sea Serpent); The Slaves in Barbary; The Two Gregories; Valentine and Orson.

Dimond, William: Abon Hassan; Adrian and Orilla; The Aethiop; The Bride of Abydos; The Broken Sword; Brother and Sister; The Doubtful Son; Englishmen in India; The Foundling of the Forest; The Hunter of the Alps; The Lady and the Devil; My Native Land; The Peasant Boy; The Young Hussar; Youth, Love, and Folly.

Donizetti, Gaetano: Lucia di Lammermoor; Marino Faliero; Parisena.

Dowler, M. Morton: Richard Savage.

Ducrow, Andrew: St. George and the Dragon.

Dumont, Frank: Love at All Corners.

Dumont, John R.: A Day in New Orleans; Washington.

Dunlap, William: Abaellino, the Great Bandit; The Blind Boy; Fraternal Discord; The Glory of Columbia, Her Yeomanry; The Stranger.

Ebsworth, Joseph: The Rival Valets.

Farquhar, George: The Inconstant.

Farrell, John: The Dumb Girl of Genoa.

Farren, George: Life in New York; The Tower of Nesle, adaptation of Frank Haynes' translation.

Faucit, John: The Miller's Maid.

Fawcett, John: La Perouse.

Field, Joseph M.: Bennett in Texas; Catharine Howard; (The Clouds); Coming Out; G-A-G; Mademoiselle de Belle Isle; Sckaggs' Family; Tourists in America;

Field, J. M.; Schinder Eller

Fielding, Thomas: Anne Boleyn.

Finn, H. J.: Kasper Hauser; Montgomery; Removing the Deposits; (The Water Witch).

Fitzball, Edward: The Burgomaster's Daughter; The Carmelites; Esmeralda; The Floating Beacon; The Flying Dutchman; Hofer, the Tell of the Tyrol; Joan of Arc; Jonathan Bradford; The Last Days of Pompeii; The Lord of the Isles; The Three Hunchbacks; Tom Cringle's Log; Walter Tyrrell; Za Ze Zi Zo Zu.

Foote, Samuel: The Liar; The Mayor of Garratt; Taste.

Galt, J.: (MyAunt).

Garrick, David: The Clandestine Marrage; The Country Girl; Gulliver in Lilliput; High Life Below Stairs; The Irish Widow; Catharine and Petruchio; The Lying Valet.

Gay, John: The Beggar's Opera.

Glover, S. E.: The Banished Provincial; The Cradle of Liberty; The Last of the Mohicans; Rake Hellies.

Goldsmith, Oliver: She Stoops to Conquer.

Gore, Mrs. Catharine Grace Frances: King O'Neil; The Maid of Croissy.

Greffulhe: Budget of Blunders.

Greenwood, T.: Death of Life in London.

Grice, C. E.: The Battle of New Orleans.

Hackett, J. H.: Jonathan in England.

Haines, James T.: Amilie; The French Spy; The Idiot Witness; Maidens Beware; The Wizard Skiff.

Harby, George Washington: The Deceived; Hard Times in New Orleans; Nick of the Woods; Tutoona.

Harby, Isaac: Alberti Contadini, the Last of the Abruzzi.

Haworth, R.: Disguises.

Haynes, Frank: Lucrece Borgia; The Tower of Nesle.

Haynes, James: Durazzo; The Man in the Iron Mask; Mary Stuart, Queen of Scots.

Hentz, Mrs. Caroline Lee: Lamorah; The Moorish Bride.

Hill, F. S.: Love and a Bunch; Opera Mad; The School of Ten Quakers; The Shoemaker of Toulouse; Six Degrees of Crime.

Herold: Zampa, the Red Corsair.

Hill, H.: Zaire.

Hoadley, Benjamin: The Suspicious Husband.

Hoare, Prince: Lock and Key; No Song, No Supper; The Prize; Three and the Duce.

Hodgkinson: The Man of Fortitude.

Holcroft, Thomas: Deaf and Dumb; The Deserted Daughter; The Road to Ruin; The Tale of Mystery.

Holland, George H.: Whims of a Comedian.

Home, John: Douglas.

Hook, Theodore Edward: Darkness Visible; Exchange No Robbery; Killing No Murder; The Soldier's Return; Tekeli.

Inchbald, Mrs. Elizabeth: Animal Magnetism; Everyone Has His
    Faults; Lovers Vows; The Midnight Hour; The Mogul Tale;
    The Wedding Day; Wives as They Were and Maids as They
    Are.
Irving Washington, with J. H. Payne: Charles the Second.

Jackman, Isaac: All the World's a Stage.
Jerrold, Douglas William: Ambrose Gwinette; Black Eyed Susan;
    Dolly and the Rat; The Drunkard's Fate; The Hazard of the
    Die; The Housekeeper; John Overy; The Mother; The Mutiny
    at the Nore; The Rent Day; The Smoked Miser; The Wedding
    Gown.
Johnson, Charles: The Farm House.
Jones, J. S.: The Adventure; The Green Mountain Boy; The
    Liberty Tree.
Jones, Richard: The Green Man; Too Late for Dinner.

Keating, E. H.: The Two Sisters.
Kemble, Charles: Plot and Counterplot; The Point of Honor;
    The Wanderer.
Kemble, Fanny: Francis the First of France.
Kemble, J. Philip: The Roman Actor ,altered from Massinger.
Kemble, Marie Therese: The Day after the Wedding; Per-
    sonation.
Kenney, James: Ella Rosenberg; The Illustrious Stranger; The
    Irish Ambassador; Matrimony; Not a World; Raising the
    Wind; Spring and Autumn; Sweethearts and Wives; Turn
    Out.
Kennicott, James H.: Irma.
Kerr, John: (Rip Van Winkle).
King, T.: Lovers' Quarrels.
Knight, E. P.: A Chip of the Old Block.
Knight, Thomas: The Honest Thieves; The Turnpike Gate.
Knowles, James Sheridan: The Beggar of Bethnal Green; Brian
    Boroihme; The Hunchback; John of Procida; Love; The
    Love Chase; The Maid of Mariendorpt; The Old Maids; Vir-
    ginius; The Wife; William Tell; Woman's Wit; The Wrecker's
    Daughter.

Lacy, Michael Rophino: Cinderella; Fra Diavolo; Love and
    Reason; Love in Wrinkles; Napoleon Bonaparte; The Two
    Friends.
Lamb, Charles: Mr. H.
Lancaster, Edward: The Manager's Daughter.
Lanfau, Mrs.: The Sons of Erin.
Le Bree, Lawrence : (Ebenezer Venture).
Lee, Nathaniel: Alexander the Great.
Lemon, Mark: Ins and Outs; The Ladies' Club; My Sister Kate;
    Out of Place; Walden, the Avenger.

Lewis, M. G.: Adelgitha; The Captive; The Castle Spectre; Timour the Tartar; The Wood Daemon.

Lillo, George: George Barnwell.

Livius, Barham: Maid or Wife.

Lovell, George W.: The Avenger; The Provest of Bruges.

Lover, Samuel: Rory O'More; The White Horse of the Peppers.

Lunn, Joseph: All on the Wing; Capers and Coronets; Family Jars; Fish Out of Water; Hide and Seek.

Lytton, Edward Bulwer: Duchess de la Valliere; The Lady of Lyons; Money; Richelieu; The Sea Captain.

MacFarren, George: Auld Robin Gray; Malvina; The March of Intellect; Winning a Husband.

Macklin, Charles: Love à la Mode.

Macready, William: The Irishman in London; The Village Lawyer; Werner.

Madden: The Triumph of Texas.

Massinger, Philip: The Fatal Dowry; A New Way to Pay Old Debts; The Roman Actor.

Mathews, Charles: Mail Coach Adventures.

Mathews, Charles James: My Wife's Mother; Truth.

Maturin, Charles R.: Bertram.

Mayer: Il Fanatico per la Musica.

Mayhew, Edward: Make Your Wills; The Wandering Minstrel.

Medina, Louisa H.: Nick of the Woods.

Mercadante: Donna Caritea.

Meyerbeer: Robert le Diable.

Mildenhall, T.: The Sentinel.

Millingen, John Gideon: The Bee Hive; Borrowed Feathers; The Illustrious Stranger; The King's Fool.

Milman, Henry Hart: Fazio.

Milner, H. M.: (The Gambler's Fate); Mazeppa; The Moorish Page; One Hundred and Two; Twelve Precisely.

Mitford, Mrs. Mary Russell: Rienzi.

Moncrieff, William Thomas; The Cataract of the Ganges; Foreign Airs and Native Graces; Giovanni in London; (Ivanhoe); The Lear of Private Life; Life in London; Monsieur Mallet; Monsieur Tonson; Old Heads Upon Young Shoulders; Paris and London; The Pickwickians; Rochester; The Secret; The Somnambulist; The Spectre Bridegroon; Wanted a Wife.

Moore, Edward: The Gamester.

Moore, Tom: M.P.

Morton, John Maddison: Chaos is Come Again; My Husband's Ghost; The Spitfire.

Morton, Thomas: The Children in the Woods; Columbus; A Cure for the Heartache; Henri Quartre; The Invincibles; A Roland for an Oliver; The School of Reform; Speed the Plough; The Sublime and Beautiful; Town and Country; The Way to Get Married.

Mozart, Wolfgang: Don Juan of Austria; The Marriage of Figaro.
Murphy, Arthur: All in the Wrong; The Citizen; The Grecian
    Daughter; Know Your Own Mind; Old Maid; Three Weeks
    After Marriage.
Murry, William Henry: No!

Noah, Mordecai Manuel: Marion; She Would Be a Soldier; The
    Wandering Boys.

O'Callaghan, P. P.: The Married Bachelor.
O'Hara, Kane: Midas; Tom Thumb.
O'Keeffe, John: The Agreeable Surprise; Castle of Andalusia;
    The Dead Alive; Fontainbleau; The Grenadier; The High-
    land Reel; Love in a Camp; Modern Antiques; The Poor
    Soldier; The Rival Soldiers; Wild Oats; The Young Quaker.
Otway, Thomas: The Orphan; Venice Preserved.
Oulton, Wally Chamberlaine: Botheration; Frightened to Death;
    The Somnambula.
Oxberry, William Henry: Actress of All Work; The Conscript;
    Matteo Falcone.
Oxenford, John: Does Your Mother Know You're Out?; My
    Fellow Clerk; Twice Killed.

Parry, J.: The Peacock and the Crow.
Parry, Thomas: Helpless Animals; P. P.
Payne, John Howard: Adeline; Brutus; Charles the Second;
    Clari, the Maid of Milan; The Fall of Algiers; The Lancers;
    Love in Humble Life; Thérèse; 'Twas I; The Two Galley
    Slaves.
Peake, Richard Brinsley: Amateurs and Actors; The Bottle Imp;
    The Climbing Boy; The Duel; The Haunted Inn; H. B.; My
    Master's Rival; One Hundred Pound Note; The Poachers.
Phillips, Jonas B.: Oranaska; The Widow's Curse.
Philips, Ambrose; The Distressed Mother.
Pilson, Frederick: He Would Be a Soldier.
Pitt, George Dibdin: The Eddystone Elf; The Last Man; The
    Last Nail; Lurline; Rookwood; The Whistler.
Planché, James Robinson: The Brigand; Charles XII; The Child
    of the Wreck; Court Favour; Der Freischutz; The Green
    Eyed Monster; Half an Hour's Courtship; The Loan of a
    Lover; The Dumb Belle; Michel Perrin; My Daughter, Sir;
    My Friend the Governor; My Schoolfellow; Olympic Devils;
    Pay to My Order; A Peculiar Position; The Printer's Devil;
    Rencontre.
Planché, Mrs. J. R.: A Handsome Husband; A Pleasant Neigh-
    bor; The Ransom; The Sledge Driver; The Welsh Girl.
Pocock, Isaac: For Freedom Ho!; Hit or Miss; Husbands and
    Wives; John of Paris; The Magpie and the Maid; The Miller
    and His Men; The Omnibus; The Robber's Wife; Robinson
    Crusoe; Rob Roy Macgregor; Sweet Home; Zembuca.

Poole, John: The Atonement; Deaf as a Post; Frederick the Great; Intrigue; Married and Single; Old and Young; Paul Pry; The Scape Goat; The Secret; Simpson and Company; The Soldier's Courtship; 'Tis She; Turning the Tables; Uncle Sam.

Power, Tyrone: Born to Good Luck; Etiquette Run Mad; Paddy Carey; St. Patrick's Eve.

Ranger, E. W.: The Gentleman and the Upstart; (The Lover Husband) ; The Romantic Widow.

Rawlinson: The Tragedians.

Raymond, Richard John: Cherry Bounce; Mrs. White; P. S. Come to Dinner.

Rayner, B. F.: The Dumb Man of Manchester.

Rede, William L.: Affair of Honor; The Foreign Prince; The Game Cock of the Wilderness; His First Champagne; The Rake's Progress; The Skeleton Witness.

Rees, James: Charlotte Temple; The Headsman; Lafitte, the Pirate of the Gulf; The Miniature; The Mistletoe Bough; Oliver Twist; (The Prairie Girls) ; The Squatter; The Unknown; Washington Preserved; (Washington at Valley Forge).

Reynolds, Frederick: The Dramatist; The Exiles of Siberia; Folly as It Flies; Laugh When You Can; Management; The Will.

Reynolds, John Hamilton: Confounded Foreigners.

Rica: Chiara de Rosemberg.

Rice, T. D.: Bone Squash Diavolo; Jim Crow in London; Jumbo Jim; Oh! Hush!; Such a Gitting up Stairs; Virginia Mummy.

Rhodes, William: Bombastes Furioso.

Rodwell, George Herbert: The Chimney Piece; I'll be Your Second; The Irish Valet; My Own Lover; Teddy the Tiler.

Rodwell, J. Thomas G.: The Young Widow.

Rossini, Giacomo: The Barber of Seville; Il Barbiere de Seviglia; La Cenerentola; La Gazza Ladra; l'Inganno Felice; Otello; Il Tancredi; Il Turco in Italia; Semiramide; Zelmira.

Rowe, Nicholas: The Fair Penitent; Jane Shore.

Ryan, Richard: Everybody's Husband.

Sargent, Epes: The Genoese.

Scott, Miss: The Old Oak Chest.

Scribe and Taglioni: La Sylphide.

Selby, Charles: Catching an Heiress; The Dancing Barber; A Day in Paris; Frank Fox Phipps; Hunting a Turtle; Jacques Strop; The Married Rake; The Rival Pages; Robert Macaire; The Unfinished Gentleman; Valet de Sham; The Widow's Victim.

Serle, Thomas James: A Ghost Story; The Shadow on the Wall; The Yeoman's Daughter.

Shakespeare, William: Antony and Cleopatra; As You Like It; Comedy of Errors; Hamlet; Henry IV; Henry VIII; Julius Caesar; King John; King Lear; Macbeth; The Merchant of

Venice; The Merry Wives of Windsor; Much Ado About
Nothing; Othello; Richard III; Romeo and Juliet; Twelfth
Night; Two Gentlemen of Verona.
Shannon, Charles: My Wife or My Place; The Youthful Queen.
Sherburne, J. H.: (Oceola.)
Sheridan, Richard Brinsley: The Critic; Pizarro; The Rivals;
Saint Patrick's Day; The School for Scandal.
Sheil, R. S.: The Apostate; Evadne.
Smith, G.: Make Your Wills.
Smith, Richard P.: The Eighth of January.
Soane, George: Aladdin; The Falls of Clyde; The Inn Keeper's
Daughter; The Young Reefer.
Somerset, Charles A.: A Day after the Fair; Jack the Giant
Killer; Maurice, the Wood Cutter; Shakespeare's Early
Days; The Wreck.
Southerne, Thomas: Isabella.
Stevens, (H. E.): The Skeleton Robber.
Stirling, Edward: Blue Jackets; The Fortunes of Smike; Nicholas
Nickleby.
Stokes, J.: The Forest of Rosenwald.
Stone, J. A.: The Knight of the Golden Fleece; Lion of the West;
Metamora.

Talfourd, Sergeant: Glencoe; Ion.
Terry, Daniel: (Guy Mannering).
Thackeray, Thomas James: The Force of Nature; The Mountain
Sylph.
Thompson, C. Pelham: An Uncle Too Many.
Thompson, E. H.: Sam Patch.
Thomson, James: Tancred and Sigismunda.
Tobin, John: The Curfew; The Honey Moon.

Walker, Benjamin: The Swiss Swains.
Walker, C. E.: Wallace; The Warlock of the Glen.
Walker, John: Napoleon, or The Emperor and the Soldier; The
Wild Boy of Bohemia.
Wallack, W. H.: Paul Jones.
Webster, Benjamin Nottingham: The Alpine Maid; The Golden
Farmer; High Ways and By Ways; My Young Wife and My
Old Umbrella; The Old Gentleman; Paul Clifford.
Wilks, Thomas Egerton: The Buckle of Brilliants; The Death
Token; He's Not A-Miss; Introduce Me; (Rafael, the Liber-
tine); The Rail Road Station; Seven Clerks; State Secrets;
The Wolf and the Lamb.
Willis, Nathaniel Parker; Bianca Visconti; Tortesa, the Usurer.
Woodworth, Samuel: The Forest Rose; The Foundling of the
Sea; Lafayette.

Young, Edward: The Revenge.